T0212194

Lecture Notes in Computer Science   13547

More information about this series at https://link.springer.com/bookseries/558

Xiaofeng Chen · Jian Shen · Willy Susilo (Eds.)

Cyberspace Safety and Security

14th International Symposium, CSS 2022
Xi'an, China, October 16–18, 2022
Proceedings

Editors
Xiaofeng Chen
Xidian University
Xi'an, China

Jian Shen 🆔
Nanjing University of Information Science
and Technology
Nanjing, China

Willy Susilo 🆔
University of Wollongong
Wollongong, NSW, Australia

ISSN 0302-9743   ISSN 1611-3349 (electronic)
Lecture Notes in Computer Science
ISBN 978-3-031-18066-8   ISBN 978-3-031-18067-5 (eBook)
https://doi.org/10.1007/978-3-031-18067-5

This Springer imprint is published by the registered company Springer Nature Switzerland AG
The registered company address is: Gewerbestrasse 11, 6330 Cham, Switzerland

Preface

This volume contains the papers selected for presentation at the 14th International Symposium on Cyberspace Safety and Security (CSS 2022), held during October 16–18, 2022, in Xi'an, China.

In response to the call for papers, 104 papers were submitted to the conference. These papers were peer reviewed and subsequently discussed based on their novelty, quality, and contribution by at least three members of the Program Committee. The submission of the papers and the review process were carried out using the EasyChair platform. Based on the reviews and the discussion, 27 papers were selected for presentation at the conference (resulting in an acceptance rate of 26 %). We note that many high-quality submissions were not selected for presentation because of the high technical level of the overall submissions, and we are certain that many of these submissions will, nevertheless, be published at other competitive forums in the future.

The CSS Symposium aims to advance the research in cyberspace safety and security communities by establishing a forum, bringing together researchers in these areas, and promoting the exchange of ideas with the developers, standardization bodies, and policy makers in related fields. Besides the technical program composed of the papers collated in these proceedings, the conference included invited talks. We were honored to have seven keynote speakers: Elisa Bertino, Xuemin Lin, Jinjun Chen, Yan Zhang, Xinghua Li, Jin Li, and Moti Yung. Their talks provided interesting insights and research directions in important research areas.

An event like CSS 2022 depends on the volunteering efforts of a host of individuals and the support of numerous institutes. There is a long list of people who volunteered their time and energy to put together and organize the conference, and who deserve special thanks. Thanks to all the members of the Program Committee and the external reviewers for their hard work in evaluating the papers. We are also very grateful to all the people whose work ensured a smooth organization process: the CSS Steering Committee, and its Chair, Yang Xiang, in particular; Honorary Chairs Jiandong Li and Jianfeng Ma; General Chairs Min Sheng, Yong Yu, and Fangguo Zhang; all of the co-chairs and the Organization Committee, for helping with organization and taking care of local arrangements. A number of institutes deserve thanks as well for supporting the organization of CSS 2022: Xidian University, the State Key Laboratory of Integrated Service Networks (ISN), NSCLab, Xi'an University of Posts and Telecommunications, and Nanjing University of Information Science and Technology. We are also grateful to Springer, for its support.

Finally, we would like to thank the authors for submitting their papers to CSS 2022. We hope that the proceedings will promote the research and facilitate future work in the field of cyberspace safety and security.

August 2022

Xiaofeng Chen
Jian Shen
Willy Susilo

Organization

Organizing Committee

Steering Committee Chair

Yang Xiang   Swinburne University of Technology, Australia

Honorary Chairs

Jiandong Li   Xidian University, China
Jianfeng Ma   Xidian University, China

General Chairs

Min Sheng   Xidian University, China
Yong Yu   Xi'an University of Posts and
                                      Telecommunications, China
Fangguo Zhang   Sun Yat-sen University, China

Program Co-chairs

Xiaofeng Chen   Xidian University, China
Jian Shen   Nanjing University of Information Science and
                                      Technology, China
Willy Susilo   University of Wollongong, Australia

Publicity Co-chairs

Jianfeng Wang   Xidian University, China
Weizhi Meng   Technical University of Denmark, Denmark

Organization Committee Members

Shichong Tan   Xidian University, China
Guohua Tian   Xidian University, China
Jiaojiao Wu   Xidian University, China

Program Committee

Cristina Alcaraz   University of Malaga, Spain
Silvio Barra   University of Naples Federico II, Italy

Chao Chen	James Cook University, Australia
Rongmao Chen	National University of Defense Technology, China
Chi Cheng	China University of Geosciences, China
Changyu Dong	Newcastle University, UK
Ashutosh Dhar Dwivedi	Technical University of Denmark, Denmark
Dieter Gollmann	Hamburg University of Technology, Germany
Fuchun Guo	University of Wollongong, Australia
Jinguang Han	Southeast University, China
Haibo Hu	The Hong Kong Polytechnic University, China
Qiong Huang	South China Agricultural University, China
Miroslaw Kutylowski	Wroclaw University of Science and Technology, Poland
Jingwei Li	University of Electronic Science and Technology of China, China
Jay Ligatti	University of South Florida, USA
Shigang Liu	Swinburne University of Technology, Australia
Ximeng Liu	Singapore Management University, Singapore
Jiqiang Lv	Beihang University, China
Xu Ma	Qufu Normal University, China
Jianting Ning	Singapore Management University, Singapore
Lei Pan	Deakin University, Australia
Claudia Peersman	University of Bristol, UK
Josef Pieprzyk	CSIRO's Data61, Australia
Saiyu Qi	Xi'an Jiaotong University, China
Jun Shao	Zhejiang Gongshang University, China
Shi-Feng Sun	Shanghai Jiao Tong University, China
Zhiyuan Tan	Edinburgh Napier University, UK
Qiang Tang	Luxembourg Institute of Science and Technology, Luxembourg
Ding Wang	Peking University, China
Yunling Wang	Xi'an University of Posts and Telecommunications, China
Jianghong Wei	State Key Laboratory of Mathematical Engineering and Advanced Computing, China
Qianhong Wu	Beihang University, China
Zhe Xia	Wuhan University of Technology, China
Peng Xu	Huazhong University of Science and Technology, China
Lei Xue	The Hong Kong Polytechnic University, China
Wun-She Yap	Universiti Tunku Abdul Rahman, Malaysia
Xingliang Yuan	Monash University, Australia
Xiaoyu Zhang	Xidian University, China

Xuyun Zhang   Macquarie University, Australia
Youwen Zhu   Nanjing University of Aeronautics and
                         Astronautics, China

Contents

Cryptography and Its Applications

Publicly Verifiable Conjunctive Keyword Search with Balanced Verification Overhead

Qitian Sheng, Jiaojiao Wu, and Jianfeng Wang[✉]

School of Cyber Engineering, Xidian University, Xi'an 710126, China
{qtsheng,jiaojiaowujj}@stu.xidian.edu.cn,
jfwang@xidian.edu.cn

Abstract. Verifiable conjunctive search in Searchable Symmetric Encryption (VSSE) allows a client to search multiple keywords with sublinear computation overhead and ensures the integrity of search results. However, the state-of-the-art VSSE schemes are either probabilistically verifiable or have significant communication overhead. In this paper, we propose an efficient VSSE scheme that achieves a balance between communication and computation overheads. Our scheme supports public and private verification for different scenarios by utilizing RSA accumulator and has constant-size public parameters. Finally, we prove that our scheme is secure against malicious servers and conclude that our scheme is efficient by comparing and analyzing the performance.

Keywords: Searchable encryption · Conjunctive keyword search · Public verification

1 Introduction

Cloud computing allows users to enjoy unlimited resources at a low maintenance cost. Although data outsourcing provides great convenience to users, it also inevitably suffers from some security risks. Since the server is not trusted, users need to encrypt data before outsourcing, which makes it challenging to search over the encrypted database.

Searchable symmetric encryption (SSE), initiated by Song *et al.*[22], supports search over the encrypted data while protecting user privacy. As a promising solution, SSE was improved in the aspects of security [5,12], functionality [16,17], and performance [8]. To cope with the complex search in the real world, Cash *et al.* [7] presented a construction named OXT, which enables users to search conjunctive keywords with sublinear performance. OXT also strikes a balance between efficiency and security, and is suitable for large-scale databases.

Furthermore, the untrusted server may return incorrect or partial data for economic reasons or information security incidents in the malicious-server model. Therefore, it is necessary to ensure the integrity of search results [9,20,24].

Wang *et al.* [26] proposed the first verifiable conjunctive keyword SSE scheme, which can verify the search results even if they are empty. However, this scheme is probabilistically verifiable and requires public parameters as large as the database size. Fan *et al.* [11] proposed an efficient scheme named VCKSCF using the cuckoo filter. In this scheme, the server does not generate the proof of search results but encases the membership relationship in an encrypted cuckoo filter. This scheme has low storage and computation costs but suffers high communication overhead. However, both above schemes only support private verification, which is unsatisfied with public verification scenarios.

Therefore, it is critical to design an efficient VSSE scheme supporting public and private verification. In this paper, we make a breakthrough toward this problem and present a communication-efficient VSSE scheme.

1.1 Our Contribution

In this paper, we investigate an effective method to construct a VSSE scheme. Our contributions are summarized as follows:

- We propose a novel VSSE scheme based on RSA accumulator, which requires only constant-size public parameters and supports both private and public verification.
- We present a formal security definition for our proposed scheme and prove that our scheme is secure against a malicious server by a series of rigorous security proof.
- We analyze the performance of our proposed scheme and compare it with other schemes [11,26]. Finally, we conclude that our scheme keeps a balanced performance between computation and communication overheads.

1.2 Related Work

The first SSE was introduced by Song *et al.* [22], and the computation overhead increases with the database capacity linearly. Goh *et al.* [13] enhanced the search performance by creating an index for each document. Curtmola *et al.* [10] initially achieved sublinear search performance using an inverted index on each keyword. They also presented a formal leakage profile called search pattern and access pattern. To improve search accuracy, Golle *et al.* [14] proposed a scheme supporting conjunctive keyword search by utilizing structured data. The communication of the scheme costs linearly with file numbers. Cash *et al.* [7] introduced the first sublinear conjunctive keyword searchable encryption scheme. They also explored a dynamic scheme [6] for handling complicated search requests (*e.g.,* boolean queries). Jarecki *et al.* [15] extended Cash *et al.*'s work for the multi-user setting while retaining the original functionality. Sun *et al.* [23] expanded the scheme into a non-interactive version.

Chai *et al.* [9] first considered the active adversary and realized *verifiable searchability* by utilizing a trie-like index. Kurosawa and Ohtaki [18] brought verifiability into SSE and formulated the security of the proposed scheme.

Later, plenty of works proposed workable solutions for verifiable SSE [4,20]. Sun et al.[24] applied an accumulation tree and designed a verifiable search scheme supporting conjunctive keyword search. However, the scheme fails to work toward an empty search result. Wang et al. [26] introduced a *sample method* to deal with this case, but the verification has a probability of failure. Fan et al. [11] used the cuckoo filter to optimize computation and storage compared to Wang et al.'s scheme. Azraoui et al. [2] then improved the construction by providing public verification. Soleimanian and Khazaei [21] proposed the publicly verifiable components with compact cryptographic primitives. Tong et al. [25] proposed a verifiable search scheme supporting fuzzy keyword search. Ali et al. [1] extended verifiable keyword search to IoT scenarios.

2 Preliminaries

In this section, we list Table 1 for notations used throughout this paper and review the cryptographic primitives and corresponding security definitions.

Table 1. Notations

Notations	Description
λ	Security parameter
$s \xleftarrow{\$} S$	Choose a uniformly randomly selected element s from set S
$H(\cdot)$	Secure hash function
$H_p(\cdot)$	Hash-to-prime function
$F(\cdot)$	A deterministic pseudo-random function (PRF)
$F_p(\cdot)$	A deterministic PRF mapped into group $\mathbb{Z}_p^*$
ind_i	Identifier of the i-th file
W	The all keywords in DB
W_i	Keywords in document ind_i
DB	The whole database $(\mathrm{ind}_i, \mathrm{W}_i)_{i=1}^T$
Stag	The search token set of all keywords
stag_w	The search token for keyword w
R_{w_1}	The result of matching keyword w_1
R	The result of matching the search query

2.1 RSA Group

An RSA group is a computational group $\mathbb{Z}_n^*$ of invertible integers modulus n, which is the product of two big primes. The equation $\gcd(e, n) = 1$ makes it easy to assert if element e belongs to group $\mathbb{Z}_n^*$. For the prime products p, q of n, the RSA group cardinality is $\varphi(n) = \varphi(pq)$. If p and q are safe primes, *i.e.*, $p = 2p' + 1, q = 2q' + 1$ for other primes p', q', the group has order $\varphi(n) = 4p' \cdot q'$.

2.2   RSA Accumulator

We present an overview of the RSA accumulator [19]. The RSA accumulator allows users to commit a set of values with a short element and to assert whether the selected elements belong to the given set through a verification algorithm.

Specifically, we define n as the RSA group modulus, where n is the product of two safe primes. The integer element set $S = \{s_1, s_2, \ldots, s_n\}$ is accumulated into an element as $Acc(S) \leftarrow g^{\Pi_{s \in S} H_p(s)} \in \mathbb{G}$, where g is the group generator. Note that neither inserting a new element s' nor modifying the present element s in set S may contaminate the accumulator value. It is tough to reconstruct the accumulator value under the strong RSA assumption.

The prover provides proof $W_{S_1} = g^{\Pi_{s \in S - S_1} H_p(s)}$ to prove the membership of $S_1 \subseteq S$. The verifier detects whether members in S_1 are all in S by testing the equality of $W_{S_1}^{\Pi_{s \in S_1} H_p(s)} = Acc(S)$.

The non-membership witness of element $s' \notin S$ is feasible through Bézout's identity. The prover computes the Bézout coefficients a and b for $\prod_{s \in S} H_p(s)$ and $H_p(s')$, then furnishes the witness tuple $\hat{W}_{s_i} = (a, g^b)$. The coefficients a, b satisfy $a \cdot \prod_{s \in S} H_p(s) + b \cdot H_p(s') = 1$ by leveraging the fact that $s' \notin S \iff \gcd(H_p(s'), \prod_{s \in S} H_p(s)) = 1$. The non-membership can be verified by checking $Acc(S)^a \cdot (g^b)^{H_p(s')} = g$.

For scenarios in which multiple elements not in S are presented, there still exists coefficients a, b satisfying $a \cdot \prod_{s \in S} H_p(s) + b \cdot \prod_{s' \notin S} H_p(s') = 1$, and the non-membership is verified if the equation holds:

$$Acc(S)^a \cdot (g^b)^{\Pi_{s' \notin S} H_p(s')} = g. \tag{1}$$

Remark 1. For consistency, we define VerMem and VerNonMem as member and non-member verification algorithms, respectively. Both algorithms take the accumulated value, elements, and witnesses as inputs and output verification results (*True* or *False*).

2.3   Hardness Assumptions

Definition 1 (DDH assumption). *Given a cyclic group $\mathbb{G}$ of prime order p, let $\mathcal{D}_1 \leftarrow \{g^a, g^b, g^{ab}\}$ and $\mathcal{D}_2 \leftarrow \{g^a, g^b, g^c\}$ as the two distributions in $\mathbb{G}$, where $a, b, c \xleftarrow{\$} \mathbb{Z}_p$. If the Decisional Diffie-Hellman(DDH) assumption holds, no efficient adversary $\mathcal{A}$ can distinguish between $\mathcal{D}_1$ and $\mathcal{D}_2$.*

Definition 2 (Strong RSA assumption). *When the security parameter is λ, we define $GGen(\lambda)$ as a algorithm generating a RSA modulus n of length λ. If the strong RSA assumption holds, there is no efficient adversary $\mathcal{A}$ to find the roots of a randomly selected group element:*

$$\Pr \left[u^l = w, l > 1 : \begin{array}{c} \mathbb{G} \xleftarrow{\$} GGen(\lambda) \\ w \leftarrow \mathbb{G} \\ (u, l) \leftarrow \mathcal{A}(\mathbb{G}, w) \end{array} \right] \leq \mathrm{negl}(\lambda)$$

2.4 Security Definitions

Similar to [23, 26], we introduce the leakage function $\mathcal{L}_{\text{VSSE}}$ (the rigid definition is introduced later), which reveals leaked information to an adversary $\mathcal{A}$ during scheme execution. We define Π as a VSSE scheme containing (VEDBSetup, KeyGen, TokenGen, Search, Verify), and $\mathcal{L}_{\text{VSSE}}$ be an algorithm. For the formal security of VSSE scheme Π, we define the real experiment $\mathbf{Real}_{\mathcal{A}}^{\Pi}(\lambda)$ and ideal one $\mathbf{Ideal}_{\mathcal{A},\mathcal{S}}^{\Pi}(\lambda)$:

$\mathbf{Real}_{\mathcal{A}}^{\Pi}(\lambda)$: $\mathcal{A}(1^{\lambda})$ selects a database DB and search queries $\mathbf{q}$. Experiment then runs the VEDBSetup(λ, DB) and outputs the results (PK, VEDB). $\mathcal{A}$ chooses a series of search keywords $\mathbf{w}$ for an authenticated user and generates SK using KeyGen$(\text{MK}, \mathbf{w})$, assuming that the conjunctive keywords $\bar{\mathbf{w}}$ are associated with $\mathbf{q}$ within the set $\mathbf{w}$. Through TokenGen$(\text{SK}, \bar{\mathbf{w}})$, $\mathcal{A}$ obtains the search token st for keywords $\bar{\mathbf{w}}$. As a result, the experiment executes the remaining algorithms Search$(\text{st}, \text{VEDB}, \text{PK})$ and Verify$(\text{stag}_{w_1}, \text{pos}, \text{R}_{w_1}, \text{proof}_{1,2})$. Then $\mathcal{A}$ receives transcript and client output and outputs the binary bit b as experiment output finally.

$\mathbf{Ideal}_{\mathcal{A},\mathcal{S}}^{\Pi}(\lambda)$: $\mathcal{A}(1^{\lambda})$ selects DB and queries $\mathbf{q}$. The experiment then runs the algorithm $S(\mathcal{L}_{VSSE}(\text{DB}))$ and outputs results(PK, VEDB). Then $\mathcal{A}$ repeatedly send query q to experiment. In return, the experiment saves q as $\mathbf{q}[i]$ ($i \in |\mathbf{q}|$), then runs $S(\mathcal{L}_{VSSE}(\text{DB}, \mathbf{q}))$ and sends the output to $\mathcal{A}$, where $\mathbf{q}$ contains all the queries sent from $\mathcal{A}$. Eventually, $\mathcal{A}$ returns b as the experiment output.

We claim scheme Π is an $\mathcal{L}$-semantically secure VSSE scheme, if there exists a simulator $\mathcal{S}$ for all efficient adversaries $\mathcal{A}$ such that:

$$\left| \Pr[\mathbf{Real}_{\mathcal{A}}^{\Pi}(\lambda) = 1] - \Pr[\mathbf{Ideal}_{\mathcal{A},\mathcal{S}}^{\Pi}] \right| \leq \text{neg}(\lambda)$$

Furthermore, we formally introduce the leakage function $\mathcal{L}_{VSSE}$, which will be employed in security analysis. For a couple of T conjunctive queries $\mathbf{q}(\mathbf{s}, \mathbf{x})$, the i-th query denotes $\mathbf{q}[i] = (\mathbf{s}[i], \mathbf{x}[i, \cdot])$, where $\mathbf{s}$ and $\mathbf{x}$ refer to *sterm* and *xterm*. Input DB and $\mathbf{q}$, the items in $\mathcal{L}_{VSSE}$ are as follows:

- $K = \bigcup_{i=1}^{d} W_i$ represents amounts of keywords in DB.
- $N = \sum_{j=1}^{d} |W_{id_j}|$ denotes the capacity of keyword-document id pairs in DB.
- $\bar{\mathbf{s}} \in [m]^{T}$ is the *equality pattern* of the sterms $\mathbf{s}$ implying which queries containing same sterms. In details, $[m]$ contains the appearance order of *sterm*. As an example, if $\mathbf{s} = (x, y, z, x, y)$ then $\bar{\mathbf{s}} = (0, 1, 2, 0, 1)$.
- SP indicates the number of documents matching *sterm* . Formally, $\text{SP}[i] = |\text{DB}(\mathbf{s}[i])|$.
- RP is the *result pattern* of the queries, it represents documents matching query $\mathbf{q}[i]$. RP returns cross set of *sterm* search result and related *xterm* in the query, *i.e.*, $\text{DB}(\mathbf{s}[i]) \cap \text{DB}(\mathbf{x}[i, \alpha])$.
- SRP represents the *search results pattern* in each query, which is the stags and corresponding **proof** related to the *sterm*. Formally, $\text{SRP}[i] = \text{DB}(\mathbf{s}[i])$.

- IP represents the *conditional intersection pattern* among in selected queries and formally $IP[i, j, \alpha, \beta]$, it represents the intersection of DB ($s[i]$) and DB ($s[j]$), where $\mathbf{x}[i, \alpha] = \mathbf{x}[j, \beta]$ and $i \neq j$.

3   Publicly Verifiable SSE Based on Accumulator

In this section, we propose a publicly verifiable conjunctive keyword search scheme VEDB by utilizing RSA accumulator. We demonstrate the detailed construction in the following.

Our scheme consists of five algorithms $\Pi =$ (VEDBSetup, KeyGen, TokenGen, Search, Verify). In this construction, every keyword w is prime, and the "hash-to-prime" statement for keywords is omitted for clarity. We employ the BLS short signature [3] $\Pi_{\mathrm{BLS}} =$ (Gen, Sign, Vrfy) to generate and verify signatures. The following are the description of our scheme.

- VEDBSetup(λ, DB): The algorithm inputs a security parameter λ and a database DB, and then outputs key pairs {MK, PK} as well as a verifiable encrypted database VEDB. Initially, the data owner selects two safe primes p, q, and computes modulo $n = pq$. For pseudo-random functions (PRF), the data owner randomly selects K_X, K_I, K_Z for a PRF F_P and K_S, K_B for a PRF F. Additionally, the data owner generates signature key pair (K_B, kb) by algorithm BLS.Gen, where kb is the public key. Then the data owner randomly selects $g_a, g_1, g_2, g_3 \xleftarrow{\$} \mathbb{Z}_n^*$, $g \xleftarrow{\$} \mathbb{G}$. Eventually, the data owner sets the system master key MK $\leftarrow \{K_X, K_I, K_Z, K_S, p, q, g_1, g_2, g_3\}$ and public key PK $\leftarrow \{n, kb, g, g_a\}$.
- KeyGen(MK, $\mathbf{w}$): If keywords $\mathbf{w} = \{w_1, w_2, \ldots, w_N\}$ is accessible for a user, the data owner set $sk_{\mathbf{w}}^{(i)} = (g_i^{1/\prod_{j=1}^{N} w_j} \mod n)$, $i \in \{1, 2, 3\}$ and delegates key SK $= \{K_S, K_X, K_Z, sk_{\mathbf{w}}\}$ to the user.
- TokenGen(SK, $\bar{\mathbf{w}}$): When searching keywords $\bar{\mathbf{w}} = (w_1, \ldots, w_d)$, the authenticated user has to generate the corresponding token st first and send it to the server, where $d \leqslant N$. In this algorithm, w_1 is marked *sterm* while the remaining keywords are marked *xterms*.
- Search(st, VEDB, PK): Once receiving a search token st, the server first searches for w_1 and gets the result R_{w_1}, then gets the final result R by cross-matching with the rest of the keywords. The server, as a prover, provides corresponding proofs for different search results.
- Verify($stag_{w_1}$, pos, R_{w_1}, $proof_{1,2}$): Anyone can verify the correctness and completeness of search results[1] by verifying the signature and non-membership witness. In this algorithm, the user regenerates xtags for public verifiability. Finally, the algorithm outputs *Accept* or *Reject* to assert the server's honesty. In algorithm Verify, the verification depends on the search results, and the details are as follows:

---

[1] The verification in authenticated users can be boost if the data owner adds $\phi(n)$ into SK in Eq. (1).

Algorithm 1: Full Construction

VEDBSetup (DB, λ)
▷ Data Owner

1. TSet, XSet, Stag $\leftarrow \emptyset$
2. for $w \in W$ do
3. $K_e \leftarrow F(K_S, w)$
4. $e_w \leftarrow \emptyset; c \leftarrow 1$
5. $stag_w \leftarrow H(K_S, g_1^{1/w} \bmod n)$
6. $Stag \leftarrow Stag \cup \{stag_w\}$
7.   for $ind \in DB(w)$ do
8. $xind \leftarrow F_p(K_I, ind)$
9. $z \leftarrow F_p(K_Z, g_2^{1/w} \bmod n \parallel c)$
10. $l \leftarrow F(stag_w, c)$
11. $e \leftarrow \mathsf{Enc}(K_e, ind); y \leftarrow xind \cdot z^{-1}$
12. $TSet[l] = (e, y); \mathbf{e}_w \leftarrow \mathbf{e}_w \cup \{e\}$
13. $x \leftarrow F_p(K_X, g_3^{1/w} \bmod n)$
14. $XSet \leftarrow XSet \cup \{g^{x \cdot xind}\}$
15. $c \leftarrow c + 1$
16. $l_0 \leftarrow F(stag_w, 0)$
17. $\sigma_w \leftarrow \mathsf{BLS.Sign}(K_B, \mathbf{e}_w)$
18. $TSet[l_0] \leftarrow h_w$
19. $Acc(Stag) \leftarrow g_a^{\prod_{stag \in Stag}(H_p(stag))}$
20. $Acc(XSet) \leftarrow g_a^{\prod_{xtag \in XSet}(H_p(xtag))}$
21. $VEDB \leftarrow \{TSet, XSet, Stag, Acc(Stag), Acc(XSet)\}$
22. $MK \leftarrow \{K_S, K_B, K_I, K_Z, K_X, p, q, g_1, g_2, g_3\}$
23. $PK \leftarrow \{g, g_a, n, kb\}$
24. return $\{VEDB, MK, PK\}$

TokenGen (SK, $\bar{\mathbf{w}}$)
▷ User

1. $st, xtoken \leftarrow \emptyset$
2. $stag_{w_1} \leftarrow H_p(K_S, (sk_{\mathbf{w}}^{(1)})^{\prod_{w \in \mathbf{w} \setminus w_1} w} \bmod n)$
   $= H_p(K_S, g_1^{1/w_1} \bmod n)$
3. for $c = 1, 2, \ldots$ do   //traversal
4. $z \leftarrow F_p(K_Z, (sk_{\mathbf{w}}^{(2)})^{\prod_{w \in \mathbf{w} \setminus w_1} w} \bmod n \parallel c)$
   $= F_p(K_Z, g_2^{1/w_1} \bmod n \parallel c)$
5.   for $i = 2, \ldots, d$ do
6. $x \leftarrow F_p(K_X, (sk_{\mathbf{w}}^{(3)})^{\prod_{w \in \mathbf{w} \setminus w_i} w} \bmod n)$
   $= F_p(K_X, g_3^{1/w_i} \bmod n)$
7. $xtoken[c, i] \leftarrow g^{z \cdot x}$
8. $xtoken[c] = \{xtoken[c, j]\}_{j=2, \cdots, d}$
9. $st \leftarrow \{stag_{w_1}, xtoken[1], xtoken[2], \ldots\}$
10. return st

Search $(st, VEDB, PK)$
▷ Server

1. $R_{w_1}, R, Y, pos \leftarrow \emptyset$ //Phase 1
2. $l_0 \leftarrow F(stag_{w_1}, 0); \sigma_{w_1} \leftarrow TSet[l_0]$
3. for $c = 1, 2, \cdots$ do   //until find all
4. $l \leftarrow F(stag_{w_1}, c); (e_c, y_c) \leftarrow TSet[l]$
5. $R_{w_1} \leftarrow R_{w_1} \cup \{e_c\}$
6. if $R_{w_1} = \emptyset$ then
7. $proof_1 \leftarrow \hat{W}_{stag_{w_1}, Stag}$
8.   return $\{stag_{w_1}, proof_1\}$
9. $proof_1 \leftarrow \sigma_{w_1}$ //Phase 2
10. for $c = 1, \cdots, |R_{w_1}|$ do
11.   for $i = 2, \ldots, d$ do
12. $xtag \leftarrow xtoken[c, i]^{y_c}$
13.   if $xtag \notin XSet$ then
14. $Y \leftarrow Y \cup \{xtag\}$
15. $pos \leftarrow pos \cup \{(c, i)\}$ and **break**
16.   if $\forall i = 2, \cdots, d : xtag \in XSet$ then
17. $R \leftarrow R \cup \{e_c\}$
18. $proof_2 \leftarrow \hat{W}_{Y, XSet}$
19. return $\{R_{w_1}, R, pos, proof_{1,2}\}$

Verify$(stag_{w_1}, pos, R_{w_1}, proof_{1,2})$
▷ Verifier

1. if $R_{w_1} = \emptyset$ then   //Case 1
2.   return $\mathsf{VerNonMem}(Acc(Stag),$ $stag_{w_1}, proof_1)$
▷ User   //Case 2
3. $K_e \leftarrow F(K_S, w_1); Y \leftarrow \emptyset$
4. for $c = 1, \ldots, |R_{w_1}|$ do
5. $ind \leftarrow \mathsf{Dec}(K_e, e_c); xind \leftarrow F_p(K_I, ind)$
6.   for $i = 2, \ldots, d$ do
7.   if $(c, i) \in pos$ then
8. $xtag \leftarrow g^{F_p(K_X, g_3^{1/w_i} \bmod n) \cdot xind}$
9. $Y \leftarrow Y \cup \{xtag\}$
10. return $\{Y\}$
▷ Verifier
11. $res_1 \leftarrow \mathsf{BLS.Vrfy}(kb, R_{w_1}, proof_1)$
12. $res_2 \leftarrow \mathsf{VerNonMem}(Acc(XSet), Y, proof_2)$
13. if $res_{1,2} = True$ then
14.   return $Accept$
15. else
16.   return $Reject$

Case 1: If the result R_{w_1} is empty, the keyword w_1 is not in the database. The server returns $proof_1$ to the verifier and exits. The non-membership witness for w_1 is represented as $\hat{W}_{stag_{w_1}, Stag} = proof_1 = (a, B)_{stag_{w_1}}$, where

$$(a, b) \xleftarrow{\text{Bezout}} (\prod_{s \in Stag} s, stag_{w_1}), (a, B)_{stag_{w_1}} \leftarrow (a, g^b) \quad (2)$$

A verifier runs VerNonMem and checks whether the server is malicious by comparing the equality of $Acc(\text{Stag})^a * B^{\text{stag}_{w1}} \equiv g \bmod N$. Eventually, the verifier returns *Accept* if the equation passes, *Reject* if not.

Case 2: If $\mathsf{R}_{\mathsf{w}_1}$ is not empty, the server first provides the BLS signature as proof_1 for the completeness of $\mathsf{R}_{\mathsf{w}_1}$. Then the server traverses every identifier $e \in \mathsf{R}_{w_1}\backslash\mathsf{R}$ and finds out the first xtag is not in XSet. Then the server stores these xtags into set Y and generates the proof $\hat{\mathsf{W}}_{\mathsf{Y,XSet}} = \mathsf{proof}_2$.

$$(a,b) \xleftarrow{\textbf{Bezout}} (\prod_{s\in\text{XSet}} s, \prod_{y\in\mathsf{Y}} y), (a,B)_{\mathsf{Y}} \leftarrow (a, g^b) \tag{3}$$

The server also needs to provide the Y's positions in R_{w_1} and saves positions into pos which is used for the user to regenerate the data set Y. Finally, the server sends $\mathsf{R}_{w_1}, \mathsf{R}, \mathsf{pos}$ to the user, and $\mathsf{stag}_{w_1}, \mathsf{proof}_{1,2}$ to the verifier. Additionally, the user has to reconstruct xtags through pos and R_{w_1} and supply them to the verifier. The verifier checks the following two equations to verify the search results:

$$res_1 \leftarrow \text{BLS.Vrfy}(kb, \mathsf{R}_{w_1}, \mathsf{proof}_1)$$

$$res_2 \leftarrow Acc(\text{XSet})^a * B^{\prod_{y\in\mathsf{Y}} y} \equiv g \bmod N$$

If both res_1 and res_2 are True, the verifier asserts that the server is honest.

4   Security Analysis

In this section, we prove the security of our scheme under non-adaptive attacks by a simulation-based method and extend the security under adaptive one.

Theorem 1. *Provided leakage function $\mathcal{L}_{\text{VSSE}}$, scheme Π is $\mathcal{L}$-semantically secure under the strong RSA assumption in $\mathbb{G}$, symmetric algorithms (Enc, Dec) are IND-CPA secure and PRFs F, F_P are secure.*

Proof. The proof is made up of a series of games similar to [23,26]. At the start of games, adversary $\mathcal{A}$ provides a database DB and all search queries q. G_0 has the same uniform distribution as $\mathbf{Real}_{\mathcal{A}}^{\Pi}(\lambda)$ (assuming no false positives). With the leakage profile, the final game is designed to be easily simulated by an efficient simulator $\mathcal{S}$. Finally, the final game is identical to $\mathbf{Ideal}_{\mathcal{A},\mathcal{S}}^{\Pi}(\lambda)$. We argue that simulator $\mathcal{S}$ meets the security by demonstrating that the distributions of all games are computationally indistinguishable from one other. Referring to [23], we build the game for a similar TSet structure and additional leakage profiles. We present a query-optimized system model in which the client sends some **xtoken** arrays (T_c) to the server and knows when to stop.

Game G_0: G_0 defines essentially the same as real game $\mathbf{Real}_{\mathcal{A}}^{\Pi}(\lambda)$, except that we keep two arrays WPerms[w] and Stag[w] to record the order of keyword/document identifier pairs and stag related to every keyword. As a public parameter of the $\mathbf{Real}_{\mathcal{A}}^{\Pi}(\lambda)$, Stag[$w$] would not leak information to stag due to the feature of one-way functions $H(\cdot), H_p(\cdot)$. By running INITIALIZE on input $(\mathsf{DB}, \mathbf{w}, \mathbf{s}, \mathbf{x})$, the experiment simulates $\mathsf{VEDBSetup}(\lambda, \mathsf{DB})$ process. To obtain the transcript array $\mathbf{t}$ for $i \in [I]$, it creates the transcript $\mathbf{t}[i]$ by calling $\mathrm{TRANSGEN}(\mathsf{VEDB}, \mathsf{sk_w}, K_X, K_Z, \mathbf{s}[i], \mathbf{x}[i], Q_{\mathrm{stag}})$ and stores $\mathbf{t}[i]$ in an array $\mathbf{t}$. Note that we record every first occurred stag value into a set and lookup it to get the subsequent stag values but recomputing them: for every first $i \in [I]$, $Q_{\mathrm{stag}} \leftarrow \mathrm{stags}[\mathbf{s}[i]]$. The array $\mathbf{t}$ distributes as same as the real game $\mathbf{Real}_{\mathcal{A}}^{\Pi}(\lambda)$ except for the different methods to compute ResInds. Instead of decrypting ciphertext Res, the experiment gets the corresponding result by scanning the query. Therefore, we conclude that game G_0 has the same distribution as $\mathbf{Real}_{\mathcal{A}}^{\Pi}(\lambda)$ if, for all probabilistic polynomial-time (PPT) adversaries $\mathcal{A}$, there is a negligible function $\mathsf{negl}(\lambda)$ such that

$$\left| \Pr[G_0 = 1] - \Pr[\mathbf{Real}_{\mathcal{A}}^{\Pi}(\lambda) = 1] \right| \le \mathsf{negl}(\lambda)$$

Game G_1: G_1 is almost the same as G_0, except that we replace $F_p(K_X, \cdot)$, $F_p(K_I, \cdot)$, $F_p(K_Z, \cdot)$ with random functions $f_X(\cdot), f_I(\cdot), f_Z(\cdot)$. Function $F(K_S, \cdot)$ only evaluates once for the same input, so we replace it with a random selection with the same input range, i.e., random selection K_e. $\mathcal{A}_{1,1}, \mathcal{A}_{1,2}$ are two efficient adversaries who can distinguish the difference between F, F_p and random function with advantages $\mathsf{Adv}_{\mathcal{A}_{1,1}, F}^{\mathrm{prf}}(\lambda)$, $\mathsf{Adv}_{\mathcal{A}_{1,2}, F_p}^{\mathrm{prf}}(\lambda)$ respectively such that:

$$\left| \Pr[G_0 = 1] - \Pr[G_1 = 1] \right| \le \mathsf{Adv}_{\mathcal{A}_{1,1}, F}^{\mathrm{prf}}(\lambda) + 3\mathsf{Adv}_{\mathcal{A}_{1,2}, F_p}^{\mathrm{prf}}(\lambda)$$

Game G_2: G_2 is transformed from G_1. In G_2, the document identifiers encryption consists of a series of encryption towards a constant string $\{0\}^{\lambda}$. Given the IND-CPA security for encryption scheme Σ run in polynomial $poly(k)$ times, we declare an efficient adversary $\mathcal{A}_2$ such that

$$\left| \Pr[G_2 = 1] - \Pr[G_1 = 1] \right| \le poly(k) \cdot \mathsf{Adv}_{\mathcal{A}_2, \Sigma}^{\mathrm{ind\text{-}cpa}}(\lambda)$$

Game G_3: G_3 is exactly the same as G_2 with the change of XSet and **xtoken**. This experiment firstly computes all possible **xtoken** combinations of keywords and document identifiers and stores them in an array H represented as $H[w, \mathrm{ind}] \leftarrow H_p(g^{f_X(g_3^{1/w} \bmod n) \cdot f_I(\mathrm{ind})})$. For **xtoken** values in transcripts but not corresponding to possible matches, the experiment generates and stores these values in another array named Y. Function $\mathrm{TRANSGEN}$ takes arrays H and Y as input and returns the same output for the same **xtoken** values, which acts as the previous game.

In G_2, function $\mathrm{TRNASGEN}(c)$ generates xtoken value **xtoken**$[c]$ with unit item $\mathbf{xtoken}[c, j] \leftarrow g^{f_Z(g_2^{1/\mathbf{s}[i]} \bmod n \| c) \cdot f_X(g_3^{1/\mathbf{x}[i,j]} \bmod n)}$, and $c \in [1, \cdots, T_c]$ and j represents the index of keyword in xterm $\mathbf{x}[i]$. In this game, function $\mathrm{TRNASGEN}$ lookups $\sigma = \mathrm{WPerms}[\mathbf{s}[i]]$, TSet and $\mathsf{DB}[\mathbf{s}[i]] = (\mathrm{ind}_1, \cdots, \mathrm{ind}_{T_s})$ firstly. For $j \in [1, \cdots, |\mathbf{x}|]$ and $c \in [1, \cdots, T_s]$, it processes $l = F(Q_{\mathrm{stag}}, c)$

and fetches (e, y) through $\text{TSet}[l]$, where $y = f_I(\text{ind}_{\sigma[c]}) \cdot f_Z(g_2^{1/\mathbf{s}[i]} \bmod n \| c)^{-1}$, then $\mathbf{xtoken}[c, j] = H[\text{ind}_{\sigma[c]}, \mathbf{x}[i, j]^{1/y}]$. For $T_s < c \leqslant T_c$, the $\mathbf{xtoken}[c, j] = Y[\mathbf{s}[i], \mathbf{x}[j], c]$. In above cases, the $\mathbf{xtoken}[c, j]$ is represents as $g^{f_Z(g_2^{1/\mathbf{s}[i]} \bmod n \| c) \cdot f_X(g_3^{1/\mathbf{x}[i,j]} \bmod n)}$, and we have

$$\Pr[G_3 = 1] = \Pr[G_2 = 1]$$

Game G_4: G_4 replaces the value $y \leftarrow \text{xind} \cdot z^{-1}$ with $y \xleftarrow{\$} \mathbb{Z}_p^*$ shown in G_3. And the uniform random function f_Z runs only once and outputs an independent distribution, so the value y depends on its randomness. Therefore, the distribution of y is not affected by the replacement and

$$\Pr[G_4 = 1] = \Pr[G_3 = 1]$$

Game G_5: In G_5, values in H and Y are sampled randomly from $\mathbb{G}$ rather than computed in G_4. In addition, both arrays can treat as DDH tuples. We assume an efficient adversary $\mathcal{A}_5$ with the advantage $\mathsf{Adv}_{\mathcal{A}_5,\mathbb{G}}^{\text{DDH}}(\lambda)$ exists, and we have

$$\left| \Pr[G_5 = 1] - \Pr[G_4 = 1] \right| \leq \mathsf{Adv}_{\mathcal{A}_5,\mathbb{G}}^{\text{DDH}}(\lambda)$$

Game G_6: G_6 replaces the XSETSETUP algorithm in G_5. In G_5, array H can be accessed by functions XSETSETUP and TRANSGEN. Note that the algorithm XSETSETUP will not repeatedly access H. For a given index (w, ind) of H, the experiment test whether TRANSGEN access the position only. Additionally, only positions of H satisfying the condition $\text{ind} \in \mathsf{DB}[\mathbf{s}[i]] \wedge \mathbf{x}[i, j] = w$ will be accessed for specific i and j, while others are assigned to random values. So the distribution will not be altered that

$$\Pr[G_6 = 1] = \Pr[G_5 = 1]$$

Game G_7: In G_7, TRANSGEN only reacts to the repetitive access to H and computes the related $\mathbf{xtoken}$. To inspect the repeated requests to H, this experiment needs to check whether XSETSETUP has accessed the given index, or TRANSGEN will request again. In G_7, the computation of $\mathbf{xtoken}$ splits into three categories. For positions in H as the first type, they satisfies $\text{ind} \in \mathsf{DB}[\mathbf{s}[i]] \wedge \mathbf{x}[i, j] = w$, the same as XSETSETUP. For the second condition, some inds are shown in different queries, utilizing the repeated access in TRANSGEN. This experiment sends random values to the remaining elements of H. Because the repeated access values are not changed, the distribution of H remains the same so that

$$\Pr[G_7 = 1] = \Pr[G_6 = 1]$$

Simulator: The simulator $\mathcal{S}$ receives leakage $\mathcal{L}_{VSSE} = (K, N, \bar{\mathbf{s}}, \mathsf{SP}, \mathsf{RP}, \mathsf{SRP}, \mathsf{IP})$ and outputs encrypted database VEDB and transcripts $\mathbf{t}$. We demonstrate that the simulator satisfies the criteria in the theorem by providing that it creates the same distribution as G_7 and associating the relationship between previous games. Note that the simulator computes a set named $\hat{\mathbf{x}}$, the restricted equality pattern of $\mathbf{x}$.

Firstly, $\mathcal{S}$ computes the restricted equality pattern $\hat{\mathbf{x}}$ with IP. Suppose there exists ind, i, j such that ind $\in \mathsf{DB}[\mathbf{s}[i]] \bigcap \mathsf{DB}[\mathbf{s}[j]]$, and $\mathcal{S}$ can learn the equivalence of $\mathbf{x}[i, \alpha]$ and $\mathbf{x}[j, \beta]$ through checking if $H[\mathbf{x}[i, \alpha], \text{ind}]$ is equivalent to $H[\mathbf{x}[j, \beta], \text{ind}]$. Then $\mathcal{S}$ can construct a lookup table $\hat{\mathbf{x}}[i, \alpha]$ as $\hat{\mathbf{x}}[i, \alpha] = \hat{\mathbf{x}}[j, \beta]$ if and only if $\mathrm{IP}[i, j, \alpha, \beta] \neq \emptyset$. We can easily obtain these two equations $\mathbf{x}[i, \alpha] = \mathbf{x}[j, \beta]$ and $\hat{\mathbf{x}}[i, \alpha] = \hat{\mathbf{x}}[j, \beta]$ by $\hat{\mathbf{x}}[i, \alpha] = \hat{\mathbf{x}}[j, \beta]$ and $(\mathbf{x}[i, \alpha] = \mathbf{x}[j, \beta]) \wedge (\mathsf{DB}(\mathbf{s}[i]) \cap \mathsf{DB}(\mathbf{s}[j]) \neq \emptyset)$ respectively. $\mathcal{S}$ builds TSet using $\hat{\mathbf{x}}$, RP and SP by populating with H, WPerms[SP[$\hat{s}$]] and Stag[$\hat{s}$]. Compared to G_7, which fills all TSet elements, $\mathcal{S}$ only records positions meeting $w \in \bar{\mathbf{s}}$ and generates the corresponding accumulator values. To be consistent with the number of keywords, $\mathcal{S}$ appends random elements into TSet(including accumulator values) till the accumulator value and the capacity of TSet reach N and K respectively. It is hard to distinguish between G_7 and $\mathcal{S}$ towards the distribution of TSet.

The setup of XSet is similar to TSet. $\mathcal{S}$ stores positions as $H(w, id)$ satisfying ind $\in \bigcup_{(i, \alpha): \hat{\mathbf{x}} = w} \mathrm{RP}[i, \alpha]$ and $w \in \hat{\mathbf{x}}$. Then it appends random values until the size of XSet reaches N. The distribution of TSet is also indistinguishable between G_7 and $\mathcal{S}$.

For search tokens, we shall demonstrate that the **xtoken** computations in G_7 and $\mathcal{S}$ are by accessing the identical places in H. Especially, G_7 and $\mathcal{S}$ access by the following conditions: (1) ind is one of the intersections of $\mathsf{DB}(\mathbf{s}[i]) \cap \mathsf{DB}(\mathbf{x}[i, j])$; (2) elements will be repeated access to another query. Analogously, $\mathcal{S}$ has restricted access of document identifiers in result R, equal to the capacity of identifiers that match conditions: (1) by using RP; (2) by using IP.

To generate the transcript, $\mathcal{S}$ computes ResInds by RP and SRP, which means that it consists of identifiers in the intersection of RP and SRP.   □

Theorem 2. *Scheme Π is $\mathcal{L}$-semantically secure against adaptive attacks under the DDH assumption in $\mathbb{G}$, while PRFs F and F_P are secure and symmetric algorithms (Enc, Dec) are IND-CPA secure.*

Proof. Similar to [7], the simulator selects several elements of XSet at first and initializes array H adaptively. Due to page constraints, we skip the description.   □

5   Performance Analysis

In this section, we compare our scheme with two existing verifiable schemes [11,26]. Without loss of generality, we focus on time-consuming operations such as exponentiation and pairing.

Table 2 demonstrates the comparison of these VSSE schemes. To begin with, these schemes support multi-user and conjunctive keyword search. All compared schemes have the exact search computation as the base scheme [23]. We assume the search results R_{w_1} and R are not empty in the verification phase. Note that

Table 2. Performance comparison

Schemes	Scheme [26]	Scheme [11]	Our Scheme
EDBSetup	$(|DB| + 3|W| + 2)E$	$(|DB| + 2|W|)E + (|DB| + |W|)C$	$|DB|(sE + H_p) + |W|(3E + H_p)$
TokenGen	$|R_{w_1}|(d-1)E + (d+1)E$	$|R_{w_1}|(d-1)E + (d+1)E$	$|R_{w_1}|dE$
Search	$|R_{w_1}|(d-1)E$	$|R_{w_1}|dE + |DB|C$	$|R_{w_1}|d(E + H_p)$
Verification	Private and Probabilistic	Private and Deterministic	Public and Deterministic
Verify(Prover)	$(|DB| - |R|)E + k|DB|E$	$(|DB| - |R|)C + |R_{w_1}|\,\|DB|E$	$|R_{w_1}|(H_p + M) + |DB|M$
Verify(Verifier)	$3E + 4P + k(2E + 2P)$	$2C + |R_{w_1}|(2E + C)$	$|R_{w_1}\backslash R|(2E + H_p) + E$

E: an exponentiation operation; P: a pairing operation; H_p: a hash-to-prime operation; $|DB|$: the capacity of all keyword-document pairs in a database; $|R_{w_1}|$: the amount of search result for w_1; $|R|$: the amount of search result for queried keywords; d: the amount of keywords searched; k: the amount of identifiers chosen for completeness verification in [26]; C: the generation (*resp.* insertion and search) operation of a Cuckoo Filter; M: the multiplication operation in RSA accumulator.

scheme [26] can fail to verify due to its sampling method. Furthermore, our scheme supports public verification with one more interaction between the client and verifier. The computation overhead in Search algorithm is mainly from multiplication operation which is much faster than exponentiation. In algorithm Verify, our computation overhead is $\mathcal{O}(|R_{w_1}\backslash R|)$, so the verification performance relies on the search results and is slower than [26]. The scheme [11] shifts the large computation overheads in the server to users, which provides a fast proof generation speed and slow verification speed. The scheme [11] shifts the server's large computation overheads to users, providing a fast proof creation speed but a poor verification time. Table 3 indicates the communication cost during the verification phase. We list the communication comparison under different search results. Our scheme and [26] achieve a low communication overhead, while [11] needs to transfer the cuckoo filters in the scheme.

Table 3. Communication comparison in verification

Schemes	Scheme [26]	Scheme [11]	Our Scheme
$R_{w_1} = \emptyset$	$3|\mathbb{G}| + 3k|\mathbb{G}|$	$|CF| + |ECF|$	$5|\mathbb{G}| + |\mathbb{Z}|$
$R_{w_1} \neq \emptyset$	$3|\mathbb{G}| + 3k|\mathbb{G}|$	$|CF| + |ECF|$	$8|\mathbb{G}| + |\mathbb{Z}|$

$|\mathbb{G}|$ (*resp.* $|\mathbb{Z}|$): the length of a element in $\mathbb{G}$ (*resp.* $\mathbb{Z}$); $|CF|$: the size of a cuckoo filter; $|ECF|$: the size of an encrypted cuckoo filter.

6   Conclusion

In this work, we present an efficient verifiable conjunctive keyword SSE scheme. Our scheme supports public and private verification for different scenarios by utilizing RSA accumulator. Moreover, our scheme enjoys constant-size public parameters. Then, we provide formal proofs that our scheme is secure against a malicious server. Finally, we comprehensively compare our scheme with others and conclude that ours achieves a balance between communication and computation overheads. To further meet dynamic requirements, it is challenging to consider both forward and backward security while supporting verification when extending to dynamic scenarios, so we leave constructing a dynamic VSSE scheme to be the future work.

Acknowledgments. This work was supported by the National Natural Science Foundation of China (No. 62072357), the Key Research and Development Program of Shaanxi (No. 2022KWZ-01), the Fundamental Research Funds for the Central Universities (Nos. JB211503 and YJS2212).

References

1. Ali, M., Sadeghi, M., Liu, X., Miao, Y., Vasilakos, A.V.: Verifiable online/offline multi-keyword search for cloud-assisted industrial internet of things. J. Inf. Secur. Appl. **65**, 103101 (2022)
2. Azraoui, M., Elkhiyaoui, K., Önen, M., Molva, R.: Publicly verifiable conjunctive keyword search in outsourced databases. In: CNS 2015, pp. 619–627. IEEE (2015)
3. Boneh, D., Lynn, B., Shacham, H.: Short signatures from the Weill pairing. J. Cryptol. **17**(4), 297–319 (2004)
4. Bost, R., Fouque, P., Pointcheval, D.: Verifiable dynamic symmetric searchable encryption: optimality and forward security. IACR Cryptol. ePrint Arch. 62 (2016)
5. Bost, R., Minaud, B., Ohrimenko, O.: Forward and backward private searchable encryption from constrained cryptographic primitives. In: CCS 2017, pp. 1465–1482. ACM (2017)
6. Cash, D., et al.: Dynamic searchable encryption in very-large databases: data structures and implementation. In: NDSS 2014. The Internet Society (2014)
7. Cash, D., Jarecki, S., Jutla, C., Krawczyk, H., Roşu, M.-C., Steiner, M.: Highly-scalable searchable symmetric encryption with support for Boolean queries. In: Canetti, R., Garay, J.A. (eds.) CRYPTO 2013. LNCS, vol. 8042, pp. 353–373. Springer, Heidelberg (2013). https://doi.org/10.1007/978-3-642-40041-4_20
8. Cash, D., Tessaro, S.: The locality of searchable symmetric encryption. In: Nguyen, P.Q., Oswald, E. (eds.) EUROCRYPT 2014. LNCS, vol. 8441, pp. 351–368. Springer, Heidelberg (2014). https://doi.org/10.1007/978-3-642-55220-5_20
9. Chai, Q., Gong, G.: Verifiable symmetric searchable encryption for semi-honest-but-curious cloud servers. In: ICC 2012, pp. 917–922. IEEE (2012)
10. Curtmola, R., Garay, J.A., Kamara, S., Ostrovsky, R.: Searchable symmetric encryption: improved definitions and efficient constructions. In: CCS 2006, pp. 79–88. ACM (2006)
11. Fan, C., Dong, X., Cao, Z., Shen, J.: VCKSCF: efficient verifiable conjunctive keyword search based on cuckoo filter for cloud storage. In: TrustCom 2020, pp. 285–292. IEEE (2020)
12. George, M., Kamara, S., Moataz, T.: Structured encryption and dynamic leakage suppression. In: Canteaut, A., Standaert, F.-X. (eds.) EUROCRYPT 2021. LNCS, vol. 12698, pp. 370–396. Springer, Cham (2021). https://doi.org/10.1007/978-3-030-77883-5_13
13. Goh, E.: Secure indexes. IACR Cryptology ePrint Archive, p. 216 (2003)

14. Golle, P., Staddon, J., Waters, B.: Secure conjunctive keyword search over encrypted data. In: Jakobsson, M., Yung, M., Zhou, J. (eds.) ACNS 2004. LNCS, vol. 3089, pp. 31–45. Springer, Heidelberg (2004). https://doi.org/10.1007/978-3-540-24852-1_3
15. Jarecki, S., Jutla, C.S., Krawczyk, H., Rosu, M., Steiner, M.: Outsourced symmetric private information retrieval. In: CCS 2013, pp. 875–888. ACM (2013)
16. Kamara, S., Moataz, T.: SQL on structurally-encrypted databases. In: Peyrin, T., Galbraith, S. (eds.) ASIACRYPT 2018. LNCS, vol. 11272, pp. 149–180. Springer, Cham (2018). https://doi.org/10.1007/978-3-030-03326-2_6
17. Kamara, S., Papamanthou, C., Roeder, T.: Dynamic searchable symmetric encryption. In: CCS 2012, pp. 965–976. ACM (2012)
18. Kurosawa, K., Ohtaki, Y.: How to construct UC-secure searchable symmetric encryption scheme. IACR Cryptology ePrint Archive, p. 251 (2015)
19. Li, J., Li, N., Xue, R.: Universal accumulators with efficient nonmembership proofs. In: Katz, J., Yung, M. (eds.) ACNS 2007. LNCS, vol. 4521, pp. 253–269. Springer, Heidelberg (2007). https://doi.org/10.1007/978-3-540-72738-5_17
20. Ogata, W., Kurosawa, K.: Efficient no-dictionary verifiable searchable symmetric encryption. In: Kiayias, A. (ed.) FC 2017. LNCS, vol. 10322, pp. 498–516. Springer, Cham (2017). https://doi.org/10.1007/978-3-319-70972-7_28
21. Soleimanian, A., Khazaei, S.: Publicly verifiable searchable symmetric encryption based on efficient cryptographic components. Des. Codes Cryptogr. **87**(1), 123–147 (2018). https://doi.org/10.1007/s10623-018-0489-y
22. Song, D.X., Wagner, D.A., Perrig, A.: Practical techniques for searches on encrypted data. In: IEEE S&P 2000, pp. 44–55. IEEE Computer Society (2000)
23. Sun, S.-F., Liu, J.K., Sakzad, A., Steinfeld, R., Yuen, T.H.: An efficient non-interactive multi-client searchable encryption with support for Boolean queries. In: Askoxylakis, I., Ioannidis, S., Katsikas, S., Meadows, C. (eds.) ESORICS 2016. LNCS, vol. 9878, pp. 154–172. Springer, Cham (2016). https://doi.org/10.1007/978-3-319-45744-4_8
24. Sun, W., Liu, X., Lou, W., Hou, Y.T., Li, H.: Catch you if you lie to me: Efficient verifiable conjunctive keyword search over large dynamic encrypted cloud data. In: INFOCOM 2015, pp. 2110–2118. IEEE (2015)
25. Tong, Q., Miao, Y., Weng, J., Liu, X., Choo, K.K.R., Deng, R.: Verifiable fuzzy multi-keyword search over encrypted data with adaptive security. IEEE Trans. Knowl. Data Eng. 1 (2022). https://doi.org/10.1109/TKDE.2022.3152033
26. Wang, J., Chen, X., Sun, S.-F., Liu, J.K., Au, M.H., Zhan, Z.-H.: Towards efficient verifiable conjunctive keyword search for large encrypted database. In: Lopez, J., Zhou, J., Soriano, M. (eds.) ESORICS 2018. LNCS, vol. 11099, pp. 83–100. Springer, Cham (2018). https://doi.org/10.1007/978-3-319-98989-1_5

A Secure and Efficient Certificateless Authenticated Key Agreement Scheme for Smart Healthcare

Yuqian Ma, Yongliu Ma, Yidan Liu, and Qingfeng Cheng[✉]

Strategic Support Force Information Engineering University,
Zhengzhou 450001, China
qingfengc2008@sina.com

Abstract. Smart healthcare plays a vital role in contemporary society while its security and privacy issues remain critical challenges. With the aim of resolving problems related to the integrity and confidentiality of information transmitted in the smart healthcare, Wang et al. designed a certificateless authenticated key agreement (CL-AKA) scheme recently. However, we analyze their protocol and prove that theirs did not satisfy forward security. Further, this paper proposes an improved authenticated key agreement (AKA) scheme based on the certificateless cryptography. The proposed CL-AKA scheme does not only satisfy the security requirements in smart healthcare networks but also performs more efficient. The performance comparison shows our scheme has comparable efficiency in terms of computation cost.

Keywords: Certificateless authenticated key agreement (CL-AKA) · Scyther · Smart healthcare

1 Introduction

More and more attention has been paid on the medical infrastructure since people ask for higher medical quality and more convenient service. As one of the most promising applications based on the Internet of Things (IoT), smart healthcare system, a self-organizing network realizes the interaction among patients, medical staff, hospitals and medical equipment. However, its communications are conducted through open wireless channels which makes the networks vulnerable to various attacks, such as man-in-the-middle attacks and ephemeral key leakage attacks.

Since users may outsource their sensitive information to servers to alleviate the heavy overheads, secure communications over the public channel are important. Aiming at secure data storage, Chenam and Ali [1] proposed an encryption scheme based on certificateless public key authentication to resist keyword guessing attacks. Besides, to aid security and efficiency, Shiraly et al. [2] first designed a security model facing multi-servers and then proposed a certificateless public key encryption scheme with keyword search proved secure under the

X. Chen et al. (Eds.): CSS 2022, LNCS 13547, pp. 17–31, 2022.
https://doi.org/10.1007/978-3-031-18067-5_2

security model they described. To tackle the problem of mutual authentication in the process of data transmission, Turkanović et al. [3] designed a user authentication and key agreement scheme focusing on the wireless sensor networks. However, Farash et al. [4] pointed out that the scheme of Turkanović et al. was susceptible to several shortcomings mainly threatening the identities of users. Further, they [4] proposed an improved protocol tackling and eliminating the security shortcomings of the previous one.

Because of the high bandwidth of mobile communication, lightweight cryptography was proposed to satisfy the urgent requirement of high communication efficiency. In 2016, Gope et al. [5] proposed a realistic lightweight anonymous user authentication protocol in wireless networks. However, in 2019, Adavoudi-Jolfaei et al. [6] showed that in Gope et al.'s scheme the adversary could obtain the session key under the Dolev-Yao model [7]. Further, they designed a lightweight and anonymous three-factor authentication and access control scheme for real-time applications. But one year later, Ryu et al. [8] found the weaknesses of Adavoudi et al.'s protocol including insider attacks, user impersonation attacks, and session key attacks. To address these problems, they proposed a three-factor authentication scheme based on hash function and XOR.

AI-Riyami and Paterson [9] firstly introduced certificateless public key cryptography (CL-PKC) in 2003. Once the concept was proposed, adopted widely has it been to expand authenticated key agreement (AKA) protocols because of the two advantages this scheme possesses. First, CL-PKC is capable of static private key leakage resistance since the full private key is composed of two parts, one generated by key generation center (KGC) and the other generated by the user. Second, few computation resource is needed by CL-PKC which is required urgently in the Internet of Things.

Mandt et al. [10] improved the efficiency of AI-Riyami et al.'s scheme based on the bilinear Diffie-Hellman problem. Wang et al. [11] also pointed out that the efficiency of AI-Riyami et al.'s scheme was low since it at least required a paring evaluation computed on-line. Thus, Wang et al. proposed a certificateless authenticated key agreement (CL-AKA) protocol for Web client/server setting. Later, Hou and Xu [12] found that the scheme could not resist key compromised impersonation attacks, man-in-the-middle attacks and key replicating attacks.

Because of the advantages of CL-PKC, it has been applied in various environments. Asari et al. [13] utilized CL-PKC in automatic dependent surveillance-broadcast (ADS-B) systems and designed a certificateless authentication protocol resolving the privacy problem. In vehicular ad hoc networks (VANETs), both privacy and efficiency are necessary. A certificateless conditional anonymous authentication scheme was investigated by Samra et al. [14] for softwares in VANETs. Also, patients' diagnosis information plays a vital role in wireless body area network (WBAN) which motivates designers to find resolutions. Cheng et al. [15] designed a CL-AKA for cloud-enabled WBAN based on ECDL assumption.

Recently, considering the drawbacks of existing AKA protocols, Wang et al. [17] designed a computation-transferable AKA scheme without an online registration center for smart healthcare networks. Nevertheless, in this paper, the shortcomings of Wang et al.'s scheme will be illustrated, proving that theirs could not satisfy the forward security.

The main contributions of this paper are summarized specifically as follows.

- Recently, Wang et al. [17] proposed an AKA protocol, denoted as WHX protocol, for smart healthcare and claimed that it satisfied security and privacy protection requirements. However, an effective attack on WHX protocol is presented, which proves that WHX protocol does not satisfy the forward security.
- To remedy the shortcoming we point out, a secure and efficient CL-AKA scheme is designed which can resist common attacks and achieve mutual authentication as well as key agreement.
- Security analysis claims that the proposed scheme can satisfy security properties required urgently in smart healthcare environment. Performance evaluation and comparison demonstrated in Sect. 6 shows that the design scheme can behave better than other related schemes.

The arrangement of this paper is following. The security model is presented in Sect. 2. In Sect. 3, a brief review of the WHX protocol is presented. Then a specific security analysis of WHX protocol is presented in this section as well. In Sect. 4, the detailed procedures of the proposed scheme are illustrated. Following is the security analysis in Sect. 5. Performance evaluation and comparison are presented in Sect. 6. Finally, Sect. 7 provides some concluding remarks.

2   Security Model

For discussing the security of the proposed scheme, here, we introduce a security model suitable for the CL-AKA setting based on [16]. In particular, let $\mathcal{A}$ and Π_Γ^φ be a probabilistic polynomial time adversary and φth instance of a participant Γ, respectively. There exist two types of adversaries, denoted as $\mathcal{A}_1$ and $\mathcal{A}_2$. The main difference between them is that $\mathcal{A}_1$ does not have the ability of knowing the master key but can replace the public keys of any participant with selected values while $\mathcal{A}_2$ has the ability of learning the master key but can not replace the public keys of participants.

The security of the proposed scheme is defined based on a game executed between $\mathcal{A}$ and a challenger $\mathcal{C}$. In the game, the abilities of $\mathcal{A}$ are described by several kinds of queries answered by $\mathcal{C}$ shown in Table 1.

After making a Test-query towards an instance Π_Γ^φ, $\mathcal{A}$ can also make queries towards Π_Γ^φ or to the matching session (if it exists) except Reveal-query and Corrupt-query towards the potential partner. Finally, $\mathcal{A}$ should output a guess result c'. If $c' = c$, then $\mathcal{A}$ wins the game.

Definition. A CL-AKA protocol is secure if any session instance Π_Γ^φ satisfies:

- achieving the same session key with its matching session.
- making sure that the advantage $Advantage_\mathcal{A}(\Pi_\Gamma^\varphi) = |2P[c' = c] - 1|$ is negligible for any $\mathcal{A}$.

Table 1. Description of the abilities of adversary

Queries	Description
H_i-query	If C receives the query with m_i, it verifies if (m_i, H_i) exists in the list L_{H_i}. If so, the challenger returns H_i to A; otherwise, C selects a random number H_i, adds (m_i, H_i) to L_{H_i}, and returns H_i to A
Create-query	If C receives the query with a party Γ's identity ID_Γ, it creates Γ's private and public key pair
Send-query	If C receives the query with a session instance Π_Γ^φ and the message m, it returns the corresponding response to A according to the proposed scheme
Reveal-query	If C receives the query with a party Γ's identity ID_Γ, it returns the session key of Π_Γ^φ to A
Corrupt-query	If C receives the query with a session instance Π_Γ^φ, it returns Γ's private key to A
Ephemeral-query	If C receives the query with a session instance Π_Γ^φ, it returns Γ's ephemeral private key to A
Test-query	If C receives the query with a session instance Π_Γ^φ, it chooses c randomly in $\{0,1\}$. If $c = 1$, it returns the session key of Π_Γ^φ to A; otherwise, it returns a random string with the same distribution of the session key to A

3   Review and Cryptanalysis of WHX AKA Protocol

In this section, we review the process of WHX AKA protocol [17] briefly, including initialization, registration, and authentication and key agreement three phases. The notations used in this paper are listed in Table 2.

3.1   Review of WHX AKA Protocol

Let q be a large prime number. The system is initialized by RC. First, it chooses a non-singular elliptic curve $E(F_q)$ and an additive group $\mathbb{G}$ over it. The generator of $\mathbb{G}$ is P whose order is q. RC then chooses s randomly in Z_q^*, computes $P_{pub} = sP$ and selects eight hash functions $H_i : \{0,1\}^* \rightarrow \{0,1\}^l$, $(i = 0, 1, ..., 7)$. Finally, it keeps the master key s as a secret and publishes the system parameters $\{q, P, \mathbb{G}, P_{pub}, H_i(i = 0, 1, ..., 7)\}$.

Before communicating, users and edge servers need to register with RC through a secure channel to get their static private key and corresponding public key. For a comprehensive process, readers can refer to the original paper [17].

After registering successfully with RC, U_i and ES can start to authenticate each other and negotiate about the session key. The detailed steps are as follows:

– U_i selects $a \in Z_q^*$ randomly and computes u, A, η. Then U_i sends the message $M_1 = \{u, A, \eta, T_i\}$ to ES where T_i is the current timestamp.

Table 2. Notations

Notation	Description
RC	The registration center responsible for the initialization and registration phases
ES	The edge server located at the edge of the network and providing service for users
U	Resource-constrained users
P	The generator of the additive group $\mathbb{G}$
s	The master key of RC
P_{pub}	The public key of RC
H_i	The hash functions, where $i = 0, ..., 7$
$ID_{U(ES)}$	The real identity of U_i/ES
$(s_{U(ES)}, x_{U(ES)})$	The static private key of U_i/ES
$(R_{U(ES)}, X_{U(ES)})$	The static public key of U_i/ES

- ES checks the freshness of T_i and the validation of η. If holds, ES chooses $b \in E_q^*$ randomly and calculates v, V, K_{ES}, SK_{ES} and ω, where the timestamp is denoted as T_j. Next, ES sends the message $M_2 = \{V, \omega, T_j\}$ to U_i.
- U_i verifies whether T_i is fresh. If successes, U_i computes K_U, SK_U. Further, U_i checks ω. If holds, it calculates λ and sends the message $M_3 = \{\lambda\}$ to ES.
- Finally, ES tests the correctness of λ.

3.2 Cryptanalysis of WHX AKA Protocol

In this subsection, we present that WHX protocol can not satisfy the requirement of forward security. If the private key of user U_i is compromised, the adversary $\mathcal{A}$ will recover the session key easily through the steps below:

Step 1. In the authentication and key agreement phase, $\mathcal{A}$ eavesdrops the message sent from U_i to ES, $M_1 = \{u, A, \eta, T_i\}$.

Step 2. $\mathcal{A}$ eavesdrops the message sent from ES to U_i, $M_2 = \{V, \omega, T_j\}$.

Step 3. After the session is completed, $\mathcal{A}$ launches Reveal-query towards the user U_i to gain its private secret keys (s_U, x_U).

Step 4. After obtaining the parameters above, $\mathcal{A}$ can easily compute $a = u - x_U$, $PID_U' = A \oplus H_3(u \cdot X_{ES})$. Then, $\mathcal{A}$ can extract K_U' by $K_U' = s_U \cdot (V - X_{ES}) + a \cdot [R_{ES} + H_2(ID_{ES} \| R_{ES}) P_{pub}]$, where X_{ES}, R_{ES}, P_{pub} are the public keys. Finally, $\mathcal{A}$ can compute the session key according to the way generating $SK_U = H_5(K_U' \| ID_{ES} \| PID_U' \| X_U \| X_{ES})$.

Thus, in this way, adversary $\mathcal{A}$ can recover the session key. According to the steps above, we can see that the adversary merely gets the private keys of user, which is accordant with the definition of weak forward security. Besides, although the real identity of the patients is unknown to the public, the PID_U can still be accessed easily, which means that WHX protocol can not resist traceability.

4   The Improved Scheme

We present a detailed description of the improved AKA scheme in this section. There are three phases involved in our scheme, which are the initialization phase, the registration phase, the authentication and key agreement phase, respectively. The details are described as follows.

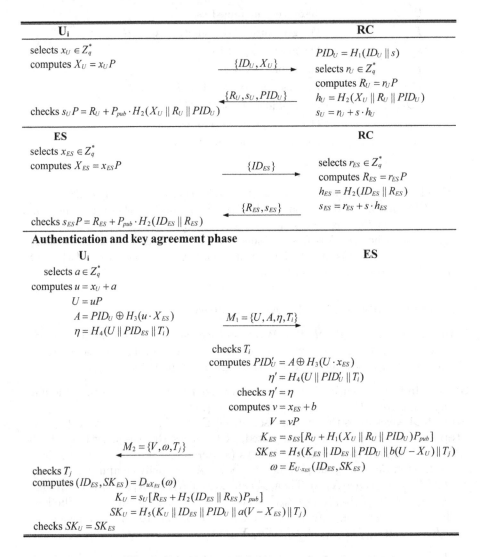

U_i		RC
selects $x_U \in Z_q^*$		$PID_U = H_1(ID_U \| s)$
computes $X_U = x_U P$	$\xrightarrow{\{ID_U, X_U\}}$	selects $r_U \in Z_q^*$
		computes $R_U = r_U P$
	$\xleftarrow{\{R_U, s_U, PID_U\}}$	$h_U = H_2(X_U \| R_U \| PID_U)$
checks $s_U P = R_U + P_{pub} \cdot H_2(X_U \| R_U \| PID_U)$		$s_U = r_U + s \cdot h_U$

ES		RC
selects $x_{ES} \in Z_q^*$		selects $r_{ES} \in Z_q^*$
computes $X_{ES} = x_{ES} P$	$\xrightarrow{\{ID_{ES}\}}$	computes $R_{ES} = r_{ES} P$
		$h_{ES} = H_2(ID_{ES} \| R_{ES})$
	$\xleftarrow{\{R_{ES}, s_{ES}\}}$	$s_{ES} = r_{ES} + s \cdot h_{ES}$
checks $s_{ES} P = R_{ES} + P_{pub} \cdot H_2(ID_{ES} \| R_{ES})$		

Authentication and key agreement phase

U_i		ES
selects $a \in Z_q^*$		
computes $u = x_U + a$		
$\quad U = uP$		
$\quad A = PID_U \oplus H_3(u \cdot X_{ES})$	$\xrightarrow{M_1 = \{U, A, \eta, T_i\}}$	
$\quad \eta = H_4(U \| PID_{ES} \| T_i)$		
		checks T_i
		computes $PID'_U = A \oplus H_3(U \cdot x_{ES})$
		$\eta' = H_4(U \| PID'_U \| T_i)$
		checks $\eta' = \eta$
		computes $v = x_{ES} + b$
		$V = vP$
		$K_{ES} = s_{ES}[R_U + H_1(X_U \| R_U \| PID_U)P_{pub}]$
	$\xleftarrow{M_2 = \{V, \omega, T_j\}}$	$SK_{ES} = H_5(K_{ES} \| ID_{ES} \| PID_U \| b(U - X_U) \| T_j)$
checks T_j		$\omega = E_{U \cdot x_{ES}}(ID_{ES}, SK_{ES})$
computes $(ID_{ES}, SK_{ES}) = D_{u X_{ES}}(\omega)$		
$\quad K_U = s_U[R_{ES} + H_2(ID_{ES} \| R_{ES})P_{pub}]$		
$\quad SK_U = H_5(K_U \| ID_{ES} \| PID_U \| a(V - X_{ES}) \| T_j)$		
checks $SK_U = SK_{ES}$		

Fig. 1. Description of the improved scheme

4.1   Initialization Phase

Let l represent the length of the session key. RC, responsible for the initialization of the system, acts as the following steps:

- Selects an additive cyclic group $\mathbb{G}$ over a non-singular elliptic curve $E(F_p)$. The order of $\mathbb{G}$ is q, a large prime number, and the generator is P.
- Chooses a random number $s \in Z_q^*$ as its master key and calculates $P_{pub} = sP$.
- Selects five one-way hash functions $H_i (i = 1, 2, ..., 5)$.
- Keeps the master key s as a secret while publishes the system parameters $\{\mathbb{G}, q, P, P_{pub}, H_i\}$.

4.2   Registration Phase

Before beginning the authentication and key agreement, both the user and the edge server need to register with the RC in the off-line channel. A user U_i with its unique identity ID_U can register with RC according to the steps below:

- Selects $x_U \in Z_q^*$ randomly as the secret key and computes $X_U = x_U P$ and sends $\{ID_U, X_U\}$ to RC through a secure channel.
- On receiving $\{ID_U, X_U\}$, RC extracts $PID_U = H_1(ID_U \| s)$. Then it randomly selects $r_U \in Z_q^*$ and computes $R_U = r_U P$, $h_U = H_2(X_U \| R_U \| PID_U)$, $s_U = r_U + s \cdot h_U$. Then RC sends $\{R_U, s_U, PID_U\}$ to U_i, where s_U is the partial private key of U_i.
- U_i checks if $s_U P = R_U + H_2(X_U \| R_U \| PID_U)P_{pub}$ is true. If so, U_i securely stores (s_U, x_U) as its full private key and publishes (R_U, X_U).

Similarly, ES registers with RC, illustrated in Fig. 1.

4.3   Authentication and Key Agreement Phase

User U_i and ES authenticate mutually and agree on a session key for a secure communication. Figure 1 shows the authentication and key agreement phase in detail and the specific process is presented below:

- User U_i selects a random value $a \in Z_q^*$, then computes $u = x_U + a$, $U = u \cdot P$, $A = PID_U \oplus H_3(u \cdot X_{ES})$, and $\eta = H_4(U \| PID_U \| T_i)$, where T_i is the current timestamp. Then U_i sends $M_1 = \{U, A, \eta, T_i\}$ to ES.
- Upon receiving the message from U_i, ES first checks the validation of timestamp T_i. Then calculates $PID_U' = A \oplus H_3(x_{ES} \cdot U)$, $\eta' = H_4(U \| PID_U' \| T_i)$. Therefore, ES can validate the user's identity through η'. If the equation holds, ES chooses a random value $b \in Z_q^*$, then calculates $v = x_{ES} + b$, $V = v \cdot P$, $K_{ES} = s_{ES} \cdot [R_U + H_1(X_U \| R_U \| PID_U)P_{pub}]$, $SK_{ES} = H_5(K_{ES} \| ID_{ES} \| PID_U \| b \cdot (U - X_U) \| T_j)$, $\omega = E_{x_{ES}U}(ID_{ES})$. Then ES sends the message $M_2 = \{V, \omega, T_j\}$ to the patient user U_i, where T_j is the current timestamp.

- After receiving M_2, U_i first checks whether T_j has expired. Then U_i computes $(ID_{ES}) = D_{u_{X_{ES}}}(\omega)$ and checks the identity of server. If it holds, then U_i continues to calculates $K_U = s_U \cdot [R_{ES} + H_2(ID_{ES} \parallel R_{ES})P_{pub}]$, $SK_U = H_5(K_U \parallel ID_{ES} \parallel PID_U \parallel a \cdot (V - X_{ES}) \parallel T_j)$. Consequently, U_i and ES complete the authentication and key agreement phase.

Finally, U_i and ES successfully achieve the same session key since:

$$\begin{aligned} K_{ES} &= s_{ES} \cdot [R_U + H_1(X_U \parallel R_U \parallel PID_U)P_{pub}] \\ &= s_{ES} \cdot s_U P \\ &= s_U \cdot [R_{ES} + H_2(ID_{ES} \parallel R_{ES})P_{pub}] \\ &= K_U, \end{aligned}$$

$$\begin{aligned} SK_{ES} &= H_5(K_{ES} \parallel ID_{ES} \parallel PID_U \parallel b \cdot (U - X_U) \parallel T_j) \\ &= H_5(K_U \parallel ID_{ES} \parallel PID_U \parallel a \cdot (V - X_{ES}) \parallel T_j) \\ &= SK_U. \end{aligned}$$

Therefore, the proposed scheme is provably correct.

5   Security Analysis of the Proposed Scheme

In this section, we analyze the security of the proposed scheme. First, we prove that the proposed scheme is secure against two types of adversaries. Then, we present the analysis result of Scyther tool claiming that our scheme is secure against common attacks.

Theorem 1. Assume that the Computational Diffie-Hellman (CDH) problem is intractable. Let $\mathcal{A}_1$ be a probabilistic polynomial time adversary against the proposed scheme Π, the advantage of $\mathcal{A}_1$ against our scheme is negligible.

Proof. Suppose there exists a probabilistic polynomial time adversary $\mathcal{A}_1$ who can win the game with a non-negligible advantage in polynomial time t. Then, we can design an algorithm $\mathcal{C}$ to solve the CDH problem using the ability of $\mathcal{A}_1$.

Suppose $\mathcal{C}$ is given an instance (aP, bP) of the CDH problem whose subject is to compute $Q = abP$. Suppose $\mathcal{A}_1$ makes at most q_{H_i} times H_i-query and creates at most q_c participants and q_s be the maximal number of sessions each participant may be involved in.

$\mathcal{C}$ sets P_0 as the system public key P_{pub}, selects the system parameter $params = \{F_p, E/F_p, G, P, P_{pub}, H_i\}$ and sends the public parameters to $\mathcal{A}_1$. $\mathcal{C}$ chooses at random $I \in [1, q_{H_2}]$, $J \in [1, q_{H_2}]$, $T \in [1, q_s]$, $s_J, x_J, h_J \in Z_q^*$, then $\mathcal{C}$ computes $R_J = s_J P - h_J P_{pub}$, $X_J = x_J P$. $\mathcal{C}$ answers $\mathcal{A}_1$'s queries as follows.

- Create(ID_j): $\mathcal{C}$ keeps an empty list L_C consisting of tuples $(ID_j, (s_j, x_j), (R_j, X_j))$. If $ID_j = ID_J$, $\mathcal{C}$ lets j's private key and public key be (s_J, x_J), and

(R_J, X_J) respectively. $\mathcal{C}$ also lets $H_2(ID_J, R_J) \leftarrow h_J$, where R_J, x_J, and h_J are the variables mentioned above. Otherwise, $\mathcal{C}$ chooses a random $x_j, s_j, h_j \in Z_q^*$ and computes $R_j = s_j P - h_j P_{pub}$ and $X_j = x_j P$. Thus, ID_j's private key is the tuple (s_j, x_j) and its public key is (R_j, X_j). At last, $\mathcal{C}$ adds the tuple (ID_j, R_j, h_j) and $(ID_j, (s_j, x_j), (R_j, Xj))$ to the list L_{H_2} and L_C, separately.

- Send($\Pi_{i,j}^n, M$): $\mathcal{C}$ keeps an empty list L_S in the form of a tuple ($\Pi_{i,j}^n, path_{i,j}^n, r_{i,j}^n$), in which $path_{i,j}^n$ is a record of session message $\Pi_{i,j}^n$ and $r_{i,j}^n$ is defined as below.
  - If $n = T, ID_i = ID_I, ID_j = ID_J$, $\mathcal{C}$ returns aP as U and updates the tuple $r_{i,j}^n = \bot$.
  - Else $\mathcal{C}$ returns the corresponding answer according to the steps.
- Reveal($\Pi_{i,j}^n$): $\mathcal{C}$ keeps an empty list L_R. If $n = T, ID_i = ID_I, ID_j = ID_J$ or $\Pi_{i,j}^n$ is the matching session of $\Pi_{I,J}^T$, $\mathcal{C}$ aborts this query; otherwise, $\mathcal{C}$ answers as follows:
  - If $ID_i \neq ID_I$, $\mathcal{C}$ searches for the list L_C and L_S for the detailed data and makes an H_5 query to compute the session key $SK_{i,j}^n$.
  - Else $\mathcal{C}$ chooses a random number $SK_{i,j}^n \in \{0,1\}^l$.
- Corrupt(ID_i): If $ID_i = ID_I$, then $\mathcal{C}$ aborts this query; otherwise, $\mathcal{C}$ searches for a tuple $\{ID_i, (s_i, x_i), (R_i, X_i)\}$ in L_C indexed by ID_i and returns (s_i, x_i).
- Replacement($ID_i, (R_i', X_i')$): $\mathcal{C}$ searches for a tuple $\{ID_i, (s_i, x_i), (R_i, X_i)\}$ in L_C which is indexed by ID_i then replaces (R_i, X_i) with (R_i', X_i').
- H_5 query: $\mathcal{C}$ keeps an empty list L_{H_5} of the tuple $(\{K_i, ID_j, PID_i, \lambda, T_j\}, h_u)$ where λ represents $a(U_j - X_j)$ or $b(U_i - Xi)$ and it answers this query as below:
  - If $(\{K_i, ID_j, PID_i, \lambda, T_j\}, h_u)$ has been in the list L_{H_5}, $\mathcal{C}$ returns h_u.
  - Else $\mathcal{C}$ looks for L_R. If there exists the record then $\mathcal{C}$ returns the correspond session key $SK_{i,j}^n$.
  - Else $\mathcal{C}$ chooses a random number $h_u \in \{0,1\}^l$ and adds the record in the list L_{H_5}.

The probability is that $\mathcal{A}_1$ chooses $\Pi_{I,J}^T$ as the $Test$ oracle and that $1/q_c^2 q_s$. In this case, $\mathcal{A}_1$ would not have made Corrupt(ID_I), Corrupt(ID_J) or Reveal($\Pi_{I,J}^T$) queries, and so $\mathcal{C}$ would not have aborted. If $\mathcal{A}_1$ can win in such a game, then $\mathcal{A}_1$ must have made the corresponding H_5 query. Therefore, $\mathcal{C}$ can find the corresponding record in the list of L_{H_5} indexed by $\{K_i, ID_j, PID_i, \lambda, T_j\}$ with the probability $1/q_{H_5}$ and output λ as the result of the CDH problem. Therefore, the probability, denoted as α that $\mathcal{C}$ tackles the CDH problem satisfies $\alpha > Adv_{\mathcal{A}_1}/q_c^2 q_s q_{H_5}$, where $Adv_{\mathcal{A}_1}$ is the advantage that $\mathcal{A}_1$ wins the game.

Theorem 2. Assume that the Computational Diffie-Hellman (CDH) problem is intractable. Let $\mathcal{A}_2$ be a probabilistic polynomial time adversary against the proposed scheme Π, the advantage of $\mathcal{A}_2$ against our scheme is negligible.

Proof. Suppose there exists a probabilistic polynomial time adversary $\mathcal{A}_2$ who can win the game with a non-negligible advantage in polynomial time t. Then, we can design an algorithm $\mathcal{C}$ to solve the CDH problem using the ability of $\mathcal{A}_2$.

Suppose $\mathcal{C}$ is given an instance (aP, bP) of the CDH problem whose subject is to compute $Q = abP$. Suppose $\mathcal{A}_2$ makes at most q_{H_i} times H_i-query and creates at most q_c participants and q_s be the maximal number of sessions each participation may be involved in.

$\mathcal{C}$ sets P_0 as the system public key P_{pub}, selects the system parameter $params = \{F_p, E/F_p, G, P, P_{pub}, H_i\}$ and sends the public parameters to $\mathcal{A}_2$. $\mathcal{C}$ chooses at random $I \in [1, q_{H_2}]$, $J \in [1, q_{H_2}]$, $T \in [1, q_s]$. $\mathcal{C}$ answers $\mathcal{A}_2$'s queries as follows.

If $\mathcal{A}_2$ makes Create(ID_i) query, $\mathcal{C}$ keeps an empty list L_C consisting of tuples $(ID_i, (s_i, x_i), (R_i, Xi))$. $\mathcal{C}$ randomly selects $s_I, h_I \in Z_q^*$ and computes $R_I = r_I P$, $s_I = r_I + sh_I$ and $X_I = x_I P$. $\mathcal{C}$ can answer other queries as Theorem 1.

The probability is that $\mathcal{A}_2$ chooses $\Pi_{I,J}^T$ as the $Test$ oracle and that $1/q_c^2 q_s$. In this case, $\mathcal{A}_2$ would not have made Corrupt(ID_I), Corrupt(ID_J) or Reveal($\Pi_{I,J}^T$) queries, and so $\mathcal{C}$ would not have aborted. If $\mathcal{A}_2$ can win in such a game, then $\mathcal{A}_2$ must have made the corresponding H_5 query. Therefore, $\mathcal{C}$ can find the corresponding record in the list of L_{H_5} indexed by $\{K_i, ID_j, PID_i, \lambda, T_j\}$ with the probability $1/q_{H_5}$ and output λ as the result of the ECDH problem. Therefore, the probability, denoted as α that $\mathcal{C}$ tackles the ECDH problem satisfies $\alpha > Adv_{\mathcal{A}_2}/q_c^2 q_s q_{H_5}$, where $Adv_{\mathcal{A}_2}$ is the advantage that $\mathcal{A}_2$ wins the game.

From the above two theorems, we can conclude that our scheme is secure against two types of adversaries.

Claim				Status	Comments
e_WHX	U	e_WHX,U1	SKR h5(sk(U),Uj,pk(ES),a,ES,PIDi,pk(U))	Ok	No attacks within bounds.
		e_WHX,U2	Alive	Ok	No attacks within bounds.
		e_WHX,U3	Weakagree	Ok	No attacks within bounds.
		e_WHX,U4	Nisynch	Ok	No attacks within bounds.
		e_WHX,U5	Niagree	Ok	No attacks within bounds.
	ES	e_WHX,ES1	SKR h5(sk(ES),ui,pk(U),b,pk(ES),A,ui)	Ok	No attacks within bounds.
		e_WHX,ES2	Alive	Ok	No attacks within bounds.
		e_WHX,ES3	Weakagree	Ok	No attacks within bounds.
		e_WHX,ES4	Nisynch	Ok	No attacks within bounds.
		e_WHX,ES5	Niagree	Ok	No attacks within bounds.

Fig. 2. The analysis result by Scyther tool

Besides proving the security of the proposed scheme under the security model, we also use Scyther tool to show the proposed scheme is secure against various attacks. The result of analysis is demonstrated in the Fig. 2. According to the

Fig. 2, we can clearly obtain that under the settings predefined, the scheme can achieve mutual authentication and secure session keys simultaneously.

6   Performance Analysis

This section presents the performance assessment of the proposed scheme on the security features, computation cost and communication cost.

6.1   Security Comparison

In this subsection, we compare the security features of the proposed scheme with other related schemes [17–20], and the result is shown in Table 3. We can see that our proposed scheme can resist various attacks and satisfies the security requirements from Table 3, which means that our scheme is superior to other previous schemes in terms of security features.

Table 3. Comparison of security features

Security features	[17]	[18]	[19]	[20]	Our scheme
Mutual authentication	√	√	√	√	√
Key agreement	√	√	√	√	√
Forward security	×	√	-	-	√
Un-traceability	√	√	√	√	√
Computation transferable	√	×	×	×	√
No online RC	√	√	√	×	√
Impersonation attack	√	√	×	√	√
Man-in-the-middle attack	√	√	×	√	√
Ephemeral secret attack	√	×	×	×	√

6.2   Computation Cost

The computation cost of the proposed scheme is compared with that of previously mentioned schemes. In terms of setting the experimental environment, we choose an additive group with the generator P and the order q, where q is 160 bits. The generator P is a base point on the Koblitz curve secp256k1: $y^2 = x^3 + 7$, denoted as E/F_p and p is 256 bits. In this paper, we mainly consider the execution time of scalar multiplication, hash function and point addition operation on an elliptic curve. Several lightweight operations, such as XOR and addition, are ignored. Table 4 shows the concrete results of these operations [17].

Table 4. The running time of related operations

Symbol	Description	Time(ms)
T_{sm}	Scalar multiplication over $\mathbb{G}_1$	1.1762
T_a	Point addition over $\mathbb{G}_1$	0.0084
T_h	Hash function	0.0019
T_{exp}	Exponentiation over $\mathbb{G}_2$	0.2332
T_{bp}	Bilinear pairing	3.3925
T_{mp}	Map to point in $\mathbb{G}_2$	3.8426
T_e	Encryption using AES	0.773
T_d	Decryption using AES	0.512

Mainly considering the authentication and key agreement phase, the comparison result is shown in Fig. 3. In our scheme, the computation time needed in user side for authentication and key agreement process is four hash function operations, four scalar multiplication operations, two point additions and one encryption while that of the server side is four hash function operations, five scalar multiplication operations, three point additions and one decryption. Therefore, the total execution time of our proposed scheme is 11.9204 ms. In the scheme of He et al. [18], the computation cost of user side is $T_{mp}+3T_{sm}+4T_h+2T_{exp} = 7.4852$ ms and server side is $2T_{bp} + 5T_h + 2T_a + T_{exp} = 7.2777$ ms. Similarly, the computation overheads of user side and server side in Liu et al.'s scheme [19] are $6T_{sm} + 5T_h + 5T_a = 7.1087$ ms and $6T_{sm} + 5T_h + 5T_a = 7.1887$ ms, respectively.

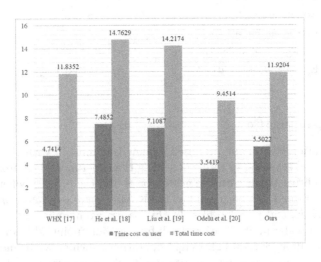

Fig. 3. The comparison result of computation cost

6.3 Communication Cost

In this subsection, the comparison of the communication cost between our proposed scheme with other related schemes is presented. We assume that the length of identity, login request and timestamp is 32 bits, marked as $|ID|$, $|L|$, $|T|$, respectively. The output length of hash function is 160 bits, expressed as $|H|$. A ciphertext block is 128 bits, expressed as $|C|$ and the lengths of p and q are 256 bits and 160 bits, respectively. In this way, a point on elliptic curve $G = (G_x, G_y)$ is 512 bits, denoted as $|G|$. Further, assume a value in Z_q^* be 160 bits, which is denoted as $\left|Z_q^*\right|$.

Table 5. Comparison of communication cost

Scheme	User side	Server side	Total
[17]	$3\left|H\right| + \left|Z_q^*\right| + \left|T\right|$	$\left|G\right| + \left|H\right| + \left|T\right|$	1376 bits
[18]	$\left|L\right| + \left|ID\right| + 2\left|G\right|$	$\left|G\right| + \left|H\right|$	1760 bits
[19]	$\left|T\right| + 2\left|G\right| + \left|H\right| + \left|Z_q^*\right|$	$2\left|G\right| + \left|ID\right| + \left|Z_q^*\right|$	2592 bits
[20]	$\left|C\right| + \left|G\right| + 2\left|H\right|$	$3\left|C\right| + 2\left|G\right| + 4\left|H\right|$	3008 bits
Ours	$\left|G\right| + 2\left|H\right| + \left|T\right|$	$\left|G\right| + \left|C\right| + \left|T\right|$	1536 bits

During the communication between U_i and ES in the proposed scheme, the message M_1 sent by user U_i, requires $|G|+2\left|H\right|+\left|T\right| = 864$ bits; and the message M_2 sent by ES, employs the cost of $|G| + |C| + |T| = 672$ bits. Therefore, the addition of all the messages is 1568 bits. In the protocol [19], the communication cost needed by user side is $|T| + 2\left|G\right| + \left|H\right| + \left|Z_q^*\right| = 1376$ bits while that by server require $2\left|G\right| + \left|ID\right| + \left|Z_q^*\right| = 1216$ bits, so the total cost is 2592 bits. The communication cost of the other related schemes can be computed similarly and the final result is shown in Table 5.

From comparison results in Table 5, it can be concluded that the communication cost of our proposed scheme generally has less communication cost than other related schemes. Although the communication cost of our proposed scheme is higher than that of WHX protocol, our scheme can satisfy more secure requirements.

7 Conclusion

In this paper, we point out that there exists forward security problem in WHX protocol. Aiming at remedy such potential risk, we propose an improved scheme based on the former one. The proposed scheme redesigns the generation of the session key without depending too much on the ephemeral keys. To comprehensively prove its security, formal analysis and informal analysis are used by combining theory and tools. Moreover, to evaluate the performance, we give comparisons on computation and communication cost with the former schemes.

The analysis results of security and performance illustrate that our scheme is exactly security-enhanced with the forward security and outperforms WHX protocol from the perspective of computation cost.

Acknowledgment. This work was supported in part by National Natural Science Foundation of China (Grant No. 61872449).

References

1. Chenam, V.B., Ali, S.T.: A designated cloud server-based multi-user certificateless public key authenticated encryption with conjunctive keyword search against IKGA. Comput. Stand. Interfaces **81**, 103603 (2022)
2. Shiraly, D., Pakniat, N., Noroozi, M., Eslami, Z.: Paring-free certificateless authenticated encryption with keyword search. J. Syst. Archit. **124**, 102390 (2022)
3. Turkanović, M., Brumen, B., Hölbl, M.: A novel user authentication and key agreement scheme for heterogeneous ad hoc wireless sensor networks, based on the Internet of Things notion. Ad Hoc Netw. **20**, 96–112 (2014)
4. Farash, M.S., Turkanović, M., Kumari, S., Hölbl, M.: An efficient user authentication and key agreement scheme for heterogeneous wireless sensor network tailored for the Internet of Things environment. Ad Hoc Netw. **36**, 152–176 (2016)
5. Gope, P., Hwang, T.: A realistic lightweight anonymous authentication protocol for securing real-time application data access in wireless sensor networks. IEEE Trans. Ind. Electron. **63**(11), 7124–7132 (2016)
6. Adavoudi-Jolfaei, A.H., Ashouri-Talouki, M., Aghili, S.F.: Lightweight and anonymous three-factor authentication and access control scheme for real-time applications in wireless sensor networks. Peer Peer Netw. Appl. **12**(1), 43–59 (2017). https://doi.org/10.1007/s12083-017-0627-8
7. Dolev, D., Yao, A.: On the security of public key protocols. IEEE Trans. Inf. Theory **29**(2), 198–208 (1983)
8. Ryu, J., Kang, D., Lee, H., Kim, H., Won, D.: A secure and lightweight three-factor-based authentication scheme for smart healthcare systems. Sensors **20**(24), 7136 (2020)
9. Al-Riyami, S.S., Paterson, K.G.: Certificateless public key cryptography. In: Laih, C.-S. (ed.) ASIACRYPT 2003. LNCS, vol. 2894, pp. 452–473. Springer, Heidelberg (2003). https://doi.org/10.1007/978-3-540-40061-5_29
10. Mandt, T.K., Tan, C.H.: Certificateless authenticated two-party key agreement protocols. In: Okada, M., Satoh, I. (eds.) ASIAN 2006. LNCS, vol. 4435, pp. 37–44. Springer, Heidelberg (2007). https://doi.org/10.1007/978-3-540-77505-8_4
11. Wang, S.B., Cao, Z.F., Wang, L.C.: Efficient certificateless authenticated key agreement protocol from pairings. Wuhan Univ. J. Nat. Sci. **11**(5), 1278–1282 (2006)
12. Hou, M.B., Xu, Q.L.: On the security of certificateless authenticated key agreement protocol. In: 2009 IEEE International Symposium on IT in Medicine Education, pp. 974–979. IEEE (2009)
13. Asari, A., Alagheband, M.R., Bayat, M., Asaar, M.R.: A new provable hierarchical anonymous certificateless authentication protocol with aggregate verification in ADS-B systems. Comput. Netw. **185**(11), 107599 (2021)
14. Samra, B., Fouzi, S.: New efficient certificateless scheme-based conditional privacy preservation authentication for applications in VANET. Veh. Commun. **34**, 100414 (2022)

15. Cheng, Q.F., Li, Y.T., Shi, W.B., Li, X.H.: A certificateless authentication and key agreement scheme for secure cloud-assisted wireless body area network. Mob. Netw. Appl. **27**, 346–356 (2022)
16. He, D.B., Chen, J.H., Hu, J.: A pairing-free certificateless authenticated key agreement protocol. Int. J. Commun. Syst. **25**(2), 221 (2011)
17. Wang, W.M., Huang, H.P., Xiao, F., Li, Q., Xue, L.Y., Jiang, J.S.: Computation-transferable authenticated key agreement protocol for smart healthcare. J. Syst. Archit. **118**, 102215 (2021)
18. He, D.B., Kumar, N., Khan, M.K., Wang, L.N., Shen, J.: Efficient privacy-aware authentication scheme for mobile cloud computing services. IEEE Syst. J. **12**(2), 1621–1631 (2018)
19. Liu, X., Jin, C., Li, F.: An improved two-layer authentication scheme for wireless body area networks. J. Med. Syst. **42**, 143 (2018)
20. Odelu, V., Das, A.K., Goswami, A.: A secure biometrics-based multi-server authentication protocol using smart cards. IEEE Trans. Inf. Forensics Secur. **10**(9), 1953–1966 (2015)

Digital Signature Scheme to Match Generalized Reed-Solomon Code over GF(q)

Yong Wang, Hao Xie$^{(\boxtimes)}$ (iD), and Ruyi Wang

School of Cyber Engineering, Xidian University, Xi'an 710126, Shaanxi, China
wangyong@mail.xidian.edu.cn, 865633089@qq.com

Abstract. Code-based public key cryptography is one of the most widely studied cryptographic algorithms against quantum computing attacks. The main issue today is determining how to choose parameters that strike a balance between security and efficiency. The key reason is that public key size is far too large to be practical. This paper is to investigate and select generalized Reed-Solomon (GRS) codes over the q-ary Galois Field (GF(q)), and attempts to build a code-based classic public key cryptographic algorithm (CFS) signature scheme and investigates its feasibility and related performance optimization, providing a full security proof and analysis. Constructing a cryptographic algorithm based on GF(q) coding can effectively reduce the size of the public key size while maintaining security. While the GRS code is preferred over GF (q), it allows for more parameter selection flexibility. It has higher security and a smaller public key size than other code-based digital signature schemes. In the case of slightly improved security, the public key size is only 4.1% of the original CFS scheme.

Keywords: Post-quantum cryptography · Code-based signature scheme · Generalized reed-solomon code · GF(q) · McEliece

1 Introduction

The most common digital signature schemes are based on RSA and ElGamal. These schemes are secure because they assume the adversary's computing power is limited. If a large quantum computer is built, it will be able to solve their related difficulty problems and render all of these signature schemes useless.

At present, post-quantum secure signature schemes mainly include lattice-based, multivariate-based, hash-based, and code-based signature schemes. The code-based signature scheme has the characteristics of fast calculation speed and good operability. According to the decoding difficulty (SD) problem and the fast decoding algorithm characteristics of GOPPA, McEliece first proposed

Supported by National Key Research and Development Program of China (No. 2018YFB0804103), Shaanxi Intelligent Social Development Strategy Research Center.

a public key cryptographic algorithm based on error correction codes in 1978 [1]. It has been subjected to various cryptographic attacks and analyses for more than 40 years. Compared with other public key cryptosystems, it has more efficient encryption and decryption performance and higher security. But there is a problem with excessive public key size.

The CFS scheme is one of the most classic code-based cryptographic algorithms [2]. Like other code-based cryptographic algorithms, it also has the defect of excessive public key size. In addition, the CFS signature scheme uses a high-rate GOPPA code to reduce the signing time. But it is mentioned in [3] that the high-rate GOPPA code is vulnerable to distinguisher attack.

In [4–6], they are suggested to use a finite field GF(q) instead of GF(2) to reduce the size of the public key. The use of GF(q)-based error-correcting codes, such as the generalized Reed-Solomon (GRS) codes, can bring more effective code design and more compact matrix representation. This paper aims to use GRS codes to build traditional CFS schemes. On the one hand, it corrects the flaw in the code-based cryptographic algorithms' large number of public key size, and on the other, it improves its security.

This paper proposes a new CFS signature scheme based on the GRS code over GF(q), analyzes its feasibility, and provides a security proof for the scheme. This scheme uses the GRS code over GF(q), and the BBCRS scheme [7,8] combined with the GRS code has anti-distinguisher characteristics, allowing the scheme to reduce the public key size while simultaneously improving security. It has a higher practicability than the original CFS scheme. We have established that the CFS scheme can be enhanced by using the GRS code over GF(q). Theoretically, if the relevant non-binary code family over GF(q) can produce valid signatures, using non-binary encoding to create a code-based digital signature technique should result in such an enhancement.

The rest of this paper is organized as follows. In the second section, we will briefly introduce two classical code-based cryptosystems –McEliece scheme and CFS scheme, and give some security concepts. In the third section, a new signature scheme based on GRS code over GF(q) is proposed. We also give a formal proof of security. The fourth section analyzes the relevant performance and proves the feasibility of the scheme. In the fifth section, the security of the proposed scheme is further analyzed. In the sixth section, compare with other schemes and give the result. The seventh section gives a conclusion.

2   Preliminary

As an asymmetric cryptosystem, the code-based public key cryptosystem should be more suitable for the creation of digital signatures. The CFS scheme is by far the most feasible code-based digital signature scheme, and it is still based on the binary GOPPA code.

2.1 Public Key Cryptosystem Based on Error Correction Codes

The classic McEliece is based on GF(2). For the sake of generality, we briefly introduce its version for any finite field. Therefore, any other cryptographic algorithms based on error correction codes (including public key cryptosystems and digital signature), which can be used for promotion. The algorithm itself is divided into three stages, the key generation stage, the encryption stage, and the decryption stage. The main contents are as follows:

- **Key generation**: Let $\mathbf{G}$ be the $k \times n$ generator matrix of the linear reduced GOPPA code C over GF(q), where $q = 2^m$, $d = 2t + 1$ and $k = n - mt$, and t is the error correction capability of the code C. plaintext $\mathbf{m} \epsilon F_q^k$, cipher $\mathbf{c} \epsilon F_q^n$. The $k \times k$ nonsingular matrix $\mathbf{S}$ and $n \times n$ permutation matrix $\mathbf{P}$ are randomly selected on the finite field GF(q) to calculate

$$\mathbf{G}' = \mathbf{SGP} \tag{1}$$

  Then $\mathbf{S}$, $\mathbf{G}$, $\mathbf{P}$ and a binary GOPPA code fast decoding algorithm φ_D are used as the private key, and $\mathbf{G}'$ is disclosed as the public key.
- **Encryption**: The sender uses the receiver's public key to encrypt the plaintext $\mathbf{m}$ with information bits k, and the following ciphertext $\mathbf{c}$ with length n is obtained

$$\mathbf{c} = \mathbf{mG}' + \mathbf{z} \tag{2}$$

  where $\mathbf{z}$ is an n-bit random error vector with weight $\leq t$ over GF(q).
- **Decryption**: When the receiver receives the ciphertext $\mathbf{c}$, it uses the private key in the hand to decrypt the ciphertext, first calculate

$$\mathbf{cP}^{-1} = \mathbf{mSG} + \mathbf{zP}^{-1} \tag{3}$$

Because $\mathbf{P}$ is a permutation matrix, $\mathbf{mS}$ can be obtained according to the fast decoding algorithm φ_D of GOPPA code, and then the plaintext $\mathbf{m}$ corresponding to the ciphertext $\mathbf{c}$ can be obtained.

The Niederreiter public key cryptosystem is a dual scheme with the McEliece public key cryptosystem. It has a smaller public key size and equivalent security than McEliece.

2.2 Digital Signature Scheme Based on Error Correction Code

The CFS signature scheme is a signature algorithm based on the GOPPA code applied to the Niederreiter scheme. The algorithm is mainly summarized as follows:

- **Key generation**: Set a $[n,k,d]$ linear reduction GOPPA code C, with a $(n-k) \times n$ parity check matrix $\mathbf{H}$, its error correction ability $t = \frac{n-k}{m} = \frac{n-k}{\log_2 n}$. Randomly select $(n - k) \times (n - k)$ non-sisngular matrix $\mathbf{S}$ and $n \times n$ permutation matrix $\mathbf{P}$. Choose a fast decoding algorithm φ_D of GOPPA code. The public key is $\mathbf{H}' = \mathbf{SHP}$, and the private key is $\{\mathbf{H,S,P},\varphi_D\}$.

- **Signature**: Choose a public hash function $h(\cdot)$ that returns a binary code-word of length $n-k$ (syndrome length), Let M be the document to be signed, first calculate $s = h(M)$, then calculate.

$$s_i = h(s|i) \tag{4}$$

where $(s|i)$ represents the connection between s and i, i is a counter with an initial value of 0, gradually increase i by 1 until a decipherable syndrome s_{i_0} is obtained. Use i_0 to represent the first index of the decodable s_i, and the syndrome $s_{i_0} = h(s|i_0)$ as the signature, and decode an error vector $\mathbf{z}$ such that $\mathbf{Hz}^T = s_{i_0}$. Then the final signature is $[\mathbf{z}|i_0]$.

- **Signature verification**: The verifier judges whether when $w(\mathbf{z}) \leq t$ there is

$$\mathbf{H'z}^T = h(h(M)|i_0) \tag{5}$$

If it is satisfied, the verification is successful, otherwise the verification fails.

As described in the above algorithm, the signature phase is an iterative process until a decodable syndrome is obtained. Because the probability that the syndrome randomly selected by the original CFS scheme can be decoded with $\frac{1}{t!}$, Therefore, the value of error correction capability t should be small enough to reduce the number of iterations. Then the GOPPA code with high rate should be used. However, the CFS signature scheme should have a large enough key size to resist decoding attacks, and a small t value cannot bring a large enough key size to meet the relevant security. In addition, it is mentioned in [3] that the high rate GOPPA code is not resistant to distinguisher attack. In short, the CFS signature scheme is insecure and inefficient due to the use of GOPPA code.

2.3 Security Concept

We will use provably secure methods to reduce the security of our scheme to one or more algorithmic problems that are considered intractable. As long as the underlying algorithmic problems are difficult, the scheme is safe. In most cases, semantic security can be provided by indistinguishable games in provable security theory. Because this paper focuses on digital signature algorithms, it can demonstrate that the core security problem is existential unforgeability in the face of adaptive chosen message attacks (EUF-CMA). Here we introduce some basic security concepts for later security proof and analysis.

Definition 1 (EUF-CMA). *When attacking the cryptographic scheme maintained by the challenger, the advantage of the adversary* A *is the absolute value of the difference between the probability of* A*'s successful attack to win the indistinguishable game and 1/2. A signature scheme* S *is* (τ, ϵ)*-EUF-CMA-secure if for any adversary* A *at polynomial time* τ:

$$Adv_S^{EUF-CMA}(A) = \left| Pr_{Succ} - \frac{1}{2} \right| \leq \epsilon \tag{6}$$

Definition 2 (q-Syndrome Decoding Problem (q-SD problem)). *Given the $r \times n$ matrix $\mathbf{H}$ on F_q, the r-dimensional vector $\mathbf{s}$, and the positive integer $t \leq n$, is there an n-dimensional vector $\mathbf{e}$ on F_q such that the weight $w(e) \leq t$ and $\mathbf{e}\mathbf{H}^T = \mathbf{s}$?*

Theorem 1. *The q-SD problem is called (τ, ϵ)-difficult, if for any decoder D runs in at most τ time there is $Succ^{qSD}(D) \leq \epsilon_{qSD}$.*

Definition 3 (GRS Code Distinguishing(GRSD)). *According to the BBCRS scheme proposed in [7], The GRS Code Distinguishing is said to be (τ, ϵ)-hard if for any distinguisher D running in time at most τ we have $Adv^{GRSD}(D) \leq \epsilon_{GRSD}$.*

Definition 4 (Security Level (SL)). *If in actual operation an adversary attacks an algorithm and requires at least 2^σ binary calculations, we call σ the security level of the algorithm. And if the security level of an algorithm reaches 80, we consider it to be security. If it reaches 128, we consider it to be strong security.*

3   The Proposed Scheme

The original CFS scheme has relatively large signature complexity, inflexible parameter selection, and has defects in resisting distinguisher attacks. Most code-based cryptographic algorithms have such shortcomings. However, in the past two decades of research progress, many secure code-based cryptographic algorithms have emerged [7,9–12], and the BBCRS scheme is one of the representatives. It effectively solves the security defect that the cryptographic algorithm based on GRS code construction is not resistant to distinguisher attacks [3,13].

The BBCRS scheme realizes anti-distinguisher attacks. If it is used in the CFS scheme, it can reduce the public key size while improving security. This paper selects the BBCRS scheme that is resistant to distinguisher attack, applies it to the CFS scheme, and proposes a new and improved GRS code-based signature scheme over GF(q), and analyzes its feasibility (see Sect. 4) And security (see Sect. 5). This scheme can be divided into three phases according to the classic code-based signature scheme, namely the key generation algorithm, the signing algorithm, and the signature verifying algorithm. The specific program content is as follows:

- **Key generation:** Using elements in GF(q) ($q = 2^m$, m is a positive integer), randomly select $(n-k) \times (n-k)$ non-singular confusion matrix $\mathbf{S}$, $(n-k) \times n$ generalized Reed-Solomon code (here in after referred to as GRS code) parity check matrix $\mathbf{H}$ (n is the code length of the code, k is the dimension of the code, and the code can correct $t = \lfloor \frac{r}{2} \rfloor = \lfloor \frac{n-k}{2} \rfloor$ errors), $n \times n$ non-singular transformation matrix $\mathbf{Q}(\mathbf{Q} = \mathbf{R} + \mathbf{T}$, $\mathbf{T}$ is sparse matrix over GF(q). The average row weight and column weight are m', and m' not necessarily integers. $\mathbf{R}$ is the dense matrix over GF(q), $\mathbf{R} = \mathbf{a}^T\mathbf{b}$, Among them, $\mathbf{a}$ and $\mathbf{b}$ are two matrices defined on GF(q), with a size of $z \times n$ and row full rank matrix). And choose a fast decoding algorithm φ. Calculate $\mathbf{H}' = \mathbf{S}^{-1}\mathbf{H}\mathbf{Q}^T$, $\mathbf{H}'$ will be released as the public key, keep $(\mathbf{S},\mathbf{H},\mathbf{Q})$ and φ as the private key.

- **Signature**: The signer hashes the plaintext to get $h(M)$, and set $i = 0$, and calculate $\mathbf{S}_x = h(h(M)|i)$. Let $\mathbf{S}_x$ be a vector of length $n-k$, finally calculated $\mathbf{S}_x' = \mathbf{S}\mathbf{S}_x$. Then the signer tries to use the fast decoding algorithm φ on $\mathbf{S}_x'$, decodes an error vector $\mathbf{e}$ with weight $\leq m't$, and calculates $\bar{\mathbf{e}} = \mathbf{e}\mathbf{Q}^{-1}$, whose weight $t_p \leq t$. If decoding fails, set $i + 1$ until a decodable syndrome $\mathbf{S}_x'$ is generated. Finally, extract the non-zero elements in $\bar{\mathbf{e}}$ as the error value, and construct the index pair $I_e = \sum_{t_p} \binom{\alpha_j}{c_j}$ of $\bar{\mathbf{e}}$ with the error position α and the error value c, that is $I_e = \binom{\alpha_1}{c_1} + \binom{\alpha_2}{c_2} + \cdots + \binom{\alpha_{t_p}}{c_{t_p}}$, And use $[I_e|i]$ as the signature of message M.

- **Signature verification**: It is first check whether the weight of I_e is satisfied $w(I_e) \leq t_p$. If it is not satisfied, the verification will fail. Otherwise, it will continue to be restored $\bar{\mathbf{e}}$ according to I_e. That is, fill with 0 at the position outside the index α_j and fill with at the position of the index c_j until the vector length reaches $n-k$. Calculate $x = \mathbf{H}'\bar{\mathbf{e}}^T$, that is, calculate the product of each column of $\mathbf{H}'$ according to the value of the corresponding row indexed by α_j and c_j. Then calculate $x' = h(h(M)|i)$, and compare x and x'. If $x = x'$ is satisfied, the verification is successful. Otherwise the verification fails.

Compared with other digital signature schemes, the signature verification process of this scheme is simple and only needs to calculate the hash twice. Efficient signature verification can lead to a more efficient data processing process, which is a distinct advantage of our scheme.

3.1   Reductionist Security Proof

We refer to the analysis methods of [12,14,15] on the modified CFS scheme, which proves our scheme is EUF-CMA.Next, we will produce a sequence of games relating the EUF-CMA game to the q-SD game. Each game is a slight modification of the preceding game, and the difference between the two games can evaluate. Because the challenger can control the oracles, the adversary has to solve the q-SD problem.

In order to prove the game sequence, we need two oracle machines, Hash oracle machine $\bar{H}$, and signature oracle machine Σ. And use three lists $\Lambda(\bar{H})$, $\Lambda(\Sigma)$ and $\Lambda(M)$. Where $\Lambda_{\bar{H}}(m,i) = (\mathbf{s}, \mathbf{e})$ is used to store m and its counter i, $\Lambda(\bar{H})$ is used to store the output syndrome $\mathbf{s}$ and its error vector $\mathbf{e}$. And $\Lambda_{\Sigma}(m) = (i, \mathbf{e})$ stores any message m's output signature $(i, \mathbf{e})$. Finally $\Lambda_M(m) = i$, used to store the index value i corresponding to any message m. If there is no value corresponding to the input in the list, we record the output as $\perp$. A adversary A can query the hash oracle machine q_H times, and the signature oracle machine q_{Σ} times, and count A's own output at the end. The total number of hash queries of A is $q_{\bar{H}} + q_{\Sigma} + 1$.

GAME 0: This is the initial attack, which can be expressed by the algorithm as follows

Algorithm 1. GAME 0: mCFS EUF-CMA game

Require: An adversary A
1: $(\mathbf{H'}, \mathbf{S}, \mathbf{H}, \mathbf{P}) \leftarrow Gen_{mCFS}(n, k)$;
2: Set the oracle $\bar{H}$ and Σ ;
3: $(m^*, \mathbf{e}^*, i^*) \leftarrow A^{\bar{H}, \Sigma}(\mathbf{H'})$;
4: **if** $\bar{H}(m^*, i^*) = \mathbf{He}^{*T}$, $wt(\mathbf{e}^*) \leq t$ and $\mathbf{e}^* \notin \Lambda(\Sigma)$ **then**
5:     A win the game;
6: **else**
7:     A lose the game;
8: **end if**

Where $m^*, \mathbf{e}^*, i^*$ is the output obtained by A querying the oracle $\bar{H}$ and Σ. The challenger generates a public key through a key generation algorithm, and provides the public key to A. A queries the hash oracle and signature oracle many times, and tries to obtain a valid signature of a certain message. Where $Pr[S_0] = Succ_{mCFS}^{EUF-CMA}(A)$ represents the probability of A wins the GAME 0.

GAME 1: In this game, challenger replace the hash oracle $\bar{H}$ with a simulated $\bar{H}'$. We use F to represent the event of $i = \Lambda(M)$, that is, when $i = \Lambda(M)$, $\bar{H}'$ creates a t-decodable syndrome and stores its decoded value in list $\Lambda_{\bar{H}}$: it first gets a random word x of weight t in F_q^n, then calculate its syndrome $\mathbf{s}$ as output. $\bar{H}'$ stores the values $\mathbf{s}$ and x in $\Lambda_{\bar{H}}$. Of course, $\bar{H}'$ will check whether the corresponding output value is stored in the list of its query.

Obviously, when the event F does not occur, the process of GAME 0 and GAME 1 are the same. Then, according to the difference lemma [16], we have

$$|Pr[S_1] - Pr[S_0]| \leq Pr[F] \tag{7}$$

the occurrence of event F obeys the binomial distribution of $\frac{1}{q^{n-k}}$ and $q_H + q_\Sigma + 1$, so

$$Pr[F] = 1 - \left(1 - \frac{1}{q^{n-k}}\right)^{q_{\bar{H}} + q_\Sigma + 1} \tag{8}$$

GAME 2: Similar to the modification of GAME 1, the challenger uses simulated Σ' to replace the signature oracle Σ on the basis of GAME 1. Because the hash query of A in GAME 2 comes from $\bar{H}'$, Σ' does not require key generation. And in order to prevent the same message from generating different signatures due to different indexes, Σ' needs to delete $\Lambda(M)$.

The difference between GAME 2 and GAME 1 is that if A queries $\bar{H}'$ for the query value in Σ', then $\bar{H}'$ will output a syndrome value described by F in GAME 1. The maximum probability of this event is $\frac{q_\Sigma}{q^{n-k}}$. So we have

$$|Pr[S_2] - Pr[S_1]| \leq 1 - \left(1 - \frac{q_\Sigma}{q^{n-k}}\right)^{q_{\bar{H}}} \tag{9}$$

GAME 3: In this GAME, the challenger uses a random GRS code parity check matrix to replace the key generation algorithm. Because neither a nor b requires a private key and a hash function, the simulation will not change, so

$$Pr[S_3] = Pr[S_2] \tag{10}$$

GAME 4: In GAME 4, we use random linear codes to replace random GRS codes. Since this article uses baldi's scheme [7], we can assume

$$|Pr[S_4] = Pr[S_3]| \leq \epsilon_{GRSD} \tag{11}$$

is negligible.

GAME 5: In this GAME, the challenger modifies the winning conditions. The condition of this game is that the adversary makes a forgery on a specific hash query: the challenger first gets a random $c \xleftarrow{R} \{1, \cdots, q_{\bar{H}} + q_\Sigma + 1\}$. If in addition to the previous winning conditions, the c-th query on $\bar{H}'$ is performed on (m^*, i^*), then A wins. This event, independent form the choice of the adversary, has probability $\frac{1}{q_{\bar{H}} + q_\Sigma + 1}$. Then, we have:

$$Pr[S_5] = \frac{Pr[S_4]}{q_{\bar{H}} + q_\Sigma + 1} \tag{12}$$

GAME 6: The challenger modifies the hash oracle to output a random syndrome to the c-th query. If the probability space is not modified, then $Pr[S_6] = Pr[S_5]$. According to the restrictions of GAME 5, the challenger knows that A will forge a hash oracle on the result s^* of the c-th query (m^*, i^*). So if A wins GAME, then

$$\begin{cases} \mathbf{H}'(\mathbf{e}^*)^T = \bar{H}'(m^*, i^*) = \mathbf{s}^* \\ wt(\mathbf{e}^*) \leq t \end{cases} \tag{13}$$

Then the adversary won the qSD-game, $Succ^{qSD}(A) = Pr[S_6]$. From Definition 2 and 1, $Succ^{qSD}(A) \leq \epsilon_{qSD}$. So

$$Pr[S_6] \leq \epsilon_{qSD} \tag{14}$$

In summary, we can conclude that for any adversary A in the polynomial time τ, our scheme has:

$$Adv^{EUF-CMA}(A) \leq (q_{\bar{H}} + q_\Sigma + 1)\epsilon_{qSD} + \epsilon_{GRSD}$$
$$+ 2 - \left(1 - \frac{1}{q^{n-k}}\right)^{q_{\bar{H}} + q_\Sigma + 1} - \left(1 - \frac{q_\Sigma}{q^{n-k}}\right)^{q_{\bar{H}}} \tag{15}$$

Because the q-SD problem is NP-difficult, and baldi's work ensures that the GRS code is indistinguishable. Hence, we claim that under the assumption that both qSD problem and the GRS code distinguishing problem are hard, our scheme is EUF-CMA security.

4   Performance Analysis of the Proposed Algorithm

4.1   Signature Complexity

To realize a feasible CFS signature scheme, the key problem is to find a decodable syndrome, construct the mapping relationship between syndrome and generate a usable signature. However, as mentioned in the CFS original scheme [2], to find a decodable syndrome, the code type used in the signature scheme needs to meet specific boundary decoding conditions. The code type that can be decoded is accounted for in all syndromes. The ratio reaches a certain level in order to get an acceptable probability of success in finding the decodable syndrome. The original CFS scheme uses the binary GOPPA code and a good estimate of the ratio between the decodable syndrome and all syndromes can be obtained, that is $\frac{1}{t!}$. It can be concluded that the value of t should not exceed 10. This paper uses GRS code, which is a non-binary code based on GF(q) (where $q = p^m$, m is an integer, p is a prime number, and $p = 2$ is used in this paper). In this section and beyond, all GRS codes are analyzed with (m, t) as the main analysis parameter.

If the GRS code is used, we can know that the number of syndromes that can be decoded is

$$N_{dec} = \sum_0^t \binom{n}{i} \times (q-1)^i \tag{16}$$

The total number of syndromes (that is, all syndrome possibilities allowed by the redundant bit length) is

$$N_{tot} = q^{n-k} = q^{2t} = 2^{2mt} \tag{17}$$

Therefore, the possibility of finding a translatable syndrome in this scheme using the GRS code over GF(q) is

$$P = \frac{N_{dec}}{N_{tot}} = \frac{\sum_{i=0}^t \binom{n}{i} \times (q-1)^i}{2^{2mt}} \tag{18}$$

Suppose the average number of searches, that is, the complexity of the signature is $Y = \frac{1}{P}$.

When using the (m, t) parameter pair in the GRS code signature scheme based on the finite field GF(q) in this paper, we must first ensure that the average number of searches is less than 10 million, otherwise the signature complexity will be too large. The computing power of the existing computer may be does not support generating a valid signature. In addition, the value of t affects the public key size and security, and is a value that cannot be small. In Fig. 1a and Fig. 1b, we calculated the relationship between the logarithm of the signature complexity ($\log_2 Y$) and the value of m and t respectively. In Fig. 1a, the mean value of m is 12. We can see that when $t = 11$, the signature complexity of the entire scheme (take the logarithmic value) has exceeded tens of millions of calculation levels. The value of t should less than or equal to 10. According to

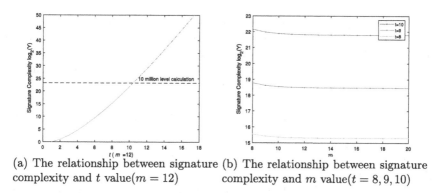

(a) The relationship between signature complexity and t value($m = 12$)

(b) The relationship between signature complexity and m value($t = 8, 9, 10$)

Fig. 1. The relationship between signature complexity and m, t value

the experimental results in Fig. 1b, the value of m also has a certain impact on the complexity of the signature. A small value of m will bring about a slightly greater complexity of the signature, but a large value of m has little effect on the complexity of the signature. Basically, when m is greater than or equal to 12, the complexity of the signature is not affected by the value of m.

In general, after the value of m is greater than or equal to 12, it will no longer affect the complexity of the signature. If the restriction is relaxed, we believe that m should satisfy $m \geq 10$ and m is an integer. The value of t should not be greater than 11, but t should be as large as possible. So, the reasonable value of t is 8, 9 or 10. Therefore, taking the above (m, t) value can bring a relatively reasonable signature complexity and achieve the basic feasibility of constructing a code-based signature scheme.

4.2 Public Key Size

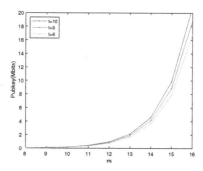

Fig. 2. The relationship between the public key size and m

Because this scheme is based on Niederreiter's scheme, a GRS code $(n - k) \times n$ parity check matrix is used. The Gaussian elimination of the parity check matrix into a row ladder type does not change its properties. Therefore, the public key quantity of this scheme can be recorded as a $(n - k) \times k$ matrix. It is a matrix over GF(q), the public key size can be defined as

$$Key_{pub} = k \times (n - k) \times \log_2(q) \qquad (19)$$

Considering that the appropriate signature complexity is satisfied, the value of t is 8, 9, or 10. This article calculates the size of the public key corresponding to the relevant (m, t) value.

Figure 2 shows the public key size (in Mbits) corresponding to different values of m when t takes 8, 9, and 10 respectively. It can be seen that the size of the public key quantity Key_{pub} is mainly determined by the size m of the finite field. Key_{pub} and m have an exponential relationship. In addition, the size of t also has a certain influence on the public key size. Considering the general defect that the public key size of code-based cryptographic algorithms is too large, the value of m should not be too large. It ensures that this scheme has an acceptable size of public keys.

4.3   Signature Length

The signature of this scheme is mainly related to the error vector. When this signature is represented by an index pair, the error location and error value of the related error need to be stored. There are t_p errors, and the error location is in $2^m - 1$. The error value is in GF(q) element. The length can be recorded as $q = 2^m$. Therefore, the index value to store the error needs to be $2 * m * t_p$, and the value of i can be estimated by the average search length of $Y = 1/P$, which requires $\log_2(Y)$ bits at most. So the total length is

$$2 * m * t_p + \log_2(Y) \qquad (20)$$

5   Security Analysis

5.1   Information Set Decoding Attack

For the solution proposed in this paper, we need to first consider the most common attack technique for cryptographic systems based on error correction codes, that is, an attack technique that attempts to perform information set decoding (ISD) on public key codes. Information Set Decoding Attack is a powerful decoding attack method, and the ISD decoding attack proposed by Stern is the most efficient decoding attack algorithm [17,18]. Stern algorithm was originally an attack algorithm against binary code-based cryptographic algorithms, but in [19] proposed its version for arbitrary finite field GF(q). The ISD attack is designed to decode random linear codes without using any structural properties (even if they exist). Its complexity mainly depends on the actual number

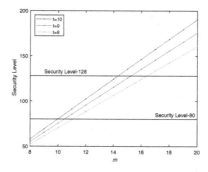

Fig. 3. The security level corresponding to different m and t values.

of errors added to the codeword (The cardinality of the field, the length and dimension of the code also determine its complexity), it does not depend on the error correction capability of the code.

The original CFS scheme used the Canteaut-Chabaud attack to analyze the security performance of the signature scheme. This attack is also a decoding attack, when it is not as efficient as Stern's scheme. We can also see that the original GOPPA code-based scheme is facing the stern version of ISD does not have significant security when attacking. Recalling the previous part, in order to obtain considerable signature complexity, the value of t will not be too large. So, a code that only corrects so few errors, a longer codeword (a bigger m) is needed to ensure its security.

In Fig. 3, we analyzed the security level of the ISD attack in this scheme according to the attack method described in [19]. It can be seen that when m is 10, only t is 10 to reach the security level of 80. m takes 11, the t-values of the three versions 8, 9, and 10 all reached the safety level of 80. In general, the safety of the entire scheme is exponentially related to the product of $m * t$. The larger the value of m and t, the more secure the whole scheme. Meanwhile, the larger the m and t, the larger the public key size of the scheme. The lower bound of (m, t) can be determined as (10,10) or (11, 8). Otherwise, higher security can only be brought at the cost of sacrificing the size of the public key. At this time, it should increase the value of m and adjust the value of t according to the situation.

5.2 Distinguisher Attack

Because the GRS code has an obvious algebraic structure, distinguisher attacks is also the first attack method that needs to be considered. In [3], for some system parameters, the distinguisher attack can be used to distinguish the matrix in the classic McEliece cryptosystem based on GOPPA code and the CFS signature scheme. In [20–22], both authors only focused on attacking GRS codes. It restricted some specific choices of GRS code-based system parameters [21,22]. It was pointed out in [23] that the distinguisher that can distinguish between the random matrix and the generation (or parity check) matrix of the common code gives clues about some possible vulnerabilities, but the attack process is not strictly defined.

According to the description in [23], using a transformation matrix $\mathbf{Q}$ can effectively cover the structure of the GRS code private key matrix. As long as the value of z and m' is not 1 (see the section 3, Attack [22] almost destroys all parameters of [7], to avoid the attack of [22], we need $m' > 1 + \frac{k}{n}$ and $z \neq 0$), an effective anti-distinguisher attack effect can be achieved. The scheme in this paper inherits this security feature and can effectively resist distinguisher attacks. It is necessary to pay attention to the choice of transformation matrix $\mathbf{Q}$. In addition, in the BBCRS scheme, the use of the transformation matrix $\mathbf{Q}$ affects the error correction performance of the private key matrix, which reduces the error correction ability t to t_p. This is a loss in the public key cryptographic algorithm. However, considering the signature scheme proposed in this paper, the loss from t to t_p brings a smaller signature size, which can also be regarded as a gain on the GRS code-based signature scheme.

6   Result

Because the original CFS scheme uses GOPPA codes over $GF(2)$, the proposed scheme uses GRS codes over $GF(q)$. Table 1 compares the proposed scheme with the original CFS scheme under the assumption that the scheme achieves a security level of 80 to demonstrate the performance improvement effect of GRS over $GF(q)$ for the CFS scheme. When the signature complexity is similar and the security is slightly better, the public key size of the proposed scheme (10,10) is only 4.1% of the original CFS scheme (15,10). In the face of ISD attacks, the original CFS signature scheme has a security level that is close to but not quite 80. The parameters must be at least (16,10), and the public key size must be around 10460 kbits to achieve this security level. The parameters for the scheme in this paper only need to be (10,10), and the public key size is around 200 kbits. In conclusion, the proposed scheme's performance and security have greatly improved when compared to previous schemes.

Table 1. Comparison of $GF(q)$-based GRS code signature and CFS signature under the same parameter pair

Scheme	Signature complexity	Security level (Logarithm)	Public key size (kbits)	Signature length (bits)
CFS (15,10)	21.79	76.89	4892.7	150
CFS (16,9)	18.46	76.92	9416.4	144
Proposed (10,10)	21.88	80.33	200.40	202
Proposed (11,8)	15.33	79.50	357.28	170

On the other hand, many improved code-based signature schemes have appeared in recent years [9,10,12]. Table 2 compares the comparison between the proposed scheme and the parallel CFS scheme [9] and the signature scheme based on RM code [10]. Compared with other schemes, the public key size of the signature scheme based on GRS code over GF(q) in this paper is very small. The calculation of the public key size and the length of the signature is calculated by selecting parameters after considering the complexity of the signature. The parameter selection of the Parallel-CFS scheme is considered in the comprehensive situation of ISD (less than 80) and GBA (satisfying 80). For details, please refer to [9, 10].

Table 2. Comparison of different code-based signature schemes under the same security

Level		Our scheme	pqsigRM [10]	Parallel-CFS [9]
80	Public key size (MB)	0.0239	0.249	20
	Signature length (bits)	202	2048	294
128	Public key size (MB)	0.5461	0.733	2.7×10^5
	Signature length (bits)	274	4096	474

The idea behind the scheme in this paper is more low-level, which means it can be applied to other improved schemes to establish a more flexible and safe CFS scheme. The proposed scheme can be applied to provable special signature schemes, such as blind signature [15], code-based ring signature scheme [24]. Based on the current cloud and big data background, the amount of data transmission and data storage is increasing. These schemes have broad application prospects.

7   Conclusions

This paper proposes a new signature scheme, which is called a signature scheme based on GRS code over GF(q). The advantage of this scheme is the high efficiency of signature verification, which is conducive to data processing. This scheme inherits the characteristics of the BBCRS scheme against distinguisher attacks, and constructs a scheme over GF(q). It can ensure security, while it effectively reduces the size of public keys. With the development of the times, there will definitely be more types of attacks in the future, and the values of m and t must be increased to resist various attacks. The public key size and the complexity of the signature must be weighed. In this case, the original CFS signature scheme parameter selection limit is relatively large. The scheme proposed in this paper has more ability of parameter selection. In addition, this scheme is more low-level. It can be combined with other highly efficient and improved code-based cryptographic algorithms and applied to special signatures such as blind signatures and ring signatures. Although the algorithm in this research is fantastic in theory, it is yet unclear how it will work in practice.

References

1. McEliece, R.J.: A public-key cryptosystem based on algebraic. Coding Thv **4244**, 114–116 (1978)
2. Courtois, N.T., Finiasz, M., Sendrier, N.: How to achieve a McEliece-based digital signature scheme. In: Boyd, C. (ed.) ASIACRYPT 2001. LNCS, vol. 2248, pp. 157–174. Springer, Heidelberg (2001). https://doi.org/10.1007/3-540-45682-1_10
3. Faugere, J.C., Gauthier-Umana, V., Otmani, A., Perret, L., Tillich, J.P.: A distinguisher for high-rate mceliece cryptosystems. IEEE Trans. Inf. Theory **59**(10), 6830–6844 (2013)
4. Berger, T.P., Loidreau, P.: How to mask the structure of codes for a cryptographic use. Des. Codes Crypt. **35**(1), 63–79 (2005)
5. Berger, T.P., Cayrel, P.-L., Gaborit, P., Otmani, A.: Reducing key length of the McEliece cryptosystem. In: Preneel, B. (ed.) AFRICACRYPT 2009. LNCS, vol. 5580, pp. 77–97. Springer, Heidelberg (2009). https://doi.org/10.1007/978-3-642-02384-2_6
6. Misoczki, R., Barreto, P.S.L.M.: Compact McEliece keys from Goppa codes. In: Jacobson, M.J., Rijmen, V., Safavi-Naini, R. (eds.) SAC 2009. LNCS, vol. 5867, pp. 376–392. Springer, Heidelberg (2009). https://doi.org/10.1007/978-3-642-05445-7_24
7. Baldi, M., Bianchi, M., Chiaraluce, F., Rosenthal, J., Schipani, D.: Enhanced public key security for the McEliece cryptosystem. J. Cryptol. **29**(1), 1–27 (2016)
8. Baldi, M., Chiaraluce, F., Rosenthal, J., Santini, P., Schipani, D.: Security of generalised Reed-Solomon code-based cryptosystems. IET Inf. Secur. **13**(4), 404–410 (2019)
9. Finiasz, M.: Parallel-CFS. In: Biryukov, A., Gong, G., Stinson, D.R. (eds.) SAC 2010. LNCS, vol. 6544, pp. 159–170. Springer, Heidelberg (2011). https://doi.org/10.1007/978-3-642-19574-7_11
10. Lee, Y., Lee, W., Kim, Y.S., No, J.S.: Modified pqsigRM: RM code-based signature scheme. IEEE Access **8**, 177506–177518 (2020)
11. Zhou, Y., Zeng, P., Chen, S.: An improved code-based encryption scheme with a new construction of public key. In: Abawajy, J.H., Choo, K.-K.R., Islam, R., Xu, Z., Atiquzzaman, M. (eds.) ATCI 2019. AISC, vol. 1017, pp. 959–968. Springer, Cham (2020). https://doi.org/10.1007/978-3-030-25128-4_118
12. Liu, X., Yang, X., Han, Y., Wang, X.A.: A secure and efficient code-based signature scheme. Int. J. Found. Comput. Sci. **30**(04), 635–645 (2019)
13. Pellikaan, R., Márquez-Corbella, I.: Error-correcting pairs for a public-key cryptosystem. In: Journal of Physics: Conference Series, vol. 855, p. 012032. IOP Publishing (2017)
14. Dallot, L.: Towards a concrete security proof of courtois, finiasz and sendrier signature scheme. In: Lucks, S., Sadeghi, A.-R., Wolf, C. (eds.) WEWoRC 2007. LNCS, vol. 4945, pp. 65–77. Springer, Heidelberg (2008). https://doi.org/10.1007/978-3-540-88353-1_6
15. Chen, S., Zeng, P., Choo, K.K.R.: A provably secure blind signature based on coding theory. In: 2016 IEEE 22nd International Conference on Parallel and Distributed Systems (ICPADS), pp. 376–382. IEEE (2016)
16. Shoup, V.: Sequences of games: a tool for taming complexity in security proofs. IACR Cryptology ePrint Archive 2004/332 (2004)
17. Kachigar, G., Tillich, J.-P.: Quantum information set decoding algorithms. In: Lange, T., Takagi, T. (eds.) PQCrypto 2017. LNCS, vol. 10346, pp. 69–89. Springer, Cham (2017). https://doi.org/10.1007/978-3-319-59879-6_5

18. Canto Torres, R., Sendrier, N.: Analysis of information set decoding for a sub-linear error weight. In: Takagi, T. (ed.) PQCrypto 2016. LNCS, vol. 9606, pp. 144–161. Springer, Cham (2016). https://doi.org/10.1007/978-3-319-29360-8_10

19. Peters, C.: Information-set decoding for linear codes over F_q. In: Sendrier, N. (ed.) PQCrypto 2010. LNCS, vol. 6061, pp. 81–94. Springer, Heidelberg (2010). https://doi.org/10.1007/978-3-642-12929-2_7

20. Couvreur, A., Gaborit, P., Gauthier-Umaña, V., Otmani, A., Tillich, J.P.: Distinguisher-based attacks on public-key cryptosystems using Reed-Solomon codes. Des. Codes Crypt. **73**(2), 641–666 (2014)

21. Gauthier, V., Otmani, A., Tillich, J.P.: A distinguisher-based attack on a variant of McEliece's cryptosystem based on Reed-Solomon codes. arXiv preprint arXiv:1204.6459 (2012)

22. Couvreur, A., Otmani, A., Tillich, J.-P., Gauthier–Umaña, V.: A polynomial-time attack on the BBCRS scheme. In: Katz, J. (ed.) PKC 2015. LNCS, vol. 9020, pp. 175–193. Springer, Heidelberg (2015). https://doi.org/10.1007/978-3-662-46447-2_8

23. Baldi, M., Bianchi, M., Chiaraluce, F., Rosenthal, J., Schipani, D.: Enhanced public key security for the McEliece cryptosystem. submitted. arXiv preprint arxiv:1108.2462 (2011)

24. Ren, Y., Zhao, Q., Guan, H., Lin, Z.: On design of single-layer and multilayer code-based linkable ring signatures. IEEE Access **8**, 17854–17862 (2020)

A Collaborative Access Control Scheme Based on Incentive Mechanisms

Yifei Li[1,2,3](✉) [ID], Yinghui Zhang[1,2,3,4] [ID], Wei Liu[1,2,3] [ID], Jianting Ning[2] [ID], and Dong Zheng[1,3,4] [ID]

[1] School of Cyberspace Security, Xian University of Posts and Telecommunications, Xian 710121, China
liyifei1116@163.com
[2] Fujian Provincial Key Laboratory of Network Security and Cryptology, Fujian Normal University, Fuzhou 350007, China
[3] National Engineering Laboratory for Wireless Security, Xian University of Posts and Telecommunications, Xian 710121, China
[4] Westone Cryptologic Research Center, Beijing 100070, China

Abstract. Aiming at the problems of the existing attribute-based collaborative decryption schemes exemplified by failures in cloud storage servers and poor enthusiasm of users for collaborative decryption, a collaborative access control scheme based on incentive mechanisms is proposed. In this scheme, users are divided into different groups and only users of the same group can collaborate to decrypt. The data is encrypted with attribute-based encryption (ABE) and is uploaded to Inter-Planetary File System (IPFS), which not only ensures the confidentiality of data but also prevents malfunctions. Through the incentive mechanism of the blockchain, the user's enthusiasm of decryption is improved. Finally, the theoretical analysis shows that the scheme is secure and efficient.

Keywords: ABE · IPFS · Collaborative decryption · Blockchain

1 Introduction

With the vigorous development of the information revolution, human society has gradually entered the era of information explosion. Therefore, more and more individuals put massive amounts of datas on cloud storage servers [1,2]. However, centralized cloud storage servers are prone to failures such as data tampering or removal [3].

Although the use of blockchain to store data can prevent data from being tampered with, removed and ensure the correctness of the ciphertext, it is not suitable for storing massive amounts of data [4]. In view of this, the Inter-Planetary File System (IPFS) was proposed [5]. IPFS has the characteristics of decentralization and non-tampering [6].

Similarly, to prevent semi-trusted IPFS from accessing sensitive data while achieving fine-grained access control, so that attribute-based encryption (ABE)

X. Chen et al. (Eds.): CSS 2022, LNCS 13547, pp. 48–55, 2022.
https://doi.org/10.1007/978-3-031-18067-5_4

was proposed [7]. The collusion resistance feature of traditional ABE technology makes it impossible for users to obtain a decryption ability greater than their own access rights by collaborating with each other. Therefore, scholars proposed an attribute-based collaborative access control scheme. However, the existing schemes have prominent problems such as cloud storage servers being prone to failures, poor enthusiasm of users for collaborative decryption. The incentive mechanism of the blockchain plays a vital role in the blockchain. A common reward is to give users a higher reputation value [8].

In order to solve the above-mentioned prominent problems, this paper proposes a collaborative access control scheme based on incentive mechanism. **The main contributions of this paper are as follows:**

(1) **Fine-grained access control and collaborative decryption.** Combining attribute-based encryption and blockchain technology, users are divided into different groups, a fine-grained cooperative access control scheme is realized.

(2) **Active collaboration and the correctness of ciphertext.** Based on the incentive mechanism of the blockchain, for the collaboration request of high reputation users, other users will give priority to process. In addition, the using of IPFS to store encrypted private data ensures the correctness of the ciphertext.

2   Related Work

In collaborative access control scenario, scholars have proposed a series of schemes for the confidentiality of data stored on IPFS [9–11]. In order to achieve fine-grained access control, ABE technology has been proposed [12]. However, the collusion resistance of traditional ABE makes it impossible for multiple users to obtain greater access rights through cooperation, which greatly restricts secure data sharing. In view of this, attribute-based collaborative access control technology arises at the historic moment.

In recent years, the attribute-based collaborative access control in the smart health scenario and dynamic user groups scenario [14,15] have attracted the attention. For the first time, Li et al. [16] will group users and only users in the same group can collaborate. However, this scheme only achieves coarse-grained access control [16]. Bobba et al. [17] proposed the concept of translation key, which provides the possibility to realize multi-user fine-grained collaborative decryption under the premise of anti-user collusion. In 2019, Xue et al. [18] constructed a fine-grained collaborative access control scheme, but this scheme is poor practicality.

The blockchain technology was first proposed by "Satoshi Nakamoto" [19]. Blockchain technologies have been used for realizing fair payments in cloud service [20] and global authentication in 5G mobile communications [21]. The incentive mechanism of the blockchain plays an important role in the efficient operation of the blockchain network [22].

3   The Proposed Scheme

The system model of our scheme is shown in the Fig. 1, which includes five entities: IPFS storage server, data owner (DO), data user (DU), center authority (CA) and blockchain.

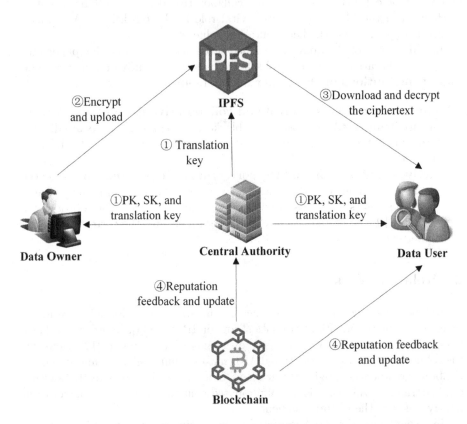

Fig. 1. System model

3.1   Setup

First, for each users group τ, CA defines the group secret key with random numbers $\mathbb{A}, \mathbb{B}, \mathbb{C} \in \mathbb{Z}_\mathbb{P}$ and then defines map $e : G \times G \to G_T$. $\mathbb{H}$ is hash function. Then, CA groups G and G_T (g is generator) are picked by CA. Next, CA selecting the secret key for each group $\theta_\tau \in \mathbb{Z}_\mathbb{P}$ and releasing unique identifier U_p to each user. Finally, CA output PK and MK.

$$PK = \left(e(g,g)^{\mathbb{A}}, \mathcal{D} = g^{\mathbb{B}}, \mathcal{F} = g^{\mathbb{C}}, J = g^{1/\mathbb{B}}, \mathcal{K} = g^{1/\mathbb{C}}, g, \mathbb{H}, G_T, G \right)$$

$$MK = \left(g^{\mathbb{A}}, \mathbb{B}, \mathbb{C}, g^{\theta_1}, \dots, g^{\theta_\tau} \right)$$

3.2   KenGey

The attribute set of user U_p is S_p. First, CA randomly selected group key θ_τ, random parameters $\sigma_p \in \mathbb{Z}_\mathbb{P}$ and $\sigma_{p,q} \in \mathbb{Z}_\mathbb{P}$. Finally, outputs the translation key $\mathbb{T}_p$ [17] used for collaborative decryption and private key SK_p.

$$SK_p = \left(M_p = g^{(\mathbb{A}+\theta_\tau)/\mathbb{B}}, M_{p,q} = g^{\sigma_p}\mathbb{H}\left(a_{p,q}\right)^{\sigma_{p,q}} M'_{p,q} = g^{\sigma_{p,q}}, 1 \le q \le w_p \right)$$

$$\mathbb{T}_p = g^{(\theta_\tau + \sigma_p)/\mathbb{C}}$$

3.3   Encryption

The data owner selects the q_x for each node in the tree T. For each non-leaf node x in the tree, the degree d_x is set to be 1 less than the threshold k_x, that is $d_x = k_x - 1$, then selects $\forall \mathbb{S} \in \mathbb{Z}_\mathbb{P}$ from the root node r, so that other points d_r of the polynomial q_r are randomly selected to fully define the polynomial q_r. Finally, for any other node x, let $q_x(0) = q_{parent(x)}(index(x))$, and q_x randomly select other points d_x to fully define the degree of q_x leaf node set to 0. Let $\mathbb{Y}$ be the set of leaf nodes in T, $\mathbb{X}$ be the set of non-leaf nodes defined in T. Then use T to construct the ciphertext CT_μ.

$$CT_\mu = \begin{pmatrix} C = \mathcal{D}^\mathbb{S}, \bar{C} = \mathcal{F}^\mathbb{S}, T, \forall x \in \mathbb{X} : \hat{C}_x = \mathcal{F}^{q_x(0)}, \\ \forall y \in \mathbb{Y} : C_y = g^{q_y(0)}, C'_y = \mathbb{H}(att(y))^{q_y(0)}, C' = \mu \cdot e(g,g)^{\mathbb{A}\mathbb{S}} \end{pmatrix}$$

3.4   Decryption

Fiest, define a recursive decryption algorithm $\mathrm{Decrypt}_{IPFS}\,(CT_\mu, \gamma, x, u_p)$, where x is the nodes of the tree T, γ is the attribute set, u_p is the user's unique identifier.

i) If x is a leaf node (attribute is p), and store the calculated values in set B_x:

$$P_x = \mathrm{Dec\,Node}\,(CT_\mu, \gamma, u_p, x) = \frac{e\left(M_{p,q}, C_x\right)}{e\left(M'_{p,q}, C'_x\right)} = \frac{e\left(g^{\sigma_p}\mathbb{H}\left(a_{p,q}\right)^{\sigma_{p,q}}, g^{q_x(0)}\right)}{e\left(g^{\sigma_p}, \mathbb{H}\left(a_{p,q}\right)^{q_x(0)}\right)} .$$

$$= e(g,g)^{\sigma_p q_x(0)}, att(x) = a_{p,q} \in S_p$$

otherwise, $P_x = \perp$.

ii) If x is a no-leaf node: when z not translation nodes (not collaborate decryption), z is child node of x and attribute is p:

$$P_z = \mathrm{DecNode}\,(CT_\mu, \gamma, u_p, z)$$

$$= \frac{e\left(M_{p,q}, C_z\right)}{e\left(M'_{p,q}, C'_z\right)} = e(g,g)^{\sigma_p q_z(0)}. \quad att(z) = a_{p,q} \in S_p; \text{ otherwise, } P_z = \perp$$

When z is translation nodes, DU can achieve multi-user collaboration decryption. First calculate the value of the child node z, and store the calculated values in set B_z:

$$P'_z = \mathrm{Dec\,Node}\,(CT_\mu, \gamma, u_p, z) = \frac{e\left(M_{p,q}, C_z\right)}{e\left(M'_{p,q}, C'_z\right)} = e(g,g)^{\sigma'_p q_z(0)}$$

Then, DU uses the translation key $\mathbb{T}_p$ of the access requester U_p and the translation key $\mathbb{T}_j$ of the decryption collaborator U_j to convert the intermediate ciphertext P'_z into the intermediate ciphertext P_z containing the identity of the access requester, so as to prepare for the local decryption of the access requester U_p.

$$P_z = P'_z \cdot e\left(\hat{C}_z, \mathbb{T}_p/\mathbb{T}'_p\right)$$
$$= e(g,g)^{\sigma'_p q_z(0)} \cdot e\left(g^{\mathbb{C}} g^{q_z(0)}, g^{(\theta_\tau + \sigma_p)/\mathbb{C}}/g^{(\theta_\tau + \sigma'_p)/\mathbb{C}}\right).$$
$$= e(g,g)^{q_z(0) \cdot \sigma_p}$$

iii) Access requestor U_p merges the user attribute private key set, and continues the decryption operation using Lagrange interpolation theorem as follows:

$$P_x = \Pi_{z \in B_x} P_z^{\Delta_{k,B'_z}(0)} = e(g,g)^{\sigma_p q_x(0)},$$

where: $k = \text{index}\ (z), B'_z = \{\text{index}\ (z) : z \in B_x\}$ and

$$\Delta_{p,S(x)} = \Pi_{q \in S, q \neq p} \frac{x - q}{p - q}.$$

Then, access requestor runs the recursive algorithm to decrypt the root node r as follows:

$$P_r = \text{Dec Node}\ (CT_\mu, \gamma, r, u_i) = e(g,g)^{\sigma_p \cdot \mathbb{S}}.$$

Continue decrypting, output:

$$P = \frac{e\left(\bar{C}, \mathbb{T}_p\right)}{P_r} = \frac{e\left(g^{\mathbb{C} \cdot q_r(0)}, g^{\theta_\tau/\mathbb{C}} \cdot g^{\sigma_p/\mathbb{C}}\right)}{e(g,g)^{\sigma_p \cdot q_r(0)}} = e(g,g)^{\theta_\tau \cdot \mathbb{S}}$$

The access requestor U_p continues decryption to find the symmetric key μ:

$$\mu = \frac{P \cdot C'}{e\left(C, M_p\right)} = \frac{e(g,g)^{\theta_\tau \cdot \mathbb{S}} \cdot \mu \cdot e(g,g)^{\text{SA}}}{e\left(g^{\mathbb{BS}}, g^{\frac{A+\theta_\tau}{\mathbb{B}}}\right)}$$

Finally, the access requester U_p recovers the plaintext.

3.5   Incentive Mechanism of Blockchain

An incentive mechanism based on the user's dynamic reputation value is introduced into the alliance chain network, which can improve the enthusiasm of other users in the same group for collaborative decryption. The interaction model of the reputation-based incentive mechanism is shown in Fig. 2, which includes three entities: the authoritative center CA, the data user DU and the alliance chain network.

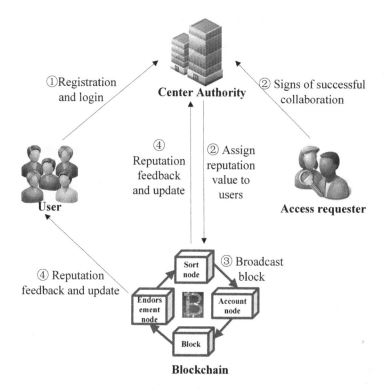

Fig. 2. Interaction model of the reputation-based incentive mechanism

4 Analysis

4.1 Security Analysis

Our scheme has the following five security requirements:

(1) **Data confidentiality.** Sensitive data is kept confidential from unauthorized users and IPFS. The adversary will accept the challenge on the ciphertext of the access policy $T*$ and can request the private key associated with any attribute set γ (not satisfied with $T*$). The security model of our scheme is similar to the scheme [7], so please follow the proof procedure of [7].

(2) **Collaborative decryption by users in the same group.** Only users in the same group are allowed to collaborate and other forms of collaboration will be resisted.

(3) **Collusion resistance.** Collaborative decryption operations from different groups of users are resisted.

(4) **Privacy of the private key.** In the process of multi-user collaborative decryption, the user's private key will not be disclosed.

(5) **One-time intermediate ciphertext.** Each collaboration is only useful for decrypting the current ciphertext.

The secrue proof shows that our scheme meets the above safety requirements.

Table 1. Theoretical analysis.

Phase	Xue et al. scheme	Our scheme
Ciphertext size	$(2W_c + 3 + |tr|)\,|p|$	$(2W_c + 3 + |tr|)\,|p|$
Secret key size	$(2W_u + 2)\,|p|$	$(2W_u + 2)\,|p|$
Communication overhead	$(|tr_\gamma| + 1)\,|p|$	$[(2W_u + 1) + 3\,(E_x + P_a)]\,|p|$

4.2 Performance Analysis

At present, only Xue et al. 's scheme and our scheme have realized the fine-grained collaborative scheme control mechanism. So, in order to evaluate the performance of our scheme, we compared Xue et al. scheme [18] with our scheme from the perspectives of theoretical analysis. Obviously, the secret key size, ciphertext size and communication overhead of the two schemes are the same. The comparison results are shown in Table 1.

5 Conclusion

In this paper, a collaborative access control scheme based on incentive mechanism is constructed by adopting the collaboration-oriented attribute-based encryption mechanism and blockchain technology in the IPFS environment. Through the introduction of the blockchain incentive mechanism, users' enthusiasm for decryption has been greatly improved. Finally, the scheme is secure and has a broad prospect in practical application.

Acknowledgement. This work is supported by the National Natural Science Foundation of China (No. 62072369, 62072371), Opening Foundation of Fujian Provincial Key Laboratory of Network Security and Cryptology Research Fund, Fujian Normal University (No. NSCL-KF2021-05), and the Innovation Capability Support Program of Shaanxi (No. 2020KJXX-052).

References

1. Bajad, R.A., Srivastava, M., Sinha, A.: Survey on mobile cloud computing. Int. J. Eng. Sci. Emerg. Technol. 1(2), 8–19 (2012)
2. Wu, J., Ping, L., Ge, X., et al.: Cloud storage as the infrastructure of cloud computing. In: 2010 International Conference on Intelligent Computing and Cognitive Informatics, pp. 380–383. IEEE (2010)
3. Stergiou, C., Psannis, K.E., Kim, B.G., et al.: Secure integration of IoT and cloud computing. Futur. Gener. Comput. Syst. **78**, 964–975 (2018)
4. Wang, Y., Zhang, A., Zhang, P., et al.: Cloud-assisted EHR sharing with security and privacy preservation via consortium blockchain. IEEE Access **7**, 136704–136719 (2019)
5. Benet, J.: IPFS-content addressed, versioned, P2P file system. arXiv preprint arXiv:1407.3561, pp. 1–11 (2014)

6. Chen, Y., Li, H., Li, K., et al.: An improved P2P file system scheme based on IPFS and blockchain. In: 2017 IEEE International Conference on Big Data (IEEE BigData), pp. 2652–2657. IEEE (2017)
7. Bethencourt, J., Sahai, A., Waters, B.: Ciphertext-policy attribute-based encryption. In: 2007 IEEE Symposium on Security and Privacy (SP 2007), pp. 321–334. IEEE (2007)
8. Ren, Y., Liu, Y., Ji, S., et al.: Incentive mechanism of data storage based on blockchain for wireless sensor networks. Mob. Inf. Syst. 1–18 (2018)
9. Zheng, Q., Li, Y., Chen, P., et al.: An innovative IPFS-based storage model for blockchain. In: 2018 IEEE/WIC/ACM International Conference on Web Intelligence (WI), pp. 704–708. IEEE (2018)
10. Yeh, S.C., Su, M.Y., Chen, H.H., et al.: An efficient and secure approach for a cloud collaborative editing. J. Netw. Comput. Appl. **36**(6), 1632–1641 (2013)
11. Ilia, P., Carminati, B., Ferrari, E., et al.: SAMPAC: socially-aware collaborative multi-party access control. In: Proceedings of the Seventh ACM on Conference on Data and Application Security and Privacy, pp. 71–82 (2017)
12. Zhang, Y., Deng, R.H., Xu, S., et al.: Attribute-based encryption for cloud computing access control: a survey. ACM Comput. Surv. (CSUR) **53**(4), 1–41 (2020)
13. Li, Q., Xia, B., Huang, H., et al.: TRAC: traceable and revocable access control scheme for mHealth in 5G-enabled IIoT. IEEE Trans. Industr. Inform. **18**, 1–12 (2021)
14. Xu, S., Ning, J., Huang, X., et al.: Server-aided bilateral access control for secure data sharing with dynamic user groups. IEEE Trans. Inf. Forensics Secur. **16**, 4746–4761 (2021)
15. Xu, S., Ning, J., Huang, X., et al.: Untouchable once revoking: a practical and secure dynamic EHR sharing system via cloud. IEEE Trans. Dependable Secure Comput. (2021). https://doi.org/10.1109/TDSC.2021.3106393
16. Li, M., Huang, X., Liu, J.K., Xu, L.: GO-ABE: group-oriented attribute-based encryption. In: Au, M.H., Carminati, B., Kuo, C.-C.J. (eds.) NSS 2014. LNCS, vol. 8792, pp. 260–270. Springer, Cham (2014). https://doi.org/10.1007/978-3-319-11698-3_20
17. Bobba, R., Khurana, H., Prabhakaran, M.: Attribute-sets: a practically motivated enhancement to attribute-based encryption. In: Backes, M., Ning, P. (eds.) ESORICS 2009. LNCS, vol. 5789, pp. 587–604. Springer, Heidelberg (2009). https://doi.org/10.1007/978-3-642-04444-1_36
18. Xue, Y., Xue, K., Gai, N., et al.: An attribute-based controlled collaborative access control scheme for public cloud storage. IEEE Trans. Inf. Forensics Secur. **14**(11), 2927–2942 (2019)
19. Nakamoto, S.: Bitcoin: a peer-to-peer electronic cash system. Decentralized Bus. Rev. **21260**, 1–9 (2008)
20. Zhang, Y., Deng, R.H., Liu, X., Zheng, D.: Outsourcing service fair payment based on blockchain and its applications in cloud computing. IEEE Trans. Serv. Comput. **14**(4), 1152–1166 (2021)
21. Zhang, Y., Deng, R.H., Elisa, B., Zheng, D.: Robust and universal seamless handover authentication in 5G HetNets. IEEE Trans. Dependable Secure Comput. **18**(2), 858–874 (2021)
22. Huang, L., Wang, L., Zhang, G.: Security model without managers for blockchain trading system. J. Commun. **41**(12), 36–46 (2020). (in Chinese)

Quartet: A Logarithmic Size Linkable Ring Signature Scheme from DualRing

Zijian Bao[iD], Debiao He[(✉)][iD], Yulin Liu[iD], Cong Peng[iD], Qi Feng[iD], and Min Luo[iD]

Key Laboratory of Aerospace Information Security and Trusted Computing, Ministry of Education, School of Cyber Science and Engineering, Wuhan University, Wuhan 430000, China
{baozijian,liuyulin,cpeng,fengqi,mluo}@whu.edu.cn, hedebiao@163.com

Abstract. Ring signature (RS) allows a user to sign a message on behalf of a group without exposing who the true signer is. In addition, linkable ring signature (LRS) allows signatures can be publicly verified whether they were generated by the same singer. In Crypto 2021, Yuen *et al.* proposed a novel construction paradigm DualRing for RS. In this paper, we first present a DualRing-type LRS scheme *Quartet*. Then, we optimize it by using *sum arguments of knowledge* to a logarithmic size LRS scheme *Quartet*$^+$. Next, we prove the security properties of our schemes, *i.e.*, unforgeability, linkability, anonymity, non-frameability. Finally, we evaluate the performance to illustrate its utility regarding communication and computation costs.

Keywords: Linkable ring signature · Logarithmic size · Sum argument

1 Introduction

Ring signature (RS) [1] allows the signer spontaneously to select multiple users as ring members and then uses his or her private key to sign a message, without revealing who the actual signer is. Ring signature achieves the goal of hiding the real signer's identity within the ring set. It thus has a variety of applications in a myriad of privacy-preserving contexts, including e-voting, privacy-preserving blockchain, *etc.* Abe *et al.* [2] proposed how to construct 1-out-of-n signatures using public keys generated by several different signature schemes. Zhang *et al.* [3] created an identity-based ring signature scheme using bilinear pairings, which can be easily deployed in the e-voting or e-cash systems.

According to the actual needs of different application scenarios, various modifications of ring signature were presented later. Bresson *et al.* [4] significantly proposed threshold ring signature and made it suitable in the multi-signer threshold setting scheme. Naor [5] proposed a deniable ring authentication that lets users to leak an authenticated secret while maintaining their identities' anonymity. Based on the literature [5], Susilo *et al.* [6] proposed a non-interactive deniable ring authentication system. Lv *et al.* [7] introduced a verifiable ring signature

X. Chen et al. (Eds.): CSS 2022, LNCS 13547, pp. 56–70, 2022.
https://doi.org/10.1007/978-3-031-18067-5_5

that the verifier could correctly determine who among the possible signers actually signed the message if the signer was willing to reveal its identity. Fujisaki and Suzuki proposed traceable ring signatures [8] to solve the uncontrolled anonymity in ring signatures.

Suffering from the complete anonymity of RS, the verifier cannot determine whether two signatures are from the same signer, which can cause attacks in some scenarios. Liu *et al.* [9] presented the linkable spontaneous anonymous group (LSAG) signature scheme for the first time. The security of LSAG was proved by the forking lemma. Using the scheme, the authors constructed a one-round registration-free e-voting system. Based on [9], Patrick *et al.* [10] proposed the separable linkable ring signature (LRS) scheme, which also supported a threshold option. Liu *et al.* [11] developed two polynomial-structured linkable ring signature methods, as well as a strong security model of [9] for practical attacker environments. Fan *et al.* [12] proposed a (linkable) ring signature with SM2 algorithm.

LRS is currently in widespread use, particularly in the realm of blockchain. A well-known blockchain Monero [13] that protects users' privacy is built on the CryptoNote protocol [14] and linkable ring signatures, which aims at hiding the transaction information and hiding the real identities [15–17]. However, the size of most existing ring signatures is directly linearly related to the ring size, which may bring many limitations to its application. For example, the communication cost is relatively large, resulting in high system latency and low throughput. Therefore, how to reduce the signature size is of paramount importance.

Many researchers are striving to realize the goal of reducing the ring signature size. Dodis *et al.* [18] constructed the ring signature by accumulators for achieving the constant signature size. For smaller signatures, several ring signature techniques based on zero-knowledge proofs [19–21] were introduced. Yuen *et al.* [22] designed a novel generic ring signature structure, called DualRing, in which the signature size can be compressed into a logarithmic size.

Synthesizing the inspiration provided by the above literature, and aiming at the existing problems, the contributions are as follows:

- We propose a DualRing-type LRS scheme called *Quartet*[1].
- Based on *Quartet*, we propose an LRS scheme with logarithmic size called *Quartet*[+].
- We analyze the schemes' security properties, which satisfy *unforgeability, linkability, anonymity, non-frameability*.
- We evaluate the performance of our schemes from *communication* and *computation* costs.

1.1 Organization

In Sect. 2, we put forward the preliminaries, such as notations, sum arguments of knowledge, the DualRing scheme. In Sect. 3, we focus on the syntax and security

---

[1] We call our scheme *Quartet* because it has a quaternionic ring structure, just as the name DualRing comes from the dual-ring structure in [22].

model. In Sect. 4, we construct *Quartet* from DualRing and further optimize it to *Quartet*$^+$ with logarithmic size. We also give their security analysis in this part. In Sect 5, we evaluate our schemems and put forward the computation and communication costs. In Sect. 6, we conclude our paper.

2   Preliminaries

2.1   Notations

To keep consistent with the parameter setting in [22], we take λ as the security parameter and $\mathbb{G}$ as a cyclic group with the order p. Let g be one generator of $\mathbb{G}$. Each letter with an overrightarrow such as $\vec{a}$ means it is a vector and $r \leftarrow_R \mathbb{Z}_p$ represents randomly selecting an element from $\mathbb{Z}_p$. We make use of $[n]$ to represent the set $\{1, 2, ..., n\}$ and PPT to represent probabilistic polynomial time. Next, an intractable problem is defined as follows:

Discrete Logarithm (DL) Problem: given any two elements $(g, g_1) \in \mathbb{G}$, it is hard for a PPT algorithm to compute a such that $g_1 = g^a$.

2.2   Sum Arguments of Knowledge

DualRing supports logarithmic size DL-based (discrete logarithm) ring signature. Under the DL-based setting, the original DualRing construction can be optimized by using a non-interactive sum argument of knowledge (NISA). Our *Quartet* will also benefit from it to achieve *logarithmic* size signatures.

Non-interactive Sum Argument for (Linkable) Ring Signature. The thing we need is a sum argument proving the following statement. For several $a_i \in \mathbb{Z}_p$, given $c \in \mathbb{Z}_p$ and $P, g_i \in \mathbb{G}$, the equation holds:

$$P = \prod_{i=1}^{n} g_i^{a_i} \wedge c = \sum_{i=1}^{n} a_i.$$

The inner product argument in [22] is a variation of the above NISA. Inspiring from it, Yuen *et al.* designed a novel approach to construct a logarithmic size proof for NISA relation. The authors also provided the theorem that NISA has *statistical witness-extended emulation* for the above relation.

2.3   The DL-Based DualRing Signature

We now review the DL-based DualRing signature scheme (abbr. DR) in [22]. It is the original construction of DualRing, which could be further transformed into a logarithmic size ring signature scheme by combining it with NISA. It has a quartet of PPT algorithms.

- DR.Setup(1^λ). Input a security parameter λ, output a set of public parameters pp. Specifically, it chooses a cyclic group $\mathbb{G}$, generates a generator g, defines a hash operation $\mathcal{H} : \{0, 1\}^n \rightarrow \mathbb{Z}_p$.

- DR.KeyGen(1^λ). Input the parameter set pp, output (pk, sk) such that $pk = g^{sk}$.
- DR.Sign(m, $\vec{pk}$, sk_π). Input a message m, a public key set $\vec{pk} = \{pk_1, .., pk_\pi, ..., pk_n\}$, a signer's secret key sk_π, output $\sigma = (s, c_1, c_2, ..., c_n)$. The detailed steps are as follows.
    1. Choose $r_\pi \in_R \mathbb{Z}_p$, $c_i \in_R \mathbb{Z}_p$, where $1 \leq i \leq n$, and $i \neq \pi$, calculate $R = g^{r_\pi} \cdot \prod_{i=1}^{n} pk_i{}^{c_i}$.
    2. Calculate $c = \mathcal{H}(m || \vec{pk} || R)$.
    3. Calculate $c_\pi = c - c_{\pi+1} - \cdots - c_n - c_1 - \cdots - c_{\pi-1}$.
    4. Calculate $s = r_\pi - c_\pi \cdot sk_\pi$.
    5. Output a signature $\sigma = (s, c_1, c_2, ..., c_n)$.
- DR. Verify(m, $\vec{pk}$, σ). Input a message m, a set $\vec{pk}$, a signature σ, output $1/0$ which denotes accept/reject. The detailed steps are as follows.
    1. Calculate $R = g^s \cdot \prod_{i=1}^{n} pk_i{}^{c_i}$.
    2. Check whether $\mathcal{H}(m || \vec{pk} || R) = \sum_{i=1}^{n} c_i$.

3 Syntax and Security Model

3.1 Syntax of LRS

The following five PPT algorithms define the syntax of LRS.

- LRS.Setup(1^λ). Given λ as input, it outputs the public parameters pp.
- LRS.KeyGen(pp). Given pp as input, it outputs a user's key pair (pk, sk).
- LRS.Sign(m, $\vec{pk}$, sk_π). Given a message m, a set $\vec{pk} = \{pk_1, .., pk_\pi, ..., pk_n\}$, a signer's secret key sk_π as input, it outputs σ.
- LRS.Verify(m, $\vec{pk}$, σ). Given a message m, a set $\vec{pk}$, a signature σ as input, it outputs $1/0$.
- LRS.Link($\vec{pk}$, m', m'', σ', σ''). Given a set $\vec{pk}$ and two message/signature pairs (m', σ') and (m'', σ'') as input, it outputs $1/0$, where 1 indicates that the signatures are "Linked" that they are created by the same secret key; otherwise, 0 indicates "Unlinked".

Correctness. For any λ and any messages m_0, m_1, we have the following equation holds:

$$\Pr \left[\begin{array}{l} \text{LRS.Verify}(m_b, \vec{pk}_b, \sigma_b) = 1, \\ \forall\, b \in \{0, 1\} \text{ and} \\ \text{LRS.Link}(\sigma_0, \sigma_1) = 1 \end{array} \middle| \begin{array}{l} \text{pp} \leftarrow \text{LRS.Setup}(1^\lambda) \\ (pk_i, sk_i) \leftarrow \text{LRS.KeyGen(pp)}, \forall i \in [n] \\ \sigma_b \leftarrow \text{LRS.Sign}(m_b, \vec{pk}_b, sk_\pi), \forall b \in \{0, 1\} \end{array} \right] = 1.$$

Different from ring signatures, the *correctness* definition of LRS considers linkability that we can link two different signatures signed by the same user (specifically, the same secret key) under the same ring set.

3.2   Security Model

In this section, we look at the security model of LRS. We start by defining two Oracles that an adversary can query. We use the symbols S and A to represent a simulator and an adversary.

- Corruption Oracle $CO(i)$: It takes a user's index i and returns the private key sk_i.
- Signing Oracle $SO(m, \vec{pk}, j)$: It takes a message m, a set $\vec{pk}$, and a signer's index j and returns a signature $\sigma \leftarrow \text{LRS.Sign}(m, \vec{pk}, sk_j)$.

Definition 1 (Unforgeability). We use Game_{Unf} to define *unforgeability*:

1. The S generates $\text{pp} \leftarrow \text{LRS.Setup}(1^\lambda)$ and delivers it to A;
2. The A adaptively queries CO, SO and the random Oracle RO;
3. The A outputs a message m^*, a forged signatures σ^* along with a set $\vec{pk} = \{pk_1, pk_2, ..., pk_n\}$.

The A wins the Game_{unf} if the requirements are met:

1. For a message m^*, the signature σ^* is valid, *i.e.*, $\text{LRS.Verify}(m^*, \vec{pk}, \sigma^*) = 1$;
2. For any $i \in [n]$, each index i has not been queried in the Oracle CO;
3. σ^* is not the output of Oracle SO.

The A's advantage is $\text{Adv}_{\text{LRS}}^{\text{Unf}}(A) = \Pr[A \text{ wins}]$. A LRS scheme is *unforgeable* if $\text{Adv}_{\text{LRS}}^{\text{Unf}}(A) \leq \text{negl}(\lambda)$.

Definition 2 (Linkability). We use $\text{Game}_{\text{Link}}$ to define *linkability*:

1. The S generates $\text{pp} \leftarrow \text{LRS.Setup}(1^\lambda)$ and delivers it to A;
2. The A adaptively queries Oracles CO and SO;
3. The A returns two tuples $(m_0^*, \vec{pk}, \sigma_0^*)$, $(m_1^*, \vec{pk}, \sigma_1^*)$ and a set $\vec{pk} = \{pk_1, pk_2, ..., pk_n\}$.

The A wins the $\text{Game}_{\text{Link}}$ if the requirements are met:

1. The A only queries the Oracle CO for $pk_i \in \vec{pk}$ once, *i.e.*, only one private key can be obtained by A, corresponding to a user's pk in $\vec{pk}$;
2. $(m_0^*, \vec{pk}, \sigma_0^*)$, $(m_1^*, \vec{pk}, \sigma_1^*)$ are valid message/signature tuples, *i.e.*, $\text{LRS.Verify}(m_b^*, \vec{pk}, \sigma_b^*) = 1, \forall b \in \{0, 1\}$;
3. $\text{LRS.Link}(\vec{pk}, m_0^*, m_1^*, \sigma_0^*, \sigma_1^*) = \text{Unlinked}$.

The A's advantage is $\text{Adv}_{\text{LRS}}^{\text{Link}}(A) = \Pr[A \text{ wins}]$. A LRS scheme is *linkable* if $\text{Adv}_{\text{LRS}}^{\text{Link}}(A) \leq \text{negl}(\lambda)$.

Definition 3 (Anonymity). We use $\text{Game}_{\text{Anon}}$ to define *anonymity*:

1. The S generates $\text{pp} \leftarrow \text{LRS.Setup}(1^\lambda)$ and delivers it to A;
2. The A adaptively queries Oracles CO and SO;
3. The A outputs a tuple $(m^*, \vec{pk}, i_0, i_1)$ and sends them to S;

4. The $\mathcal{S}$ selects $b \in \{0,1\}$ and computes $\sigma \leftarrow$ LRS.Sign$(m^*, \vec{pk}, sk_{i_b})$;
5. The $\mathcal{A}$ returns $b' \in \{0,1\}$. If $b' = b$, the $\mathcal{A}$ wins the Game.

The $\mathcal{A}$'s advantage is $\mathsf{Adv}_{\mathsf{LRS}}^{\mathsf{Anon}}(\mathcal{A}) = | \Pr[\mathcal{A} \text{ wins}] - 1/2 |$. A LRS scheme is *anonymous* if $\mathsf{Adv}_{\mathsf{LRS}}^{\mathsf{Anon}}(\mathcal{A}) \leq \mathsf{negl}(\lambda)$.

Definition 4 (Non-frameability). We use $\mathsf{Game}_{\mathsf{Frame}}$ to define *non-frameability*:

1. The $\mathcal{S}$ generates pp $\leftarrow$ LRS.Setup(1^λ) and delivers it to $\mathcal{A}$;
2. The $\mathcal{A}$ sends $(m, \vec{pk}, i)$ to $\mathcal{S}$, the $\mathcal{S}$ computes $\sigma \leftarrow$ LRS.Sign$(m, \vec{pk}, sk_i)$ and sends σ to $\mathcal{A}$;
3. The $\mathcal{A}$ adaptively queries Oracles $\mathcal{CO}$ and $\mathcal{SO}$;
4. The $\mathcal{A}$ returns $(m_0^*, \vec{pk}, \sigma^*)$.

The $\mathcal{A}$ wins the $\mathsf{Game}_{\mathsf{Frame}}$ if the requirements are met:

1. For a message m^*, the σ^* is valid, *i.e.*, LRS.Verify$(m^*, \vec{pk}, \sigma^*) = 1$, and σ^* is not the Oracle $\mathcal{SO}$'s output;
2. The index i has not been queried in the Oracle $\mathcal{CO}$;
3. LRS.Link$(\vec{pk}, m, m^*, \sigma, \sigma^*) = $ Linked.

The $\mathcal{A}$'s advantage is $\mathsf{Adv}_{\mathsf{LRS}}^{\mathsf{Frame}}(\mathcal{A}) = \Pr[\mathcal{A} \text{ wins}]$. A LRS scheme is *non-frameable* if $\mathsf{Adv}_{\mathsf{LRS}}^{\mathsf{Frame}}(\mathcal{A}) \leq \mathsf{negl}(\lambda)$.

4   The Proposed Linkable Ring Signatures

We first present a LRS scheme *Quartet* under the construction of DualRing. Then, we optimize it by using NISA to a logarithmic size linkable ring signature scheme *Quartet*$^+$.

4.1   *Quartet*: a Basic Version

We first appoint notations to be used in Table 1. Then, we present *Quartet* as follows:

1. Setup. Given λ as input, it returns a set of public parameters pp, where pp $= \{\mathbb{G}, p, g, \mathbb{Z}_p, \mathcal{H}^s, \mathcal{H}^p\}$.
2. KeyGen. Given the parameter set pp as input, it returns a key pair (pk, sk) such that $pk = g^{sk}$.
3. Sign. Given a message $m \in \{0,1\}^*$, a set $\vec{pk} = \{pk_1, .., pk_\pi, ..., pk_n\}$, a signer's secret key sk_π as input, it returns a signature σ.
   (a) According to the $\vec{pk}$, Compute the signer's linking tag I, namely, $h = \mathcal{H}^p\left(\vec{pk}\right)$, $I = h^{sk_\pi}$.
   (b) Randomly choose $r_\pi \in_R \mathbb{Z}_p$, $c_i \in_R \mathbb{Z}_p$, where $1 \leq i \leq n$, and $i \neq \pi$.

Table 1. Notations.

Notation	Description
$\mathbb{G}$	A cyclic group
p	The order of $\mathbb{G}$
g	A generator of $\mathbb{G}$
n	Number of ring members
$[n]$	The set $\{1, 2, ..., n\}$
π	The signer's index, where $1 \le \pi \le n$
pk_π, sk_π	The signer's key pair
λ	The security parameters
pp	The public parameters
$\mathbb{Z}_p$	$\{1, 2, ..., p\}$
$\mathcal{H}^s$	$\{0, 1\}^* \to Z_p$
$\mathcal{H}^p$	$\{0, 1\}^* \to \mathbb{G}$
m	A message
I	A linking tag
NISA	Non-interactive sum argument
$\vec{pk}$	The public key set, $\vec{pk} = (pk_1, \ldots, pk_n)$

(c) Compute $L = g^{r_\pi} pk_{\pi+1}{}^{c_{\pi+1}} \cdots pk_n{}^{c_n} pk_1{}^{c_1} \cdots pk_{\pi-1}{}^{c_{\pi-1}}$, and $R = h^{r_\pi} I^{c_{\pi+1}} \cdots I^{c_n} I^{c_1} \cdots I^{c_{\pi-1}}$.

(d) Compute $c = \mathcal{H}^s \left(m, \vec{pk}, L, R \right)$.

(e) Compute $c_\pi = c - c_{\pi+1} - \cdots - c_n - c_1 - \cdots - c_{\pi-1}$. Then, we have $\mathcal{H}^s \left(m, \vec{pk}, L, R \right) = c_1 + \cdots + c_n$.

(f) Compute $s = r_\pi - c_\pi \cdot sk_\pi$.

(g) Output the signature $\sigma = (s, c_1, \cdots, c_n, I)$.

4. **Verify.** Given a message m, a set $\vec{pk}$, a linkable ring signature $\sigma = (s, c_1, \cdots, c_n, I)$ as input, it returns $1/0$.

(a) Compute $h = \mathcal{H}^p \left(\vec{pk} \right)$.

(b) Compute $L = g^s pk_1{}^{c_1} \cdots pk_n{}^{c_n}$, and $R = h^s I^{c_1} \cdots I^{c_n}$.

(c) Compute $c = c_1 + \cdots + c_n$.

(d) Check whether c and $\mathcal{H}^s \left(m, \vec{pk}, L, R \right)$ are equal. If it is equal, then σ is a legal signature, the algorithm outputs accept; Otherwise, the signature is invalid, the algorithm outputs reject.

5. **Link.** Given a set $\vec{pk}$ and two pairs (m', σ') and (m'', σ'') as input, it returns $1/0$, where 1 indicates that the signatures are "Linked" that they are produced with the same secret key; otherwise, 0 indicates "Unlinked".

(a) For a $\vec{pk} = (pk, \cdots, pk_n)$, given two signatures $\sigma' = (s', c_0', \cdots, c_n', I')$ for m' and $\sigma'' = (s'', c_0'', \cdots, c_n'', I'')$ for m'', we can check whether $I' \stackrel{?}{=} I''$. If it is equal, they come from the same signer, i.e., Linked; otherwise, Unlinked.

Correctness. Let $\sigma = (s, c_1, \cdots, c_n, I)$ from *Quartet*.Sign, then in the *Quartet*.Verify algorithm, we have:

$$L = g^s pk_1^{c_1} \cdots pk_n^{c_n}$$
$$= g^{r_\pi} g^{-c_\pi \cdot sk_\pi} pk_1^{c_1} \cdots pk_n^{c_n}$$
$$= g^{r_\pi} pk_{\pi+1}^{c_{\pi+1}} \cdots pk_n^{c_n} pk_1^{c_1} \cdots pk_{\pi-1}^{c_{\pi-1}}.$$

$$R = h^s I^{c_1} \cdots I^{c_n}$$
$$= h^{r_\pi} h^{-c_\pi \cdot sk_\pi} I^{c_1} \cdots I^{c_n}$$
$$= h^{r_\pi} I^{-c_\pi} I^{c_1} \cdots I^{c_n}$$
$$= h^{r_\pi} I^{c_{\pi+1}} \cdots I^{c_n} I^{c_1} \cdots I^{c_{\pi-1}}.$$

Then, $c = \mathcal{H}^s\left(m, \vec{pk}, L, R\right)$ is satisfied, which completes the proof.

4.2 Security Analysis of *Quartet*

Theorem 1. *Quartet is unforgeable under the random oracle model, if DL problem is hard.*

Proof. The general idea is that if an adversary $\mathcal{A}$ have the ability to forge a ring signature, then a simulator $\mathcal{S}$ can make use of the above ability to solve DL problem. We briefly describe the proof. In the Setup phase, given a DL problem (g, g_1), $\mathcal{S}$ runs pp $\leftarrow$ Setup(λ), and for $i \in [n]/i^*$, $\mathcal{S}$ runs $(pk_i, sk_i) \leftarrow$ LRS.KeyGen(pp), for $i = i^*$, $\mathcal{S}$ returns $pk^* := g_1$, sends pp and $\vec{pk} = \{pk_1, pk_2, ..., pk_n\}$ to $\mathcal{A}$. In the Oracle Simulation phase, $\mathcal{A}$ queries $\mathcal{CO}$, $\mathcal{SO}$ and the random Oracle $\mathcal{RO}$ to $\mathcal{S}$. Finally, $\mathcal{A}$ returns a forged signature σ, and $\mathcal{S}$ can rewind to obtain another forgery σ'. Since $\sigma = (s, c_1, \cdots, c_n, I)$ and $\sigma' = (s', c_1', \cdots, c_n', I')$ are valid signatures for the same L, we have:

$$L = g^s pk_1^{c_1} \cdots pk_n^{c_n} = g^{s'} pk_1^{c_1'} \cdots pk_n^{c_n'}.$$

Then, we are able to find $j \in [n]$ where $c_j \neq c_j'$, which implys $g^s pk_j^{c_j} = g^{s'} pk_j^{c_j'}$. Therefore, $\mathcal{S}$ can extract the secret key $\frac{s-s'}{c_j'-c_j}$ to solve the DL problem.

Theorem 2. *Quartet is linkable under the random oracle model, if DL problem is hard.*

Proof. The general idea is that if an adversary $\mathcal{A}$ can break *linkability*, then a simulator $\mathcal{S}$ can make use of the above ability to solve DL problem. First, $\mathcal{S}$ runs pp $\leftarrow$ Setup(λ), and for $i \in [n]$, $\mathcal{S}$ runs $(pk_i, sk_i) \leftarrow$ LRS.KeyGen(pp), sends pp and $\vec{pk} = \{pk_1, pk_2, ..., pk_n\}$ to $\mathcal{A}$. Note that $\mathcal{A}$ can only obtain only one private key sk_π in $\vec{pk}$. In the Output phase, $\mathcal{A}$ returns two valid signatures $(m_0^*, \vec{pk}, \sigma_0^*)$, $(m_1^*, \vec{pk}, \sigma_1^*)$ where $I \neq I'$. It implys $\mathcal{A}$ only knowing the sk_π successfully forges a signature, which breaks the *unforgeability*, thereby solving the DL problem.

Theorem 3. *Quartet is prefect anonymous under the random oracle model.*

Proof. We create a simulator $\mathcal{S}$ that provides *perfect anonymity*. In the Setup phase, $\mathcal{S}$ generates pp $\leftarrow$ Setup(λ) and $(pk_i, sk_i) \leftarrow$ LRS.KeyGen(pp) for $i \in [n]$, then sends pp and $\vec{pk} = \{pk_1, pk_2, ..., pk_n\}$ to $\mathcal{A}$. In the Oracle Simulation phase, $\mathcal{A}$ queries $\mathcal{CO}$, $\mathcal{SO}$ to $\mathcal{S}$. Finally, $\mathcal{A}$ returns $(m^*, \vec{pk}, i_0, i_1)$ to $\mathcal{S}$. If the hash value is already queried in $\mathcal{RO}$, $\mathcal{S}$ fails and exits. Then, $\mathcal{S}$ chooses $b \in \{0,1\}$, calculates $\sigma \leftarrow$ LRS.Sign($m^*, \vec{pk}, sk_{i_b}$), and then sends it to $\mathcal{A}$. In the Output phase, $\mathcal{A}$ outputs $b' \in \{0,1\}$. We briefly analyse the probability of success. After the first q_s queries to $\mathcal{SO}$, the probability of success is $1 - \frac{q_h}{q}$. Then, after q_s queries to $\mathcal{SO}$, the probability is $\left(1 - \frac{q_h}{q}\right)\left(1 - \frac{q_h+1}{q}\right)...\left(1 - \frac{q_h+q_s-1}{q}\right) \geq 1 - \frac{q_s(q_h+q_s-1)}{q}$. We have $q >> 1 - \frac{q_s(q_h+q_s-1)}{q}$, thus, there is no PPT adversary who has a non-negligible chance of winning more than half.

Theorem 4. *Quartet is non-frameable under the random oracle model, if DL problem is hard.*

Proof. According to Theorem 1, we know no PPT adversary can successfully forge a signature. Here, for *non-frameability*, we consider an $\mathcal{A}$ who wants to forge a signature linked with a given signature. In the Setup phase, $\mathcal{S}$ runs pp $\leftarrow$ Setup(λ), and for $i \in [n]$, $\mathcal{S}$ runs $(pk_i, sk_i) \leftarrow$ LRS.KeyGen(pp), sends pp and $\vec{pk} = \{pk_1, pk_2, ..., pk_n\}$ to $\mathcal{A}$. Finally, $\mathcal{A}$ returns $(m, \vec{pk}, i)$ to $\mathcal{C}$, the $\mathcal{C}$ calculates $\sigma \leftarrow$ LRS.Sign($m, \vec{pk}, sk_i$) and sends σ to $\mathcal{A}$. In the Oracle Simulation phase, $\mathcal{A}$ queries $\mathcal{CO}$, $\mathcal{SO}$ to $\mathcal{S}$. In the Output phase, $\mathcal{A}$ returns a tuple $(m_0^*, \vec{pk}, \sigma^*)$. As we know, LRS.Link($\vec{pk}, m, m^*, \sigma, \sigma^*$) = Linked implys $I = I^*$, then $h^{sk_i} = h^{sk_i^*}$ where $h = \mathcal{H}^p\left(\vec{pk}\right)$. Immediately, $\mathcal{A}$ has $sk_i = sk_i^*$. Since, the index i has not been queried in the Oracle $\mathcal{CO}$. Then, we know σ^* is valid for the message m_0^*, which breaks the unforgeability, thereby solving the DL problem.

Correctness. As the NISA and *Quartet* are *correct*, it is easy to reach *Quartet*$^+$ is *correct*.

4.3   *Quartet*$^+$: An Improved Version with Logarithmic Size

In this section, we use NISA to prove that the verifier knows the vector $\vec{a} = (c_1, \cdots, c_n)$ such that $\mathcal{H}^s\left(m, \vec{pk}, L, R\right) = \sum_{i=1}^{n} c_i$ without revealing $\vec{a}$, which can reduce the signature size from *linear* level to *logarithmic* level. The Setup, KeyGen algorithms are almost the same in *Quartet* and *Quartet*$^+$, the only difference is the public paremeters pp in *Quartet*$^+$.Setup contains an additional common reference string crs for NISA, so we ignore them here.

1. Sign.
   (a) Invoke *Quartet*.Sign($m, \vec{pk}, sk_\pi$) to get the signature $\sigma = (s, c_1, \cdots, c_n, I)$, and store the intermediate results (c, L, R) in *Quartet*.
   (b) Let $\vec{a} = (c_1, \cdots, c_n)$.

    (c) Compute $P = L \cdot (g^s)^{-1} \cdot R \cdot (h^s)^{-1}$.

    (d) Compute $\pi \leftarrow$ NISA.Proof$(\mathsf{pp}, \vec{pk}, I, P, c, \vec{a})$.

    (e) Output the signature $\sigma = (s, L, R, I, \pi)$.

2. Verify.

    (a) Compute $h = \mathcal{H}^p\left(\vec{pk}\right)$.

    (b) Compute $c = \mathcal{H}^s\left(m, \vec{pk}, L, R\right)$.

    (c) Compute $P = L \cdot (g^s)^{-1} \cdot R \cdot (h^s)^{-1}$.

    (d) Check whether NISA.Verify $\left(\mathsf{pp}, \vec{pk}, I, P, c, \pi\right) \overset{?}{=} 1$. If the equation holds, then σ is a legal signature, the algorithm outputs accept; Otherwise, the signature is invalid, the algorithm outputs reject.

3. Link.

    (a) For a $\vec{pk} = (pk, \cdots, pk_n)$, given two signatures $\sigma' = (s', L', R', I', \pi')$ for m' and $\sigma'' = (s'', L'', R'', I'', \pi'')$ for m'', we can check whether $I' \overset{?}{=} I''$. If it is equal, they come from the same signer, *i.e.*, Linked; otherwise, Unlinked.

4.4   Security Analysis of *Quartet*$^+$

Theorem 5. *Quartet*$^+$ *is unforgeable If Quartet is unforgeable and the NISA has statistical witness-extended emulation.*

Proof. The basic idea is that we assume if an $\mathcal{A}$ can break the *unforgeability* of *Quartet*, then we can build an algorithm $\mathcal{B}$ breaking the *unforgeability* of *Quartet*$^+$. $\mathcal{B}$ is given the public parameters pp from the simulator $\mathcal{S}$ in Game$_{\mathsf{Unf}}$, then $\mathcal{B}$ generates pp' which contains pp and an additional crs. $\mathcal{B}$ sends pp' to $\mathcal{A}$. When $\mathcal{A}$ queries $\mathcal{SO}$, $\mathcal{B}$ first queries its $\mathcal{SO}$ to get $\sigma = (s, c_1, \cdots, c_n, I)$ and then converts it to $\sigma' = (s, L, R, I, \pi)$. $\mathcal{B}$ returns σ' to $\mathcal{A}$ as the result of $\mathcal{SO}$ queries. Finally, $\mathcal{A}$ returns a forgery σ^*. By using the properties of NISA, $\mathcal{B}$ can extract $(c_1^*, c_2^*, ..., c_n^*)$ from σ^*. Then, $\mathcal{B}$ returns a forgery $\sigma' = (c_1^*, c_2^*, ..., c_n^*, z^*)$ to $\mathcal{A}$.

Theorem 6. *Quartet*$^+$ *is linkable If Quartet is linkable and the NISA has statistical witness-extended emulation.*

Proof. The proof strategy is the same as that of *unforgeability*. In the Setup and Oracle Simulation phases, $\mathcal{B}$ simulates it as the *unforgeability*'s proof. In the Output phase, $\mathcal{A}$ outputs two valid signatures. Then, by using the properties of NISA, $\mathcal{B}$ can extract two valid signatures and sends them to its challenger.

Theorem 7. *Quartet*$^+$ *is prefect anonymous If Quartet is prefect anonymous.*

Proof. We assume if an $\mathcal{A}$ can break the *anonymity* of *Quartet*, then we can build an algorithm $\mathcal{B}$ breaking the *anonymity* of *Quartet*$^+$. First, $\mathcal{B}$ is given the public parameters pp from the simulator $\mathcal{S}$ in Game$_{\mathsf{Unf}}$, then $\mathcal{B}$ generates pp' which contains pp and an additional crs. $\mathcal{B}$ sends pp' to $\mathcal{A}$. In the Oracle Simulation phase, $\mathcal{B}$ simulates it as the *unforgeability*'s proof. Finally, $\mathcal{A}$ outputs a tuple $(m^*, \vec{pk}, i_0, i_1)$ and sends them to $\mathcal{B}$. And $\mathcal{B}$ delivers it to its challenger. Then, upon receiving the $\sigma = (s, L, R, I, \pi)$ from the $\mathcal{B}$'s challenger, $\mathcal{B}$ converts it to $\sigma' = (s, L, R, I, \pi)$ and sends σ' to $\mathcal{A}$. In the Output phase, $\mathcal{B}$ outputs the same result of the $\mathcal{A}$'s output.

Theorem 8. *Quartet$^+$ is non-frameable If Quartet is non-frameable and the NISA has statistical witness-extended emulation.*

Proof. We assume if an $\mathcal{A}$ can break the *non-frameability* of *Quartet*, then we can build an algorithm $\mathcal{B}$ breaking the *non-frameability* of *Quartet$^+$*. The proof is similar to that of *linkability*. We ignore it here.

5   Evaluation and Analysis

The performance of our schemes is measured in terms of communication and computation costs.

5.1   Communication Cost

Firstly we analyze the communication cost. We set $|q|$ as the bits of order q, $|\mathbb{G}|$ as the bits of group $\mathbb{G}$. In Table 2, we make a comparison between the signature size of LSAG [9] and that of our schemes. We can know that LSAG and *Quartet* have the same signature size.

Assuming that $|q| = 160$ bits, $|\mathbb{G}| = 512$ bits. We present the communication cost of the three protocols in different ring sizes as shown in Fig. 1. The communication cost in [9] and *Quartet* both have a linear relationship with the ring size. While in *Quartet$^+$*, the signature size is proportional to the number of members in the ring. It can be seen our scheme is slightly worse than [9] at the beginning. When the ring size is greater than 32, the communication cost of *Quartet$^+$* grows slower and remains lower than [9].

Table 2. Communication cost in comparison to LSAG

Schemes	Signature	Size
LSAG[9]	$(c_1, s_1, \cdots, s_n, I\ )$	$(n+1)|q| + |\mathbb{G}|$
Quartet	$(s_1, c_1, \cdots, c_n, I\ )$	$(n+1)|q| + |\mathbb{G}|$
Quartet$^+$	(s, L, R, I, π)	$3|q| + (2log_2 n + 3)|\mathbb{G}|$

5.2   Computation Cost

This paper focuses on the computation cost in algorithms including Sign, Verify. Suppose that the number of ring members is n, T_{ga} is the time of additive operation on group $\mathbb{G}$, T_{gm} indicates the time of multiplication operation on group $\mathbb{G}$, T_{za} indicates the time of modular addition over $\mathbb{Z}_q$, T_{zm} indicates the

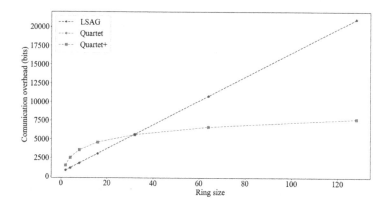

Fig. 1. Practical comparison of communication cost

time of modular multiplication over $\mathbb{Z}_q$. In addition, T_{hs} is the time of hash function for $\{0,1\}^* \to \mathbb{Z}_q$, and T_{hp} represents the time of hash function for $\{0,1\}^* \to \mathbb{G}$.

We analyze and compare [9] with our schemes, the results are shown in Table 3. Further, We implement our proposed schemes in Python, using the Fastecdsa library. In the practical evaluation, the personal computer is configured with an operating system with Ubuntu 18.04. The practical comparison result is shown in Fig. 2. We find that the communication cost of Sign in $Quartet^+$ is slightly heavier than that in [9] but it is acceptable, and $Quartet$ has the shortest running time. While the communication cost of Verify in $Quartet^+$ has an advantage over that in both [9] and $Quartet$. To sum up, we know that $Quartet^+$ is more *efficient* from the comparison.

Table 3. Computation cost in comparison to LSAG

Schemes	Sign	Verify
LSAG [9]	$(4n-1)T_{gm} + (2n-2)T_{ga} + T_{za}$ $+nT_{hs} + T_{hp}$	$4nT_{gm} + 2nT_{ga} + nT_{hs}$
$Quartet$	$(2n+1)T_{gm} + (2n-2)T_{ga}$ $+(n-1)T_{za} + T_{hs} + T_{hp}$	$(2n+2)T_{gm} + 2nT_{ga} + (n-1)T_{za}$ $+T_{hs} + T_{hp}$
$Quartet^+$	$(6n+2log_2n)T_{gm} + (3n+2log_2n)T_{ga}$ $+(3n-2)T_{za} + (4n-3)T_{zm}$ $+(log_2n+2)T_{hs} + T_{hp}$	$(2log_2n+n+4)T_{gm} + (n+5)T_{ga}$ $+2T_{zm} + T_{za} + (log_2n+1)T_{hs}$

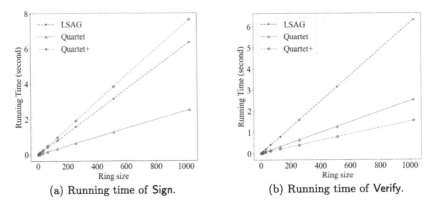

(a) Running time of **Sign**.　　　　(b) Running time of **Verify**.

Fig. 2. Practical comparison of computation cost

6   Conclusion

In this paper, we concentrate on constructing a DualRing-type LRS scheme $Quartet$ and an LRS scheme with logarithmic size $Quartet^+$. Then, we prove the security of the proposed schemes. Finally, we evaluate the performance for *communication* and *computation* costs. In the future, we can focus on more *efficient* (linkable) ring signature constructions, and study *functional* ring signatures such as traceable/recoverable ring signatures.

Acknowledgement. The work was supported by the National Key Research and Development Program of China (No. 2021YFA1000600), the National Natural Science Foundation of China (Nos.U21A20466, 62172307, 61972294, 61932016), the Special Project on Science and Technology Program of Hubei Provience (No. 2020AEA013), the Natural Science Foundation of Hubei Province (No. 2020CFA052) and the Wuhan Municipal Science and Technology Project (No. 2020010601012187).

References

1. Rivest, R.L., Shamir, A., Tauman, Y.: How to leak a secret. In: Boyd, C. (ed.) ASIACRYPT 2001. LNCS, vol. 2248, pp. 552–565. Springer, Heidelberg (2001). https://doi.org/10.1007/3-540-45682-1_32
2. Abe, M., Ohkubo, M., Suzuki, K.: 1-out-of-n signatures from a variety of keys. In: Zheng, Y. (ed.) ASIACRYPT 2002. LNCS, vol. 2501, pp. 415–432. Springer, Heidelberg (2002). https://doi.org/10.1007/3-540-36178-2_26
3. Zhang, F., Kim, K.: ID-based blind signature and ring signature from pairings. In: Zheng, Y. (ed.) ASIACRYPT 2002. LNCS, vol. 2501, pp. 533–547. Springer, Heidelberg (2002). https://doi.org/10.1007/3-540-36178-2_33
4. Bresson, E., Stern, J., Szydlo, M.: Threshold ring signatures and applications to. In: Yung, M. (ed.) CRYPTO 2002. LNCS, vol. 2442, pp. 465–480. Springer, Heidelberg (2002). https://doi.org/10.1007/3-540-45708-9_30

5. Naor, M.: Deniable ring authentication. In: Yung, M. (ed.) CRYPTO 2002. LNCS, vol. 2442, pp. 481–498. Springer, Heidelberg (2002). https://doi.org/10.1007/3-540-45708-9_31

6. Susilo, W., Mu, Y.: Non-interactive deniable ring authentication. In: Lim, J.-I., Lee, D.-H. (eds.) ICISC 2003. LNCS, vol. 2971, pp. 386–401. Springer, Heidelberg (2004). https://doi.org/10.1007/978-3-540-24691-6_29

7. Lv, J., Wang, X.: Verifiable ring signature. In: Proceedings of Third International Workshop on Cryptology and Network Security (CANS 2003) (2003), pp:663–665. https://www.researchgate.net/publication/265929579

8. Fujisaki, E., Suzuki, K.: Traceable ring signature. In: Okamoto, T., Wang, X. (eds.) PKC 2007. LNCS, vol. 4450, pp. 181–200. Springer, Heidelberg (2007). https://doi.org/10.1007/978-3-540-71677-8_13

9. Liu, J.K., Wei, V.K., Wong, D.S.: Linkable spontaneous anonymous group signature for ad hoc groups. In: Wang, H., Pieprzyk, J., Varadharajan, V. (eds.) ACISP 2004. LNCS, vol. 3108, pp. 325–335. Springer, Heidelberg (2004). https://doi.org/10.1007/978-3-540-27800-9_28

10. Liu, J.K., Wei, V.K., Wong, D.S.: Linkable spontaneous anonymous group signature for ad hoc groups. In: Wang, H., Pieprzyk, J., Varadharajan, V. (eds.) ACISP 2004. LNCS, vol. 3108, pp. 325–335. Springer, Heidelberg (2004). https://doi.org/10.1007/978-3-540-27800-9_28

11. Liu, J.K., Wong, D.S.: Linkable ring signatures: security models and new schemes. In: Gervasi, O., et al. (eds.) ICCSA 2005. LNCS, vol. 3481, pp. 614–623. Springer, Heidelberg (2005). https://doi.org/10.1007/11424826_65

12. Fan, Q., He, D.B., Luo, M., Huang, X.Y., Li, D.W.: Ring signature schemes based on SM2 digital signature algorithm. J. Cryptol. Res. **8**(4), 710–723 (2021). https://doi.org/10.13868/j.cnki.jcr.000472

13. "Monero," [Online]. https://www.getmonero.org/

14. Van Saberhagen N.: "CryptoNote v2.0," (2013). [Online]. https://cryptonote.org/whitepaper.pdf

15. Sun, S.-F., Au, M.H., Liu, J.K., Yuen, T.H.: RingCT 2.0: a compact accumulator-based (linkable ring signature) protocol for blockchain cryptocurrency monero. In: Foley, S.N., Gollmann, D., Snekkenes, E. (eds.) ESORICS 2017. LNCS, vol. 10493, pp. 456–474. Springer, Cham (2017). https://doi.org/10.1007/978-3-319-66399-9_25

16. Sun, S.-F., Au, M.H., Liu, J.K., Yuen, T.H.: RingCT 2.0: a compact accumulator-based (linkable ring signature) protocol for blockchain cryptocurrency Monero. In: Foley, S.N., Gollmann, D., Snekkenes, E. (eds.) ESORICS 2017. LNCS, vol. 10493, pp. 456–474. Springer, Cham (2017). https://doi.org/10.1007/978-3-319-66399-9_25

17. Zhang, F., Huang, N.N., Gao, S.: Privacy data authentication schemes based on Borromean ring signature. J. Cryptol. Res. **5**(5), 529–537 (2018). https://doi.org/10.13868/j.cnki.jcr.000262

18. Dodis, Y., Kiayias, A., Nicolosi, A., Shoup, V.: Anonymous identification in *Ad Hoc* groups. In: Cachin, C., Camenisch, J.L. (eds.) EUROCRYPT 2004. LNCS, vol. 3027, pp. 609–626. Springer, Heidelberg (2004). https://doi.org/10.1007/978-3-540-24676-3_36

19. Bootle, J., Cerulli, A., Chaidos, P., Ghadafi, E., Groth, J., Petit, C.: Short accountable ring signatures based on DDH. In: Pernul, G., Ryan, P.Y.A., Weippl, E. (eds.) ESORICS 2015. LNCS, vol. 9326, pp. 243–265. Springer, Cham (2015). https://doi.org/10.1007/978-3-319-24174-6_13

20. Esgin, M.F., Steinfeld, R., Liu, J.K., Liu, D.: Lattice-based zero-knowledge proofs: new techniques for shorter and faster constructions and applications. In: Boldyreva, A., Micciancio, D. (eds.) CRYPTO 2019. LNCS, vol. 11692, pp. 115–146. Springer, Cham (2019). https://doi.org/10.1007/978-3-030-26948-7_5
21. Esgin, M.F., Steinfeld, R., Sakzad, A., Liu, J.K., Liu, D.: Short lattice-based one-out-of-many proofs and applications to ring signatures. In: Deng, R.H., Gauthier-Umaña, V., Ochoa, M., Yung, M. (eds.) ACNS 2019. LNCS, vol. 11464, pp. 67–88. Springer, Cham (2019). https://doi.org/10.1007/978-3-030-21568-2_4
22. Yuen, T.H., Esgin, M.F., Liu, J.K., Au, M.H., Ding, Z.: *DualRing*: generic construction of ring signatures with efficient instantiations. In: Malkin, T., Peikert, C. (eds.) CRYPTO 2021. LNCS, vol. 12825, pp. 251–281. Springer, Cham (2021). https://doi.org/10.1007/978-3-030-84242-0_10

Updatable Hybrid Encryption Scheme with No-Directional Key Update for Cloud Storage

Zhenhua Liu[1,2], Yuanju Ma[1(✉)], Yaxin Niu[1], Jingwan Gong[1], and Baocang Wang[3]

[1] School of Mathematics and Statistics, Xidian University, Xi'an 710071, China
`1803739732@qq.com`
[2] State Key Laboratory of Cryptology, P. O. Box 5159, Beijing 100878, China
[3] State Key Laboratory of Integrated Services Networks, Xidian University, Xi'an 710071, China
`bcwang79@aliyun.com`

Abstract. Updatable encryption (UE) plays an important role in mitigating the impact of key compromise on ciphertext in the scenario of cloud storage. Nevertheless, most of the existing UE schemes focus on making symmetric encryption updatable. In this paper, to give play to advantages of symmetric and asymmetric encryption, we present an updatable hybrid encryption (UHE) scheme. By setting the REACT transform as the underlying encryption scheme and using the indistinguishable obfuscation to convert the private key into a public key encryption program, the synchronous update of public/private key pair and ciphertext can be realized. More importantly, the generation and update of private key are stored locally in hybrid encryption, the update token is not used to derive the private key, and thus the no-directional key update can be achieved. Furthermore, considering for the adversarial attack behaviors, we build a reasonable security model. Finally, since the decryption ability of the punctured keys is limited at the punctured points, the adversary can be allowed to access to all oracles at the full epochs, and then under the proposed security framework the confidentiality of the proposed scheme can be proven based on the indistinguishability between pseudorandom functions, where the confidentiality can capture forward and post-compromise security.

Keywords: Updatable encryption · Hybrid encryption · t-puncturable pseudorandom function · Forward security · Post-compromise security

---

Supported by the Natural Science Basic Research Plan in Shaanxi Province of China under Grant No. 2022JZ-38.

X. Chen et al. (Eds.): CSS 2022, LNCS 13547, pp. 71–85, 2022.
https://doi.org/10.1007/978-3-031-18067-5_6

1   Introduction

With the rise and development of cloud computing, cloud storage has been providing ample space, flexible access, and reasonable price for the clients. Since cloud storage can guarantee the durability, availability and security of data, individuals and businesses are willing to store their data in the cloud in order to reduce storage costs and access data anytime and anywhere. Cloud storage is used in many application scenarios due to the above advantages.

For data confidentiality, data owners encrypt the data and then store them in the cloud. However, it is unavoidable that their private keys would be lost, stolen or compromised. This situation would cause data leakage in the cloud. Recent research [27] showed that out of 1,609,983 mobile apps in leakscope and 15,098 backend servers could be attacked by data breaches. An unsecured mobile app backend database reportedly leaked around 280 million sensitive user records, including usernames, passwords, phone numbers, locations [24]. Thus it is urgent to exploit a kind of technique of key and ciphertext update for cloud storage.

In the beginning, key rotation is an obvious approach that downloads and decrypts the ciphertext, and then re-encrypts the message with the new key. Actually, key rotation is mandated by regulation in some contexts. For example, under the PCI-DSS standard [7], the encrypted credit card data needs to be replaced periodically, i.e., transforming the encrypted data from an old key to a fresh one. Similarly, this strategy is used by many cloud storage providers, such as Google [13] and Amazon [2]. However, key rotation is only suitable for local storage due to heavy computation and bandwidth consumption.

Subsequently, Boneh et al. [3] introduced the concept of updatable encryption (UE) and proposed the first UE scheme based on symmetric-key proxy re-encryption from key homomorphic pseudorandom functions. Compared with the original encryption scheme (*KeyGen, Enc, Dec*), UE scheme has two additional algorithms *ReKeyGen* and *ReEnc*, where the client only needs to generate a token via *ReKeyGen* and the cloud server uses the token to update the ciphertext via *ReEnc*. In fact, the token is used to update the client's secret key and the ciphertext stored in the cloud, and thus computation cost and bandwidth consumption are acceptable for the client and the cloud server. Due to the above advantages, UE could be optimal for cloud storage to resist key compromise. Since the concept of updatability was introduced, many important advances [1, 16, 20] have been made in updatable encryption.

1.1   Our Motivations and Contributions

Most of the existing UE schemes concentrated on the updatability of symmetric encryption schemes. Nevertheless, the updatable symmetric encryption has some limitations due to key distribution in cloud storage scenario. Fortunately, hybrid encryption can combine the advantages of symmetric and asymmetric encryption, which motivates us to explore updatable hybrid encryption.

The existing research results [16, 20] indicated that no-directional key update discloses less information than uni-/bi-directional key update, and is the optimal option for constructing UE schemes. Furthermore, the combination of no-directional key update and uni-directional ciphertext update can achieve forward and post-compromise security [20]. Thus, it is significant to propose an updatable hybrid encryption scheme with no-directional key update.

The major contributions of this paper are follows.

1. The reasonable security notions is modeled for UHE. Based on the security model proposed by Chen et al. [8], we consider the following attack behaviors: chosen-ciphertext attack, malicious update query attack and the corrupt attack, and define the decryption oracle, update oracle and corrupt oracle. The t-puncturable pseudorandom function can be utilized to limit the decryption ability at the punctured points, so that the restrictions on the existing ciphertext-dependent UE schemes [5,8,10] can be eliminated. Thus, in the proposed security notions, the adversary can be allowed to access to the oracles at all epochs.

2. The UHE scheme with no-directional key update is putted forward.
   - The t-puncturable pseudorandom function with private key is used to construct an encryption function, the public key is represented as the indistinguishable obfuscation of the encryption function, and thus the synchronous update of the public and secret key pair can be achieved.
   - Furthermore, we consider the update of the key and the ciphertext via utilizing the key generation method in the underlying hybrid encryption scheme. During the process of updating the asymmetric encryption that is constructed by key encapsulation mechanism (KEM), the updated public key and auxiliary elements are exploited to update the ciphertext and keys generated by KEM. Then, the ciphertext generated in the symmetric encryption that is constructed by data encapsulation mechanism (DEM) can be updated through updating the encapsulated key in KEM due to the homomorphism of series functions. Therefore, the ciphertext and key can be updated synchronously.
   - The update tokens only contain the update variable of the key generated via KEM to achieve the purpose of updating the ciphertexts, rather than derive the private keys, as a result that no-directional key update can be realized.

3. The *UP-IND-CCA* security of the proposed UHE scheme is proven on the basis of the indistinguishability among a series of pseudorandom functions. Even if the update oracle in the *UP-IND-CCA* security model provides the adversary with the updated/upgraded and degraded ciphertexts at the challenge-equal epochs from the key corruption epochs, the punctured keys cannot decrypt the ciphertexts containing the punctured points due to the t-puncturable pseudorandom function. Thus, the confidentiality can imply the forward and post-compromise security.

1.2   Related Works

In 2013, Boneh et al. [3] explicitly proposed the concept of UE from incremental cryptography [6] and defined a security notion for UE. Furthermore, Ananth et al. [1] presented a systematic study of updatable cryptographic primitives through adding updatability into various cryptographic schemes, such as signature, encryption, and classical protocols, and introduced updatable randomized encodings to incorporate updatability features.

There are two flavors of current UE: ciphertext-dependent updatable encryption (CDUE) [5,8,10] and ciphertext-independent updatable encryption (CIUE) [3,4,16–19]. The developments of CDUE mainly focused on updatable authenticated encryption (UAE) schemes. Everspaugh et al. [10] systematically studied updatable authenticated encryption and proposed two CDUE schemes KSS and Recrypt, where Recrypt satisfied a set of strengthened security notions, such as a new security notion for confidentiality *UP-IND*, a security notion for ciphertext integrity *UP-INT*, and a new notion called re-encryption indistinguishability *UP-REENC*. To hide the update number, Boneh et al. [5] defined a stronger confidentiality property that a re-encrypted ciphertext is required to be computationally indistinguishable from a freshly generated ciphertext, and proposed two efficient constructions: Nested UAE and RLWE-based UAE.

CIUE schemes [3,4,17,19] concentrated on the security of bi-directional update. Lehmann et al. [19] introduced the concepts of key and ciphertext update direction, which consisted of uni- and bi-directional update, and presented RISE scheme that achieved post-compromise security via uni-directional key update and uni-directional ciphertext update in the case of excluding the trivial winning. Jiang [16] closed the gap via increasing the no-directional key updates, analyzing the relationship between the security notions with uni- and bi-directional updates, and proving that confidentiality and integrity of UE schemes are not influenced by uni-/bi-directional updates. In addition, Jiang showed that the confidentiality notions with no-directional key updates are obviously stronger than the other two updates. Nishimaki [20] refuted Jiang's view [16] that the update direction is not important through defining a new definition of backward-leak uni-directional key update and showing that it is strictly stronger than those of bi-directional and forward-leak uni-directional key updates. Nishimaki's view [20] showed that the fewer the update directions, the higher the security of UE scheme. Therefore, the update directionality is very vital.

2   Preliminaries

Basic Notations. For $n \in \mathbb{N}$, let $[n] := \{1, \cdots, n\}$ and $\lambda \in \mathbb{N}$ be the security parameter. For a finite set S, the process of sampling x uniformly from S is denoted by $x \leftarrow S$. Let s be a random value of arbitrary length, $\mathcal{K}$ be key space of length l that is consistent with the message length, and $\mathcal{M}$ be message space of length l. The symbol $\perp$ indicates that an algorithm terminates with an error. A function $f(\lambda)$ is negligible in λ, denoted by $\mathbf{negl}(\lambda)$, if $f(\lambda) = o(1/\lambda^c)$ for all $c \in \mathbb{N}$. The $poly(\cdot)$ denotes a polynomial whose value is linear with λ.

t-Puncturable Pseudorandom Function (PRF). t-puncturable PRF [15] is an extended puncturable PRF, where $t(\cdot)$ is a polynomial and it is possible to derive a punctured key at any set S of size at most t. A PRF $F_t : \mathcal{K} \times \mathcal{X} \rightarrow \mathcal{Y}$ is a *t-puncturable PRF* if there is an additional punctured key space $\mathcal{K}_p$ and three polynomial-time algorithms: $F_t.$**Setup**, $F_t.$**Puncture** and $F_t.$**Eval**, as follows.

1. $F_t.$**Setup**(1^λ) is a randomized algorithm that takes the security parameter λ as input and outputs a description of the key space $\mathcal{K}$, the punctured key space $\mathcal{K}_p$ and the PRF F_t.
2. $F_t.$**Puncture**(k, S) is a randomized algorithm that takes as input a PRF key $k \in \mathcal{K}$ and $S \in \mathcal{X}$, $|S| \leq t(\cdot)$, and outputs a t-punctured key $k_S \in \mathcal{K}_p$, where S is the set of punctured points.
3. $F_t.$**Eval**(k_S, x') is a deterministic algorithm that takes as input a t-punctured key $k_S \in \mathcal{K}_p$ and $x' \in \mathcal{X}$. Let $k \in \mathcal{K}, S \in \mathcal{X}$ and $k_S \leftarrow F_t.$**Puncture**(k, S). For correctness, the following property holds:

$$F_t.\textbf{Eval}(k_S, x) = \begin{cases} PRF(k, x), & \text{if } x \notin S; \\ \perp, & \text{otherwise.} \end{cases}$$

Indistinguishability Obfuscation. A uniform PPT machine $i\mathcal{O}$ is called an *indistinguishability obfuscation* [23] for a circuit class C_λ if the following conditions are satisfied:

1. For all $C \in C_\lambda$ and any input x, $\Pr[C'(x) = C(x) : C' \leftarrow i\mathcal{O}(\lambda, C)] = 1$.
2. For any (not necessarily uniform) PPT distinguisher $\mathcal{D}$, there exists a negligible function $\textbf{negl}(\cdot)$ such that the following holds: for all pairs of circuit $C_0, C_1 \in C_\lambda$, we have that if $C_0(x) = C_1(x)$ for all inputs x, then

$$\big| \Pr[\mathcal{D}(i\mathcal{O}(\lambda, C_0)) = 1 - \Pr[\mathcal{D}(i\mathcal{O}(\lambda, C_1)) = 1] \big| \leq \textbf{negl}(\lambda).$$

Key-Homomorphic Pseudorandom Function. Let $(\mathcal{K}, \oplus)$ and $(\mathcal{Y}, \otimes)$ be groups. A keyed function $F : \mathcal{K}_\lambda \times \mathcal{X}_\lambda \to \mathcal{Y}_\lambda$ is a *key-homomorphic pseudorandom function* [3] if F is a secure pseudorandom function, which satisfies that for any key $k_1, k_2 \in \mathcal{K}$ and any input $x \in \mathcal{X}$, we have $F(k_1, x) \otimes F(k_2, x) = F(k_1 \oplus k_1, x)$.

Seed-Homomorphic Pseudorandom Generator (PRG). An efficient computable function $PRG : \mathcal{X} \to \mathcal{Y}$, where $(\mathcal{K}, \oplus)$ and $(\mathcal{Y}, \otimes)$ are groups, which is said to be seed homomorphic if PRG is secure and satisfies $PRG(s_1) \otimes PRG(s_2) = PRG(s_1 \oplus s_2)$.

Homomorphic Hash Function. A homomorphic hash function [8] $\textbf{H}_{\text{hom}}$ is a linear function that maps a vector of starting group elements $\vec{v} = (v_1, \cdots, v_n)$ in the starting group $\mathbb{G}_{HS}^n$ into a target group element $u \in \mathbb{G}_{HT}$ as the following two algorithms:

1. *HomHash.***Setup**(1^λ): on input the security parameter λ, output an evaluation key hk.
2. *HomHash.***Eval**$(hk, \vec{v})$: on input the evaluation key hk and a vector of starting group elements $\vec{v} = (v_1, \cdots, v_n) \in \mathbb{G}_{HS}^n$, output a target group element $u \in \mathbb{G}_{HT}$.

Given an evaluation key hk, let $\mathbf{H_{hom}}(\vec{v}) = HomHash.\mathbf{Eval}(hk, \vec{v}) = u$. Specifically, a *homomorphic hash function* should satisfy the following properties:

1. **Collision resistance:** the probability that any PPT adversary generates two vectors $\vec{v}, \vec{v}' \in \mathbb{G}_{HS}^n$ such that $\mathbf{H_{hom}}(\vec{v}) = \mathbf{H_{hom}}(\vec{v}')$ is negligible.
2. **Homomorphism:** $\mathbf{H_{hom}}(\vec{v}) + \mathbf{H_{hom}}(\vec{v}') = \mathbf{H_{hom}}(\vec{v} + \vec{v}')$.

Homomorphic Commitment Protocol. A commitment protocol $Com = (\mathbf{Init}, \mathbf{Com}, \mathbf{Open})$ [22] includes three algorithms as follows:

1. **Init:** generate the public parameter pp.
2. **Com:** output a commitment value com that is bounded to m.
3. **Open:** check whether the protocol satisfies the *hiding* and *binding* properties.

The *hiding* property requires the distributions of the commitment values for different messages cannot be distinguished by the adversary, while the *binding* property requires the commitment value cannot be opened to two different messages. Furthermore, homomorphic commitment protocol satisfies the following properties:

1. $\mathcal{M}_{COM} \times \mathcal{O}_{COM} = \mathcal{C}_{COM}$, that is to say, message $m \in \mathcal{M}_{COM}$, public parameter $hopen \in \mathcal{O}_{COM}$, commitment value $hcom \in \mathcal{C}_{COM}$.
2. $\mathbf{Com}(m_1, hopen_1) \oplus \mathbf{Com}(m_2, hopen_2) = \mathbf{Com}(m_1 \oplus m_2, hopen_1 \oplus hopen_2)$.

3   Formal Updatable Hybrid Encryption

3.1   Syntax

In hybrid encryption, the ciphertext generated via key-encapsulation mechanism KEM = $(Encaps, Decaps)$ should be regarded as the auxiliary information of the ciphertext generated via data-encapsulation mechanism DEM = (Enc', Dec'). Therefore, in ciphertext-dependent updatable hybrid encryption, the ciphertext of KEM can be viewed as the header of complete ciphertext and used to generate a token.

An UHE scheme consists of the following six algorithms UHE = (**Setup, KeyGen, Encrypt, Next, Update, Decrypt**).

– **Setup**(1^λ): The algorithm inputs a security parameter λ and outputs the public parameter pp that is contained implicitly in the following algorithms.
– **KeyGen**(e): The algorithm takes an epoch index e as input and outputs a pair of public and secret keys (pk_e, sk_e) related to the epoch e.
– **Encrypt**(pk_e, m): At the epoch e, the algorithm takes the public key pk_e and a message m as inputs, runs $Encaps_{pk_e}(pp)$ to generate one partial ciphertext (c_{e,k_e}, k_e), and implements $Enc'_{k_e}(m)$ to get the other partial ciphertext c'_e. Let c_{e,k_e} be a ciphertext header $\tilde{c}_e$ and c'_e be a ciphertext body $\bar{c}_e$. Finally, this algorithm outputs a complete ciphertext $c_e = (\tilde{c}_e, \bar{c}_e)$.

- **Decrypt**(sk_e, c_e): The algorithm takes the secret key sk_e and the ciphertext $c_e = (\tilde{c}_e, \bar{c}_e)$ as inputs, implements $Decaps_{sk_e}(\tilde{c}_e)$ to recover the key k_e, and executes $Dec'_{k_e}(\bar{c}_e)$ to output a message m or a symbol $\perp$.
- **Next**$(sk_e, sk_{e+1}, \tilde{c}_e)$: The algorithm takes the ciphertext header $\tilde{c}_e$, the secret key sk_e at the previous epoch e, and the secret key sk_{e+1} at the current epoch $e + 1$ as inputs, and outputs an update token $\Delta_{e,\tilde{c}_{e+1}}$ or a symbol $\perp$.
- **Update**$(\Delta_{e,\tilde{c}_{e+1}}, c_e)$: The algorithm takes the update token $\Delta_{e,\tilde{c}_{e+1}}$ and the ciphertext $c_e = (\tilde{c}_e, \bar{c}_e)$ as inputs and outputs an updated ciphertext $c_{e+1} = (\tilde{c}_{e+1}, \bar{c}_{e+1})$ for the current epoch $e + 1$.

Correctness: After performing properly these algorithms **Setup**(1^λ), **Key-Gen**(e), **Encrypt**(pk_e, m), **Next**$(sk_e, sk_{e+1}, \tilde{c}_e)$, and **Update**$(\Delta_{e,\tilde{c}_{e+1}}, c_e)$, the decryption operation would output m, that is to say,

$$\Pr[\textbf{Decrypt}(sk_{e+1}, c_{e+1}) \neq m] \leq \textbf{negl}(\lambda).$$

3.2 Instantiation Scheme

The proposed UHE scheme consists of the underlying hybrid encryption scheme REACT transform [21] and the update process in UE scheme ReCrypt$^+$ [8].

Let PRG be a pseudorandom generator that maps $\{0,1\}^\lambda$ to $\{0,1\}^{2\lambda}$, F_t be a t-puncturable pseudorandom function that takes as input 2λ bit strings and outputs l bit strings. We suppose that G is a homomorphic hash function, which maps $\mathcal{K}_{SE}$ to $\mathbb{G}_{HT}$. F is a key-homomorphic pseudorandom function that maps $\mathcal{K}_{PRF}$ and $\mathcal{M}_{PRF}$ to $\mathcal{G}_{PRF}$. In particular, $\mathbb{G}_{HS}$ contains $\mathcal{K}_{SE}$ and $\mathcal{G}_{PRF}$. We assume that H is collision-resistant hash function that output l bits. At the same time, denote H_1 as a collision-resistant homomorphic hash function with the outputs of l bits, and define the message space $|\mathcal{M}_{PRF}| = \{0,1\}^l$ and the key space $|\mathcal{K}| = \{0,1\}^l$, which includes two types of key spaces $\mathcal{K}_{PRF}$ and $\mathcal{K}_{SE}$. Finally, define a homomorphic commitment protocol $HCOM = (HCOM.\textbf{Init},$ $HCOM.\textbf{Com}$ and $HCOM.\textbf{Open})$, where the message space, opening randomness space and commitment value are $\mathcal{M}_{COM}$, $\mathcal{O}_{COM}$, and $\mathcal{C}_{COM}$, respectively, and the message space $\mathcal{M}_{COM}$ is required to contain the key space $\mathcal{K}$. The detailed construction is as follows.

- **Setup**(1^λ): Run $HCOM.\textbf{Init}$ to generate the public parameter $hopen$ for the *homomorphic commitment protocol*, and operate $HomHash.\textbf{Init}$ to generate the public parameter hk for the collision-resistant homomorphic hash function. Publish the public parameter $UHE.pp = (hopen, hk)$.

- **KeyGen**(e): The algorithm proceeds in the following.
  1. Select randomly a value r from the set $\mathcal{K}_{PRF}$ as a secret key at the epoch e.
  2. Initialize the punctured set $S^* \subseteq \{0,1\}^{2\lambda}$ at the punctured points t_e^* corresponding to the seed s_e^* of PRG, and generate a punctured secret key as $r^*(\{S^*\})$.

Table 1. The description of circuit C_{enc}

Encryption circuit $C_{enc}[r](s, a)$
Hardwired: r
Input: s, a
Output: $ct = (\underbrace{PRG(s)}_{c_1}, \underbrace{F_t(r, PRG(s)) \oplus a}_{c_2})$

3. Perform the public key program $i\mathcal{O}(C_{enc}[r_e])$ with the real secret key r_e, and generate the corresponding public key pk_e, where the circuit C_{enc} is described in Table 1.

– **Encrypt**(pk_e, m): The algorithm proceeds in the following.
  1. Select a random number $R \in \mathcal{M}_{PRF}$, two symmetric encryption keys $z, y \in \mathcal{K}_{SE}$, and a seed s of the pseudorandom generator.
  2. Run the public key program $i\mathcal{O}(C_{enc}[r_e])$, encrypt the random value R to generate a ciphertext $c_{e,1} = i\mathcal{O}(C_{enc}[r_e])(s, R)$, where R is regarded as a key seed of KEM and a key $k = R \oplus G(z)$ is generated for DEM.
  3. Map the message m into n group elements $m_1, m_2, \cdots, m_n \in \mathcal{G}_{PRF}$, encrypt each element m_i to generate a ciphertext $c_{e,2,i} = m_i \oplus F(k, i)$, and set $c_{e,2} = (c_{e,2,1}, c_{e,2,2}, \cdots, c_{e,2,n}) \in G^n_{PRF}$.
  4. Utilize hash function H and homomorphic hash function $HomHash_{hk}$ that is abbreviated to H_1 to generate a verification value $c_{e,3} = H(R, m) \oplus H_1(c_{e,1}, c_{e,2})$ about $R, m, c_{e,1}, c_{e,2}$ due to the property $\mathcal{G}_{PRF} \subseteq \mathcal{G}_{HS}$.
  5. Generate a commitment $HCOM.\mathbf{Com}(y, c_{e,3}, hopen) = hcom_e \in \mathcal{C}_{COM}$ for y, where $hopen \in \mathcal{O}_{COM}$ is the corresponding open randomness.
  6. Compute the other sharing element $x \in \mathcal{K}_{SE}$ of z such that $x = z \oplus y$, and generate a ciphertext $ct_e = i\mathcal{O}(C_{enc}[r_e])(s, x)$.
  7. Set the ciphertext is $c_e = (\tilde{c}_e, \bar{c}_e)$, where the ciphertext header is $\tilde{c}_e = (ct_e, hcom_e, c_{e,1}, c_{e,3})$, and the ciphertext body is $\bar{c}_e = (y, c_{e,2}, hopen)$.

– **Next**$(sk_e, sk_{e+1}, \tilde{c}_e)$: The algorithm parses the ciphertext header $\tilde{c}_e = (ct_e, hcom_e, c_{e,1}, c_{e,3})$, decrypts the ciphertext ct_e, and verifies the results x'. If the verification does not pass, it returns $\perp$. Otherwise, the algorithm does as follows.
  1. Choose randomly a value $\Delta r \in \mathcal{K}_{PRF}$, set $r_{e+1} = r_e \oplus \Delta r$, and store $sk_{e+1} = r'$ at the new epoch $e + 1$ in local storage. Furthermore, run the public key program $i\mathcal{O}(C_{enc}[\cdot])$ to generate an updated public key $pk_{e+1} \leftarrow i\mathcal{O}(C_{enc}[r_{e+1}])$ for the new epoch $e + 1$, and choose random values $\Delta z, \Delta y \in \mathcal{K}_{SE}$.
  2. Randomly select the seed $\Delta s \in \{0,1\}^\lambda$ that is the update variable. Calculate $c_{e+1,1,1} = c_{e,1,1} \oplus PRG(\Delta s)$. Utilize the difference Δ between the values of the puncturable pseudorandom function $F_t(r_{e+1}, c_{e+1,1,1})$ and $F_t(r_e, c_{e,1,1})$ to update $c_{e,1}$.

3. Calculate $\Delta c_{e,e+1,1} = (\Delta s, \Delta)$, and update $c_{e+1,1} = (c_{e+1,1,1}, c_{e,1} \oplus \Delta c_{e,e+1,1}) = (c_{e+1,1,1}, c_{e+1,1,2})$.

4. Compute $\Delta k = G(\Delta z)$ and $\Delta c_{e,e+1,2,i} = F(\Delta k, i)$ for $i = 1, \cdots, n$, and set $\Delta c_{e,e+1,2} = (\Delta c_{e,e+1,2,1}, \Delta c_{e,e+1,2,2}, \cdots, \Delta c_{e,e+1,2,n}) \in \mathcal{G}_{PRF}^n \subseteq \mathbb{G}_{HS}$.

5. Enumerate $\Delta c_{e,e+1,3} = H(\Delta c_{e,e+1,1}, \Delta c_{e,e+1,2})$ and update $c_{e+1,3} = c_{e,3} \oplus \Delta c_{e,e+1,3}$.

6. Select randomly an opening value $\Delta hopen \in \mathcal{O}_{COM}$, and compute a new commitment value $hcom_{e+1} = hcom_e \oplus HCOM.\mathbf{Com}(\Delta y, \Delta c_{e,e+1,3}, \Delta hopen)$.

7. Compute $\Delta x = \Delta y \oplus \Delta z$ and $\Delta ct_{e,e+1} = (\Delta s, \Delta, \Delta x)$ and update ct_e in the ciphertext header to $ct_{e+1} = (ct_{e,1} \oplus PRG(\Delta s), ct_{e,2} \oplus \Delta \oplus \Delta x) = (ct_{e+1,1}, ct_{e+1,2})$.

8. Set the updated ciphertext header as $\tilde{c}_{e+1} = (ct_{e+1}, hcom_{e+1}, c_{e+1,1}, c_{e+1,3})$ at the next epoch, and return the updated token $\Delta_{e,\tilde{c}_{e+1}} = (\tilde{c}_{e+1}, (\Delta c_{e,e+1,2}, \Delta y, \Delta hopen))$.

– **Update**$(\Delta_{e,\tilde{c}_{e+1}}, c_e)$: After parsing the ciphertext header $\tilde{c}_e = (ct_e, hcom_e, c_{e,1}, c_{e,3})$, the ciphertext body $\bar{c}_e = (y, c_{e,2}, hopen)$, and the update token $\Delta_{e,\tilde{c}_{e+1}} = (\tilde{c}_{e+1}, \Delta c_{e,e+1,2}, \Delta y, \Delta hopen)$, then proceed as follows.
  1. Verify whether $hcom_e$ is a valid commitment value of $y \in \mathcal{K}_{SE}$ through calling the opening algorithm $HCOM.\mathbf{Open}(hcom_e, y, c_{e,3})) == 1$.
  2. Compute $c_{e+1,2} = c_{e,2} \oplus \Delta c_{e,e+1,2}$.
  3. Calculate $y' = y \oplus \Delta y$ and $hopen' = hopen \oplus \Delta hopen$.
  4. Generate a new ciphertext body $\bar{c}_{e+1} = (y', c_{e+1,2}, hopen')$.
  5. Obtain a new ciphertext $c_{e+1} = (\tilde{c}_{e+1}, \bar{c}_{e+1})$.

– **Decrypt**(sk_e, c_e): The decrypt algorithm first parses the ciphertext c_e into the header $\tilde{c}_e = (ct_e, hcom_e, c_{e,1}, c_{e,3})$ and the body $\bar{c}_e = (y, c_{e,2}, hopen)$.
  1. Verify whether $hcom_e$ is a valid commitment value of $y \in \mathcal{K}_{SE}$ through calling the opening algorithm $HCOM.\mathbf{Open}(hcom_e, y, c_{e,3})) == 1$.
  2. If the verification holds, then the secret key $sk_e = r$ is used to decrypt $c_{e,1}$ to obtain $R = PRF(r, PRG(s)) \oplus c_{e,1,2}$ and the share element $x = PRF(r, PRG(s)) \oplus ct_{e,2}$.
  3. Compute $z = x \oplus y$ and $k = R \oplus G(z)$, which is the key of DEM, restore the message $m_i = c_{e,2,i} \oplus F(k, i)$ for $i = 1, \cdots, n$, and recover the complete message m such that $m = (m_1, m_2, \ldots, m_n)$.
  4. Generate a new verification value $c_0 = H(R, m) \oplus H_1(c_{e,1}, c_{e,2})$.
  5. Verify whether $c_0 == c_{e,3} \in \mathcal{M}_{COM}$. If the verification holds, the message m would be recovered successfully.

3.3   Correctness

The decryption algorithm can recover correctly the message as follows. For the ciphertext $c_e = (\tilde{c}_e, \bar{c}_e)$ and the secret key $sk_e = r$ at the epoch e, compute $R = F_t(r, PRG(s)) \oplus c_{e,1,2}$, $x = F_t(r, PRG(s)) \oplus ct_{e,2}$, and $z = x \oplus y$, generate the key $k = R \oplus G(z)$ of DEM, and recover the message $m \leftarrow (c_{e,2,1} \oplus F(k, 1), c_{e,2,2} \oplus F(k, 2), \ldots, c_{e,2,n} \oplus F(k, n))$.

Furthermore, at the next epoch $e + 1$, for the update ciphertext $c_{e+1} = (\tilde{c}_{e+1}, \bar{c}_{e+1})$, which is the output of $\mathbf{Update}(\Delta_{e,\tilde{c}_{e+1}}, c_e)$, the update secret key $sk_{e+1} = r' = r \oplus \Delta r$ can recover the message m.

3.4 UP-IND-CCA Security

In order to prove the security of UHE, we adopt a similar proof method in the dual system encryption [25]. The ciphertexts at the punctured points and the punctured keys can be regarded as the semi-functional ciphertexts and the semi-functional keys, where the punctured points and the punctured keys are in the t-puncturable pseudorandom function. The punctured points as well as their update version are recorded in the list $\mathbf{P.P}$.

Theorem 1. *The proposed updatable hybrid encryption scheme UHE is UP-IND-CCA security if the hybrid encryption HE is IND-CCA security, the homomorphic commitment HCOM is statistic hiding and computation binding, and the key-homomorphic F and PRG are pseudorandom.*

Proof. The proof consists of a sequence of indistinguishable experiments. In the following experiment sequence, Suc_i indicates that the adversary $\mathcal{A}$ succeeds in the experiment $\mathbf{Expt}_i (i = 1, 2, \cdots, 7)$.

$\mathbf{Expt}_1$: This experiment is the *UP-IND-CCA* experiment that is described as follows. During the initialization phase, the challenger generates the public and secret key pair $(pk_0, sk_0) \leftarrow \mathbf{KeyGen}$, and sends the public key pk_0 to $\mathcal{A}$. The public key pk_0 is $pk_0 \leftarrow i\mathcal{O}(C_{enc}[r_0^*])$, and the secret key is $sk_0 = r_0^*(\{S^*\})$. $\mathcal{A}$ can query to the following oracles at any epochs in the experiment. The challenger maintains the list $\mathbf{P.P}$ when $\mathcal{A}$ queries oracles.

1. *Advance epoch queries.* On input a trigger bit of the oracle $\mathcal{O}.\text{Next}()$, the challenger invokes **Next** and **Update** to induce $\mathcal{O}.\text{Next}()$, and completes the epoch increment in the experiment.
2. *Secret key queries.* On input an epoch e, the challenger generates the pair of public and secret key $(i\mathcal{O}(C_{enc}[r_e^*]), r_e^*(\{S^*\})) \leftarrow \mathbf{KeyGen}(e)$ and returns the secret key $r_e^*(\{S^*\})$.
3. *Update token queries.* On input an epoch e and a ciphertext header $\tilde{c}_e$, the challenger parses $\tilde{c}_e$ as $(ct_e, hcom_e, c_{e,1}, c_{e,3})$ and generates an update token $\Delta_{e,\tilde{c}_{e+1}} = (\tilde{c}_{e+1}, \Delta c_{e,e+1,2}, \Delta y, \Delta hopen)) \leftarrow \mathbf{Next}(r_e^*, r_{e+1}^*, \tilde{c}_e)$. It returns the update token $\Delta_{e,\tilde{c}_{e+1}}$ that are produced via the punctured keys.
4. *Update queries.* On input an epoch e and a ciphertext c_e, the challenger parses c_e as $\tilde{c}_e = (ct_e, hcom_e, c_{e,1}, c_{e,3})$ and $\bar{c}_e = (y, c_{e,2}, hopen)$. If $c_{e,1,1} \in S^* \subset \mathbf{P.P}$, the challenger updates the list $\mathbf{P.P}$ through the ciphertext updates. The challenger computes $(\tilde{c}_{e+1}, \bar{c}_{e+1}) \leftarrow \mathbf{Update}(\Delta_{e,\tilde{c}_{e+1}}, c_e)$ and returns it. Meanwhile, the challenger updates the list $\mathbf{P.P} \leftarrow \mathbf{P.P} \cup \{c_{e+1,1,1}\}$.
5. *Decrypt queries.* On input a ciphertext c_e, the challenger parses c_e as $\tilde{c}_e = (ct_e, hcom_e, c_{e,1}, c_{e,3})$ and $\bar{c}_e = (y, c_{e,2}, hopen)$. The challenger computes $m \leftarrow \mathbf{Decrypt}(r_e^*, c_e)$. If $c_{e,1,1} \in \mathbf{P.P}$, the challenger returns $\bot$.

After querying the oracles, $\mathcal{A}$ submits a pair of challenge messages $(m_0, m_1) \in \{0,1\}^l \times \{0,1\}^l$, and the challenge epoch e^*. The challenger proceeds as follows:

1. Select a challenge bit $b \in \{0,1\}$ randomly.
2. Pick the punctured point $t_{e^*}^* \in \mathbf{P.P}$, which is the image of $PRG(s^*)$ and also be regarded as $c_{e^*,1,1}$.
3. Compute the challenge ciphertext $c_e^* \leftarrow \mathbf{Encrypt}(pk_{e^*}, m)$, and return c_e^* to $\mathcal{A}$.

The above oracles can still be adaptively queried at any epoch before $\mathcal{A}$ finally outputs a guess bit b'. The challenger returns 1 if $b = b'$, that is, $\mathcal{A}$ guesses successfully. In this case, the probability of success of $\mathcal{A}$ can be expressed as follows,

$$\left| \Pr[\mathbf{Exp}_{UP\text{-}IND\text{-}CCA,\ UHE}^{\mathcal{A}} = 1] \right| = \left| \Pr[Suc_1] \right|.$$

$\mathbf{Expt_2}$: The challenger replaces the ciphertext ct of the asymmetric encryption used by honest x with the randomly chosen-ciphertext related to x. After querying $\mathcal{O}.\text{Next}$, $\mathcal{O}.\text{Corrupt}$ and $\mathcal{O}.\text{Upd}$, the challenger will request with the randomly chosen ciphertext. Additionally, the challenger in $\mathbf{Expt_2}$ will build a table $\mathbf{T_{HE}}$ when $\mathcal{A}$ queries $\mathcal{O}.\text{Next}$, $\mathcal{O}.\text{Corrupt}$ and $\mathcal{O}.\text{Upd}$, where the table is used to request the query with $\mathcal{O}.\text{Dec}$ and $\mathcal{O}.\text{Upd}$, instead of directly invoking the decryption algorithm. The indistinguishability between $\mathbf{Expt_1}$ and $\mathbf{Expt_2}$ can be reduced to the pseudorandomness of the key homomorphic pseudorandom function F. Due to the pseudorandomness, we have

$$\left| \Pr[Suc_1] - \Pr[Suc_2] \right| = \left| \Pr[\mathcal{A}^{F(r,\cdot)}(1^\lambda) : r \xleftarrow{R} \{0,1\}^\lambda] \right.$$

$$\left. - \Pr[\mathcal{A}^{f(\cdot)}(1^\lambda) = 1] : f \xleftarrow{R} Funs[\cdot] \right|$$

$$\leq \mathbf{negl}_1(\lambda).$$

$\mathbf{Expt_3}$: The experiment is similar to $\mathbf{Expt_2}$, except that way to deal with the commitment $hcom$ in the header: when $\mathcal{A}$ queries $\mathcal{O}.\text{Next}$, $\mathcal{O}.\text{Corrupt}$ and $\mathcal{O}.\text{Upd}$, the challenger generates $hcom$ in UHE headers $\tilde{C} = (ct_{e^*}, hcom_{e^*}, c_{e^*,1}, c_{e^*,3})$ by selecting a random commitment value $hcom_{e^*}$. Moreover, the challenger in $\mathbf{Expt_3}$ will build a table $\mathbf{T_{Hcom}}$ to record all the tuples of the UHE ciphertext, the commitment, its message and opening according to the epoch indexes. When $\mathcal{A}$ queries $\mathcal{O}.\text{Dec}$ and $\mathcal{O}.\text{Upd}$, the challenger checks the commitment by looking up the table $\mathbf{T_{Hcom}}$. The indistinguishability of $\mathbf{Expt_2}$ and $\mathbf{Expt_3}$ can be reduced to the hiding property of the commitment. Therefore, the following inequality can be derived,

$$\left| \Pr[Suc_2] - \Pr[Suc_3] \right| = \left| \Pr[HCOM.\mathbf{Init} \leftarrow \mathbf{Init}(1^\lambda, y_0) \leftarrow \{0,1\}^\lambda, \right.$$

$$\left. (r_1, hcom) \leftarrow HCOM(1^\lambda, hopen)|b \leftarrow \mathcal{A}] - \frac{1}{2} \right|$$

$$\leq \mathbf{negl}_2(\lambda).$$

Expt$_4$: The experiment is similar to **Expt$_3$**, except that way to deal with the commitment $c_{e^*,3}$ in the header: when $\mathcal{A}$ queries $\mathcal{O}$.Next, $\mathcal{O}$.Corrupt and $\mathcal{O}$.Upd, the challenger generates $c_{e^*,3}$ in the header $\tilde{c} = (ct_{e^*}, hcom_{e^*}, c_{e^*,1}, c_{e^*,3})$ by selecting a random hash value instead of invoking the hash generation algorithm. Through this process, the challenger builds a table $\mathbf{T_{hash}}$ of entries indexed by epoch, hash values and their corresponding values $R, m, c_{e^*,1}, c_{e^*,2}$. When $\mathcal{A}$ queries $\mathcal{O}$.Upd and $\mathcal{O}$.Dec, $c_{e^*,3}$ and the corresponding values could be choose from this table. The indistinguishability of **Expt$_3$** and **Expt$_4$** can be reduced to the pseudorandomness of the hash function. Therefore, we have

$$\big|\Pr[Suc_3] - \Pr[Suc_4]\big| \leq \mathbf{negl}_3(\lambda).$$

Expt$_5$: The experiment is similar to **Expt$_4$**, except that way to deal with the decryption oracle $\mathcal{O}$.Dec: when $\mathcal{A}$ queried $\mathcal{O}$.Dec for all epoch, the challenger in **Expt$_5$** will look up the corresponding message value from the table $\mathbf{T_{hash}}$ that is indexed by the epoch instead of the original generation of $c_{e^*,1}$. The indistinguishability of **Expt$_4$** and **Expt$_5$** can be reduced to the $OW\text{-}PCA$ security.

$$\big|\Pr[Suc_4] - \Pr[Suc_5]\big| \leq Adv_{KEM}^{OW\text{-}PCA} \leq \mathbf{negl}_4(\lambda).$$

Expt$_6$: The experiment is similar to **Expt$_5$**, except that way to deal with the decryption oracle $\mathcal{O}$.Dec: when $\mathcal{A}$ queries $\mathcal{O}$.Dec for the full epochs, the challenger in **Expt$_6$** will look up the corresponding message value from the table $\mathbf{T_{hash}}$ that is indexed by the epoch instead of the original generation of $c_{e^*,2}$. The indistinguishability of **Expt$_5$** and **Expt$_6$** can be reduced to the OT security.

$$\big|\Pr[Suc_5] - \Pr[Suc_6]\big| \leq Adv_{DEM}^{OT} \leq \mathbf{negl}_5(\lambda).$$

Expt$_7$: The experiment is similar to **Expt$_6$**, except that the challenger encrypts a random string instead of the challenge message. $\mathcal{A}$ can not distinguish **Expt$_6$** and **Expt$_7$** due to the fact that random values are indistinguishable from random values. Therefore, the probability of success in the **Expt$_7$** is $\frac{1}{2}$. In a conclusion, we have that

$$\big|\Pr[Suc_6] - \Pr[Suc_7]\big| = \big|\Pr[Suc_6] - \frac{1}{2}]\big| \leq \mathbf{negl}_6(\lambda).$$

Using the conclusions of the above facts, we can prove that the advantage of the PPT adversary $\mathcal{A}$ in attacking UHE scheme is negligible, that is

$$Adv_{Adaptive}^{UP\text{-}IND\text{-}CCA}(\lambda)$$

$$=\big|\Pr[\mathbf{Exp}_{UP\text{-}IND\text{-}CCA,\,UHE}^{\mathcal{A}} = 1] - \frac{1}{2}\big|$$

$$\leq\big|\Pr[Suc_1] - \Pr[Suc_2]\big| + \big|\Pr[Suc_2] - \Pr[Suc_3]\big| + \cdots + \big|\Pr[Suc_6] - \frac{1}{2}\big|$$

$$\leq\mathbf{negl}_1(\lambda) + \cdots + \mathbf{negl}_6(\lambda).$$

Therefore, the Theorem 1 is proven.

Post-compromise and Forward Security. Both the forward and post-compromise security require that the confidentiality of ciphertext is not affected by ciphertext and key updates during the honest epoch. Take the post-compromise security as the example, in the case that the key for the epoch $e^* - 1$ is corrupted, $\mathcal{A}$ has no advantage in decrypting the ciphertext for the epoch e^*. This security is mainly composed of the following two aspects of reasons, which are

1. The key update in the UHE scheme satisfies the no-directional key update. The reason is that the update token does not contain the update part of the key, so that the update token cannot derive the keys for the old and new epochs. Therefore, the key for the epoch $e^* - 1$ cannot be updated to the epoch e^*.
2. The ciphertext update in the UHE scheme meets the bi-directional update. If $\mathcal{A}$ uses the update token to downgrade the ciphertext for the epoch e^* to the epoch $e^* - 1$, the puncture point $t^*_{e^*} = c_{e^*,1,1}$ in the ciphertext will also be downgraded. Due to the maintenance of list **P.P**, the degraded point $t^*_{e^*-1} = c_{1,1,e^*-1}$ is still the puncture point. Combined with the limitation of the decryption ability of the punctured key at the punctured point, the ciphertext c_{e^*-1} still cannot be decrypted correctly.

To sum up, the proposed scheme UHE satisfies the post-compromise security. In the same way, the UHE scheme satisfies forward security.

3.5 Evaluation of the Proposed UHE Scheme

We evaluate the implementation of the proposed scheme UHE based on the six algorithms (**Setup, KeyGen, Encrypt, Next, Update, Decrypt**). In the **Setup** algorithm, the process undertakes the initialization process of the homomorphic commitment protocol and the homomorphic hash function. During the **KeyGen** algorithm, this process uses the indistinguishability obfuscation to generate the public key. The **Encrypt** algorithm of the proposed scheme UHE performs the indistinguishable obfuscation for one time, the homomorphic commitment protocol operation for one time, and XOR operations for $n+4$ times. In the **Next** algorithm, the computational overhead consists of the homomorphic commitment protocol operation for one time, the homomorphic function operation for one time, the indistinguishable obfuscation programs for one times, the key-homomorphic pseudorandom function for n times, and XOR operation for eight times. The **Update** algorithm of the proposed scheme UHE includes the homomorphic commitment protocol verification process for one time and XOR operation for two times. During the **Decrypt** algorithm, the computational overhead contains the homomorphic commitment protocol operation for one time, the hash function operation for one time, the homomorphic hash function operation for one time, and XOR operations for $n + 6$ times.

4 Conclusions

In this paper, we have proposed an updatable hybrid encryption scheme that plays out the advantages of asymmetric encryption, symmetric encryption, and updatable encryption. More importantly, the proposed UHE scheme can support no-directional key update that means less information leakage. Furthermore, we have built a formal definition of confidentiality for updatable hybrid encryption and proven the proposed scheme to be *UP-IND-CCA* that can achieve both post-compromise and forward security.

References

1. Ananth, P., Cohen, A., Jain, A.: Cryptography with updates. In: Coron, J.-S., Nielsen, J.B. (eds.) EUROCRYPT 2017. LNCS, vol. 10211, pp. 445–472. Springer, Cham (2017). https://doi.org/10.1007/978-3-319-56614-6_15
2. AWS: Protecting data using client-side encryption. http://docs.aws.amazon.com/AmazonS3/latest/dev/UsingClientSideEncryption.html
3. Boneh, D., Lewi, K., Montgomery, H., Raghunathan, A.: Key homomorphic PRFs and their applications. In: Canetti, R., Garay, J.A. (eds.) CRYPTO 2013. LNCS, vol. 8042, pp. 410–428. Springer, Heidelberg (2013). https://doi.org/10.1007/978-3-642-40041-4_23
4. Boyd, C., Davies, G.T., Gjøsteen, K., Jiang, Y.: Fast and secure updatable encryption. In: Micciancio, D., Ristenpart, T. (eds.) CRYPTO 2020. LNCS, vol. 12170, pp. 464–493. Springer, Cham (2020). https://doi.org/10.1007/978-3-030-56784-2_16
5. Boneh, D., Eskandarian, S., Kim, S., Shih, M.: Improving speed and security in updatable encryption schemes. In: Moriai, S., Wang, H. (eds.) ASIACRYPT 2020. LNCS, vol. 12493, pp. 559–589. Springer, Cham (2020). https://doi.org/10.1007/978-3-030-64840-4_19
6. Bellare, M., Goldreich, O., Goldwasser, S.: Incremental cryptography: the case of hashing and signing. In: Desmedt, Y.G. (ed.) CRYPTO 1994. LNCS, vol. 839, pp. 216–233. Springer, Heidelberg (1994). https://doi.org/10.1007/3-540-48658-5_22
7. Bradley, M., Dent, A.: Payment card data security standard. https://www.pcicomplianceguide.org/faq/
8. Chen, L., Li, Y., Tang, Q.: CCA updatable encryption against malicious re-encryption attacks. In: Moriai, S., Wang, H. (eds.) ASIACRYPT 2020. LNCS, vol. 12493, pp. 590–620. Springer, Cham (2020). https://doi.org/10.1007/978-3-030-64840-4_20
9. Cini, V., Ramacher, S., Slamanig, D., Striecks, C., Tairi, E.: Updatable Signatures and Message Authentication Codes. In: Garay, J.A. (ed.) PKC 2021. LNCS, vol. 12710, pp. 691–723. Springer, Cham (2021). https://doi.org/10.1007/978-3-030-75245-3_25
10. Everspaugh, A., Paterson, K., Ristenpart, T., Scott, S.: Key rotation for authenticated encryption. In: Katz, J., Shacham, H. (eds.) CRYPTO 2017. LNCS, vol. 10403, pp. 98–129. Springer, Cham (2017). https://doi.org/10.1007/978-3-319-63697-9_4
11. Garg, S., Gentry, C., Halevi, S., Raykova, M., Sahai, A., Waters, B.: Candidate indistinguishability obfuscation and functional encryption for all circuits. In: IEEE 54th Annual Symposium on Foundations of Computer Science, FOCS 2013, pp. 40–49, IEEE (2013)
12. Goldreich, O., Goldwasser, S., Micali, S.: On the cryptographic applications of random functions (extended abstract). In: Blakley, G.R., Chaum, D. (eds.) CRYPTO 1984. LNCS, vol. 196, pp. 276–288. Springer, Heidelberg (1985). https://doi.org/10.1007/3-540-39568-7_22

13. Google: Managing data encryption. https://cloud.google.com/storage/docs/encryption
14. Garg, S., Gentry, C., Halevi, S., Sahai, A., Waters, B.: Attribute-based encryption for circuits from multilinear maps. In: Canetti, R., Garay, J.A. (eds.) CRYPTO 2013. LNCS, vol. 8043, pp. 479–499. Springer, Heidelberg (2013). https://doi.org/10.1007/978-3-642-40084-1_27
15. Hohenberger, S., Koppula, V., Waters, B.: Adaptively secure puncturable pseudorandom functions in the standard model. In: Iwata, T., Cheon, J.H. (eds.) ASIACRYPT 2015. LNCS, vol. 9452, pp. 79–102. Springer, Heidelberg (2015). https://doi.org/10.1007/978-3-662-48797-6_4
16. Jiang, Y.: The direction of updatable encryption does not matter much. In: Moriai, S., Wang, H. (eds.) ASIACRYPT 2020. LNCS, vol. 12493, pp. 529–558. Springer, Cham (2020). https://doi.org/10.1007/978-3-030-64840-4_18
17. Kloog, M., Lehmann, A., Rupp, A.: (R)CCA secure updatable encryption with integrity protection. In: Ishai, Y., Rijmen, V. (eds.) EUROCRYPT 2019. LNCS, vol. 11476, pp. 68–99. Springer, Cham (2019). https://doi.org/10.1007/978-3-030-17653-2_3
18. Katz, J., Lindell, Y.: Introduction to Modern Cryptography, 3rd edn., Taylor & Francis Group, Boca Raton (2021)
19. Lehmann, A., Tackmann, B.: Updatable encryption with post-compromise security. In: Nielsen, J.B., Rijmen, V. (eds.) EUROCRYPT 2018. LNCS, vol. 10822, pp. 685–716. Springer, Cham (2018). https://doi.org/10.1007/978-3-319-78372-7_22
20. Nishimaki, R.: The direction of updatable encryption does matter. In: Hanaoka, G., Shikata, J., Watanabe, Y. (eds.) PKC 2022, LNCS 13178, pp. 194–224. Springer, Heidelberg (2022). https://doi.org/10.1007/978-3-030-97131-1_7
21. Okamoto, T., Pointcheval, D.: REACT: rapid enhanced-security asymmetric cryptosystem transform. In: Naccache, D. (ed.) CT-RSA 2001. LNCS, vol. 2020, pp. 159–174. Springer, Heidelberg (2000). https://doi.org/10.1007/3-540-45353-9_13
22. Pedersen, T.P.: Non-interactive and information-theoretic secure verifiable secret sharing. In: Feigenbaum, J. (ed.) CRYPTO 1991. LNCS, vol. 576, pp. 129–140. Springer, Heidelberg (1992). https://doi.org/10.1007/3-540-46766-1_9
23. Sahai, A., Waters, B.: How to use indistinguishability obfuscation: deniable encryption, and more. SIAM J. Comput. **50**, 857–908 (2021)
24. Spring, T.: Insecure backend database blamed for leaking 43tb of app data. https://threatpost.com/insecure-backend-databases-blamed-for-leaking-43tb-of-app-data
25. Waters, B.: Dual system encryption: realizing fully secure IBE and HIBE under simple assumptions. In: Halevi, S. (ed.) CRYPTO 2009. LNCS, vol. 5677, pp. 619–636. Springer, Heidelberg (2009). https://doi.org/10.1007/978-3-642-03356-8_36
26. Yan, Z., Deng, R.H., Varadharajan, V.: Cryptography and data security in the cloud computing. Inf. Sci. **387**, 53–55 (2017)
27. Zuo, C., Lin, Z., Zhang, Y.: Why does your data leak? Uncovering the data leakage in cloud from mobile apps. In: 2019 IEEE Symposium on Security and Privacy, S&P 2019, pp. 1296–1310, IEEE (2019)

Data Security

FDLedger: Dynamic and Efficient Anonymous Audit for Distributed Ledgers

Yao Liu[✉], Zhonghao Yuan, and Yunhan Hu

School of Cyber Engineering, Xidian University, Xi'an 710126, China
yliu_61@stu.xidian.edu.cn

Abstract. Distributed ledger schemes supporting users privacy protection have been proposed recently to provide users with better anonymity. However, their schemes made compromises in users addition or deletion, calculation efficiency, and storage overhead. How to implement a work that supports users dynamic addition and deletion with low computational and storage overhead in multi-user scenarios remains a challenging problem. This work introduces our scheme, a more efficient and dynamic user-supported auditing private ledger system. Computational overhead in our scheme is far less than the previous schemes. The storage overhead is independent of the number of transactions, thus only a minimal storage space can store large ledger. Specifically, we firstly propose a new authentication data structure, Sparse Prefix Symbol Tree (SPST), which can be used as an accumulator to implement ledger pruning. Secondly, we introduce a new encryption primitive Order-Revealing Encryption (ORE) to complete cipher text comparison, which reduces the computational overhead and storage space caused by zero-knowledge proof in the original schemes. Thirdly, our scheme use ledger pruning technology and a weighted random sampling algorithm to reduce storage overhead. We provide a formal security concept and conduct a security analysis of our program.

Keywords: Distributed ledger · Privacy-preserving · Auditability · dynamic

1 Introduction

The emergence of blockchain technology solves the problems of trust and value transmission at low cost, reshapes the form of financial activities, and gradually becomes an essential infrastructure of the 'value Internet'. At the same time, blockchain has decentralization, unalterable, traceability and permanent verification so that it has a wider application in trusted storage, market transactions, and financial audit. Nevertheless, many of these applications compromise identity information and ownership, which requires additional privacy protection.

© The Author(s), under exclusive license to Springer Nature Switzerland AG 2022
X. Chen et al. (Eds.): CSS 2022, LNCS 13547, pp. 89–108, 2022.
https://doi.org/10.1007/978-3-031-18067-5_7

In unlicensed systems, all transaction information including the public key of the transaction party is permanently recorded on the public blockchain, such as bitcoin scheme. Attack schemes such as Dust Attacks [24] can track user behavior and obtain additional information (user's real identity). Recently, several data disclosure events have proved the importance of meeting these requirements. At the same time, the privacy of the payment system in the consortium blockchain is still prominent. They should not reduce the cost of verification and reconciliation by sharing transaction data because recent regulations also stipulate this.

Presently, MiniLedger [7] and others have constructed a payment scheme that meets privacy protection and auditability. However, there are several problems in these schemes such as supporting account scalability and the amount of computational and storage overhead. Besides, the deletion of old or unnecessary transactions from classified accounts directly damages auditability because auditor cannot audit data that no longer exist in classified accounts. If multi-users' dynamic addition and deletion are considered, the challenge of designing scheme becomes more complex.

1.1   Our Contributions

In this paper, we focus on ledger audit that support privacy protection. Motivated by the above observations, we propose the first distributed bank payment system. To evaluate our scheme, we implement the prototype system and conduct multiple experiments. Our main contributions can be summarized as follows:

- We propose a new authenticated data structure SPST that provide proof of membership and proof of non-membership.
- We first use ORE to compare data range size in ciphertext, which greatly reduces computational overhead and storage space.
- We use account pruning techniques and weighted random sampling algorithms to reduce storage space.

1.2   Related Work

In this section, we briefly review the work of auditing privacy-protected ledgers in distributed ledgers.

Privacy-Preserving Distributed Payment System. Confidential Transactions and Confidential Assets [22] hide assets in transactions and support all participants to verify transactions. However, auditor need to access all transactions in plaintext to ensure integrity. Leakage in trading relationships can provide substantial privacy information [1,17,20,23]. Zcash [25] is a permissionless protocol concealing transaction amounts and parties using zero knowledge proofs. Other systems like the Monero cryptocurrency [26], based on anonymous transaction inputs and ring signatures to provide transactions privacy. Quisquis [11] provides the same anonymity class to Monero but consider a more compact sized ledger. Zether [3] is payment system based on smart contract which only conceal theamounts of transactions. Solidus [4] achieved confidential transactions in public ledgers, it hides access patterns in publicly verifiable encrypted Bank memory blocks by Oblivious RAM techniques. This approach allow users to transact anonymously in the system, and the Banks played a intermediaries roles. The schemes [7,14,19] use zero knowledge proof to conceal the transaction amount and relationship.

Distributed Payment System with Audit. Zcash and its extensions [12,13] enable a designated authority to perform accountability functionalities by adding additional ancillary information. Zcash need for strong computational assumptions and trusted setup. Monero [15] is similar to the use of cash, allowing for tracing the source or destination of transactions by linking anonymous transactions to participants. PRCash [27] use threshold encryption to send credentials to trading users, who must use their real names to continue trading if the volume exceeds the threshold for a period of time. ZkLedger [19] proposed the use of tokens to audit, which can achieve a variety of interactive audit types, but it destroys the whole purpose of its construction by using private swaps [5]. MiniLedger [7] proposes a private audit system that relies on trusted third parties to perform audits.

2 Preliminaries

2.1 Notation

As show in Table 1, we will define the notation that be using throughout this work.

Table 1. Notations and descriptions

Notations	Description
λ	Security prime
pp	Public parameters
$\mathbb{G}$	Schnorr group with prime order p
$\mathbb{Z}_p$	Group with prime order p
g	The generators of $\mathbb{G}$
h	The generators of $\mathbb{Z}_p$
F	Secure PRF
H	Hash function
n	The message of n bits
D_0	The accumulator initial state
w_x^t	The accumulator witness
R	The sparse prefix symbol tree root
k_i	The sparse prefix symbol tree leaf node

2.2 ElGamal Encryption Variant

Our scheme uses a variant of ElGamal encryption (called 'twisted ElGamal' (TEG)[8]). Compared with the standard ElGamal, in the public parameter PP, TEG needs an additional generator of the group (denoted by h belo), which enables it to homomorphically add ciphertexts com_2 and com_2' to generate different public keys pk and PK' and intentionally leak the relationship information between encrypted messages m and m' as follows. This variant works when the message space is small because lookup tables are needed when decrypting. TEG is secure against a chosen-plaintext attack. It works as follows:

- pp $\leftarrow$ TEG.Set(1^λ). Outputs PP = ($\mathbb{G}$,g,h,p) Where g,h are generators of the cyclic group $\mathbb{G}$ with prime order p.
- (pk,sk) $\leftarrow$ TEG.Gen(pp). Outputs sk $\leftarrow$ $\mathbb{Z}_p$, pk = h^{sk}.
- (com_1, com_2) $\leftarrow$ TEG.Enc(pk,u). Sample $r \leftarrow \mathbb{Z}_P$, computer $com_1 = \text{pk}^r$, $com_2 = g^u h^r$ and output $Com = (com_1, com_2)$.
- $u \leftarrow$ TEG.Dec(sk,(com_1, com_2)). Compute $g^u = com_2/com_1^{(1/\text{sk})}$ and recover u from the lookup table assuming the message space is relatively small.

TEG encryption is additively homomorphic:

$$\text{TEG.Enc}(\text{pk},u_1) \cdot \text{TEG.Enc}(pk.u_2) = \text{TEG.Enc}(\text{pk},u_1 + u_2)$$

Also if (com_1,com_2) $\leftarrow$ TEG.Enc(pk,m) and (com_1',com_2') $\leftarrow$ TEG.Enc(pk',u'), then $com_2 \cdot com_2'$ contains an encryption of $m + m'$. This indicates if $com_2 \cdot com_2' = 1$, then any external observer could deduce that $u = -u'$ for properly chosen r,r'.

2.3 Order-Revealing Encryption

In this part, we give a construction of an ORE scheme [9] for the set of n-bit. Set a security parameter λ. Take an integer number $M \geqslant 3$. Let $F : k \times ([n] \times \{0,1\}^{n-1}) \longrightarrow \mathbb{Z}_M$ be a secure PRF. A ORE scheme consists of four algorithms $\Pi_{ore} = (ORE.KGen, ORE.Enc, ORE.Cmp)$ as follows:

- ORE.KGen(1^λ). On input the security parameter λ, the key generation algorithm ORE.KGen outputs secret key sk of each bank.
- ORE.Enc(sk,m). Let $b_1...b_n$ be the binary representation of m and let $sk = k$. For each $i \in [n]$, the encryption algorithm computes $u_i = F(k, (i, b_1 b_2...b_i - 1||0^{n-i})) + b_i (mod\ M)$, and outputs the tuple $(u_1, u_2, ..., u_n)$.
- ORE.Cmp(ct_1,ct_2). The compare algorithm first parses $ct_1 = (u_1, u_2, \cdots, u_n)$ and $ct_2 = (u_1', u_2', \cdots, u_n')$, Where $u_1, \cdots, u_n, u_1', \cdots, u_n' \in \mathbb{Z}_M$. Let i be the smallest index where $u_i \neq u_i'$. If no such index exists, output 0. If such an index exists, output 1 if $u_i' = u_i + 1(mod\ M)$, and 0 otherwise.

2.4   Consensus

Consensus protocol (represented by CN) allows a set of S_{CN} decentralized individuals to agree in the presence of faults. We assume that the date is published on the ledger L by consensus. Only authenticated individuals have privilege of write in the ledger. We define consensus protocol: $Conscus(u, L) := L'$ which allows all system participants given an input value u and ledger state L, to agree on a new state L'. We also assume that it satisfies two basic properties:

- Consistency: an honest participant's view of the ledger on some round j is a prefix of an honest node's view of the ledger on some round $j + l, l > 0$.
- Liveness: an honest party inputing a value x, system will output a view of the ledger that includes x after a certain number of rounds.

3   System Model

3.1   Architecture

In this paper, we consider the following system participants: a central bank CB, which is also an *Auditor*, a dynamic set of n Banks with IDs defined by $[B_j]_{j=1}^n$ (known to everyone). Each Bank has an initial asset value $[u_j]_{j=1}^n$. We save transactions in a public ledger L maintained by a consensus layer CN and stored by all banks. We use tx_i to represent transaction where i is the transaction's index in the ledger.

We summarize the roles of each participant in the scheme and present the scheme model in Fig. 1. Then, we will introduce the specific work of each participant:

System Participants: There are n banks that issue transactions with transferring digital assets $(Bank_1 \cdots Bank_n)$, and an auditor *Auditor*, that verifies certain operational aspects of transactions performed by the banks.

Distributed Ledger: Distributed ledger stores transaction data in pure text, maintained by all peers and shared by participating banks. Ledger is composed of an $N \times M$ table, including N organizations. Each organization has a column to record its transaction information. The remaining three columns are transaction time, transaction identifier, and hash information of each row of transactions. A three-tuple represents each transaction information. Each row in the distributed ledger represents a piece of transaction information. In order to facilitate the accounting of participating banks, they can first record transaction information on their private ledgers for calculation. However, our scheme does not recognize the legitimacy of private ledgers.

3.2   Assumptions

We focus on the trading layer, and consider the basic consensus and network layer of the scheme and their mitigation orthogonal to this work. At the network level, we assume that malicious banks cannot prevent the view of another bank (Eclipse

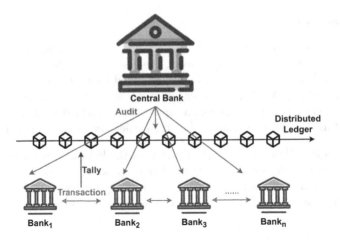

Fig. 1. xxxx.

attack). In addition, we assume that the transaction is sent to all banks through anonymous communication channels to maintain the anonymity of sending and receiving banks. We do not need out-of-band communication between banks.

The 'competitive condition' problem in $CreateTx()$ is considered orthogonal to our work, where different transactions may be created simultaneously. We can assume that all transactions are submitted to the agreement in a synchronous manner for verification (that is, there is no 'mempool' function), and we can also use the existing solution proposed in using atomic exchange protocol. Finally, for simplicity, we assume that the collection of participating banks is static, but it is easy to extend the system to dynamically add or delete banks. We also assume that the random oracle model converts our ZK proof to non-interactive.

3.3   Security Goals

Our scheme contains the following properties which are defined in a game-based fashion.

Theft Prevention and Balance: When initiating a transaction, the scheme can achieve: a) the bank who initiates the transaction cannot create more asset, and b) the initiating transaction amount should be less than the total balance of the bank.

Dynamic Additions or Deletions: When a bank is added or deleted, the ledger needs to prune, which is performed by the user designated, and finally outputs a digest of the ledger information. Ledger pruning must to do two things: a) contain the right trades and orders, and b) contain no wrong trades. A final safe trim prevents tampering with the history of the ledger.

Sound Auditability: An honest bank that follows the protocol will always be able to give the correct audit and convince the auditor. Besides, auditors always reject claims from malicious banks.

Ledger Correctness: The distributed ledger accepts only valid transactions and pruning operations.

4   FDLedger Construction

In this section, we first describe the formal definition of our scheme. Then, we expound on the main idea of the scheme. We introduce our new data structure - Sparse Prefix Symbol Tree. Finally, we present the specific scheme. The main functions of our scheme are defined as follows:

- Setup(1^λ,n). Given security parameters λ, the number of banks n. Then, the algorithm outputs each bank's public and private key pairs (pk, sk) for TEG and the private key (sk_{ore}) for ORE encryption.
- Transaction creation($sk_{B_k}, [u_{ij}]_{j=1}^n$). The transaction-initiated bank creates the transaction information. TEG is used to hide the transaction amount, ORE is used to encrypt the transaction amount, and the hash function binds the transaction information. Finally, a three-tuple has been generated. At the same time, in order to hide the transaction relationship, the transaction sponsor uses the weighted random sampling algorithm to select t banks for redundant padding. The transaction initiator sends the generated transaction information to other participating banks.
- Transaction pruning(st_j). The transaction-initiated bank prunes ledger. It uses SPST to calculate all transaction information from the last pruning to this pruning. Digest message D and its signature α are sent to SN.
- Consensus protocol(tx, D). SN verifies the correctness of transaction tx and summary D by verification algorithm, updates account L.
- Auditing(L). Auditor calculate the correctness of the transaction amount, and the algorithm outputs 1 or 0, where 1 represents the success of this round of audit and 0 represents failure.
- Adding or removing banks(q, D). When a new bank joins or leaves, CB sends information to the following banks to conduct transactions. The bank uses the transaction pruning algorithm to prune the accounts, and the consensus layer verifies this pruning. CB actively audits the transaction information after the previous audit to confirm the accuracy of these transactions.

4.1   Main Idea

Our scheme mainly aims at the problem that the participating banks cannot be dynamically added or deleted in the previous scheme. We propose an efficient audit scheme for ledger data that supports participating bank's dynamic addition and deletion. The main idea is to use the Sparse Prefix Symbol Tree proposed by our scheme to achieve ledger pruning and real-time audit to achieve dynamic addition or deletion of users. Specifically, when participating banks need to join or exit, CB will require the following participating banks to use a sparse prefix symbol tree to prune all the ledger information to this time from the previous pruning. At the same time, CB audits the current ledger information to ensure that the current ledger information is correct. The next book is equivalent to new for all participants so that the participating banks could be added or deleted. In order to reduce the computational and storage overhead, we replace the range proof in the original scheme with the order-revealing encryption. We also use the weighted random sampling algorithm to reduce the redundant filling in the ledger.

4.2 Sparse Prefix Symbol Tree

We use the accumulator-based ledger pruning technology proposed in Miniledger [7] to delete the ledgers in this scheme. In MiniLedger, their scheme analyzed and compared various accumulators, and concludes that Merkle Tree is better than RSA-based accumulator in computing efficiency and storage overhead. However, the author described the shortcomings of Merkle Tree mainly because it cannot prove non-member information. In the FastVer [2], we see that the sparse Merkle tree [6,21] can provide non-member proof. The sparse Merkle tree has a leaf key-value entry for each key domain (which can be unbounded) and an exceptional value null for non-existent keys (after this referred to as empty keys). The sparse Merkle tree uses linear spatial representation on the number of non-empty keys by exploiting the sparsity of non-empty keys.A famous implementation [6,21] constructs Patricia trie [18] on the non-empty key. It expands this data structure by storing encrypted hash points to each pointer node. We have improved and proposed a sparse prefix symbol tree.

In order to facilitate the recording, we encode the sparse prefix symbol tree in $< key, value >$ format, each node of the tree has only one $value$. Bank B_k takes the commitment value of each transaction in the ledger that needs to be trimmed as a $value$, its hash value as a key. We use the key as a prefix to build the tree, the $root$ node is the ancestor of all keys and our tree structure also has get/put operations.

Algorithm 1: SparsePrefixSymbolTreeAlgorith

Input : each transactions hash value h_i
Output: SPST Root: R
1 **Function Sparse Prefix Symbol Tree Build:**
2   **for** *each transactions hash value h_i* **do**
3   *Expand h_i as a bit string, expressed in hexadecimal for every 4 bits*
4       $k_i \leftarrow h_i$
5       $node_i \leftarrow inset(k_i)$
6   ***Update*** *root:* R
7   **return** R

Input : need to verify h
Output: Member witness w or Non-membership wn
1 **Function Verify node:**
2    $k \leftarrow h$
3   **for** traversal SPST data **do**
4   **if** $h = h'$ **then**
5   The sibling and parent nodes of h' until the root
6   **else**
7   The longest node h' matching h and its sibling and parent nodes until the root
8   **return** w OR wn

4.3 Our Construction

We assume the following building blocks: ORE (ORE.KGen, ORE,Enc, ORE.Cmp), Sparse Prefix Symbol Tree (SPSTSetup, SPSTBuild, SPSTVerify), a consensus protocol Conscus. The phases of construction work as follows:

Setup:

1. $SysSetup(1^\lambda, n, u_j)$. The agreement is implemented between CB and a set of n banks. CB sets the number of bits representing a transaction amount to p and verifies each bank's initial asset value v. BankSetup () is the algorithm for initial setting of each bank. By running TEG.Gen() to generate their public and private key pairs (pk_{teg}, sk_{teg}) for TEG encryption. ORE.Setup() is executed to generate the key sk_{ore} for ORE encryption. Bank sends (sk_{ore}) to CB through the secure channel. Then the bank runs runs ORE.Enc() to generate the encryption value of its initial amount. Then CB initializes a public account beginning with $Q_{0j} = C_{0j}$, and the vector $[Q_{0j}, C_{0j}]_{(j=1)}^n$ is composed of the 'initial' state of the distributed account L, the system parameter pp containing key parameters and all bank public keys. We assume that all banks (whether they participate in the consensus layer or not) store L, where the consensus participants all agree on a distributed ledger L.

Algorithm 2: FDLedger Construction

$\mathbf{SystemSetup}\Big(1^\lambda, n, u_j\Big)$

    ▷ CBSetup$\Big(1^\lambda, n\Big)$

1    $H() \leftarrow SPSTSet()$

2    $pp(G, g, h, p) \leftarrow TEG.Set(1^\lambda, n)$

3    $CB \longrightarrow \mathcal{B}_j : pp$

    ▷ BankSetup(pp)

4    $\mathcal{B}_j$ computes:

5    $Com_{0j} = Com(u_{0j}, r_{0j}) = g^{u_{0j}} h^{r_{0j}}$

6    $C_{0j} \leftarrow ORE.Enc(u_{0j}) \parallel H(u_{0j})$

7    $\mathcal{B}_j \longrightarrow CB$:

8   Com_{0j} and C_{0j}

9   CB verify u_{1j} and C_{0j}

$\mathbf{Transactioncreation}\Big(sk_{B_k}, v_{j=1}^n\Big)$

    ▷ B$_k$ For Oneself$\big(sk_{B_k}\big)$

1    $\mathcal{B}_k$ computes:

2    $Com_{ik} = Com(u_{ik}, r_{ik}) = g^{u_{ik}} h^{r_{ik}}$

3    $C_{ik} \leftarrow ORE.Enc(b_{ik}) \parallel H(b_{ik})$

4    $C_k = pk^{r_{ik}}$

    ▷ B$_k$ For Others$\big(sk_{B_k}\big)$

5    $\mathcal{B}_k$ for $\mathcal{B}_j$ computes:

6    $Com_{ij} = Com(u_{ij}, r_{ij}) = g^{u_{ij}} h^{r_{ij}}$

7    $C_{ij} \leftarrow ORE.Enc(u_{ij}) \parallel H(u_{ij})$

8    $\mathcal{B}_k \longrightarrow L$:

9    $tuple(Com_{ij}, C_{ij}, Token_j, H)$

$\mathbf{Transaction\ pruning}(st_j)$

    ▷ B$_j$

1    $\mathcal{B}_j$ fetch D$_{\alpha j}$ in previous digest

2   for $i = \alpha, i \leq \beta, i+1$ do

3        $\mathcal{B}_j$ execute SPST Build :

4        $D_{Bj} \leftarrow SPST_{node}\ Inset(H)$

5        $\sigma_j \leftarrow Sign(D_{Bj})$

6    $\mathcal{B}_j \longrightarrow CN : \sigma_j$

7   CN verify :

8    $D'_{\beta j} \overset{?}{=} D_{\beta j}$

Consensus protocol(tx, D, σ)

    ▷ CN

1    $\mathcal{B}_k \longrightarrow CN$:

2    $tuple(Com_{ik}, C_{ik}, C_k)$

3    $\mathcal{B}_j$ verify : $tuple(Com_{ij}, C_{ij}, C_j)$

4   CB computers :

5    $ORE.Enc_{B_k}(0)$ andORE.Enc$_{B_j}(0)$

6   S_{CN} execute ORE.Cmp :

7   S_{CN} verify tx or D

8    $\mathcal{B}_j$ update L

Auditing(C_{ij}, tx_{ij})

    ▷ Auditior

1    $\mathcal{A}$ Audit to tx :

2    $u_{ik} \leftarrow \mathcal{B}_k$ decrypts C_{ik}

3    $\mathcal{A}$ compare :

4    $H(u_{ik}) \overset{?}{=} H(u_{ik})$

5    $\mathcal{A}$ Audit to Balance $\sum_{i=\alpha}^{\beta} u_{ik}$:

6    $u_{ik} \leftarrow \mathcal{B}_k$ computes $\sum_{i=\alpha}^{\beta} Com_{ik}$

7    $\mathcal{A}$ Audit to :

8    $S_C N$ verify txor D

9    $\mathcal{B}_j$ update L

Dynamic Adding or Remove Bank(R)

    ▷ CB

1   if *When banks are added or removed* then

2        $CB \longrightarrow \mathcal{B}_k$

3        $D_k, \sigma_k \leftarrow \mathcal{B}_k$ execute Prune()

4        $CB \longrightarrow$ **Auditor**

5   **Auditor** execute PruneAud()

6   Adding or removed banks

Transaction Creation:

2. $CreateTx(sk_{B_k}, [u_{ij}]_{j=1}^n)$. For each B_j (including itself) in L, B_k executes $C_{ij} \leftarrow TEG.Enc(pk_B, u_{ij})$, calculates $[Ore]_{ij} \leftarrow ORE.Encrypt(sk_{B_k}, u_{ij})$, $Q_{ij} \leftarrow Q_{(i-1)j} \cdot C_{ij}$. To verify the value of each row, B_k should choose a random value for r_{ij} so that $\sum_{j=1}^n r_{ij} = 0$.

3. $VerifyTx(tx_i)$. Other banks B_j check that $\prod_{j=1}^n c_2^{(ij)} = 1$ (proof of balance) and that $Q_{ij} = Q_{(i-1)j} \cdot C_{ij}$ When output 1 is successfully verified, else output $\perp$.

Transaction Pruning:

4. $Prune(st_j)$. When CB wants to save more storage compression transaction history, the algorithm notifies B_k to execute SPST() and 'compress' it as the

accumulator summary $D_{\beta j}$, where the pruning depth of the account is $q = \beta - \alpha$, α is the latest summary, β is the current line number usually the bank will prune all the content between the last pruning and the latest transaction in L. It parses C_{ij} from each tx_{ij}. It obtains the previous summary $D_{\alpha j}$ if $\alpha = 1$, then set $D \to D_{\alpha j}$ as the initial accumulator value, where A is defined by pp. Then $\forall C_{ij}$, $i \in [\alpha, \beta]$ it continuously runs the accumulator addition $Add(D_{(i-1)j}, (i||C_{ij}))$ pay attention to the inclusion of index i, which retains the order of pruning transactions in D_j. Finally, B_k stores all transactions encrypted $[i, C_{ij}]_{i=\alpha}^{\beta}$ into its local memory, updates st_j to st_{0j}, calculates $\sigma j \leftarrow signature(D_{\beta j})$ and sends $D_{\beta j}$, σ_j to CN.

Consensus Protocol:

5. Our consensus protocol is similar to the basic blockchain consensus. The consensus protocol needs to initiate the corresponding verification algorithm to verify the effectiveness of the transaction when the participants initiate the transaction to the account. The participants only use new tx or D to update the account L.

Auditing:

6. $Audit\{A(C_{ij}) \leftrightarrow B_j(sk_j)\}$. Our audit agreement below includes a basic audit of the transaction value v deleted or not deleted and the sum of values which may be all past transactions, thereby auditing the bank's total assets. These audits are interactive and require the bank's consent.

Dynamic Adding or Removing Banks

7. Whenever a new bank joins the system, CB will notify the initiator of the next transaction to prune the Ledger. So this algorithm is executed by B_j when it receives notification from CB, to prune its transaction history of depth $q = \beta\alpha$ and 'compact' it to an digest $D_{\beta j}$, where α is the latest digest and β is a currently posted row number usually a Bank will prune everything between its last pruning and the latest transaction that appeared in L.

4.4   Discussions and Comparisons

In order to save storage space and improve computational efficiency, we introduce weighted random sampling algorithm [10]. In this algorithm, we require that the sampling probability of each unselected bank depends on the weight of this bank. The weight w of a single bank. The sum of ownership weights are W. B for many participating banks, $B.C$ returns current bank of all bank sets. $B.W$ returns weight of current banks, $B.Next$ advances bank to next position. Q is the new min priority queue. The power operator is represented by $\wedge$. We considered that Q needs the follow supports:

5   Security Analysis

In this section, we evaluate the security of an ORE-based dynamic ledger audit scheme. Meanwhile, we believe that the tools and cryptographic primitives used in our solution are secure.

Algorithm 3: WeightedRandomSamplingAlgorithms

Input : $B[1, ..., n]$
Output: $Q[1, ..., k]$

1 **while** B has data and $Q.C < k$ **do**
2 | $r := random()^{1/B.W}$ // random() selects homogeneous distribution in (0,1)
3 | $Q.Insert(r, B.C)$
4 | $B.Next$

5 $i := log(random())/log(Q.Min)$
6 **while** B has data **do**
7 | $i := i - B.W$
8 | **if** $i <= 0$ **then**
9 | | $j := Q.Min^{B.W}$ // returns minimum key value of all items
10 | | $r := random(j, 1)^{1/B.W}$
11 | | $Q.Extract - Min()$ // Remove the item with minimum key
12 | | $Q.Insert(r, B.C)$ // Adds item with specified key
13 | | $i := log(random())/log(Q.Min)$
14 | $B.Next$

15 **return** items in Q

Security Definitions. To define security, we first describe oracle provided to rival A. We assume that challenger CH maintains a damaged bank list T_c and performs some 'ledgerkeeping' for honest *banks* $\notin T_c$ in oracle query, where the total asset of honest bank is u^{CH}. This bookkeeping includes the following contents : a) for $CreateTx()$, it adds the output transaction tx to the ledger L ; b) For $Prune()$, it replaces the transaction history of honest banks with summary D on L, and updates the state of banks to st_{0j}. Please note that for the following security definition involving auditability, we only consider the basic audit of transaction value u for simplicity, we omit the security definition involving more complex audit.

- O_c A malicious bank B_c and completely controlled it. O_c Record B_c to T_c. This prediction reveals that adversary A can erode honest banks.
- O_{tx} A query O_{tx} creates a transaction that transfers u_c from Bank c (where $c \notin T_c$) to the recipient Bank(s) B_k. If Bank c has at least assets u_c, O_{tx} performs $CreateTx()$ to output tx_i and carry out accounting, otherwise it outputs $\perp$. This prediction indicates that A can instruct honest banks to conduct specific but effective transactions according to their own choices.

– O_{prn} Query O_{prn} to prune the transaction history of $B_c \notin T_c$. O_{prn} generates summary D and runs the bookkeeping. This prediction indicates that A can delete the transaction history of honest banks.

Definition 1 (Theft prevention and balance). For all security parameters λ, for all adversaries A accessing a through O_c, O_{tx} prophet in polynomial time:

$$\Pr \left[\begin{array}{c} pp \leftarrow \mathsf{SysSetup}\{\lambda, [B_c]_{c=1}^n\}, u_t = \sum_{c=1}^n u_i \\ tx* \leftarrow A^{O_c, O_{tx}}(pp) : \\ (B_c \notin T_c) \vee (u* \neq u_t) \vee \\ (B_c \in T_c, B_k \notin T_c, u* > u^A) \wedge \\ \mathbf{VerifyTx(tx^*)} = 1 \end{array} \right] \leq negl(\lambda)$$

Where $tx*$ is a transaction spending u^* from B_c to B_k, u^A the adversary's total assets before tx^* and u_t, u_t^* the system's total value before and after tx^* respectively.

This definition states that the owner can use their assets. When a transaction occurs, the assets of sender decrease correspondingly and should not exceed the value of their assets.

Definition 2 (Ledger Correctness). For all security parameters λ, for all adversaries A accessing a through O_c, O_{tx}, O_{prn} prophet in polynomial time:

$$\Pr \left[\begin{array}{c} pp \leftarrow \mathsf{SysSetup}\{\lambda, [B_c]_{c=1}^n\} \\ tx^* \div D^* \leftarrow A^{O_c, O_{tx}, O_{prn}}(pp) : \\ \left\{ \begin{array}{l} \mathsf{VerifyTx}(tx^*) = 0 \wedge tx^* \in L \\ \mathsf{PruneVrfy}(D^*) = 0 \wedge D^* \in L \end{array} \right\} \end{array} \right] \leq negl(\lambda)$$

An adversary creates a transaction via query functions O_c, O_{tx}, but our scheme can already prove that the bank's assets are safe. Therefore, the illegal transactions cannot be verified and will not be recorded in the distributed ledger, which ensures the correctness and security of transactions in the ledger.

Definition 3 (Corret Auditability). For all security parameters λ, for all adversaries A accessing a through O_c, O_{tx} prophet in polynomial time and for any honest auditor A:

$$\Pr \left[\begin{array}{c} pp \leftarrow \mathsf{SysSetup}\{\lambda, [B_j]_{j=1}^n\} \\ A^O(pp) : \\ \exists B_c \notin T_c \wedge \exists tx_{B_c} \wedge \\ \mathsf{Audit}\{A(tx_{B_c}) \Longleftrightarrow B_c(u)\} := \pi^{Aud} \wedge \\ \mathsf{AuditVrfy}(\pi^{Aud}) := 0 \end{array} \right] \leq negl(\lambda)$$

where tx_{B_j} is a transaction spending where B_j is involved in and v is input of $\mathsf{CreateTx}()$ which outputs tx_{B_j} from B_j to B_k, v^A the adversary's total assets before tx^* and u_t, v_t^* the system's total value before and after tx^* respectively.

Lemma 1. Assuming that the ORE encryption and TEG encryption schemes are secure and under the discrete logarithm hard problem, FDLedger can guarantee the security of the bank's assets.

Prove:

- Assuming that the adversary A can obtain the private key encrypted by the bank's TEG from the public parameter PP, the adversary can use the private key to initiate transactions and steal the bank's assets. At this point, the adversary's behavior can solve the discrete log-hard problem, contradicting the assumptions in the theorem.
- Suppose that the adversary A constructs an ORE encryption $C*$ that can pass the verification of the transaction amount range and change the total assets of the ledger $v*_t$, indicating that the adversary can obtain the ORE encrypted private key of the bank B_j. At this time, the adversary has broken the ORE encryption scheme security, contradicting the assumptions in the theorem.
- Assuming that the total assets of the ledger are u_t, the adversary A can construct a verified transaction $tx*$ to change the total assets of the ledger $v*_t \neq u_t$. It means that the transaction $tx*$ contains $\prod_{j=1}^{n} Com_2^{(ij)} = 1 \longrightarrow g^{u_1+u_2+\cdots+u_n+e}h^{r_1+r_2+\cdots+r_n} = 1$, where $e \neq 0$, which means that the adversary A can find $r* = r_1 + r_2 + \cdots + r_n \neq 0$, so that $h^{r*} = 1/g^{v_i^*}$, the adversary's behavior can solve the discrete Logarithmic hard problem, contradicting assumptions in the theorem.

In summary, FDLedger can prevent adversaries from creating assets and illegal transactions out of thin air, thus ensuring the safety of bank assets.

Lemma 2. Assuming that the stability of the accumulator and the consistency of the consensus layer can be guaranteed, which satisfies the correctness of the ledger.

Prove:

- The adversary A creates a transaction $tx*$ through the query function O_c, O_{tx}, but in Lemma 1, we can already prove that the bank's assets are safe, and the illegal transactions created by the adversary cannot pass the verification. Therefore, illegal transactions will not be recorded in the distributed ledger L, which ensures the security of transactions in the ledger.
- The adversary A generates a ledger pruned summary information $D*$ through three query functions O_c, O_{tx}, O_{prn}. However, an adversary A trying to pass the verification of the digest message D means breaking the safety of the accumulator. This is because the adversary A needs to forge the membership proof of the illegal transaction, while other honest nodes in the distributed network can use the sparse prefix symbol tree to provide the non-membership proof of the illegal transaction. Therefore, the security of the pruned ledger is guaranteed.
- The adversary A creates a transaction $tx*$ through three query functions O_c, O_{tx}, O_{prn} and generates a pruned summary information $D*$ to the distributed network. Due to the limited resources of the adversary, it cannot control more than 51% nodes in the network. Therefore, due to the consistency of consensus, these illegal data cannot be added to the distributed ledger L, which ensures the security and consistency of the ledger.

Lemma 3. Assuming that TEG encryption and ORE encryption schemes are secure, this scheme satisfies audit correctness.

Prove:

- First, for the transaction data ciphertext Com encrypted with TEG, where $com_1 = pk^r = h^{sk*r}$, $com_2 = g^v h^r$ the auditor decrypts using the authorized private key to get:

$$com_2 \cdot (com_1^{1/sk})^{-1} = g^v h^r \cdot (pk^{r/sk})^{-1} = g^v h^r \cdot h^{-r} = g^v \qquad (1)$$

  The auditor can get the value of the transaction amount v from the cache table. If the audit amount is correct, the output result is 1, otherwise, the output result is 0. The auditor can determine whether the transaction amount v is correct by decrypting the value of the transaction.
- Secondly, in the above proof, the correctness of the transaction amount v cannot be completely guaranteed, because the adversary A can pass the proof by $com_2' = g^v h^r = g^{(v+p)} h^r$ forging com_2 to pass the proof and destroy the correctness of the audit. The transaction amount v is encrypted by ORE to get $C(v)$, and the range of the transaction amount can be obtained by using the ORE.Cmp algorithm, preventing the adversary from launching malicious attacks. In summary, the correctness of the audit has been proved.

6 Performance Evaluation

In this section, we conduct a thorough experimental evaluation of the audit scheme proposed by us. We first describe the configuration of the experimental environment and the selection of parameters. After that, we will evaluate our scheme by comparing it with the miniledger scheme [7].

6.1 Experiment Setup

This section describes the performance evaluation of our scheme, and since we are focusing on the transaction layer. We deployed all our experiments on a personal laptop computer with Ubuntu 18.04, Intel Core i7-6700K @ 4.0 GHz, and 16 GB RAM employing a single-thread. We implement a prototype of the transaction layer of Ledger in Python using the *petlib*[1] library to support cryptographic operations over the secp256k1 elliptic curve. We use $fast - ore$[2] to implement ORE encryption.

6.2 Experiment Evaluation

In this section, we make a comparative analysis between our scheme and the existing scheme, mainly comparing with miniledger scheme to evaluate our scheme. We compare proof generation, validation, and proof size. As shown in

---

[1] https://github.com/gdanezis/petlib/.
[2] https://github.com/collisionl/fast_ore.

the Table 2, we list in detail the comparison of our scheme with previous schemes, and set the same parameters in each scheme to the same size for ease of comparison. ZkLedger performs better than other schemes in many aspects because of the Borromean ring signatures [16] used in zkLedger for zero-knowledge proofs and the Bulletproofs used in other schemes for range proofs. But we used ORE encryption to replace the range proof used in the previous scheme, and we significantly improved the efficiency from the initial millisecond level to the microsecond level, about a thousand-fold increase in efficiency.

Table 2. The efficiency of contrast

Scheme	Transaction creat	Transaction verify	Transaction audit	Ledger storage	Ledger pruning
zkLedger [19]	6.8 ms	5.7 ms	6 ms	4 KB	N
FabZK [14]	152 ms	2 ms	300 ms	120 KB	N
MiniLedger [7]	53 ms	49 ms	4.8 ms	68 KB	2 KB
FDLedger (This work)	4.3 ms	2 ms	4 ms	50 KB	1.8 KB

Note: We set the parameters of different scenarios to the same situation. After adopting the weighted random sampling algorithm and sparse prefix symbol tree, we have better performance in storage space.

Transaction Creation, Verification and Audit. Each transaction in FDLedger includes the commitment value of the transaction, ORE-encrypted ciphertext and other information, which leads to a linear increase in the computational cost of transaction creation and verification with the number of banks, as shown in Fig. 2, The blue line represents the transaction creation stage, and the red line represents the transaction verification stage, both of which show a clear linear relationship. The cost of creating and validating each transaction in the FDLedger scheme is 4.3 ms and 2 ms, respectively. As shown in Fig. 3, it takes about 4 ms to audit any single transaction in the distributed ledger, which is the cost of the full audit protocol, i.e. the bank's decryption time and proof verification time and the auditor's verification cost. Since the audit of this scheme is only for both parties involved in the transaction, the audit cost is constant and is not affected by the number of banks or the number of previous transactions.

The FDLedger scheme mainly uses ORE encryption for transaction encryption, decryption and comparison. We use the blue line to describe our scheme and the red line to describe the miniLedger scheme. As shown in Fig. 4, our scheme takes about 12 μs to encrypt 64-bit plaintext, and the miniLedger scheme takes about 55 ms, which is a great improvement. As shown in Fig. 5, this scheme takes about 0.35 μs to verify the 64-bit plaintext size, and the miniLedger scheme takes about 3.5 ms. Our scheme does not lower the security requirements than the miniLedger scheme, so our scheme has high computational efficiency. As shown in Fig. 6, in terms of storage overhead, for 64-bit plaintext, our storage size is slightly larger than that of the miniLedger scheme, but this does not affect the practical use of our scheme.

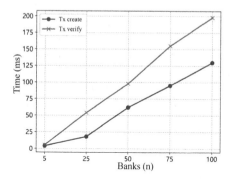

Fig. 2. Transaction create and verify

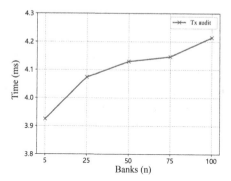

Fig. 3. Transaction audit

Transaction Pruning. FDLedger evaluates the computational requirements of the pruning operation, including executing Prune and PruneVerfy to create a summary D_j. The results of the scheme in Fig. 7 show that it takes less than a second to prune 10,000 transactions using the SPST and Merkle tree of this scheme, and our scheme is more efficient than the Merkle tree. Using the RSA accumulator in about 2 h is not practical for a practical use case. In Fig. 7, this scheme compares the establishment efficiency of SPST with Merkle tree and RSA accumulator. By comparison, the efficiency of this scheme in the establishment process is far lower than the calculation time of the RSA accumulator and the establishment time of the Merkle Tree. In Fig. 8, this scheme compares the time it takes for the RSA accumulator to generate proofs, since Merkle Tree cannot generate non-member proofs. Through comparative analysis, the RSA accumulator has reached the second level when generating the proof, but the SPST of this scheme still remains at the millisecond level. This program is much more practical than other programs.

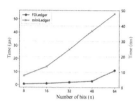

Fig. 4. Proof generation

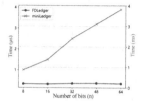

Fig. 5. Proof verify

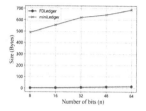

Fig. 6. Proof size

Storage Costs. Specifically, in FDLedger's implementation, the communication and storage cost per transaction is 50 KB per bank, including TEG encryption, ORE encryption, and total runs. Note that this scheme provides the actual memory footprint (which depends on the efficiency of the underlying library), not the theoretical lower bound, including summaries of common parameters, transactions, and ledger pruning, requiring only 50 KB of storage per bank. The storage cost of the distributed ledger L is capped at $64n$ bytes for TEG encryption (representing the running total Q). For the storage required for summary D and parameters pp, assuming all n banks delete their transaction history, the distributed ledger consists of one row. When the system is running, the actual storage exceeds the minimum value due to the increase in transaction volume. Through certain reward and punishment measures, the storage cost of the ledger can be minimized, which can save huge storage costs.

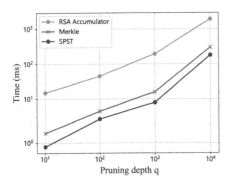

Fig. 7. Ledger pruning cost

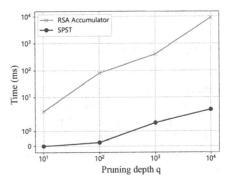

Fig. 8. SPST cost

7   Conclusion

We propose the first private and auditable payment system which is independent of the number of transactions and supports user dynamic addition and deletion. Our scheme uses the existing encryption tool ORE, and uses a sparse prefix symbol tree to solve the dynamic addition and deletion of important users in auditable private payments. In addition, we provide a formal definition of security, auditability and security pruning in private and auditable payment systems. Compared with the previous work of storing information for each transaction, we have achieved great storage savings. Using our pruning technology, no matter how many transactions happened, the overall size of each bank's storage can be impressively compressed to 50 KB. Our scheme can currently serve a small consortium composed of banks (such as the World Central Bank or CB of various countries), any number of customers, or build a hierarchical structure composed of a large number of banks and customers. Implementing its attributes without permission is an interesting direction for future work.

Acknowledgment. This work is supported by the Fundamental Research Funds for the Central Universities (No. JB211503).

References

1. Ahn, G.J., Shehab, M., Squicciarini, A.: Security and privacy in social networks. IEEE Internet Comput. **15**(3), 10–12 (2011)
2. Arasu, A., et al.: FastVer: making data integrity a commodity. In: Proceedings of the 2021 International Conference on Management of Data, pp. 89–101 (2021)
3. Bünz, B., Agrawal, S., Zamani, M., Boneh, D.: Zether: towards privacy in a smart contract world. In: Bonneau, J., Heninger, N. (eds.) FC 2020. LNCS, vol. 12059, pp. 423–443. Springer, Cham (2020). https://doi.org/10.1007/978-3-030-51280-4_23
4. Cecchetti, E., Zhang, F., Ji, Y., Kosba, A., Juels, A., Shi, E.: Solidus: confidential distributed ledger transactions via PVORM. In: Proceedings of the 2017 ACM SIGSAC Conference on Computer and Communications Security, pp. 701–717 (2017)
5. Centelles, A., Dijkstra, G.: Extending zkLedger with private swaps. In: 15th USENIX Symposium on Networked Systems Design and Implementation (2018)
6. Chase, M., Deshpande, A., Ghosh, E., Malvai, H.: SEEMless: sSecure end-to-end encrypted messaging with less trust. In: Proceedings of the 2019 ACM SIGSAC conference on Computer and Communications Security, pp. 1639–1656 (2019)
7. Chatzigiannis, P., Baldimtsi, F.: MINILEDGER: compact-sized anonymous and auditable distributed payments. In: Bertino, E., Shulman, H., Waidner, M. (eds.) ESORICS 2021. LNCS, vol. 12972, pp. 407–429. Springer, Cham (2021). https://doi.org/10.1007/978-3-030-88418-5_20
8. Chen, Yu., Ma, X., Tang, C., Au, M.H.: PGC: decentralized confidential payment system with auditability. In: Chen, L., Li, N., Liang, K., Schneider, S. (eds.) ESORICS 2020. LNCS, vol. 12308, pp. 591–610. Springer, Cham (2020). https://doi.org/10.1007/978-3-030-58951-6_29
9. Chenette, N., Lewi, K., Weis, S.A., Wu, D.J.: Practical Order-Revealing Encryption with Limited Leakage. In: Peyrin, T. (ed.) FSE 2016. LNCS, vol. 9783, pp. 474–493. Springer, Heidelberg (2016). https://doi.org/10.1007/978-3-662-52993-5_24
10. Efraimidis, P.S., Spirakis, P.G.: Weighted random sampling with a reservoir. Inf. Process. Lett. **97**(5), 181–185 (2006)
11. Fauzi, P., Meiklejohn, S., Mercer, R., Orlandi, C.: Quisquis: a new design for anonymous cryptocurrencies. In: Galbraith, S.D., Moriai, S. (eds.) ASIACRYPT 2019. LNCS, vol. 11921, pp. 649–678. Springer, Cham (2019). https://doi.org/10.1007/978-3-030-34578-5_23
12. Garman, C., Green, M., Miers, I.: Accountable privacy for decentralized anonymous payments. In: Grossklags, J., Preneel, B. (eds.) FC 2016. LNCS, vol. 9603, pp. 81–98. Springer, Heidelberg (2017). https://doi.org/10.1007/978-3-662-54970-4_5
13. Jiang, Y., Li, Y., Zhu, Y.: Auditable zerocoin scheme with user awareness. In: Proceedings of the 3rd International Conference on Cryptography, Security and Privacy, pp. 28–32 (2019)
14. Kang, H., Dai, T., Jean-Louis, N., Tao, S., Gu, X.: FabZK: supporting privacy-preserving, auditable smart contracts in hyperledger fabric. In: 2019 49th Annual IEEE/IFIP International Conference on Dependable Systems and Networks (DSN), pp. 543–555. IEEE (2019)

15. Li, Y., Yang, G., Susilo, W., Yu, Y., Au, M.H., Liu, D.: Traceable monero: anonymous cryptocurrency with enhanced accountability. IEEE Trans. Depend. Secure Comput. **18**, 679–691 (2019)
16. Maxwell, G., Poelstra, A.: Borromean ring signatures. https://raw.githubusercontent.com/Blockstream/borromean_paper/master/borromean_draft_0.01_34241bb.pdf
17. Meiklejohn, S., et al.: A fistful of bitcoins: characterizing payments among men with no names. In: Proceedings of the 2013 Conference on Internet Measurement Conference, pp. 127–140 (2013)
18. Morrison, D.R.: Patricia-practical algorithm to retrieve information coded in alphanumeric. J. ACM **15**(4), 514–534 (1968)
19. Narula, N., Vasquez, W., Virza, M.: zkLedger: privacy-preserving auditing for distributed ledgers. In: 15th USENIX Symposium on Networked Systems Design and Implementation NSDI 2018), pp. 65–80 (2018)
20. Ober, M., Katzenbeisser, S., Hamacher, K.: Structure and anonymity of the bitcoin transaction graph. Future internet **5**(2), 237–250 (2013)
21. Oprea, A., Bowers, K.D.: Authentic time-stamps for archival storage. In: Backes, M., Ning, P. (eds.) ESORICS 2009. LNCS, vol. 5789, pp. 136–151. Springer, Heidelberg (2009). https://doi.org/10.1007/978-3-642-04444-1_9
22. Poelstra, A., Back, A., Friedenbach, M., Maxwell, G., Wuille, P.: Confidential assets, 2017. In: 4th Workshop on Bitcoin and Blockchain Research (2017)
23. Ron, D., Shamir, A.: Quantitative analysis of the full bitcoin transaction graph. In: Sadeghi, A.-R. (ed.) FC 2013. LNCS, vol. 7859, pp. 6–24. Springer, Heidelberg (2013). https://doi.org/10.1007/978-3-642-39884-1_2
24. Saad, M., et al.: Exploring the attack surface of blockchain: a systematic overview. arXiv preprint arXiv:1904.03487 (2019)
25. Sasson, E.B., et al.: Zerocash: Decentralized anonymous payments from bitcoin. In: 2014 IEEE Symposium on Security and Privacy, pp. 459–474. IEEE (2014)
26. Van Saberhagen, N.: Cryptonote v 2.0 (2013). https://cryptonote.org/whitepaper.pdf
27. Wüst, K., Kostiainen, K., Čapkun, V., Čapkun, S.: PRCash: fast, private and regulated transactions for digital currencies. In: Goldberg, I., Moore, T. (eds.) FC 2019. LNCS, vol. 11598, pp. 158–178. Springer, Cham (2019). https://doi.org/10.1007/978-3-030-32101-7_11

A Method of Traceless File Deletion for NTFS File System

Shujiang Xu[1]([✉]), Fansheng Wang[1], Lianhai Wang[1], Xu Chang[2], Tongfeng Yang[2], and Weijun Yang[3]

[1] Shandong Provincial Key Laboratory of Computer Networks, Shandong Computer Science Center (National Supercomputer Center in Jinan), Qilu University of Technology (Shandong Academy of Science), Jinan 250014, China
xushj@sdas.org
[2] School of Cyber Security, Shandong University of Political Science and Law, Jinan 250014, China
[3] First Research Institute of the Ministry of Public Security of PRC, Beijing 100044, China

Abstract. NTFS is the most widely used disk partition format today, especially in personal computers and mobile storage devices, for its high security, excellent performance, and good convenience. After a file is normally deleted in NTFS file system, it can be still recovered by analyzing the file records and properties in MFT, and the deletion leave traces in the operation system which can be detected by the forensic tools. If the computer/USB device is lost or stolen, files on the hard disk, including the files that has been deleted, can be leaked which leaves a huge security risk. To securely and completely delete a file, this paper proposes a method of traceless file deletion for Windows NTFS file system. Experimental results show that the deleted file cannot be recovered and the deletion operation leaves no trace even by the forensic tools.

Keywords: Traceless file deletion · Secure data destruction · NTFS file system

1 Introduction

With the rapid development of network and information technology, data has become an important fundamental strategic resource, which plays an increasingly important role in improving production efficiency, and has become the most important production factor of the times. As the core engine of the development of digital economy, data is constantly giving rise to new industrial forms and injecting strong power into the rapid development of economy and society. To ensure social stability and national security, we must keep the factors of data production secure. Therefore, data security is particularly important [1, 2].

In daily work and life, interactions in social networks, purchases of goods and services, various types of monitoring devices generate a large amount of data. All such data is stored on hard drives of servers and computer, or mobile storage devices. With the improvement of informatization and network, the network attack technology aiming at data theft is more advanced and diversified, and the problem of data security is becoming increasingly serious. Some hackers, viruses, trojans constantly intrude on our computers to steal business secrets and personal information. As a result, there is a huge risk of information leakage, which may bring huge economic, political, military and other losses to individuals, institutions and countries [3]. We must ensure the security of the data on the computer.

Usually, the hard disk of computers and mobile storage devices should be formatted into one or more file systems so as to manage the stored files conveniently. NTFS (New Technology File System) is the most widely used file system and disk partition format for its high security, excellent performance, and good convenience [4]. Compared with FAT (File Allocation Table) file system, NTFS file system has the advantage of big volume size, increased fault tolerance and enhanced security [5].

If your computer or data storage devices are obtained by data thieves, data stored in them can be copied. It is worth noting that the file not deleted completely also can be recovered by the tools of data recovery. If a hacker gains read and write access of your computer over the Internet, the files that have not been completely erased on your hard drive can also be recovered by data recovery technology. Therefore, it is necessary to clear it completely when important data needs to be deleted. The most ideal effect is that hackers detect no trace of deletion and find that no data has been deleted.

This paper propose a method of traceless file deletion for NTFS file system to ensure the data we want to delete is completely cleared. The file deleted by this method leaves no trace of deletion operation and can resist security audits. It has achieved the ideal result, a file in NTFS file system has been removed and left no trace of the deletion in the operation system. So the operation system does not notice that a file has been deleted and the deleted file cannot recover. Experimental results show that the cleared files cannot recover and the deletion operation leaves no trace in the operation systems.

The rest of this paper is organized as follows. Section 2 summarizes the related work. The brief introduction for NTFS file system is given in Sect. 3. Section 4 presents the mechanism and the method of data deletion for NTFS file system. Section 5 analyzes the performance of the proposed method and Sect. 6 concludes this paper.

2 Related Work

In the past, most of the researches focused on data recovery for NTFS. Wang and Ju [6] analyzed the structure of NTFS file system in Windows NT, including the basic data structure of MFT (master file table), MFT record, file and fold structure, and described data recovery method by logging file system. Oommen and Sugathan [7] gave the structure of the NTFS file system and presented a scheme to recover deleted files from NTFS file system. The scheme analyzed the MFT entry to detect the directory of the deleted file. To recover the deleted file used NTFS compression which makes it difficult to obtain the deleted data in a digital forensic investigation, Yoo et al. [8] draw a carving method for the continuously allocated compressed files with more than 16 clusters. Peng et al. [9] introduced the structure of NTFS files system and gave a scheme to recover deleted data in NTFS file system. Feng et al. [10] designed and implemented a data recovery system for NTFS file system. Zhang et al. [11] described the recovery process of deleted files and formatted files in FAT32 file system, and introduced the recovery process of deleted files in NTFS file system according to the different storage characteristics of file records, file attributes and running lists on NTFS.

US DoD 5220.22-M (E, ECE) US DoD 5220.22-M (E) is a data wiping method that is commonly known as 'three-pass'. The method first overwrites the data once with a certain value, then overwrites the data with its complement [12], and then, overwrites the data with random data finally. Most data clear tools default follow the US DoD 5220.22-M (E) standard. But US DoD 5220.22-M (8-306./ECE) employs 'seven-pass' operation, which firstly performs a three-pass operation, then overwrites with a random hex value, and then performs the three-pass operation again.

In recent years, the methods to find execution traces in Windows have attracted widespread attention. Employing NTFS transaction features and a machine learning algorithm, Dong et al. [13] proposed a method to effectively recognize wiped partitions and files in the NTFS file system and identify tools used in data sanitization. Park et al. [14] checked the installation and execution of data clearing tools with the indicators of anti-forensics. Zareen et al. (2015) suggested criteria for validating file wiping software. They observed that NTFS transaction metadata have many artifacts of user file system actions but are difficult for most tools to wipe out. In 2019, Horsman [15] presented a digital tool marks (DTM) to detect file wiping software for Windows NTFS and FAT32. In 2020, Karresan et al. [16] studied the NTFS allocation algorithm and its behavior empirically using two virtual machines in Windows 7 and 10 on NTFS formatted fixed size virtual hard disks.

3   Brief Introduction for NTFS File System

NTFS is a widely used computer file system with the advantage of good fault tolerance, convenience and security [4, 5]. It is usually employed in personal computers, servers, mobile storage devices, especially in the computer with Windows operation systems. Furthermore, NTFS supports a big volume size (a max file size of 16 EB). All of the above advantages make NTFS the preferred file system for Windows.

Boot area	MFT area	Data area	MFT mirror area	Data area	DBR mirror area

Fig. 1. The structure of NTFS file system

The structure of NTFS file system is shown in Fig. 1 which composes of the boot area, MFT area, MFT mirror area, data area and DBR mirror area [11]. The 0th sector of the NTFS file system is the $Boot sector including DBR (DOS boot record). This sector contains the BPB and extended BPB parameters, which can be parsed to obtain the volume size, number of heads, sector size, cluster size, the starting logical cluster number of the MFT and other parameters. Among them, MFT Start Address = Start Cluster of MFT * Bytes per Sector * Sectors per cluster [7].

MFT includes $MFT, $MFTMirr, $LogFile, $Volume, $AttrDef, $Root, $Bitmap, $Boot, $BadCius, $Secure, $Upcase, and $Extend. The MFT records each file on the partition by 2 sectors (1024 bytes). The file record consists of two parts, one is the file record header (48 bytes) and the other is the properties list. The record header includes the start flag "FILE", the offset of the first attribute, the file characteristics (00H indicates the file is deleted, 01H indicates the normal file, 02H indicates the deleted directory), the actual length of the file record, and the allocated record size for file. Each file record has several relatively independent properties with their own types and names. Each attribute consists of an attribute header and an attribute body. The first four bytes of the attribute header are the type of the attribute. There are two types of attributes: resident and non-resident. When a file is very small, all of its attribute bodies can be stored in the file record, and these attributes stored in the meta-file of MFT are called resident attributes. If a file is much larger than a 1 KB, file record cannot store all of its attributes, the file system stores other file record attributes of the file in an area outside the meta-file of MFT, also called the data stream. Records stored in a non-MFT meta-file are called non-resident attributes. The MFT also has its own record, and record 0 in the MFT is the record of itself.

Because MFT is so important, the system also prepares a mirror file $MFTMirr for it. The record 1 of the MFT is $MFTMirr, which typically mirrors only the first four file records in $MFT. The record 6 is a Bitmap file $Bitmap, in which the allocation status of NTFS cluster is recorded in the Bitmap file. Each bit records a cluster in the cluster, which is used to identify whether the cluster is free or allocated.

4   A Method of Traceless Data Deletion for NTFS File System

4.1   The Requirements of Traceless Data Deletion

Let's first consider the normal file deletion. After we delete a file in NTFS file systems, its file characteristics in the file head at the offset 16H byte is changed into 00H which indicates the file is deleted. At the same time, the file index entry in the file directory index buffer is deleted, and the corresponding cluster in the Bitmap file $Bitmap is released (filled with 0). Although the MFT number, data cluster and directory entry are withdrawn by the file system after the deletion operation, the important information (including data index), such as file name in 30H, file size in 80H, creation time and data, is still intact in the MFT record, the data area is also not changed yet, so the deleted file can be recovered. Because the important attributes such as the file name, file size, and Run List of the deleted file have not changed, the contents of the data area have not changed either, the deleted file can be recovered if its file data is stored in continuous cluster. If the discontinuous clusters are used to store its file data, only part of the file data of the first cluster can be recovered. Once the corresponding data area of the deleted file has been overwritten by new data, the file is difficult to recover.

After a file is deleted, its index entry in the root directory is reclaimed by the system, and the index entry of the recorded file is modified. Therefore, the MFT reference number of the file cannot be found by looking up the index entry in the directory. However, the file's record, which exists in the form of index entries and records the MFT reference number of the file in the $LOGFILE file, still exists, and there is one more record which extra records the change of the record for $LOGFILE file. Though the time value is different from the original record, but the MFT reference number is the same as the original record, thus providing a reference for finding the MFT item.

Figure 2, 3, and 4 respectively show the deletion trace detected by the forensics tools before and after normal deletion in Windows NTFS file system. From them, we can find that normal deletion left trace of deletion operation which can be detected by forensics tools, such as FinalData, WinHex. As a result, both the normal "Del" operation and the "Shift+Del" operation cannot completely deletes a file to make it unrecoverable since the deletion operation is recorded by the operating system. Employing the deletion trace, the deleted files can be recovered by forensics tools.

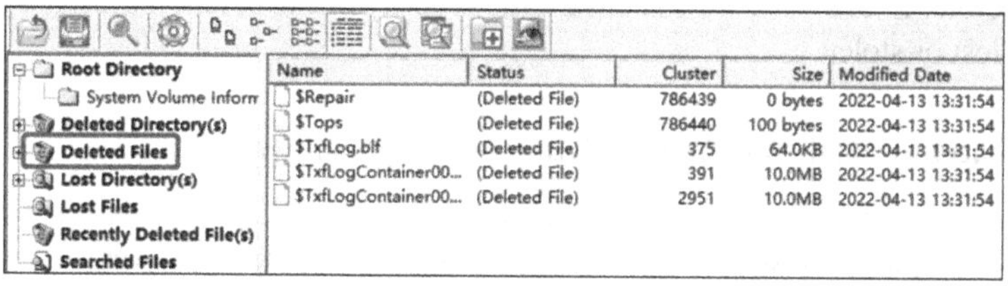

Fig. 2. Trace of deletion operation before deletion by FinalData

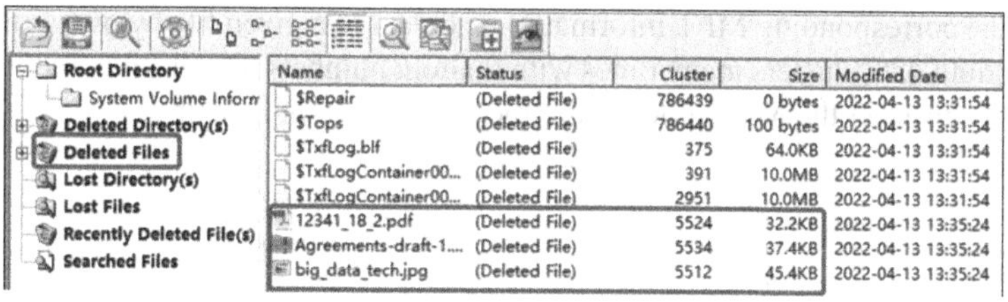

Fig. 3. Trace of deletion operation after deletion by FinalData

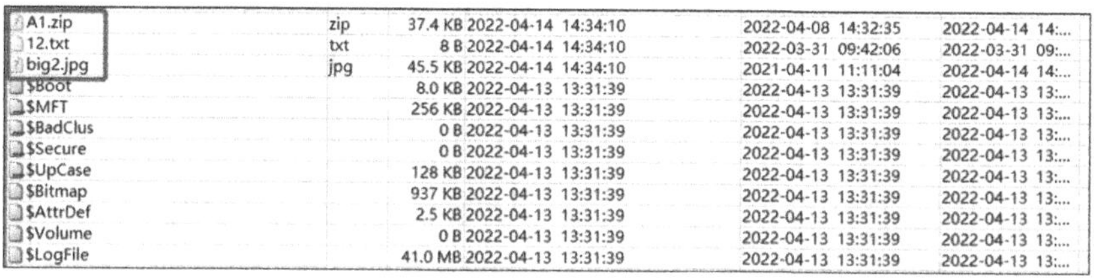

Fig. 4. Trace of deletion operation after deletion by WinHex

We must ensure that the deleted file cannot be recovered and cannot leave any operation trace to delete a file completely. To make sure the deleted file cannot be restored even by the professional data recovery tools, the residual data including the information in its corresponding MFT and the corresponding data in data area after normal deletion should be cleared completely. For NTFS file system, normal deletion operation has already cleared some related contents of the deleted file, but the important information including file name in 30H, and file size in 80H are still in MFT.

These related information including the additional record in $LOGFILE should be cleared at the same time of deleting file. It's important to emphasize that the data stored in the data area and its related information in MFT must be overwritten for multiple times according to US DoD 5220.22-M (E) standard, so that any content of the deleted file cannot be recovered even by forensics tools.

Furthermore, the files deletion operation leaves no trace so as to resist the security audit of Windows operating system and detection of professional forensics tools. If no trace left of the file deletion is detected, even a hacker will assume that no file has been deleted in the past. Therefore, we need to reconstruct the MFT after cleaning up the file data and its associated information, so that it looks exactly as it was never used to store any file before. In this way, we can ensure the security of file deletion even if a storage device is lost or stolen.

4.2 A Traceless Method of Data Deletion for NTFS File System

A traceless method of file deletion for NTFS file system is proposed in this subsection, which can completely destroy file data and makes it impossible to recover a deleted file. The method load hard disks as physical files to attract no attention of Windows operating system. The disks are locked to avoid the audit of the operating system. So no operation record is left when erasing and overwriting data. This presented method completely destroys the corresponding MFT information and data of a given file by overwriting the corresponding data clusters many times with random numbers to make it unrecoverable, and then reconstruct the MFT to leave no trace of erasing and writing.

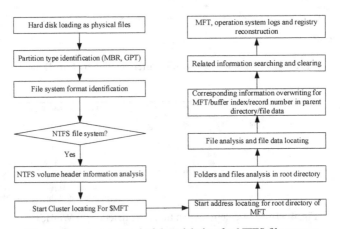

Fig. 5. Traceless method of data deletion for NTFS file system

The proposed method shown in Fig. 5 is described below.

Step 1. Load the hard disk that stores the given file as physical files.

Step 2. Identify the partition type of the disk that stores the given file: MBR (Main boot record) or GPT (GUID partition Table)?

Step 3. Identify the file system format that stores the given files. If it is NTFS formation, then turn to next step.

Step 4. Analyze the header information of the NTFS volume, locate the start address of DBR (DOS boot record) and find the BPB (BIOS parameter block), and then read BPB structure information to get the start cluster address of the $MFT.

Step 5. Locate the start cluster address for the root directory of MFT which is at $MFT start address offset $0 \times 05 * 2 *$ the number of bytes per sector.

Step 6. Analyze the folders and files in the root directory, obtain the attribute 0×30, and find the MFT file name. Based on the storage path of the given file, the given file can be located.

Step 7. Locate the file data. Note that there are two types of attributes: resident and non-resident. The permanent resident files exist in the MFT header file. For the non-resident attribute, the starting cluster address and its length of the data can be obtained by analyzing the attribute 0×80.

Step 8. Overwriting the corresponding information in MFT/buffer index/record number in parent directory/file data of the given file.

Step 9. Search the related information of the given file, and clear it by the above method.

Step 10. Reconstruct the MFT to make the deleted file looks like it never existed in the disk. If there is related information about the given file in the operation system logs and registry, we also need to clear it and reconstruct the corresponding log and registry.

5 Performance Analysis

5.1 Experiment Result

We perform the experiment in Intel(R) Core(TM) i7-10510U CPU @ 1.80 GHz 2.30 GHz, 8 G memory Windows 10. And the given files are stored in a mobile USB device which is formatted into NTFS file system.

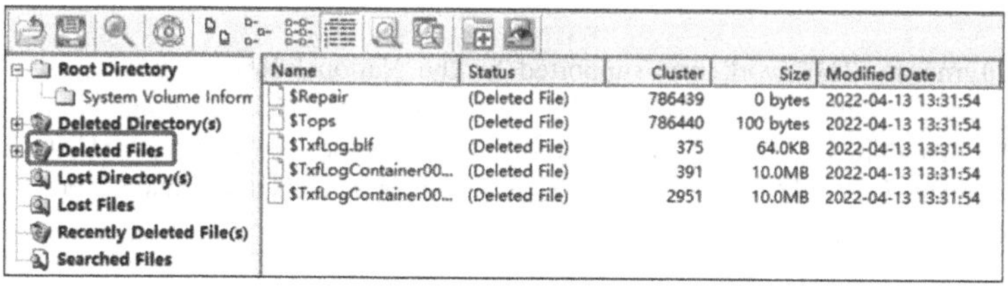

Fig. 6. The trace detection result after deletion by FinalData

In the experiment, 3 files with different file types and sizes, big1.jpg (46K), 12.txt (1K) and A1.zip (38K) are utilized to test the performance of the proposed method. After file deletion, we use the forensic tools FinalData and WinHex to detect the deletion trace of them. The trace detection result is show in Fig. 6 and Fig. 7 respectively by the forensic tool FinalData and Winhex. Comparing them with Fig. 3 and Fig. 4, we can find that there is no trace of the deletion operation. It looks like the deleted files had never been on the NTFS file system.

$SLogFile	41.0 MB 2022-04-13 13:31:39	2022-04-13 13:31:39	2022-04-13 13:...
$Volume	0 B 2022-04-13 13:31:39	2022-04-13 13:31:39	2022-04-13 13:...
$AttrDef	2.5 KB 2022-04-13 13:31:39	2022-04-13 13:31:39	2022-04-13 13:...
$Bitmap	937 KB 2022-04-13 13:31:39	2022-04-13 13:31:39	2022-04-13 13:...
$Boot	8.0 KB 2022-04-13 13:31:39	2022-04-13 13:31:39	2022-04-13 13:...
$BadClus	0 B 2022-04-13 13:31:39	2022-04-13 13:31:39	2022-04-13 13:...
$Secure	0 B 2022-04-13 13:31:39	2022-04-13 13:31:39	2022-04-13 13:...
$UpCase	128 KB 2022-04-13 13:31:39	2022-04-13 13:31:39	2022-04-13 13:...
$MFTMirr	4.0 KB 2022-04-13 13:31:39	2022-04-13 13:31:39	2022-04-13 13:...
$MFT	256 KB 2022-04-13 13:31:39	2022-04-13 13:31:39	2022-04-13 13:...

Fig. 7. The trace detection result after deletion by Winhex

5.2 Performance Analysis

In the above subsection, the experiment results show that the deletion method leaves no trace of deletion operation. In this subsection, the irrecoverability of deleted files is examined.

Data recovery tools employ the residual information of the deleted files from the MFT to get the important information including file name in 30H, and file size in 80H, and then obtains the location of file data in data area. In this method, the corresponding data in MFT and data area has already been overwritten many times after deletion operation. Therefore, both the related information about the deleted files in MFT and the data in data area cannot be gained. As a result, deleted files are impossible to recover because the file looks like never existing in the disk.

6 Conclusion

This paper presents a method of traceless and complete file deletion For NTFS file system files. The method can secure deleted files quickly and tracelessly which leaves no possibility of recovery even using forensic tools such as WinHex. This method loads disk as physical files and bypasses the access control permission of the operating system, so it leaves no trace of deletion operation, which ensures the security and confidentiality of deletion of important files.

Acknowledgments. This work was supported by the National Key Research and Development Program of China (2018YFB0804104), National Natural Science Foundation of China (62102209), Shandong Provincial Key Research and Development Program (2021CXGC010107, 2020CXGC010107, 2019JZZY020715), the Shandong Provincial Natural Science Foundation of China (ZR2020KF035).

References

1. Govindarajan, M.: Challenges for big data security and privacy. Encyclopedia of Information Science and Technology. 4th edn, pp. 373–380. IGI Global, New York, NY (2018)
2. Gahi, Y., Guennoun, M., Mouftah, H.T.: Big data analytics: security and privacy challenges. In: IEEE Symposium on Computers and Communication, pp. 952–957. IEEE, Messina, Italy (2016)
3. Chen, L., Liu, F., Yao, D.: Enterprise data breach: causes, challenges, prevention, and future directions: enterprise data breach. Wiley Interdiscip. Rev. Data Mining Knowl. Discov. **7**(C), e1211 (2017)

4. Microsoft Corporation: The NTFS File System (2008)
5. Microsoft Corporation: Choosing Between File Systems (2014)
6. Wang, L.Y., Ju, J.W.: Analysis of NTFS file system structure. Comput. Eng. Des. **27**(3), 418–420 (2006)
7. Oommen, R.R., Sugathan, P.: Recovering deleted Files from NTFS. Int. J. Sci. Res. **51**(6), 205–208 (2016)
8. Yoo, B., Park, J., Bang J., Lee S.: A study on a carving method for deleted NTFS compressed files, In: 3rd International Conference on Human-Centric Computing, pp. 1–6. IEE, Cebu, Philippines (2010)
9. Peng, Z., Feng, X., Tang, L., Zhai, M.: A data recovery method for NTFS files system. In: Niu, W., Li, G., Liu, J., Tan, J., Guo, L., Han, Z., Batten, L. (eds.) ATIS 2015. CCIS, vol. 557, pp. 379–386. Springer, Heidelberg (2015). https://doi.org/10.1007/978-3-662-48683-2_34
10. Feng, F.J., Li, X.J., Yao, J.P.: Design and implementation of data recovery system based on NTFS. DEStech Trans. Comput. Sci. Eng. **291**, 240–244 (2018)
11. Zhang, N., Jiang, Y., Wang, J.: The research of data recovery on Windows file systems. In: International Conference on Intelligent Transportation, Big Data & Smart City, pp. 644–647, IEEE, Vientiane, Laos (2020)
12. Frields, J.: National Industrial Security Program. Operating manual supplement technical report, Department of defense Washington DC (1995)
13. Dong, B.O., Park, K.H., Kim, H.K.: De-wipimization: detection of data wiping traces for investigating NTFS file system. Comput. Secur. **99**, 102034 (2020)
14. Park, K.J., Park, J.M., Kim, E.J., Cheon, C.G., James, J.I.: Anti-forensic trace detection in digital forensic triage investigations. J. Dig. Foren. Secur. Law **12**(1), 8–15 (2017)
15. Horsman, G.: Digital tool marks (DTMs): a forensic analysis of file wiping software. Aust. J. Forensic Sci. **53**(1), 1–16 (2019)
16. Karresand, M., Axelsson, S., Dyrkolbotn, G.O.: Disk cluster allocation behavior in Windows and NTFS. Mobile Networks Appl. **25**(3), 248–258 (2020)

Efficient and Collusion Resistant Multi-party Private Set Intersection Protocols for Large Participants and Small Sets Setting

Lifei Wei[1,2], Jihai Liu[1], Lei Zhang[1(✉)], and Wuji Zhang[1]

[1] College of Information Technology, Shanghai Ocean University,
Shanghai 201306, China
{lfwei,Lzhang}@shou.edu.cn
[2] College of Information Engineering, Shanghai Maritime University,
Shanghai 201306, China

Abstract. Multi-party private set intersection (MP-PSI) allows m participants with private sets to calculate their intersection without revealing any information, which is quite different from the traditional two-party PSI. Although some efficient MP-PSI protocols already exist, the efficiency of these protocols decreases significantly in the scenarios with the increasing number of participants for the small sets setting. In this paper, we propose efficient MP-PSI protocols based on one-round two-party key agreement embedding with unconditional zero sharing technique and prove secure by resisting up to $m-2$ parties collision in the semi-honest model and $m-1$ parties collision in the malicious model. Compared with the current efficient MP-PSI, our protocol performs better in terms of the communication round, communication cost and the running time in small sets setting. Extensive experiments show that as the number of participants m increases from 5 to 50 and the upbound of the set size n scales from 2^8 to 2^{10}, the running time of our MP-PSI protocol is faster than those of the most efficient MP-PSI protocol [14] and the recent work [4]. Take the set size at 2^7 for example, as the number of the participants increases from 10 to 50, our protocol only requires 4–26× less running time and 8–11× less communication cost than those of [14], respectively. We conclude that our protocols are practical solutions suitable for the scenarios in small set setting with increasing participants.

Keywords: Private set intersection · Collusion resistant · Large participants · Small sets · Malicious secure

This work is supported in part by National Natural Science Foundation of China under Grant 61972241, in part by Natural Science Foundation of Shanghai under Grant 22ZR1427100 and 18ZR1417300, and in part by Luo-Zhaorao College Student Science and Technology Innovation Foundation of Shanghai Ocean University.

X. Chen et al. (Eds.): CSS 2022, LNCS 13547, pp. 118–132, 2022.
https://doi.org/10.1007/978-3-031-18067-5_9

1   Introduction

Private Set Intersection (PSI) is a specific problem in secure multi-party computation, allowing a set of parties to input their private sets and output their intersection without revealing any additional information. PSI is always defined as a fundamental protocol used in the distributed private data protection for further exploring the potential value of these data. In the past years, the researchers from academia and industry pay attention to the two party PSI with large set scenarios. According to the various distributed private data discovery scenarios, the traditional PSI can be also divided into *three* types based on the data size of the participants: *large-to-large, large-to-small,* and *small-to-small* set settings.

Large-to-Large Set Settings. Each party holds millions of data with huge computational resource and high-speed networks, such as the human genome testing [1] and the effectiveness of online advertisement measuring [2] carried out by two high-performance servers. Concentrating on the efficiency in terms of the running time and communication costs, the researchers have constructed several cryptographic primitive, named as Oblivious Transfer Extension (OTE) [6–8] with high computational efficiency in running time. OTE succeeds in fast execution of two-party PSI in the large set scenarios [9–14].

Large-to-Small Set Settings. As the emergence of the cloud computing, an unbalanced PSI is presented, named as *asymmetric* PSI [15,16] for the *large-to-small* set scenarios. It uses in the classic client-server scenario with the different set sizes as well as the unbalanced computational resource between two parties. In this scenario, the researchers focus on whether the communication complexity of the PSI protocol is determined by the set size, especially by the size of the small set. Since the communication costs of OTE-based PSI always grow linearly in the number of the items in the largest sets among the parties, it is unacceptable in the client-server scenarios. Chen *et al.* [15] construct a homomorphic encryption (HE) based PSI protocols achieving the optimal communication complexity that only relys on the set size of the weak client.

Small-to-Small Set Settings. Both of the participants hold the private sets with the similar size less than one thousand even several hundreds, in which it is important to consider both of the communication and computation overhead according to the capability of the participants. The most intuitive idea is to directly carry out the most efficient PSI protocol in large set scenarios. However, as we all known, the OTE-based PSI brings the communication cost and HE-based PSI brings the computation overhead. Rosulek et al. [17] proved that the two-party PSI protocol by the key agreement technique has better both in communication and computational efficiency than those by OTE and HE in a small-to-small set settings.

MP-PSI allows parties take in private sets to jointly calculate the intersection and not to obtain any other information except intersection which is quite different from the traditional two-party PSI. Although some efficient MP-PSI protocols already exist [14,21,22,26], few of the work consider the MP-PSI protocols in the *small set scenarios* and scale well with a growing number of parties.

The efficiency of these protocols decreases significantly in the scenarios with the increasing number of participants for the small sets setting. This kind of applications includes PrivateDrop [3], anonymous voting and consensus [5], criminal activities on smart roads and identifying the high risk individuals in the spread of diseases [4] in which the participants hold the private sets with the similar size less than one thousand even one hundred, in which it is important to consider both of the communication cost and computation overhead according to the capability of the participants.

After that, Bay *et al.* [4] find that the existing MP-PSI protocols are not applicable in the scenario where the number of parties is large and the size of sets is small and then propose a concrete MP-PSI protocol based on Threshold Public Key Encryption (TPKE) and Bloom Filter (BF). However, the experiments show that their protocol is only efficient in the small sets (less than 2^6) and become inefficient in the communication load and running time when the set size is larger than 2^6 compared with the MP-PSI protocols [14], the most efficient MP-PSI in the large set settings. Furthermore, compared with OTE-based PSI, the method in [17] using the key agreement for PSI is only efficient under the two-party scenarios with small sets (less than 500). However, it fails to be generalized to MP-PSI in the small set settings.

Therefore, this paper focuses on the problem whether it is possible to design a practical MP-PSI protocol with optimal running time and communication load under small sets ($n < 500$) and further adaptable to the small sets with increasing number of parties. The target of is paper includes following two aspects.

1. We consider the MP-PSI scenario that the number of parties is much smaller than the size of the sets especially for the small sets, which focuses on the running time efficiency as the traditional MP-PSI protocols.
2. We consider another MP-PSI scenario that the number of parties is increasing to large in the small set scenarios which is not considered by traditional MP-PSI protocols.

1.1   Contributions

Compared with the related work, Kolesnikov *et al.* [14] employs secret sharing technique to defend collusion attack but to generate additional overhead by Oblivious Programmable Pseudo-Random Function (OPPRF) operations and both the communication load and the computational complexity grow linearly with the number of parties, which does not fit well to our scenarios since the number of the parties is large. In addition, Bay *et al.* [4] overcome the shortcoming and propose MP-PSI based on TPKE with no additional overhead. However, in their protocol, each items of the server is encrypted once that is only suitable for situations with many parties and very few items and bring the high running time and communication load by encrypting the Bloom Filter bits.

In summary, the contributions of this paper are summarized as follows:

1. We design the first MP-PSI protocol suitable for small sets by embedding unconditional zero-sharing to the one-round two-party key agreement.

Our MP-PSI protocol is proven secure defending against up to $m - 2$ corrupted parties in the semi-honest model and $m - 1$ corrupted parties in the malicious model.

2. The analysis shows that our MP-PSI protocol achieves the theoretically optimal communication rounds, the best communication complexity depending on the statistical security parameters rather than the computational security parameters among the known MP-PSI protocol for small sets. The computational complexity is only related to the set size, which can be effectively applied to two scenarios under the small sets.

3. Extensive experiments show that as the number of participants m increases from 5 to 50 and the upbound of the set size n scales from 2^8 to 2^{10}, the running time of our MP-PSI protocol is faster than those of the most efficient MP-PSI protocol [14] and the recent work [4].

2   Related Work

In this section, we give an overview of the existing efficient MP-PSI protocol, from the fundamental primitives in the traditional PSI protocols and the multi-party collusion resistance technology in MP-PSI protocol.

2.1   Traditional PSI

The fundamental cryptographic primitives of the PSI protocols always fall into four main categories: Diffie-Hellman (DH), OTE, HE, Garbled Circuits (GC). In general, single DH and OTE primitives are computed exponentially faster than HE and GC primitives in PSI construction.

OTE-Based PSI. Pinkas *et al.* [20] first propose a PSI protocol by employing the IKNP-OT technique [6], which significantly reduces the computational overhead but increases the communication cost. Kolesnikov *et al.* [9] constructs a batched OPRF based on OTE [7], which improves the computational efficiency by 2.3–3.6×, and become the fastest two-party PSI protocol in a high speed network up to now. The works [10] and [12] construct a new tool, named as *multi-point OPRF* based on OTE, allowing the receiver to randomly select k subsets from n secrets. The communication cost only depends on the size of subsets k and makes [10] and [12] as the optimal two-party PSI protocol for computation and communication under normal bandwidth networks. Rindal *et al.* [13] present a new construction for PSI based on *Silent-OT* [8], which significantly reduces the communication complexity. However, OTE is efficient achieved by a few basic OTs and a number of the symmetric key based operations. As a result, the basic OT using in [6,7] needs to consume 5κ and the Silent OT [8] only needs to consume 3κ where κ is the security parameters.

DH-Based PSI. The DH cryptographic primitive is more advantageous in the small sets for PSI design. The DH-based PSI protocol has lower communication cost as well as the constant rounds whereas the OTE-based PSI protocol has efficient computational efficiency. The DH-based PSI protocol was originally derived from Meadows [18] and Bernardo [19], which perfectly follows the two-party key agreement to achieve computationally efficient PSI protocols. Meadows [18] demonstrated that the elliptic curve based PSI protocol has faster computational efficiency and lower communication complexity than those of the finite field based PSI protocol. Rosulek *et al.* [17] upgrade DH-based PSI protocols from semi-honest security to malicious security and reduce the communication and computation cost by embedding a key agreement into polynomial instead of embedding the private equivalence test into polynomial, which achieves the most efficient two-party PSI protocol for small sets ($n < 500$) in the malicious security model at present.

2.2   Collusion Resisting MP-PSI

The existing techniques for resisting collusion in MP-PSI protocols can be divided into two categories: *secrete sharing* and *threshold encryption*.

Kolesnikov *et al.* [14] achieves $m-1$ party collusion in the semi-honest security model through the conditional zero-sharing. Each party P_i uses the share as a programmable value during performing the OPPRF with another party P_j. It is guaranteed that the parties can obtain the zero share only if they use the correct keys and can not guess the correct zero shares by collusion. In addition, Kolesnikov *et al.* [14] consider unconditional zero sharing and achieve to $m-2$ party collusion in the semi-honest security model in which the party P_i randomly selects a key and distributes to other party P_j, and locally computes the secret share of each element by using the same key. Obviously, unconditional secret sharing only transmits the keys and achieves more efficient computation and lower communication load. However, how to guess the correct zero-sharing value depends on whether the colluding parties can use the corresponding element to decode *oblivious key-value store* (OKVS) [25]. Chandran *et al.* [21] implements $(m+1)/2$ parties collusion in the semi-honest security model based on unconditionally secure circuit evaluation protocol. P_i obtains a linear secret sharing of a random value by secure circuit random sharing that is used to mask the OPPRF value sending to the server.

The work [4] and [22] realize semi-honest security of $m-1$ party collusion resisting based on TPKE. A TPKE scheme shares the secret key and distribute among m parties and each of the parties holds a share of the secret key which is corresponding to the same public key. In the decryption, it is possible for m parties to jointly decrypt ciphertext and combine to final plaintext. It avoids additional overhead and achieves client communication complexity depending on the number of parties.

3   Preliminaries

3.1   Diffie-Hellman Key Agreement

Rosulek *et al.* [17] proposed a compact and malicious secure two-party PSI using one-round Diffie-Hellman key agreement (DHKA) protocol based on elliptic curve group with elligator encoding mechanism *et al.* [24]. Since the conventional elliptic curves are compact but the encoded uniform strings are easily distinguishable, this kind of DHKA messages do not provide pseudo-randomness in the security proof. The elligator encoding mechanism [24] overcomes the above problem by providing efficient encoding/decoding functions, in which *enc* encodes an elliptic curve points to a strings with pseudo-randomness, *dec* decodes to an elliptic curve points. The Elligator DHKA protocol in Rosulek *et al.* [17] as a one-round key agreement protocol defines as follows:

- $KA.R = \{r \in \mathbb{Z}_q | g^r \in im(dec)\}$, defines the space of randomness number.
- $KA.M = \{0,1\}^t$, defines the space of messages, $t = 256$.
- $KA.K = \{0,1\}^\gamma$, defines the space of keys, $\gamma = \lambda + 2 \log n$.
- $KA.msg(a) = enc(g^a)$, computes the key agreement message.
- $KA.key(a, s_b) = dec(s_b)^a$, computes the shared key.

Due to the properties of the elligator encoding, the messages are distributed uniform in the image of *enc* and hence as a pseudo-randomness in $\{0,1\}^t$. The security of above DHKA against eavesdropper from the CDH assumption if the adversary acquires $KA.key$ and $KA.K$, they are indistinguishable, as well as those of $KA.msg$ and $KA.M$.

3.2   Zero Sharing Technique

Zero sharing technique can be divided into two kinds: *unconditional zero sharing* and *conditional zero sharing*. The former refers to the scenarios that without a trusted third party, the functionality secretly splits zero and assigns a share to each party. Conditional zero sharing refers to the absence of a trusted third party, the functionality assigns a shared value to the parties who can get the shares if they satisfy some pre-defined conditions. Otherwise, they obtain a random number. However, it is difficult for the parties to distinguish a share from a random number. In [14], the authors propose conditional zero sharing with additional $O(n^2)$ times by OPPRF operations, which increases a lot of additional communication and computing overhead. Each participant P_i randomly chooses numbers $t_{i,j}$ for each element $x_{i,j}$ in the private set satisfying $\oplus_i \sum_{j=1}^m t_{i,j} = 0$. P_i and P_j execute OPPRF protocol in pairs. If X_i and X_j have the same element, the share of the corresponding element is obtained. Subsequently, authors in [14] propose an unconditional zero sharing and further design an augmented MP-PSI, at the cost of weakening the collusion conditions at most corrupted $m - 2$ participants. Unconditional zero sharing obviously reduces the communication and computation overhead, but it still needs additional communication costs.

This paper uses Hao *et al.*'s method [23] to generate an unconditional zero sharing. P_i generates and broadcasts a random value x_i. After receiving the values from others, P_i computes $y_i = \sum_{t=1}^{i-1} x_t - \sum_{t=i+1}^{n} x_t$ and sets $x_i y_i$ as zero sharing value. A simple verification shows that zero shares of all parties add by $\sum_{i=1}^{n} x_i y_i = 0$.

4   Security Model

4.1   Functionality

The ideal functionality of MP-PSI protocols F_{MP-PSI} is shown in Definition 1.

Definition 1 (Ideal Functionality of MP-PSI F_{MP-PSI}).

Parameters: There are m parties $P_1, P_2, ..., P_m$ and each P_i owns a private set $X_i = \{x_{i,1}, x_{i,2}, ..., x_{i,n}\}$, where $i \in \{1, 2, ..., m\}$. $P_1, P_2, ..., P_{m-1}$ denote the clients and P_m denotes the server.

Functionality: All parties jointly compute the intersection $I = \bigcap_{i=1}^{m} X_i$. Except for the intersection generated by the server P_m, no other information is leaked.

4.2   Security Definitions

Inspired by the security definition of secure multi-party computation, the security models of MP-PSI can be classified into two categories according to the behaviors of adversaries attacking capabilities. The one type is *semi-honest* security model, allowing the adversary to control the honest parties' executions by actively collecting the input and the output of the MP-PSI protocol from the interaction and further infer the additional elements not in the intersection. The other type is *malicious* security model, allowing the adversary to control parties' deviating from the protocol execution for gaining the additional element not in the intersection. In this paper, we consider m-party case, which can resist $m - 2$ parties collusion in the semi-honest security model and $m - 1$ parties collusion in malicious security model.

The semi-honest security model is defined according to the ideal model *vs* real model as follows. Let the view of semi-honest adversaries by executing realistic protocols π_{MP-PSI} be $View_\pi(input(X, Y), out(X, Y))$ with the realistic input and output. Let the view of semi-honest adversaries by executing the ideal protocols be $Sim(input(X, Y), F_{MP-PSI}(X, Y))$ with the realistic input and ideal functionality F_{MP-PSI} generated by a simulator. The semi-honest security model is formally defined by the computational indistinguishability between the above two views within a Probabilistic Polynomial Time (PPT) simulator, that is:

$$View_\pi(input(X, Y), out(X, Y)) \approx Sim(input(X, Y), F_{MP-PSI}(X, Y)).$$

5 Concrete Protocols

Inspired by the two-party PSI [17] which achieves the optimal efficiency for small sets through one-round key agreement, we present a practical MP-PSI protocol for the small sets. The detailed description of our protocol π_{MP-PSI} is shown in Fig. 1.

5.1 System Initialization Step

The system parameter are set as follows. Set elligator-DHKA protocol parameters: $KA.M = \mathbb{F}$, $|KA.K| \geq 2^{\lambda+2logn}$, an ideal permutation $\Psi : \mathbb{F} \to \mathbb{F}$ and its inverse $\Psi^{-1} : \mathbb{F} \to \mathbb{F}$.

5.2 Key Agreement Step

Each party P_i in the clients generates a random number $a_i \leftarrow KA.R$ where $i \in [m-1]$ and broadcasts the key agreement message msg_i by $msg_i = KA.msg(a_i)$.

The server P_m uses each element $x_{m,j}$ in the set X_m where $j \in [n]$ and performs as follows.

- P_m generates n random numbers $b_j \leftarrow KA.R$ and generates the corresponding key agreement message $msg_{m,j}$ by $msg_{m,j} = KA.msg(b_j)$.
- P_m uses ψ^{-1} to map $msg_{m,j}$ to f_j, that is, $\psi(f_j) = msg_{m,j}$.
- P_m encoding these key-value pairs $\{(x_{m,j}, f_i)|x_{m,j} \in X_m\}$ into a polynomial $P(\cdot)$ and broadcasts the polynomial to all the clients P_i.

5.3 Zero Sharing Step

Each party P_i in the clients generates a conditional zero share for each element $x_{i,j}$ in the private set X_i where $i \in [m-1]$ and $j \in [n]$ as follows:

- Each party P_i computes a value S_i according to the key agreement messages msg_t from other clients, that is,

$$S_i = \prod_{t=1}^{i-1} msg_t \bigg/\!\!\!\!\bigg/ \prod_{t=i+1}^{m-1} msg_t.$$

- P_i performs the polynomial $P(x_{i,j})$ for each element $x_{i,j}$ in X_i and computes the message $msg_{i,j}$ by using the ideal permutation ψ, that is,

$$msg_{i,j} = \psi(P(x_{i,j})).$$

- P_i gets the zero shares on the element $x_{i,j}$ by

$$k_{i,j} = KA.key(a_i, S_i/msg_{i,j}).$$

- P_i encoding the key-value pairs $\{(x_{i,j}, k_{i,j})|x_{i,j} \in X_i\}$ into a polynomial $Pol_i(\cdot)$ and sends the polynomial to the server P_m.

The server P_m can also aggregate the key agreement message by $S_m = \prod_{t=1}^{m-1} msg_t$. In addition, P_m generates its zero share for each element $x_{m,j}$ in the private set X_m by

$$k_{m,j} = KA.key(b_j, S_m/msg_{m,j}).$$

5.4 Intersection Calculation Step

Finally, the server P_m gets the intersection as follows.

- P_m computes the values $k_{i,j} = Pol_i(x_{m,j})$ for each element $x_{m,j} \in X_m$ on the polynomials $Pol_i(\cdot)$ from P_i where $i \in [m-1]$ and $j \in [n]$.
- $x_{m,j}$ is in the intersection if $\prod_{i=1}^{m} k_{i,j} = 1$.

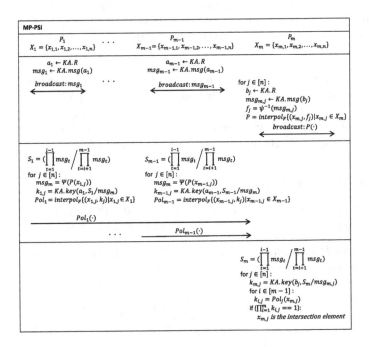

Fig. 1. π_{MP-PSI} formalized description

6 Security Analysis

6.1 Correctness

The protocol π_{MP-PSI} is correct with an overwhelming probability. For each element $x_{m,j} \in X_m$ in the server P_m, if the client P_i has the same element,

P_i can get the key agreement message $msg_{m,i}$ and further obtain the zero shares in part of $k_{i,j}$ as well as those in $k_{m,j}$ in the server. The client P_i locally computes zero share by $KA.key(a_i, \prod_{t=1}^{i-1} msg_t / \prod_{t=i+1}^{m-1} msg_t / msg_{m,j})$. According to [23], the server multiplies all $k_{m,j}$ to aggregates the zero shares and exactly recover the value when all of the parties own a common element, that is, the item $a_i \cdot b_j$ occurs exactly twice and $\prod_{i=1}^{m} k_{i,j} = 1$. It is obviously that if $x_{i,j} \in X_m$, it satisfies the condition to get zero sharing value $k_{i,j}$. Otherwise, $k_{i,j}$ is a random value. Finally, $x_{m,j}$ is an intersection element among all of the parties.

We also analyze the false positive probability as follows.

- If P_i does not own the element $x_{m,i}$, it can obtain $msg_{m,j}$ from one round key agreement with pseudo randomness by the polynomial $P(\cdot)$ with the probability is $2^{-\phi}$. ϕ is the element size in Elliptic Curve.
- If P_m obtain $k_{m,j}$ from the $Pol_i(\cdot)$ where P_i does not have the element $x_{m,j}$, since the one round key agreement with pseudo randomness and the length of $k_{m,j}$ is $\lambda + 2 \log n$, the probability $2^{-\lambda}$.

6.2   Security Proof

Theorem 1. *The protocol π_{MP-PSI} is secure against up to $m-2$ collision in a semi-honest model, if KA is a pseudorandom-message elligator $- DHKA$ and ψ and ψ^{-1} are a pair of ideal permutations.*

Proof. Please refer the full version for the security proof due to limited space.

6.3   Malicious Secure MP-PSI

In order to design MP-PSI protocols with stronger security, we need to solve the challenges caused by the possible malicious behavior of the clients and the server. We need to prevent the malicious parties from influencing honest parties by adding additional elements. Rosulek *et al.* [17] only resort to the honest party extracting the data sent by the malicious party through random oracle, and promote a two-party PSI in semi-honest security model to a two-party PSI protocol in malicious security model. Our semi-honest secure MP-PSI protocol also can be extended to a maliciously secure MP-PSI protocol by adding two random oracles inspired by Rosulek *et al.* [17]. Our MP-PSI protocol perfectly follows the one-round key agreement as well as the two-party PSI protocol by using random oracle H_1 to act as the generation of server's polynomial $P(\cdot)$ and random oracle H_2 to act as the generation of the client's polynomial $Pol_i(\cdot)$. In this way, the malicious secure MP-PSI protocol is achieved.

Theorem 2. *The protocol π^*_{MP-PSI} is secure against up to $m-1$ collision in a malicious model, if KA is a pseudorandom-message elligator-DHKA, H_1, H_2 are two anti-collision hash functions and ψ and ψ^{-1} are a pair of ideal permutations.*

Proof. Please refer our full version for the detailed security proofs.

Table 1. Theoretical comparison of MP-PSI protocol. λ is statistical security parameters, κ is computational security parameters. Each party holds a set with a size n and t of m parties collude. The size of the ciphertext is $log|X|$.

Protocol	Communication		Computation		Threshold	Rounds	Security
	Server	Client	Server	Client			
Ref [22]	$O(nm\lambda)$	$O(n\lambda)$	$O(nm\log n\kappa)$	$O(n\kappa)$	$t < m$	4	Semi-honest
Ref [22]	$O((m^2 + nm\log n\lambda)\kappa)$	$O((m + n\log n\lambda)\kappa)$	$O(n^2)$	$O(n^2)$	$t < m$	7	Malicious
Ref [14]	$O(nm(\lambda + \kappa))$	$O(n(\lambda + \kappa))$	$O(m\kappa)$	$O(n\kappa)$	$t < m - 1$	3	Semi-honest
		$O(nt(\lambda + \kappa))$		$O(nt\kappa)$	$t < m$	4	Semi-honest
Ref [21]	$O(nm(\lambda + \kappa + \log n))$	$O(n(\lambda + \kappa + \log n))$	$O(nm\kappa)$	$O(n\kappa)$	$t < (m + 1)/2$	8	Semi-honest
Ref [4]	$O(nm\log|X|)$	$O(n\lambda \log|X|)$	$O(n)$	$O(n\lambda)$	$t < m$	5	Semi-honest
Ref [26]	$O(n\kappa max\{t, m - t\})$	$O(n\lambda)$	$O(n\kappa(m - t))$	$O(n\kappa t)$	$t < m$	4	Malicious
Ours	$O(nm\lambda)$	$O(n\lambda)$	$O(n(\log n)^2)$	$O(n(\log n)^2)$	$t < m - 1$	2	Semi-honest
							Malicious

Table 2. Communication complexity comparison of MP-PSI protocol. Statistical security parameters is λ, computational security parameters is κ, and $log|X|$. The size of Elliptic Curve elements is ϕ. $|baseOT| = 5\kappa$.

Protocol	Communication	
	Server	Client
Ref [14]	$(46n(\lambda + \log n) + 4.5n\kappa + |baseOT|)(nt + 2n - 1)$	$(46n(\lambda + \log n) + 4.5n\kappa + |baseOT|)(2t + 3)$
Ref [14]-aug	$(46n(\lambda + \log n) + 4.5n\kappa + |baseOT|)(m - 1) + m\kappa$	$46n(\lambda + \log n) + 4.5n\kappa + |baseOT| + m\kappa$
Ref [21]	$n(m - 1)(35(\lambda + \log n) + 4.5\kappa + 140 + |baseOT|)$	$n(64(\lambda + \log n) + 4.5\kappa + |baseOT| + 256)$
Ref [4]	$(m - 1)(\lambda + 2)n \log|X|$	$(\lambda + 2)n \log|X|$
Ours	$\phi(n + m - 1) + (\lambda + 2\log n)n(m - 1)$	$\phi(n + m - 1) + (\lambda + 2\log n)n$
Ours-mal	$2n\kappa(m - 1) + \phi(n + m - 1)$	$2n\kappa + \phi(n + m - 1)$

7   Performance and Performance

7.1   Complexity Analysis

Communication Rounds and Complexity. A theoretical comparison of our protocol with the related MP-PSI protocols is shown in Table 1. It shows that the communication complexity of our MP-PSI only depends on the statistical security parameter as a constant. The computational complexity relying on to the size of the private set, can be effectively applied to the scenarios in the small sets. Our MP-PSI protocol have least number of communication rounds of any known MP-PSI protocol.

Computational Complexity. The complete communication complexity is shown in Table 2. Our computational complexity is sublinear in OKVS. However, the computational cost of the polynomial interpolation or other linear OKVS under small sets is little compared to the cost of elliptic curve exponential operation.

7.2 Experimental Implementation

Setup. In order to evaluate the computational efficiency of our MP-PSI proto-col, we implement it in the C++ environment. Our benchmarks are performed on a server with 256 GB RAM equipping a 64-bit Ubuntu 18.04. The instantiated components of this experiment are mainly from the two-party PSI protocol of Rosulek *et al.* [17], such as DHKA based on ellipse group, Elliptic curve encoding/decoding based on libsodium, and ideal permutations based on Rijndal-256. We also use GMP and NTL to implement large arithmetic operations.

We compare our MP-PSI protocol against Kolesnikov *et al.* [14] and Bay *et al.* [4]. The size of each parties private set is n. Our computation security parameters $\kappa = 128$ while the security parameters in Bay *et al.* [4] set as the public key security parameters up to $\kappa = 2048$ for Paillier based Encryption. Our WAN setting is a 200 Mbps network. Similar to [14], to ensure parallelism in our protocol, each client communicates with the server using an independent thread.

For the semi-honest MP-PSI protocol of [14] and the MP-PSI protocol of [4], the computational efficiency is affected by the number of colluding parties. However, the augmented semi-honest MP-PSI protocol in [14] and our MP-PSI protocol are not affected by the number of colluding parties, but only resist up to $m - 2$ party collusion. Therefore, we report the running time and communication load comparison of small set size $n = \{2^7, 2^8, 2^9, 2^{10}\}$ and resistance to up to $m - 2$ party collusion $(m, t) = \{(5, 3), (10, 8)\}$ in Table 3.

By analyzing [14] and our MP-PSI protocol, it can be seen that the intersection computation step of our MP-PSI protocol involves most of the running time of the protocol. Unlike [14], their intersection computation step is negligible for the entire protocol. We consider the methods in parallel and in non-parallel when the server verifies whether the element belongs to the intersection.

7.3 Experiment Results

Small Set Setting with a Small Number of Participants. As shown in Table 3 by running time in milliseconds (ms) of the MP-PSI protocols for m parties with corruption threshold t on sets with size n, it is found that when the parameters set $(m, t) = (5, 3)$ and $n \leq 2^8$, the running time of the client and the server in our protocol outperforms one of the previous most efficient MP-PSI protocols [14]. Our advantage is more pronounced as the set is small. Our protocol is faster $2\times$ than those of [14] when $n = 2^7$. When the parameters set $(m, t) = (10, 8)$ and $n \leq 2^{10}$, the running time of the client and the server in our protocol outperforms the MP-PSI protocols [14].

Small Set Setting with a Large Number of Participants. As shown in Table 4 of MP-PSI protocols for large number of parties m with corruption threshold t on sets of size n, it is found that the client performs from $3.7\times$ faster in $m = 10$ to $27\times$ faster in $m = 50$ than those of [14] when $n = 2^7$. The running time of the server computing the intersection in parallel from $4\times$ faster

Table 3. Running time (ms) of the MP-PSI protocols for m parties with corruption threshold t on sets with size n. Server(P) stands for the intersection computing in parallel by the server.

Protocol	(m, t)	$(5, 3)$				$(10, 8)$			
	n	2^7	2^8	2^9	2^{10}	2^7	2^8	2^9	2^{10}
Ref [14]-aug	Client	181	199	**192**	**248**	297	357	384	477
	Server	191	209	**222**	**254**	340	367	404	513
Ref [14]	Server	483	484	555	681	2994	3221	3570	4309
Ref [4]	Server	5648	12395	29075	77359	6335	15168	40497	–
Ours	Client	**78**	**168**	266	467	**79**	**168**	**267**	**468**
	Server	143	341	537	931	205	510	793	1414
	Server(P)	**82**	**176**	281	486	**83**	**176**	**282**	**490**

Table 4. Running time (ms) of MP-PSI protocols for *large* m and t on the small sets with size n. Server(P) stands for the intersection computing in parallel.

Protocol	n	2^7			2^8			2^{10}		
	(m, t)	(10, 8)	(30, 28)	(50, 48)	(10, 8)	(30, 28)	(50, 48)	(10, 8)	(30, 28)	(50, 48)
Ref [4]	Server	6335	9524	16113	15168	27637	47112	–	–	–
Ref [14]-aug	Client	297	1248	2319	357	1552	2699	477	2248	4437
	Server	340	1327	2421	367	1552	2809	513	2290	4517
Ours	Client	**79**	**81**	**83**	168	171	174	468	470	471
	Server	**205**	451	681	510	1183	1855	1414	3146	4917
	Server(P)	**83**	**87**	**90**	176	182	187	490	493	497

in $m = 10$ to $26\times$ faster in $m = 50$ than those of [14]. As the increasing number of the participants, the advantage of our protocol becomes more efficient.

8   Conclusion

We have proposed the first MP-PSI protocol suitable for small sets by embedding unconditional zero-sharing to the two-party key agreement without additional overhead. Our MP-PSI protocols are proven secure defending against up to $m - 2$ corrupted parties in the semi-honest model and $m - 1$ in the malicious model, respectively. Theoretical analysis and extensive experiments show that our MP-PSI protocol achieves the theoretically optimal communication rounds, communication load and running time compared with the state-of-the-art MP-PSI protocols in the typical scenarios for the small sets.

References

1. Baldi, P., Baronio, R., De Cristofaro, E., Gasti, P., Tsudik, G.: Countering GATTACA: efficient and secure testing of fully-sequenced human genomes. In: Proceedings of the 18th ACM Conference on Computer and Communications Security (ACM CCS 2011), pp. 691–702. ACM (2011)

2. Miao, P., Patel, S., Raykova, M., Seth, K., Yung, M.: Two-sided malicious security for private intersection-sum with cardinality. In: Micciancio, D., Ristenpart, T. (eds.) CRYPTO 2020. LNCS, vol. 12172, pp. 3–33. Springer, Cham (2020). https://doi.org/10.1007/978-3-030-56877-1_1
3. Heinrich, A., Hollick, M., Schneider, T., Stute, M., Weinert, C.: PrivateDrop: practical privacy-preserving authentication for apple airdrop. In: 30th USENIX Security Symposium (USENIX Security 2021), pp. 3577–3594. USENIX Association (2021)
4. Bay, A., Erkin, Z., Alishahi, M., Vos, J.: Practical multi-party private set intersection protocols. IEEE Trans. Inf. Forensics Secur. **17**, 1–15 (2022). https://doi.org/10.1109/TIFS.2021.3118879
5. Bay, A., Erkin, Z., Alishahi, M., Vos, J.: Multi-party private set intersection protocols for practical applications. IEEE Trans. Inf. Forensics Secur. (2021). (SECRYPT 2021), pp. 515–522. SciTePress
6. Ishai, Y., Kilian, J., Nissim, K., Petrank, E.: Extending oblivious transfers efficiently. In: Boneh, D. (ed.) CRYPTO 2003. LNCS, vol. 2729, pp. 145–161. Springer, Heidelberg (2003). https://doi.org/10.1007/978-3-540-45146-4_9
7. Kolesnikov, V., Kumaresan, R.: Improved OT extension for transferring short secrets. In: Canetti, R., Garay, J.A. (eds.) CRYPTO 2013. LNCS, vol. 8043, pp. 54–70. Springer, Heidelberg (2013). https://doi.org/10.1007/978-3-642-40084-1_4
8. Schoppmann, P., Gascón, A., Reichert, L., Raykova, M.: Distributed vector-OLE: improved constructions and implementation. In: 26th ACM Conference on Computer and Communications Security (ACM CCS 2019), pp. 1055–1072. ACM (2019)
9. Kolesnikov, V., Kumaresan, R., Rosulek, M., Trieu, N.: Efficient batched oblivious PRF with applications to private set intersection. In: 23rd ACM Conference on Computer and Communications Security (ACM CCS 2016), pp. 818–829. ACM (2016)
10. Pinkas, B., Rosulek, M., Trieu, N., Yanai, A.: SpOT-Light: lightweight private set intersection from sparse OT extension. In: Boldyreva, A., Micciancio, D. (eds.) CRYPTO 2019. LNCS, vol. 11694, pp. 401–431. Springer, Cham (2019). https://doi.org/10.1007/978-3-030-26954-8_13
11. Pinkas, B., Rosulek, M., Trieu, N., Yanai, A.: PSI from PaXoS: fast, malicious private set intersection. In: Canteaut, A., Ishai, Y. (eds.) EUROCRYPT 2020. LNCS, vol. 12106, pp. 739–767. Springer, Cham (2020). https://doi.org/10.1007/978-3-030-45724-2_25
12. Chase, M., Miao, P.: Private set intersection in the internet setting from lightweight oblivious PRF. In: Micciancio, D., Ristenpart, T. (eds.) CRYPTO 2020. LNCS, vol. 12172, pp. 34–63. Springer, Cham (2020). https://doi.org/10.1007/978-3-030-56877-1_2
13. Rindal, P., Schoppmann, P.: VOLE-PSI: fast OPRF and circuit-psi from vector-OLE. IACR Cryptology ePrint Archive 2021/266 (2021)
14. Kolesnikov, V., Matania, N., Pinkas, B., Rosulek, M., Trieu, N.: Practical multi-party private set intersection from symmetric-key techniques. In: 24th ACM Conference on Computer and Communications Security (ACM CCS 2017), pp. 1257–1272. ACM (2017)
15. Chen, H., Laine, K., Rindal, P.: Fast private set intersection from homomorphic encryption. In: 24th ACM Conference on Computer and Communications Security (ACM CCS 2017), pp. 1243–1255. ACM (2017)
16. Davi Resende, A.C., de Freitas Aranha, D.: Faster unbalanced Private Set Intersection in the semi-honest setting. J. Cryptogr. Eng. **11**(1), 21–38 (2020). https://doi.org/10.1007/s13389-020-00242-7

17. Rosulek, M., Trieu, N.: Compact and malicious private set intersection for small sets. In: 28th ACM Conference on Computer and Communications Security (ACM CCS 2021), pp. 1166–1181. ACM (2021)
18. Meadows, C.A.: A more efficient cryptographic matchmaking protocol for use in the absence of a continuously available third party. In: IEEE Symposium on Security and Privacy (IEEE S&P 1986), pp. 134–137. IEEE (1986)
19. Huberman, B.A., Franklin, M., Hogg, T.: Proceedings of the 1st ACM Conference on Electronic Commerce, pp. 78–86 (1999)
20. Pinkas, B., Schneider, T., Zohner, M.: Faster private set intersection based on OT extension. In: 23rd USENIX Security Symposium (USENIX Security 2014), pp. 797–812. USENIX Association (2014)
21. Chandran, N., Dasgupta, N., Gupta, D., Obbattu, S.L.B., Sekar, S., Shah, A.: Efficient linear multiparty PSI and extensions to circuit/quorum PSI. In: 28th ACM Conference on Computer and Communications Security (ACM CCS 2021), pp. 1182–1204. ACM (2021)
22. Hazay, C., Venkitasubramaniam, M.: Scalable multi-party private set-intersection. In: Fehr, S. (ed.) PKC 2017. LNCS, vol. 10174, pp. 175–203. Springer, Heidelberg (2017). https://doi.org/10.1007/978-3-662-54365-8_8
23. Hao, F., Zieliński, P.: A 2-round anonymous veto protocol. In: Christianson, B., Crispo, B., Malcolm, J.A., Roe, M. (eds.) Security Protocols 2006. LNCS, vol. 5087, pp. 202–211. Springer, Heidelberg (2009). https://doi.org/10.1007/978-3-642-04904-0_28
24. Bernstein, D.J., Hamburg, M., Krasnova, A., Lange, T.: Elligator: elliptic-curve points indistinguishable from uniform random strings. In: 20th ACM Conference on Computer and Communications Security (ACM CCS 2013), pp. 967–980. ACM (2013)
25. Garimella, G., Pinkas, B., Rosulek, M., Trieu, N., Yanai, A.: Oblivious key-value stores and amplification for private set intersection. In: Malkin, T., Peikert, C. (eds.) CRYPTO 2021. LNCS, vol. 12826, pp. 395–425. Springer, Cham (2021). https://doi.org/10.1007/978-3-030-84245-1_14
26. Nevo, O., Trieu, N., Yanai, A.: Simple, fast malicious multiparty private set intersection. In: 28th ACM Conference on Computer and Communications Security (ACM CCS 2021), pp. 1151–1165. ACM (2021)

Multi-user Verifiable Database with Efficient Keyword Search

Meixia Miao$^{(\boxtimes)}$, Panru Wu, and Yunling Wang

School of Cyberspace Security, Xi'an University of Posts and Telecommunications,
Xi'an 710121, China
miaofeng415@163.com

Abstract. The notion of Verifiable database (VDB) allows data owners with limited resources to outsource large databases to powerful but untrusted cloud servers, ensuring the integrity of the database when performing index-based query operations. In recent years, researchers have extended the index-based query method to propose VDB scheme supporting keyword search. However, the existing VDB schemes supporting keyword search only allow the data owner to generate the search token based on the private key to perform search. In order to extend this single-user setting to the multi-user setting, we first propose a new multi-user VDB scheme which allows the data owner to authorize keyword search ability to other users. Specifically, different users have different search permissions, that is, they can only perform search operations under the keywords authorized by the data owner. In addition, we also give a new construction which supports conjunctive keyword search. Finally, efficiency analysis and security proof ensure the feasibility and security of our VDB scheme.

Keywords: Verifiable database · Multi-client · Searchable encryption

1 Introduction

Enterprises or individuals outsource their database to the cloud server to obtain better performance and larger storage space. However, the cloud server is untrusted who may tamper with the database. Therefore, it is very crucial to ensure the integrity of database and the integrity and correctness of query results. In recent decades, researches on these issues have emerged, including verifiable computing [1–4] and verifiable storage [5–8].

Benabbas et al. [9] proposed a method to solve the above problems, named verifiable database (VDB), which allows clients to store, query and update data stored on the server. In addition, any wrong behavior trying to modify the database can be found by the client to ensure the correctness and integrity of the database records. However, this scheme only supports private verification of outsourced database. In order to realize the public verification, Katalano et al. [6] designed vector commitment to build a publicly verifiable VDB scheme. After these two

© The Author(s), under exclusive license to Springer Nature Switzerland AG 2022
X. Chen et al. (Eds.): CSS 2022, LNCS 13547, pp. 133–146, 2022.
https://doi.org/10.1007/978-3-031-18067-5_10

schemes are proposed, many related researches on VDB structure have emerged in recent years, such as [7, 8, 10–13].

All the above VDB schemes only support index-based queries, that is, the client queries index x, server returns the data d_x on the location x and the corresponding proof to verify the integrity and correctness of d_x. Miao et al. [14] first extended the query method and proposed a VDB scheme supporting effective keyword search. However, in this scheme, the data owner owns the private key, so only he can use it to generate a keyword search token to retrieve all relevant documents. However, in the real world, there are often multiple users accessing a database and they have different permissions to access the database.

In the multi-user scenario, a simple idea is that each time an authorized user searches a database, he asks the database owner for a search token for the data to be queried. However, in this way, their communication costs are very high and owner must always be online to serve users. Sun et al. [15] skillfully canceled the interaction process in the multi-client searchable encryption scheme, they use the search token constructed by the RSA function for the authorized user. However, it is still challenge to construct a multi-client VDB. As far as we know, there is no VDB construction in a multi-user scenario supporting keyword search.

1.1 Our Contribution

This paper solves the problem of effective keyword search of VDB in multi-user scenario. The contributions are summarized as follows:

- By combining VDB and multi-user searchable encryption to achieve our concrete construction. In our scheme, users only need to obtain their own private key from the owner and then use the private key to generate their own search token, which saves communication costs. Specifically, the data owner sends an authorized key to the user, and the user can generate search tokens based on the authorized key.
- We extend our construction to support conjunctive keyword search. That is, the user can obtain the documents containing all the queried keywords in the VDB structure.

1.2 Related Work

Verifiable Database. With this primitive, the data owner can safely outsource the database to an untrusted server, and the correctness of the query data and the integrity of the database can be guaranteed during subsequent queries. This primitive was originally defined by Benabbas et al. [9]. Their scheme requires private key to perform the verify operation, that is, it does not support public verification. To support public validation, Catalano et al. [6] presented a new scheme based on vector commitment. After these two pioneering works, there are many VDB schemes have been put forward continuously [7, 8, 10–13, 16]. However, the main feature of these schemes is that they are VDB schemes based on index query. That is, the client submits the query index x to the server who then returns the search result d_x and the corresponding proof, and finally, this evidence enables the client to determine whether d_x is valid. To support keyword search, Miao et al. [14] added keyword retrieval function to VDB for the first, which only supports replacement operations, then they [17] extended the scheme to support all update operations, such as add, replace and delete.

Searchable Encryption. This concept was given by Song et al. [18]. Golle et al. [19] first extended this to conjunctive keyword search. However, when using them to perform retrieval operations, the time complexity is linearly related to the database size. After that, cash et al. [20] did a lot of research and gave the first sublinear conjunctive keyword query scheme (OXT). Wang et al. [21] proposed conjunctive keyword search with search patter hidden. The above schemes can only be used in single user scenarios. In a multi-user scenario, any user authorized by the data owner can access the owner's database. Curtmola et al. [22] proposed a multi-user structure which adopts broadcast encryption on a single reader scheme. Unfortunately, the efficiency of broadcast encryption is very low. Then, Jarecki et al. [23] borrowed the ideas of cash et al. [20] and extended them to multi-user scenarios but with multiple interaction. Sun et al. [15] also extended it [20] to the multi-user scenario, by skillfully using RSA functions. Some other work [24–26] also extended the Sun et al.'s scheme [15].

1.3 Organization

Section 2 gives some preliminary information required in the paper. Section 3 gives the construction of specific VDB schemes supporting search in multi-user scenarios. In Sect. 4, we present the security and efficiency of our proposed VDB. Finally, we summarize this paper in Sect. 5.

2 Preliminaries

2.1 Mathematical Assumption

Definition 1 (CDH problem). The Computational Diffie-Hellman (CDH) Problem in group $\mathbb{G}_1$ is that: Inputs a triple (g, g^x, g^y), where g is the generator of $\mathbb{G}_1$ and $x, y \in_R \mathbb{Z}_p$, and outputs g^{xy}. The CDH assumption holds that any probabilistic polynomial time adversary $\mathcal{A}$ has a non-negligible probability to output g^{xy}, i.e.,

$$\Pr[\mathcal{A}(1^k, g, g^x, g^y) = g^{xy}] \leq \text{negl}(k)$$

where $\text{negl}(\cdot)$ is a negligible function with security parameter k.

Definition 2 (DDH problem). The decisional Diffie-Hellman (DDH) problem means that it is difficult to distinguish tuples (g, g^x, g^y, g^{xy}) from (g, g^x, g^y, g^z), where $\mathbb{G}_1$ be a cyclic group of prime order p, $g \in \mathbb{G}_1$ and randomly chooses $x, y, z \in \mathbb{Z}_p$. The advantage for any probabilistic polynomial time (PPT) distinguisher $\mathcal{D}$ is defined as:

$$\text{Adv}_{\mathcal{D},\mathbb{G}}^{\text{DDH}} = \Pr[\mathcal{D}(g, g^x, g^y, g^{xy}) = 1] - \Pr[\mathcal{D}(g, g^x, g^y, g^z) = 1]$$

The DDH assumption holds if for any PPT distinguisher $\mathcal{D}$, its advantage $\text{Adv}_{\mathcal{D},\mathbb{G}}^{\text{DDH}}(k)$ is negligible in k.

Definition 3 (Strong RSA Problem). Let a and b be two k-bit prime numbers such that $a = 2a' + 1$ and $b = 2b' + 1$, where a', b' are primes and $N = ab$. If it receives as input the tuple (N, g) and outputs two elements (z, e) such that $z^e = g \bmod N$, where g be a random element in $\mathbb{Z}_N^*$, the strong RSA assumption holds.

2.2 Verifiable Database (VDB)

VDB can effectively solve the problems of database verification and data update when users outsource data, its definition is as follows [4].

Definition 4. The four specific algorithms of **VDB = (Setup, Query, Verify, Update)** are defined as follows:

- **Setup**$(1^k, DB)$: The data owner inputs parameter k, the output private key SK is kept by him, public key PK and database DB for the server.
- **Query**(x, PK): The server executes the algorithm by inputting index x and PK, returns (d_x, τ), where d_x represents the document at location x and τ is the related proof.
- **Verify**(PK, x, τ): The user runs this algorithm to test the validity of the returned document using the PK, index x and proof τ.
- **Update**(SK, PK, x, d_x'): The data owner is in possession of the updating algorithm. It takes SK, x and d_x as inputs, generates a new public key PK based on the most recent database, and alters d_x to d_x' at position x.

3 Multi-user Verifiable Database with Efficient Keyword Search

3.1 Framework

A Multi-user Verifiable Database with Efficient Keyword search scheme **MUVDB = (Setup, Share, Query, Verify, Update)** consists of five algorithms.

- **Setup**$(1^k, DB)$: The data owner runs this algorithm by inputting parameter k to generate the key sk secretly held by the data owner, hand over the database VDB to server, distribute the public key PK to users.
- **Share**(SK, w_S): A user is allowed to search for keywords $w_s = (w_1, w_2, ..., w_n)$. On input the secret key SK, keywords $w_s \subseteq W$, where W is the keyword set of DB, output key sk and send it to the user together with w_S.
- **Query**(sk, x, PK, w): User inputs keyword w and key sk, server produces (v_x, τ), where v_x is hash value of all documents in keyword w and τ is proof.

- **Verify**(PK, x, τ): User runs it to verify the validity of the document returned by the server, including correctness and integrity. Take PK, index x and proof τ as input. If τ is right with regard to x, returns value v_x; otherwise returns error $\perp$.
- **Update**(SK, PK, x, v_x'): The data owner runs this algorithm. It takes SK, x and v_x as inputs, generates a new public key PK based on the most recent database, and changes v_x to v_x' at position x.

3.2   High Level Description

The idea of adding keyword retrieval operation to VDB scheme is to add an additional layer on vector commitment [14]. Specifically, through the key value pair feature of vector commitment, when the index x is input, all document identifiers DB_w contained in the keyword w in this position will be searched. However, the document can be only retrieved using the private key by data owner. In real life, the data owner would like to authorize the search ability to other users. As a result, we expand the existing VDB scheme [14] based on keyword search to a multi-user scenario and propose a multi-user VDB scheme based on keyword search (the scheme idea is shown in Fig. 1).

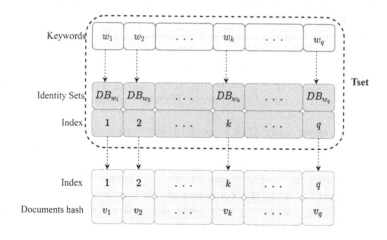

Fig. 1. The main idea of MUVDB scheme.

In the case of multi-user search operations, a simple idea is that users must ask the data owner every time they want to perform a database search operation. That is, the data owner inputs private key and then generates search token for the user's query keywords through function operation, which is sent to the user to execute the query on the server. Finally, server provides the user the search results (the encrypted document identifier DB_w corresponding to the keyword w). The user can retrieve the matching document identification DB_w after decryption. However, this way will increase the cost of communication between them. In order to make VDB support multi-user operation, we give a specific scheme to realize this operation. The main idea is to use RSA function [15] to skillfully eliminate the interaction between users and data owners to generate search tokens. Users only need to earn the key sk from the data owner and then they can use the key sk to generate a search token for keyword query. It is worth noting that users can only search in the subset of the authorized keywords shared by the data owner.

3.3 A Concrete MUVDB Scheme

We first give some definitions of notations. A database DB $= (id_i, W_i)_{i=1}^d$ consists of two parts: document identifier and keyword, where d refers to the total number of documents in the database. Our scheme uses RSA function to construct search token, so we need to make all keywords W_i in DB using 'keyword to prime' function [15] to get a corresponding prime w_i and $W = \cup_{i=1}^d w_i$ refers to the set of all keywords contained in the database. Let DB_w represents the set of all document identifiers contained in w. F is a pseudorandom function. $\mathbb{G}_1$ and $\mathbb{G}_2$ are two groups of order q and g is a generator of $\mathbb{G}_1$. e is bilinear map, $\mathcal{H}$ is hash function in $\mathbb{G}_1$.

- **Setup**$(1^k, DB)$: The data owner runs this algorithm. It inputs parameter k, database DB $= (\mathrm{id}_i, \mathrm{W}_i)_{i=1}^d$, generates key K_S for a PRF F and primes a, b to make $ab = N$. It chooses q elements $z_i \in_R \mathbb{Z}_p$ and computes $h_i = g^{z_i}, h_{i,j} = g^{z_i z_j}$, where $1 \leq i \neq j \leq q$. Then, it chooses $y \in {}_R\mathbb{Z}_p$ and computes $Y = g^y$. The secret key $SK = (a, b, g_1, K_S, y)$ and the parameter $PP = (Y, N, p, q, \mathbb{G}_1, \mathbb{G}_2, \mathcal{H}, H, e, g, \{h_i\}_{1\leq i\leq q}, \{h_{i,j}\}_{1\leq i,j\leq q, i\neq j})$, $g_1 \leftarrow \mathbb{Z}_N^*$. Then it runs Algorithm 1 to initialize an array TSet and generate the corresponding VDB.
  1. It initializes an array TSet to perform keyword search on VDB, a bloom filter (BF) to provide search verifiability and a Merkle hash tree(MHT) to assure search result completeness.
  2. It generates a vector commitment to ensure the correctness of search result. C_R is the commitment on the original database vector $(1||v_1, ..., q||v_q)$, where v_x represents keyword w_x hash value of ciphertexts of document sets, $C^{(T)}$ is a commitment on by updating T times, $T = 0$ is the initial counter, $C^{(0)} = C_R$. C_{T-1} is the last commitment of the latest commitment value, when T $= 0$, $C_{T-1} = C_{-1} = C_R$.
- **Share**(SK, w_s): The data owner runs it. it generates a key $sk = (K_S, sk_w)$ for the user, Where the keywords sets $w_s = (w_1, w_2, ..., w_n) \subseteq W$ and $sk_w = g_1^{1/\prod_{j=1}^n w_j} \bmod N$.
- **Query**(sk, PK, w, i): Users can find all documents contained in the keyword by inputting the keyword $w \in w_s$, sk. The algorithm calculates the search token $stag_w = F(K_S, (sk)^{\prod_{w_j \in w_s \backslash w} w_j} \bmod N) = F(K_S, g_1^{1/w} \bmod N)$ and sends it to the server. The operation is then detailed as follows:
  1. The server searches in TSet and returns the search results $e' = $ TSet$[stag_w]$ to the user who performs the search operation.

Algorithm 1: Setup($1^k, DB$)

input : $1^k, DB$
output: PK,SK,VDB

1 TSet, STAG, TR← ∅, $T = 0$
2 **for** each $w \in W$ **do**
3 | $e_{w_i} = \textbf{Enc}(i||DB_{w_i})$
4 | $stag_{w_i} = F(K_S, g_1^{1/w_i} \bmod N)$
5 | $TSet[stag_{w_i}] \leftarrow e_{w_i}$
6 | $STAG \leftarrow STAG \cup \{stag_{w_i}\}$
7 | $|DB_w| = n_i, h = H(i||w_i||n_i)$
8 | $TR \leftarrow TR \cup h$
9 **end**
10 **Compute Merkle hash tree:**
11 MHT(TR) and $root = \emptyset$
12 **Compute Bloom filter:** BF(STAG)
13 **Compute vector commitment:**
14 $C_R \leftarrow \prod_{i=1}^{q} h_i^{v_i}$
15 $C^{(T=0)} = C_R$
16 $C_{-1} = C_R$
17 $H_0 \leftarrow \mathcal{H}(C_{-1}, C^{(0)}, 0)^y$
18 $aux \leftarrow (H_0, C_{-1}, C^{(0)}, 0)$
19 Set VDB← $\{TSet, aux\}$
20 PK= $(PP, C_R, C_0, BF(STAG), \emptyset)$
21 SK= (y, K_S, a, b, g_1, msk)
22 **Return** {VDB,PK,SK}

2. After decrypting e', the user obtains index i and returns it to the server, then the server calculates relevant evidence to prove the correctness of the documents stored at index i. The specific calculation of evidence is $\pi_i^{(T)} = \prod_{1 \leq j \leq q, j \neq i} h_{x,j}^{v_j^{(T)}}$ and sends back $\tau = (v_i^{(T)}, \pi_i^{(T)}, H_T, C_{T-1}, C^{(T)}, T)$ to the user, where $H_T = \mathcal{H}(C_{T-1}, C^{(T)}, T)^y$.

- **Verify**(PK, i, τ): We will implement our verify algorithm in two stages:
  1. The user verifies the integrity of the results returned by the server is mainly divided into two parts: if the server does not return any documents, the user checks whether $BF(stag_w) = 0$ is true. If established, users will accept the search results. Otherwise, reject. If the server returns specific documents, verifies the integrity of the returned result by calculating $H(i||w_i||n_i)$ and checking the root of MHT $\emptyset$.
  2. The user verifies the integrity of the entire database and the correctness of the data by checking τ. The verification is through checking the equality of the two equations, as follows: $e(H_T, g) = e(\mathcal{H}(C_{T-1}, C^{(T)}, T), Y)$ and $e(C_T/H_T h_i^{v_i^{(T)}}, h_i) = e(g, \pi_i^{(T)})$. If so, it outputs $v_i^{(T)}$. Otherwise, returns a terminator $\perp$.

- **Update**(SK, PK, i, w, v_i'): The data owner replaces v_i with v_i'. He queries the record v_i and the proof τ by sending keyword w_i to the server. If **Verify**(PK, i, τ) $= v_i$ holds, he increases T by 1, computes $C^{(T)} = \frac{C_{T-1}}{H_{T-1}} h_i^{v_i'-v_i}$ and $t_i' = H_T = \mathcal{H}(C_{T-1}, C^{(T)}, T)^y$. (t_i', v_i') is sent to the server. If t_i' is valid, the server generates $C_T = H_T C^{(T)}$ and updates $PK = (PP, C_R, C_0, BF, \emptyset')$. The server replaces v_i by v_i' at position i, updates $e_w' = \textbf{Enc}(mpk, i||DB_w')$ and inserts $(t_i' = H_T, C_{T-1}, C^{(T)}, T)$ into aux.

3.4 Extended Construction: Support Conjunctive Keyword Search

In our basic scheme, users can only perform simple single keyword search. In order to make it more widely used in the real world, we use the OXT protocol [20] to expand the basic construction, so that our scheme can realize multiple keyword search. The search index in the OXT scheme has two structures: TSet and XSet (as shown in Fig. 2). The following are the specifics of the proposed construction:

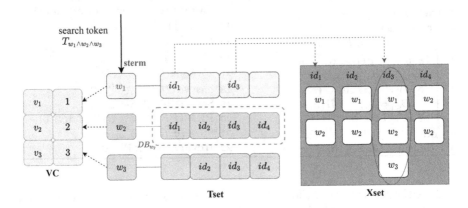

Fig. 2. Overview of the enhanced construction.

Algorithm 2: Setup($1^k, DB$)

---

input : $1^k, DB$
output: PK,SK,VDB

1 TSet,XSet,STAG$\leftarrow \varnothing$
2 **for** $w \in W$ **do**
3 $\quad C_w \leftarrow \varnothing; c \leftarrow 1; T \leftarrow 0; M \in \mathbb{Z}_p^*$
4 $\quad stag_w \leftarrow F(K_S, g_1^{1/w} \bmod N); STAG \leftarrow STAG \cup \{stag_w\}$
5 $\quad$**for** $id \in DB_w$ **do**
6 $\quad\quad xid \leftarrow F_p(K_I, id); z \leftarrow F_p(K_Z, g_2^{1/w} \bmod N || c); y \leftarrow xid \cdot z^{-1}$
7 $\quad\quad l \leftarrow F(stag_w, c); e \leftarrow \textbf{Enc}(x_w || id || M)$
8 $\quad\quad TSet[l] = (e, y); C_w \leftarrow C_w \cup \{e\}; c \leftarrow c + 1$
$\quad\quad xtag_w \leftarrow g^{F_p(K_X, g_3^{1/w} \bmod N) \cdot xid}; XSet \leftarrow XSet \cup \{xtag_w\}$
9 $\quad$**end**
10 $\quad$**Bloom filter:** $BF(C_w)$
11 $\quad d_w = H(M) \oplus BF(C_w) \oplus c; l \leftarrow F(stag_w, 0); TSet[l] \leftarrow d_w$
12 **end**
13 $BF(XSet), BF(Token)$
14 $C_R \leftarrow \prod_{i=1}^q h_i^{v_i}; C^{(0)} = C_R; C_{-1} = C_R; H_0 \leftarrow \mathcal{H}(C_{-1}, C^{(0)}, 0)^y;$
$\quad aux \leftarrow (H_0, C_{-1}, C^{(0)}, 0)$
15 Set VDB$\leftarrow \{TSet, XSet, aux\}$
16 PK= $(PP, C_R, C_0, BF(XSet), BF(Token))$
17 SK= $(y, K_S, K_X, K_I, K_Z, a, b, g_1, g_2, g_3)$
18 **Return** {VDB,PK,SK}

- **Setup**$(1^k, DB)$: The data owner runs it, inputting security parameter k and the database $DB = \{id_i, W_i\}_{i=1}^d$, then makes key K_S for PRF F, K_X, K_I, K_Z for PRF F_p, big primes a, b to make $ab = N$, q elements $z_i \in_R \mathbb{Z}_p$ and computes $h_i = g^{z_i}, h_{i,j} = g^{z_i z_j}$. then it chooses key $y \in_R \mathbb{Z}_p$, computes $Y = g^y$. the parameter is $PP = (Y, N, p, q, \mathbb{G}_1, \mathbb{G}_2, \mathcal{H}, e, g, \{h_i\}_{1 \leq i \leq q}, \{h_{i,j}\}_{1 \leq i,j \leq q, i \neq j})$ and the secret key is $SK = (y, K_S, K_X, K_I, K_Z, a, b, g_1, g_2, g_3)$, where $g_i \leftarrow \mathbb{Z}_N^*$ for $i \in [3]$. At last, it generates VDB with Algorithm 2.
- **Share**$(\mathbf{w}, SK)$: The data owner authorizes a user to query the keyword set $\mathbf{w} = (w_1, w_2, ..., w_n)$. He runs it to create key $sk = (K_S, K_I, K_Z, K_X, sk_w)$, which sk_w consists of three parts $(sk_w^{(1)}, sk_w^{(2)}, sk_w^{(3)})$ is computed as $sk_w^{(i)} = (g_i^{1/\prod_{j=1}^n w_j} \mod N)$ for $i \in [3]$.
- **TokenGen**$(\bar{w}, sk)$: A user wants to perform search over a given set of keywords $\bar{w} = (w_1, ..., w_n) \subseteq \mathbf{w}$, It inputs keywords w and key sk, outputs the search token $T_{\bar{w}}$(stags and xtokens). For ease of use, w_1 can be used as the sterm, and $T_{\bar{w}}$ is generated in Algorithm 3.

Algorithm 3: TokenGen$(\bar{w}, sk)$

    input : $\bar{w}, sk$
    output: $T_{\bar{w}}$

1   $stag \leftarrow F(K_S, (sk_w^{(1)})^{\prod_{w \in \mathbf{w} \setminus \{w_1\}} w} \mod N) = F(K_S, g_1^{1/w_1} \mod N)$
2   **for** $c=1,2,...$ **do**
3   **for** $i = 2, ..., n$ **do**
4        $xtoken[c, i] \leftarrow$
         $g^{F_p(K_Z, (sk_w^{(2)})^{\prod_{w \in \mathbf{w} \setminus \{w_1\}} w} \mod N||c) \cdot F_p(K_X, (sk_w^{(3)})^{\prod_{w \in \mathbf{w} \setminus \{w_1\}} w} \mod N)}$
5        $= g^{F_p(K_Z, g_2^{1/w_1} \mod N||c) F_p(K_X, g_3^{1/w_1} \mod N)}$
6   **end**
7      $xtoken[c] = xtoken[c, 2], ..., xtoken[c, n]$
8   **end**
9   $T_{\bar{w}} \leftarrow (stag, xtoken[1], xtoken[2], ...)$
10   **return** $T_{\bar{w}}$

- **Query**$(T_{\bar{w}}, VDB, PK)$: The server receives the user's search token $T_{\bar{w}}$, runs this algorithm to get the query result R and proof of the result to ensure the integrity and correctness. The specific construction is in the Algorithm 4.
- **Verify**(R_{w_1}, R, τ): The user firstly checks the integrity and correctness of document identifiers after getting the evidence given by the server; next it checks the integrity of document contents. Algorithm 5 shows the details of this process.
- **Update**(SK, PK, w, x, v'_x): The data owner runs it, which is similar to the one used in the basic construction. As a result, we've left it out.

Algorithm 4: $\text{Query}(T_{\tilde{w}}, VDB, PK)$

---

input : $(T_{\tilde{w}}, VDB, PK)$
output: $R_{w_1}, R, proof$

1 **Server:**
2 $R_{w_1}, R \leftarrow \varnothing; l \leftarrow F(stag, 0)$
3 $TSet[l] \leftarrow d_w$
4 **for** $c = 1, 2, ...$ **do**
5 $\quad\big|\quad l \leftarrow F(stag, c); (e_c, y_c) \leftarrow$
   $\quad\quad\quad TSet[l]; R_{w_1} = R_{w_1} \cup \{e_c\}$
6 $\quad\big|\quad$ **Return** $\{R_{w_1}, d_w\}$ to client
7 **end**
8 **Client:**
9 **if** $R_{w_1} = \varnothing$ **then**
10 $\quad\big|\quad \text{BFVerify}_{Token}(stag_{w_1}) = 1$
11 $\quad\big|\quad$ **Return** reject and exit
12 **else**
13 $\quad\big|\quad x_w \| M \| c \leftarrow \mathbf{Dec}(e)$
14 $\quad\big|\quad$ **Return** x_w to server

15 **end**
16 **Server:**
17 computing:
18 $\pi_{x_w}^{(T)} \leftarrow \prod_{1 \leq j \leq q, j \neq x_w} h_{x_w, j}^{v_j^{(T)}}$
19 $\tau = (v_{x_w}^{(T)}, \pi_{x_w}^{(T)}, H_T, C_{T-1}, C^{(T)}, T)$
20 **for** $c = 1, ..., |R_{w_1}|$ **do**
21 $\quad\big|\quad$ **for** $i = 2, ..., n$ **do**
22 $\quad\big|\quad\big|\quad b[c, i] \leftarrow xtoken[c, i]^{y_c}$
23 $\quad\big|\quad$ **end**
24 $\quad\big|\quad$ **if** $\forall i = 2, ..., n : b[c, i] \in XSet$
   $\quad\quad\quad$ **then**
25 $\quad\big|\quad\big|\quad R \leftarrow R \cup \{e_c\}$
26 $\quad\big|\quad$ **end**
27 $\quad\big|\quad$ **Return** $\{R, \tau\}$
28 **end**

---

4   Security and Efficiency Analysis

4.1   Security

Theorem 1. *The MUVDB scheme supporting keyword search is secure, assuming that the Squ-CDH assumption holds.*

Proof. Our scheme is an extension of Miao et al.'s scheme [14] in the multi-user scenario and also uses the vector commitment constructed based on squ-CDH assumption to ensure the correctness of the database. They use the reduction method to give the security proof, which is also applicable to our scheme. Therefore, our MUVDB scheme can realize secure keyword search under the assumption of squ-CDH.

Theorem 2. *By assuming that the DDH assumption holds, the TSet instantiation Σ is L-semantically secure against adaptive attacks, F, F_p are secure PRFs.*

Proof. The structure of Tset in our scheme adopts RSA function of sun et al. [15], which is secure under the above assumptions. Their proof is carried out through a series of games, and finally they complete the proof of the theorem by proving that the distribution (in calculation) of all games is difficult to distinguish from each other.

Algorithm 5: Verify(R_{w_1}, R, τ)

---

input : R_{w_1}, R, τ
output: Accept / Reject

1 **Verify the document identifiers:**
2 $BF_w(C_w) = d_{w_1} \oplus H(M) \oplus c$
3 **if** $BF_w(R_{w_1}) = 0$ **then**
4 | Reject and exit
5 **end**
6 **if** $R = \varnothing$ **then**
7 | **for** $i = 1, 2, ..., |R_{w_1}|$ **do**
8 | | $id \leftarrow \mathbf{Dec}(e_c)$
9 | | **for** $j = 2, ..., n$ **do**
10 | | | $xid \leftarrow F_p(K_I, id_i)$
11 | | | $xtag[i,j] \leftarrow g^{F_p(K_X, (sk_w^{(3)})^{\prod_{w \in \mathbf{w} \setminus \{w_1\}} w}} \mod N) \cdot xid$
12 | | | $xtag[i] \leftarrow xtag[i] \cup xtag[i,j]$
13 | | **end**
14 | | **if** $BF_X(xtag[i] = 1)$ **then**
15 | | | **return** Reject
16 | | **end**
17 | **end**
18 **else**
19 | The client select all $id \in R_{w_1} - R$
20 | Other operations are the same as above.
21 **end**
22 **Verify**
23 $e(H_T, g) = e(\mathcal{H}(C_{T-1}, C^{(T)}, T), Y); e(C_T / H_T h_x^{v_x^{(T)}}, h_x) = e(\pi_x^{(T)}, g)$
24 **return** Accept or Reject

Theorem 3. *In our construction, when the strong RSA assumption is true, the search token is unforgeable for adaptive attacks.*

Proof. When retrieving some keywords $w' \notin w_S$, the user cannot generate the correct search token. The reason lies in the feature of PRFs, where w_S refers to all keyword sets that the user can search, unless he can properly predict the value $(g_1^{1/w'} \mod N)$. Assume there is an adversarial $\mathcal{A}$, and he can generate a valid search token $g_1^{1/w'} \mod N$ for some keyword $w' \notin w_S$. In this instance, we may utilize $\mathcal{A}$ to build an algorithm $\mathcal{B}$ to solve strong RSA problem. (The RSA function of sun et al. [15], which is secure under the strong RSA assumption). Therefore, user cannot generate a correct search token when he does not have access to the keyword.

4.2 Comparison

Our scheme is a multi-user version of Miao et al.'s scheme [14], and it primarily uses the TSet structure of Cash et al. [20] in VDB to realize keyword search

Table 1. Efficiency comparison.

Schemes	Scheme [14]	Our scheme
Model	Amortized	Amortized
Multi-user	No	Yes
Keyword Search	Yes	Yes
Querycost (owner)	$F + D$	$E + D$
Querycost (user)	–	$(n - 1)M + E + D$
Querycost (Server)	$(q - 1)(E + M) + H$	$(q - 1)(E + M) + H$
Verifycost (Verifier)	$2E + 2M + 4P + \mathcal{O}(\log_2 q)H$	$2E + 2M + 4P + \mathcal{O}(\log_2 q)H$
Updatecost (Owner)	$2E + 2M + 2H$	$2E + 2M + 2H$

operations. Our goal is to tackle the problem of users needing to obtain the search trapdoor from the data owner every time they search in a multi-user situation, so that users can search documents without having to contact with the data owner, and can only search some of the data owner's documents.

In the query phase, scheme [14] requires the data owner to use the private key to generate the search token of the query, that is, only the data owner can query the database. In a multi-user scenario, other users can not only share the database of the data owner, but also enable users to search only some keywords in the database. Most importantly, inspired by the scheme of sun et al. [15], our scheme avoids the interaction between the owner and the user (except in the sharing stage, the data owner sends the private key of search authorization to the user, and then the user can use the private key for keyword search).

Finally, we compared our proposed scheme with Miao et al.'s scheme [14] (as shown in Table 1). In terms of efficiency, the Setup is a one-time operation and can be completed offline, which is beneficial to lightweight client users with limited computing resources and communication bandwidth. In the verification stage, since our scheme is the extension of Miao's scheme in the multi-user scenario, the framework of VDB constructed by vector commitment technology. The verification overhead is basically the same, and the cost of proof generation is independent of the size of the database. We compare their differences in Table 1. M is the multiplication operation of group $\mathbb{G}_1, \mathbb{G}_2$, E is the modular index operation in $\mathbb{G}_1$, D is the decryption operation of symmetric encryption, H is the hash operation, P is the pairing operation, F is the pseudo random calculation, n represents the number of key words shared by the data owner to the user, – indicating that this scheme does not have this function. Some lightweight operations are omitted here.

5   Conclusion

VDB plays a role in the research of verifiable storage outsourcing. It can be used to query documents (keyword based and index based queries) and verify the integrity of databases. However, the existing VDB scheme based on keyword search only supports the query operations for the data owner. In this paper, we propose a VDB structure that supports keyword search in multi-user scenarios and we also extend the above scheme to support conjunctive keyword search. Finally, we provide the evaluation of security and efficiency of our proposed schemes.

Acknowledgments. This work is supported by National Natural Science Foundation of China (Nos. 61902315 and 62102313).

References

1. Atallah, M.J., Frikken, K.B.: Securely outsourcing linear algebra computations. In: Proceedings of the 5th ACM Symposium on Information, Computer and Communications Security (ASIACCS 2010), pp. 48–59. ACM (2010)
2. Atallah, M.J., Pantazopoulos, K.N., Rice, J.R., Spafford, E.H.: Secure outsourcing of scientific computations. Adv. Comput. **54**, 215–272 (2001)
3. Atallah, M.J., Li, J.: Secure outsourcing of sequence comparisons. Int. J. Inf. Secur. **4**(4), 277–287 (2005). https://doi.org/10.1007/s10207-005-0070-3
4. Chen, X., Li, J., Susilo, W.: Efficient fair conditional payments for outsourcing computations. IEEE Trans. Inf. Forensics Secur. **7**(6), 1687–1694 (2012)
5. Backes, M., Fiore, D., Reischuk, R.M.: Verifiable delegation of computation on outsourced data. In: Proceedings of the 2013 ACM SIGSAC Conference on Computer & Communications Security, pp. 863–874. ACM (2013)
6. Catalano, D., Fiore, D.: Vector commitments and their applications. In: Kurosawa, K., Hanaoka, G. (eds.) PKC 2013. LNCS, vol. 7778, pp. 55–72. Springer, Heidelberg (2013). https://doi.org/10.1007/978-3-642-36362-7_5
7. Chen, X., Li, J., Ma, J., Tang, Q., Lou, W.: New algorithms for secure outsourcing of modular exponentiations. IEEE Trans. Parallel Distrib. Syst. **25**(9), 2386–2396 (2014)
8. Chen, X., Li, J., Huang, X., Ma, J., Lou, W.: New publicly verifiable databases with efficient updates. IEEE Trans. Dependable Secur. Comput. **12**(5), 546–556 (2015)
9. Benabbas, S., Gennaro, R., Vahlis, Y.: Verifiable delegation of computation over large datasets. In: Rogaway, P. (ed.) CRYPTO 2011. LNCS, vol. 6841, pp. 111–131. Springer, Heidelberg (2011). https://doi.org/10.1007/978-3-642-22792-9_7
10. Chen, X., Li, J., Weng, J., Ma, J., Lou, W.: Verifiable computation over large database with incremental updates. IEEE Trans. Comput. **65**(10), 3184–3195 (2016)
11. Miao, M., Ma, J., Huang, X., Wang, Q.: Efficient verifiable databases with insertion/deletion operations from delegating polynomial functions. IEEE Trans. Inf. Forensics Secur. **13**(2), 511–520 (2018)
12. Miao, M., Wang, J., Ma, J., Susilo, W.: Publicly verifiable databases with efficient insertion/deletion operations. J. Comput. Syst. Sci. **86**, 49–58 (2017)
13. Zhang, Z., Chen, X., Li, J., Tao, X., Ma, J.: HVDB: a hierarchical verifiable database scheme with scalable updates. J. Ambient. Intell. Humaniz. Comput. **10**(8), 3045–3057 (2018). https://doi.org/10.1007/s12652-018-0757-8
14. Miao, M., Wang, J., Wen, S., Ma, J.: Publicly verifiable database scheme with efficient keyword search. Inf. Sci. **475**, 18–28 (2019)

15. Sun, S.-F., Liu, J.K., Sakzad, A., Steinfeld, R., Yuen, T.H.: An efficient non-interactive multi-client searchable encryption with support for Boolean queries. In: Askoxylakis, I., Ioannidis, S., Katsikas, S., Meadows, C. (eds.) ESORICS 2016. LNCS, vol. 9878, pp. 154–172. Springer, Cham (2016). https://doi.org/10.1007/978-3-319-45744-4_8

16. Wang, Q., Zhou, F., Zhou, B., Xu, J., Wang, Q.: Privacy-preserving publicly verifiable databases. IEEE Trans. Dependable Secure Comput. **19**(3), 1639–1654 (2022)

17. Miao, M., Wang, Y., Wang, J., Huang, X.: Verifiable database supporting keyword searches with forward security. Comput. Stand. Interfaces **77**, 103491 (2021)

18. Pitigalaarachchi, P., Gamage, C.: Efficiency enhancements for practical techniques for searches on encrypted data. In: ICCSP 2020, pp. 13–18. ACM (2020)

19. Golle, P., Staddon, J., Waters, B.: Secure conjunctive keyword search over encrypted data. In: Jakobsson, M., Yung, M., Zhou, J. (eds.) ACNS 2004. LNCS, vol. 3089, pp. 31–45. Springer, Heidelberg (2004). https://doi.org/10.1007/978-3-540-24852-1_3

20. Cash, D., Jarecki, S., Jutla, C., Krawczyk, H., Roşu, M.-C., Steiner, M.: Highly-scalable searchable symmetric encryption with support for Boolean queries. In: Canetti, R., Garay, J.A. (eds.) CRYPTO 2013. LNCS, vol. 8042, pp. 353–373. Springer, Heidelberg (2013). https://doi.org/10.1007/978-3-642-40041-4_20

21. Wang, Y., Sun, S.-F., Wang, J., Liu, J.K., Chen, X.: Achieving searchable encryption scheme with search pattern hidden. IEEE Trans. Serv. Comput. **15**(2), 1012–1025 (2022)

22. Curtmola, R., Garay, J.A., Kamara, S., Ostrovsky, R.: Searchable symmetric encryption: improved definitions and efficient constructions. In: Proceedings of the 2006 ACM SIGSAC Conference on Computer & Communications Security (CCS 2006), pp. 79–88. ACM (2006)

23. Jarecki, S., Jutla, C.S., Krawczyk, H., Rosu, M.-C., Steiner, M.: Outsourced symmetric private information retrieval. In: Proceedings of the 2013 ACM SIGSAC Conference on Computer & Communications Security (CCS 2013), pp. 875–888. ACM (2013)

24. Wang, Y., Wang, J., Sun, S.-F., Liu, J.K., Susilo, W., Chen, X.: Towards multi-user searchable encryption supporting Boolean query and fast decryption. In: Okamoto, T., Yu, Y., Au, M.H., Li, Y. (eds.) ProvSec 2017. LNCS, vol. 10592, pp. 24–38. Springer, Cham (2017). https://doi.org/10.1007/978-3-319-68637-0_2

25. Wang, Y., et al.: Towards multi-user searchable encryption supporting Boolean query and fast decryption. J. Univers. Comput. Sci. **25**(3), 222–244 (2019)

26. Wang, J., Chen, X., Sun, S.-F., Liu, J.K., Au, M.H., Zhan, Z.-H.: Towards efficient verifiable conjunctive keyword search for large encrypted database. In: Lopez, J., Zhou, J., Soriano, M. (eds.) ESORICS 2018. LNCS, vol. 11099, pp. 83–100. Springer, Cham (2018). https://doi.org/10.1007/978-3-319-98989-1_5

A Blockchain-Based Collaborative Auditing Scheme for Cloud Storage

Jie Xiao[1], Hui Huang[1,2(✉)], Chenhuang Wu[3], Qunshan Chen[1,2],
and Zhenjie Huang[4]

[1] School of Computer Science, Minnan Normal University, Zhangzhou, Fujian, China
[2] Key Laboratory of Data Science and Intelligence Application,
Fujian Province University, Zhangzhou, Fujian, China
hhui323@163.com
[3] Key Laboratory of Applied Mathematics of Fujian Province University,
Putian University, Putian, Fujian, China
[4] Fujian Key Laboratory of Granular Computing and Application,
Minnan Normal University, Zhangzhou, Fujian, China

Abstract. Cloud storage system has brought great convenience but also brings serious security problems. To ensure data security in the cloud, users usually authorize a third-party auditor (TPA) to verify their data integrity regularly. However, TPA may lead to security threats such as data disclosure and tampering. Fortunately, blockchain makes up for the lack of TPA. But there exists the problem of interaction difficulties and expensive deployment of smart contracts in the blockchain scenario. This paper proposes a blockchain-based collaborative public auditing scheme for remote data. In the proposed scheme, the cloud service provider (CSP) completes the challenge and verification work independently, reducing the communication overhead in the proof stage and improving the overall system efficiency. In addition, we consider allowing users to seek partners to reduce the cost of personal audits. Through the EigenTrust model evaluating the credibility of users, the users can select a high-quality partner to complete public auditing work, effectively avoiding collusion among malicious users. The proposed scheme can be proved secure and efficient according to the complete security analysis and comprehensive performance evaluation.

Keywords: Public auditing · Blockchain · Collaborative auditing · Reputation system

1 Introduction

With the development of cloud computing, cloud storage has been widely used in various industries in recent years [1]. CSP provides an effective data management model for users, which frees enterprises from maintaining IT infrastructure and focuses more on core business development. Compared with traditional storage technology, the distributed storage technology dramatically meets the massive scale and high scalability data processing needs [2].

© The Author(s), under exclusive license to Springer Nature Switzerland AG 2022
X. Chen et al. (Eds.): CSS 2022, LNCS 13547, pp. 147–159, 2022.
https://doi.org/10.1007/978-3-031-18067-5_11

However, the development of cloud storage is currently facing many problems. Among them, security is the primary issue [3]. The separation of data ownership and management rights in cloud storage services significantly threatens cloud data security. The cloud server may suffer data loss or service interruption caused by external factors, such as natural disasters, hardware failure, software bugs, etc. [4]. Moreover, the CSP may be a malicious entity, for instance, accessing user data for his benefit or concealing data loss to maintain his reputation [5]. Facing this situation, users need to audit the data on the cloud to confirm integrity. Data integrity verification is the key technology to solve this problem.

Traditional methods for data integrity verification [6,7], such as hash functions and message authentication codes, are unsuitable for outsourced storage environments. These methods need to download the entire data to the local when users want to verify the integrity of the data, which will consume a large number of bandwidth resources and bring a heavy burden to users. Therefore, we need a remote data integrity verification scheme that does not require the whole data while maintaining the minimum computing cost. Fortunately, Ateniese et al. [8] proposed the first provable data possession (PDP) model to solve the problem of remote data audit. Then, there have been many public auditing schemes based on PDP model [9–11]. However, there are some problems with the centralized public audit. First, neither CSP nor a third-party auditor (TPA) can be a fully trusted entity, and there is the possibility of doing evil for their interests. Secondly, the audit system will be directly endangered once the centralized TPA is down or attacked. Finally, a single TPA cannot simultaneously handle large-scale audit requests from multiple users.

To solve the single point of failure and performance problems, some researchers suggest using blockchain technology in cloud storage audit solutions [12–15]. Blockchain technology was first proposed in the bitcoin white paper published by Nakamoto in 2008 [16]. The characteristics of blockchain, such as decentralization, tamper proof, and traceability, have inspired the cloud audit scheme greatly.

Currently, in the articles that apply blockchain to audit schemes, the role of blockchain is to replace the audit function of TPA. The audit has changed from a single centralized manner to a decentralized manner. Their common way is to deploy the audit-related code on the blockchain in advance by using smart contracts. This method can automatically, effectively, and safely complete the audit requirements. However, there are several problems in the application of smart contracts. One point is smart contracts are usually initiated by a third party sending blockchain transactions. However, in the audit scenario, we hope that the smart contract will actively audit CSP, which is not in line with the operating habits of smart contracts. For the interaction problem between smart contracts and CSP, Wang et al. [17] proposed the notion of non-interactive public provable data possession (NI-PPDP). NI-PPDP allows CSP to generate challenge sets and proofs independently, so CSP does not need to interact with smart contracts many times in the audit process, which greatly reduces the communication overhead. This non-interactive idea also inspired many articles in the follow-up

[18,19]. Another point is that the use of smart contracts is too expensive. For example, the deployment cost of a smart contract in Ethereum is about \$40–\$70, which is more than ten times the basic operation cost. This is unbearable for ordinary users. Therefore, the collaborative audit can reduce the cost pressure of a single user and improve the efficiency of the whole system. Li et al. [20] proposed a blockchain-based cross-user data shared auditing scheme, allowing users to find partners and cooperate through the password-authenticated key exchange to share individual audit costs and improve overall system efficiency. However, Li et al. did not consider the credibility of users' partners. If malicious users participate in the cooperation, it will lead to errors in the audit results of both sides, which will not only waste computing resources but also make the audit system inefficient.

1.1 Our Contribution

We propose a public auditing scheme based on a blockchain network for collaboration to address the above challenges. We design the CSP independently to generate the challenge set and send the proof to the smart contract, which reduces the communication cost in the audit stage. In our scheme, users find another partner to deploy smart contracts on the blockchain to achieve a collaborative data audit. To get a reliable audit partner, we introduce the EigenTrust model [21], which considers the transactions between users and evaluates the trust value of each user. We use the Diffie-Hellman protocol to establish a cooperative audit relationship between trust users so that users can audit efficiently based on sharing audit costs. In general, the main contributions of this paper are summarized as follows:

- We propose a non-interactive public auditing scheme based on blockchain for collaboration, allowing users to find partners to share audit costs. The CSP directly interacts with the blockchain to complete the audit work, which is more efficient and secure.
- We introduce an EigenTrust reputation model to construct groups of users with trustworthiness. The reputation model can prevent users with low trust value from participating in auditing, improving auditing efficiency and reducing the frequency of malicious events.
- We set up smart contracts in cooperation scenarios in a reasonable way. The smart contract manages the deposit of the data owner and CSP as a service fee or compensation. The smart contracts minimize the gas consumption while ensuring a smooth audit process.

2 Public Provable Data Possession Scheme

2.1 System Model

The scheme proposed in this paper consists of three different roles: data owner, cloud service provider, and miners, as shown in Fig. 1. Each role is defined as follow:

- Data Owner (DO): The DO is the entity that uploads the file data to the cloud server. DO generates tags on data blocks to ensure the integrity of data stored in the cloud.
- Cloud Service Provider (CSP): The CSP provides storage services to do and charges according to the service conditions.
- Miners: Miners are the fundamental entities that drive the operation of the entire blockchain network. Miners can be any node on the blockchain network.

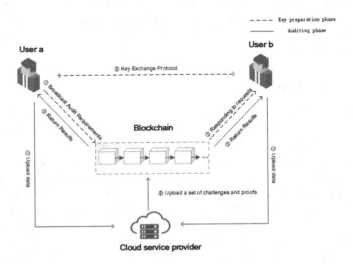

Fig. 1. The system model.

2.2   Adversary Model and Design Goals

We assume that CSP may delete some data stored long ago because more storage space is reserved to obtain more economic benefits. In addition, the CSP may hide data loss caused by external problems to ensure its reputation. Moreover, we reasonably assume that some malicious DOs participate in collaborative audits in an attempt to destroy the audit process. Besides, we presume that miners may hinder the broadcast of audit smart contract calculation results and delay the release of audit results. In the context of such attacks, our proposed scheme is expected to meet the following security requirements.

- *Soundness (Data integrity)*: If and only if the CSP can maintain the integrity of outsourcing data well, it can pass the audit of the smart contract.
- *Privacy preserving*: The scheme ensures that malicious third parties will not obtain data information during the audit process.
- *Automatic auditing*: After CSP receives the data, it triggers the audit smart contract for regular verification.

- *Public auditability*: Random nodes on the blockchain can remotely audit the integrity of data.
- *Collaborative auditing*: The EigenTrust model evaluates the reputation value of DO to reduce the cost of the personal audit and improve efficiency.

2.3   EigenTrust Model

EigenTrust [21] is a trust model proposed by Stanford University in 2003. It is the first typical model that dynamically calculates the global trust value of nodes, which proficiently evaluates the trust value of each node. EigenTrust model recording the satisfaction level of inter-node transactions obtains a global trust value for each node in the system.

Local Trust Values. When nodes trade with each other, EigenTrust needs to evaluate the transaction. For example, if node i downloads a file from node j, the served node i needs to evaluate the service provider for this transaction. Let $sat(i, j)$ represents the number of times that node i thinks node j provides resources or services correctly, $unsat(i, j)$ indicates the number of times that node i thinks node j provides resources or services incorrect. In the algorithm, $S(i, j)$ is defined to the local trust of node i to node j:

$$S(i, j) = sat(i, j) - unsat(i, j)$$

To aggregate local trust values, it is necessary to normalize them in the way of normalization. Otherwise, the malicious node can assign any high local trust value to other malicious nodes and any low local trust value to good nodes. The algorithm defines the symbol $C(i, j)$ as the normalized local trust value of node i to node j.

$$C(i, j) = \begin{cases} \frac{max(S(i,j),0)}{\sum_j max(S(i,j),0)}, & if \sum_j max(S(i,j),0) \neq 0; \\ p_i, & \text{otherwise} \end{cases}$$

In EigenTrust algorithm, a trusted node-set P is defined. If the node i belongs to the set of trusted nodes, then defined $p_i = \frac{1}{|P|}$ if $i \in P$, otherwise $p_i = 0$. So that all $C(i, j)$ is between zero and one. Each node gives a local trust normalization value to the other nodes with direct transaction records. This value indicates the trust degree of the other nodes j in front of the node i.

Recommended Trust Value. When node i and node k have no direct transaction, node i can calculate the trust value of node k by asking the recommended information of nodes $k_1, k_2, k_3, ..., k_n$ that have direct transactions with node k. Thus, the recommended trust value of i to k is established, where j refers to the node that has a direct transaction with node i.

$$t(i, k) = \sum_j C(i, j)C(j, k)$$

Let C be a matrix $[C(i,j)]$, $\overrightarrow{t}_i = C^T \overrightarrow{c}_i$ and $\overrightarrow{t}_i$ to be vector containing the values $t(i,k)$. However, the trust values of node i only reflect by his friends. If node i wishs to get a wider view by asking his friends' friends $(t = (C^T)^2 c_i)$. Finally, node i will have a complete view of the network $(t = (C^T)^n c_i)$. Therefore, t can be seen as a global trust in EigenTrust model. The vector t_j can quantify the trust of the whole system to j.

2.4   A Concrete Scheme

- **Setup:** Let G_1, G_2 and G_T be multiplicative cyclic groups of prime order p, and $e : G_1 \times G_2 \rightarrow G_T$ be a bilinear map as introduced in preliminaries. Let g be a generator of G_2, select two hash functions $h(\cdot) : \{0,1\}^* \rightarrow Z_p$, $H(\cdot) : \{0,1\}^* \rightarrow G_1$. The pseudorandom function $\zeta : \{0,1\}^* \rightarrow [1,2n]$ is defined for generate challenged data blocks. The DO U_i selects a random $sk_i \in Z_p^*$ for private key and computes the public key $pk_i = g^{sk_i}$. The CSP selects a random $ssk \in Z_p^*$ for private key and computes the public key $spk = g^{ssk}$.

- **Trust testing and Key sharing:** Before uploading file to the CSP, the DO U_a wants to save audit costs by broadcasting a message to find a partner on the blockchain. When a partner U_b responses the message, U_a will first evaluate the trust value of U_b by EigenTrust model to prevent malicious DO participating in collaborative audits. If the trust value falls below the preset threshold, U_a continues to broadcast the message. Otherwise, U_a accepts. The specific steps are described in Sect. 2.3. After passing the trust test, U_a and U_b execute a Diffie-Hellman key exchange protocol to generate public-private key pairs over an insecurity communications channel as follow.

$$k = (g^{sk_a})^{sk_b} = (g^{sk_b})^{sk_a} = g^{sk_a \cdot sk_b}.$$

sk_a and sk_b are the private keys of the DOs. Then, they use the hash function to compute the shared private key $SK = h(k)$ and the shared public key $PK = g^{SK}$. Then, U_a chooses a random element $u \leftarrow G_1$, and computes $e(u, PK)$. The public parameters are $Para = (PK, g, u, e(u, PK), h(\cdot), H(\cdot))$.

- **Data upload:** Using the sharing key pair (SK,PK), the DO U_a firstly divides F_a into $F_a = m_1 \parallel m_2 \parallel m_3 \parallel ... \parallel m_n$. Then, u_a calculates tags σ_i for each file data block.

$$\sigma_i = (H(W_i) \cdot u^{m_i})^{SK}, i \in [1,n]$$

Denote the set of authenticators by $\psi_a = \{\sigma_1, \sigma_2, ..., \sigma_n\}$. Here, $W_i = name_a \parallel i$ and $name_a \in Z_p$ is chosen randomly by the DO U_a as the identifier of file F_a. To make sure the integrity of the unnique file identifier $name_a$, the user U_a computes $t_a = name_a \parallel Sig_{sk_a}(name_a)$ as the file tag for F_a, where $Sig(\cdot)$ is a signature algorithm. Finally, the data owner U_a uploads the file F_a and tags $\phi_a = \{\psi_a, t_a\}$ to the CSP. Meanwhile, U_a sends tags about file $\phi_a = \{\psi_a, t_a\}$ to the blockchain. The DO U_b do in the same way to send the file

$F_b = m'_1 \parallel m'_2 \parallel m'_3 \parallel \dots \parallel m'_n$ and tags $\phi_b = \{\psi_b, t_b\}$. Before the CSP stores data, the DO U_a, U_b and the CSP will simultaneously sign a smart contract SC_a for the deposit. The role of SC_a is to obtain the deposit from three parties and return or detain the deposit after receiving the audit results. The deposit can ensure data security, and the results can also reflect on the EigenTrust reputation system. The initialized SC_a input contains $\{cycletime, price\}$, where $cycletime$ is a preset audit cycle, $price$ is the deposit amount set in advance. As shown in Algorithm 1, the deposit deposited by the three parties shall be used as a follow-up service fee or compensation. Since U_a and U_b have reached a collaborative audit, they can share half of the designated deposit. The destination of the deposit is determined by the results of the audit smart contract SC_b. If the SC_b returns that the audit is correct, the deposit of U_a and U_b will be sent to the CSP address as a service fee. Otherwise, the deposit of the CSP will be sent to the U_a and U_b address as compensation. After the CSP receives the data and tags sent by U_a and U_b and confirms their correctness, it reassembles them in order. After finishing the above process, the CSP obtain $F = \{F_a \parallel F_b\}, \phi = \{(\psi_a, \psi_b), (t_a, t_b)\}$.

Algorithm 1. Initialization payment Smart Contract SC_a.

Input: $cycletime$, $price$
Output: void
```
 1: TimeStamp=System.time;
 2: msg.value=price;
 3: require( msg.value==Deposit_CSP, "Deposit of the CSP is effective");
 4: require( msg.value/2==Deposit_Ua, "Deposit of the Ua is effective");
 5: require( msg.value/2==Deposit_Ub, "Deposit of the Ub is effective");
 6: while System.time==TimeStamp+cycletime do
 7:     TimeStamp+=cycletime;
 8:     if Addr_SCb.response==1 then
 9:         send (Deposit_Ua, Deposit_Ub) to Addr_CSP;
10:     else
11:         Perform corresponding punishment measures;
12:     end if
13: end while
```

- **Challenge:** In our scheme, the work of generating the challenge set is done by the CSP. The CSP and blockchain can reduce one interaction to improve efficiency and reduce gas consumption. The CSP will trigger audit smart contract SC_b for launch audit challenges circularly after the data file received. Specifically, the CSP chooses an integer c randomly, $c \in [1, 2n]$, computes $s_i = \zeta(\tau \parallel time \parallel i), i \in [1, c]$, where τ is the lastest block hash in the blockchain, $time$ is the current timestamp. So, S is the current challenge set, $S = \{s_1, s_2, s_3, ..., s_c\}$.

154   J. Xiao et al.

Algorithm 2. Audit smart contract SC_b.

Input: $(\mu, \sigma, R, \tau, c)$
Output: result
1: Boolean Result;
2: **if** $R \cdot e(\sigma^\gamma, g) == e((\prod_{i=1}^{c} H(W_{s_i})^{\nu_i})^\gamma \cdot u^\mu, PK)$ **then**
3:     result=1;
4: **else**
5:     result=0;
6: **end if**
7: Assess the credibility of all parties;
8: Return result;

- **Prove:** According to the multiset S computed in Challenge phase, the CSP computes $\nu_i = h(\tau \parallel time \parallel i), i \in [1, c]$. Then, it computes $\sigma = \prod_{i=1}^{c} \sigma_{s_i}^{\nu_i}$ and $\mu' = \sum_{i=1}^{c} \nu_i \cdot m_{s_i}$, m_{s_i} refers to a data block in the integrated file F. Specifically, the CSP chooses a random element, $r \in Z_p$, and calculates $R = e(u, PK)^r, R \in G_T$, Then, it computes $\mu = r + \gamma\mu'$, where $\gamma = h(R) \in Z_p$. The CSP will send $prove = (\mu, \sigma, R, \tau, c)$ to the audit smart contract SC_b as the response proof of storage correctness.
- **Verify:** With the response, audit smart contract SC_b automatically run verification algorithm to verify the integrity of challenge set. First, SC_b verifies status information τ via blockchain, reconstructs challenge set $S = \{\zeta(\tau \parallel time \parallel 1), \zeta(\tau \parallel time \parallel 2), ..., \zeta(\tau \parallel time \parallel c)\}$ and computes $\gamma = h(R)$. The verified equation is as follows:

$$R \cdot e(\sigma^\gamma, g) \overset{?}{=} e((\prod_{i=1}^{c} H(W_{s_i})^{\nu_i})^\gamma \cdot u^\mu, PK)$$

Then, SC_b outputs 1 or 0, sends the results to smart contract SC_a in Data Upload phase. The specific audit smart contract process is shown in Algorithm 2. After this transaction, the U_a, U_b shall evaluate the reputation value of both parties for this transaction.

3   Security Analysis and Efficiency Analysis

3.1   Correctness

If the CSP completely stores user data, it can be proved by the following:

$$R \cdot e(\sigma^\gamma, g) = e(u, PK)^r \cdot e((\prod_{i=1}^{c} \sigma_{s_i}^{\nu_i})^\gamma, g)$$

$$= e(u, PK)^r \cdot e((\prod_{i=1}^{c} ((H(W_{s_i}) \cdot u^{m_{s_i}})^{SK})^{\nu_i})^\gamma, g)$$

$$= e(u, PK)^r \cdot e((\prod_{i=1}^{c} (H(W_{s_i})^{\nu_i} \cdot u^{m_{s_i} \cdot \nu_i})^\gamma, g)^{SK}$$

$$= e(u, PK)^r \cdot e((\prod_{i=1}^{c} (H(W_{s_i})^{\nu_i})^\gamma \cdot u^{\mu' \cdot \gamma}, g)^{SK}$$

$$= e(u^r, g)^{SK} \cdot e((\prod_{i=1}^{c} (H(W_{s_i})^{\nu_i})^\gamma \cdot u^{\mu' \cdot \gamma}, g)^{SK}$$

$$= e((\prod_{i=1}^{c} (H(W_{s_i})^{\nu_i})^\gamma \cdot u^{\mu' \cdot \gamma + r}, g)^{SK}$$

$$= e((\prod_{i=1}^{c} H(W_{s_i})^{\nu_i})^\gamma \cdot u^\mu, PK)$$

It can be seen from the above mathematical proof that if CSP stores data correctly, it can pass the proof, otherwise the data is incomplete.

3.2 Security Analysis

Theorem 1. *The proposed scheme satisfies the property of soundness.*

Proof. Suppose there is a malicious CSP that will retain the proof of the previous challenge and forge the proof of the current challenge set with a non negligible probability. Assume that malicious CSP can generate $\gamma^* \neq \gamma$ and outputs $(\mu^*, \sigma', R, \tau)$ when a forge signature σ' can pass the verification, we have that:

$$R \cdot e(\sigma^{\gamma*}, g) = e((\prod_{i=1}^{c} H(W_{s_i})^{\nu_i})^{\gamma*} \cdot u^{\mu*}, PK)$$

Let $\mathcal{A}$ be a CDH promble attacker. Suppose g^x and g^y are the elements of CDH problem, $\mathcal{A}$ can set $PK = g^x, u = g^y$. If we define $\Delta\mu_i = \mu_i^* - \mu_i, i = 1, 2, ..., c$, there is at least one $\Delta\mu_i$ is nonzero. We know that if $\mathcal{A}$ can forge an aggregate signature σ' in probabilistic polynomial time, then $\mathcal{C}$ would break the CDH problem by the same probability. $\mathcal{C}$ can computes the equation as follows:

$$e(\sigma'/\sigma, g) = e(\prod_{i=1}^{c} u^{\Delta\mu_i}, PK) = e(g^{\sum_{i=1}^{c} \Delta\mu_i \cdot x \cdot y}, g)$$

Therefore, $\mathcal{C}$ can calculate $g^{x \cdot y} = (\sigma'/\sigma)^{\frac{1}{\sum_{i=1}^{c} \Delta\mu_i}}$. By doing so, $\mathcal{C}$ can solve CDH problem using $\mathcal{A}$'s forge signature. However, the CDH problem is a difficult problem, $\mathcal{A}$ cannot forge a valid aggregate signature in probabilistic polynomial time.

Theorem 2. *The proposed scheme satisfies the property of privacy preserving.*

Proof. The third party cannot disclose DO's data information in the process of verifying data integrity. In our scheme, CSP sends $prove = (\mu, \sigma, R, \tau, c)$ to the smart contract, where $\mu = r + \gamma\mu'$, μ' and σ contain data blocks. On the one hand, an attacker could not recover $u^{m_{s_i}}$ from $\sigma = \prod_{i=1}^{c} \sigma_{s_i}^{\nu_i}$ and $\sigma_{s_i} = (H(W_{s_i}) \cdot u^{m_{s_i}})^{SK}$ because he does not know the SK. The attacker also cannot recover m_{s_i} from $u^{m_{s_i}}$ even if SK is leaked due to the user's negligence. Otherwise, the attacker can solve the discrete logarithm problem. On the other hand, CSP randomly selects r and calculates $\gamma = h(R) = h(e(u, PK)^r)$. Here γ is used to hide μ' to prevent data leakage. A malicious adversary obtains μ without knowing r, trying to obtain m_{s_i} from μ, which is equivalent to solving the discrete logarithm problem. Moreover, an attacker can get the random number r and recover μ' from μ. ν_i is known, and $\mu' = \sum_{i=1}^{c} \nu_i \cdot m_{s_i}$ is a C-Variables linear equation. This equation has infinite solutions m_{s_i}. Therefore, the attacker also cannot obtain data information from the *prove*. To sum up, our scheme satisfies the property of privacy preserving.

Theorem 3. *The proposed scheme satisfies the property of automatic auditing, public auditability, and collaborative auditing.*

Proof. Only when the CSP generates challenge set and proof within the specified time can it pass the verification. We replace the semi-honest TPA to complete the audit with a smart contract that comes with consensus property. The proofs and results of the audits are stored publicly. The CSP in our scenario uses the latest information on the blockchain to generate a set of challenges. If the adversary wants to control the generation of a set of challenges, it needs to change the blockchain information. It is not possible to tamper with the information on the blockchain unless more than 51% of the nodes in the entire blockchain network are malicious. However, the cost of this tampering differs significantly from the value derived from the act of tampering.

4   Performance Evaluation

4.1   Functionality Comparisons

Table 1 shows the functional comparison of the five schemes, consisting of Wang et al.'s scheme [9], Wang et al.'s scheme [17], Xu et al.'s scheme [13], Fan et al.'s scheme [18] and our scheme.

All schemes guarantee probabilistic audit for reducing the resource cost of the audit process. Wang et al.'s scheme [9] uses the TPA to audit, and users interact with CSP through the TPA. Wang et al.'s scheme [9] cannot provide privacy protection because the unreliability of TPA is not considered. Besides Wang et al.'s scheme [9], smart contracts are used to replace the audit role of TPA in other schemes. The essence of the smart contract is a piece of written code. Once the smart contract is successfully deployed on the blockchain, no one can change it.

Only our scheme and the Wang et al.'s scheme [17] can reach automatic auditing, which enables regular auditing mode by setting up the specific details of the smart contract. Although the Fan et al.'s scheme [18] also generates challenge elements from smart contracts, CSP needs further calculates the set of challenges. This does not generate a challenge set in one step. In our scheme, the CSP generates their challenge set and proofs to save interactive challenge communication costs. Further, our scheme uses collaborative auditing to reduce individual audit costs and increase efficiency. Trusted users evaluated by the EigenTrust model cooperate to mitigate wasted audit resources.

Table 1. Comparisons between several schemes

Scheme	Probabilistic audit	No semi-honest TPA	Fair arbitration	Automatic auditing	Collaboration audit
[9]	√	×	×	×	×
[13]	√	√	√	×	×
[18]	√	√	√	×	×
[17]	√	√	√	√	×
Our	√	√	√	√	√

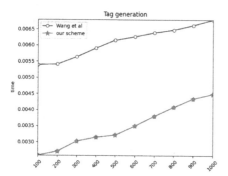

Fig. 2. The comparison of tag generation

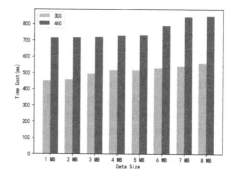

Fig. 3. Computation costs of proof generation (300 and 460 challenged blocks)

4.2 Implementation

To comprehensively evaluate the performance of our scheme, we conduct an experimental evaluation. We perform on a computer with Intel(R) Core(TM) i7-10710U, CPU 1.1 GHz, and 4 GB RAM on the Ubuntu system. The prototype is based on an existing open-source project called the pairing-based cryptography (PBC) library.

As is shown in Fig. 2, we compare the time spent in the tag generation phase of our scheme and Wang et al.'s scheme [17] is compared. The scenario we set up corresponds to tag generation times in the case of equal file sizes. Because in this scheme, users who have reached cooperation can generate labels of their own data blocks at the same time. Compared with the scheme of Wang et al., when CSP stores the same amount of data, the time of label generation in this scheme can be reduced about half. Our scheme performs best when the number of blocks of generated labels is 500, with a time of 0.0032s.

Figure 3 shows the comparison of proof generation time under the influence of two different tampered data detection criteria. A common standard is to detect with 95% probability when each set of random challenge data blocks is 300. Another higher standard requires that tampering be prevented with a 99% probability when the evidence contains 460 blocks of data. As shown in Fig. 3, with the continuous increase of data block capacity, it is proved that the time cost of generation increases gently under the standards of 300 and 460, and the gap between the two is less than 40%.

5   Conclusion

The combination of cloud servers and blockchain is the trend of future development and a remedy to solve the problem of secure data storage for public audits. In this paper, we propose a multi-user public audit scheme based on the EigenTrust model. In our scheme, high-quality users are obtained through a reputation model to improve the efficiency and security of subsequent collaborative audits. Using smart contracts instead of traditional third-party auditors improves auditing while circumventing the disadvantages of smart contracts that are unsuitable for multiple interactions. This scheme is based on the security of the Ethereum mechanism, and the experimental results also show the scheme's effectiveness. The scheme proposed in this paper aims to provide an efficient and economic audit framework for static data based on blockchain. However, the common audit of dynamic data based blockchain is rarely discussed. For dynamic data management methods on the cloud, it is often infeasible to put them on the blockchain because of capacity problems. Therefore, an efficient, economical, and safe storage audit of dynamic data based on blockchain is our future work.

Acknowledgements. This work is supported in part by the National Social Science Fund of China (No. 21XTQ015), the Natural Science Foundation of Fujian Province of China under Grant (Nos. 2019J01752, 2020J01905, 2020J01814); Science and Technology Project of Putian City (No. 2021R4001-10); and the presidential research fund of Minnan Normal University (No. KJ18024).

References

1. He, Q., Li, Z., Zhang, X.: Study on cloud storage system based on distributed storage systems. In: International Conference on Computational and Information Sciences, Chengdu, pp. 1332–1335. IEEE (2010)

2. Hashem, I.A.T., Yaqoob, I., Anuar, N.B., Mokhtar, S., Gani, A., Khan, S.U.: The rise of "big data" on cloud computing: review and open research issues. Inf. Syst. **47**, 98–115 (2015)
3. Singh, A., Chatterjee, K.: Cloud security issues and challenges: a survey. J. Netw. Comput. Appl. **79**, 88–115 (2017)
4. Kandukuri, B.R., Rakshit, A., et al.: Cloud security issues. In: 2009 IEEE International Conference on Services Computing, Chengdu, pp. 517–520. IEEE (2009)
5. Wang, C., Ren, K., Lou, W.: Toward publicly auditable secure cloud data storage services. IEEE Netw. **24**(4), 19–24 (2010)
6. Katz, J., Lindell, A.Y.: Aggregate message authentication codes. In: Malkin, T. (ed.) CT-RSA 2008. LNCS, vol. 4964, pp. 155–169. Springer, Heidelberg (2008). https://doi.org/10.1007/978-3-540-79263-5_10
7. Liu, B., Lu, J., Yip, J.: XML data integrity based on concatenated hash function. arXiv preprint arXiv:0906.3772 (2009)
8. Ateniese, G., Burns, R., Curtmola, R., et al.: Provable data possession at untrusted stores. In: Proceedings of the 14th ACM Conference on Computer and Communications Security, pp. 598–609. ACM, New York (2007)
9. Cong, W., Chow, S.S.M., Qian, W., Ren, K., Lou, W.: Privacy-preserving public auditing for secure cloud storage. IEEE Trans. Comput. **62**(2), 362–375 (2011)
10. Wang, B., Li, B., Hui, L.: Oruta: privacy-preserving public auditing for shared data in the cloud. IEEE Trans. Cloud Comput. **2**(1), 43–56 (2014)
11. Yang, K., Jia, X.: An efficient and secure dynamic auditing protocol for data storage in cloud computing. IEEE Trans. Parallel Distrib. Syst. **24**(9), 1717–1726 (2012)
12. Huang, L., Zhang, G., Yu, S., Fu, A., Yearwood, J.: SeShare: secure cloud data sharing based on blockchain and public auditing. Concurr. Comput. Pract. Exp. **31**(22), e4359 (2012)
13. Xu, Y., Ren, J., Zhang, Y., Zhang, C., Shen, B., Zhang, Y.: Blockchain empowered arbitrable data auditing scheme for network storage as a service. IEEE Trans. Serv. Comput. **13**(2), 289–300 (2019)
14. Yu, Y., Li, Y., Yang, B., Susilo, W., Yang, G., Bai, J.: Attribute-based cloud data integrity auditing for secure outsourced storage. IEEE Trans. Emerg. Top. Comput. **8**(2), 377–390 (2020)
15. Xue, J., Xu, C., Zhao, J., et al.: Identity-based public auditing for cloud storage systems against malicious auditors via blockchain. Sci. China Inf. Sci. **62**(3), 1–16 (2019)
16. Nakamoto, S.: Bitcoin: a peer-to-peer electronic cash system (2008). https://bitcoin.org/bitcoin.pdf. Accessed 1 July 2015
17. Wang, H., Qin, H., Zhao, M., Wei, X., Shen, H., Susilo, W.: Blockchain-based fair payment smart contract for public cloud storage auditing. Inf. Sci. **519**, 348–362 (2020)
18. Fan, K., Bao, Z., Liu, M., Vasilakos, A.V., Shi, W.: Dredas: decentralized, reliable and efficient remote outsourced data auditing scheme with blockchain smart contract for industrial IoT. Futur. Gener. Comput. Syst. **110**, 665–674 (2020)
19. Zhang, C., Xu, Y., Hu, Y., et al.: A blockchain-based multi-cloud storage data auditing scheme to locate faults. IEEE Trans. Cloud Comput. (2021) https://doi.org/10.1109/TCC.2021.3057771. Early access 8 Feb 2021
20. Li, A., Tian, G., Miao, M., Gong, J.: Blockchain-based cross-user data shared auditing. Connect. Sci. **34**(1), 83–103 (2022)
21. Kamvar, S.D., Schlosser, M.T., Garcia-Molina, H.: The EigenTrust algorithm for reputation management in P2P networks. In: Proceedings of the 12th International Conference on World Wide Web, pp. 640–651. ACM, New York (2003)

Attack and Defense Techniques

High Quality Audio Adversarial Examples Without Using Psychoacoustics

Wei Zong[(✉)], Yang-Wai Chow[ⓘ], and Willy Susilo[ⓘ]

Institute of Cybersecurity and Cryptology (iC2), School of Computing and
Information Technology, University of Wollongong, Wollongong, NSW, Australia
wz630@uowmail.edu.au, {caseyc,wsusilo}@uow.edu.au

Abstract. In the automatic speech recognition (ASR) domain, most, if
not all, current audio AEs are generated by applying perturbations to
input audio. Adversaries either constrain norm of the perturbations or
hide perturbations below the hearing threshold based on psychoacoustics.
These two approaches have their respective problems: norm-constrained
perturbations will introduce noticeable noise while hiding perturbations
below the hearing threshold can be prevented by deliberately removing inaudible components from audio. In this paper, we present a novel
method of generating targeted audio AEs. The perceptual quality of
our audio AEs are significantly better compared to audio AEs generated by applying norm-constrained perturbations. Furthermore, unlike
approaches that rely on psychoacoustics to hide perturbations below the
hearing threshold, we show that our audio AEs can still be successfully
generated even when inaudible components are removed from audio.

Keywords: Audio adversarial examples · Automatic speech
recognition · Deep learning · Machine learning

1 Introduction

These days, deep learning techniques are becoming increasingly popular as they
have achieved tremendous success across many domains, such as image recognition [20], automatic speech recognition (ASR) [5,13], natural language processing
(NLP) [6], and so on. However, deep learning models are vulnerable to adversarial examples (AEs), which were first defined in the image recognition domain
[17]. Given a correctly classified benign (normal) image, an image AE is generated by adding small or even imperceptible perturbations to the benign image,
such that the resulting AE will mislead or fool a target model into misclassifying
the image.

Research interest on AEs has extended to the ASR domain. In initial work
on audio AEs, Cisse et al. [3] proposed a novel loss function, called Houdini,
for generating AEs. However, when used for audio AEs, the limitation was that
the method required input audio to phonetically resemble the target adversarial

X. Chen et al. (Eds.): CSS 2022, LNCS 13547, pp. 163–177, 2022.
https://doi.org/10.1007/978-3-031-18067-5_12

phrase. In other work, Carlini and Wagner [1] applied maximum norm constrained perturbations to benign audio to generate audio AEs that could be transcribed into arbitrary target phrases. Although perturbations in their AEs are generally quiet, there is still some noticeable noise. Qin et al. [14] argued that psychoacoustics should be incorporated to improve the quality of audio AEs. They proposed a masking loss function to hide perturbations in the masking threshold of input audio.

However, although audio AEs generated using psychoacoustics can successfully hide perturbations in the masking threshold, research has shown that in doing so the power of perturbations may actually increase [19]. In fact, a recent study by Eisenhofer et al. [4] proposed the deliberate removal of inaudible parts from audio based on psychoacoustics to prevent adversaries from hiding perturbations in the masking threshold. In that sense, methods which hide perturbations below hearing thresholds will fail to converge.

This paper investigates the generation of audio AEs using a novel method that is not based on applying perturbations to input audio. The resulting audio AEs are targeted attacks, which mean they are transcribed by an ASR model into predetermined target phrases. We call our method adversarial convolution, because it is based on the convolution operation. We also propose a regularization term that theoretically and empirically lowers the power of noise to improve the quality of the resulting audio AEs. This new line of attack aims to inspire further development in ASR security. Our main contributions are summarized as follows:

- Unlike other audio AE generation techniques that are based on adding perturbations to input audio, we propose a novel approach of using convolution operations with an impulse response with different weights for generating audio AEs.
- We theoretically and empirically show that decreasing power of input audio improves the quality of our audio AEs, because the power of noise is decreased.
- Compared with the state-of-the-art audio AEs proposed by Carlini and Wagner [1], which are generated via applying norm-constrained perturbations, the perceptual quality of our audio AEs are significantly better in terms of their PESQ results.
- We show that temporal dependency (TD) detection [21], which was proposed as an effective method to detect audio AEs, performs poorly on detecting our audio AEs.
- Our audio AEs can be successfully generated when inaudible components from audio are deliberately removed and the number of queries is limited. In contrast, the generation of audio AEs by Qin et al. [14], which hides perturbations below hearing thresholds, fail to converge when inaudible components from audio are removed.

2   Related Work

Carlini and Wagner [1] proposed a method of generating targeted audio AEs, which could be transcribed into arbitrary target phrases via applying max norm constrained perturbations. DeepSpeech was the target ASR model used in their research. A drawback of their method is that perturbations are applied to all input audio samples, so noise is apparent in audio sections that are relatively quiet. A potential solution to this can be found in recent work by Li et al. [9], in which they performed a preliminary study on injecting multiple short perturbations into audio to generate audio AEs. Nevertheless, it should be mentioned that this work focused on fooling automatic speaker verification and speech command recognition models, instead of ASR models [9].

Compared to limiting the norm of perturbations, it is better to incorporate psychoacoustics to constrain perturbations [14,16]. In particular, Qin et al. [14] split the generation process into two stages. During the first stage, they generated audio AEs using the same method as in [1]. Then, they used a masking loss function for minimization during the second stage. Minimizing the masking loss has the effect of making perturbations imperceptible. Similarly, Schöenherr et al. [16] used the MP3 compression mechanism to make adversarial perturbation imperceptible.

Nonetheless, a recent study proposed a defense method based on the removal of inaudible components from audio using psychoacoustics [4]. The purpose of this deliberate removal is so that adversaries can no longer hide perturbations in the masking threshold. As such, the audio AE generation methods, which hide perturbations below the hearing threshold, either fail to converge or generate audio AEs with audible noise. Their experiments showed that the removal of inaudible components from audio effectively defended the audio AEs by [16], which used MP3 compression mechanism to hide perturbations.

3   Problem Definition

In this research, we explore the generation of targeted audio AEs. Given a benign audio x, we generate x' by modifying x such that x' is perceived to be semantically the same as x by humans. In addition, x' will fool a target ASR model into outputting a predetermined target phrase. Formally, if $y = f(x)$, where y is the transcript of the original unmodified audio and $f(\cdot)$ represents the ASR model, we want $y' = f(x')$, where y' is the target phrase and $y' \neq y$.

3.1   Threat Model and Assumptions

In this study, we assume a white-box threat model, which is similar to most prior work [1,9,11,14]. Under this threat model, an adversary has full access to a target ASR model's architecture, weights, etc. In addition, this means that gradients of the loss function with respect to input audio can be calculated explicitly.

While a white-box threat model may not be practical when it comes to commercial products, as companies do not generally release the inner workings of their products, recent studies [2,8] have shown that adversaries can train a surrogate model that is similar to the target model. Adversaries can then generate white-box audio AEs using the surrogate model and use these to attack the target model.

3.2 Evaluation Metrics

In the ASR domain, there is no unified agreement on the metrics to evaluate the quality of audio AEs. For example, Carlini and Wagner [1] measured distortion in decibels (dB) by defining their own function, while Signal-to-Noise Ratio (SNR) has been used in other work [11,22]. Furthermore, other metrics like hearing thresholds and frequency masking, which only apply to the specific methods being investigated in other work [14,16], have also been used. In this research, we use the following standard metrics in the field to measure the quality of our audio AEs.

Signal-to-Noise Ratio (SNR). SNR is a means of ascertaining the power of noise introduced by distortion. Larger SNR values indicate less distortion. The formula is given as follows:

$$SNR = 10\log_{10}\frac{P_s}{P_n}, \tag{1}$$

where P_s is the power of the original audio signal and P_n is the power of the distortion.

Perceptual Evaluation of Speech Quality (PESQ). PESQ was originally proposed as an automatic evaluation metric for measuring speech degradation in the context of telephony [15]. PESQ values range from 1.0 to 4.5, with higher values representing better quality. Although this metric was not designed to be a universal measurement, experimental results show that PESQ values aligned with the perception of our audio AEs.

4   Method

In this section, we present our proposed method for generating audio AEs.

4.1   Adversarial Convolution

Let $\theta \in \mathbb{R}^L$ be a vector representing parameters to optimize, $x \in \mathbb{R}^N$ be a benign audio with $||x||_\infty \leq 1$, $r \in \mathbb{R}^M$ be an impulse response and t be a target phrase. It is required that $L = M + N - 1$. The generation of audio AEs can be formulated as solving the following optimization problem:

$$\underset{\theta}{\text{minimize}}\ \ell_{adv}(g_\theta(x,r),t) + \lambda\ell_{reg}(\theta)$$
$$\text{such that: } f(g_\theta(x,r)) = t, \tag{2}$$

where $g_\theta(x, r)$ is a function to modify x using r parameterized by θ, $\ell_{adv}(\cdot)$ is the loss function of the target ASR model and $f(\cdot)$ is the target ASR model. Minimizing $\ell_{adv}(\cdot)$ causes the modified audio to be misclassified as the target phrase t. The $\ell_{reg}(\theta)$ term is used for regularizing θ with λ as its weight. Regularization is discussed in the next subsection. $g_\theta(x, r)$ is defined as follows:

$$g_\theta(x, r)[n] \triangleq \sum_{i=0}^{L-1} [x * (\theta'_i \cdot r)][n] \cdot \Delta_i[n], \tag{3}$$

where θ'_i is the clamped i^{th} element of θ, and $*$ denotes the convolution operation. θ'_i is defined as: $\theta'_i \triangleq \max(\alpha, \min(\beta, \theta_i))$, where $\alpha, \beta \in \mathbb{R}$ are predefined constants. $\Delta_i[n]$ is a shifted Dirac delta function $\delta[n]$ with its domain limited to $\{0, 1, \ldots, L-1\}$. Specifically, $\Delta_i[n] = \delta[n-i]$ for $n \in \{0, 1, \ldots, L-1\}$, where $\delta[n]$ $(n \in \mathbb{Z})$ is defined as:

$$\delta[n] \triangleq \begin{cases} 1, \text{for } n = 0 \\ 0, \text{for } n \neq 0 \end{cases} \tag{4}$$

Equation 3 results in a vector of length $M + N - 1$, since x and r are both of finite-length. The length of θ is the same as the convolution result, because $L = M + N - 1$ as defined above. As illustrated in Fig. 1, $g_\theta(x, r)$ performs a convolution between x and r, L times, with r being multiplied by the clamped θ_i each time. This results in L vectors where one element from each vector is extracted by $\Delta_i[n]$ to form the final output.

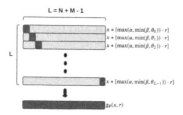

Fig. 1. $g_\theta(x, r)$ is equivalent to extracting one element per convolution among multiple convolution results. The impulse response is weighted by a different value for each convolution operation.

It should be noted that, to be a valid audio, $g_\theta(x, r)$ is implicitly constrained by $\|g_\theta(x, r)\|_\infty \leq 1$. Thus, elements of $g_\theta(x, r)$ are clipped into the range $[-1, 1]$ before further processing. In practice, by constraining θ and using appropriate x and r, elements of $g_\theta(x, r)$ will already be within $[-1, 1]$ prior to clipping. For conciseness, we omit this implicit constraint in this paper.

To accelerate computation, Eq. 3 can be calculated as:

$$\begin{aligned} g_\theta(x, r) &= (x * r) \cdot \theta' \\ &= \mathcal{F}^{-1}\{\mathcal{F}\{x\} \cdot \mathcal{F}\{r\}\} \cdot \theta', \end{aligned} \tag{5}$$

where $\mathcal{F}$ and $\mathcal{F}^{-1}$ are the Fourier transform and inverse Fourier transform, respectively. They can be calculated efficiently via the fast Fourier transform algorithm. It should be mentioned that to lower the convolution boundary effects and to make the output length the same as the input, M is required to be an odd number and only the middle N elements of output are kept.

To generate audio AEs that are perceived to be semantically the same as their original counterparts, we must ensure that the convolution between x and r results in audio that is perceived to be the same as x. How to appropriately choose r will be discussed later.

4.2   Regularization

Let us first discuss the intuition behind designing the regularization term $\ell_{reg}(\theta)$. We do not consider maximizing PESQ directly, because PESQ was originally designed for evaluating quality degradation in the context of telephony. Thus, maximizing PESQ directly via gradient ascent does not necessarily improve the quality of audio AEs, even though our experiments showed that PESQ aligns well with the perception of our audio AEs.

Instead, we attempt to maximize SNR, because SNR is a measurement that universally evaluates the power of noise in a signal. It should be noted that SNR measures the overall power of noise, so improving SNR does not necessarily improve the quality of audio AEs either. However, PESQ can be calculated during the generation process, and if PESQ and SNR both improve, this gives an indication that minimizing $\ell_{reg}(\theta)$ improves the quality of audio AEs. In a nutshell, minimizing $\ell_{reg}(\theta)$ should maximize SNR, while PESQ is calculated to indicate whether the perceptual speech quality of audio AEs has really improved. Our experimental results show that SNR and PESQ indeed align with each other when minimizing $\ell_{reg}(\theta)$.

To simplify analysis, we assume that θ is bounded within $[\alpha, \beta]$ such that $\theta = \theta'$. We also assume that convolution between x and r does not impair its perception. Distortion in audio AEs, which does impair their perception, then comes from variations in elements of θ. This is because when $\theta_i = c$, where $c \in [\alpha, \beta]$ and $i \in [0, L-1]$, we have $g_\theta(x, r) = c \cdot (x * r)$, so that $g_\theta(x, r)$ is equivalent to multiplying $x * r$ by a scalar. If we can decrease the variation in θ, SNR is expected to increase.

Theorem 1. *Let $c \in [\alpha, \beta]$ be a constant and $\eta \in \mathbb{R}_{>0}$ with $c - \eta, c + \eta \in [\alpha, \beta]$. Let θ^η denote a vector whose elements are i.i.d. random variables: $\theta_i^\eta \sim \mathcal{U}(c - \eta, c + \eta)$. Let x and r be random vectors such that $(x * r)_i$ are i.i.d. random variables with $\mathbb{E}[(x * r)_i^2] \neq 0$. $SNR(s, s') = 10 \log_{10} \frac{P_s}{P_{s'-s}}$ calculates SNR by comparing a real signal s with its distorted version s'. Then, $SNR(g_{\theta^0}(x, r), g_{\theta^\eta}(x, r)) = 10 \log_{10} \frac{3c^2}{\eta^2}$, where $g_\theta(x, r)$ is defined in Eq. 3.*

Considering $g_{\theta^0}(x, r)$ as the undistorted audio, Theorem 1 demonstrates that SNR of $g_{\theta^\eta}(x, r)$ is a decreasing function of $\eta \in \mathbb{R}_{>0}$. In addition, SNR of $g_{\theta^\eta}(x, r)$ does not depend on the contents of x and r.

Assuming that θ_i, in Eq. 3, are i.i.d. random variables uniformly distributed in $[\alpha, \beta]$, from Theorem 1 we know that SNR of audio AEs are higher if we consider $c \cdot (x * r)$ as the undistorted audio and bound θ_i within a smaller range around c. Considering $c \cdot (x * r)$ as the undistorted audio, instead of x, is reasonable because it is not necessary for audio AEs to be acoustically indistinguishable from their original counterparts, and $g_\theta(x, r) = c \cdot (x * r)$ when there are no variations in θ. Intuitively, bounding θ_i within a small range is preferred as it would let samples in the output audio be generated by similarly weighted r. When $\theta_i = c$ for all i, then SNR will be $+\infty$.

Based on the above discussion, we define $\ell_{reg}(\theta)$ as a hinge loss as follows:

$$\ell_{reg}(\theta) \triangleq \sum_{i=0}^{L-1} max(|\theta_i - c| - \eta, 0), \tag{6}$$

where θ_i is the ith element of θ, $c \in [\alpha, \beta]$ is a predefined constant, and $\eta \in \mathbb{R}_{>0}$ is a variable such that $c - \eta, c + \eta \in [\alpha, \beta]$. Minimizing $\ell_{reg}(\theta)$ causes all θ_i to be bounded around c by η. If all θ_i are bounded and uniformly distributed, then smaller η leads to larger SNR according to Theorem 1. It should be mentioned that a trade-off exists in that a lower η value will make it more difficult to generate audio AEs, since the constraint is stronger. In practice, we initially set η to a relatively large value and gradually decrease it.

4.3   Impulse Response

As previously discussed, the key requirement for choosing r is to make sure the convolution between x and r results in audio that is perceived to be semantically the same as x. If we only consider this criterion, r can potentially be a room impulse response, an impulse response of low-pass filters, etc. In the following, we will show a strategy to select r that can improve the quality of audio AEs by reducing the power of noise.

Corollary 1. *Let $c \in [\alpha, \beta]$ be a constant and $\eta \in \mathbb{R}_{>0}$ be a variable, where $c - \eta, c + \eta \in [\alpha, \beta]$. Let θ^η denote a vector whose elements are i.i.d. random variables: $\theta_i^\eta \sim \mathcal{U}(c - \eta, c + \eta)$. Let x and r be random vectors such that $(x * r)_i$ are i.i.d. random variables with $\mathbb{E}[(x * r)_i^2] \neq 0$. Let $D_{\theta^\eta}(x, r) = g_{\theta^\eta}(x, r) - g_{\theta^0}(x, r)$, where $g_\theta(x, r)$ is defined in Eq. 3. Then, the power of $D_{\theta^\eta}(x, r)$ decreases if the power of $g_{\theta^0}(x, r)$ decreases when c and η are fixed.*

In Corollary 1, $D_{\theta^\eta}(x, r)$ represents noise if we consider $g_{\theta^\eta}(x, r)$ to be the distorted $g_{\theta^0}(x, r)$. Corollary 1 shows that we can lower the power of noise by lowering the power in $x * r$. This can easily be proven, since Theorem 1 shows that the ratio between the power of $g_{\theta^0}(x, r)$ and $D_{\theta^\eta}(x, r)$ is fixed when c and η are fixed.

In this research, the input audio is human speech, so a large amount of power is usually concentrated in its low frequency components. It is a well-known fact that speech filtered by a high-pass filter with a small cutoff frequency can still be correctly perceived. Therefore, it is better to choose r as an impulse response of a high-pass filter with a small cutoff frequency. In this manner, we can remove power from $x * r$ without impairing its perception, hence, decreasing the power of noise in audio AEs. In general, this will result in better quality audio AEs.

4.4   Two-Stage Generation Process

The regularization in Eq. 6 tries to constrain θ to be within a small range, which empirically makes the generation difficult if η is small. Thus, we split the generation process into 2 stages. Stage 1 generates an initial audio AE with low quality, which is followed by stage 2 that focuses on improving the quality.

During stage 1, η from Eq. 6 is initialized to a relatively large value with $c + \eta \in [\alpha, \beta]$. Instead of using a fixed learning rate, we adaptively change the learning rate to accelerate convergence. Stage 1 concludes when the transcript matches the target phrase. At the beginning of stage 2, the learning rate is fixed at a small value. If the audio AE's transcript successively matches the target phrase, η decreases. The audio AE with the highest SNR value is returned as the final result.

5   Experimental Results

This section presents experimental results of our proposed generation method.

5.1   Setup

Similar to previous research on audio AEs [1,16,18], we used DeepSpeech [5] as the target ASR model for our experiments. More specifically, we used Deep-Speech 0.8.2 implemented by Mozilla[1], which is the latest release at the time of writing. The LibriSpeech [12] dataset was used to generate the audio AEs as Mozilla released a pre-trained model for this dataset. In addition, the open source PESQ implementation[2] was used in wide band mode to evaluate the perceptual quality of speech in the resulting audio AEs. The experiments were conducted on a computer with 16G RAM, an Intel i7-8750H CPU and an Nvidia GeForce GTX 1060 graphic card.

All experiments, if not otherwise indicated, were based on the following settings. We used 801 taps for the impulse responses and fixed α and β in Eq. 3 as -1.0 and 3.0. θ was initialized as a vector of 1s. λ in Eq. 2 was set to 0.2. The initial learning rate was set to $1e^{-2}$ and adaptively increased to its maximum value of $1e^{-1}$ if the transcript did not change for some iterations. At the beginning of stage 2, the learning rate was fixed at $1e^{-3}$. In Eq. 6, c was set to 1.0, which caused θ_i to be bounded around 1. η was initially set to 0.2 and adaptively decreased during stage 2 via being multiplied by 0.8. The Adam method [7] was used for optimization.

---

[1] https://github.com/mozilla/DeepSpeech.

[2] https://github.com/ludlows/python-pesq.

5.2   Regularization

We first demonstrate the ideal scenario by sampling each element of θ from an uniform distribution $\mathcal{U}(1 - \eta, 1 + \eta)$. We used $g_\theta(x, r)$ to transform an audio with r as the impulse response of high-pass filters with cutoff frequencies of 100 Hz, 200 Hz, 300 Hz and 400 Hz. A cutoff frequency that is too large would significantly decrease the quality. Thus, 400 Hz is the largest cutoff frequency we consider in this research. Figure 2 presents the average SNR and PESQ results of 50 randomly selected audio. Figure 2a shows that SNR increases as η decreases. This is expected since smaller η leads to larger SNR as discussed above. Figure 2b compares PESQ of audio filtered using different cutoff frequencies. We can see that larger cutoff frequencies generally result in higher PESQ values, while PESQ of non-filtered audio is the lowest. As previously discussed, this is because filters with larger cutoff frequencies remove more power from audio, such that the power of noise decreases.

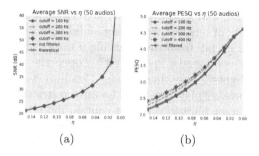

(a)   (b)

Fig. 2. Average SNR and PESQ results for 50 audio. In general, SNR and PESQ values increase as η decreases and larger cutoff frequencies lead to higher PESQ values. (a) SNR results; (b) PESQ results.

To examine the actual effect of our strategy, we show the SNR and PESQ trends obtained from two audio samples that underwent the generation process using a 400 Hz cutoff frequency in Fig. 3. It can be seen that the SNR and PESQ trends correlated with one another throughout the generation process. After stage 2 begins, which is indicated by the vertical green bar in each figure, η is gradually decreased so that θ is encouraged to be within a smaller range around 1. From the figures, we can see that both SNR and PESQ values significantly increase despite some fluctuations. This implies that our strategy of minimizing the regularization term $\ell_{reg}(\theta)$ during stage 2 does indeed increase the quality of the resulting audio AEs.

5.3   Adversarial Example Generation

In this experiment, we generated 50 audio AEs using a high-pass filter with a 400 Hz cutoff frequency. We randomly selected input audio with a duration

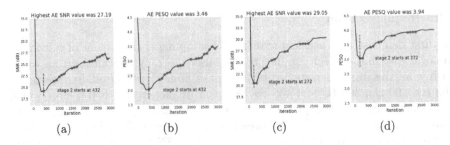

Fig. 3. SNR and PESQ values decrease during stage 1 and increase during stage 2. The red dots indicate iterations where audio AEs were successfully generated. Transcript of the original audio for (a) and (b) was "it's a stock company and rich", the target phrase was "open the door". Transcript of the original audio for (c) and (d) was "he knows them both", the target phrase was "power off". (Color figure online)

between 2 and 4 s from the "test-clean" set. According to the report in [9], audio commands in the real world are not long. Thus, it is enough to demonstrate practical threats of our methods using audio with length 2 to 4 s. Target phrases were selected evenly from the following 9 target phrases that represent potentially malicious commands: "power off", "open the door", "visit danger dot com", "turn off lights", "use silent mode", "call my wife", "navigate to my home", "take a picture", "play music". The only restriction placed on target phrases was that a target phrase could not contain more letters than the input audio's transcript. This is because it is overly challenging to make a short audio clip be incorrectly transcribed by an ASR model into a much longer phrase.

We ran the generation for 5,000 iterations, which was the same as in [1]. The initial success rate of our UAAE generation process was 96%, where 2 audio AEs failed to generate. We then increased the initial value of η from 0.2 to 0.3, and re-ran the two failed cases. The success rate then increased to 100%.

Table 1. Comparison between our audio AEs and audio AEs based on [1].

	Our audio AE	Audio AE [1]
Iterations	5,000	5,000
Success rate	100%	100%
Median PESQ	3.11	2.62

To compare our audio AEs with audio AEs produced using the method proposed by Carlini and Wagner [1], we implemented their method of adding max norm constrained perturbations to input audio. Using their method, we generated 50 audio AEs using the same set of input audio and target phrases that were used in the generation of our audio AEs. Results comparing our audio AEs with audio AEs based on [1] are presented in Table 1. The table shows that the median PESQ of our audio AEs is significantly better than the audio AEs in [1], an overall improvement of greater than 18%. This indicates the better perceptual quality of our AEs. A potential explanation for this is that our audio AEs are generated by multiplying audio samples with a vector, as shown in Eq. 5. Samples with small values will remain small, because elements of θ are encouraged to be bounded around 1. This is in contrast to the audio AEs based on [1], where perturbations are applied in a non-selective manner. As such, noise in relatively quiet sections are generally more audible, which adversely affects the overall quality of the audio AEs.

5.4 Robustness

In this section, we first present and discuss experimental results regarding robustness of our audio AEs against temporal dependency (TD) detection. We then show that our audio AEs can still be successfully generated when inaudible components of input audio are deliberately removed.

Table 2. Detection of our audio AEs using temporal dependency. Results for AEs based on [1] are in the parentheses.

	WER	CER	LCP
$k = 1/2$	0.667 (0.771)	0.424 (0.438)	0.678 (0.747)
$k = 2/3$	0.693 (0.632)	0.424 (0.380)	0.750 (0.695)
$k = 3/4$	0.673 (0.703)	0.484 (0.510)	0.810 (0.842)
$k = 4/5$	0.593 (0.702)	0.397 (0.412)	0.766 (0.840)
$k = 5/6$	0.703 (0.718)	0.455 (0.415)	0.769 (0.807)

Temporal Dependency Detection. TD was proposed by Yang et al. [21] as an important property to detect audio AEs. The key assumption is that benign audio preserves TD, while audio AEs do not. Their experimental results showed that TD was effective to detect audio AEs proposed by [1]. We used the TD method to try to detect our audio AEs from Sect. 5.3. Detection method was based on the same metrics as [21]: word error rate (WER), character error rate (CER) and the longest common prefix (LCP). Table 2 shows that our audio AEs are robust against TD detection, as indicated by the low AUC scores. In comparison, the audio AEs by [1] are also robust against TD detection, which appears to contradict the conclusion in [21].

Nevertheless, we suggest that this is due to a major change in DeepSpeech's architecture compared to the version used by Yang et al. [21]. Specifically, the version used in [21] was a biRNN based model, while the recent version used in this paper has replaced the biRNN with LSTM, which is not bidirectional. This means that the prediction of hidden states only depends on previous hidden states. Therefore, it is reasonable that audio AEs will preserve temporal dependency if we truncate the input audio from the beginning. This should explain why we obtained contradictory detection results for audio AEs by [1].

Table 3. Detection of our audio AEs using a modified temporal dependency method. Results for AEs based on [1] are in the parentheses.

	WER	CER	LCP
k = 1/2	0.762 (0.917)	0.654 (0.787)	0.788 (0.933)
k = 2/3	0.837 (0.883)	0.714 (0.815)	0.861 (0.902)
k = 3/4	0.812 (0.945)	0.767 (0.831)	0.882 (0.965)
k = 4/5	0.837 (0.978)	0.731 (0.867)	0.907 (0.970)
k = 5/6	0.904 (0.977)	0.752 (0.852)	0.903 (0.959)

Although this paper focuses on attacking ASR models, we propose a simple and effective method to empirically improve the current TD detection when the target model is not biRNN based. This will be beneficial for further study. Instead of truncating the input from the beginning, we discard the first 20 ms of input audio. This part normally does not contain meaningful utterances so it can be safely discarded. Results demonstrating the effectiveness of this modified TD detection method are shown in Table 3. We can see that the overall AE detection performance has greatly improved. Overall, our audio AEs are still robust against TD detection because the maximum AUC score achieved is only 0.907 while most AUC scores are below 0.9. A potential reason is that the values of samples at the beginning are normally small, as such, our generation method does not greatly modify them. Thus, discarding these samples does not significantly affect TD for our audio AEs.

Removal of Inaudible Components. Inspired by Eisenhofer et al. [4], we consider the scenario where the number of queries made by adversaries is limited to 1,000 and inaudible components of input audio are deliberately removed before audio is input to the ASR model. We used the method in [10] to calculate hearing thresholds given an input audio and remove inaudible components. We generated 30 audio AEs using our method with η initially set to 0.4 instead of 0.2. Again, the impulse response of a high-pass filter with a 400 Hz cutoff frequency was used. 30 audio AEs using the method proposed by Qin et al. [14] were generated for comparison. It should be mentioned that, Qin et al. [14] split the generation process into 2 stages. The first stage is identical to the method in [1] and stage 2 focuses on hiding perturbations below the hearing threshold while making audio AEs adversarial. Due to the number of queries being limited to 1,000, it is impractical to run the method by Carlini and Wagner [1] first and then run stage 2. Thus, we directly ran their stage 2 to generate audio AEs.

Table 4. Success rates of generating audio AEs with limited queries and inaudible components removed.

	Our audio AE	Audio AE [14]
1,000 queries	73.33%	80.00%
1,000 queries & removed*	60.00%	6.67%

*: the number of queries were limited to 1,000 and inaudible components of input audio were removed during preprocessing.

For reference, also we considered the case when inaudible components were not removed, where the number of queries were limited to 1,000. Experimental results are shown in Table 4. The results clearly show that the success rate of our method is slightly affected by removing the inaudible components, while the method by Qin et al. [14] mostly fails. This is as expected, because our method does not rely on psychoacoustics. Whereas adversarial perturbations based on [14] are easily destroyed if inaudible components are deliberately removed, because the method requires perturbations to be hidden below the hearing threshold.

6 Conclusion and Future Work

This paper proposes a novel method of generating high perceptual quality audio AEs without relying on the use of psychoacoustics. Experimental results show that PESQ of our audio AEs is significantly better than the state-of-the-art method in [1]. In the scenario where the number of queries is limited and inaudible components of input audio are deliberately removed, the generation of our audio AEs can still be successful, whereas the method in [14], which hides perturbations below the hearing threshold, fails to converge in most cases. In future work, we intend to examine whether our audio AEs can be modified to attack automatic speaker verification and speech command recognition models.

References

1. Carlini, N., Wagner, D.: Audio adversarial examples: targeted attacks on speech-to-text. In: 2018 IEEE Security and Privacy Workshops (SPW), pp. 1–7. IEEE (2018)
2. Chen, Y., et al.: Devil's whisper: a general approach for physical adversarial attacks against commercial black-box speech recognition devices. In: 29th USENIX Security Symposium (USENIX Security 2020) (2020)
3. Cisse, M., Adi, Y., Neverova, N., Keshet, J.: Houdini: fooling deep structured visual and speech recognition models with adversarial examples. In: Proceedings of the 31st International Conference on Neural Information Processing Systems, pp. 6980–6990 (2017)

4. Eisenhofer, T., Schönherr, L., Frank, J., Speckemeier, L., Kolossa, D., Holz, T.: Dompteur: taming audio adversarial examples. arXiv preprint arXiv:2102.05431 (2021)
5. Hannun, A., et al.: Deep speech: scaling up end-to-end speech recognition. arXiv preprint arXiv:1412.5567 (2014)
6. Jia, R., Liang, P.: Adversarial examples for evaluating reading comprehension systems. In: Palmer, M., Hwa, R., Riedel, S. (eds.) Proceedings of the 2017 Conference on Empirical Methods in Natural Language Processing, EMNLP 2017, Copenhagen, Denmark, 9–11 September 2017, pp. 2021–2031. Association for Computational Linguistics (2017)
7. Kingma, D.P., Ba, J.: Adam: a method for stochastic optimization. In: Bengio, Y., LeCun, Y. (eds.) 3rd International Conference on Learning Representations, ICLR 2015, San Diego, CA, USA, 7–9 May 2015, Conference Track Proceedings (2015)
8. Li, J., Qu, S., Li, X., Szurley, J., Kolter, J.Z., Metze, F.: Adversarial music: real world audio adversary against wake-word detection system. In: Advances in Neural Information Processing Systems, pp. 11931–11941 (2019)
9. Li, Z., Wu, Y., Liu, J., Chen, Y., Yuan, B.: AdvPulse: universal, synchronization-free, and targeted audio adversarial attacks via subsecond perturbations. In: Ligatti, J., Ou, X., Katz, J., Vigna, G. (eds.) CCS 2020: 2020 ACM SIGSAC Conference on Computer and Communications Security, Virtual Event, USA, 9–13 November 2020, pp. 1121–1134. ACM (2020)
10. Lin, Y., Abdulla, W.H.: Principles of psychoacoustics. In: Lin, Y., Abdulla, W.H. (eds.) Audio Watermark, pp. 15–49. Springer, Cham (2015). https://doi.org/10.1007/978-3-319-07974-5_2
11. Liu, X., Wan, K., Ding, Y., Zhang, X., Zhu, Q.: Weighted-sampling audio adversarial example attack. In: The Thirty-Fourth AAAI Conference on Artificial Intelligence, AAAI 2020, The Thirty-Second Innovative Applications of Artificial Intelligence Conference, IAAI 2020, The Tenth AAAI Symposium on Educational Advances in Artificial Intelligence, EAAI 2020, New York, NY, USA, 7–12 February 2020, pp. 4908–4915. AAAI Press (2020)
12. Panayotov, V., Chen, G., Povey, D., Khudanpur, S.: LibriSpeech: an ASR corpus based on public domain audio books. In: 2015 IEEE International Conference on Acoustics, Speech and Signal Processing (ICASSP), pp. 5206–5210. IEEE (2015)
13. Park, D.S., et al.: SpecAugment: a simple data augmentation method for automatic speech recognition. In: Kubin, G., Kacic, Z. (eds.) Interspeech 2019, 20th Annual Conference of the International Speech Communication Association, Graz, Austria, 15–19 September 2019, pp. 2613–2617. ISCA (2019)
14. Qin, Y., Carlini, N., Cottrell, G.W., Goodfellow, I.J., Raffel, C.: Imperceptible, robust, and targeted adversarial examples for automatic speech recognition. In: Proceedings of the 36th International Conference on Machine Learning, ICML 2019, Long Beach, California, USA, 9–15 June 2019, pp. 5231–5240 (2019)
15. Rix, A.W., Beerends, J.G., Hollier, M.P., Hekstra, A.P.: Perceptual evaluation of speech quality (PESQ)-a new method for speech quality assessment of telephone networks and codecs. In: IEEE International Conference on Acoustics, Speech, and Signal Processing, ICASSP 2001, Salt Palace Convention Center, Salt Lake City, Utah, USA, 7–11 May 2001, Proceedings, pp. 749–752. IEEE (2001)
16. Schönherr, L., Kohls, K., Zeiler, S., Holz, T., Kolossa, D.: Adversarial attacks against automatic speech recognition systems via psychoacoustic hiding. In: 26th Annual Network and Distributed System Security Symposium, NDSS 2019, San Diego, California, USA, 24–27 February 2019. The Internet Society (2019)

17. Szegedy, C., et al.: Intriguing properties of neural networks. In: Bengio, Y., LeCun, Y. (eds.) 2nd International Conference on Learning Representations, ICLR 2014, Banff, AB, Canada, 14–16 April 2014, Conference Track Proceedings (2014)
18. Taori, R., Kamsetty, A., Chu, B., Vemuri, N.: Targeted adversarial examples for black box audio systems. In: 2019 IEEE Security and Privacy Workshops (SPW), pp. 15–20. IEEE (2019)
19. Wang, Q., Guo, P., Xie, L.: Inaudible adversarial perturbations for targeted attack in speaker recognition. In: INTERSPEECH 2020 (2020)
20. Xie, Q., Luong, M., Hovy, E.H., Le, Q.V.: Self-training with noisy student improves ImageNet classification. In: 2020 IEEE/CVF Conference on Computer Vision and Pattern Recognition, CVPR 2020, Seattle, WA, USA, 13–19 June 2020, pp. 10684–10695. IEEE (2020)
21. Yang, Z., Li, B., Chen, P., Song, D.: Characterizing audio adversarial examples using temporal dependency. In: 7th International Conference on Learning Representations, ICLR 2019, New Orleans, LA, USA, 6–9 May 2019. OpenReview.net (2019)
22. Yuan, X., et al.: CommanderSong: a systematic approach for practical adversarial voice recognition. In: 27th USENIX Security Symposium (USENIX Security 2018), pp. 49–64 (2018)

Working Mechanism of Eternalblue and Its Application in Ransomworm

Zian Liu[1,3(✉)], Chao Chen[2], Leo Yu Zhang[4], and Shang Gao[4]

[1] Swinburne University of Technology, Hawthorn, VIC, Australia
zianliu@swin.edu.au
[2] Royal Melbourne Institute of Technology, Melbourne, VIC, Australia
[3] Data61, CSIRO, Sydney, Australia
[4] Deakin University, Geelong, VIC, Australia

Abstract. After the leaking of exploit Eternalblue, some ransomworms utilizing this exploit have been developed to sweep over the world in recent years. Ransomworm is a global growing threat as it blocks users' access to their files unless a ransom is paid by victims. Wannacry and Notpetya are two of those ransomworms which are responsible for the loss of millions of dollar, from crippling U.K. national systems to shutting down a Honda Motor Company in Japan. Many dynamic analytic papers on Wannacry were published, however, static analytic papers about Wannacry were limited. Our aim is to present readers an systematic knowledge about exploit Eternalblue, from a high– leveled semantic view to the code details. Specifically, the working mechanism of Eternalblue, the reverse engineering analysis of Eternalblue in Wannacry, and the comparison with the Metasploit's Eternalblue exploit are presented. The key finding of our analysis is that the code remains almost the same when Eternalblue is transplanted into Wannacry, which indicates its potential for signatures and thus detection.

Keywords: Cyber threat · Ransomworm · Static analysis · Wannacry

1 Introduction

With computers and networks being applied more and more widely in daily life, enterprise and organizations tend to store large scale data digitally. However, those information management systems often contain vulnerabilities and are prone to be exploited by attackers. There are many academic work analysing malware such as malware static classification [8,14,15,17], malware traffic classification [7,13,22,23], and etc. However, there lack work analysing malware behaviour in depth. We aim to present an in-depth analysis on one exploitation module shared in many recent year malware.

In May 2017, a ransomworm called *Wannacry* bursts out worldwide. It caused massive infection and enormous economic losses by infecting various industrial and government internal networks, such as UK's National Health Service and etc. [2]. The average attack the other organizations suffer is 14,300 per day according

X. Chen et al. (Eds.): CSS 2022, LNCS 13547, pp. 178–191, 2022.
https://doi.org/10.1007/978-3-031-18067-5_13

to [6]. It is reported to derive from an NSA exploit tool [21]. Once Wannacry infects a system, it encrypts copies of various file types and deletes the originals. The encrypted files cannot be accessed without a decryption key.

A lot of work has been done to analyze Eternalblue and Wannacry. Most of the papers on Wannacry focused on the dynamical analysis. D.Y. KAO et al. analyzed Wannacry dynamically, from the aspects of process name, Registry, file system, and Network activity, respectively. They also applied the features to these aspects to create Yarra rules for pattern-matching detection [11]. Qian et al. also dynamically analyzed Wannacry for testing the performance of an automatic dynamical analysis tool [9]. As to the static analysis, D.Y. KAO et al. provided a detailed analysis based on different phases. Critical files and strings participating in those phases were highlighted [12]. Hirokazu statically analyzed Wannacry based on the Eternalblue and DoublePulsar modules. He also applied the discoveries into Snort rules to defend future network attacks based on those two modules [16].

Even though those works helped investigate the working mechanism of Wannacry and Eternalblue, there lacks the study on the comparison between Wannacry's Eternalblue module and the original Eternalblue module. To bridge this research gap, we proceed with our analysis by first studying the exploit's working mechanism that applied in *Wannacry*. Then we use code analytic tools and network capture tools to compare Wannacry's Eternalblue module and the original Eternalblue module. After a detailed study, we find that the exploit utilized in Wannacry shares a very similar pattern to the original exploit, which can be used as features for signature extraction.

The remainder of this paper is organized as follows. In Sect. 2, the original Eternalblue module's working mechanism is introduced. Section 3 analyzes the Eternlablue module in *Wannacry* and Sect. 4 concludes this paper.

2 Eternalblue's Working Mechanism in Metasploit

Assume we have two computers: an attacking machine and a victim machine. At the very beginning, Eternalblue is a piece of code on the attacking machine. Once executed, it will send multiple SMB (Server Message Block) requests to the victim machine through the SMB protocol. As a result, the victim machine must respond to these requests. In this SMB communication phase, the attacking machine plays the role of client and the victim machine plays the role of server, which is the reason we refer them to attacking machine and victim machine respectively. Among these SMB requests, the Transaction SMB commands are essential because they are utilized to tamper the data on the server (victim) with a buffer overflow bug, which further leads to the execution of the ransomworm on the victim machine.

Hence, prior to introducing details of the working mechanism of Eternalblue, in this section we will firstly introduce the normal usage of Transaction SMB. According to MSDN [3], Transaction SMB commands enable the client to access advanced features on the server. Specifically, the three transaction messages are:

– SMB_COM_TRANSACTION (or *Trans*),

- SMB_COM_TRANSACTION2 (or *Trans2*),
- SMB_COM_NT_TRANSACT (or *NT Trans*).

It is also noted in [4] that, SMB_COM_NT_TRANSACT subcommands enable the transfer of very large data chunks. And SMB_COM_TRANSACTION2 subcommands provide richer file system services such as allowing clients to set and retrieve Extended Attribute key/value pairs, to make use of long file names, and to perform directory searches, etc.

The information above summarizes the legitimate usage of the Transaction SMB commands. However, in Eternalblue, they are not applied for the original legitimate purposes, but for a buffer overflow bug. Specifically, when responding to these crafted requests, the server will convert the payload contained in these requesting Transaction SMB packets, i.e., the original Os2Fea [1] list, to the currently used NtFea [1] format (result type), as Os2Fea (the original type) is outdated [18]. The NtFea list will be stored into a *result list buffer*. This process is also referred to the conversion process. Under some mild conditions, the server can be fooled by allocating a result list buffer smaller than the NtFea list to be stored. Thus the NtFea list can overwrite the next buffer. And the original list with a specific length will satisfy such mild conditions.

In more detail, the "next buffer" is a Srvnet.sys [1] buffer, which is allocated on the server for the attacker's SMB request. Once allocated, this buffer will wait for another data package to be sent to the server. There are two parameters in the header of this Srvnet.sys buffer: one decides where to map the data package on this server upon receiving the data package and another decides what function to execute when the Srvnet connection is disconnected. So if these two parameters are modified to the same address, the payload will be mapped and be executed upon closing the connection.

To trigger the overflow of Srvnet.sys and thus inject the malicious codes to the victim, Eternalblue covers three essential steps: *crafting original list, buffer grooming*, and *sending the payload*. We proceed our discussion of Eternalblue by first showing a high-level description of the three steps, then dive into details of each step.

From a high-level point of view, in step *crafting original list*, an original list is crafted. In the second step, multiple grooming packages are sent in a deliberate order which changes the server's buffer status to a point that is vulnerable to overflow. Then, sending the complete original list results in the overflow. In the final step, the payload is sent to the server's Srvnet.sys buffer. Because of the overflow, the payload can be mapped to the desired location and executed upon closing the connection.

2.1   Crafting Original List

To understand crafting of the original list, we firstly recall the normal conversion process on the server machine.

As shown in Algorithm 1, in the Os2Fea format, there is a parameter *ULONG SizeOfList* prior to the actual records describing the total bytes of the original list.

The server's legitimate conversion process is shown in Algorithm 2. In step *Compute S1*, the algorithm will go through the original list and discard the records that exceed the boundary set by SizeOfList, and the remaining original list (Os2Fea) size is S2, as shown in Fig. 1a. S1 is the result list (NtFea) size corresponding to the remaining original list with size S2. Hence, in the third line of Algorithm 2, the server allocates the result list buffer with size S1.

Back into the second line of Algorithm 2, S2 needs to be assigned to the original list's parameter SizeOfList, as this parameter will be used later in the while loop. In the *while* statement of Algorithm 2, the server calls a subfunction repeatedly to convert the original list block by block and stores the result list into this result list buffer. The number of the loop is determined by the SizeOfList's value. The original_list_initial_address in this algorithm points to the beginning of the original list. It is later assigned to variable *Current_pointer*, which will increase after each iteration.

Above is the server's conversion process. The bug occurs when assigning S2 to the original list's parameter SizeOfList if the SizeOfList is no less than 2^{16} (0×10000 in hexadecimal) and the actual original list's record exceeds the boundary set by SizeOfList [19], like shown in Fig. 1a.

In more detail, when parsing S2 to SizeOfList, only the LOWORD (low-order word) bytes of the DWORD (double word) variable SizeOfList is updated because of a wrong casting instruction. Hence the End_pointer in Algorithm 2 will be miscalculated, which leads to an unexpected conversion time. This corresponds to a different time to execute the *while* statement in Algorithm 2. For example, as occurred in this Eternalblue exploit, the SizeOfList is initiated with 0×10000. After discarding, the remaining original list size S2 is 0xff5d. However, when executing the second line of Algorithm 2 (i.e., assigning S2 to SizeOfList), only the LOWORD bytes of SizeOfList is updated, which turns SizeOfList from 0×10000 to $0 \times 1ff5d$ rather than 0xff5d, hence enlarge this SizeOfList.

Algorithm 1. Os2Fea list structure

Struct Os2FeaList{
ULONG SizeOfList
UCHAR Os2FeaList⌈SizeOfList − 4⌉
}

Based on the discussion above, the crafted list is as follows. The forged original list is of the Os2Fea type, its parameter SizeOfList is with value 2^{16} (0×10000 in hexadecimal), followed by a list of Os2Fea data, as demonstrated in Algorithm 1. There are 607 pieces of data included in this crafted list and garbage data at the end which confines the request packet to a particular size. The first 605 pieces of records are empty, the 606th record is not empty and can be filled with arbitrary data of a certain length. The 607th record contains the fake Srvnet.sys header and this 607th record exceeds the boundary set by

---

Algorithm 2. The legitimate server's conversion process

   Compute S1
   S2 assigned to SizeOfList
   Allocate buffer (result list buffer) with size S1
   End_pointer = original_list_initial_address + SizeOfList
   Current_pointer = original_list_initial_address
   while Current_pointer<End_pointer **do**
      convert(Current_pointer)
      Current_pointer+ = each_record_size
   end while

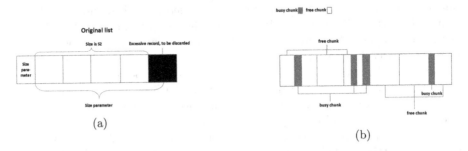

(a)

(b)

Fig. 1. (a) Server discards the out-of-boundary records and calculates the result list size S1 based on the remaining records. (b) Server machine's buffer initial status. Busy chunks lay among free chunks.

SizeOfList [18]. As analog in Fig. 1a, the 607th record is the black section, followed by some garbage data. After discarding, only the first 606 records should be converted.

When converting this crafted list on the server, as demonstrated in Algorithm 2, after discarding, S1 and S2 are calculated representing the first 606 records of the result list and the original list. Then, the SizeOfList should be assigned to S2 but in fact assigned to an enlarged value because of the wrong casting (assigned $0 \times 1ff5d$ rather than $0 \times ff5d$). Hence the *End_pointer* is also enlarged. Afterwards, the result list buffer that can only store the first 606 result records will be allocated. Later, the conversion begins, and the loop will be executed for extra times as the *End_pointer* is enlarged. Hence the server will convert and store 607 records in the buffer for 606 records. This is the reason why this 607th record shall be crafted with a forged Srvnet.sys buffer header and the preceding records can be filled with arbitrary data of a certain size.

As mentioned earlier, once the Srvnet.sys buffer is allocated on the server, it waits for another data packet. There are two critical fields in the Srvnet.sys buffer header for processing the data packet: one is called *memory descriptor list* (MDL) which points to a virtual address that the data package shall be mapped to once received the other one is called *pSrvNetWskStruct*. It points to a function which shall be called when the Srvnet connection is closed. Therefore, overwriting these two fields with the same address can make the server map the shellcode to the desired location and execute the shellcode after closing the Srvnet connection.

Finally, it should be noted that the crafted data in the 607th record should be differentiated from the shellcode since the crafted 607th record is used to overwrite the Srvnet.sys buffer's header, which paves the way for sending the shellcode. The sending process of the shellcode is to be discussed later.

2.2   Buffer Grooming

We have discussed how the crafted list will lead to the buffer overflow in Srvnet.sys. If the buffer Srvnet.sys is not allocated exactly after the result list buffer, the attack fails. This *buffer grooming* process aims to improve the success rate of overflowing the Srvnet.sys buffer. Table 1 shows all the grooming packages sent by Eternalblue in timeline. We have validated the packets by analyzing the packets sent by the samples from 2 sources [20] and [10]. The ultimate goal of the grooming procedure is to make the server allocate a *Srvnet.sys buffer* immediately following the *result list buffer*. Only when this goal is achieved, the excessive data from the *result list buffer* can overwrite the *Srvnet.sys buffer*'s header later. The order of the packages sent in Table 1 can increase the possibility of achieving our ultimate goal. However, the proof is complicated and out of the scope of this paper.

The following paragraphs introduce the packages sent in each step listed in Table 1. To validate the buffer grooming process, we reproduce the spreading process in a virtual environment and check the captured network packages listed in Table 1. The samples are created based on scripture on the exploit-db website [20] and Metasploit Eternalblue module [10]. The baseline of the virtual environment and experiment tools are shown below:

- Virtual Machine: VMWare Workstation
- Client (attacker) machine OS: Windows 7×64 SP1
- Client (attacker) machine IP address: 10.10.10.151
- Server (victim) machine OS: Windows 7×64 SP1
- Server (victim) machine IP address: 10.10.10.152
- Analysis tools: Wireshark

Firstly the exploit from the client (attacker) machine establishes a connection and determines the target operating system's version and architecture based on the SMB and DCE/RPC (Distributed Computing Environment/Remote Procedure Calls [5]) reply, respectively. Figure 1b shows the server (victim) machine's buffer initial status before receiving any packages from the client (attacker) machine.

Then the exploit sends the original list to the target machine through connection No. 1. However, the legitimate usage of the Transaction SMB request is to send Trans2 Secondary Request after Trans2 Request or to send the NT Trans Secondary Request after the NT Trans Request. Here in this exploit, the purpose of sending Trans2 Secondary Requests packets after the initial NT Trans

Table 1. Eternalblue package sent in timeline

No.	Type	Description
1	Srv	Anonymous login and IPC$ tree connect, then send the crafted original list except the last segment to the server through an NT Trans Request and multiple Trans2 Secondary Requests. An Echo package is followed to ensure the list was sent successfully
2	1st reserve	Send malformed Negotiate Protocol Request and Session Setup AndX Request to reserve buffer (0×10000 bytes) with size smaller than the result list buffer in NonPagedPool on the server
3–15	Srvnet	Send multiple TCP packages to establish Srvnet connections which fill up the slot before the result list buffer
16	2nd reserve	Send malformed Negotiate Protocol Request and Session Setup AndX Request to reserve buffer (0×11000) slightly bigger than the result list buffer. This reserved buffer serves as a place holder for the result list buffer
2	1st reserve	Send a FIN TCP package to free the 1st reserved buffer
17–22	Srvnet	Send TCP packages to establish extra Srvnet connections. One of them is expected to be allocated next to the 2nd reserved buffer
16	2nd reserve	Send a FIN TCP package to free the 2nd reserved buffer
1	Srv	Send the last segment of the original list through a Trans2 Secondary Request. So the Srv.sys will convert the list. To store the result list with size $0 \times 10fe8$ (S1), the server allocates 0×11000 bytes. Because of Windows memory's last-in-first-out working fasion, the 2nd reserved buffer just being freed should be allocated here
3–15 and 17–22	Srvnet	Send the shellcode through Mutiple TCP packages. The overflow ensures the shellcode be mapped to a desired location. Then close the connections

Request is to utilize another data parsing bug, which permits the attacker to send the payload in a Trans2 request that is bigger than its limit, e.g. $0 \times ffff$ [18]. To ensure the original buffer is received correctly by the target machine, the exploit on the client machine sends an echo package to the server machine. After receiving those packages, the server machine's buffer status changes to the one depicted in Fig. 2a.

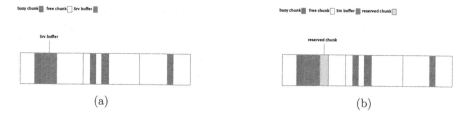

Fig. 2. (a) Server machine's buffer state after receiving echo packets. (b) Server machine's buffer state after receiving grooming packet.

Then in connection No. 2, to reserve a buffer chunk which is used for grooming, another request is sent from the client to the server. After receiving the request, the server's buffer status is updated as shown in Fig. 2b.

Next, in order to keep grooming the buffer, as in connection No. 3–15 in Table 1, multiple Srvnet requests are sent to allocate multiple Srvnet.sys buffer chunks on the server. This is the first series of the Srvnet request packages which fill up the slot before the second reserved buffer. Figure 3a demonstrates the server's buffer status after receiving these Srvnet requests. Srvnet connections in this step increase the probability that the Srvnet buffer allocated in connections No. 17–22 be allocated immediately following the *result list buffer* because connections No. 3–15 fill up the slot between the two reserved Srv buffer (connection 2 and connection 16).

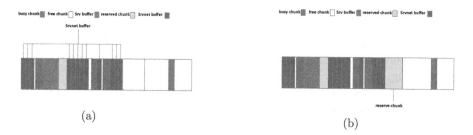

Fig. 3. (a) Server machine's buffer state after receiving Srvnet requests to allocate multiple Srvnet.sys buffer chunks. (b) Server machine's buffer state after receiving NonPagedPool allocation packets.

As in connection No. 16 in Table 1, the second reserving buffer chunk is reserved as a placeholder (to be replaced with the *result list buffer* later). Afterwards, the first reserved buffer chunk through connection No. 2 shall be freed. The first and second buffer reserving packets also utilize a bug by setting special parameters in the request to make the large NonPagedPool allocation [18], which is much greater than it is permitted to. After these two steps, the server's buffer status changes to the one depicted in Fig. 3b.

Next, in connection No. 17–22, extra Srvnet request packages are sent to the server. It is expected that one Srvnet.sys buffer allocated by these requests can be immediately after the *result list buffer*, hence the overflow in the *result list buffer* can overwrite the following Srvnet.sys buffer's header. Figure 4a shows the server buffer status after receiving the extra Srvnet requests.

(a)

(b)

Fig. 4. (a) Server machine's buffer state after receiving the extra Srvnet requests. One Srvnet.sys buffer should follow the result list buffer. (b) Server machine's buffer state after receiving the overwriting packet.

In connection No. 16, the second reserved buffer is freed. And in connection No. 1, the last segment of the original list is sent to the server, making the system start the conversion.

To start the conversion process, the server tries to allocate a *result list buffer* with size S1. Since the second reserved buffer, which has the size slightly greater than the result list, is just freed, Windows memory's last-in-first-out working fashion guarantees this buffer be allocated as the *result list buffer*. During the conversion process, as introduced before, the data in the result buffer can overwrite the following Srvnet.sys buffer. The server buffer status changes to the one shown in Fig. 4b.

Finally, the exploit sends the shellcode through each of the previously established Srvnet connections (i.e., connection No. 3–15, and 17–22).

2.3 Sending the Shellcode

The payload is a piece of executable code that is sent after the target machine is penetrated. Once the payload is executed, the attacker can leverage the vulnerability and do whatever he wants to do. In previous discussion, we have explained that by sending the grooming packages, multiple Srvnet connections are established and one of these corresponding Srvnet.sys buffes is expected to be overflown. According to the Check Point Reseach paper [1], after the Srvnet connections are established, these connections wait for another data packages and upon receiving the data packet, it will map the data according to the parameter *pMdl* contained in the Srvnet buffer's header. Also, upon closing the Srvnet connection, the function pointed by *HandlerFunction* in the *pSrvnetWskStruct* will be called. The Srvnet.sys buffer has a structure as shown in Algorithm 3.

Algorithm 3. Srvnet.sys buffer structure

Struct Srvnet_header{

......

$MDL * pMdl1$

......

*Srvnet_receive * pSrvnetWskStruct{*

......

$PVOIDHandleFunction$

 }

......

}

In this section, we have introduced the *shellcode sending process*. However, the detailed code analysis on the shellcode is not discussed in this paper as it is beyond the scope of this paper.

3 Code Analysis

As described in Sect. 1, *Wannacry* utilizes the famous exploit Eternalblue in its spreading process. In this section, we provide a static analysis on Wannacry's exploit module to investigate how this exploit is utilized. The baseline of the analysis tools are shown below:

- *Wannacry* SHA256 hash: 24d004a104d4d54034dbcffc2a4b19a11f39008a575a a614ea04703480b1022c
- Static analysis tool: IDA 6.8

3.1 Summary of Wannacry's Network Behaviour

Wannacry creates local network spreading threads and Internet spreading threads to propagate through the network. Both threads use the same exploit Eternalblue to infect other systems.

In the local network spreading process, Wannacry creates a target IP address table and tries to attack the potential victims in the table exhaustively. In the Internet spreading process, Wannacry generates a random IP address and tries to attack the system sharing the same network segment. Like Eternalblue, the spreading process in Wannacry also consists of 3 essential steps: *crafting original list, buffer grooming* and *sending the payload*. Table 2 depicts the summery of Wannacry's package caption after we analyzed the network traffic during the infection. This table describes almost the same process as shown in Table 1, except for several differences. Even though the general process described in Table 2 is similar to the process given in Table 1, some of the packets are not introduced in Table 1, as they are unique in Wannacry. Due to the page limit, we summarise each step's behaviour with no assembly code demonstrated.

Through the static analysis of Wannacry by using IDA 6.8, we discovered a function crafts the fake original list and prepares the grooming packages, which is discussed in Sect. 2.1 and 2.2. These fake original list, grooming packages, and the shellcode mentioned above are embedded into the ransomworm by the ransomworm author. During the runtime, they are extracted and pasted into a buffer chunk in the same order as listed in Table 1. Then data in this buffer chunk will be sent later to the server, which spreads the ransomworm and executes the ransomworm on the server. All the data is in plain-text format and is barely different from the Metasploit's exploit. We will discuss the particulars in the following paragraphs.

3.2   Detailed Analysis of Wannacry Network Behaviour

Table 2. Summery of package caption of Wannacry

Step	Attempt	Packages
1	Detect the existence of MS17_010 and DoublePulsar	PeekNamedPipe Request and Trans2 Request
2	Send the original list except the last segment	A NT Trans Request and multiple Trans2 Secondary Requests
3	Ensure the package in last step were sent successfully	Echo Request
4	Reserve the first buffer	Negotiate Protocol Request and Session Setup Andx Request
5	Reserve Srvnet.sys buffers	Multiple TCP packages
6	Reserve the second buffer	Negotiate Protocol Request and Session Setup Andx Request
7	Free the first reserved buffer	A FIN TCP package
8	Reserve extra Srvnet.sys buffers	Multiple TCP packages
9	Ensure the packages sent in last step were sent successfully	Echo Request
10	Free the second reserved buffer	A FIN TCP package
11	Send the last segment of the original list	A Trans2 Secondary Request
12	Send the shellcode	Mutiple TCP packages

Prior to preparing the grooming packages and the shellcode, Wanancry sends a PeekNamePipe package and a Trans2 Request package to detect the existence of MS17_010 and backdoor Doublepulsar respectively [11]. As step 1 listed in Table 2, the PeekNamePipe package data is embedded into the ransomworm. It is used when the ransomworm needs to send it After sending this package, the ransomworm waits for the response from the server. If the data in the response package equal to *STATUS_INSUFF_SERVER_RESOURCES* that denotes the MS17_010 vulnerability resides on the server.

The Trans2 package data is also embedded into the ransomworm. The ransomworm waits for the response from the server. If the *Multiplex ID* field in the response package equals to *0x51*, that denotes the server is infected with Doublepulsar, whereas if the field equals to *0x41*, that denotes the server is not infected.

To establish the connection to the server (victim) machine, the first Negotiate Protocol package is crafted. The Session Setup AndX and Tree Connect AndX Request packages are crafted in the similar way.

Next, in step 2 of Table 2, an NT Trans Request package, and multiple Trans2 Secondary Request packages containing the crafted Os2Fea list without the last segment are prepared. In step 3, to ensure the original list is received completely, an echo package is prepared.

In step 4, a package which reserves the first buffer chunk on the target is prepared. To continue the buffer grooming process, in step 5, multiple Srvnet connection requests should be sent to reserve Srvnet.sys buffer chunks on the target system. In step 6, the second reserving package shall be sent to the server. The crafting process includes Negotiate Protocol Request and Session Setup AndX Request. In step 7, the first reserving buffer allocated previously shall be freed.

In step 8, extra 5 Srvnet connection requests are crafted. Later they are sent to the target machine to reserve Srvnet.sys buffers. It is expected that one Srvnet.sys buffer allocated in this step is immediately after the second reserved buffer, which will be replaced with the *result list buffer* later. In step 9, an Echo package is crafted. In step 10, the second reserved buffer shall be freed and in step 11, the last segment of the crafted original list shall be sent to the target. Once this last segment is received, the target's conversion process (converting the original list to the result list) begins. In step 12, multiple packages that contain the same shellcode Later they will be sent through the Srvnet connections established earlier.

4   Conclusion

The wide application of exploit Eternalblue is a meaningful security incident. The massive infection based on Eternalblue spurs everyone to raise the awareness of patching computers to current status. This paper introduced the underlying mechanism of exploit Eternalblue, as well as the reverse engineering result of Eternalblue. The code of Eternalblue applied in Wannacry is compared with the original exploit based on the reverse engineering results. The analysis reveals that the exploit Eternalblue is slightly modified when applied in Wannacry. Our work gathered much-known knowledge of Eternalblue to provide readers with a clear picture of this exploit. We have concluded the similarity and the difference of Eternalblue's code in Wannacry. We have also analyzed Notpetya and found the exploit in Notpetya is encrypted and only decrypted while the shellocode is executed. After decrypting it, the Notepetya exploit is almost identical to the original Eternalblue exploit. Due to the length constrains of the paper, the analysis details are not included here. It is possible to extend our work to the code analysis for ransomworm detection.

References

1. EternalBlue – Everything There Is To Know (2017). https://research.checkpoint.com/eternalblue-everything-know/. Accessed 15 Apr 2018
2. Investigation: Wannacry Cyber Attack and the NHS (2018). https://www.nao.org.uk/report/investigation-wannacry-cyber-attack-and-the-nhs/. Accessed 18 Mar 2018
3. (2019). https://msdn.microsoft.com/en-us/library/ee441928.aspx. Accessed 16 May 2018
4. (2019). https://msdn.microsoft.com/en-us/library/ee441720.aspx. Accessed 16 May 2018
5. (2019). https://www.dcerpc.org/documentation/rpc-porting.pdf. Accessed 18 Mar 2018
6. Alterson, G.: Confronting One of Healthcare's Biggest Challenges: Cyber Risk (2019). https://www.forbes.com/sites/insights-intelai/2019/02/11/confronting-one-of-healthcares-biggest-challenges-cyber-risk/amp/. Accessed 11 Feb 2019
7. Anderson, B., McGrew, D.: Machine learning for encrypted malware traffic classification: accounting for noisy labels and non-stationarity. In: Proceedings of the 23rd ACM SIGKDD International Conference on Knowledge Discovery and Data Mining, pp. 1723–1732 (2017)
8. Chakraborty, T., Pierazzi, F., Subrahmanian, V.: EC2: ensemble clustering and classification for predicting android malware families. IEEE Trans. Dependable Secure Comput. **17**(2), 262–277 (2017)
9. Chen, Q., Bridges, R.A.: Automated Behavioral Analysis of Malware A Case Study of WannaCry Ransomware (2017). https://arxiv.org/abs/1709.08753. Accessed 3 Apr 2018
10. Dillon, S., Jennings, L.: ms17_010_eternalblue (2017). https://github.com/rapid7/metasploit-framework/blob/master/modules/exploits/windows/smb/ms17_010_eternalblue.rb. Accessed 24 Apr 2018
11. Kao, D.Y., Hsiao, S.C.: The dynamic analysis of WannaCry ransomware. In: International Conference on Advanced Communications Technology (ICACT) (2018). https://www.dcerpc.org/documentation/rpc-porting.pdf. Accessed 18 Apr 2018
12. Kao, D.Y., Hsiao, S.C.: The static analysis of WannaCry ransomware. In: International Conference on Advanced Communications Technology (ICACT) (2018). https://ieeexplore.ieee.org/document/8323679/. Accessed 18 Apr 2018
13. Marín, G., Casas, P., Capdehourat, G.: Deep in the dark-deep learning-based malware traffic detection without expert knowledge. In: 2019 IEEE Security and Privacy Workshops (SPW), pp. 36–42. IEEE (2019)
14. McLaughlin, N., et al.: Deep android malware detection. In: Proceedings of the Seventh ACM on Conference on Data and Application Security and Privacy, pp. 301–308 (2017)
15. Milosevic, N., Dehghantanha, A., Choo, K.K.R.: Machine learning aided android malware classification. Comput. Electr. Eng. **61**, 266–274 (2017)
16. Murakami, H.: Reverse Engineering of WannaCry Worm and Anti Exploit Snort Rules (2018). https://www.sans.org/reading-room/whitepapers/malicious/paper/38445. Accessed 7 July 2018

17. Pai, S., Troia, F.D., Visaggio, C.A., Austin, T.H., Stamp, M.: Clustering for malware classification. J. Comput. Virol. Hacking Tech. **13**(2), 95–107 (2016). https://doi.org/10.1007/s11416-016-0265-3
18. Kulkarni, P., Sameer Patil, P.K., Dolas, A.: EternalBlue: A prominent threat actor of 2017–2018 (2018). https://www.virusbulletin.com/uploads/pdf/magazine/2018/201806-EternalBlue.pdf. Accessed 23 May 2018
19. Sanchez, W.G.: MS17-010: EternalBlue's Large Non-Paged Pool Overflow in SRV Driver (2017). https://blog.trendmicro.com/trendlabs-security-intelligence/ms17-010-eternalblue. Accessed 16 Mar 2018
20. sleepya: Microsoft Windows Windows 7/2008 R2 (×64) - 'Eternalblue' SMB Remote Code Execution (MS17-010) (2017). https://www.exploit-db.com/exploits/42031/. Accessed 12 Apr 2018
21. Thomson, I.: Leaked NSA Point-and-pwn Hack Tools Menace Win2k to Windows 8 (2017). https://www.theregister.co.uk/2017/04/14/latest_shadow_brokers_data_dump/. Accessed 5 Mar 2018
22. Wang, W., Zhu, M., Zeng, X., Ye, X., Sheng, Y.: Malware traffic classification using convolutional neural network for representation learning. In: 2017 International Conference on Information Networking (ICOIN), pp. 712–717. IEEE (2017)
23. Yu, K.F., Harang, R.E.: Machine learning in malware traffic classifications. In: MILCOM 2017–2017 IEEE Military Communications Conference (MILCOM), pp. 6–10. IEEE (2017)

Substitution Attacks Against Sigma Protocols

Yuliang Lin, Rongmao Chen$^{(\boxtimes)}$, Yi Wang$^{(\boxtimes)}$, Baosheng Wang$^{(\boxtimes)}$, and Lin Liu

School of Computer, National University of Defense Technology, Changsha, China
{linyuliang21,chromao,wangyi14,bswang,liulin16}@nudt.edu.cn

Abstract. Inspired by the Snowden revelations, Bellare, Paterson, and Rogaway proposed the notion of Algorithm Substitution Attack (ASA) where the attacker could subvert cryptographic algorithms to leak secret information stealthily. Since their work, there have been several ASAs proposed for various cryptographic schemes such as encryption schemes and digital signatures. In this work, we investigate the first study of ASA against Σ protocols which are widely considered as an important and useful cryptographic tool. Concretely, we formally define the ASA models for subverting Σ protocols and propose two concrete attacks that are mainly inspired by the attacks by Bellare *et al.* (CRYPTO'14) and Chen *et al.* (ASIACRYPT'20). In our proposed attacks, a subverted prover could leak the secret witness to the outside world in undetectable way by generating biased commitment, and a subverted verifier could break the knowledge soundness by choosing a biased challenge. Several concrete Σ protocols are also provided to demonstrate the feasibility of our proposed attack. Our work shows that ASAs have powerful impacts on Σ protocols, and thus it is highly desirable for the research community to design new Σ protocols that could resist ASAs.

Keywords: Algorithm substitution attack · Sigma protocols · Witness recovery

1 Introduction

The Snowden revelations in 2013 showed that provably secure cryptographic algorithms might not provide security guarantees in the real world. The main reason is that typical security models implicitly assume that cryptographic implementations always follow the specifications, while in the real world the attacker might have the ability to tamper with the implementations to embed backdoors. In fact, over two decades ago, similar attacks (i.e., embedding backdoors into the cryptographic algorithms) had been raised by Young and Yung [23,24]. Particularly, they formalized such an attack as *Secretly Embedded Trapdoor with Universal Protection* (SETUP) [23]. Subsequently, Young and Yung conducted a series of studies [24–27] of SETUP attacks on different cryptographic schemes.

ALGORITHM SUBSTITUTION ATTACK. In 2014, inspired by the Snowden revelations and the emergence of mass surveillance, Bellare, Paterson, and Rogaway [10]

X. Chen et al. (Eds.): CSS 2022, LNCS 13547, pp. 192–208, 2022.
https://doi.org/10.1007/978-3-031-18067-5_14

formalized a new attack called *algorithm substitution attacks* (ASAs). Roughly, the adversary in an ASA aims at subverting the cryptographic implementation to destroy the security of the algorithm while not being perceived by users. In [10], two different ASAs called IV-replacement attack and biased ciphertext attack were proposed against symmetric encryption algorithms. In 2015, Degabriele, Farshim, and Poettering [16] investigated a further study of the ASA notion defined by Bellare *et al.*, and proposed stronger ASAs on symmetric encryption schemes. Bellare, Jaeger, and Kane [9] improved the previous work in [10] by proposing stateless ASAs that could subvert all randomized symmetric encryption schemes with stronger undetectability. In 2015, Ateniese, Magri, and Venturi [5] studied ASAs in the context of signature schemes and show that signature schemes with certain properties suffer from powerful substitution attacks. Since then, the research community turns to exploring ASAs against other cryptographic primitives including message authentication [3], authenticated encryption with associated data [4], unified zero-knowledge [22], and practical cryptographic protocols [13,18].

Recall that Σ protocols, a well-known class of zero-knowledge proof, are widely considered as an important and useful tool in constructing advanced cryptographic systems. Surprisingly, ASAs against such a useful protocol have not been fully investigated yet. In this work, we focus on ASAs against Σ protocols. In particular, we intend to formalize the ASA model for Σ protocols and explore potential ASAs.

Since Σ protocols involve the interaction of prover and verifier, the definitions of ASA models should capture this feature carefully. Also, it is natural to consider the subversion of the prover, as it holds the secret witness of the statement. However, the challenge sent by the verifier might also act as a subliminal channel to leak private information to the adversary.

CONTRIBUTIONS. In this work, we first proposed the ASA model for Σ protocols by providing formal definitions of subverting prover and verifier respectively and then presented two kinds of ASAs against Σ protocols.

1. As for subverting the prover, the main goal is to leak the secret witness. To show how to achieve this via ASAs, we provide both stateful and stateless biased-commitment attacks where one can completely recover the witness from a series of transcripts. Our idea is inspired by the works of Bellare *et al.* [9] and Chen *et al.* [15]. To show the effectiveness of the proposed attacks, we defined two properties to capture the attack's undetectability and the witness recovery.
2. As for subverting the verifier, we propose a biased-challenge attack. This attack is designed to help the adversary (i.e., the malicious prover) owning the backdoor predict the challenge returned by the subverted verifier and pass the verification with non-negligible probability. Besides the property of undetectability, we introduce a new property called *challenge distinguishability* to capture the ability of the adversary to predict the challenge sent by the subverted verifier.

We show that these attacks can be applied to several Σ protocols. Concretely, we demonstrate the effectiveness of our proposed attack on Schnorr's Identification Protocol [21] and Okamoto's Protocol [20].

It is worth noting that while Teşeleanu also conducted a similar study of substitution attacks on Σ protocols [22], our attacks are different from Teşeleanu's in the following respects.

- At the core of Teşeleanu's attack is the previously known SETUP [23] while we study the ASA where each bit of the witness is encoded into the commitments to achieve stealthy leakage.
- Our attack is of high efficiency and feasibility. To extract the witness, the proposed attacks only requires the commitments sent by prover, while Teşeleanu's work needs two full transcripts.
- Teşeleanu's attack mainly aims at subverting the prover in a Σ protocol while we also consider ASAs against the verifier.

OTHER RELATED WORK. Some other works also studied ASAs on zero-knowledge proof protocols. In [12], Ben-Sasson et al. considered subverted common reference string (CRS), and provided a distributed scheme to securely generate CRS. Bellare, Fuchsbauer and Scafuro [8] analyzed the security of non-interactive zero-knowledge proofs (NIZKs) with subverted CRS, and described properties of subversion soundness, subversion witness indistinguishability, and subversion zero knowledge. They also discussed the attributes of non-interactive witness indistinguishable (NIWI) with some assumptions.

In light of [8], Abdolmaleki et al. [1] achieved computationally knowledge-soundness and perfectly composable subversion-resistant zero-knowledge equipped with the extractable CRS trapdoor and the publicly verifiable CRS.

2 Preliminaries

2.1 Notations and Definitions

Notations. For a string $x \in \{0,1\}^*$, we denote the binary length of x as $|x|$. For $n \in \mathbb{N}$, $[n]$ denotes set $\{0,1,...,n-1\}$. For $i \in [|x|]$, $x[i]$ denotes the i-th bit of x. For two strings x_0 and x_1, $x = x_0\|x_1$ is the concatenation of x_0 and x_1. Let C be a finite set and B be a probabilistic function, $c \leftarrow_s C$ denotes that c is chosen randomly from the set C while $c \leftarrow_s B(\lambda)$ denotes that c is generated randomly by the function B with the parameter λ. For an efficient algorithm A and an oracle DO, $b \leftarrow A^{DO}(x)$ denotes that with input x, A queries the oracle DO multiple times and outputs b. Let $\mathsf{negl}(n)$ denote the negligible function with $n \in \mathbb{N}$. For any $c \in \mathbb{N}$, there exists $n_0 \in \mathbb{N}$ such that $\mathsf{negl}(n) < n^{-c}$ for all $n \geq n_0$. Let $\mathsf{noti}(n)$ denote the noticeable function with $n \in \mathbb{N}$. There exists $c, n_0 \in \mathbb{N}$ such that $\mathsf{noti}(n) \geq n^{-c}$ for all $n \geq n_0$.

Pseudo-Random Functions (PRFs). Let $\mathsf{FUNS}[A, B]$ be the set of all functions mapping A to B. PRF is defined over $[(K \times \{0,1\}^*), R]$ where K is the key space and R is the range of PRF.

Definition 1 (Secure PRF). *Consider the game in Fig. 1. We say the* PRF F *is secure if for any* PPT PRF *adversary* $\mathcal{A}$ *in the game* $\mathsf{IND}_\mathsf{F}^\mathcal{A}(n)$,

$$\mathsf{Adv}_{\mathcal{A},\mathsf{F}}^{\mathsf{ind}}(n) := \left| 2 \cdot \Pr\left[\mathsf{IND}_\mathsf{F}^\mathcal{A}(n) = 1\right] - 1 \right| \leq \mathsf{negl}(n).$$

$\mathsf{IND}_\mathsf{F}^\mathcal{A}(n)$	$\mathcal{O}(s)$
1 : $\quad k \leftarrow_\$ \mathcal{K}$	1 : $\quad$ **if** $b = 0$, $r \leftarrow \mathsf{F}(k,s)$
2 : $\quad f \leftarrow_\$ \mathsf{FUNS}[(\mathcal{K} \times \{0,1\}^*), \mathcal{R}]$	2 : $\quad$ **else** $r \leftarrow f(s)$
3 : $\quad b \leftarrow_\$ \{0,1\}$	3 : $\quad$ **return** r
4 : $\quad b' \leftarrow \mathcal{A}^{\mathcal{O}(\cdot)}(n)$	
5 : $\quad$ **return** $(b = b')$	

Fig. 1. Definition of game $\mathsf{IND}_\mathsf{F}^\mathcal{A}(n)$

2.2 Σ Protocols

Zero-knowledge proofs of knowledge have found great applications in both theoretical and applied cryptography. Σ protocol is a well-known kind of zero-knowledge proof which is firstly proposed by Schnorr [21]. It is commonly used in authentication scenarios where some private information is held. Up to now, research in this direction has been very mature. Various types of Σ protocols and their conversion to other schemes have emerged [2,6,7,11,17,19,20].

A Σ protocol defined over a relation $\mathcal{R}$ is an interactive two-party protocol with a prover Σ.Pro and a verifier Σ.Ver. For two parties Σ.Pro and Σ.Ver, $(t, c, z) \leftarrow \Sigma$.Pro $\rightleftharpoons \Sigma$.Ver indicates that the transcript of one run of the protocol between Σ.Pro and Σ.Ver is a tuple (t, c, z). With only one party Σ.Ver, we write $c \leftarrow \Sigma$.Ver(t) to denote that with input t, Σ.Ver would give a result c.

Let $\mathcal{R}: \mathcal{X} \times \mathcal{Y} \rightarrow \{0,1\}$ be a relation defined over two sets $\mathcal{X}$ and $\mathcal{Y}$ where $\mathcal{Y}$ is the set of statements and $\mathcal{X}$ is the set of witnesses related to $\mathcal{Y}$. Let $(x, y) \in \mathcal{R}$ indicate $\mathcal{R}(x, y) = 1$. Let $\Sigma = (\Sigma$.Pro$(x, y), \Sigma$.Ver$(y))$ be a basic Σ protocol for the relation $\mathcal{R}$ in which (x, y) is the secret key and y is the verification key, as shown in Fig. 2. Let Com be the space of commitments and $\mathcal{C}$ be the room of challenges. After three-round interaction, the verifier examines the tuple (t, c, z) and outputs accept or reject. Many well-known protocols including Schnorr's Identification Protocol [21], Okamoto's Protocol for Representations [20], Chaum-Pedersen Protocol [14] are derived from this basic Σ protocol.

A crucial property of Σ protocol is *knowledge soundness*. Roughly, any adversary needs two transcripts (t_1, c_1, z_1) and (t_2, c_2, z_2) with $t_1 = t_2$ and $c_1 \neq c_2$ to extract the witness. Another way of thinking about it, this property binds the prover. Interacting with an verifier, an honest prover can easily pass the verification, while a malicious one without the witness cannot.

Definition 2 (Knowledge Soundness). *Consider (P, V) provided by a Σ protocol for $\mathcal{R}$. We say that (P, V) has knowledge soundness if there exists an efficient algorithm which could output $x \in \mathcal{X}$ such that $(x, y) \in \mathcal{R}$, given a statement $y \in \mathcal{Y}$, together with two correct transcripts (t_1, c_1, z_1) and (t_2, c_2, z_2) for y where $t_1 = t_2$ and $c_1 \neq c_2$.*

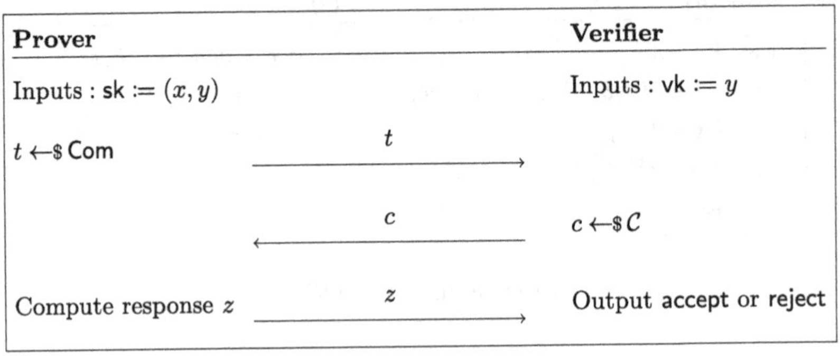

Prover		**Verifier**
Inputs : sk := (x, y)		Inputs : vk := y
$t \leftarrow\!\!{\scriptstyle\$}\ \mathsf{Com}$	$\xrightarrow{\quad t \quad}$	
	$\xleftarrow{\quad c \quad}$	$c \leftarrow\!\!{\scriptstyle\$}\ \mathcal{C}$
Compute response z	$\xrightarrow{\quad z \quad}$	Output accept or reject

Fig. 2. The basic Σ protocol

3   ASA Models for Σ Protocols

Let $\Sigma = (\Sigma.\mathsf{Pro}, \Sigma.\mathsf{Ver})$ be a Σ protocol for the relation $\mathcal{R} = \{(x, y)\}$, the ASA on protocol atk $= (\mathcal{BK}, \tilde{\Sigma} = (\tilde{\Sigma}.\mathsf{Pro}, \tilde{\Sigma}.\mathsf{Ver}))$ is defined as follows.

- $\mathcal{BK}$: the space of symmetric subversion backdoor bd;
- $\tilde{\Sigma} = (\tilde{\Sigma}.\mathsf{Pro}, \tilde{\Sigma}.\mathsf{Ver})$: consists of a subverted prover $\tilde{\Sigma}.\mathsf{Pro}$ with a backdoor bd_1 and a pair $(x, y) \in \mathcal{R}$, and a subverted verifier $\tilde{\Sigma}.\mathsf{Ver}$ with another backdoor bd_2 and the statement y.

3.1   Subverting Prover

In this case, we define two properties of subversion against the prover: undetectability and witness recoverability. In the game of undetectability, if the verifier could not distinguish whether the prover is honestly implemented, the detector could not distinguish from the transcript (t, c, z) either. In the game of witness recoverability, the adversary could only eavesdrop, extract the witness from the transcripts and then interact proactively.

Definition 3 (Undetectability for Subverted Prover). *Consider the undetectable game between $\Sigma.\mathsf{Pro}$ and $\tilde{\Sigma}.\mathsf{Pro}$ provided by detector $\mathcal{D}$ in Fig. 3. We say that $\tilde{\Sigma}.\mathsf{Pro}$ is undetectable if for any PPT detector $\mathcal{D}$ in the game $\mathsf{UND}^{\mathcal{D}}_{\Sigma, \tilde{\Sigma}}(n)$,*

$$\mathsf{Adv}^{\mathsf{und}}_{\mathcal{D}, \Sigma, \tilde{\Sigma}}(n) := \left| 2 \cdot \Pr\left[\mathsf{UND}^{\mathcal{D}}_{\Sigma, \tilde{\Sigma}}(n) = 1 \right] - 1 \right| \leq \mathsf{negl}(n).$$

$\mathrm{UND}^{\mathcal{D}}_{\Sigma,\tilde{\Sigma}}(n)$	$\mathcal{DO}_{\mathsf{eav}}(\cdot)$
1 : $(x,y) \leftarrow_\$ \mathcal{R}$	1 : **if** $b = 0$, $(t,c,z) \leftarrow \tilde{\Sigma}.\mathsf{Pro}(x,y,bd_1) \rightleftharpoons \Sigma.\mathsf{Ver}(y)$
2 : $bd_1 \leftarrow_\$ \mathcal{BK}$	2 : **else** $(t,c,z) \leftarrow \Sigma.\mathsf{Pro}(x,y) \rightleftharpoons \Sigma.\mathsf{Ver}(y)$
3 : $b \leftarrow_\$ \{0,1\}$	3 : **return** (t,c,z)
4 : $b' \leftarrow \mathcal{D}^{\mathcal{DO}_{\mathsf{eav}}(\cdot)}(y)$	
5 : **return** $(b = b')$	

Fig. 3. Definition of game for undetectability for prover

$\mathrm{WR}^{\mathcal{A}}_{\tilde{\Sigma}.\mathsf{Pro}}(n)$	$\mathcal{DO}_{\mathsf{eav}}(\cdot)$
1 : $(x,y) \leftarrow_\$ \mathcal{R}$	1 : $(t,c,z) \leftarrow \tilde{\Sigma}.\mathsf{Pro}(x,y,bd_1) \rightleftharpoons \Sigma.\mathsf{Ver}(y)$
2 : $bd_1 \leftarrow_\$ \mathcal{BK}$	2 : **return** (t,c,z)
3 : $x' \leftarrow \mathcal{A}^{\mathcal{DO}_{\mathsf{eav}}(\cdot)}(y,bd_1)$	
4 : **return** $(x = x')$	

Fig. 4. Definition of game for witness recoverability

Definition 4 (Witness Recoverability). *Consider the game between adversary $\mathcal{A}$ and $\tilde{\Sigma}.\mathsf{Pro}$ provided by adversary $\mathcal{A}$ in Fig. 4. We say that the adversary $\mathcal{A}$ can recover witness from the transcripts of $\Sigma' = (\tilde{\Sigma}.\mathsf{Pro}, \Sigma.\mathsf{Ver})$ if for any PPT adversary $\mathcal{A}$ in the game $\mathrm{WR}^{\mathcal{A}}_{\tilde{\Sigma}.\mathsf{Pro}}(n)$,*

$$\mathsf{Adv}^{\mathsf{wr}}_{\mathcal{A},\tilde{\Sigma}.\mathsf{Pro}}(n) := \Pr\left[\mathrm{WR}^{\mathcal{A}}_{\tilde{\Sigma}.\mathsf{Pro}}(n) = 1\right] \le \mathsf{noti}(n).$$

3.2 Subverting Verifier

We also introduce two properties of subversion against the verifier: undetectability and challenge distinguishability. The undetectable one is similar to that in Sect. 3.1. For the challenge distinguishability game, if the adversary could identify the challenge generated by the subverted verifier, the adversary $\mathcal{A}$ would determine the right challenge c for a future, compute the response z previously and pass the verification with non-negligible probability for further attacks. Therefore, the adversary $\mathcal{A}$ could interact with the verifier independently.

Definition 5 (Undetectability for Subverted Verifier). *Consider the undetectable game between $\Sigma.\mathsf{Ver}$ and $\tilde{\Sigma}.\mathsf{Ver}$ provided by detector $\mathcal{D}$ in Fig. 5. We say that $\tilde{\Sigma}.\mathsf{Ver}$ is undetectable if for any PPT detector $\mathcal{D}$ in the game $\mathrm{UND}^{\mathcal{D}}_{\Sigma,\tilde{\Sigma}}(n)$,*

$$\mathsf{Adv}^{\mathsf{und}}_{\mathcal{D},\Sigma,\tilde{\Sigma}}(n) := \left|2 \cdot \Pr\left[\mathrm{UND}^{\mathcal{D}}_{\Sigma,\tilde{\Sigma}}(n) = 1\right] - 1\right| \le \mathsf{negl}(n).$$

Definition 6 (Challenge Distinguishability). *Consider the game between $\Sigma.\mathsf{Ver}$ and $\tilde{\Sigma}.\mathsf{Ver}$ provided by adversary $\mathcal{A}$ in Fig. 6. We say that the adversary*

$\mathrm{UND}_{\Sigma,\tilde{\Sigma}}^{\mathcal{D}}(n)$	$\mathcal{DO}_{\mathsf{eav}}(\cdot)$
1: $(x,y) \leftarrow_{\$} \mathcal{R}$	1: **if** $b=0$, $(t,c,z) \leftarrow \Sigma.\mathsf{Pro}(x,y) \rightleftharpoons \tilde{\Sigma}.\mathsf{Ver}(y,bd_2)$
2: $bd_2 \leftarrow_{\$} \mathcal{BK}$	2: **else** $(t,c,z) \leftarrow \Sigma.\mathsf{Pro}(x,y) \rightleftharpoons \Sigma.\mathsf{Ver}(y)$
3: $b \leftarrow_{\$} \{0,1\}$	3: **return** (t,c,z)
4: $b' \leftarrow \mathcal{D}^{\mathcal{DO}_{\mathsf{eav}}(\cdot)}(y)$	
5: **return** $(b=b')$	

Fig. 5. Definition of game for undetectability for verifier

$\mathrm{CD}_{\Sigma,\tilde{\Sigma}}^{\mathcal{A}}(n)$	$\mathcal{DO}_{\mathsf{atk}}(t_i)$
1: $(x,y) \leftarrow_{\$} \mathcal{R}$	1: **if** $b=0$, $c_i \leftarrow \tilde{\Sigma}.\mathsf{Ver}(y,bd_2,t_i)$
2: $b \leftarrow_{\$} \{0,1\}$	2: **else** $c_i \leftarrow \Sigma.\mathsf{Ver}(y,t_i)$
3: $bd_2 \leftarrow_{\$} \mathcal{BK}$	3: **return** c_i
4: $b' \leftarrow \mathcal{A}^{\mathcal{DO}_{\mathsf{atk}}(\cdot)}(y,bd_2)$	
5: **return** $(b=b')$	

Fig. 6. Definition of game for challenge distinguishability

$\mathcal{A}$ can distinguish the challenges from $\Sigma.\mathsf{Ver}$ or $\tilde{\Sigma}.\mathsf{Ver}$ if for any PPT adversary $\mathcal{A}$ in the game $\mathrm{CD}_{\Sigma,\tilde{\Sigma}}^{\mathcal{A}}(n)$,

$$\mathsf{Adv}_{\mathcal{A},\Sigma,\tilde{\Sigma}}^{\mathsf{cd}}(n) := \left| 2 \cdot \Pr\left[\mathrm{CD}_{\Sigma,\tilde{\Sigma}}^{\mathcal{A}}(n) = 1 \right] - 1 \right| \leq \mathsf{noti}(n).$$

4 Mounting ASAs on Σ Protocols

In this section, we propose two concrete ASAs subverting the prover and verifier respectively. The undetectability and effectiveness of those attacks are rigorously analyzed according to the formalization in the previous section. In all attacks, PRFs are used as backdoor functions to help adversaries achieve some purposes.

4.1 The Biased-Commitment Attack

We first present an ASA subverting the prover to steal the secret witness. The proposed attack can be stateful and stateless. In the stateful one, the adversary could extract the witness from the transcripts in polynomial time of $O(\ell_x)$ where $\ell_x = |x|$. However, in the stateless one, with the principle of inclusion-exclusion, the adversary could extract the witness with a very significant probability and $O(\ell_x \ln \ell_x)$ time complexity, unlike the original method to guess the witness with a almost negligible probability $\frac{1}{|\mathcal{X}|}$.

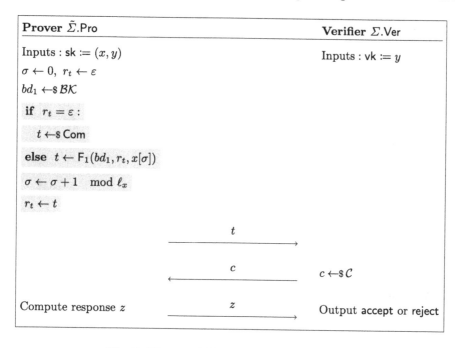

Fig. 7. The stateful biased-commitment attack

Details of the Attack. Let $\ell_x = |x|$ and $F_1\colon \mathcal{BK} \times \mathsf{Com} \times \{0,1\} \to \mathsf{Com}$ be a PRF and ε be a symbol for *null*. The stateful biased-commitment attack against the basic Σ protocol is shown in Fig. 7. In particular, the subverted prover $\tilde{\Sigma}.\mathsf{Pro}$ maintains a counter σ that increments by itself and an array register r_t to store the last output.

To build the stateless biased-commitment attack, let $F_2\colon \mathcal{BK} \times \mathsf{Com} \to [\ell_x]\|\{0,1\}$ be a PRF. Thus, we replace the if structure in the generation of commitments to convert the stateful one to the stateless one as Fig. 8. With this modification, the attack does not need to use σ however knowledge of probability theory is used. How to apply the Principle of Inclusion-Exclusion will be described in the following analysis.

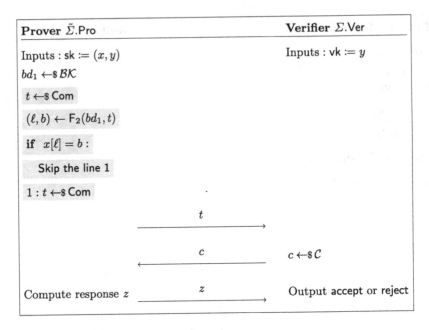

Fig. 8. The stateless biased-commitment attack

Formal Analysis. Next, we will explain how destructive the above-mentioned adversaries are in the environment we set up. Each attack will be given two advantages based on the previously defined attack games in Sect. 3.1.

Theorem 1. *Let Σ protocol $(\Sigma.\mathsf{Pro}, \Sigma.\mathsf{Ver})$ be an honest two-party protocol, and let $\tilde{\Sigma}.\mathsf{Pro}$ be the subverted prover which is embedded with the stateful biased-commitment attack algorithm. Let $\mathsf{F}_1 : \mathcal{BK} \times \mathsf{Com} \times \{0,1\} \to \mathsf{Com}$ be a PRF and $f \in \mathsf{FUNS}[(\mathcal{BK}, \mathsf{Com}, \{0,1\}), \mathsf{Com}]$ be randomly chosen. If F_1 is a secure PRF, we have $\mathsf{Adv}^{ind}_{\mathcal{F},\mathsf{F}_1} \le \epsilon_1$ where ϵ_1 is negligible for all PPT PRF adversary $\mathcal{F}$. Then,*

1. *For any efficient detector $\mathcal{D}$, we have $\mathsf{Adv}^{und}_{\mathcal{D},\Sigma,\tilde{\Sigma}} \le 2 \cdot \mathsf{Adv}^{ind}_{\mathcal{F},\mathsf{F}_1} \le 2 \cdot \epsilon_1$, where ϵ_1 is negligible.*
2. *For any efficient adversary $\mathcal{A}$, we have $\mathsf{Adv}^{wr}_{\mathcal{A},\tilde{\Sigma}.\mathsf{Pro}} = 1$, when $\mathcal{A}$ can make q times of eavesdropping where $q > \ell_x$. Otherwise, $\mathsf{Adv}^{wr}_{\mathcal{A},\tilde{\Sigma}.\mathsf{Pro}} \ge \frac{1}{2^{\ell_x - q}}$.*

Proof. Let G_i be the game i and W_i denotes the event that the detector $\mathcal{D}$ or the adversary $\mathcal{A}$ wins G_i.

(1). Let G_0 be the initial undetectable game in Fig. 3 and through the definition we have

$$\mathsf{Adv}^{und}_{\mathcal{D},\Sigma,\tilde{\Sigma}}(n) := |2 \cdot \Pr[W_0] - 1|.$$

In game G_1, we replace the PRF F_1 with a randomly chosen function f. $\mathcal{F}$ simulates the challenger for $\mathcal{D}$ and chooses a bit $\hat{b}$ to decide which interaction to simulate. If $\mathcal{D}$ can distinguish the tuples generated by different functions, especially commitments t, then we can construct a PRF adversary $\mathcal{F}$ to identify the different PRFs by returning $(\hat{b} = b')$ where b' is $\mathcal{D}$'s output. Thus, by the Difference Lemma, we can have

$$|\Pr[W_1] - \Pr[W_0]| \leq \mathsf{Adv}^{\mathsf{ind}}_{\mathcal{F},\mathsf{F}_1}(n).$$

Consider the game G_1. Because f is randomly chosen, t is like being produced at random after the first one. Thus, we could view the tuple (t, c, z) generated in $(\tilde{\Sigma}.\mathsf{Pro}, \Sigma.\mathsf{Ver})$ as the ones generated by the honest one are identically distributed because the tuple (t, c, z) in the subverted one is generated completely randomly through the function f. In such a situation, the detector $\mathcal{D}$ wins the game only by purely guessing with the probability $\frac{1}{2}$. Finally, we have

$$\begin{aligned}
\mathsf{Adv}^{\mathsf{und}}_{\mathcal{D},\Sigma,\tilde{\Sigma}}(n) &:= |2 \cdot \Pr[W_0] - 1| \\
&= |2 \cdot \Pr[W_0] - 2 \cdot \Pr[W_1] + 2 \cdot \Pr[W_1] - 1| \\
&\leq |2 \cdot \Pr[W_0] - 2 \cdot \Pr[W_1]| + |2 \cdot \Pr[W_1] - 1| \\
&\leq 2 \cdot \mathsf{Adv}^{\mathsf{ind}}_{\mathcal{F},\mathsf{F}_1}(n) \leq 2 \cdot \epsilon_1
\end{aligned}$$

(2). In the witness recovery game as Fig. 4, we need to have a categorical discussion.

Firstly, when $q \geq \ell_x + 1$, by the definition of the stateful $\tilde{\Sigma}.\mathsf{Pro}$ itself, we consider that the adversary $\mathcal{A}$ gets the tuple (t, c, z) with exfiltrated information more than ℓ_x times. $\mathcal{A}$ could extract the witness completely by telling whether $t = \mathsf{F}_1(bd_1, r_t, 0)$ and setting $x[\sigma]$ with a symmetric backdoor bd_1 and PRF F_1. The reason is that $\mathcal{A}$ can make use of σ to traverse every bit of the witness x. Therefore, we have

$$\mathsf{Adv}^{\mathsf{wr}}_{\mathcal{A},\tilde{\Sigma}.\mathsf{Pro}}(n) = 1.$$

Secondly, let us discuss the situation in which $q \leq \ell_x$. In any case, with the state σ, the adversary $\mathcal{A}$ can traverse only $q - 1$ bits of the witness. Then, $\mathcal{A}$ needs to guess the remaining $\ell_x - q + 1$ bits of the witness x with the probability $\frac{1}{2^{\ell_x - q + 1}}$. In a word, we have

$$\mathsf{Adv}^{\mathsf{wr}}_{\mathcal{A},\tilde{\Sigma}.\mathsf{Pro}}(n) \geq \frac{1}{2^{\ell_x - q + 1}}.$$

$\square$

Theorem 2. *Let Σ protocol $(\Sigma.\mathsf{Pro}, \Sigma.\mathsf{Ver})$ be an honest two-party protocol, and let $\tilde{\Sigma}.\mathsf{Pro}$ be the subverted prover which is embedded with the stateless biased-commitment attack algorithm. Let $\mathsf{F}_2 \colon \mathcal{BK} \times \mathsf{Com} \to [\ell_x]\|\{0,1\}$ be a PRF. Then,*

1. *For any efficient detector $\mathcal{D}$, we have $\mathsf{Adv}^{\mathsf{und}}_{\mathcal{D},\Sigma,\tilde{\Sigma}} \leq \mathsf{negl}$.*
2. *For any efficient adversary $\mathcal{A}$, we have $\mathsf{Adv}^{\mathsf{wr}}_{\mathcal{A},\tilde{\Sigma}.\mathsf{Pro}} \geq 1 - \ell_x \cdot e^{-\frac{q}{2 \cdot \ell_x}}$, where q is the number of times $\mathcal{A}$ eavesdrops.*

Proof. In this proof, we analyze the advantages through textual descriptions and calculations from probabilistic theory.

(1). Consider the subverted prover $\tilde{\Sigma}$.Pro in Fig. 8. The existence of PRF F_2 does not affect the distribution of the commitment t including the challenge c and response z. Everyone views the tuple (t, c, z) between $\tilde{\Sigma}$.Pro and Σ.Ver just the same as honest Σ generates. Thus, we can have

$$\mathsf{Adv}^{\mathsf{und}}_{\mathcal{D}, \Sigma, \tilde{\Sigma}}(n) \leq \mathsf{negl}(n).$$

(2). In the witness recovery game as Fig. 4, we need to use the knowledge of probability theory and the Principle of Inclusion-Exclusion. To recover the witness, $\mathcal{A}$ does not need to know if it skipped the line 1, simply uses F_2 to obtain (ℓ, b) and do the replacement $x[\ell] = b$. Successful extraction just relies on knowledge of statistics.

From a holistic view, we can view the if condition as an event that a bit is exfiltrated with the probability $\frac{1}{2}$. By computing, We can obtain an ideal number $q = O(\ell_x \log_2 \ell_x)$ of eavesdropping by statistics. More precisely, we can compute the ideal number q to extract the complete witness as:

$$E(q) = \ell_x \cdot \left(\frac{1}{1 \cdot \frac{1}{2}} + \frac{1}{2 \cdot \frac{1}{2}} + \dots + \frac{1}{\ell_x \cdot \frac{1}{2}} \right) = \frac{\ell_x}{\frac{1}{2}} \cdot \left(\frac{1}{1} + \frac{1}{2} + \dots + \frac{1}{\ell_x} \right) \approx 2n \ln \ell_x$$

But in the set of the witness-recovery game, ignoring the ideal number to achieve recovery, we are concerned about only how many useful bits of the witness can be obtained under q times of eavesdropping, and how much advantage can be achieved. If we set that there are i bits of the witness exfiltrated never, the event that for one time of eavesdropping any of the i bits is not exfiltrated, happens with the probability $1 - \frac{i}{2 \cdot \ell_x}$. So we can obtain the probability $(1 - \frac{i}{2 \cdot \ell_x})^q$ for q times. According to the Principle of Inclusion-Exclusion, we can compute the probability that $\mathcal{A}$ extracts a full witness as follows.

$$\mathsf{Adv}^{\mathsf{wr}}_{\mathcal{A}, \tilde{\Sigma}.\mathsf{Pro}}(n) = \sum_{i=0}^{\ell_x} (-1)^i \binom{n}{i} \left(1 - \frac{i}{2 \cdot \ell_x} \right)^q$$

$$\geq 1 - \ell_x \cdot \left(1 - \frac{1}{2 \cdot \ell_x} \right)^q \geq 1 - \ell_x \cdot e^{-\frac{q}{2 \cdot \ell_x}}$$

$\square$

4.2   The Biased-Challenge Attack

This section provides an algorithm substitution attack, called a biased-challenge attack. In this attack, the adversary could tell whether the verifier is honest through challenges returned by the verifier. With a secure PRF F_3, we construct a subverted verifier $\tilde{\Sigma}$.Ver. When the adversary could access $\tilde{\Sigma}$.Ver multiple times, it will pass the verification with a probability of convergence to 1 even not knowing the witness which is contrary to knowledge soundness. After a successful verification, the adversary will carry out subsequent attacks more calmly while $\tilde{\Sigma}$.Ver still shows honesty for some honest provers.

Details of the Attack. Before giving the details of the attack, we first define some concepts. Let $F_3\colon \mathcal{BK} \times \mathsf{Com} \to \mathcal{C}$ be a PRF and ε be a symbol for *null*. In the attack, the subverted verifier $\tilde{\Sigma}$.Ver maintains a register r_t just like $\tilde{\Sigma}$.Pro does in Fig. 7. Through the above definitions, we could construct a biased-challenge attack as Fig. 9 to achieve subversion effect.

Prover Σ.Pro		Verifier $\tilde{\Sigma}$.
Inputs : sk $:= (x, y)$		Inputs : vk $:= y$
		$bd_2 \leftarrow\!\!\$\ \mathcal{BK}$
		$r_t \leftarrow \varepsilon$
$t \leftarrow\!\!\$\ \mathsf{Com}$	$\xrightarrow{\hspace{2cm} t \hspace{2cm}}$	
		if $r_t = \varepsilon$:
		$\quad c \leftarrow\!\!\$\ \mathcal{C}$
		else $c \leftarrow F_3(bd_2, r_t)$
		$r_t \leftarrow t$
	$\xleftarrow{\hspace{2cm} c \hspace{2cm}}$	
Compute response z	$\xrightarrow{\hspace{2cm} z \hspace{2cm}}$	Output **accept** or **reject**

Fig. 9. The biased-challenge attack

Formal Analysis. Then, we will explain how destructive the above-mentioned adversary is in the environment we set up. We discuss this attack through two attack models in Sect. 3.2.

Theorem 3. *Let Σ protocol (Σ.Pro, Σ.Ver) be an honest two-party protocol, and let $\tilde{\Sigma}$.Ver be the subverted verifier which is embedded with the biased-challenge attack algorithm. Let $F_3\colon \mathcal{BK} \times \mathsf{Com} \to \mathcal{C}$ be a PRF and $f \in \mathsf{FUNS}[(\mathcal{BK}, \mathsf{Com}), \mathcal{C}]$ be randomly chosen. If F_3 is a secure PRF, we have $\mathsf{Adv}^{\mathsf{ind}}_{\mathcal{F}, F_3} \le \epsilon_3$ where ϵ_3 is negligible for all PPT PRF adversary $\mathcal{F}$. Then,*

1. *For any efficient detector $\mathcal{D}$, we have $\mathsf{Adv}^{\mathsf{und}}_{\mathcal{D}, \Sigma, \tilde{\Sigma}} \le 2 \cdot \mathsf{Adv}^{\mathsf{ind}}_{\mathcal{F}, F_3} \le 2 \cdot \epsilon_3$, where ϵ_3 is negligible.*
2. *For any efficient adversary $\mathcal{A}$, we have $\mathsf{Adv}^{\mathsf{cd}}_{\mathcal{A}, \Sigma, \tilde{\Sigma}} \approx 1$, when $\mathcal{A}$ can make q inquiries where $q \ge 2$ and $|\mathcal{C}|$ is super-poly. Otherwise, $\mathsf{Adv}^{\mathsf{cd}}_{\mathcal{A}, \Sigma, \tilde{\Sigma}} \le \mathsf{negl}$.*

Proof. In this proof, we analyze the advantages through the previous example and the subverted algorithm content.

(1). As the previous proof in Theorem 1, as long as the PRF F_3 is secure, then we can have

$$\mathsf{Adv}^{\mathsf{und}}_{\mathcal{D},\Sigma,\tilde{\Sigma}}(n) \leq 2 \cdot \mathsf{Adv}^{\mathsf{ind}}_{\mathcal{F},F_3}(n) \leq 2 \cdot \epsilon_3.$$

(2). In the challenge distinguishability game, we need to have a categorical discussion. In this game, the adversary $\mathcal{A}$ can interact with $\Sigma.\mathsf{Ver}$ or $\tilde{\Sigma}.\mathsf{Ver}$. Firstly, case 1 is that $q \geq 2$. $\mathcal{A}$ can store the last accessed commitment u_L and send a randomly chosen commitment u_N every time after the first query. If the challenge c_N satisfies the condition that $c_N = F_3(bd_2, u_L)$, $\mathcal{A}$ can consider that the verifier has been subverted with the error probability only $\frac{1}{|\mathcal{C}|}$. Therefore, $\Sigma.\mathsf{Ver}$ simulates the same as $\tilde{\Sigma}.\mathsf{Ver}$ with the probability $(\frac{1}{|\mathcal{C}|})^{q-1}$ when $\mathcal{A}$ can ask q inquiries. Finally, when $|\mathcal{C}|$ is super-poly, we have

$$\mathsf{Adv}^{\mathsf{cd}}_{\mathcal{A},\Sigma,\tilde{\Sigma}}(n) = 1 - (\frac{1}{|\mathcal{C}|})^{q-1} \approx 1.$$

Then, case 2 is that $q = 1$. Obviously, in $\tilde{\Sigma}.\mathsf{Ver}$, when the first query, the challenge is chosen randomly as honest $\Sigma.\mathsf{Ver}$ does. Only with a single purely random pair (t, c), $\mathcal{A}$ can only guess whether the verifier is honest with the probability $\frac{1}{2}$. So, we have

$$\mathsf{Adv}^{\mathsf{cd}}_{\mathcal{A},\Sigma,\tilde{\Sigma}}(n) \leq \mathsf{negl}(n).$$

$\square$

5   Instantiations of Subvertible Σ Protocols

In this section, we describe two instantiations to describe the proposed attacks on the basic Σ protocol. We choose two better-known examples of Σ protocols, the *Schnorr's identification Protocol* and the *Okamoto's Protocol for Representations*. Through practical examples, clarify the undetectability and effectiveness of the attacks under these Σ protocols.

5.1   Schnorr's Identification Protocol

In 1991, Schnorr proposed the first efficient example of Σ protocols. It is based on the Discrete Logarithm Problem (DLP) and has been applied widely. In the protocol, let p be a super-poly prime and $\mathcal{X} = \mathbb{Z}_p^*$ be the set $\{1, 2, 3, ..., p-1\}$. Then, let $\mathcal{C}$ be a subgroup of $\mathbb{Z}_p^*$. Com$= \mathbb{G}$ denotes a circular group produced by a generator g where $|\mathbb{G}| = p$. Thus, response z is generated from $\mathbb{Z}_p^*$. Define the relation $\mathcal{R}$ as $\{(x,y)|x \in \mathcal{X} \wedge y = g^x \in \mathbb{G}\}$. This relation determines the generation of commitments and responses, and the computation of the final authentication result. With these concepts, the Schnorr's identification Protocol is shown in Fig. 10.

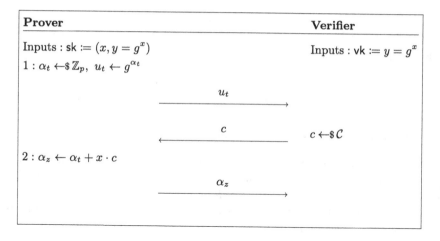

Fig. 10. Schnorr's identification protocol

Then let us analyze three attacks. We ignore the undetectable property of three attacks which has been proven above reduced to the indistinguishability of the different PRFs, and focus on the substantial effect of the attacks. We also ignore the special cases in the attack analysis, for example, $q < \ell_x$ in the biased-commitment attack and $q = 1$ in the biased-challenge attack. Obviously, any adversary wants to extract the witness from the transcripts of an honest prover with only the probability $\frac{1}{|\mathcal{X}|} = \frac{1}{|\mathbb{Z}_p^*|} = \frac{1}{p-1}$ by guessing randomly, and to pass the verification interacting with an honest verifier with the probability $\frac{1}{|\mathcal{C}|}$ to guess the challenge returned and compute the right transcript.

For the subverted prover, we discuss two attacks. For the stateful biased-commitment attack, with the state σ and a PRF $F_1 \colon \mathcal{BK} \times \mathbb{G} \times \{0,1\} \to \mathbb{G}$, the adversary $\mathcal{A}$ could recover the witness x with only $\ell_x + 1 = \log_2(p-1) + 1$ times of eavesdropping. Thus, when $q \geq \log_2(p-1) + 1$, we have a significantly improved advantage that

$$\mathsf{Adv}^{\mathsf{wr}}_{\mathcal{A},\tilde{\Sigma}.\mathsf{Pro}} = 1 \gg \frac{1}{p-1}(n).$$

In the stateless biased-commitment attack, according to the Theorem 2, we know that a PRF F_2 is defined over $[(\mathcal{BK} \times \mathbb{G}), [\ell_x] \| \{0,1\}]$ and the adversary $\mathcal{A}$ needs the average times $2\ell_x \ln \ell_x$ to ensure the witness recovered fully where $\ell_x = \log_2(p-1)$ is the binary length of the witness x. Based on Sect. 4.1, we have

$$\mathsf{Adv}^{\mathsf{wr}}_{\mathcal{A},\tilde{\Sigma}.\mathsf{Pro}}(n) \geq 1 - \ell_x \cdot e^{-\frac{q}{2 \cdot \ell_x}} \gg \frac{1}{p-1}.$$

It is obvious that if $q = 2 \times 2n \ln \ell_x = 4\ell_x \ln \ell_x$, $\mathsf{Adv}^{\mathsf{wr}}_{\mathcal{A},\tilde{\Sigma}.\mathsf{Pro}}(n) \approx 1 - \frac{1}{\ell_x}$ which is considerable when p is super-poly.

As for the subverted verifier, with only analyzing the biased-challenge attack, because $\mathcal{C}$ is the subgroup of $\mathbb{Z}_p^*$ and a PRF $\mathsf{F}_3\colon \mathcal{BK} \times \mathbb{G} \to \mathcal{C}$, we have $\frac{1}{|\mathcal{C}|} \geq \frac{1}{p}$. Using the proof in Sect. 4.2, when q is big enough, we have

$$\mathsf{Adv}^{cd}_{\mathcal{A},\Sigma,\tilde{\Sigma}} = 1 - (\frac{1}{|\mathcal{C}|})^{q-1} \leq 1 - (\frac{1}{p})^{q-1} \approx 1 \text{ and } \mathsf{Adv}^{cd}_{\mathcal{A},\Sigma,\tilde{\Sigma}} = 1 - (\frac{1}{|\mathcal{C}|})^{q-1} \gg \frac{1}{|\mathcal{C}|}.$$

5.2 Okamoto's Protocol for Representations

For Okamoto's Protocol, with the same symbols above, we use the same groups $\mathbb{Z}_p^*$ and $\mathbb{G}$, however set $\mathcal{X} = \mathbb{Z}_p^{*2}$ and $\mathsf{Com} = \mathbb{G}$ respectively. The relation $\mathcal{R}$ is the set $\{(x,y)|x = (\alpha,\beta) \in \mathcal{X} \wedge (y = g^\alpha h^\beta \wedge g, h \in \mathbb{G})\}$. Under these concepts, the prover needs to choose two random values α_t and β_t in line 1 and compute two responses α_z and β_z in line 2 in Fig. 10. Next, we will briefly analyze the effect of three attacks on it.

Considering that there are two witnesses, we need to merge them by $\alpha' = \alpha \| \beta$. Thus, let $\ell_x = 2 \cdot \log_2(p-1)$ be the binary length of the new witness. Without subversions, in Okamoto's Protocol, any adversary has the probability $\frac{1}{|\mathcal{X}|} = \frac{1}{(p-1)^2}$ to guess the witness and the probability $\frac{1}{|\mathsf{Com}|} = \frac{1}{|\mathbb{G}|}$ to pass the verification. In the biased-commitment attacks, we can use the same PRFs F_1 and F_2 defined in Sect. 5.1 for both the stateful one and the stateless one. For the stateful attack, we do the same analysis. As for the stateless attack, we have a remarkable advantage that

$$\mathsf{Adv}^{wr}_{\mathcal{A},\tilde{\Sigma}.\mathsf{Pro}}(n) \geq 1 - \ell_x \cdot e^{-\frac{p}{2\cdot\ell_x}} \gg \frac{1}{(p-1)^2}$$

where p perhaps needs to be nearly twice as much as the one in Sect. 5.1 to achieve a similar advantage.

The definitions of $\mathcal{C}$ and PRF F_3 are the same as before in Sect. 5.1. Therefore, for the biased-commitment attack, the analysis are identical in which the advantage is much greater than $\frac{1}{|\mathbb{G}|}$.

6 Conclusion

Again before, algorithm substitution attacks are designed to target encryption schemes, signature schemes and some other protocols. This work applies the attack to the basic Σ protocol. With both prover and verifier as targets, we innovatively propose two biased attacks of the ASAs which not only improve the ability of the mass surveillance adversaries to gain access to the prover's secret witness but helps the adversaries pass the authentication with non-negligible advantage. Though this work is based on a basic structure for design, the feasibility of the attacks on specific Σ protocols has been demonstrated by two examples. As for how to mitigate the attacks, it is a meaningful area of research that needs further study.

Acknowledgements. This work is support by National Natural Science Foundation of China (Grant No. 62122092, 62032005). Lin Liu is support by the National Natural Science Foundation of China (Grant No. 62102430) and the Natural Science Foundation of Hunan Province, China (Grant No. 2021JJ40688), and the Science Research Plan Program by NUDT (Grant No. ZK22-50).

References

1. Abdolmaleki, B., Baghery, K., Lipmaa, H., Zając, M.: A subversion-resistant SNARK. In: Takagi, T., Peyrin, T. (eds.) ASIACRYPT 2017. LNCS, vol. 10626, pp. 3–33. Springer, Cham (2017). https://doi.org/10.1007/978-3-319-70700-6_1
2. Abe, M., Ambrona, M., Bogdanov, A., Ohkubo, M., Rosen, A.: Non-interactive composition of sigma-protocols via share-then-hash. In: Moriai, S., Wang, H. (eds.) ASIACRYPT 2020. LNCS, vol. 12493, pp. 749–773. Springer, Cham (2020). https://doi.org/10.1007/978-3-030-64840-4_25
3. Armour, M., Poettering, B.: Substitution attacks against message authentication. In: Cryptology ePrint Archive (2019)
4. Armour, M., Poettering, B.: Subverting decryption in AEAD. In: Albrecht, M. (ed.) IMACC 2019. LNCS, vol. 11929, pp. 22–41. Springer, Cham (2019). https://doi.org/10.1007/978-3-030-35199-1_2
5. Ateniese, G., Magri, B., Venturi, D.: Subversion-resilient signatures: definitions, constructions and applications. Theoret. Comput. Sci. **820**, 91–122 (2015)
6. Attema, T., Cramer, R., Rambaud, M.: Compressed σ-protocols for bilinear group arithmetic circuits and application to logarithmic transparent threshold signatures. In: Tibouchi, M., Wang, H. (eds.) ASIACRYPT 2021. LNCS, vol. 13093, pp. 526–556. Springer, Cham (2021). https://doi.org/10.1007/978-3-030-92068-5_18
7. Bangerter, E., Camenisch, J., Krenn, S.: Efficiency Limitations for σ-Protocols for Group Homomorphisms. In: Micciancio, D. (ed.) TCC 2010. LNCS, vol. 5978, pp. 553–571. Springer, Heidelberg (2010). https://doi.org/10.1007/978-3-642-11799-2_33
8. Bellare, M., Fuchsbauer, G., Scafuro, A.: NIZKs with an untrusted CRS: security in the face of parameter subversion. In: Cheon, J.H., Takagi, T. (eds.) ASIACRYPT 2016. LNCS, vol. 10032, pp. 777–804. Springer, Heidelberg (2016). https://doi.org/10.1007/978-3-662-53890-6_26
9. Bellare, M., Jaeger, J., Kane, D.: Mass-surveillance without the state: Strongly undetectable algorithm-substitution attacks (2015)
10. Bellare, M., Paterson, K.G., Rogaway, P.: Security of symmetric encryption against mass surveillance. In: Garay, J.A., Gennaro, R. (eds.) CRYPTO 2014. LNCS, vol. 8616, pp. 1–19. Springer, Heidelberg (2014). https://doi.org/10.1007/978-3-662-44371-2_1
11. Bellare, M., Ristov, T.: Hash functions from sigma protocols and improvements to VSH. In: Pieprzyk, J. (ed.) ASIACRYPT 2008. LNCS, vol. 5350, pp. 125–142. Springer, Heidelberg (2008). https://doi.org/10.1007/978-3-540-89255-7_9
12. Ben-Sasson, E., Chiesa, A., Green, M., Tromer, E., Virza, M.: Secure sampling of public parameters for succinct zero knowledge proofs. In: 2015 IEEE Symposium on Security and Privacy, pp. 287–304 (2015). https://doi.org/10.1109/SP.2015.25
13. Berndt, S., Wichelmann, J., Pott, C., Traving, T.H., Eisenbarth, T.: ASAP: algorithm substitution attacks on cryptographic protocols. Cryptology ePrint Archive, Report 2020/1452 (2020)

14. Chaum, D., Pedersen, T.P.: Wallet databases with observers. In: Brickell, E.F. (ed.) CRYPTO 1992. LNCS, vol. 740, pp. 89–105. Springer, Heidelberg (1993). https://doi.org/10.1007/3-540-48071-4_7

15. Chen, R., Huang, X., Yung, M.: Subvert KEM to break DEM: practical algorithm-substitution attacks on public-key encryption. In: Moriai, S., Wang, H. (eds.) ASIACRYPT 2020. LNCS, vol. 12492, pp. 98–128. Springer, Cham (2020). https://doi.org/10.1007/978-3-030-64834-3_4

16. Degabriele, J.P., Farshim, P., Poettering, B.: A more cautious approach to security against mass surveillance. In: Leander, G. (ed.) FSE 2015. LNCS, vol. 9054, pp. 579–598. Springer, Heidelberg (2015). https://doi.org/10.1007/978-3-662-48116-5_28

17. Guillou, L.C., Quisquater, J.-J.: A practical zero-knowledge protocol fitted to security microprocessor minimizing both transmission and memory. In: Barstow, D., et al. (eds.) EUROCRYPT 1988. LNCS, vol. 330, pp. 123–128. Springer, Heidelberg (1988). https://doi.org/10.1007/3-540-45961-8_11

18. Marchiori, D., Giron, A.A., do Nascimento, J.P.A., Custódio, R.: Timing analysis of algorithm substitution attacks in a post-quantum TLS protocol. In: Anais do XXI Simpósio Brasileiro em Segurança da Informação e de Sistemas Computacionais. pp. 127–140 (2021)

19. Maurer, U.: Zero-knowledge proofs of knowledge for group homomorphisms. Des. Codes Crptogr. **77**, 663–676 (2015). https://doi.org/10.1007/s10623-015-0103-5

20. Okamoto, T.: Provably secure and practical identification schemes and corresponding signature schemes. In: Brickell, E.F. (ed.) CRYPTO 1992. LNCS, vol. 740, pp. 31–53. Springer, Heidelberg (1993). https://doi.org/10.1007/3-540-48071-4_3

21. Schnorr, C.P.: Efficient signature generation by smart cards. J. Crptogr. **4**, 161–174 (1991). https://doi.org/10.1007/BF00196725

22. Teşeleanu, G.: Unifying kleptographic attacks. In: Gruschka, N. (ed.) NordSec 2018. LNCS, vol. 11252, pp. 73–87. Springer, Cham (2018). https://doi.org/10.1007/978-3-030-03638-6_5

23. Young, A., Yung, M.: The dark side of "Black-Box" cryptography or: should we trust capstone? In: Koblitz, N. (ed.) CRYPTO 1996. LNCS, vol. 1109, pp. 89–103. Springer, Heidelberg (1996). https://doi.org/10.1007/3-540-68697-5_8

24. Young, A., Yung, M.: Kleptography: using cryptography against cryptography. In: Fumy, W. (ed.) EUROCRYPT 1997. LNCS, vol. 1233, pp. 62–74. Springer, Heidelberg (1997). https://doi.org/10.1007/3-540-69053-0_6

25. Young, A., Yung, M.: Malicious cryptography: kleptographic aspects. In: Menezes, A. (ed.) CT-RSA 2005. LNCS, vol. 3376, pp. 7–18. Springer, Heidelberg (2005). https://doi.org/10.1007/978-3-540-30574-3_2

26. Young, A., Yung, M.: The prevalence of kleptographic attacks on discrete-log based cryptosystems. In: Kaliski, B.S. (ed.) CRYPTO 1997. LNCS, vol. 1294, pp. 264–276. Springer, Heidelberg (1997). https://doi.org/10.1007/BFb0052241

27. Young, A., Yung, M.: A space efficient backdoor in RSA and its applications. In: Preneel, B., Tavares, S. (eds.) SAC 2005. LNCS, vol. 3897, pp. 128–143. Springer, Heidelberg (2006). https://doi.org/10.1007/11693383_9

A Multi-stage APT Attack Detection Method Based on Sample Enhancement

Lixia Xie[1], Xueou Li[1], Hongyu Yang[1,2(✉)], and Liang Zhang[3]

[1] School of Computer Science and Technology, Civil Aviation University of China,
Tianjin 300300, China
yhyxlx@hotmail.com
[2] School of Safety Science and Engineering, Civil Aviation University of China,
Tianjin 300300, China
[3] School of Information, The University of Arizona, Tucson, AZ 85721, USA

Abstract. In order to solve the problems that the current Advanced Persistent Threat (APT) attack detection methods lack the detection of potential APT attack threats, and are difficult to obtain high detection accuracy in the case of smaller APT attack samples, a Sample Enhanced Multi-Stage APT Attack Detection Network (SE-ADN) is proposed. Sequence Generative Adversarial Network (seq-GAN) is used to simulate the generative attack encoder sequences, which are constructed by malicious traffic. The samples of multi-stage APT attack sequences are enhanced to increase the number of samples and improve the diversity of sample traffic features. A multi-stage APT attack detection network is proposed, which uses the attack features of each stage to enhance the detection awareness ability and improve the detection accuracy of the potential APT attack. The experimental results show that SE-ADN performs well on two benchmark datasets, and is better than the comparison methods in detecting multiple types of potential APT attacks.

Keywords: APT attack detection · Multi-stage · Sample enhancement

1 Introduction

Advanced Persistent Threat (APT) attack has become one of the most difficult attack methods to prevent in network attacks. Compared with traditional attacks, APT can be described from three perspectives: advanced, persistent, and threat [1]. Advanced means that APT attackers often master a variety of zero-day vulnerabilities that bypass system detection to achieve the ideal attack effect. Persistence refers to a long attack cycle. Attackers usually seek high priority and continue to attack them. Threats refer to the ability of attackers to cause certain losses and damages to key components in the target organization's systems and networks. The APT attack is not only a direct destructive behavior, but also gradually acquires more information, privileges, and resources in multiple stages, infiltrating the target system more subtly and persistently, to form an internal foothold and achieve the goal. APT attacks are generally divided into five stages: reconnaissance, foothold establishment, lateral movement, exfiltration or impediment, and post-exfiltration or post-impediment [2].

Due to the large scale and long duration of the APT attack, the current research on APT attack detection mostly uses public datasets for simulation experiments. There are smaller attack samples collected in public datasets and APT attack traffic features are single and lacking diversity. In addition, most detection studies of APT attacks only consider the completed APT attack sequences in the entire attack cycle, and no potential APT attack threat is detected.

To address the above issues, this paper proposes a Sample Enhanced Multi-Stage APT attacks Detection Network (SE-ADN): (1) Sequence Generative Adversarial Network (seqGAN) is used to generate attack samples at various stages. It can not only increase the number of multi-stage sequence samples of APT attacks but also improve the diversity of sample features. (2) A multi-stage APT attack detection network (ADN) based on stage awareness is proposed. The multi-stage awareness mechanism is used to explore the dependencies between the stages of the APT sequence to improve the detection accuracy of APT attacks. Experimental results show that SE-ADN exhibits good results on two benchmark datasets and outperforms existing detection methods.

2 Related Work

Common APT attack detection mainly includes host detection and traffic detection. The former mainly analyzes the communication between hosts, detects infected hosts, and predicts potential paths of APT attacks [3, 4]. The latter extracts the features of abnormal behaviors in the network traffic data and analyzes them to conclude. Among them, the current research on APT attack sequence detection methods is mainly based on traffic analysis.

With the deepening of the current research on APT attacks and the continuous development of emerging technologies, the use of deep learning methods to detect APT attacks has gradually become a current research hotspot [5]. Liu et al. [6] proposed an APT attack detection method, which generated APT attack samples and considers the timing of APT attacks. Dong [7] proposed a method to generate and detect of APT attack sequence with Long Short-Term Memory (LSTM), which is used to expand the APT dataset and detect the APT attack. Joloudari et al. [8] proposed a six-layer deep learning method to automatically extract the hidden layer features of the neural network, which achieved a good accuracy on the NSL-KDD dataset. However, the dataset was too old to lack detection of new attack methods. Do et al. [9] used Bi-directional Long Short-Term Memory (Bi-LSTM) and Graph Convolutional Network (GCN) to detect APT attacks. However, the detection effect of this method was not good for high concealment attacks.

Compared with the above research methods, this paper innovatively uses the multi-stage feature of the APT attack through the sample enhancement process as detection information to enhance the awareness of the detection network. Then detect the potential APT attack sequence containing multiple attack stages. To improve the diversity of attack samples, the seqGAN network is used as the sample enhancement model, which is more conducive to discrete long-sequence samples.

3   Multi-stage APT Attack Detection Method Based on Sample Enhancement

The multi-stage APT attack detection network based on sample enhancement consists of two parts: multi-stage sample enhancement and multi-stage APT attack detection. The detection architecture is shown in Fig. 1.

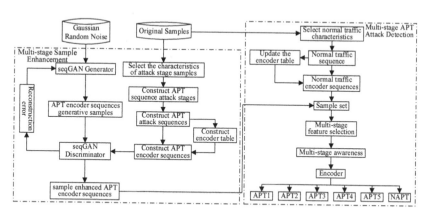

Fig. 1. The detection architecture.

3.1   Multi-stage Sample Enhancement

Multi-stage sample enhancement firstly constructs the APT encoder sequence by reconstructing the original sample. Then, the seqGAN generator is used to learn the probability distribution features of Gaussian random noise and generate the APT encoder sequence generative samples. Finally, the seqGAN discriminator is used to identify and simulate the generated samples and the original samples. The reconstruction error guides the generator to generate the APT encoder sequence samples which are more consistent with the probability distribution of the original sample.

To construct the APT attack sequence, the original sample needs to be preprocessed. Firstly, according to the traffic features of the multi-stage, select the features of attack stage samples. Secondly, construct APT sequence attack stages separately. Then, with the attack steps, the features of each stage are sequentially spliced to construct five types of APT sequences. Since SE-ADN needs to code each element in the sequence for the APT sequence, this paper constructs an encoder table to reconstruct the attack sequence into an encoder sequence to improve the efficiency of network training.

The sample enhancement module in the multi-stage detection of APT attacks proposed in this paper uses seqGAN to generate simulated samples. Figure 2 shows the structure of sample enhancement based on seqGAN. Firstly, under the premise of the known likelihood function, the Gaussian random noise is randomly sampled as the input of the seqGAN generator. The generator uses the Gated Recurrent Unit (GRU) to generate multi-stage APT attack encoder sequences. Then, the coding sequence is successively passed through the convolution layer, Relu, pooling layer, and linear layer to determine whether the current sequence is the generative sequence or the original sample. It is best to reconstruct error and update generator parameters by gradient strategy. After several iterations, the generative APT attack encoder sequence will be subject to the distribution of the real samples most likely.

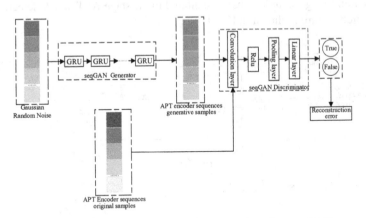

Fig. 2. The structure of sample enhancement based on seqGAN.

3.2 Multi-stage APT Attack Detection

The multi-stage detection network for APT attacks proposed in this paper is based on the Transformer encoder and a multi-stage awareness mechanism. By selecting normal traffic features, the normal traffic sequences are constructed. The normal traffic encoder sequences are generated with the updated encoder table. By selecting the network traffic features of multi-stage, each attack stage feature is aware to guide the detection of network learning and improve detection accuracy. The structure of this attack network is shown in Fig. 3. The specific steps are designed as follows.

Multi-stage Feature Selection
Feature selection can learn the key information of the original sample, which can not only reduce the size of the original feature vector but also help optimize the performance of the detection network. First of all, the multi-stage traffic features are mapped by vector. The traffic at different stages is filled into sequences with the same length, and the phase traffic matrix M is obtained by splicing. Then, the convolution layer is used to select the feature of the matrix, and the max pooling layer is used to obtain the key features. Finally, the key features of multi-stages mf_i are combined to obtain the traffic features of multiple stages MF, which are defined as follows:

$$MF = concat(mf_1, mf_2, mf_3, mf_4, mf_5),$$
$$mf_i = max(f_i(Relu(M * C) + b)) \qquad (1)$$

where $concat()$ is splicing operation, $Relu()$ represents the nonlinear activation function, * represents the inner product operation of the convolution kernel, C is the convolution kernel, and b is the bias term.

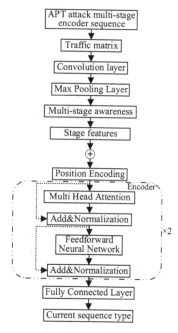

Fig. 3. The structure of multi-stage APT attack detection network.

Multi-stage Awareness

Since APT attacks have staged features, this paper proposes a stage awareness mechanism to calculate the correlation between the encoder sequence and *MF*. Taking the correlation as supplementary knowledge can improve the awareness of multi-stage features, thereby improving the accuracy of staged detection. First, according to the multi-stage feature *MF*, and attack encoder sequence in calculating the dot product contribution score and convert to the attention coefficient. The stage awareness is calculated by the weighted summation of *MF* according to the attention coefficient. Finally, the stage feature generated by the stage awareness is spliced with the APT attack encoder sequence as the input of the multi-stage attack detection model.

Encoder Construction

The multi-stage APT attack detection network adopts Transformer model encoder with position encoder. The detection network is composed of two coding layers, each coding layer consists of a self-attention layer and a feedforward neural network. The self-attention layer uses multi-head attention (MHA) mechanism to capture the global information in the sequence to effectively improve the multi-stage APT attacks detection ability. MHA can connect any two locations of the hidden state and find connections between different locations in the attack sequence. In order to solve the problem of gradient disappearance and speed up the training speed, residual connection, add and normalization are used between each sub-layer. Finally, according to the APT attack detection task corresponding to ADN, the fully connected layer is constructed to detect the current sequence type.

4 Experimental Results

4.1 Environment and Evaluation Metrics

The hardware environment of this experiment is Intel(R) Xeon(R) Silver processor, 32 GB main memory, 16G memory, and NVIDIA Quadro RTX5000. Experiments were carried out on the Ubuntu operating system with Python 3.8 and Pytorch 1.7. The experiment sample is selected from the CICIDS2017 [10] and the DAPT2020 [11].

The F1-score (F1) comprehensively considers the method's precision and recall. Precision refers to the proportion of true positive samples detected as positive samples. Recall refers to the ratio of true positive samples to detected positive samples. F1 can be expressed as

$$F1 = \frac{2TP}{2TP + FN + FP} \tag{2}$$

The macro average (Macro_avg) comprehensively considers the F1 scores of the classification results of different categories and calculates the F1 arithmetic average of multiple categories, which can be expressed as

$$Macro\_avg = \frac{1}{n}\sum_{i=0}^{n} F1_i \tag{3}$$

where TP (True Positive) is the number of samples detected as normal samples by normal samples, FP (False Positive) is the number of samples detected by attack samples as normal samples, and FN (False Negative) is the number of samples detected by normal samples as attack samples number of cases.

4.2 Experimental Results and Analysis

The set is divided into three parts: 60% are used as the training set, 20% are used as the validation set, and 20% are used as the testing set. Each stage type is recorded as APT1, APT2, APT3, APT4, APT5, and NAPT respectively. The normal sequence length is the same as the APT5 sequence length.

The SE-ADN, TextRCNN, DPCNN, and LSTM are used as multi-stage APT attack detection methods respectively. The sequence sample sets are generated by the CICIDS2017 and DAPT2020. Table 1 and Table 2 show the F1 result pairs of multi-stage APT attack detection of the four methods, and the comparison of the Macro_avg results is shown in Fig. 4.

In the APT attack detection, the LSTM has limited ability to deal with long-term dependencies, because of the slow parameter training and the disappearance of gradients occurs. DPCNN can extract long-term dependencies by continuously deepening the network, but the method does not consider the features of the APT attack sequence and has pool results in NAPT detection. TextRCNN uses the cyclic network structure to extract long-distance semantic information as much as possible, but the method needs to analyze the information in the sequence one by one. It cannot effectively solve the long-sequence dependency problem. SE-ADN makes full use of the multi-stage APT attack feature. The Macro_avg on the two datasets is better than the other three methods and obtains better results in APT5 and NAPT detection.

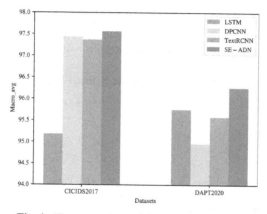

Fig. 4. The comparison of the Macro_avg results.

Table 1. F1 of the four methods in the CICIDS2017 dataset.

Method	F1/%					
	APT1	APT2	APT3	APT4	APT5	NAPT
LSTM	100	100	100	100	85.86	85.24
DPCNN	100	99.96	99.96	99.93	92.44	92.30
TextRCNN	100	100	99.96	99.96	92.35	91.96
SE-ADN	100	99.96	99.93	99.93	92.77	92.78

Table 2. F1 of the four methods in the DAPT2020 dataset.

Method	F1/%					
	APT1	APT2	APT3	APT4	APT5	NAPT
LSTM	99.89	99.89	100	99.86	86.79	88.08
DPCNN	99.47	99.14	96.62	95.75	89.25	89.55
TextRCNN	96.60	96.51	99.86	99.64	91.01	89.89
SE-ADN	99.54	99.32	99.39	99.50	89.82	89.99

5 Conclusion

Current APT attack detection methods have a small number of attack samples and the unitary sample form. Therefore, APT attack detection is ineffective and cannot distinguish unfinished APT attack threats. To solve the above problems, this paper proposes a sample enhanced multi-stage APT attack detection network (SE-ADN). The APT attack sequences are generated using seqGAN network to enhance the samples. In addition, a multi-stage APT attack detection network is proposed. The attack features of each stage are used as auxiliary information to enhance the detection network's awareness of different attack stages and improve detection accuracy. The detection results are better than the current method on two benchmark datasets.

Acknowledgment. This work was supported by the National Natural Science Foundation of China (No. U1833107).

References

1. Stojanović, B.F., Hofer-Schmitz, K.S., Kleb, U.T.: APT datasets and attack modeling for automated detection methods: a review. Comput. Secur. **92**, 101734–101752 (2020)
2. Alshamrani, A.F., Myneni, S.S., Chowdhary, A.T.: A survey on advanced persistent threats: techniques, solutions, challenges, and research opportunities. IEEE Commun. Surv. Tutorials **21**(2), 1851–1877 (2019)
3. Coulter, R.F., Zhang, J.S., Pan, L.T., Xiang, Y.F.: Domain adaptation for Windows advanced persistent threat detection. Comput. Secur. **112**, 102496–102510 (2022)
4. Coulter, R.F., Zhang, J.S., Pan, L.T., Xiang, Y.F.: Unmasking windows advanced persistent threat execution. In: Wang, G.F., Ko, R.S. (eds.) Proceedings of 19th International Conference on Trust, Security and Privacy in Computing and Communications 2020. LNCS, vol. 19, pp. 268–276. IEEE, Piscataway (2020)
5. Lin, G.F., Wen, S.S., Han, Q.L.: Software vulnerability detection using deep neural networks: a survey. Proc. IEEE **108**(10), 1825–1848 (2020)
6. Liu, H.F., Wu, T.S., Shen, J.T.: Advanced persistent threat detection based on generative adversarial networks and long short-term memory. Comput. Sci. **47**(1), 281–286 (2020)
7. Dong, J.F.: Research on generation and detection of APT attack sequence based on GAN. Harbin Engineering University, pp. 857–916 (2020)
8. Joloudari, J.F., Haderbadi, M.S., Mashmool, A.T.: Early detection of the advanced persistent threat attack using performance analysis of deep learning. IEEE Access **8**(8), 186125–186137 (2020)
9. Do, X.F., Dao, M.S., Nguyen, H.T.: APT attack detection based on flow network analysis techniques using deep learning. J. Intell. Fuzzy Syst. **39**(3), 4785–4801 (2020)
10. Sharafaldin, I.F., Lashkari, A.S., Ghorbani, A.T.: Toward generating a new intrusion detection dataset and intrusion traffic characterization. In: ICISSP, vol. 1, pp. 108–116 (2018)
11. Myneni, S., et al.: DAPT 2020 - constructing a benchmark dataset for advanced persistent threats. In: Wang, G., Ciptadi, A., Ahmadzadeh, A. (eds.) MLHat 2020. CCIS, vol. 1271, pp. 138–163. Springer, Cham (2020). https://doi.org/10.1007/978-3-030-59621-7_8

VDHGT: A Source Code Vulnerability Detection Method Based on Heterogeneous Graph Transformer

Hongyu Yang[1]([⊠]), Haiyun Yang[2], and Liang Zhang[3]

[1] School of Safety Science and Engineering, Civil Aviation University of China,
Tianjin 300300, China
yhyxlx@hotmail.com
[2] School of Computer Science and Technology, Civil Aviation University of China,
Tianjin 300300, China
[3] School of Information, The University of Arizona, Tucson, AZ 85721, USA

Abstract. Vulnerability detection is still a challenging problem. The source code representation method used by the existing vulnerability detection methods cannot fully contain the context information of the vulnerability occurrence statement, and the vulnerability detection model does not fully consider the importance of the context statement to the vulnerability occurrence statement. Aiming at the problems raised above, this paper proposes a source code vulnerability detection method based on the heterogeneous graph transformer. The method proposed in this paper adopts a novel source code representation method—**the vulnerability dependence representation graph**, which includes the control dependence of the vulnerability occurrence statement and the data dependence of the variables involved in the statement. At the same time, this paper builds a graph learning network for vulnerability dependence representation graph based on the heterogeneous graph transformer, which can automatically learn the importance of contextual sentences for vulnerable sentences. To prove the effectiveness of the method in this paper, experiments were carried out on the SARD data set, and the average accuracy rate was 95.4% and the recall rate was 92.4%. The average performance is improved by 4.1%–62.7%.

Keywords: Vulnerability detection · Code representation · Heterogeneous graph transformer · Graph neural network · Code representation graph

1 Introduction

In the past decades, a large number of vulnerability detection methods have been proposed [1]. Most of the methods rely on vulnerability characteristics or template rules manually defined by security experts. These methods not only have a high false positive rate, but also cover a limited number of vulnerabilities, but also template rules need to be dynamically updated with the emergence of new vulnerability patterns [2, 3].

Sequence-Based Method. Russell et al. [4] used the feature extraction method of sentence emotion classification based on CNN and RNN to detect function-level source code vulnerabilities. Li et al. [5] believe that whether a line of code contains vulnerabilities is related to the context, and the parameters of function calls in the program are often affected by the early or middle, and late stages of the program. Therefore, [5] selects bidirectional long short-term memory (BLSTM) to model the source code. The SySeVR method proposed in reference [2] believes that not every line in the source code is related to the vulnerability characteristics. It selects four points of interest (function call, array index, expression calculation, pointer reference) for code slicing, and then selects neural network models such as bidirectional gate recurrent unit (BGRU), BLSTM, CNN, and so on to model the source code slicing.

Graph-Based Method. Allamanis et al. [6] believe that using the natural language processing (NLP) method for source code vulnerability detection can not solve the problem of long dependence caused by using the same variables and functions far away from the statements where the vulnerability occurs. Therefore, the source code is represented as a joint graph of abstract syntax code (AST), data flow graph (DFG), and control flow graph (CFG). Based on the gated graph neural network [7] (GGNN), the effectiveness of using a graph to represent source code is proved in two scenarios: variable name prediction and variable name misuse detection. The Devign method proposed in [8] adds a natural sequence edge of the code to encode the natural sequence of the source code and uses the code representation of the GGNN learning program joint graph with the convolution module for vulnerability detection.

In the above two methods, sequence-based methods either do not contain syntactic-semantic information or do not explicitly maintain any dependencies in source code slices, making it difficult to learn and reason about source code semantic information. The graph-based method simply uses one or more representation graphs of the source code to represent the source code and does not further analyze the nodes and edges related to the vulnerability statement in the representation graph, so that the model cannot comprehensively learn and reason about the relevant information of the vulnerability statement.

This paper proposes a source code vulnerability detection method based on the heterogeneous graph transformer (VDHGT). VDHGT has the following characteristics:

(1) we believe that the source code statements with vulnerabilities are closely related to the data dependence of variables in the statements and the control structure corresponding to the statements. Therefore, this paper proposes a code representation method named Vulnerability Dependence Representation Graph (VDRG). VDRG distinguishes the dependent edges related to vulnerabilities and the unrelated edges.

(2) VDRG is a heterogeneous graph. Considering that the four different edges may have different characteristic dimension distributions, And there are differences in the importance of VDRG, so heterogeneous graph transformer (HGT) [9] is used to learn and infer the relationship between source code nodes.

2   Overview

The proposed method VDHGT is divided into four stages: VDRG generation stage, nodes embedding stage, graph learning network stage, and vulnerability detection stage. The overall framework of VDHGT is shown in Fig. 1.

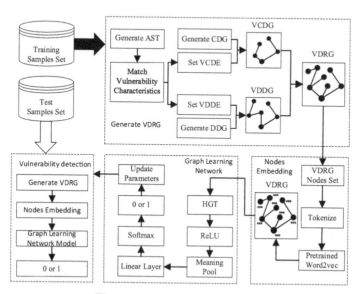

Fig. 1. The framework of VDHGT.

3   VDHGT Method

3.1   Generation of VDRG

The representation of VDRG for function-level source code proposed in this paper can be formally recorded as $f_{vdrg} = (V, E, X, D)$, where V represents the node set and E represents the edge set. X represents the attribute of the node set and saves the node type. The node type can be divided into two types by whether it contains SyVC [2] or not. D represents the attribute of the edge set and saves the edge type. The edge types are divided into four types.

Algorithm1 gives a high-level description of the VDRG generation process. The main idea of algorithm1 is to generate the corresponding VDRG by analyzing the control dependence and data dependence of each SyVC in the function code slice. The input of the algorithm is the function code slice, and the output is the VDRG set.

Algorithm 1 VDRG generation algorithm

Input: Funciton $f = \{s_1, ..., s_n\}$, s_i Represents a source code statement

Output: A set S with VDRG as element

1: $S \leftarrow \emptyset$;
2: Generate the f_{ast} corresponding to f
3: Generate the SyVC set S_{SyVC} corresponding to f_{ast} by matching vulnerability syntax features
4: Generate f_{cdg} corresponding to f
5: Generate f_{cdg} corresponding to f
6: **for** each $SyVC \in S_{SyVC}$ **do**
7:     Calculate the statement s_{pvs} where SyVC is located
8:     $f_{vcdg} \leftarrow f_{cdg}$
9:     $f_{vddg} \leftarrow f_{ddg}$
10:    $S_{pvs} \leftarrow \emptyset$
11:    $S_{pvs} \leftarrow S_{pvs} \cup s_{pvs}$
12:    **while** S_{pvs} **do**
13:        Remove element s_{pvs} from S_{pvs}
14:        **for** each $edge_{vcdg} \in f_{vcdg}$ **do**
15:            **if** $edge_{vcdg}.dst == s_{pvs}.dst$ and $edge_{vcdg}.label \neq$ 'vcde' **then**
16:                $S_{pvs} \leftarrow S_{pvs} \cup edge_{vcdg}.src$;
17:                $edge_{vcdg}.label \leftarrow$ 'vcde'
18:            **else if** $edge_{vcdg}.label \neq$ 'vcde' **then**
19:                $edge_{vcdg}.label \leftarrow$ 'cde'
20:            **end if**
21:        **end for**
22:    **end while**
23:    **for** each $var \in s_{pvs}$ **do**
24:        **for** each $edge_{vddg} \in f_{vddg}$ **do**
25:            **if** $var.name == edge_{vddg}.label$ and $edge_{vddg}.label \neq$ 'vdde' **then**
26:                $edge_{vddg}.label \leftarrow$ 'vdde'
27:            **else if** $edge_{vddg}.label \neq$ 'vdde' **then**
28:                $edge_{vddg}.label \leftarrow$ 'dde'
29:            **end if**
30:        **end for**
31:    **end for**
32:    $f_{vdrg} \leftarrow f_{vcdg} \cup f_{vddg}$;
33:    $S \leftarrow S \cup f_{vdrg}$
34: **end for**

3.2 Node Embedding

The goal of the node embedding stage is to generate an initial representation vector for each node of the VDRG graph. The node embedding phase takes VDRG as the input and goes through the following steps:

(1) Tokenization: in this step, each source code in the data set is divided into a combination of single coincidence numbers. In order not to let the variable name and function name affect the learning of semantic relationships in the program, the variables in each sample are uniformly named *var1*, *var2*, ..., The functions are uniformly named *fun1*, *fun2*, ...

(2) Training word2vec: The phrase generated by the marked function slice is used as the input of word2vec to train a word2vec word encoder.

(3) Generate the node vector representation of VDRG: input the code statement corresponding to each node into the pre-trained word2vec, and obtain the initial vector representation of the node according to the determined parameters through calculation.

3.3 Graph Learning Network and Vulnerability Detection

This paper designs a VDRG graph learning network for source code vulnerability detection based on the heterogeneous graph transformer. The VDRG graph learning network minimizes the loss through the training set and obtains the optimal parameters by fitting the model. After the VDRG generation and node embedding stage, the test sample is input into the pre-trained VDRG graph learning network model in the vulnerability detection stage to obtain the detection result, that is, whether there is a vulnerability in the function slice. Algorithm 2 gives the calculation of VDRG.

Algorithm 2 Calculate the VDRG global representation

Input: $G_{VDRG} = \{V, E, X, D\}$
Output: VDRG global representation H_{VDRG}

1: $h \leftarrow 2$
2: **for** each $t \in V$ **do**
3:     **for** $s \in N(t)$ **do**
4:         **for** $i = 0; i <= h; i + +$ **do**
5:             $K^i(s) \leftarrow K\_Linear^i_{\tau(s)}(H^{init}[s])$
6:             $Q^i(t) \leftarrow Q\_Linear^i_{\tau(t)}(H^{init}[t])$
7:             $e \leftarrow (s, t)$
8:             $ATT\_head^i(s, e, t) \leftarrow (K^i(s)W^{ATT}_{\phi(e)}Q^i(t)^T) \cdot \frac{\mu_{<\tau(s),\phi(e),\tau(t)>}}{\sqrt{d}}$
9:         **end for**
10:         $\mathbf{Attention}_{HGT}(s, e, t) \leftarrow \underset{\forall s \in N(t)}{Softmax}(\underset{i \in [1,h]}{\|} ATT\_head^i(s, e, t))$
11:         **for** $i = 0; i <= h; i + +$ **do**
12:             $MSG\_head^i(s, e, t) \leftarrow M\_Linear^i_{\tau(s)}(H^{init}[s])W^{MSG}_{\phi(e)}$
13:         **end for**
14:         $\mathbf{Message}_{HGT}(s, e, t) \leftarrow \underset{i \in [1,h]}{\|} MSG\_head^i(s, e, t))$
15:     **end for**
16:     $\tilde{H}[t] \leftarrow \underset{\forall s \in N(t)}{\oplus}(\mathbf{Attention}_{HGT}(s, e, t) \cdot \mathbf{Message}_{HGT}(s, e, t))$
17:     $H[t] \leftarrow A\_Linear_{\tau(t)}(\sigma(\tilde{H}[t])) + H^{(init)}[t]$
18:     $H[t] \leftarrow Relu(H[t])$
19: **end for**
20: $H_{VDRG} \leftarrow \underset{\forall t \in V}{\oplus} H[t]$

---

4 Experiment and Result Analysis

4.1 Experimental Dataset

The dataset used in this paper is the Software Assurance reference dataset [10] (SARD). The experiment designed in this paper selects the following types of vulnerability datasets from SARD. The specific information is shown in Table 1.

Table 1. Types of source code vulnerabilities contained in the experimental dataset.

CWE type	Name	Counts
CWE78	OS injection	17000
CWE80	XSS	3400
CWE89	SQL injection	14000
CWE129	Improper array index validation	11000
CWE190	Integer overflow	25000
CWE400	Resource exhaustion	7800
CWE789	Out of control memory allocation	7300

4.2 Experimental Results and Analysis

The results of the comparative experiment are shown in Table 2. From the results, it can be seen that the VDHGT method proposed in this paper is superior to other methods in four indexes. The method proposed by Russell et al. processes the source code text into character sequences without considering the context of source code statements. At the same time, it uses the method based on NLP to model the source code, which loses the structured syntax and semantic information in the source code. Therefore, the index value corresponding to the experimental results is the lowest. Vuldeepecker also processes the source code as a sequence model, but it uses BLSTM to build a vulnerability detection model. BLSTM will consider the impact of the pre and post-code statements, which makes its experimental indicators better than those of Russell et al. SySeVR put forward the concepts of program interest points and vulnerability syntax features for the first time and eliminates the statements irrelevant to the vulnerability. Although it also uses the sequence model, it filters the invalid information to a great extent and obtains a more accurate model by learning the dependence information of the vulnerability. Devign is a classic method of modeling the source code as a graph and then using GNN for vulnerability detection. It integrates the AST, CFG, DFG, and natural sequence information of the source code into the program representation diagram, which greatly improves the performance of vulnerability detection.

The reason why the VDHGT method proposed in this paper is superior to other methods is that it not only considers the control dependence and data dependence information of source code statements but also distinguishes the control dependence edges related to and unrelated to vulnerability statements through SyVC so that the later neural network can learn the context of vulnerability more accurately. At the same time, this paper uses the heterogeneous graph transformer to exchange neighbor information of VDRG. It maintains proprietary linear transformation for each VDRG edge type and node type, which greatly enhances the expression ability of the model.

Table 2. Comparison of detection and evaluation indexes between VDHGT method and classical methods

Methods	A	P	R	F1
Russell et al.	78.3	70.6	47.4	56.8
VulDeePecker	84.4	83.2	60	69.8
SySeVR	86.1	84.9	65.1	73.7
Devign	93.4	89.9	87.8	88.8
VDHGT	95.4	91.4	93.3	92.4

5 Conclusion

This paper proposes a vulnerability detection method based on the heterogeneous graph transformer. It obtains the potential vulnerability statements by matching the vulnerability syntax features on the abstract syntax tree corresponding to the function slice and then constructs the vulnerability control dependence graph by analyzing the control dependence of the potential vulnerability statements and the data dependence of the variables contained therein. This source code representation method accurately depicts the context of the vulnerability statement and provides sufficient data basis for the training of the neural network. At the same time, this paper constructs the graph neural network based on the heterogeneous graph transformer. It can maintain different feature dimension distribution for different edge types and node types and learn the key context affecting vulnerability statements through the multi-head attention mechanism, to further improve the accuracy of vulnerability detection.

References

1. Lin, G.J.F., Wen, S.S., Han, Q.L.T.: Software vulnerability detection using deep neural networks: a survey. Proc. IEEE **108**(10), 1825–1848 (2020)
2. Li, Z.F., Zou, D.Q.S., Xu, S.H.T.: SySeVR: a framework for using deep learning to detect software vulnerabilities. IEEE Trans. Depend. Secure Comput. 1–15 (2021)
3. Russell, R.F., Kim, L.S., Hamilton, L.T.: Automated vulnerability detection in source code using deep representation learning. 17th IEEE International Conference on Machine Learning and Applications 2018, ICMLA, vol. 122018, pp. 757–762. IEEE, Piscataway (2018)
4. Wang, H.T.F., Ye, G.X.S., Tang, Z.Y.T.: Combining graph-based learning with automated data collection for code vulnerability detection. IEEE Trans. Inform. Foren. Secur. **16**, 1943–1958 (2021)
5. Li, Z.F., Zou, D.Q.S., Xu, S.H.T.: Vuldeepecker: A Deep Learning-Based System for Vulnerability Detection. arXiv preprint arXiv 1801, pp. 1681–1695 (2018)
6. Allamanis, M.F., Brockschmidt, M.S., Khademi, M.T.: Learning to Represent Programs with Graphs. arXiv preprint arXiv 1711, pp. 740–756 (2017)
7. Li, Y.J.F., Tarlow, D.S., Brockschmidt, M.T.: Gated Graph Sequence Neural Networks. arXiv preprint arXiv 1511, pp. 5493–5512 (2015)

8. Zhou, Y.Q.F., Liu, S.Q.S., Siow, J.K.T.: Devign: effective vulnerability identification by learning comprehensive program semantics via graph neural networks. Adv. Neural Inf. Process. Syst. **32**, 1–11 (2019)
9. Hu, Z.N.F., Dong, Y.X.S., Wang, K.S.T.: Heterogeneous graph transformer. In: Proceedings of The Web Conference 2020, WWW, vol. 04202020, pp. 2704–2710. Association for Computing Machinery, New York (2020)
10. NVD: Software assurance reference dataset (2018). https://samate.nist.gov/SRD/index

Anomalous Network Traffic Detection Based on CK Sketch and Machine Learning

Yaping Chi[1,2], Defan Xue[1(✉)], Ziyan Yue[1], Zhiqiang Wang[1], and Liang Jiaming[1]

[1] Beijing Electronic Science and Technology Institute, Beijing RPC 100070, China
bjutxuedefan@163.com
[2] University of Science and Technology of China, Hefei 230027, China

Abstract. The rapid development of the explosive growth of the network traffic and new networks, such as cloud computing and IoT have challenged the traditional network measurement techniques with limited memory resources and computational resources. The measurement method based on sketch structure can compress and store massive traffic data by hash calculation, which facilitates statistical analysis in limited memory and has a greater impact on anomalous traffic detection. Current researches show that using sketch structure to store network traffic and combining it with machine learning to detect anomalous traffic in network traffic can solve the above problem effectively. However, the classical sketch structure has some problems such as hash collision and low memory usage, etc., which in turn affect the accuracy of machine learning models for anomalous traffic detection. In this paper, an improved sketch structure is proposed based on the cuckoo hash and CK Sketch structure which replaces the hash function in the classical sketch with the mechanism of cuckoo hash to avoid hash conflict, adds Bloom filter, and can self-adaption allocate the number of Hash buckets. By storing the anomalous traffic data as CK Sketch structure and classical sketch structure respectively, and conducting the anomalous traffic detection comparison experiments with machine learning respectively, the experimental results show that the CK sketch structure proposed in this paper can effectively improve the accuracy of machine learning to determine the anomalous traffic, the utilization rate of hash buckets and the network throughput.

Keywords: Sketch · Cuckoo hash · Machine learning · Anomalous network traffic detection

1 Introduction

The traffic of the Internet in China has increased dramatically in recent years. In 2021, the total amount of network traffic in the country reached 221.6 billion GB, an increase of 33.9% compared to previous years, of which the average monthly traffic generated by each user on the Internet is about 13.36 GB [1]. With the rapid growth of network traffic, the statistical analysis of network traffic has become more complicated [2], and the storage, transmission, and so on of traffic require a lot of resources. It is necessary to ensure high efficiency and accuracy when measuring and recording the massive traffic

X. Chen et al. (Eds.): CSS 2022, LNCS 13547, pp. 225–243, 2022.
https://doi.org/10.1007/978-3-031-18067-5_17

data without negligence and omission. Network security risks are generalized and security risks are emerging, so how efficiently and accurately detecting anomalous traffic in massive network traffic is one of the important tasks to ensure network security. By detecting anomalous traffic promptly, network maintainers can determine security policy to prevent further security incidents effectively.

In order to meet the above high efficiency and high accuracy network measurement requirements, the following three techniques are mainly used: (1) Network traffic measurement technique on the basis of sampling [3] refers to the selection of a representative part of the traffic from the massive network traffic data, and all the characteristics of the massive network traffic are deduced from the characteristics of that traffic [4]. It mainly includes group sampling and stream sampling. Group sampling refers to grouping network traffic individually without considering the correlation between individual groups. Stream sampling refers to the selection of data streams for correlation grouping at a fixed time, which means the different characteristics of each group are considered and then analyzed. Sampling-based network traffic measurement techniques can alleviate the pressure of resource mobilization to a certain extent and reduce the data used for storage and analysis. However, features of some data sets do not perfectly fit the original data thus leading to sampling measurements cannot accurately obtain the required features, and the real-time performance is poor [5]; (2) Network measurement technique on the basis of counters [6] provides a counter for each traffic containing key values and frequencies, and when the traffic arrives, the counter updates the frequencies and key values in the counter according to the current traffic. This method can effectively achieve high accuracy requirement, which is suitable for dealing with small network traffic, but causes huge space loss when faced with excessive network traffic data; (3) Network measurement technique on the basis of sketch structure, which uses the count_all strategy [7] to compress all traffic data by hash calculation, facilitates statistical analysis in limited memory. Under the situation of the rapid growth of network traffic and limited memory resources as well as computational resources for network measurement, the measurement technique on the basis of sketch structure is a breakthrough to solve the problem of degraded network measurement performance in recent years. Sketch structure which mainly contains two parts, hash function, and hash buckets, can ensure the low space consumption while providing a high accuracy rate. It is a hot research topic in the field of network measurement and anomalous network traffic detection.

Currently, in the field of anomalous network traffic detection, different sketch structures are heavily used to count, analyze, and judge anomalous traffic. When the classical CM (Count Min) Sketch proposed in [8] is used for anomalous network traffic detection, users usually set different thresholds for each feature in the traffic on the basis of their experience, and when the network traffic is compressed and stored in the CM Sketch, they need to manually determine whether the current CM Sketch structure contains anomalous traffic that exceeds the threshold value. However, this method can only issue warnings but not reverse tracing when anomalous traffic is found. A structure called k-ary Sketch is designed in [9] to compress and count network traffic which in turn notify the amount of anomalous traffic in it to reduce security risks. The structure mainly contains a sketch module, prediction module, and change detection module. The sketch structure is similar to the classical CM Sketch; the prediction module is mainly used by users to predict the threshold values of network traffic features that will lead to security risks; the change detection module is mainly responsible for warning when a feature value in the current sketch structure exceeds a predefined range. Replacing the hash function in the classical CM Sketch with a modulo operation using the Chinese Remainder Theorem, and setting the number of hash buckets in each layer to a large prime number P_i, $i = (0, 1, 2,..., n)$ is proposed by [10]. When issuing an anomalous network traffic warning, it can obtain the anomalous key value by backtracking through the Chinese residual theorem. MLR (Multi-Layer Reversible) Sketch is designed by [11]. It can be combined with CM Sketch to backtrack key values with security risks.

However, the above methods have the following three shortcomings: 1. Due to the unpredictability and variability of network traffic, users usually cannot accurately predict the appropriate threshold value. 2. The above structures require multiple hash calculations for all network traffic, which takes up a large amount of computing resources and reduces information processing throughput. 3. The above sketch structures contain a fixed number of hash buckets, as a result, when compressing and counting a large amount of network traffic, hash conflicts are very likely to occur, thus triggering wrong judgments. This paper summarizes and analyzes the existing sketch structures and their improvement methods, and explores the sketch structure improvement methods that can enhance the efficiency and performance of network anomalous network traffic detection.

2 Related Work

2.1 Sketch Structure

Network traffic is gradually characterized by high speed and non-uniform distribution [12], and the excessive amount of network traffic data makes it exceptionally difficult to accurately measure network characteristics, which will inevitably cause a decrease in throughput if the statistical measurement method has a delay. In the field of network traffic statistical analysis, sketch structure summarizes the network traffic compression by constructing hash functions. Sketch structure usually contains two parts, one is the hash function, which calculates the hash value corresponding to the key in the network traffic as the index for data compression, aggregation, and storage. Second is the hash buckets, sketch structure is usually set a certain number of hash buckets for storing the required feature values of the network traffic. Sketch has been widely used in several directions such as flow analysis, stream size change measurement, large stream detection, persistent stream measurement, etc. It can improve statistical accuracy while compressing, aggregating, and storing network traffic [13]. Several typical sketch structures and their performance are presented and analyzed below.

The classical CM Sketch was introduced in [8], and many subsequent studies have used this structure for network traffic statistics, traffic analysis, etc., which is the basis for many variants of sketch structures. The structure of CM Sketch is shown in Fig. 1, which contains n hash functions and n * m two-dimensional arrays T for compressing and counting network traffic. When using this structure to perform network traffic analysis, it is necessary to use a feature of the network traffic such as source IP, destination IP, etc., as a key value, and the rest of the required statistical features such as flow duration, average packet size, flow packets/s, etc. as value. N hash functions are used to calculate loc$_i$ = H$_i$(Key) to get the location of each network traffic, each network traffic is mapped to n hash buckets, and then the values in the network traffic are added to the values in the hash buckets.

$$T[i][hi(key)] = T[i][hi(key)] + Value. \tag{1}$$

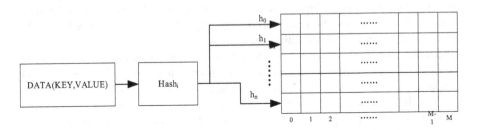

Fig. 1. CM sketch data structure

C(Count)Sketch is proposed by [14]. C Sketch adds a set of hash functions S1,......Sn that take values in the range {+1, −1} concerning CM Sketch. This structure, when adding data, is similar to CM in finding the location of the hash bucket where the data should be stored, and then add Si[key] to the hash bucket at the corresponding location. When it comes to query, the value in the n-row hash buckets needs to be multiplied by Si[k] and the median is the final result. Since the network traffic of high-frequency items is often more meaningful for statistical analysis in network traffic measurement analysis, this method mainly uses the probabilistic operation of adding and subtracting one from the values in the hash bucket to offset the influence of low-frequency items on high-frequency items and in turn, reduces the error of high-frequency stream statistics. CU (Conservative update) Sketch is proposed by [15], which is more conservative in data update operation compared with CM Sketch, and when the structure compresses and counts the statistics of new network traffic, only the one with the smallest value among the n matching hash buckets is inserted. When querying, the same method selects the smallest one among the n matching hash buckets as the resulting output. This method can improve the accuracy to some extent, however, if the element is deleted directly, it will not only affect the element but also affect the other elements sharing the bucket. CSM (Counter sum estimation) Sketch is proposed by [16], which randomly selects one of the n-matching hash buckets for insertion in the statistical stage of compressing and counting network traffic. The values in n matching hash buckets are summed at query time and output after subtracting a predetermined amount of noise.

A (Augmented) Sketch structure is proposed by [17]. The authors pointed out that CM Sketch is less accurate for network traffic statistics, especially the inability to accurately measure high-frequency data and the recording of low-frequency data as high-frequency data due to hash conflicts, which can have a more serious impact on the subsequent statistical analysis using the sketch structure. Augmented Sketch consists of two data structures: filter and CM Sketch. The filter stores several high-frequency items and two associated parameters, the new_count and old_count of each item it monitors, and the difference between the two represents the cumulative frequency of a particular item in that period. When dealing with network traffic (key, num), the key represents its key value and the num represents its number of occurrences. The structure performs a filtering operation on the network traffic, adding num directly to the new_count if the filter contains this element while leaving the old_count unchanged. If the filter does not contain the element and there is a free space, the network traffic (key, num) is added to the filter, and new_count = num, old_count = 0. If the filter does not contain the element and there is no free space, the element is added to the sketch structure and if the sketch structure estimates the frequency of its occurrence to be greater than the minimum value in the filter, the element is swapped with the minimum value in the filter, and both new_count and old_count are set to the estimated frequency of occurrence. This method effectively avoids the collision between low-frequency and high-frequency flows and improves detection accuracy and efficiency. A multi-layer sketch structure is proposed by [18], which can build a multi-layer sketch self-adaption when a hash conflict occurs in the hash buckets section, effectively avoiding the error caused by the hash conflict.

2.2 Sketch Improvement Structure on the Basis of Cuckoo Hash

To solve the hash conflict problem, the cuckoo hash algorithm is proposed by [19], which is adaptive and utilizes less computation in exchange for a larger space. The principle is similar to that of the perfect hash function, but relatively cuckoo hash has the advantages of faster processing speed and lower space consumption. The traditional cuckoo hash contains two hash functions as well as two one-dimensional hash tables.

When cuckoo hash processes data (Key, Value), it will first calculate the primary hash value $H_1(Key)$ as the primary position, if the primary position is empty, the data will be inserted, otherwise, it will calculate the secondary hash value $H_2(Key)$ as the secondary position, if the secondary position is empty, the data will be inserted. When the data is not available in both hash tables, it will randomly kick out the original data from the corresponding position in the primary or secondary hash table and replace it with new data. The kick-out mechanism allows Cuckoo Hash to resolve conflicts more efficiently and flexibly than other hash algorithms and increases the utilization of the hash buckets.

An example of a traditional cuckoo hash is shown in Fig. 2, which contains two hash functions and one-dimensional hash tables of capacity 6 and shows the different strategies of cuckoo hash in data insertion respectively.

It contains three cases:

1. No hash conflict. The data is inserted into the main hash table after the main hash calculation and no hash conflict occurs.
2. One hash conflict. When data (Key, Value) is inserted into the main hash table, a hash conflict occurs, the data is put into the secondary hash function for computation and then inserted into the secondary hash table.
3. Both hash conflict. When data(Key, Value) is inserted into both main and secondary hash tables, hash conflicts occur, and a cuckoo hash mechanism is used to randomly kick out the original data that has a hash conflict in the primary or secondary hash table and insert the new data (Key, Value) into it.

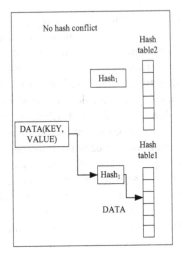
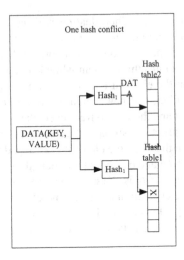
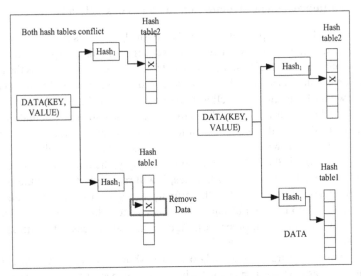

Fig. 2. Cuckoo hash insert items

3   Anomalous Network Traffic Detection Solution on the Basis of Machine Learning and CK Sketch

3.1   Design of the Anomalous Network Traffic Detection Process

Determining whether the network traffic is anomalous is a machine learning binary classification problem, which can be effectively solved by combining sketch structure with the various machine learning models such as Logistic Regression, Decision tree, Bayesian, etc. [20]. For example, in traditional CM Sketch, the source IP of network traffic is used as the key, and flow duration, average packet size, flow packets/s, etc. are used as the value, and when the network traffic is stored in the sketch structure, the data in the hash buckets is raised to obtain a two-dimensional array containing the key and value. Each hash bucket corresponds to an IP address. According to whether the IP address is a security risk or not, the corresponding label is given as the training and testing set for machine learning. Figure 3 shows the process of machine learning combined with the sketch to detect anomalous network traffic.

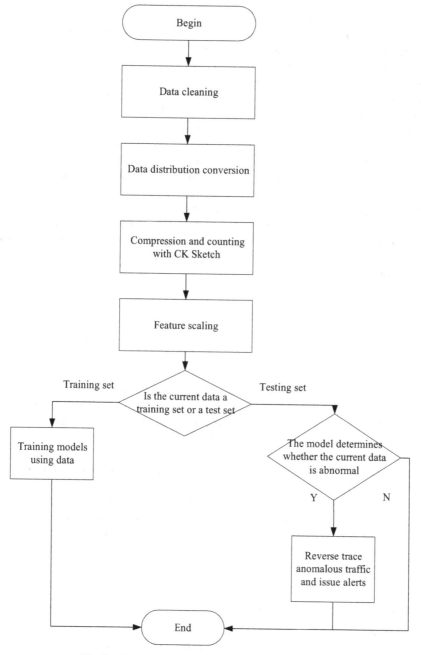

Fig. 3. Anomalous network traffic detection flow chart

Usually, the network traffic data obtained through network acquisition cannot be directly put into the machine learning model for model training, which contains a variety of anomalies, such as feature clutter, key value vacancy, the presence of noise, and data distribution is too concentrated, etc. The preprocessing of the detection process in this paper contains four main stages: data cleaning, data distribution conversion, statistical compression of the sketch module, and feature scaling.

In the data cleaning phase, the data usually set samples to contain some nonsensical characters that cannot be transformed into values for machine learning model training, so such data needs to be removed in the cleaning phase.

In the data distribution conversion stage, some anomalous data in the data set are converted for the problem of too concentrated distribution. For example, the DDoS attack data in the CICIDS2017 data set are from two IP addresses: 192.168.10.50, and 172.16.0.1. After the data is compressed by sketch structure, it only contains two data with Label as DDoS, which reduces the accuracy of machine learning detection. If the Source IP is used as the Key, the Key does not affect determining whether the data is a DDoS attack. Therefore, changing the distribution pattern of keys in the data set can better show the experimental comparison effect.

In the feature scaling phase, the data set contains various features corresponding to different numerical magnitudes, some of which include features that can reach over a million, while others are in the range of $(0, 1)$. Therefore, the solution uses a normalization scheme for each feature to improve the accuracy of model training and shorten the time required for model training.

$$X' = \frac{X - mean(X)}{max(X) - min(X)} \tag{2}$$

There are two problems in using classical sketch structure data for machine learning model training.

1. The traditional sketch is lack self-adaption because the number of hash buckets in the traditional sketch is fixed. When the traditional sketch is oriented to the large network traffic, hash conflicts will inevitably occur. As a result, the value of a hash bucket and the label corresponding to multiple IP Addresses, which greatly reduces the accuracy of machine learning detection.
2. In the traditional sketch, multiple hash functions and multi-layer hash buckets are usually introduced to improve the statistical accuracy, so each network traffic stored in the sketch needs to go through multiple sash operations thus leading to a decrease in the throughput of traffic processing. Therefore, at this stage, this paper improves the sketch structure on the basis of the Cuckoo Hash principle and applies the improved sketch structure (CK Sketch) to compress and store the network traffic, which solves the above problems.

3.2   CK Sketch Structure Improvement

Traditional sketch (e.g. Count Sketch, CM Sketch, etc.) cannot predict the size of network traffic during network traffic analysis, and usually set the number of hash buckets to a predefined value to detect anomalous network traffic. However, when the network traffic is large, the hash conflict will occur, and when the network traffic is small, the predefined hash buckets cannot be fully utilized, resulting in the waste of memory resources and computational resources. The improved structure of CK (Cuckoo) Sketch in this paper effectively contains a multi-layer sketch structure with different hash functions and hash buckets, where the creation of different layers of the sketch is based on the principle of Cuckoo hash to resolve hash conflicts. The structure will adaptively adjust the number of hash functions and the number of hash buckets according to the size of network data traffic when performing compressing and counting, to improve the throughput and reduce hash conflicts.

Data Structure

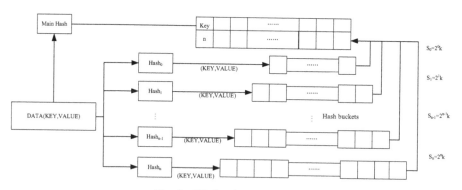

Fig. 4. CK sketch data structure

To achieve the ideal network traffic statistics analysis, the CK Sketch data structure established in this paper is shown in Fig. 4, which contains a multi-layer hash table and a bloom filter that records the number of network traffic storage layers.

- (1) Sketch. It consists of hash functions and hash buckets. The newly arrived network traffic is a set of (key, value) key-value pairs, according to the specific statistical needs of the application, the key is used as the index for statistics (e.g. Source IP destination IP), and the value is the feature value that needs to be analyzed statistically. The $hash_n$ function of each layer operates the key in the network traffic, and maps the corresponding (KEY, VALUE) to the back hash buckets according to the calculated value.

$$loc = hash_n(key). \tag{3}$$

The result of the hash function operation differs for each layer, and to fully consider the variability of network traffic, the number of hash buckets in the layer n+1 is twice the number of the layer n, i.e.

$$Sn + 1 = 2Sn \tag{4}$$

234 Y. Chi et al.

- (2) Bloom filter. This structure contains a main hash function as well as a two-dimensional vector. The main hash function is used to map the network traffic into the two-dimensional vector, and the key value is recorded to the first line of the corresponding position of the mapping. After the data insertion is completed, the number of layers where the data is located is recorded in the second row of the corresponding position of the mapping.

The process of compressing and counting the statistical network traffic (Key, Value) is shown in Fig. 5 and consists of the following steps.

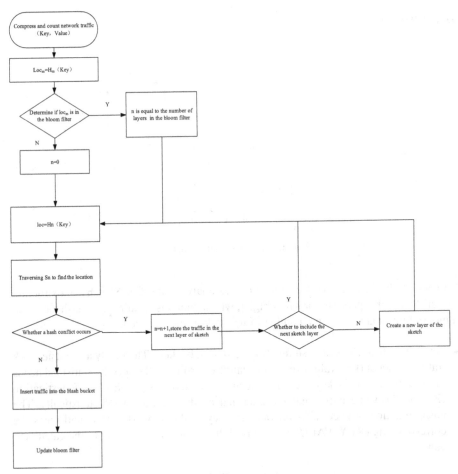

Fig. 5. CK Sketch compressing and counting flow chart

1. Determine whether the current network traffic is already located in the sketch. The key in the network traffic (Key, Value) is calculated by the main hash function to get $Loc_m = H_m(Key)$. Querying whether the loc location in the Bloom filter contains the element can correspond to the following three cases. 1) If there is no data at that location, the element is added to the Loc_m in the bloom filter and the element is stored in a multi-layer sketch starting from the first level. 2) If there is data at that location but the corresponding Key value is different from the Key corresponding to the current data, the element will be stored in a multi-layer sketch starting from the first level.3) If there is data at that location and the corresponding Key value is the same as the corresponding key value with the current data, the element is directly stored in the corresponding layer of the multi-layer sketch according to the layer in the bloom filter.

2. Calculate the location of the hash bucket where the network traffic is stored. The Key in the network traffic (Key, Value) is put into the k (0, 1, 2,..., n) layer according to (1), and calculate $loc_k = hash_k(Key)$, i.e., determine its corresponding hash bucket position in each layer of the sketch.

3. Determine whether a hash conflict occurs. If the loc_k position in the hash buckets does not contain any data means no hash conflict. If there is already data in it and the data is the same as the data to be inserted, there is no hash conflict, if it is different, there is a hash conflict.

4. Counting characteristics. The process is shown in Fig. 6. If there is no hash conflict, the key in the network traffic is recorded, and add the value to the corresponding position in the hash buckets. If a hash conflict occurs, innovate a different hash function H_{k+1} and a layer hash buckets S_{k+1}, where the number of hash buckets S_{k+1} is twice the number of S_k, calculate $loc_{k+1} = H_{k+1}(Key)$ and insert this network traffic into the layer k + 1 hash buckets according to the above steps.

5. Count the number of hash buckets layers where the network traffic (Key, Value) is located. Record the number of layers where the network traffic is located after the completion of the compression statistics in the bloom filter.

4 Experience

4.1 Experimental Environment and Data Set

Hardware Environment
All experiments are run on a quad-core (Intel(R) Core(TM) i7-7700HQ) OC, all hash algorithms are implemented in Python, and the main framework is Sklearn.

Data Set
The experimental data are obtained from the CICIDS2017 data set. The data set mainly contains benign and various common network attack network traffic, such as DoS, DDoS, infiltration, botnet, etc. This experiment mainly selects the DDoS attack part. The data set contains a total of 225746 traffic entries, of which the attack accounted for 56.8%,

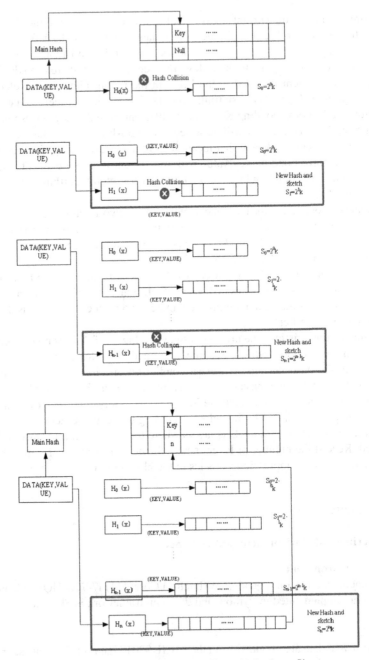

Fig. 6. Compressing and counting with hash conflict

recorded a variety of features corresponding to the IP, Flow Duration, Average Packet Size, Flow Packets/s, protocol, and so on.

Experimental Setup

The experiment selects Logistic Regression as the machine learning model to determine the anomalous network traffic. All sketch structures use Source IP as a key, and its value uses five features: Flow Bytes/s, Flow Duration, Average Packet Size, Flow Packets/s, and Entropy of Protocol (EOP). Sketch structures mainly contain CK Sketch and CM Sketch with different hash buckets. The CK Sketch structure is adaptive, the number of the hash function is 1 and the number of hash buckets at the first layer l is 3000 at the beginning, assuming that the final number of hash functions in CK Sketch is n. The rest of the CM Sketch schemes all set the number of hash functions to 5, and the number of single-level hash buckets and total hash buckets is set to 3000,5000,10000, 20000, and 50000. The specific settings are shown in Table 1.

Table 1. Experiment parameters setting

Structures	CK sketch	CM Sketch_3000	CM Sketch_5000	CM Sketch_10000	CM Sketch_20000	CM Sketch_50000
Hash functions	n	5	5	5	5	5
One layer hash Buckets	3000, 3000 * 2...3000 * (2^n)	3000	5000	10000	20000	50000
Total hash buckets	3000 + 3000*2 +... + 3000 * (2^n)	15000	25000	50000	100000	250000

4.2 Metrics

1. Hash buckets utilization: It is the ratio of the hash buckets used in compressing and counting network traffic to the predefined hash buckets. When the same number of network traffic is deposited, the higher the utilization rate of the hash buckets means the less memory waste and the better the performance.
2. Accuracy: The accuracy rate of model training is the percentage of the total test data set that the model can correctly identify after a certain number of training sessions.

$$Accuracy = \frac{TP + TN}{TP + FP + TN + FN} \tag{5}$$

TP (True Positive) denotes samples that actually attack traffic and are correctly detected as anomalous; TN (True Negative) denotes samples that are actually normal traffic and are correctly detected as normal traffic; FP (False Positive) denotes samples that are normal traffic but are incorrectly detected as anomalous traffic; FN (False Negative) denotes samples that are actually anomalous traffic but are incorrectly detected as normal traffic. When the same number of network traffic is detected, the higher the accuracy rate, the better the performance is represented.

3. Throughput: It is the number of successfully processed data per unit time. The experimental part uses the number of packets successfully deposited into the sketch structure per second as the throughput. Higher throughput means faster and shorter processing time for network traffic and better performance.

4.3 Experimental Comparison Analysis

Hash Buckets Utilization

Table 2. Non-null hash buckets statistics.

Network traffic	10000	20000	50000	100000	150000	200000
CK Sketch hash buckets	6000	6000	9000	9000	9000	9000
CK Sketch Non-null hash buckets	482	719	809	883	962	1192
CM Sketch_10000 Non-null hash buckets	472	703	784	859	919	1134
CM Sketch_20000 Non-null hash buckets	477	711	798	880	943	1183
CM Sketch_50000 Non-null hash buckets	485	720	805	891	965	1195

Table 2 shows the change in the number of CK Sketch hash buckets and the number of buckets used by CK Sketch and CM Sketch after compressing the statistics of the traffic with a different number of entries in the CICIDS2017 data set. It can be found that CK Sketch can dynamically adjust the number of hash buckets and the CK Sketch has high utilization of hash buckets. The specific detection results are shown below.

This experiment compares the hash buckets utilization rate of CK Sketch with the classical CM Sketch with a different number of hash buckets for compressing and counting network traffic. The experience uses the CICIDS2017 DDoS attack data set. The experimental results are shown in Fig. 7, where the horizontal coordinate represents the number of network traffic and the vertical coordinate represents the hash buckets utilization rate. The experimental results show that the hash buckets utilization rates of all four methods are increasing as the number of data entries increases. And the hash bucket utilization rate of CK Sketch is always much higher than classical CM Sketch methods with different numbers of hash buckets. The reason is that for the CM Sketch method, since the number of network traffic is unpredictable, the designer often needs to set a

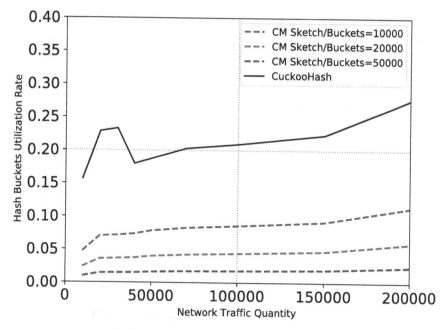

Fig. 7. Hash buckets utilization rate comparison

high number of hash buckets, and when the network traffic is too small, the hash buckets utilization rate of the sketch structure is very low, and when the network traffic is too large, the hash conflict is very likely to affect the accuracy of the subsequent machine learning detection of DDoS attacks. The method in this paper can increase the number of sketch layers adaptively according to the number of network traffic to ensure that the hash buckets utilization rate is increased as much as possible while avoiding hash conflicts. The point in Fig. 2 where the hash bucket utilization rate decreases indicate that a hash conflict has occurred and a new layer of sketch structure needs to be built, which contains a large number of empty hash buckets leading to a decrease in the hash buckets utilization rate.

Machine Learning Detection Accuracy

Table 3. Hash conflict statistics

Network traffic	50000	100000	150000	200000
CK Sketch hash conflict	0	0	0	0
CM Sketch_3000 hash conflict	285	348	483	561
CM Sketch_5000 hash conflict	127	186	226	375
CM Sketch_10000 hash conflict	65	82	145	198

Table 3 shows the number of hash conflicts between CK Sketch and CM Sketch after CK Sketch and CM Sketch compressing and counting the CICIDS2017 dataset. It can be found that CK Sketch can dynamically adjust the number of hash buckets to effectively avoid hash conflicts, while CM Sketch has hash conflicts of different degrees.

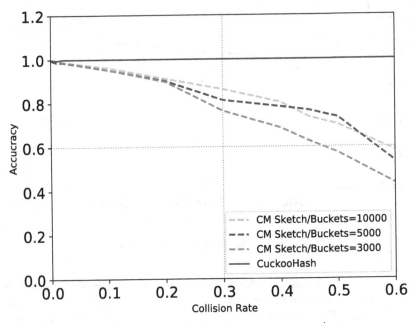

Fig. 8. Anomalous traffic detection accuracy comparison

This experiment compares the accuracy of CK Sketch and CM Sketch with a different number of hash buckets for machine learning detection of DDoS attacks. This experiment uses the CICIDS2017 DDoS attack data set, and Logistic Regression machine learning model. The experimental results are shown in Fig. 8, where the horizontal coordinate represents the percentage of hash conflicts in the sketch structure and the vertical coordinate represents the accuracy rate of DDoS attack detection. The experimental results show that, as the proportion of hash conflicts increases, different numbers of classical CM Sketch will lead to a decrease in the accuracy of subsequent machine learning detection of DDoS attacks, while CK Sketch can still guarantee a high accuracy of machine learning detection of DDoS attacks. The reason is that when different proportions of hash conflicts occur in classical CM Sketch, a single hash bucket contains feature information of multiple IPs and only contains one label, so it will bring some errors to model training. However, CK Sketch can effectively avoid the error situation that data streams of different IPs enter the same hash bucket through the mechanism of cuckoo hash when hash conflict occurs, which improves the accuracy of machine learning to detect DDoS attacks.

Throughput

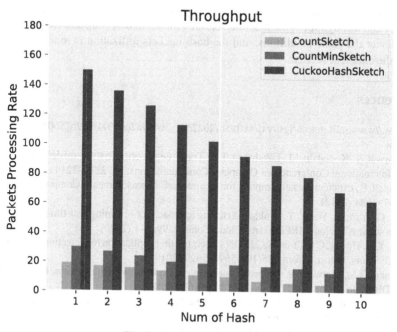

Fig. 9. Throughput comparison

To compare the difference in processing efficiency of network traffic between the different Sketch structures, this experiment compares the throughput of CK Sketch, CM Sketch, and Count Sketch when compressing and counting network traffic. The experimental results are shown in Fig. 9, where the horizontal coordinate indicates: the number of hash functions contained in different sketch structures. The vertical coordinate indicates the number of packets being processed per second. It shows that the processing efficiency of all methods for network traffic data decreases as the number of hash functions increases, while CK Sketch has a significant advantage over other methods for processing network traffic. The reason is that CM Sketch and Count Sketch need to bring the network traffic into all the hash functions to find the corresponding location, while CK Sketch only requires multiple hash calculations when a hash conflict occurs, which avoids a lot of unnecessary hash operations and saves a lot of time.

5 Conclusion

An improved sketch structure (CK Sketch) is proposed in this paper aiming for the problem of low detection accuracy due to hash conflict in the process of classical sketch combined with machine learning to detect anomalous network traffic. The CK sketch structure replaces the hash function part of the classical sketch with a cuckoo hash to avoid hash conflict and improve the throughput at the same time. It could also adaptively create multi-layer hash buckets to improve the utilization of the hash buckets. Finally, the CK sketch is compared with the classical sketch structure on the CICIDS2017 data set for experiments, and the results show that CK Sketch can effectively improve the accuracy and throughput of the machine learning model in detecting anomalous network traffic under the same conditions, and the hash buckets utilization is much larger than that of the classical sketch.

References

1. https://www.miit.gov.cn/jgsj/yxj/xxfb/art/2022/art_3b457a2cda504fe89b75605fe7235492.html
2. Agarwal, S., Kodialam, M., Lakshman, T.V.: Traffic engineering in software defined networks. In: International Conference on Computer Communications, pp. 2211–2219 (2013)
3. Raspall, F.: Efficient packet sampling for accurate traffic measurements. Comput. Netw. 56(6), 1667–1684 (2012)
4. Wu, G., Yun, X., Wang, Y., et al.: A sketching approach for obtaining real-time statistics over data streams in cloud. IEEE Trans. Cloud Comput. 99, 1–1 (2020)
5. Lin, Y.B., Huang, C.C., Tsai, S.C.: SDN soft computing application for detecting heavy hitters. IEEE Trans. Indust. Inform. 15(10), 5690–5699 (2019)
6. Manku, G.S., Motwani, R.: Approximate frequency counts over data streams. Proceedings of VLDB Endow., vol. 5, 12 (August 2012), p. 1699 (2012)
7. Wu, M., Huang, H., Sun, Y.-E., Du, Y., Chen, S., Gao, G.: ActiveKeeper: an accurate and efficient algorithm for finding top-k elephant flows. IEEE Commun. Lett. 25(8), 2545–2549 (2021). https://doi.org/10.1109/LCOMM.2021.3077902
8. Cormode, G., Muthukrishnan, S.: An improved data stream summary: the count-min sketch and its applications. J. Algor. 55(1), 58–75 (2005)
9. Salem, O., Makke, A., Tajer, J., et al.: Flooding attacks detection in traffic of backbone networks. In: Local Computer Networks. IEEE (2011)
10. Jing, X., Yan, Z., Liang, X., et al.: Network traffic fusion and analysis against DDoS flooding attacks with a novel reversible sketch. Inf. Fus. 51, 100–113 (2019)
11. Salem, O., Vaton, S., Gravey, A.: A scalable, efficient and informative approach for anomaly-based intrusion detection systems: theory and practice. John Wiley & Sons, Ltd. 20(5), 271–293 (2010)
12. Kim, M.S., Kang, H.J., Hong, S.C., et al.: A flow-based method for abnormal network traffic detection. In: Managing Next Generation Convergence Networks and Services, IEEE/IFIP Network Operations and Management Symposium, NOMS 2004, Seoul, Korea, pp. 19–23 April 2004, Proceedings. IEEE, 2004
13. Tang, J., Cheng, Y., Hao, Y., et al.: SIP flooding attack detection with a multi-dimensional sketch design. IEEE Trans. Depend. Secure Comput. 11(6), 582–595 (2014)
14. Shi, Y., Anandkumar, A.: Higher-order count sketch: dimensionality reduction that retains efficient tensor operations. 2020 Data Compression Conference (DCC), pp. 394–394 (2020). https://doi.org/10.1109/DCC47342.2020.00045
15. Liu, C.H., Kind, A., Vasilakos, A.V.: Sketching the data center network traffic. IEEE Network 27(4), 33–39 (2013). https://doi.org/10.1109/MNET.2013.6574663
16. Tao, L., Shigang, C., et al.: Per-flow traffic measurement through randomized counter sharing. IEEE/ACM Trans. Network. (2012)
17. Zhang, M., Wang, H., Li, J., et al.: Learned sketches for frequency estimation. Inf. Sci. 507, 365–385 (2020)

18. Huang, Q., Lee, P.P.C., Bao, Y.: Sketchlearn: relieving user burdens in approximate measurement with automated statistical inference. In: The 2018 Conference of the ACM Special Interest Group. ACM (2018)
19. Pagh, R., Rodler, F.F.: Cuckoo hashing. J. Algorithms **51**(2), 122–144 (2004)
20. Jiang, J., Fu, F., Ya, T., et al.: SketchML: Accelerating distributed machine learning with data sketches. In: The 2018 International Conference (2018)

FedMCS: A Privacy-Preserving Mobile Crowdsensing Defense Scheme

Mengfan Xu[1(✉)] and Xinghua Li[2]

[1] School of Computer Science, Shaanxi Normal University, Xi'an, China
cybersecurityxu@snnu.edu.cn
[2] School of Cyber Engineering, Xidian University, Xi'an 710071, China
xhli1@mail.xidian.edu.cn

Abstract. Mobile crowdsensing (MCS) provides a promising avenue for distributed data sharing. However, the increased privacy of workers and the existence of malicious workers have been verified to affect the normal performance of sensing tasks. Although the existing researches on federated learning against poisoning attacks to protect local data privacy while reducing the influence of malicious attackers on the global model, none of the existing researches consider the difficulty of obtaining benign benchmark gradients in MCS, which leads to the difficulty of malicious gradient elimination. To solve this problem, we propose a federated crowdsensing privacy-preserving method against poisoning attacks. The method can protect the gradient privacy of workers' sensing data and eliminate the poisoning behavior of malicious workers without the benchmark gradient. We further design a dynamic gradient aggregation algorithm to mitigate the effects of poisoning gradients on sensing tasks. In each epoch of gradient aggregation, the gradients uploaded by different workers are clustered. The sensing sub-gradients uploaded in each epoch are dynamically divided. We proved the security of the scheme theoretically, and verified the effectiveness of the scheme through experiments. The accuracy of the proposed scheme is at least 150% higher than that of the scheme without anti-poisoning measures.

Keywords: Mobile crowdsensing · Federated learning · Privacy-preserving · Poisoning attacks

1 Introduction

Relying on the crowdsourcing which proposed in 2006 [10], Raghu et al. proposed the mobile crowdsensing framework in 2011 [8]. With the rapid development of mobile communication and wireless sensing technology, the mobile crowdsensing (MCS) framework has gradually become a emerging sensing paradigm for largescale information dissemination and services. However, with the enactment and implementation of General Data Protection Regulation (GDPR) by European Union and Personal Information Protection Law of China [6], it would be illegal to simply transmit and process data related to sensing tasks. In addition, in MCS based on machine learning training tasks, attackers may disguise themselves as ordinary workers to participate in sensing. They upload interference data to affect the normal progress of sensing tasks. For example, during the COVID-19 pandemic, attackers can disrupt the normal epidemic management order by tampering with nucleic acid test results (the negative/positive test results are tampered with positive/negative), while causing the panic among the people in the corresponding area, or causing infection patients cannot be diagnosed in time. Delaying the opportunity to seek medical treatment and further spreading the epidemic.

Fortunately, the proposal of federated learning (FL) provides a promising way to protect the privacy of user data in distributed systems [4,7,15,18]. In FL, local users no longer need to upload the raw sensing data, but instead upload gradients to iteratively update the global model. In this process, different users can collaboratively train a global model without revealing the privacy of the raw data. Furthermore, in the existence of malicious workers, the existing researches calculate the similarity between different local gradients and benchmark benign gradients. To ensure the accuracy of the global model, the weight of gradients with low similarity is directly reduced [20,23,24].

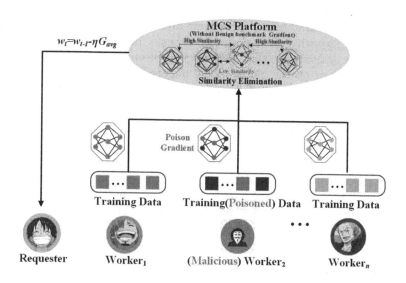

Fig. 1. The challenge arise without benign benchmark gradient.

The existing schemes can effectively protect the privacy of the raw data while ensuring the performance of the aggregated global model. However, none of them considers the difficulty of obtaining benign benchmark gradients in MCS. As shown in Fig. 1, the requester only submits the task information such as model requirements and budget to the platform [16,17,27,28,30]. The platform does not have the features of trusted data. Therefore, there is no benign benchmark gradient in MCS for detecting malicious gradients.

In order to solve above problems, this paper proposes a privacy-preserving method for federated crowdsensing against poisoning attacks. Specifically, we introduce the FL framework into MCS, and design a secure protocol (*Sec*DBSCAN) to eliminate malicious gradients. The gradient privacy of workers sensing data can still be protected and the poisoning behavior of malicious workers can be eliminated without reference gradients. To the best of our knowledge, this paper is the first to study the privacy-preserving of FL without benchmark gradients in MCS. The main contributions of our work are as follows.

- We propose a privacy-preserving crowdsensing framework (FedMCS) based on Pailliar homomorphic encryption for FL gradient. Specifically, through the interactive aggregation of workers and platforms on ciphertext gradients, malicious workers cannot use poisoned gradients to interfere with the accuracy of the global model. During this process, sensing gradients uploaded by workers will not be leaked.
- We further design a dynamic gradient aggregation algorithm to mitigate the influence of malicious poisoning gradients on sensing tasks. Specifically, in each epoch of gradient aggregation, the similarity is no longer calculated pairwise, but the gradients uploaded are clustered. The sensing sub-gradients uploaded in each epoch are dynamically divided. We further distinguish malicious and benign gradients to iteratively update the optimal global model.
- We prove the security of the proposed scheme. In addition, experiments on real datasets demonstrate that FedMCS can effectively resist the influence of malicious workers on the global model under the premise of no benchmark benign gradients, and the performance is improved by at least 150% compared with the scheme without anti-poisoning measures.

The rest of the paper is structured as follows: in Sect. 2, we introduce the system and threat model and design goals of this paper. In Sect. 3, we introduce the mathematical notation and preliminaries used in this paper. In Sect. 4, we introduce the scheme design in detail. In Sect. 5, we provide a rigorous proof of the security of the proposed scheme. In Sect. 6, we experimentally evaluate the proposed gradient privacy-preserving framework and analyze the computational and communication overhead. In Sect. 7, a summary of this paper is made.

2   Related Works

To defense the poisoning attacks, Yin et al. [29] proposed a distributed learning algorithms that are provably robust against such failures, with a focus on achieving optimal statistical performance. A sharp analysis of two robust distributed gradient descent algorithms based on median and trimmed mean operations, respectively. Blanchard et al. [1] formulate a resilience property of the aggregation rule capturing the basic requirements to guarantee convergence despite f Byzantine workers. They proposed Krum, an aggregation rule that satisfies our resilience property, which we argue is the first provably Byzantine-resilient algorithm for distributed SGD. Cao et al. [2] bridge the gap via proposing FLTrust.

In particular, the service provider itself collects a clean small training dataset for the learning task and the service provider maintains a model based on it to bootstrap trust. In each iteration, the service provider first assigns a trust score to each local model update from the clients, where a local model update has a lower trust score if its direction deviates more from the direction of the server model update. Then, the service provider normalizes the magnitudes of the local model updates such that they lie in the same hyper-sphere as the server model update in the vector space. Finally, the service provider computes the average of the normalized local model updates weighted by their trust scores as a global model update, which is used to update the global model. Mhamdi et al. [9] introduce Bulyan, and prove it significantly reduces the attackers leeway to a narrow bound. They empirically show that Bulyan does not suffer the fragility of existing aggregation rules and, at a reasonable cost in terms of required batch size, achieves convergence as if only non-Byzantine gradients had been used to update the model. Karimireddy et al. [11] designed new attacks which circumvent current defenses, leading to significant loss of performance. Then they proposed a simple bucketing scheme that adapts existing robust algorithms to heterogeneous datasets at a negligible computational cost. Karimireddy et al. [12] presented two surprisingly simple strategies: a new robust iterative clipping procedure, and incorporating worker momentum to overcome time-coupled attacks. Sun et al. [22] propose a client-based defense, named White Blood Cell for Federated Learning (FL-WBC), which can mitigate model poisoning attacks that have already polluted the global model. The key idea of FL-WBC is to identify the parameter space where long-lasting attack effect on parameters resides and perturb that space during local training. Zhao et al. [31] proposed a privacy-preserving MCS system called CROWDFL by seamlessly integrating federated learning into MCS. At a high level, in order to protect participants' privacy and fully explore participants' computing power, participants in CROWDFL locally process sensing data via FL paradigm and only upload encrypted training models to the server. To this end, we design a secure aggregation algorithm (SecAgg) through the threshold Paillier cryptosystem to aggregate training models in an encrypted form.

Table 1. Comparison of the existing works and FedMCS

Scheme	PGP	WBG
FL against poisoning attacks [1,2,9,11,12,22,29]	✗	✗
CrowdFL [31]	✓	✗
FedMCS	✓	✓

Note: **PGP**: Protect gradient privacy; **WBG**: Without benign gradient. ✗ indicates that the challenge was not considered or could not be addressed by the solution. ✓ means that the solution completely solves the challenge.

In summary, the current research on federal learning privacy protection based on anti-poisoning attacks has made some progress. However, none of them

considers the difficulty of obtaining benign benchmark gradients Coarse-grained
pairs of existing works are shown in Table 1.

3   Problem Formulation

3.1   System Model

In this paper, we consider a federated learning architecture for dynamic baseline
gradient privacy protection, as shown in Fig. 2. Our proposed system model
consists of four entities/classes: including key management center, local users,
cloud platform, and privacy service provider. The role of each entity/class is as
follows.

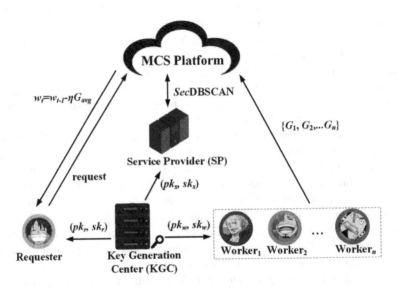

Fig. 2. System model.

- Key Generation Center (KGC): The KGC is an independent and trusted
  authority that distributes and manages all public and private keys. In the
  scheme, it is used to generate and issue public-private key pairs (pk_r, sk_r),
  (pk_w, sk_w) and (pk_s, sk_s) to requester, workers and privacy service providers,
  respectively.
- Requester: The requester is the party who initiates the sensing task in the
  MCS. It has no model training capability or data collection capability. Therefore, it is necessary to apply for specific requirements to the MCSP and pay
  for the purchase of machine learning models.
- Worker: The worker is the data source of the MCS sensing task. Different
  workers use the sensing data collected by themselves to iteratively train a
  sub-model, and upload the sub-gradient encryption in the process of training
  the sub-model to the MCS platform.

- MCS Platform (MCSP): The MCSP collects the perceptual gradients uploaded by different workers. The MCSP iteratively aggregates to obtain the optimal global model and returns it to the requester.
- Privacy Service Provider (PSP): In this article, PSP works with MCSP to weed out potential poisoning gradients.

3.2 Threat Model

In this system, the requester does not want any entity to acquire the complete model while paying for the model. Workers do not want any entity other than themselves to acquire the full sub-gradient. Among them, MCSP and PSP are regarded as honest but curious adversaries. They perform the aggregation process honestly according to the designed rules. However, they may be interested in intermediate parameters such as gradients uploaded by workers and the global model of the requested task. Furthermore, consistent with the existing scheme assumptions, malicious poisoning behaviors only occur among workers [3,21].

3.3 Design Goals

FedMCS has the following two design goals.

- Correctness: Malicious poisoning will lead to the wrong classification of the global model, so this paper needs to ensure that the accuracy of the global model is within a reasonable range.
- Security: Prevents the adversary from obtaining the true distribution of users through gradients and prevents the adversary from obtaining a complete global model. Therefore, the intermediate parameters such as the gradient of workers and the global model should be kept confidential.

4 Preliminaries

4.1 Notations

All the symbol definitions covered in this article are described in Table 2.

4.2 Poisoning Attack

Poisoning attack is a malicious behavior that modifies the data in the training stage and causes the model classification error in the reasoning stage. As shown in Fig. 3, assuming that an institution urgently needs to train the NUCLEIC acid testing model for COVID-19 to test residents, but limited by the lack of relevant data, medical resources and technology, it needs to purchase relevant data from other institutions to train the nucleic acid testing model, and the seller can tamper with the relevant data of a certain group of people. As a result, the gradient deviation of the buyer in the training process leads to the detection model trained by the buyer in the inference stage will not be able to effectively detect the virus infection. Such an attack could be used by a purposeful attacker to cause the rapid spread of COVID-19 in a specific area, seriously compromising national security.

Table 2. Notations.

Notation	Description
pk	Public key
sk	Secret key
G_k	Sensing gradient of workers
C_{max}	The benign gradient set
R	The random vector
α	Poisoning rate
η	Learning rate
w_0	Initial model parameters
n	The number of workers
l	The number of iterations

4.3   Paillier Encryption System

This scheme uses the Paillier encryption system to keep the intermediate parameters such as the perceptual gradient and the global model secret. For details of the Paillier encryption system, please refer to [19]. This chapter mainly introduces its additive homomorphism.

Additive homomorphism: The result of multiplying two ciphertext messages encrypted by Paillier is decrypted to obtain the result of adding the two messages. For two ciphertexts $c_1 = g^{m_1} r_1^n (\text{mod} n^2)$ and $c_2 = g^{m_2} r_2^n (\text{mod} n^2)$

$$c_1 \cdot c_2 = g^{m_1} \cdot g^{m_2} \cdot r_1^n \cdot r_2^n \text{mod} n^2 = g^{m_1+m_2} \cdot (r_1 \cdot r_2)^n \text{mod} n^2 \qquad (1)$$

where r_1 and r_2 are both elements in $Z_{n^2}^*$, so $r_1 \cdot r_2$ also belong to $Z_{n^2}^*$, and have the same properties, so $c_1 \cdot c_2$ can be regarded as the ciphertext encrypted by $m = m_1 + m_2$, and the decryption result of $c_1 \cdot c_2$ is m.

5   Proposed Scheme

In this section, we introduce FedMCS in detail, as shown in Fig. 4. It is mainly divided into three stages: request task publishing, sensing gradient uploading, and model secure aggregating.

5.1   Request Task Publishing

After the requester sends the request task to MCSP, KGC uses the Paillier encryption system to generate and issue public and private key pairs (pk_s, sk_s), (pk_w, sk_w) and (pk_u, sk_u) for the requester, the worker and PSP, respectively.

5.2   Sensing Gradient Uploading

The initial parameters w_0 and η of the model were generated by MCSP and sent to the workers participating in the task. Different workers trained the model on

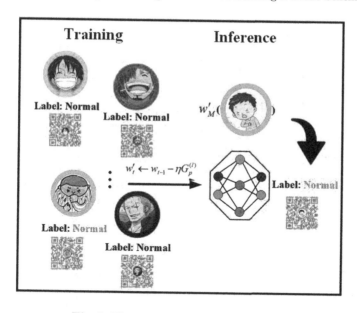

Fig. 3. The process of poisoning attack.

plaintext using the collected perceptual data and uploaded the sub gradient G_t obtained in the training process to MCSP using pk_s encryption. After interaction with PSP, MCSP returned the average gradient $[[G_{avg}^{(l)}]]_{pk_w}$ of this round and sent it to the local users. Workers use private key sk_w decryption and then combine with the FedAvg [14] algorithm recognized by current gradient aggregation to update the submodel, and iteratively train to obtain G_{k+1}. The above steps are iterated until the optimal global model is obtained and pk_r is used. Encryption is returned to the requester. Finally, the requester uses the private key sk_r to decrypt and get the global model of the request.

5.3   Model Secure Aggregation

At this stage, the MCSP interacts with the PSP to remove the perceived gradient of malicious workers and aggregate the optimal global model.

The worker upload the encrypted perceptual gradient $[[G_k]]_{pk_s}$ to the MCSP, which collaborates with the PSP to eliminate the malicious gradient. To achieve this goal, we designed the SecDBSCAN protocol, and the formalization process of SecDBSCAN is shown in Fig. 5. First, MCSP generates a random vector R, uses the additive property of the Paillier homomorphic encryption system, confuses $[[G_k]]_{pk_s}$, obtains $\{[[G_k + R]]_{pk_s}, k \in (1, n)\}$ and sends it to PSP. Then PSP decrypts all the perception gradients sent by MCSP and marks them as unvisited state. One perceptual gradient is randomly selected and marked as a visited state and classified as cluster C_1. The adjacent perception gradient of $G_k + R$ is found in the radius of ε, and the set N is obtained. In addition,

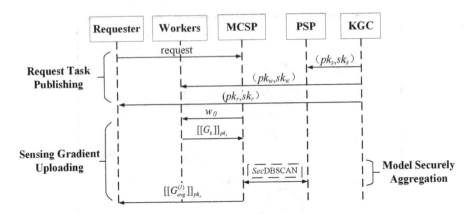

Fig. 4. The process of FedMCS.

further select the perceptual gradient $G_j + R$ in the N set to iterate the above search. Finally, the potential of all clusters was calculated, and the cluster with the largest potential was judged to be the set of benign perception gradient, which was encrypted and returned to MCSP to eliminate confusion. After several iterations of updating the model, it was finally sent to the requester to complete the perception task.

The potential of each cluster was calculated. Based on the assumption that the current working poisoning rate $\alpha < 50\%$ [5,25,26], the set with the largest potential was considered as the set of benign perception gradient, and the average gradient $G_{avg}^{(l)} + R$ was further calculated to update the model w_{t-1} to w_t. Gradients that do not belong to any cluster by the end of the iteration will be directly marked as malicious. Finally, the requester decrypts the global plaintext model using the sk_r private key.

6 Safety Certificate

We will rigorously prove the theorem using a simulation example. We construct a simulator using the inputs and outputs of relevant parties to prove that the information sequence obtained during simulation is computationally indistinguishable from the information sequence obtained during real execution.

Case 1. We will build a simulator Sim_{MCSP}, to generate computationally indistinguishable sequences of information. In real execution, the view of MCSP is $View_{MCSP}(\wedge, \wedge) = \{\wedge, R, [[G_k]](k \in [1, n])\}$, where $\wedge$ indicates that the input of MCSP and PSP is an empty set, and R represents a set of random numbers (vectors). The simulator Sim_{MCSP} does the following: it randomly selects the gradient vector $\{G_k', k \in [1, n]\}$ and computes $[[G_k']]$ using the public key pk_s. Then, based on $[[G_k']]$ and R_{CP} performs the subsequent process, that is, the information sequence generated by MCSP during the simulation is: $Sim_{MCSP}(\wedge, \lambda) = \{\wedge, R_{MCSP}, [[G_k']](k \in [1, n])\}$.

Input: $[[G_k]]_{pk}$.

Output: $[[G^{(l)}_{avg}]]_{pk}$.

Procedure:

MCSP:

1. Generating a random vector R.

2. Calculating $\{[[G_k + R]]_{pk}, k \in (1,n)\}$.

3. Sending $\{[[G_k + R]]_{pk}, k \in (1,n)\}$ to PSP.

PSP:

1. Decrypting $\{[[G_k + R]]_{pk}, k \in (1,n)\}$, Do

2. Randomly select an unvisited $G_k + R$, and mark $G_k + R$ as visited

3. If the ε neighborhood of $G_k + R$ has at least MinPts gradients

4.   Create a new cluster Ci and add $G_k + R$ to C_i

5.   Let N be the set of gradients of ε neighborhood of

6.   For $(G_j + R) \in N$

7.   If $State_{(G_j + R)} = unvisited$

8. $State_{(G_j + R)} = visited$

9. $G_j + R \in C_i$

10.   End for

11. Else $Label_{G_k + R} = abnormal$

12. Until $\max |C_i| > \dfrac{n}{2}$ $i \in (1,I)$ and $|State_{G_k + R}| = 0$

13. Return $C^{(l)}_{max}$

14. Calculating $G^{(l)}_{avg} + R \xleftarrow{Fedavg} C_{max}$.

15. If $w_t = w_{t-1}$

16. Send $[[G^{(l)}_{avg} + R]]_{pk}$ to MCSP

Fig. 5. *Sec*DBSCAN: A model aggregation protocol without disclosing workers privacy.

In $View_{MCSP}$ and Sim_{MCSP}, $[[G_k]]$ and $[[G'_k]]$ are ciphertext encrypted by the Paillier cryptosystem, and MCSP does not have the private key sk_s of the Paillier cryptosystem. Therefore, it can be known from the semantic security of the Paillier cryptosystem that $[[G_k]]$ and $[[G'_k]]$ are computatively indistinguishable.

In summary, $View_{MCSP}$ and Sim_{MCSP} are computationally indistinguishable: $View_{MCSP}(\wedge, \wedge) \overset{c}{\equiv} Sim_{MCSP}(\wedge, \lambda)$.

Case 2. Next, we construct the simulator Sim_{PSP}. In real execution, the $View$ of PSP is $View_{PSP}(\wedge, \wedge) = \{\wedge, R_{PSP}, [[G_k + R]](t \in [1,n]), G_k + R(t \in [1,n])\}$.

In order to simulate $View_{PSP}$, the simulator Sim_{PSP} performs the following operations: Firstly, gradient vector $\{G'_k, (k \in [1,n])\}$ and random number set R' are randomly selected to make $G'_k + R' = G_k + R$. And iterative calculation is performed based on DBSCAN until all sub-gradients are traversed.

That is, the information sequence generated by PSP during the simulation is
$Sim_{PSP}(\wedge, G_{avg}^{(l)} + R) = \{\wedge, R_{PSP}, [[G_k^{'} + R^{'}]](t \in [1, n]), G_k^{'} + R^{'} (t \in [1, n])\}$.

In $View_{PSP}$ and Sim_{PSP}, $[[G_k + R]], k \in [1, n]$ and $[[G_k^{'} + R^{'}]], k \in [1, n]$ are computationally indistinguishable from the semantic security of Paillier's cryptographic system. According to the randomness of the random vectors $R^{'}$ and R, $G_k + Rk \in [1, n]$ and $G_k^{'} + R^{'}, k \in [1, n]$ are computationally indistinguishable.

To sum up, $View_{PSP}$ and Sim_{PSP} are indistinguishable in calculation, namely: $View_{PSP}(\wedge, \wedge) \overset{c}{\equiv} Sim_{PSP}(\wedge, G_{avg}^{(l)} + R)$.

7   Performance Evaluation

7.1   Experimental Settings

In order to evaluate the effectiveness and safety of this scheme, two data sets were selected for the experiment. MNIST dataset is a handwritten font image dataset published by the National Institute of Standards and Technology (NIST) of the United States, which contains 10 categories of black and white image data from 0 to 9. It is the universally recognized benchmark data set in the current field of machine learning [26]. EMNIST is an extended dataset of MNIST, which not only adds handwritten Digits, but also includes handwritten letters and Digits [13].

In the establishment of federated learning and training environment, we assume that there are n clients participating in the federated learning process, and each client locally adopts stochastic gradient descent (SGD) to update the local model. We further adopted the StepLR method to adjust the learning rate, which is a common method to adjust the learning rate according to the training times of epoch [24, 25].

The experimental device is a personal desktop PC with dual-channel Zhike E5 2680 CPU, 256 GB 1333 MHz DDR3 memory, NVIDIA GeForce GTX 3090 GPU and 1 TB SSD. The operating system is Windows 10. The programming language is Python 3.7 and programming libraries such as PyTorch.

7.2   Experiment Results

Effectiveness Analysis

First, the proposed scheme was compared with the global model before and after poisoning and tested on MNIST (Fig. 6(a)) and EMNIST (Fig. 6(b)) datasets. As shown in Fig. 6, the model accuracy drops to about 70% on the MNIST dataset without defenses. The model accuracy stays above 85% after using our scheme. After defenses, the accuracy is improved by more than 150% on the EMNIST dataset (20% to 50%). This is due to the design of the security aggregation algorithm in this scheme, which uses multiple iterations to calculate the gradient center and divide the benign and toxic gradient set, minimizing the influence of the poisoned model on the global model. The detection performance of our scheme is lower than that of the model without poisoning, which is mainly caused

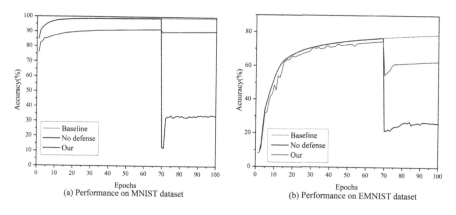

Fig. 6. The effectiveness of FedMCS on 2 datasets.

by the optimization of the clustering algorithm, which will also be the focus of our next work. In addition, the overall accuracy of the scheme is less than 80% on the EMNIST data set, which is caused by the selection of benchmark model, and the model optimization problem on the EMNIST data set is also not within the scope of this paper.

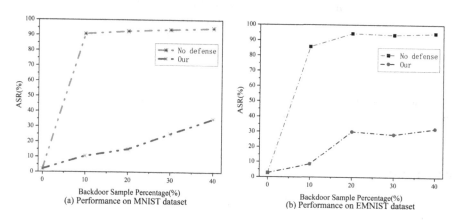

Fig. 7. The attack success rate with different backdoor sample on 2 datasets.

The Influence of Different Byzantine Nodes on the Attack Success Rate. With the increasing Byzantine nodes, the attack success rate is greatly improved. As shown in Fig. 7, under the premise of no defense measures, when the percentage of Byzantine nodes is higher than 10%, the success rate of the attacker on the two datasets reaches 90% and 85%, respectively. In this scheme, when the percentage of Byzantine nodes is higher than 20%, the attack success rate can only be improved to a certain extent. Even when the percentage of Byzantine nodes is equal to 40%, the attack success rate is less than 35%.

It indicates that the SecMCS protocol designed by this scheme can effectively eliminate malicious gradients from the gradient set, and iteratively select the optimal benign gradients and aggregate them. Therefore, in this paper, the Byzantine node percentages of 20% and 25% are selected for experiments which can ensure the robustness of the global model.

Efficiency Analysis. In this paper, we assume that the gradient vector is γ dimensional. In protocol SecDBSCAN, MCSP encrypts a γ-dimensional random vector R. That is, CP needs to perform γ encryption operations. PSP needs to decrypt $\{[[G_k + R]]_{pk_s}, k \in (1, n)\}$, i.e., performing γ decryption operations. $G_{avg}^{(l)} + R$ also needs to be encrypted, that is, γ encryption operations need to be performed. Therefore, it can be seen that Paillier encryption and decryption require running two modular exponential operations once, and the protocol SecDBSCAN needs to perform $2(n+2)\gamma$ modular exponentiations with a computational complexity $O(n\gamma)$. Since MCSP and PSP interact only once during SecDBSCAN, their communication complexity is $O(2)$.

8   Conclusion

This paper proposes an FL gradient privacy protection framework (FedDBG) based on HE. This ensures that malicious initial users and subsequent users cannot interfere with the accuracy of the global model by uploading a toxic gradient. Theoretical analysis proves that FedDBG is safe, and experimental results show that FedDBG improves the global model accuracy by at least 80%, and the computational complexity and communication complexity are greatly reduced compared with existing methods.

Acknowledgment. This work was supported by the National Natural Science Foundation of China (62125205), the Natural Science Basic Research Plan in Shaanxi Province (2022JQ-594).

References

1. Blanchard, P., El Mhamdi, E.M., Guerraoui, R., Stainer, J.: Machine learning with adversaries: Byzantine tolerant gradient descent. In: 31st Conference Advances in Neural Information Processing Systems, p. 30 (2017)
2. Cao, X., Fang, M., Liu, J., Gong, N.Z.: FLTrust: byzantine-robust federated learning via trust bootstrapping. In: NDSS (2021)
3. Cao, X., Jia, J., Gong, N.Z.: Data poisoning attacks to local differential privacy protocols. In: 30th USENIX Security Symposium (USENIX Security 21), pp. 947–964 (2021)
4. Chen, F., Li, P., Miyazaki, T., Wu, C.: FedGraph: federated graph learning with intelligent sampling. IEEE Trans. Parallel Distrib. Syst. **33**(8), 1775–1786 (2021)
5. Chen, J., Zhang, X., Zhang, R., Wang, C., Liu, L.: De-Pois: an attack-agnostic defense against data poisoning attacks. IEEE Trans. Inf. Forensics Secur. **16**, 3412–3425 (2021)

6. Consulting, I.: General data protection regulation–official (2016). https://gdpr-info.eu/

7. Deng, Y., et al.: Auction: automated and quality-aware client selection framework for efficient federated learning. IEEE Trans. Parallel Distrib. Syst. **33**(8), 1996–2009 (2021)

8. Ganti, R.K., Ye, F., Lei, H.: Mobile crowdsensing: current state and future challenges. IEEE Commun. Mag. **49**(11), 32–39 (2011)

9. Guerraoui, R., Rouault, S., et al.: The hidden vulnerability of distributed learning in byzantium. In: International Conference on Machine Learning, pp. 3521–3530. PMLR (2018)

10. Howe, J., et al.: The rise of crowdsourcing. Wired Mag. **14**(6), 1–4 (2006)

11. Karimireddy, S.P., He, L., Jaggi, M.: Byzantine-robust learning on heterogeneous datasets via bucketing. In: International Conference on Learning Representations (2021)

12. Karimireddy, S.P., He, L., Jaggi, M.: Learning from history for byzantine robust optimization. In: International Conference on Machine Learning, pp. 5311–5319. PMLR (2021)

13. LeCun, Y., Bottou, L., Bengio, Y., Haffner, P.: Gradient-based learning applied to document recognition. Proc. IEEE **86**(11), 2278–2324 (1998)

14. Li, X., Huang, K., Yang, W., Wang, S., Zhang, Z.: On the convergence of fedAvg on non-IID data. arXiv preprint arXiv:1907.02189 (2019)

15. Lim, W.Y.B., et al.: Decentralized edge intelligence: a dynamic resource allocation framework for hierarchical federated learning. IEEE Trans. Parallel Distrib. Syst. **33**(3), 536–550 (2021)

16. Liu, Y., Feng, T., Peng, M., Guan, J., Wang, Y.: Dream: online control mechanisms for data aggregation error minimization in privacy-preserving crowdsensing. IEEE Trans. Depend. Secure Comput. **19**, 1266–1279 (2020)

17. Liu, Y., Wang, H., Peng, M., Guan, J., Wang, Y.: An incentive mechanism for privacy-preserving crowdsensing via deep reinforcement learning. IEEE Internet Things J. **8**(10), 8616–8631 (2020)

18. Mills, J., Hu, J., Min, G.: Multi-task federated learning for personalised deep neural networks in edge computing. IEEE Trans. Parallel Distrib. Syst. **33**(3), 630–641 (2021)

19. Paillier, P.: Public-key cryptosystems based on composite degree residuosity classes. In: Stern, J. (ed.) EUROCRYPT 1999. LNCS, vol. 1592, pp. 223–238. Springer, Heidelberg (1999). https://doi.org/10.1007/3-540-48910-X_16

20. Schwarzschild, A., Goldblum, M., Gupta, A., Dickerson, J.P., Goldstein, T.: Just how toxic is data poisoning? A unified benchmark for backdoor and data poisoning attacks. In: International Conference on Machine Learning, pp. 9389–9398. PMLR (2021)

21. Severi, G., Meyer, J., Coull, S., Oprea, A.: {*Explanation − Guided*} backdoor poisoning attacks against malware classifiers. In: 30th USENIX Security Symposium (USENIX Security 21), pp. 1487–1504 (2021)

22. Sun, J., Li, A., DiValentin, L., Hassanzadeh, A., Chen, Y., Li, H.: FL-WBC: enhancing robustness against model poisoning attacks in federated learning from a client perspective. Adv. Neural. Inf. Process. Syst. **34**, 12613–12624 (2021)

23. Suya, F., Mahloujifar, S., Suri, A., Evans, D., Tian, Y.: Model-targeted poisoning attacks with provable convergence. In: International Conference on Machine Learning, pp. 10000–10010. PMLR (2021)

24. Wang, Y., Mianjy, P., Arora, R.: Robust learning for data poisoning attacks. In: International Conference on Machine Learning, pp. 10859–10869. PMLR (2021)

25. Weerasinghe, S., Alpcan, T., Erfani, S.M., Leckie, C.: Defending support vector machines against data poisoning attacks. IEEE Trans. Inf. Forensics Secur. **16**, 2566–2578 (2021)
26. Wen, J., Zhao, B.Z.H., Xue, M., Oprea, A., Qian, H.: With great dispersion comes greater resilience: efficient poisoning attacks and defenses for linear regression models. IEEE Trans. Inf. Forensics Secur. **16**, 3709–3723 (2021)
27. Wu, D., Yang, Z., Yang, B., Wang, R., Zhang, P.: From centralized management to edge collaboration: a privacy-preserving task assignment framework for mobile crowdsensing. IEEE Internet Things J. **8**(6), 4579–4589 (2020)
28. Xiong, J., Zhao, M., Bhuiyan, M.Z.A., Chen, L., Tian, Y.: An AI-enabled three-party game framework for guaranteed data privacy in mobile edge crowdsensing of IOT. IEEE Trans. Industr. Inf. **17**(2), 922–933 (2019)
29. Yin, D., Chen, Y., Kannan, R., Bartlett, P.: Byzantine-robust distributed learning: towards optimal statistical rates. In: International Conference on Machine Learning, pp. 5650–5659. PMLR (2018)
30. Zhang, X., Lu, R., Shao, J., Wang, F., Zhu, H., Ghorbani, A.A.: FedSky: an efficient and privacy-preserving scheme for federated mobile crowdsensing. IEEE Internet of Things J. **9**, 5344–5356 (2021)
31. Zhao, B., Liu, X., Chen, W.N., Deng, R.: CrowdFL: privacy-preserving mobile crowdsensing system via federated learning. IEEE Trans. Mobile Comput. Early Access (2022)

Membership Inference Attacks Against Robust Graph Neural Network

Zhengyang Liu[1], Xiaoyu Zhang[1(✉)], Chenyang Chen[1], Shen Lin[1], and Jingjin Li[2]

[1] State Key Laboratory of Integrated Service Networks (ISN), Xidian University, Xi'an 710071, People's Republic of China
xiaoyuzhang@xidian.edu.cn, {cychen_1,linshen}@stu.xidian.edu.cn
[2] College of Science and Engineering, James Cook University, Townsville, QLD 4811, Australia
ginger.li@my.jcu.edu.au

Abstract. With the rapid development of neural network technologies in machine learning, neural networks are widely used in artificial intelligence tasks. Due to the widespread existence of graph data, graph neural networks, a kind of neural network specializing in processing graph data, has become a research hotspot. This paper firstly studies the relationship between adversarial attacks and privacy attacks on graphs, *i.e.*, whether a robust model trained on graph adversarial can improve the attack effect of graph membership inference attacks. We also find the different performance of the robust model's loss function on the training set and the test set is a critical reason for the increasing membership inference attack success rate. Extensive experimental evaluations on Cora, Cora-ml, Citeseer, Polblogs and Pubmed demonstrate that the robust model obtained by adversarial training can significantly improve the attack success rate of membership inference attacks.

Keywords: Graph neural network · Membership inference attack · Robust model · Adversarial training

1 Introduction

With the increasing volume of big data and decentralized information sharing technology boosting, machine learning have developed rapidly in the last decades [1]. Machine learning is to learn feature from large amounts of data to build a model and then gradually improves the model's accuracy. Nowadays, machine learning is applied to almost every aspect of our daily lives. However, among those data resources that can be obtained by researchers, a lot of them are non-Euclidean data [2]. Hamilton et al. [3] pointed out that non-Euclidean data are those that are not translation invariant. This kind of data takes one of them as a node, and the number of its neighbor nodes may be different. Common types of data include knowledge graphs, social networks, chemical molecular structures.

X. Chen et al. (Eds.): CSS 2022, LNCS 13547, pp. 259–273, 2022.
https://doi.org/10.1007/978-3-031-18067-5_19

Euclidean data refers to a class of data with good translation invariance. For this type of data, one of the pixels is used as a node, and the number of its neighbor nodes is the same. Common types of data include images, text, and languages. non-Euclidean data cannot be used in models derived from Euclidean data because they do not satisfy translation invariance [4]. Figure 1 presents the differences between Euclidean data and non-Euclidean data. Graph neural network (GNN) [3] have been proposed to specifically process the typical type of non-Euclidean data, *i.e.*, graph data [5], which has been widely deployed into many applications, such as malicious user detection in social networks, traffic flow detection in urban traffic routes, classification of chemical molecules [5].

Fig. 1. Left: Euclidean data; right: non-Euclidean data.

While massive data resources enrich machine learning technology, attacks on users' private data are inevitable. There are two types of attack methods on machine learning models [6]. The first type is the attack happens at the training stage, for example, the poisoning attack; the second type is the attack happens at the testing stage, for example, evasion attack, membership inference attack (MIA), attribute inference attack, and model inversion attack [7]. The training set has a big impact on the machine learning model [8]. Comprehensive and authentic private datasets are important assets to every organization [9]. The valuable training data has always been the target of membership inference attacks. Thus, this paper focuses on membership inference attacks on graph data. There has been a lot of research on membership inference attacks [10] in the image and text domains [11]. We summarize the previous work, as shown in Table 1 to highlight our contributions.

Table 1. Summary of previous work.

Ref.	Year	Graph	Image	MIA	Adversarial training
[10]	2017	✗	✔	✔	✗
[11]	2019	✗	✔	✔	✗
[13]	2019	✗	✔	✔	✔
[20]	2021	✔	✗	✔	✗
[21]	2021	✔	✗	✔	✗
[18]	2018	✔	✗	✗	✔
[19]	2019	✔	✗	✗	✔
Our	2022	✔	✗	✔	✔

Many researchers have revealed why membership inference attacks are feasible and proposed lots of schemes to implement membership inference attacks. Still, there are very few studies on membership inference attacks in the field of graph data [12]. Furthermore, there is no research on the relationship between privacy attack and adversarial attack in the field of graph data. Therefore, the research on membership inference attack targeting graph data has significant meaning for data security and privacy [13]. The main contributions can be summarized as follows:

- We firstly build the connection between privacy attack and robust model in the domain of graph data. In addition, we find that a robust model after adversarial training can improve the attack success rate of membership inference.
- We perform extensive experiments on Cora, Cora-ml, Citeseer, Polblogs and Pubmed and the results demonstrate that the robust model after adversarial training can improve the success rate of membership inference attacks. We also conclude that the loss function difference in distribution between training set and test set feeding into the robust model is the main reason why a robust model can improve the success rate of membership inference attacks.

2 Related Work

In this section, we will introduce research developments in graph convolutional networks, graph adversarial training, and graph inference attacks.

2.1 Graph Convolutional Networks

In 2017, Kipf et al. [14] proposed the graph convolutional network (GCN). He also proposed a two-layer GCN model which becomes the most commonly used graph neural network (GNN) model. Kipf et al. pointed out two limitations that restricted GCN from being as deep as CNN: 1) Smooth transition: after using multiple convolutional layers, node features tend to converge to the same or similar vectors, making them difficult to distinguish; 2) over-compression: the number of neighbors exponentially increases after using a multi-layer graph network. To compress a large amount of node information into one node, there will be a problem of over-compression.

In subsequent research, Hamilton et al. [15] used the graphSAGE model of random collection nodes for aggregation. Velickovic et al. [16] applied the attention mechanism to GCN; Niepert et al. [17] used the CNN structure to design a new model framework PATCHY-SAN.

2.2 Graph Adversarial Training

Adversarial training is to incorporate adversarial samples into the training stage of the model, thereby making the model more robust. Graph adversarial training is divided into two parts: 1) generate adversarial examples; 2) use adversarial examples for adversarial training. Dai et al. [18] generated adversarial samples through a simple technique of randomly deleting edges for adversarial training. Although the result can only increase by 0.01, the cost of adversarial training is meager; on this basis, Jin et al. [19] proposed a scheme to add perturbation in the middle layer of the GCN.

2.3   Graph Inference Attacks

Membership inference attack was first proposed by Shokri [10]. Olatunji et al. [20] first migrated membership inference attack to graph data, using a shadow training technique. Shadow training is to train several shadow models to imitate the behavior of the target model. And then we train an attack model with the data generated by the shadow models. The proposed scheme in [10] is based on node-level tasks performed on graph data. He et al. [21] proposed a scheme for membership inference attack using 0-hop subgraph and 2-hop subgraph, which combined the membership inference attack with the structure of the graph.

3   Background

This section will briefly introduce the background of the graph data, membership inference attack in graph neural networks, and graph adversarial training.

3.1   Graph Convolutional Network

GCN mainly uses the principle of message aggregation. For each node is in a layer of GCN, it will aggregate the information of its one-hop neighbors to update the node itself. That is to say, there are several layers of GCN nodes that will aggregate its several hops of neighbors to update the node itself. The following formula is a GCN propagation formula:

$$H^{l+1} = \sigma(\hat{D}^{-\frac{1}{2}} \hat{A} \hat{D}^{-\frac{1}{2}} H^l W^l). \tag{1}$$

The H^l in the formula represents the feature matrix of the l layer, and the W^l in the formula represents the parameters that can be learned by layer l. $\hat{A} = A + I$, A represents the adjacency matrix, D represents the degree matrix, and I represents the identity matrix. The degree matrix is expressed as $D_{ii} = \sum_j A_{ij}$. σ is the activation function, and ReLU is often chosen as the activation function in GCN.

3.2   Graph Membership Inference Attacks

Membership inference attacks is an attack technique proposed by Shokri et al. in 2017 [10]. The membership inference attack is used to infer whether a given data is in the ML model's training set. Iyiola E. Olatunji [20] applied the membership inference attack to the graph data.

Graph membership inference attacks can cause significant threat to users privacy. For example, a hospital wants to predict who will be infected with COVID19 on a social network graph of COVID19 patients. The training set consists of patients who are infected with COVID19. The membership inference attack towards the social network graph will reveal the information of those patients who have had COVID19, which could cause serious privacy information leakage.

3.3   Graph Adversarial Training

The adversarial training is to incorporate adversarial samples into the model's training phase to improve the model's robustness after training. Adversarial training is divided into two parts: 1) it generates adversarial samples; 2) using the generated adversarial samples with correct labels to train the model. Its training mode is in the form of min-max. The following formula is a unified formula for graph adversarial training:

$$\min_{\theta} \max_{\epsilon \in \Delta} \sum_i L(f_\theta(A, X, \epsilon), y_i). \tag{2}$$

In the formula, ϵ is the noise, and Δ is the disturbance set; i is the number of nodes in training set; A is the topology matrix representing the structure of the graph; X is the feature matrix representing the attributes of the nodes; y_i is the true label in the training set; L is the loss function, generally using the cross-entropy loss function to proceed; θ is a learnable parameter; f is the GNN model. We list below two graph adversarial training algorithms for generating robust models.

Random Remove Adversarial Training. Dai et al. [18] proposed adversarial training with adversarial examples generated by randomly removing edges. Thus, our first adversarial training method is to delete edges randomly. Dai mentioned that deleting one edge will affect multiple edges. Because when calculating the GCN normalized Laplacian, once one edge is deleted, the normalized Laplacian needs to be recalculated all over again. The calculated one is different from the previous one, which will affect the final accuracy.

LATGCN Adversarial Training. Jin et al. [19] proposed an adversarial training method for node features and graph structure. The author believed that graph data can be approximated as word data, so the embedding layer in word data is analogous to the embedding layer of graph data.

The author stated that since the first layer aggregates the feature structure and the topology structure of the graph, adding perturbations to the first layer is equivalent to adding perturbations to the feature structure and topology at the same time. They named this approach latent adversarial training (LAT-GCN). The loss function of LATGCN is:

$$\min_{\theta} \max_{\epsilon \in \Delta} f_\theta(H^{(1)} + \epsilon). \tag{3}$$

In the loss function, $H^{(1)}$ represents the embedding layer, f is the LATGCN model, θ is the parameters of the GCN. ϵ is the imperceptible perturbation, Δ is the set of allowed perturbations. The author mentioned that since the perturbation is added to the embedding layer, the computational cost is too high, so the author used a form of regularization, and the loss function is as follows:

$$\min_{\theta} L_{\theta}(\hat{A}, X) := f_{\theta}(H^{(1)}) + rR_{\theta} \max_{\epsilon \in \Delta} ||\hat{A}(H^{(1)} + \epsilon)W^{(2)} - \hat{A}H^{(1)}W^{(2)}||_F^2, \quad (4)$$

where $r \geq 0$ is a trade-off parameter, $|| \cdot ||_F^2$ is defined as the Frobenius distance, R_{θ} is defined as the distance between the output of the original model and the output of the added perturbation.

4   Membership Inference Attacks Against GCN

In this section, we explore the relationship between the robust graph model and the success rate of the membership inference attack.

4.1   Overview

In this section, we briefly explain our process. As shown in Fig. 2, we first use the perturbed graph data for adversarial training, and the trained model is robust; we then use the clean graph data to input the robust model and the clean model, the output results are used to conduct membership inference attacks respectively. By comparing the attack success rates of membership inference attacks, we conclude that a robust model after adversarial training can improve the attack success rate of membership inference attacks.

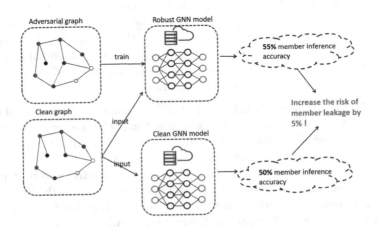

Fig. 2. Robust GNN model against membership inference attack.

4.2 Node-Level Membership Inference Strategy

In this section, we will describe the node membership inference attack and its performance. Through node membership inference attack, the adversary determine a node is a member node (from the training set) or a non-member node (from the test set).

For simplicity, we use $Z = (A, X, Y)$ to represent the output of a graph neural network model, A represents the adjacency matrix of the input, X represents the feature matrix of the input, and Y represents the true label of the model. As for the attack model, we denote the confidence node membership inference attack model as $M(f_\theta, Z)$. f_θ is our target GNN model. $M()$ represents a sign function. Then the accuracy of our node-level membership inference attack can be represented as:

$$Acc. = \frac{\sum_{Z \in D_{train}} M_{train}(f_\theta, Z)}{2|D_{train}|} + \frac{\sum_{Z \in D_{test}} M_{test}(f_\theta, Z)}{2|D_{test}|}. \tag{5}$$

In this formula, D_{train} is training set, D_{test} is test set, M_{train} represents the membership status of a node in the training set of the attack model. M_{test} represents the membership status of a node in the test set of the attack model. The value of M_{test} is 1 if a test node is a member and the value is 0, otherwise. The term 2 in the denominator means the assumption that the adversary selects the target node from the training set and the test set with a probability of 1/2. The training and test sets are entirely disjointed (there are no overlaps between training set and test set). We improved it in a unified form as follows:

$$Acc. = \frac{\sum_{Z \in D_{train}} M(f_\theta, Z)}{2|D_{train}|} + \frac{1 - \sum_{Z \in D_{test}} M(f_\theta, Z)}{2|D_{test}|}. \tag{6}$$

If the target node is the member node then the value of $M(f_\theta, Z)$ is 1, and if it is the non-member node then the value of $M(f_\theta, Z)$ is 0.

4.3 Node-Level MIA Based on Confidence Threshold

The confidence membership inference attack was proposed by Song et al. [13]. We adopt the node confidence membership inference attack strategy in this paper. If the prediction confidence of a node is larger than a specified threshold, we turn it into a training set node (member node). If the prediction confidence is less than this specified threshold, we turn it into a test set node (non-member nodes). The formula representing this process can be expressed as follows:

$$Acc._{train} = \frac{\sum_{Z \in D_{train}} M(f_\theta, Z > k)}{|D_{train}|}. \tag{7}$$

$$Acc._{test} = \frac{\sum_{Z \in D_{test}} M(f_\theta, Z < k)}{|D_{test}|}. \tag{8}$$

In the formula, k is a set threshold, and in the experiment, we evaluate the worst-case reasoning, the maximum reasoning risk. We choose k under the maximum inference risk as to the set threshold, expressed in k_{max}. We use Eq. (9) to merge and optimize these two formulas:

$$Acc. = \frac{\sum_{Z \in D_{train}} M(f_\theta, Z > k_{max})}{2|D_{train}|} + \frac{1 - \sum_{Z \in D_{test}} M(f_\theta, Z > k_{max})}{2|D_{test}|}. \quad (9)$$

4.4   Node-Level MIA Against Robust GCN Model

We conduct a node confidence inference attack with a robust model obtained via adversarial training. We first generate adversarial examples for the input (A, X) under attack constraint Δ. We generate adversarial examples in two ways. In graph adversarial attacks, we can attack the adjacency matrix which is the topology, attack the feature matrix which is the eigenstructure, and attack both the adjacency matrix and the feature matrix simultaneously. The graph adversarial training can be divided into two types according to the adversarial samples that are generated: topological adversarial training (Eq. (10), brief introduction can refer to Sect. 3.2), such as random adversarial training and topological feature structure adversarial training (Eq. (11), brief introduction can refer to Sect. 3.2), such as LATGCN adversarial training. The following two formulas represent the two adversarial training:

$$\min_\theta \max_{\epsilon \in \Delta} \sum_i L(f_\theta(A + \epsilon, X), y_i), \qquad \epsilon \in \Delta. \quad (10)$$

$$\min_\theta \max_{\epsilon \in \Delta} \sum_i L(f_\theta(A + \epsilon 1, X + \epsilon 2), y_i), \qquad \epsilon_1 + \epsilon_2 \in \Delta. \quad (11)$$

For the sake of simplicity, we denote the above two robust models after adversarial training as F_{adv}, and the output of the model as Z_{adv}, so the membership inference attack of our robust model is expressed as:

$$Acc. = \frac{\sum_{Z_{adv} \in D_{train}} M(f_{\theta adv}, Z_{adv} > k_{max})}{2|D_{train}|}$$
$$+ \frac{1 - \sum_{Z_{adv} \in D_{test}} M(f_{\theta adv}, Z_{adv} > k_{max})}{2|D_{test}|}, \quad (12)$$

where $f_{\theta adv}$ represents an robust model with adversarial training.

5   Experimental Evaluation

5.1   Datasets

Table 2 provides the detailed information for each dataset, we use the Deeprobust [22] graph neural network attack algorithm framework.

Table 2. Detailed information for datasets.

Datasets	#Nodes	#Edges	#Features	#Classes
Cora	2485	5249	1433	7
Cora-ML	2810	7981	2,879	7
Citeseer	2,100	3,668	3,703	6
Polblogs	1222	19090	1490	2
Pubmed	19,717	44,324	500	3

Cora. The Cora dataset is a citation network dataset. Each node represents a paper, and each edge represents the citation relationship in the paper. The graph formed by the Cora dataset is undirected and unweighted. Each edge is bidirectional, and each edge weights are 1. The dataset has 2485 articles, which constitutes to 2485 nodes, and 5429 edges. The articles in the dataset are divided into seven categories: case-based, genetic algorithm, neural network, probabilistic method, reinforcement learning, rule learning and theory. Each node in the dataset has a 1433 dimensional feature vector.

Cora-ML. Similar to the Cora dataset, it is also a citation network data set, but there are 2810 nodes, and each node has 2879 feature vectors. The articles in this database also has seven categories.

Citeseer. The Citeseer data set is also the data set of the citation network. The graph is also undirected and unweighted. There are 2100 nodes on the graph, that is, 2100 articles, with 3668 edges. Each node has 3703 feature vectors, which are also in one-hot form. The data set is a six classification problem. The type of the problems are: agents, AI, DB, IR, ML, and HCI.

Polblogs. The dataset is an American political blog dataset containing 1222 blog pages and 19,090 hyperlinks. Each page is equivalent to a node, and each hyperlink is equal to an edge so that the dataset can be used as a social network dataset. Each page has many attributes, and the final result is two kinds: conservative view and liberal view. So this dataset is a dataset for a binary classification task.

Pubmed. It is a dataset containing medical papers. It is a three-classification task. There are 19,717 papers in the data set. That is, it has 19,717 nodes, and each node has 500 feature vectors, which can be considered as a big graph.

We conduct experiments with two data set distributions. The first one we use graph neural network regular dataset distribution, named Dataset-Z. The ratio of the training set, validation set, and test set is 0.1, 0.1, and 0.8. We divide the second dataset into training set, valid set, and test set with a ratio of 0.45, 0.1, and 0.45. The second dataset is denoted as Dataset-G.

5.2 Robustness Analysis

In this section, we analyze the robust performance of the adversarial training against two types of adversarial attacks.

Mettack [23]. In the first test method, we used Mettack, which adds perturbation through meta-gradient and uses the perturbed adjacency matrix as input data for retraining. The verification method is to evaluate the defense effect through the model's accuracy.

Nettack [24]. For the second test method, we used the Nettack. Since it is a target attack, there is no way to use the accuracy of the model as the evaluation index of the robust model, so we use the evaluation metric of the target attack proposed by Zügner [24]. We randomly select 20 nodes to be the attack goals. We first subtract the most significant label from the true label in the probability output by each node, and then take the average of the 20 nodes. The evaluation metric is as follows:

$$Score = \frac{1}{20} \sum_{i=1}^{20} lnZ_{c_{ture}} - max_{c \neq c_{ture}} lnZ. \tag{13}$$

The Z in the formula represents the output, c represents the label, and c_{ture} represents the true label. The larger the score of the verification method represents the better defense effect.

Table 3 shows the experimental results of the robust model under random adversarial training, and Table 4 shows the experimental results of the robust model under LATGCN adversarial training. Mk(.) is the Mettack verification method, and Nk(.) is the Nettack verification method.

Table 3. Random adversarial training.

Datasets	Clean	Adv	Mk (Clean)	Mk (Adv)	Nk (Clean)	Nk (Adv)
	Model accuracy (%)				Score	
Cora	81.84	80.38	73.34	80.33	−0.9993	−0.9000
Cora-ml	85.36	83.14	N/A	N/A	−0.5668	−0.2988
Citeseer	71.27	69.14	64.28	68.48	−0.9999	−0.7000
Polblogs	95.30	95.71	77.40	95.40	−0.9999	−0.0326
Pubmed	86.05	78.38	N/A	N/A	−0.9999	−0.9807

Table 4. LATGCN adversarial training.

Datasets	Clean	Adv	Mk (Clean)	Mk (Adv)	Nk (Clean)	Nk (Adv)
	Model accuracy (%)				Score	
Cora	83.40	82.85	73.34	82.65	−0.9993	−0.0032
Cora-ml	85.28	85.05	N/A	N/A	−0.5668	−0.0004
Citeseer	75.08	74.64	64.28	73.70	−0.9999	−0.0036
Polblogs	95.60	95.71	77.40	91.50	−0.9999	−0.0005
Pubmed	86.14	83.40	N/A	N/A	−0.9999	−0.0009

The above tables shows that random adversarial training has good test performance on the Mettack attack algorithm but poor performance on the Nettack attack algorithm. Because random adversarial training is a simple defense method, and the Nettack algorithm is a powerful attack algorithm, makes the less evident effect of random adversarial training.

In the LATGCN adversarial training, we found that the effects of the Nettack attack algorithm and the Mettack attack algorithm are apparent. We think LATGCN is an added perturbation in the middle embedding layer. After all, the embedding layer is closer to the output than to the input layer, so the effect of adversarial training in the embedding layer is better than that in the input layer. However, we found that all the results on the Nettack attack algorithm are negative, which means that most of the nodes are still classified incorrectly. We think this is because the Nettack attack algorithm perturbs the topology and the feature structure. That is, the Nettack attack algorithm is a powerful adversarial attack algorithm which brings about these negative results.

5.3   Results of MIA Against Robust GCN Model

Random Adversarial Training. We perform adversarial training of randomly removing edges according to the setting of Dai et al. [18], the number of changed edges is the number of nodes/2*0.01, with a total of 100 iterations. The adversarial samples generated in each iteration are trained for another 50 times. We use a 2-layer GCN. Table 5 and 6 show the experimental results using Dataset-Z and Dataset-G respectively.

Table 5. Performance of graph membership inference attack under Dataset-Z in random adversarial training (%).

Datasets	Clean	Adv.	MIA-clean	MIA-adv.	Increased ASR
	Model accuracy		Attack success rate (ASR)		
Cora	83.60	80.38	69.12	71.83	**2.71**
Cora-ml	85.36	83.14	64.73	72.57	**7.84**
Citeseer	71.27	69.14	76.98	78.73	**1.75**
Polblogs	94.99	95.71	71.00	57.87	−13.13
Pubmed	86.05	78.38	53.88	62.49	**8.61**

Table 6. Performance of graph membership inference attack under Dataset-G in random adversarial training (%).

Datasets	Clean	Adv.	MIA-clean	MIA-adv.	Increased ASR
	Model accuracy		Attack success rate (ASR)		
Cora	87.67	83.29	58.48	63.04	**4.56**
Cora-ml	87.98	85.30	55.05	61.89	**6.84**
Citeseer	77.26	69.58	64.00	70.10	**6.10**
Polblogs	96.00	90.00	61.89	58.63	−3.26
Pubmed	87.66	86.70	50.34	52.14	**1.80**

It can be seen from the above tables that the robust model on four of the five datasets promote the success rate of graph membership inference attack, which is between 0.01 and 0.08. Only in the Polblogs data the accuracy decreases. We suppose this is due to the difference of the characteristic attribute types of Polblogs and others.

LATGCN Adversarial Training. We conducted 100 epochs with the perturbation parameter set to 0.1. Then we run experiments under two dataset distributions using the graph membership inference attack that used the confidence threshold method. Table 7 and 8 are the experimental results using Dataset-Z and Dataset-G respectively.

Table 7. Performance of graph membership inference attack under Dataset-Z in LAT-GCN adversarial training (%).

Datasets	Clean	Adv.	MIA-clean	MIA-adv.	Increased ASR
	Model accuracy		Attack success rate (ASR)		
Cora	82.04	82.84	61.15	68.03	**6.88**
Cora-ml	85.49	82.47	60.05	68.10	**8.05**
Citeseer	73.34	72.92	63.17	73.02	**9.85**
Polblogs	94.68	94.58	52.86	65.07	**12.21**
Pubmed	85.71	84.16	51.09	51.88	**0.79**

Table 8. Performance of graph membership inference attack under Dataset-G in LAT-GCN adversarial training (%).

Datasets	Clean	Adv.	MIA-clean	MIA-adv.	Increased ASR
	Model accuracy		Attack success rate (ASR)		
Cora	88.11	87.76	54.24	60.83	**6.59**
Cora-ml	89.17	85.53	52.15	55.95	**3.80**
Citeseer	76.63	76.10	54.29	57.71	**3.42**
Polblogs	96.55	96.36	50.63	55.34	**4.71**
Pubmed	86.14	83.40	50.60	50.84	**0.24**

We found that the improvement effect is evident on the citation network dataset but not on the Pubmed dataset. We deduce it is caused by the excessive number of nodes on the Pubmed dataset.

Results Analysis. The loss function value of the test set is higher than that of the training set. We found that the difference between the loss function of the test set and the training set of the robust model is more significant than that of the clean model. We deduce this is an essential factor that leads to robust models that can improve the attack success rate of MIA. The effect is as shown in Fig. 3. The horizontal axis represents the loss function value, and the vertical axis represents the frequency of each loss function value, expressed as a percentage shape.

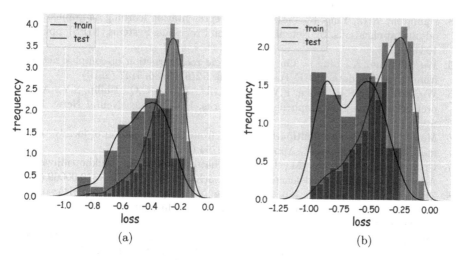

(a)   (b)

Fig. 3. GCN in Dataset-G, On the left is the loss function values for the clean model; on the right is the loss function values for the robust model.

6   Conclusion

In this paper, we investigated whether the robust model trained using graph data can effectively resist membership inference attacks. To evaluate membership inference attacks, we migrated confidence membership inference attacks from the image domain to the graph data domain. Supplementing this point filled up a gap in the graph data domain and the adversarial field in the graph neural networks. The experimental evaluations are carried out on five datasets and two adversarial training algorithms. The graph neural network model trained by using adversarial training method has been found to be vulnerable to membership inference attacks. And the reason why the robust model can improve the attack effect of membership inference attacks is analyzed. Therefore, when designing defensive adversarial examples in the future, it is necessary to consider the risk of member privacy leakage.

Acknowledgment. This work is supported by the National Nature Science Foundation of China (No. 62102300).

References

1. Jordan, M.I., Mitchell, T.M.: Machine learning: trends, perspectives, and prospects. Science **349**(6245), 255–260 (2015)
2. Wu, K., Wang, C., Liu, J.: Evolutionary multitasking multilayer network reconstruction. IEEE Trans. Cybern. (2021)
3. Hamilton, W.L., Ying, R., Leskovec, J.: Representation learning on graphs: methods and applications. In: Neural Information Processing Systems (NIPS), pp. 1024–1034 (2017)
4. Wu, K., Hao, X., Liu, J., Liu, P.H.: Online reconstruction of complex networks from streaming data. IEEE Trans. Cybern. **52**(6), 5136–5147 (2020)
5. Wu, Z.H., Pan, S.R., Chen, F.W., Long, G.D., Zhang, C.Q., Philip, S.Y.: A comprehensive survey on graph neural networks. IEEE Trans. Neural Netw. Learn. Syst. **32**(1), 4–24 (2020)
6. Ma, X., et al.: Secure multiparty learning from the aggregation of locally trained models. J. Netw. Comput. Appl. **167**, 102754 (2020)
7. Chakraborty, A., Alam, M., Dey, V., Chattopadhyay, A., Mukhopadhyay, D.: Adversarial attacks and defences: a survey. arXiv preprint arXiv:1810.00069 (2018)
8. Zhang, X.Y., Chen, X.F., Liu, J.K., Xiang, Y.: DeepPAR and DeepDPA: privacy preserving and asynchronous deep learning for industrial IoT. IEEE Trans. Ind. Inf. **16**(3), 2081–2090 (2019)
9. Zhang, X.Y., Chen, X.F., Yan, H.Y., Xiang, Y.: Privacy-preserving and verifiable online crowdsourcing with worker updates. Inf. Sci. **548**, 212–232 (2021)
10. Shokri, R., Stronati, M., Song, C.Z., Shmatikov, V.: Membership inference attacks against machine learning models. In: IEEE Symposium on Security and Privacy (SP), pp. 3–18 (2017)
11. Melis, L., Song, C.Z., De, C.E., Shmatikov, V.: Exploiting unintended feature leakage in collaborative learning. In: IEEE Symposium on Security and Privacy (SP), pp. 691–706 (2019)
12. Sun, L.C., et al.: Adversarial attack and defense on graph data: a survey. arXiv preprint arXiv:1812.10528 (2018)
13. Song, L.W., Shokri, R., Mittal, P.: Privacy risks of securing machine learning models against adversarial examples. In: Proceedings of the 2019 ACM SIGSAC Conference on Computer and Communications Security, pp. 241–257 (2019)
14. Kipf, T.N., Welling, M.: Semi-supervised classification with graph convolutional networks. In: International Conference on Learning Representations (ICLR) (2017)
15. Hamilton, W., Ying, Z.T., Leskovec, J.: Inductive representation learning on large graphs. In: Advances in Neural Information Processing Systems (2017)
16. Veličković, P., Cucurull, G., Casanova, A., Romero, A., Lio, P., Bengio, Y.: Graph attention networks. In: International Conference on Machine Learning (2017)
17. Niepert, M., Ahmed, M., Kutzkov, K.: Learning convolutional neural networks for graphs. In: International Conference on Machine Learning, pp. 2014–2023 (2016)
18. Dai, H.J., et al.: Adversarial attack on graph structured data. arXiv preprint arXiv:1806.02371 (2018)
19. Jin, H.W., Zhang, X.H.: Latent adversarial training of graph convolution networks. In: ICML Workshop on Learning and Reasoning with Graph Structured Representations (2019)
20. Olatunji, I.E., Nejdl, W., Khosla, M.: Membership inference attack on graph neural networks. arXiv preprint arXiv:2101.06570 (2021)

21. He, X.L., Wen, R., Wu, Y.X., Backes, M., Shen, Y., Zhang, Y.: Node-level membership inference attacks against graph neural networks. arXiv preprint arXiv:2102.05429 (2021)
22. Wu, H.J., Wang, C., Tyshetskiy, Y., Docherty, A., Lu, K., Zhu, L.M.: Adversarial examples on graph data: deep insights into attack and defense. In: International Joint Conference on Artificial Intelligence (IJCAI) (2019)
23. Zügner, D., Günnemann, S.: Adversarial attacks on graph neural networks via meta learning. arXiv preprint arXiv:1902.08412 (2019)
24. Zügner, D., Akbarnejad, A., Günnemann, S.: Adversarial attacks on neural networks for graph data. In: Proceedings of the 24th ACM SIGKDD International Conference on Knowledge Discovery, pp. 2847–2856 (2018)

Network Security and Its Applications

A Distributed Threshold Additive Homomorphic Encryption for Federated Learning with Dropout Resiliency Based on Lattice

Haibo Tian[1]([✉]), Yanchuan Wen[1], Fangguo Zhang[1], Yunfeng Shao[2], and Bingshuai Li[2]

[1] School of Computer Science and Engineering, Sun Yat-Sen Univeristy, Guangzhou 510275, China
{tianhb,zhangfg}@mail.sysu.edu.cn, wenych3@mail2.sysu.edu.cn
[2] Huawei Noahs Ark Lab, Beijing 100085, China
{shaoyunfeng,libingshuai}@huawei.com

Abstract. In federated learning, a parameter server needs to aggregate user gradients and a user needs the privacy of their individual gradients. Among all the possible solutions, additive homomorphic encryption is a natural choice. As users may drop out during a federated learning process, and an adversary could corrupt users and the parameter server, a dropout-resilient scheme with distributed key generation is required. We present a lattice based distributed threshold additive homomorphic encryption scheme with provable security that could be used in the federated learning. The evaluation shows that our proposal has a lower communication overhead among all lattice based proposals when the number of users in FL exceeds 26.

Keywords: Federated learning · Privacy protection · Additive homomorphic encryption

1 Introduction

Federated learning (FL) is intended to train better machine learning models on decentralized real-world data. The models then could be used to build more intelligent equipments for people, such as cars, wearable devices or browsers. McMahan et al. [27] proposed a well known FL protocol. The players in their protocol include users who owned data and a parameter server that aggregates model information of users. The running time of the protocol is divided into epoches. In each epoch, the parameter server randomly selects some users to upload their local model parameters, and averages the parameters to update a global learning model. A user in an epoch downloads the global learning model, feeds their local data, runs a deep learning network locally and gets updated local model parameters, the information of which is sent to the parameter server.

© The Author(s), under exclusive license to Springer Nature Switzerland AG 2022
X. Chen et al. (Eds.): CSS 2022, LNCS 13547, pp. 277–292, 2022.
https://doi.org/10.1007/978-3-031-18067-5_20

In different epoches the server may select different users, and within an epoch some of the selected users may drop out.

As real-world data are usually sensitive, an important problem in FL is data privacy. Although user data are not directly sent to the parameter server in FL, information of local model parameters may leak the raw data of users. Fredrikson et al. [15] show how to recover train samples from prediction results of a model. Rubaie and Chang [2] exploit feature vectors to reconstruct raw input data of a model. Chai et al. [12] show how to recover preferences of users by model gradient data. Zhu et al. [40] demonstrate that a malicious server could reconstruct raw data of a user from the gradients uploaded by the user. Zhao et al. [38] improve the label recovery algorithm in [40] to improve the reconstruction ability. Jonas et al. [17] prove that any input to a fully connected layer can be reconstructed analytically independent of the remaining architecture. Yin et al. [36] show how to recover a batch of images from average gradients with the help of a fully connected layer.

There are several approaches to protect user gradients. Martin et al. [1] propose to use differential privacy on gradients. Bonawitz et al. [6] propose to mask gradients with outputs of a pseudo random generator (PRG). Zhu et al. [39] use a distributed threshold additive homomorphic encryption (DTAHE) to encrypt gradients. Mo et al. [28] use trusted execution environment to aggregate gradients.

We focuses on the approach of using DTAHE schemes. There are few known methods to construct a DTAHE scheme with dropout resiliency. The first method relies on secret sharing schemes with general access structure. Bendlin and Damgård [5] and Boneh et al. [7] propose schemes in this way. The second method is to use the Shamir secret sharing with a large modulus. Boneh et al. [7] and Kim et al. [22] propose schemes in this way. The third method is to use the ElGamal encryption as a basic building tool [18,31]. The fourth method is to share and reconstruct secrets when some users dropout [4]. We evaluate the performance of the first three methods and give a new lightweight DTAHE scheme with provable security.

1.1   Related Works

There are some proposals to use distributed homomorphic encryption in FL. Damgård and Jurik [11] propose a threshold version of the Paillier encryption [30], which is integrated into the privacy preserving FL solutions in [21,23,34]. Bresson et al. [9] propose a public-key encryption scheme based on the Paillier encryption [30] where each user has their own private keys. The scheme [9] is used in a privacy preserving FL solution [24]. Christian et al. [29] propose lattice based multiparty homomorphic encryption schemes. Their proposal is used in privacy preserving FL solutions [14,16,32]. The same scheme is adapted in [20] with the Shamir secret sharing. Chen et al. [10] propose a multi-key homomorphic encryption scheme, which is adapted as xMK-CKKS in a privacy preserving FL solution in [26]. Pedersen [31] propose a threshold ElGamal encryption scheme and Gennaro et al. [18] gave a secure distributed key generation protocol for discrete-log encryption schemes. Their proposal are used in a privacy preserving FL solution [39].

The Paillier encryption based proposals generally need a trusted dealer [11] or a private key generation server [9]. The lattice based schemes [29] use an additive secret sharing so that all share holders are needed for decryption. The same problem exists in [10]. These limitations mean that they are not suitable to the original proposal of FL [27]. An effort to solve the problem shows in [20]. However, they need the parameter server to determine a user set for decryption before the server knows who survive in the decryption phase. In other words, they assume that users selected do not drop out.

The scheme of Pedersen [31] could be used in FL as shown in [39]. Since ElGamal encryption is multiplicative homomorphic, one has to take messages as exponentiations, which means that a discreet logarithm problem has to be solved in the decryption phase. Comparatively, lattice based schemes have no such limitation. Bendlin and Damgård [5] and Boneh et al. [7] proposed such schemes. The scheme in [5] relies on secret sharing schemes with general access structure. As the number of users increases, the computation overhead increases exponentially. Two schemes are proposed in [7]. Their first scheme relies on a secret sharing schemes constructed by a monotone formulae. The second scheme uses the Shamir secret sharing. The communication overhead of the first scheme is smaller than the scheme in [5] but is still unbearable in FL when the number of users increases. The second scheme needs a large modulus in the underlying lattice based encryption scheme, which leads to a slower computation time, which is followed in [22]. Asharov et al. [4] provide the idea to share and reconstruct individual secrets if their owners dropout. We show a different design choice to integrate the Shamir secret sharing into the lattice based encryption to get a lightweight DTAHE. The original idea is embedded in our preprint work [33]. We notice a recent work [35] containing a threshold fully homomorphic encryption where a distributed noise generation algorithm is used, which has the same effect on the partial decryption procedure.

1.2 Contributions

We show a new design method to combine the Shamir secret sharing and a lattice based homomorphic encryption scheme. Our basic idea is to share a noise whose shares are used to hide secret key shares of a user in the partial decryption phase. Since the secret recovery phase of the Shamir secret sharing is linear, the sum of the secret key and a noise could be recovered correctly.

We give a concrete DTAHE scheme based on the BFV homomorphic encryption scheme [8,13] with a security proof in a security model adapted from [7]. We also implement our DTAHE scheme and the schemes in [5,7,31]. They are evaluated in a FL scenario. Our scheme shows a good balance about the communication and computation costs.

2   Preliminaries

2.1   Basic Notations

For any set X, we denote by $|X|$ the number of elements of the set X. If x is a string, $|x|$ denotes its bit length. And if x is a vector, $|x|$ denotes the dimension of the vector. $x||y$ denotes the bit catenation of two strings x and y.

Let $R = \mathbb{Z}[x]/(f(x))$ be a polynomial ring where $f(x)$ is a monic irreducible polynomial of degree d. Elements of the ring R is denoted by vectors. For $\boldsymbol{a} \in R$, the coefficients of $\boldsymbol{a}$ is denoted by a_i such that $\boldsymbol{a} = \sum_{i=0}^{d-1} a_i \cdot x^i$. The infinity norm of $||\boldsymbol{a}||$ is defined as $max_i|a_i|$ and the expansion factor of R is defined as $\delta_R = max\{||\boldsymbol{a} \cdot \boldsymbol{b}||/(||\boldsymbol{a}|| \cdot ||\boldsymbol{b}||) : \boldsymbol{a}, \boldsymbol{b} \in R\}$.

Let $h > 1$ be an integer. Then $\mathbb{Z}_h$ denotes a set of integers $(-\frac{h}{2}, \frac{h}{2}]$. The symbol $\mathbb{Z}/q\mathbb{Z}$ denotes a ring on integers $\{0, \ldots, q-1\}$. For $x \in \mathbb{Z}$, $[x]_h$ denotes the unique integer in $\mathbb{Z}_h$ with $[x]_h = x \bmod h$. For $\boldsymbol{x} \in R$, $[\boldsymbol{x}]_h$ denotes the element in R obtained by applying $[\cdot]_h$ to all its coefficients. For $x \in \mathbb{R}$, $\lfloor x \rceil$ denotes rounding to the nearest integer and $\lfloor x \rfloor$, $\lceil x \rceil$ denote rounding up or down.

Let λ be an integer as the security parameter. A function $negl(\lambda)$ is negligible in λ if $negl(\lambda) = o(1/\lambda^c)$ for every $c \in \mathbb{N}$. An event occurs with negligible probability if the probability of the event is $negl(\lambda)$. An event occurs with overwhelming probability if its complement occurs with negligible probability.

Given a probability distribution $\mathcal{D}$, we use $x \leftarrow \mathcal{D}$ to denote that x is sampled from $\mathcal{D}$. For a set X, $x \leftarrow X$ denotes that x is sampled uniformly from X. A distribution χ over integers is called B-bounded if it is supported on $[-B, B]$.

2.2   DTAHE

Boneh et al. [7] give a definition of distributed threshold fully homomorphic encryption (DTFHE). We refine it as a DTAHE definition for the FL scenario. A DTAHE scheme is a tuple of probabilistic polynomial time (PPT) algorithms $DTAHE = (Setup, KeyGen, Share, CombKey, Enc, Eval, ParDec, FinDec)$.

1. $Setup(1^\lambda) \rightarrow parm$: It takes as input a security parameter λ, outputs system parameters $parm$.
2. $KeyGen(parm) \rightarrow (sk_u, pk_u)$: It takes as input the system parameter $parm$ to produce public and private keys for a user u.
3. $Share(parm, \{pk_v\}_{v \in U \backslash \{u\}}, t, sk_u) \rightarrow \{e_{v,u}\}_{v \in U \backslash \{u\}}$: It takes as input the system parameter $parm$, public keys of users in a set U excluding the user u, a threshold value t and private keys sk_u of the user u, to produce encrypted shares $e_{v,u}$ for each user $v \in U \backslash \{u\}$.
4. $CombKey(parm, \{pk_u\}_{u \in U}) \rightarrow pk$: It takes as input the system parameter $parm$, public keys of a set of users in U, and produces an encryption key pk.
5. $Enc(parm, pk, m_u) \rightarrow c_u$: It takes as input the system parameter $parm$, a public key pk and a message m_u from a user u, and produces a ciphertext c_u.

6. $Eval(parm, \{c_u\}_{u \in U}, \{\alpha_u\}_{u \in U}) \to \hat{c}$: It takes as the system parameter $parm$, ciphers $\{c_u\}_{u \in U}$ and coefficients $\{\alpha_u\}_{u \in U}$, and produces an evaluated cipher $\hat{c} = \sum_{u \in U} \alpha_u \cdot c_u$.

7. $ParDec(parm, \hat{c}, \{e_{u,v}\}_{v \in U}) \to \hat{m}_u$: It takes as input the system parameter $parm$, the cipher $\hat{c}$, and a set of encrypted shares $\{e_{u,v}\}_{v \in U \setminus \{u\}}$ to the user u, and produces a partially decrypted value $\hat{m}_u$.

8. $FinDec(parm, t, \hat{c}, \{\hat{m}_u\}_{u \in V}) \to m$: It takes as input the system parameter $parm$, the threshold value t, the cipher $\hat{c}$ and partially decrypted ciphers $\{\hat{m}_u\}_{u \in V}$ from users in a set V with $|V| \geq t$, and produces a plaintext m.

One could simply give an ElGamal based DTAHE instance following the constructions in [31], which justifies the correctness of the DTAHE definition.

2.3   DTAHE Model

We adapt the model of DTFHE in [7] for the DTAHE. The first definition is evaluation correctness.

Definition 1 *(Evaluation Correctness). A DTAHE scheme for a set of users U satisfies evaluation correctness if for all λ and t, the following holds:*
For an evaluated cipher

$$\hat{c} \leftarrow Eval(parm, \{c_u\}_{u \in U}, \{\alpha_u\}_{u \in U})$$

the probability

$$Pr\left[FinDec\left(\begin{array}{l} parm, t, \hat{c}, \\ \{ParDec(parm, \hat{c}, \{e_{u,v}\}_{v \in U})\}_{u \in V} \end{array} \right) = \sum_{u \in U} \alpha_u \cdot m_u \right]$$

is overwhelming where $c_u \leftarrow Enc(parm, pk, m_u)$,

$$(\{e_{v,u}\}_{v \in U}) \leftarrow Share(parm, \{pk_v\}_{v \in U \setminus \{u\}}, t, sk_u),$$

$(sk_u, pk_u) \leftarrow KeyGen(parm)$, $pk \leftarrow CombKey(parm, \{pk_u\}_{u \in U})$, *and* $parm \leftarrow Setup(1^\lambda)$.

The second definition is sematic security. It captures the privacy of messages.

Definition 2 *(Sematic Security). We say that a DTAHE scheme for a user set U satisfies sematic security if for all λ, the following holds:*
For any PPT adversary $\mathcal{A}$, the following experiment $Expt_{\mathcal{A},Sem}(1^\lambda)$ outputs 1 with probability $\frac{1}{2} + negl(\lambda)$:

- $Expt_{\mathcal{A},Sem}(1^\lambda)$:
    1. *The adversary outputs U and V where $|U| = n$ and $|V| = t$ specify an access structure.*

2. *The challenger runs* $parm \leftarrow Setup(1^\lambda)$, $(sk_u, pk_u) \leftarrow KeyGen(parm)$,

$$\{e_{v,u}\}_{v\in U\setminus\{u\}} \leftarrow Share\left(\begin{array}{c} parm, \{pk_v\}_{v\in U\setminus\{u\}}, \\ t, sk_u \end{array}\right),$$

$pk \leftarrow CombKey(parm, \{pk_u\}_{u\in U})$, *and provides* $\mathcal{A}$

$$(parm, pk, \{\{e_{v,u}\}_{v\in U\setminus\{u\}}\}_{u\in U}).$$

3. $\mathcal{A}$ *outputs a set* $S \subseteq U$ *such that* $|S| < t$. *It submits message vectors* $\{m_{u,0}, m_{u,1}\}_{u\in U}$ *and* S *to the challenger.*
4. *The challenger provides* $\mathcal{A}$ *the shares* $\{\{s_{u,v}\}_{v\in U}\}_{u\in S}$ *and a cipher set*

$$\{c_u \leftarrow Enc(parm, pk, m_{u,b})\}_{u\in U}, \text{ for } b \in \{0,1\}.$$

5. $\mathcal{A}$ *outputs a guess bit* b'. *The experiment outputs* 1 *if* $b = b'$.

The last definition is simulation security. It captures the privacy of shared secrets and private keys of users.

Definition 3 *(Simulation Security). A DTAHE scheme satisfies simulation security if for all* λ, *the following holds:*
   There is a stateful PPT algorithm $\mathcal{C} = (\mathcal{C}_1, \mathcal{C}_2)$ *such that for any PPT adversary* $\mathcal{A}$, *the following experiments* $Expt_{\mathcal{A},Real}(1^\lambda)$ *and* $Expt_{\mathcal{A},Ideal}(1^\lambda)$ *are indistinguishable:*

- $Expt_{\mathcal{A},Real}(1^\lambda)$:
  1. *The adversary outputs* U *and* V *where* $|U| = n$ *and* $|V| = t$ *specify an access structure.*
  2. *The challenger runs* $parm \leftarrow Setup(1^\lambda)$, $(sk_u, pk_u) \leftarrow KeyGen(parm)$,

$$(\{e_{v,u}\}_{v\in U}) \leftarrow Share\left(\begin{array}{c} parm, \{pk_v\}_{v\in U\setminus\{u\}}, \\ t, sk_u \end{array}\right),$$

   and $pk \leftarrow CombKey(parm, \{pk_u\}_{u\in U})$, *provides* $(parm, pk, \{\{e_{v,u}\}_{v\in U}\}_{u\in U})$ *to* $\mathcal{A}$.
  3. $\mathcal{A}$ *outputs a set* $S^* \subseteq U$ *with* $|S^*| = t - 1$ *and messages* $\{m_u\}_{u\in U}$.
  4. *The challenger provides* $\mathcal{A}$ *the shares* $\{\{s_{u,v}\}_{v\in U}\}_{u\in S^*}$ *in* $\{\{e_{u,v}\}_{v\in U}\}_{u\in S^*}$ *and a cipher set*

$$\{c_u \leftarrow Enc(parm, pk, m_u)\}_{u\in U}.$$

  5. $\mathcal{A}$ *issues a polynomial number of adaptive queries of the form* $(S \subseteq U, \{c_u\}_{u\in U^*}, \{\alpha_u\}_{u\in U^*})$ *where* $U^* \subseteq U$. *For each query, the challenger computes* $\hat{c} \leftarrow Eval(parm, \{c_u\}_{u\in U^*}, \{\alpha_u\}_{u\in U^*})$ *and provides* $\mathcal{A}$

$$\{\hat{m}_u \leftarrow ParDec(parm, \hat{c}, \{e_{u,v}\}_{v\in U})\}_{u\in S}.$$

  6. *At the end of the experiment,* $\mathcal{A}$ *outputs a distinguishing bit* b.

- $Expt_{\mathcal{A}, Ideal}(1^\lambda)$:
  1. The adversary outputs U and V where $|U| = n$ and $|V| = t$ specify an access structure.
  2. The challenger runs $(parm, pk, \{\{e_{v,u}\}_{v \in U}\}_{u \in U}, st) \leftarrow \mathcal{C}_1(1^\lambda, U, t)$ and provides $(parm, pk, \{\{e_{v,u}\}_{v \in U}\}_{u \in U})$ to $\mathcal{A}$.
  3. $\mathcal{A}$ outputs a set $S^* \subseteq U$ with $|S^*| = t - 1$ and messages $\{m_u\}_{u \in U}$.
  4. The challenger provides $\mathcal{A}$ shares $\{\{s_{u,v}\}_{v \in U}\}_{u \in S^*}$ and ciphers

$$\{c_u \leftarrow Enc(parm, pk, m_u)\}_{u \in U}.$$

  5. $\mathcal{A}$ issues a polynomial number of adaptive queries of the form $(S \subseteq U, \{c_u\}_{u \in U^*}, \{\alpha_u\}_{u \in U^*})$ where $U^* \subseteq U$. For each query, the challenger runs

$$\{\hat{m}_u\}_{u \in S} \leftarrow \mathcal{C}_2 \begin{pmatrix} S, \{c_u\}_{u \in U^*}, \{\alpha_u\}_{u \in U^*}, \\ \{m_u\}_{u \in U}, \{c_u\}_{u \in U}, st \end{pmatrix}$$

  and provides $\{\hat{m}_u\}_{u \in S}$ to $\mathcal{A}$.
  6. At the end of the experiment, $\mathcal{A}$ outputs a distinguishing bit b.

3   A DTAHE Instance

We show our design method to produce a lattice based DTAHE scheme based the BFV scheme [8,13].

3.1   The Instance

We need a sematic secure hybrid encryption scheme $HPKE$ [19] to encrypt shares.

$$HPKE = (HPKE.Gen, HPKE.Enc, HPKE.Dec).$$

A post quantum secure $HPKE$ instance such as the code based scheme in [37] will give us a post quantum secure DTAHE. The Shamir secret sharing scheme is $SS = (SS.Split, SS.Recover)$.

1. $Setup(1^\lambda) \rightarrow parm$: It takes as input a security parameter λ, produces a parameter set $parm = (d, f(x), h, R, R_h, \chi, \mu, \boldsymbol{a}, l, \lambda)$, where d is the degree depending on λ of a cyclotomic polynomial $f(x)$, $h \geq 2$ is an integer depending on λ, R is a ring $R = \mathbb{Z}[x]/(f(x))$, R_h is the set of polynomials in R with coefficients in $\mathbb{Z}_h$, χ here is in fact defined as discrete Gaussian distribution, μ is a uniform distribution, $\boldsymbol{a}$ is uniformly selected from R_h as $\boldsymbol{a} \leftarrow R_h$, and l is an integer depending on λ.
2. $KeyGen(parm) \rightarrow (sk_u, pk_u)$: It selects $\boldsymbol{s}_u \leftarrow R_3$ and samples $\boldsymbol{e}_u \leftarrow \chi$. It sets $sk_{u,0} = \boldsymbol{s}_u$ and $pk_{u,0} = [-(\boldsymbol{a} \cdot \boldsymbol{s}_u + \boldsymbol{e}_u)]_h$. It runs $(pk_{u,1}, sk_{u,1}) \leftarrow HPKE.Gen(1^\lambda)$. The output is $sk_u = (sk_{u,0}, sk_{u,1})$ and $pk_u = (pk_{u,0}, pk_{u,1})$.

3. $Share(parm, \{pk_v\}_{v \in U \setminus \{u\}}, t, sk_u) \rightarrow \{e_{v,u}\}_{v \in U \setminus \{u\}}$: It samples $e_{u,2} \leftarrow \chi$, computes $n = |\{pk_v\}_{v \in U \setminus \{u\}}| + 1$, sets $ss_u = \{sk_{u,0}, e_{u,2}\}$, and for each coefficient $ss_{u,i}$ of the elements in ss_u, computes

$$\{s_{v,u,i}\}_{v \in U} \leftarrow SS.Split(ss_{u,i}, n, t, h).$$

For all the shares to $v \in U \setminus \{u\}$, it computes a cipher

$$e_{v,u} = HPKE.Enc(pk_{v,1}, \{s_{v,u,i}\}_{i \in \{0,\ldots,|ss_u|*d-1\}}).$$

4. $CombKey(parm, \{pk_u\}_{u \in U}) \rightarrow pk$: It computes $pk = [\sum_{u \in U} pk_{u,0}]_h$.
5. $Enc(parm, pk, m_u) \rightarrow c_u$: It selects $u_u \leftarrow R_3$, $e_{u,0}, e_{u,1} \leftarrow \chi$, computes $c_{u,0} = [a \cdot u_u + e_{u,0}]_h$ and $c_{u,1} = [pk \cdot u_u + e_{u,1} + \lfloor h/l \rfloor \cdot m_u]_h$. It sets $c_u = (c_{u,0}, c_{u,1})$.
6. $Eval(parm, \{c_u\}_{u \in U}, \{\alpha_u\}_{u \in U}) \rightarrow \hat{c}$: It computes $\hat{c}_0 = [\sum_{u \in U} \alpha_u c_{u,0}]_h$, $\hat{c}_1 = [\sum_{u \in U} \alpha_u c_{u,1}]_h$ and sets $\hat{c} = (\hat{c}_0, \hat{c}_1)$.
7. $ParDec(parm, \hat{c}, \{e_{u,v}\}_{v \in U}) \rightarrow \hat{m}_u$: It decrypts the shares for the user $u \in U$ from the user $v \in U$ as $s_{u,v} \leftarrow HPKC.Dec(sk_{u,1}, e_{u,v})$. It parses the shares of coefficients as shares of elements in R, sets $(se_{u,v}, ssk_{u,v}) = s_{u,v}$, then computes $\hat{m}_u = [\hat{c}_0 \cdot \sum_{v \in U} ssk_{u,v} + \sum_{v \in U} se_{u,v}]_h$.
8. $FinDec(parm, t, \hat{c}, \{\hat{m}_u\}_{u \in V}) \rightarrow m$: It recovers $cs = [\sum_{u \in V} li_u \hat{m}_u]_h$ where li_u is the Lagrange coefficient of the user u with respect to the user set V, and computes the final output $m = [\lfloor \frac{l \cdot [\hat{c}_1 + cs]_h}{h} \rceil]_l$.

Remark 1. If the data dimension of the message m_u is greater than d, the number of noise samples $e_{u,2} \in R$ increases.

3.2 Security Analysis

The security of our scheme could be reduced to a variant of the classical ring version decisional learning with errors (RLWE) problem [13,25]. The variant is named n-Decision-RLWE problem.

Definition 4 *(n-Decision-RLWE). For a random set $\{s_i \in R_h\}_{i \in \{1,\ldots,n\}}$ and a distribution χ over R, denote with $A_{\{s_i \in R_h\}_{i \in \{1,\ldots,n\}}, \chi, \mu}$ the distribution by choosing a uniformly random element $a \leftarrow R_h$ and n noise term $\{e_i \leftarrow \chi\}_{i \in \{1,\ldots,n\}}$ and outputting $(a, \{[a \cdot s_i + e_i]_h\}_{i \in \{1,\ldots,n\}})$. The problem is then to distinguish between the distribution $A_{\{s_i \in R_h\}_{i \in \{1,\ldots,n\}}, \chi, \mu}$ and a uniform distribution μ over R_h^{n+1}.*

By a hybrid argument, one could conclude that if an adversary has an advantage at least $\epsilon_{n\text{-}RLWE}$ to solve the n-Decision-RLWE problem, the adversary has an advantage at least $\frac{1}{n}\epsilon_{n\text{-}RLWE}$ to solve the classical RLWE problem in [13,25].

The first proof is about the evaluation correctness in the Definition 1.

Theorem 1. *Assume that U is the user set, χ is B-bounded and the maximal infinity norm of elements in the set $\{\alpha_u\}_{u \in U}$ is A, the evaluation of the DTAHE is correct with probability 1 if $|U|B(1 + \delta_R A(1 + 2\delta_R|U|)) < \frac{h}{2l}$.*

Proof. Since $\hat{m}_u = [\hat{c}_0 \cdot \sum_{v \in U} \boldsymbol{ssk}_{u,v} + \sum_{v \in U} \boldsymbol{se}_{u,v}]_h$, we have the Eq. (1) due to the Lagrange interpolation.

$$
\begin{aligned}
cs &= [\sum_{u \in V} li_u \cdot (\hat{c}_0 \cdot \sum_{v \in U} \boldsymbol{ssk}_{u,v} + \sum_{v \in U} \boldsymbol{se}_{u,v})]_h \\
&= [\sum_{u \in V} li_u \cdot (\hat{c}_0 \cdot \sum_{v \in U} \boldsymbol{ssk}_{u,v}) + \sum_{u \in V} li_u \cdot (\sum_{v \in U} \boldsymbol{se}_{u,v})]_h \\
&= [\hat{c}_0 \cdot (\sum_{u \in V} li_u \cdot (\sum_{v \in U} \boldsymbol{ssk}_{u,v})) + \sum_{u \in U} \boldsymbol{e}_{u,2}]_h \\
&= [\hat{c}_0 \cdot \sum_{u \in U} sk_{u,0} + \sum_{u \in U} \boldsymbol{e}_{u,2}]_h
\end{aligned}
\tag{1}
$$

Let $X = [\hat{c}_1 + cs]_h$. Since $\hat{c}_0 = [\sum_{u \in U} \alpha_u c_{u,0}]_h$, $\hat{c}_1 = [\sum_{u \in U} \alpha_u c_{u,1}]_h$, $c_{u,0} = [\boldsymbol{a} \cdot \boldsymbol{u}_u + \boldsymbol{e}_{u,0}]_h$, $c_{u1} = [pk \cdot \boldsymbol{u}_u + \boldsymbol{e}_{u,1} + \lfloor h/l \rfloor \cdot \boldsymbol{m}_u]_h$, $pk = [\sum_{u \in U} pk_{u,0}]_h$, and $pk_u = [-(\boldsymbol{a} \cdot sk_{u,0} + \boldsymbol{e}_u)]_h$, we have the Eq. (2).

$$
\begin{aligned}
X &= [\hat{c}_1 + \hat{c}_0 \cdot \sum_{u \in U} sk_{u,0} + \sum_{u \in U} \boldsymbol{e}_{u,2}]_h \\
&= [\sum_{u \in U} \alpha_u (pk \cdot \boldsymbol{u}_u + \boldsymbol{e}_{u,1} + \lfloor h/l \rfloor \cdot \boldsymbol{m}_u) \\
&\quad + \sum_{u \in U} \alpha_u (\boldsymbol{a} \cdot \boldsymbol{u}_u + \boldsymbol{e}_{u,0}) \cdot (\sum_{u \in U} sk_{u,0}) + \sum_{u \in U} \boldsymbol{e}_{u,2}]_h
\end{aligned}
\tag{2}
$$

Let

$$
NS_0 = \sum_{u \in U} \alpha_u \boldsymbol{e}_{u,1} + (\sum_{u \in U} \alpha_u \boldsymbol{e}_{u,0}) \cdot (\sum_{u \in U} sk_{u,0}) + \sum_{u \in U} \boldsymbol{e}_{u,2},
$$

and $MP = \sum_{u \in U} \alpha_u \lfloor h/l \rfloor \cdot \boldsymbol{m}_u$, then $Y = [X - NS_0 - MP]_h$. We have the Eq. (3).

$$
\begin{aligned}
Y &= [\sum_{u \in U} \alpha_u (pk \cdot \boldsymbol{u}_u) + \sum_{u \in U} \alpha_u (\boldsymbol{a} \cdot \boldsymbol{u}_u) \cdot (\sum_{u \in U} sk_{u,0})]_h \\
&= [\sum_{u \in U} \alpha_u (\boldsymbol{u}_u \cdot (\sum_{u \in U} -(\boldsymbol{a} \cdot sk_{u0} + \boldsymbol{e}_u))) + \boldsymbol{a} \cdot (\sum_{u \in U} \alpha_u \boldsymbol{u}_u) \cdot (\sum_{u \in U} sk_{u,0})]_h \\
&= [-\sum_{u \in U} \alpha_u \boldsymbol{u}_u \cdot \sum_{u \in U} \boldsymbol{e}_u]_h
\end{aligned}
\tag{3}
$$

Let $NS = NS_0 - \sum_{u \in U} \alpha_u \boldsymbol{u}_u \cdot \sum_{u \in U} \boldsymbol{e}_u$, then $X = [NS + MP]_h$. We then have the Eq. (4).

$$m = [\lfloor \frac{l \cdot [\hat{c}_1 + cs]_h}{h} \rceil]_l$$

$$= [\lfloor \frac{l \cdot X}{h} \rceil]_l$$

$$= [\lfloor \frac{l \cdot (NS + \sum_{u \in U} \alpha_u \lfloor h/l \rfloor \cdot m_u)}{h} \rceil]_l \tag{4}$$

$$= [\sum_{u \in U} \alpha_u m_u]_l + [\lfloor \frac{l \cdot NS}{h} \rceil]_l$$

If $NS < \frac{h}{2l}$, the above decryption is correct. Since $u_u, sk_{u0} \leftarrow R_3$, e_{u0}, e_{u1}, $e_u, e_{u2} \leftarrow \chi$, the maximal infinity norm of elements in the set $\{\alpha_u\}_{u \in U}$ is A, the infinity norm of NS is

$$\|NS\| \leq \delta_R A |U| B + \delta_R^2 A |U|^2 B + |U| B + \delta_R^2 A |U|^2 B \tag{5}$$
$$= |U| B (1 + \delta_R A (1 + 2\delta_R |U|))$$

The second proof is for the privacy of messages in the Definition 2.

Theorem 2. *If there is an adversary $\mathcal{A}$ with advantage ϵ_{sem} to make the experiment $Expt_{\mathcal{A},Sem}(1^\lambda)$ output 1, one could construct a challenger to break the n-decision-RLWE problem with an advantage $\frac{1}{2}\epsilon_{sem}$ under the condition that the secret sharing scheme SS has the privacy property [7] and the hybrid encryption scheme HPKE is sematic secure.*

Proof. With $|U|$ and t, the challenger samples a $|U|$-decision-RLWE instance $(x_0, \{x_u\}_{u \in U})$. It embeds the problem instance into the DTAHE instance as follows. $parm \leftarrow Setup(1^\lambda)$, $parm = parm \backslash \{a\} \cup \{x_0\}$, $(sk_u, pk_u) \leftarrow KeyGen(parm)$, $sk_{u,0} = 0; pk_{u,0} = x_u$, $\{e_{v,u}\}_{v \in U \backslash \{u\}} \leftarrow Share(parm, \{pk_v\}_{v \in U \backslash \{u\}}, t, sk_u)$, $pk \leftarrow CombKey(parm, \{pk_u\}_{u \in U})$. It then provides $(parm, pk, \{\{e_{v,u}\}_{v \in U \backslash \{u\}}\}_{u \in U})$ to $\mathcal{A}$.

The challenger plays with $\mathcal{A}$ by $\{sk_{u,1}\}_{u \in U}$ until $\mathcal{A}$ outputs b'.

If the $HPKE$ scheme is sematic secure, the ciphers $\{e_{v,u}\}_{v \in U \backslash \{u\}}$ leak nothing about shares. Then from the privacy property of the SS scheme, if $|S| < t$, $\mathcal{A}$ can not distinguish a secret $sk_{u,0}$ from zero. So $\mathcal{A}$ should produce an educated guess b'.

The strategy of the challenger is to use the guess of $\mathcal{A}$. If the $Expt_{\mathcal{A},Sem}(1^\lambda)$ outputs 0, the challenger believes that the $|U|$-decision-RLWE instance is a uniform random sample from R_h^{n+1}.

When the input is indeed a uniform random sample from R_h^{n+1}, the advantage of $\mathcal{A}$ is simple negligible since the messages are masked by random values. Otherwise, the adversary has an advantage ϵ_{sem} by assumption. So the advantage of the challenger is $\frac{1}{2}\epsilon_{sem}$.

The third proof is for the privacy of secret keys and shares in the Definition 3.

Theorem 3. *If the secret sharing scheme SS has the privacy property [7] and the hybrid encryption scheme HPKE is sematic secure, the adversary $\mathcal{A}$ has negligible advantage to distinguish experiments $Exp_{\mathcal{A},Real}(1^\lambda)$ and $Expt_{\mathcal{A},Ideal}(1^\lambda)$.*

Proof. The proof needs a serial of hybrid experiments between an adversary $\mathcal{A}$ and a challenger.

- H_0: This is the experiment $Exp_{\mathcal{A},Real}(1^\lambda)$ in the Definition 3.
- H_1:Same as H_0, except that the challenger simulates the $ParDec$ algorithm to produce $\tilde{m}_u$ for queries of $\mathcal{A}$. Note that $\mathcal{A}$ has given the challenger a set S^* with the size $|S^*| = t - 1$. From S^*, the challenger could construct a set $S_C = S \backslash S^*$. For each party $u \in S_C$, $|S^* \cup \{u\}| = t$. The challenger sets $\tilde{m}_u$ as

$$\tilde{m}_u = [li_u^{-1}(\lfloor h/l \rfloor \sum_{v \in U} \alpha_v m_v + NS - \hat{c}_1 - \sum_{v \in S^*} li_v \hat{m}_v)]_h$$

where NS is defined in the Theorem 1. If $u \in S^*$, the challenger computes $\tilde{m}_u$ as in the game H_0.

The correctness of the simulation is obviously since

$$\tilde{m}_u = [li_u^{-1}(MP + NS - (\hat{c}_1 + \sum_{v \in S^*} li_v \hat{m}_v))]_h$$
$$= [li_u^{-1}(MP + NS - (\hat{c}_1 + cs - li_u \hat{m}_u))]_h \qquad (6)$$
$$= [li_u^{-1}(MP + NS - X + li_u \hat{m}_u)]_h$$
$$= \hat{m}_u$$

- H_2: Same as H_1, except that the challenger shares zero as

$$\{e_{v,u}\}_{v \in U \backslash \{u\}} \leftarrow Share(parm, \{pk_v\}_{v \in U \backslash \{u\}}, t, 0).$$

By the privacy property [7] of the SS scheme and the sematic security of the $HPKE$ scheme, H_2 and H_1 are indistinguishable.
- H_3: Same as H_2, except that NS is replaced by $\tilde{NS}$ as

$$\tilde{NS} = NS - (\sum_{u \in U} sk_{u,0})(\sum_{u \in U} \alpha_u e_{u,0}) + (\sum_{u \in U} u_{u,0})(\sum_{u \in U} \alpha_u e_{u,0}) \qquad (7)$$

where $u_{u,0} \leftarrow R_3$.

Since $sk_{u,0} \leftarrow R_3$, H_3 and H_2 have the same distribution. In fact, $\tilde{NS}$ may appear in an experiment when the $\{u_{u,0}\}_{u \in U}$ happens to be part of the secret keys of users. Now the challenger does not use the private keys of users $\{sk_u\}_{u \in U}$ or secret shares of users in U. So the ideal experiment $Expt_{\mathcal{A},Ideal}(1^\lambda)$ could be simulated indistinguishably.

4 Performance

4.1 Communication

We have stated that there are mainly three methods [5,7,31] to construct a DTAHE. We concrete the method in [31] based on an elliptic curve version ElGamal (EC-ElGamal) scheme, and other methods based on the BFV [8,13] scheme.

Table 1. Main communication overheads of DTAHE schemes in FL

	$e_{v,u}$	c_u	$\hat{m}_u$
Pedersen [31]	head+32	$66 * |m_u|$	$33 * |m_u|$
BD [5]	$head + LR * SN$	$2 * LR * LN$	$LR * LN * SN$
BGGJK-1 [7]	$head + LR * n^4$	$2 * LR * LN$	$LR * LN * n^4$
BGGJK-2 [7]	$head + LR'$	$2 * LR' * LN'$	$LR' * LN'$
Ours	$head + LR(1 + LN)$	$2 * LR * LN$	$LR * LN$

It is straightforward to apply a DTAHE scheme to FL following the framework in [6]. Basically, a user should upload public keys in the $KeyGen$ step, secret shares $e_{v,u}$ in the $Share$ step, ciphers c_u in the Enc step and the partially decrypted result $\hat{m}_u$ in the $ParDec$ step. The dropout resiliency requirement is satisfied by the Shamir secret sharing scheme with a threshold t among n users.

Table 1 shows the main communication cost of a user. The security parameter λ is 128. An element in EC-ElGamal takes 33 bytes where one byte is for y-coordinate. $head$ denotes the hybrid encryption cost of the $HPKE$. LR denotes the size of a ring element in R_h, SN the number of shares to each user and LN the number of ciphers to encrypt user's input m_u. n denotes the number of users in the FL. LR' and LN' have the same meaning as LR and LN with $LR \neq LR'$ and $LN \neq LN'$. The method to use Shamir secret sharing in [7] is denoted as BGGJK-2, and the other is denoted as BGGJK-1.

Figure 1 shows the main communication overhead of the protocol on user side with different DTAHE constructions when the number of user increases. We set $head = 33$ since when the $HPKE$ is implemented on ECC, only an extra ECC point is needed. Let $|m_u| = 10^5$ as the dimension of user data for all instances. Let $d = 2048$ and $|h| = 54$ so that $LR = d * |h|/8 = 13824$ bytes and $LN = \lceil |m_u|/d \rceil = 49$. We set the threshold of the Shamir secret sharing as $t = \lceil n * 2/3 \rceil$ and compute $SN = \binom{n-1}{t-1}$. The values of LR' and LN' are relative to the number of users since the noise element in the $ParDec$ algorithm should be multiplied by $(n!)^2$ [7], which are limited by the Theorem 1 and the Eq. (6) in [13].

Figure 1 shows that the BD [5] and BGGJK-1 [7] has a high communication cost as the user number increases. Our method is better than the BGGJK-2 [7] when the user number is greater than 26. The EC-ElGamal method has the best communication performance when the number of users is greater than 20. Note that the schemes in [5,7] and our proposal may be used in the post quantum era while the EC-ElGamal scheme could not.

4.2 Computation

We give Table 2 to show the time cost of some DTAHE schemes. We set the user number as $n = 35$ and implement three DTAHE schemes for comparison.

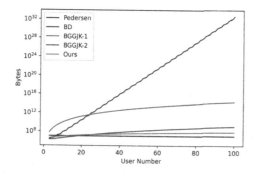

Fig. 1. Main communication overheads of different DTAHE schemes in the protocol

Table 2. Computation time of some DTAHE algorithms with 35 users

	Share	*CombKey* and *Enc*	*Eval*	*ParDec*	*FinDec*
Pedersen [31]	0.03	6.95	14.62	6.32	441.25
BGGJK-2 [7]	4.03	15.48	2.40	17.29	2.98
Ours	17.46	7.50	1.52	51.17	1.64

The schemes are implemented in Python. The "pyOpenSSL" is used to implement the EC-ElGamal based DTAHE. The small discrete logarithm of a group element is found by the well-known "Baby-Step-Giant-Step" method. An open source library "bfv-python" is adapted to implement our scheme and the BGGJK-2 method in [7]. For simplicity, we use a public python module "eciespy" as an instance of the $HPKE$ scheme. The CPUs are Intel(R) Core(TM) i7-8550U (1.80 GHz, 1.99 GHz) and the RAM is 16 GB.

We use the "secp256r1" curve as the parameter set to implement the EC-ElGamal based DTAHE. For the security parameter $\lambda = 128$, we set $d = 2048$, $|h| = 54$ and $|l| = 17$ for our DTAHE scheme. When $n = 35$, the scheme constructed by the BGGJK-2 method in [7] requires $|h| \geq 426$. So we set $d = 16384$ according to the parameter table in [3]. Each data element in m_u in our test occupies 8 bits. The time costs of the three implementations are listed in the table II, which are measured in seconds.

Apparently, the EC-ElGamal based DTAHE takes the least time on user side. Our lattice based DTAHE scheme takes the least time on the server side.

In summary, we show a DTAHE scheme suitable for FL even in the post quantum era. It is a new design choice to share noise in a lattice based homomorphic encryption scheme. We give detailed security proof and performance analysis.

Acknowledgement. Thanks to Huawei Noah's Ark Lab for funding this research.

References

1. Abadi, M., Chu, A., Goodfellow, I., McMahan, H.B., Mironov, I., Talwar, K., Zhang, L.: Deep learning with differential privacy. In: Proceedings of the 2016 ACM SIGSAC Conference on Computer and Communications Security. pp. 308–318. CCS 2016, Association for Computing Machinery, New York, NY, USA (2016). https://doi.org/10.1145/2976749.2978318
2. Al-Rubaie, M., Chang, J.M.: Reconstruction attacks against mobile-based continuous authentication systems in the cloud. IEEE Trans. Inf. Forensics Secur. $11(12)$, 2648–2663 (2016). https://doi.org/10.1109/TIFS.2016.2594132
3. Albrecht, M.,et al.: Homomorphic encryption security standard. Technical report, HomomorphicEncryption.org, Toronto, Canada, November 2018
4. Asharov, G., Jain, A., López-Alt, A., Tromer, E., Vaikuntanathan, V., Wichs, D.: Multiparty computation with low communication, computation and interaction via threshold FHE. In: Pointcheval, D., Johansson, T. (eds.) EUROCRYPT 2012. LNCS, vol. 7237, pp. 483–501. Springer, Heidelberg (2012). https://doi.org/10.1007/978-3-642-29011-4_29
5. Bendlin, R., Damgård, I.: Threshold decryption and zero-knowledge proofs for lattice-based cryptosystems. In: Micciancio, D. (ed.) TCC 2010. LNCS, vol. 5978, pp. 201–218. Springer, Heidelberg (2010). https://doi.org/10.1007/978-3-642-11799-2_13
6. Bonawitz, K., et al.: Practical secure aggregation for privacy-preserving machine learning. In: Proceedings of the 2017 ACM SIGSAC Conference on Computer and Communications Security, pp. 1175–1191. CCS 2017, Association for Computing Machinery, New York, NY, USA (2017). https://doi.org/10.1145/3133956.3133982
7. Boneh, D., Gennaro, R., Goldfeder, S., Jain, A., Kim, S., Rasmussen, P.M.R., Sahai, A.: Threshold cryptosystems from threshold fully homomorphic encryption. In: Shacham, H., Boldyreva, A. (eds.) CRYPTO 2018. LNCS, vol. 10991, pp. 565–596. Springer, Cham (2018). https://doi.org/10.1007/978-3-319-96884-1_19
8. Brakerski, Z.: Fully homomorphic encryption without modulus switching from classical GapSVP. In: Safavi-Naini, R., Canetti, R. (eds.) CRYPTO 2012. LNCS, vol. 7417, pp. 868–886. Springer, Heidelberg (2012). https://doi.org/10.1007/978-3-642-32009-5_50
9. Bresson, E., Catalano, D., Pointcheval, D.: A simple public-key cryptosystem with a double trapdoor decryption mechanism and its applications. In: Laih, C.-S. (ed.) ASIACRYPT 2003. LNCS, vol. 2894, pp. 37–54. Springer, Heidelberg (2003). https://doi.org/10.1007/978-3-540-40061-5_3
10. Chen, H., Dai, W., Kim, M., Song, Y.: Efficient multi-key homomorphic encryption with packed ciphertexts with application to oblivious neural network inference. In: Proceedings of the 2019 ACM SIGSAC Conference on Computer and Communications Security. p. 395–412. CCS 2019, Association for Computing Machinery, New York, NY, USA (2019). https://doi.org/10.1145/3319535.3363207
11. Damgård, I., Jurik, M.: A generalisation, a simplification and some applications of Paillier's probabilistic public-key system. In: Kim, K. (ed.) PKC 2001. LNCS, vol. 1992, pp. 119–136. Springer, Heidelberg (2001). https://doi.org/10.1007/3-540-44586-2_9
12. Di, C., Leye, W., Kai, C., Qiang, Y.: Secure federated matrix factorization. In: FML 2019 : The 1st International Workshop on Federated Machine Learning for User Privacy and Data Confidentiality (2019)

13. Fan, J., Vercauteren, F.: Somewhat practical fully homomorphic encryption. Cryptology ePrint Archive, Report 2012/144 (2012). https://eprint.iacr.org/2012/144
14. Fereidooni, H., et al.: Secure aggregation for private federated learning. In: 2021 IEEE Security and Privacy Workshops (SPW), pp. 56–62 (2021). https://doi.org/10.1109/SPW53761.2021.00017
15. Fredrikson, M., Jha, S., Ristenpart, T.: Model inversion attacks that exploit confidence information and basic countermeasures. In: Proceedings of the 22Nd ACM SIGSAC Conference on Computer and Communications Security, pp. 1322–1333. CCS 2015, ACM, New York, NY, USA (2015). https://doi.org/10.1145/2810103.2813677
16. Froelicher, D., et al.: Scalable privacy-preserving distributed learning. Proc. Priv. Enhanc. Technol. **2021**(2), 323–347 (2021)
17. Geiping, J., Bauermeister, H., Drge, H., Moeller, M.: Inverting gradients - how easy is it to break privacy in federated learning? (2020). http://arxiv.org/abs/2003.14053v1
18. Gennaro, R., Jarecki, S., Krawczyk, H., Rabin, T.: Secure distributed key generation for discrete-log based cryptosystems. In: Stern, J. (ed.) EUROCRYPT 1999. LNCS, vol. 1592, pp. 295–310. Springer, Heidelberg (1999). https://doi.org/10.1007/3-540-48910-X_21
19. Herranz, J., Hofheinz, D., Kiltz, E.: Some (in)sufficient conditions for secure hybrid encryption. Inf. Comput. **208**(11), 1243–1257 (010). https://doi.org/10.1016/j.ic.2010.07.002
20. Hosseini, E., Khisti, A.: Secure aggregation in federated learning via multiparty homomorphic encryption. In: 2021 IEEE Globecom Workshops (GC Wkshps), pp. 1–6 (2021). https://doi.org/10.1109/GCWkshps52748.2021.9682053
21. Jiang, Z.L., Guo, H., Pan, Y., Liu, Y., Wang, X., Zhang, J.: Secure neural network in federated learning with model aggregation under multiple keys. In: 2021 8th IEEE International Conference on Cyber Security and Cloud Computing (CSCloud)/2021 7th IEEE International Conference on Edge Computing and Scalable Cloud (EdgeCom), pp. 47–52. IEEE (2021)
22. Kim, E., Jeong, J., Yoon, H., Kim, Y., Cho, J., Cheon, J.H.: How to securely collaborate on data: decentralized threshold he and secure key update. IEEE Access **8**, 191319–191329 (2020). https://doi.org/10.1109/ACCESS.2020.3030970
23. Li, Y., Li, H., Xu, G., Huang, X., Lu, R.: Efficient privacy-preserving federated learning with unreliable users. IEEE Internet Things J. 1 (2021). https://doi.org/10.1109/JIOT.2021.3130115
24. Liu, Y., et al.: Boosting privately: federated extreme gradient boosting for mobile crowdsensing. In: 2020 IEEE 40th International Conference on Distributed Computing Systems (ICDCS), pp. 1–11 (2020). https://doi.org/10.1109/ICDCS47774.2020.00017
25. Lyubashevsky, V., Peikert, C., Regev, O.: On ideal lattices and learning with errors over rings. In: Gilbert, H. (ed.) EUROCRYPT 2010. LNCS, vol. 6110, pp. 1–23. Springer, Heidelberg (2010). https://doi.org/10.1007/978-3-642-13190-5_1
26. Ma, J., Naas, S.A., Sigg, S., Lyu, X.: Privacy-preserving federated learning based on multi-key homomorphic encryption. Int. J. Intell. Syst. (2022)
27. McMahan, H.B., Moore, E., Ramage, D., y Arcas, B.A.: Federated learning of deep networks using model averaging. CoRR abs/1602.05629 (2016). http://arxiv.org/abs/1602.05629
28. Mo, F., Haddadi, H., Katevas, K., Marin, E., Perino, D., Kourtellis, N.: PPFL: privacy-preserving federated learning with trusted execution environments (2021). https://doi.org/10.48550/ARXIV.2104.14380, https://arxiv.org/abs/2104.14380

29. Mouchet, C., Troncoso-Pastoriza, J., Bossuat, J.P., Hubaux, J.P.: Multi-party homomorphic encryption from ring-learning-with-errors. Cryptology ePrint Archive, Report 2020/304 (2020). https://ia.cr/2020/304

30. Paillier, P.: Public-key cryptosystems based on composite degree residuosity classes. In: Stern, J. (ed.) EUROCRYPT 1999. LNCS, vol. 1592, pp. 223–238. Springer, Heidelberg (1999). https://doi.org/10.1007/3-540-48910-X_16

31. Pedersen, T.P.: A threshold cryptosystem without a trusted party. In: Davies, D.W. (ed.) EUROCRYPT 1991. LNCS, vol. 547, pp. 522–526. Springer, Heidelberg (1991). https://doi.org/10.1007/3-540-46416-6_47

32. Sav, S., et al.: POSEIDON: privacy-preserving federated neural network learning. arXiv preprint arXiv:2009.00349 (2020)

33. Tian, H., Zhang, F., Shao, Y., Li, B.: Secure linear aggregation using decentralized threshold additive homomorphic encryption for federated learning (2021). https://doi.org/10.48550/ARXIV.2111.10753, https://arxiv.org/abs/2111.10753

34. Truex, S., et al.: A hybrid approach to privacy-preserving federated learning. In: Proceedings of the 12th ACM Workshop on Artificial Intelligence and Security, pp. 1–11. AISec 2019, Association for Computing Machinery, New York, NY, USA (2019). https://doi.org/10.1145/3338501.3357370

35. Urban, A., Rambaud, M.: Share & shrink: Ad-hoc threshold FHE with short ciphertexts and its application to almost-asynchronous MPC. Cryptology ePrint Archive, Paper 2022/378 (2022). https://eprint.iacr.org/2022/378

36. Yin, H., Mallya, A., Vahdat, A., Alvarez, J.M., Kautz, J., Molchanov, P.: See through gradients: Image batch recovery via gradinversion (2021). http://arxiv.org/abs/2104.07586

37. Zhang, F., Zhang, Z., Guan, P.: ECC2: error correcting code and elliptic curve based cryptosystem. Inf. Sci. **526**, 301–320 (2020). https://doi.org/10.1016/j.ins.2020.03.069, https://www.sciencedirect.com/science/article/pii/S0020025520302498

38. Zhao, B., Mopuri, K.R., Bilen, H.: IDLG: Improved deep leakage from gradients (2020). http://arxiv.org/abs/2001.02610

39. Zhu, H., Wang, R., Jin, Y., Liang, K., Ning, J.: Distributed additive encryption and quantization for privacy preserving federated deep learning. Neurocomputing **463**, 309–327 (2021)

40. Zhu, L., Liu, Z., Han, S.: Deep leakage from gradients (2019). http://arxiv.org/abs/1906.08935

A Defect Level Assessment Method Based on Weighted Probability Ensemble

Lixia Xie[1], Siyu Liu[1], Hongyu Yang[1,2(✉)], and Liang Zhang[3]

[1] School of Computer Science and Technology, Civil Aviation University of China,
Tianjin 300300, China
yhyxlx@hotmail.com
[2] School of Safety Science and Engineering, Civil Aviation University of China,
Tianjin 300300, China
[3] School of Information, The University of Arizona, Tucson, AZ 85721, USA

Abstract. In order to solve the problems that the existing defect prediction methods lack the assessment of the potential defect level of samples and do not fully consider the cost impact of misclassification, a defect level assessment method based on weighted probability ensemble (DLA-WPE) is proposed. Firstly, the greedy selection method is used to select features. Then, according to the number of samples in different categories, the unequal punishment of different misclassification is calculated to obtain the misclassification punishment (MP). The weighted probability ensemble (WPE) model is built. Finally, the voting weight of each base classifier is calculated according to the MP. According to the dichotomous probability of base classifiers, the defective quantification value is calculated to obtain the defect assessment results, and the potential defects of modules are assessed. The experimental results show that the defective quantitative values and defect levels are consistent with the actual situation of the samples.

Keywords: Defect level assessment · Weighted probability ensemble · Misclassification penalty

1 Introduction

The quality and safety problems faced by the software are becoming increasingly prominent leading to the decline of software reliability, such as high development costs, maintenance difficulties, and code vulnerability [1]. Before the software is put on the market, whether the module has defects is predicted one by one, and the defective modules are processed in disorder according to the predicted defect tendency results [2, 3].

Due to the complexity of software code and limited testing resources, it takes time and effort to predict and deal with defect modules one by one. Therefore, it is of great significance to assess the defect levels of the modules and allocate an equal amount of testing resources.

To solve the above deficiencies, this paper proposes a defect level assessment method based on weighted probability ensemble (DLA-WPE): (1) Higher cost weights are given to the misclassification of defective categories to improve the sensitivity of the defective samples to the assessment model. (2) To produce defect processing priority and allocate limited testing resources reasonably, a weighted probability ensemble (WPE) model is proposed. The model has good interpretability, which can quantify the degree of software defects to assess the defect levels of the modules effectively and provide decision support for software testers.

2   Related Work

In the field of software security, software defect prediction methods based on deep learning have become a popular research topic. Wang et al. [4] proposed a software defect prediction method based on deep belief network (DBN) automatic learning semantic features. Li et al. [5] proposed a method of software defect prediction via a convolutional neural network (DP-CNN). The above methods generally have some weaknesses, such as uncertainty of hyperparameters and poor interpretability.

The software defect prediction methods based on machine learning have been widely used. Zhou et al. [6] proposed a deep forest for defect prediction (DPDF) method, but a multi-granularity scanning strategy would produce a large number of redundant features. Issam et al. [7] proposed an average probability ensemble (APE) method and verified that the feature selection of samples is of great significance to the accurate classification of defects. Chen et al. [8] proposed a software defect number prediction method based on code metrics and synthetic minority sampling technology.

Compared with the above methods, this paper gives higher punishment to the misclassification of defect samples on the premise of feature selection. The misclassification penalty (MP) is creatively converted into the voting weight of each base classifier. The software defect levels are generated to effectively assess the defect risks by analyzing the mathematical basis of the WPE model.

3   A Defect Level Assessment Method

The defect level assessment method based on weighted probability ensemble is divided into three parts: multi-source sample treatment, misclassification penalty quantization, and defect level assessment. The assessment framework is shown in Fig. 1.

3.1   Multi-source Sample Treatment

Duplicate noise samples are deleted directly to effectively reduce the redundancy of samples on the premise of ensuring the integrity of samples. To avoid the wrong deletion of important samples and excessive time and space complexity, the average value of the remaining features of all samples is used to replace the fuzzy and abnormal noise to retain the feature data of the source samples.

According to comparing the evaluation index size of the Min-Max and Z-Score methods on different classifiers, the Z-Score method is used to normalize the discrete features. It is of great significance to use different feature selection methods to calculate the importance of features and eliminate redundant features. Four feature selection methods are analyzed and compared, which include Pearson correlation (Pearson), Fisher discriminant analysis (FDA), distance correlation (DC), and greedy selection (GS).

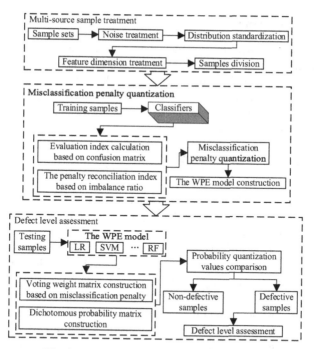

Fig. 1. The defect level assessment framework.

3.2 Misclassification Penalty Quantization

Due to the different cost effects caused by misclassification, the penalty reconciliation index is calculated by the adaptive quantification of the total number of samples.

Firstly, multiple confusion matrices are obtained. For the confusion matrix of dichotomous problems, the samples can be divided into true positive (TP), false positive (FP), true negative (TN), and false negative (FN).

Then, the MP is calculated through the false negative rate, false positive rate, and their penalty reconciliation index (i.e., a_i and b_i). The MP_k of the k_{th} classifier can be expressed as:

$$MP_k = \frac{IR_i}{IR_i + 1} \times \frac{FN_k}{TP_k + FN_k} + \frac{1}{IR_i + 1} \times \frac{FP_k}{TN_k + FP_k}, (IR_i = Ni^-/Ni^+) \quad (1)$$

where FN_k, FP_k, TP_k, and TN_k refer to the sample number of FN, FP, TP, and TN of the k_{th} classifier respectively. IR_i represents the imbalance ratio of the i_{th} sample set, and N_i^- and N_i^+ represent the majority and minority sample numbers respectively.

Finally, the misclassification penalty matrix is constructed through MP_k. From Formula (1), the smaller FN_k and FP_k, the smaller MP_k, and the better performance of classifiers.

Therefore, the performance of each base classifier is obtained by comparing the size of sorted MP_k. Therefore, the base classifiers of the WPE model include random forest (RF), logistic regression (LR), gradient boosting (GB), k-nearest neighbor (KNN), support vector machine (SVM), and Gaussian naïve Bayes (GNB).

3.3 Defect Level Assessment

The WPE model calculates the voting weight of each base classifier through the MP. According to the high voting weight of RF and GB classifiers, the classification performance of GNB, KNN, LR, and SVM can be balanced effectively.

The voting weight W_{1k} of the k_{th} classifier in the WPE model is calculated according to the complementary of MP_k in the range of [0, 1] to construct the voting weight matrix. W_{1k} can be expressed as:

$$W1_k = (\sum_k MP_k - MP_k)/ \sum_k MP_k \tag{2}$$

The dichotomous probability matrix of each classifier is output, which includes the non-defective probability $(P_{k(Y=0)})$ and defective probability $(P_{k(Y=1)})$ predicted by the k_{th} base classifier predicts.

Referring to the asset importance level and risk assessment specification [9], the value range of $P_{k(Y=1)}$ divides the defect probability level. The value range of $P_{k(Y=1)}$ is 0 to 1, which is divided equally into five intervals within the range. The ascending order of the five intervals is lower, low, medium, high, and higher respectively showing that defects have a corresponding impact on the module.

The probability quantization matrix is obtained by multiplying the dichotomous probability matrix and the voting weight matrix, which includes the non-defective quantization value $(label_{(Y=0)})$ and the defective quantization value $(label_{(Y=1)})$. By comparing the values of the $label_{(Y=0)}$ and $label_{(Y=1)}$, the assessment result is obtained.

To give priority to the defect modules with higher criticality in time the value range of $label_{(Y=1)}$ (see Proof 1 for details) to generate the defect assessment level referring to the asset importance level and risk assessment specification [9]. The $label_{(Y=1)}$ is divided equally into five intervals within the range. The ascending order of the five intervals is lower, low, medium, high, and higher respectively showing that if there is a defective, it will cause the corresponding damage to the assets.

Proof 1 $MP_k \in [0, 1]$, $W_{1k} \in [0, 1]$, $label_{(Y=1)} \in [0, 5]$.
It can be known from Formula (1) that the a_i and $b_i \in [0, 1]$, and thus the false positive rate and false negative rate are 0 to 1. The value range of the MP_k is 0 to 1. Therefore, the W_{1k} is 0 to 1 from Formula (2), and thus $\sum_k^6 P_{k(Y=1)} \geq (\sum_k^6 MP_k P_{k(Y=1)})/ \sum_k MP_k$, $label_{(Y=1)} \geq 0$. Besides, the maximum value of $P_{k(Y=1)}$ is 1, $max\{\sum_k P_k(Y=1)\} = 6$ can obtain, so $label_{(Y=1)} \leq 5$. Therefore, the range of the $label_{(Y=1)}$ is 0 to 5.

4 Experiments and Results

4.1 Experimental Samples and Evaluation Index

The experimental sample sets include four public project databases including NASA MDP [10], Promise [11], AEEEM [12], and Relink [13]. Different evaluation indexes are used to measure the assessment results. Evaluation indexes include accuracy (Acc), F-measure (F1), which can be expressed as:

$$Acc = \frac{TP + TN}{TP + FP + TN + FN} \tag{3}$$

$$F1 = \frac{2TP}{2TP + FN + FP} \tag{4}$$

4.2 Feature Selection Methods Comparative Experiment

The AUC of different feature selection methods is calculated on the RF classifier for different sample sets, as shown in Fig. 2.

Experiments show that the defect sample sets after noise processing still have high redundancy. For different sample sets, compared with other methods, GS can search the best feature subset fastest and require the least number of features and the highest AUC. The EQ sample set uses the GS to select the optimal features in RF and reaches the peak AUC when selecting the eighth features, as shown in Fig. 2(b).

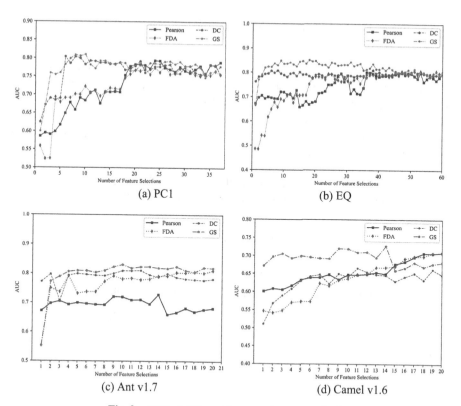

(a) PC1   (b) EQ

(c) Ant v1.7   (d) Camel v1.6

Fig. 2. AUC of different feature selection methods.

4.3 Defect Level Assessment Experiment

To prove the superiority of DLA-WPE, the Acc and F1 are calculated to compare DLA-WPE with three traditional methods and two ensemble methods, as shown in Fig. 3. The Acc and F1 are calculated to compare DLA-WPE with five advanced methods, as shown in Tables 1 and 2.

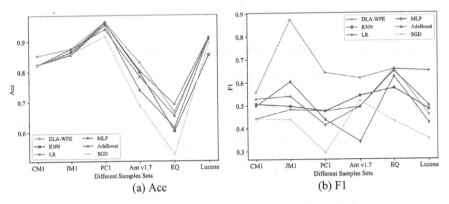

(a) Acc   (b) F1

Fig. 3. Acc and F1 with traditional and ensemble methods.

Experiments show that the Acc of DLA-WPE is slightly higher than other methods in most sample sets. DLA-WPE obtains the highest Acc in CM1, JM1, PC1, and Ant v1.7 sample sets. DLA-WPE gets the highest F1 in JM1 and PC1 sample sets. DLA-WPE obtains the highest Acc and F1. DLA-WPE can give higher punishment to the misclassification of defective samples on the premise of feature dimensionality reduction to obtain excellent assessment results.

To further prove the advantages of the defect level assessment method, the $label_{(Y=1)}$ is analyzed and calculated in different sample sets. The defect level assessment results of some samples in the Ant v1.7 sample set are shown in Table 3.

Table 1. Acc with advanced methods.

Method	JM1	PC1	Ant v1.7	Camel v1.6	EQ	Apache
DLA-WPE	**0.876**	**0.965**	**0.832**	**0.830**	**0.667**	**0.750**
CNN	0.853	0.909	0.805	0.790	0.627	0.624
DBN	0.839	0.913	0.777	0.805	0.606	0.648
DP-CNN	0.862	0.923	0.820	0.820	0.657	0.644
DPDF	**0.876**	0.925	**0.832**	0.808	0.608	0.726

Table 2. F1 with advanced methods.

Method	JM1	PC1	Ant v1.7	Camel v1.6	EQ	Apache
DLA-WPE	**0.580**	**0.643**	**0.619**	**0.300**	0.658	**0.750**
CNN	0.440	0.300	0.460	0.190	0.560	0.640
DBN	0.410	0.338	0.439	0.200	0.570	0.580
DP-CNN	0.440	0.350	0.480	0.290	0.590	0.650
DPDF	0.510	0.370	0.556	0.190	**0.660**	0.730

Table 3. Defect level assessment results of some samples.

Sample	DLA-WPE		Actual situation	
	$label_{(Y=1)}$	Defect level	$label$	Defective or Non-defective
1	3.840	High	1	Defective
2	1.627	Low	0	Non-defective
3	2.322	Medium	1	Defective
4	0.713	Lower	0	Non-defective
5	4.726	Higher	1	Defective
6	3.213	High	1	Defective
7	0.890	Lower	0	Non-defective
8	2.066	Medium	1	Defective
9	4.008	Higher	1	Defective

Experimental results show that the defect levels produced by DLA-WPE correspond to the actual situation and assess the potential defects. The allocation of software resources can be effective according to the proportion of defect level assessment.

5 Conclusion

To effectively divide the potential risk levels of defect modules and reasonably allocate limited testing resources, a defect level assessment method based on weighted probability ensemble is proposed. Based on the machine learning methods, considering the different cost effects caused by misclassification, the dichotomous probabilities of base classifiers with different performances are used for voting weight, and then the defective quantization value is calculated to assess the defect level. Through the verification experiments with ten methods in the multi-source samples environment, the feasibility and effectiveness of DLA-WPE are verified. Compared with other methods, this method can give higher weights to the base classifiers with better performance. The quantitative value can calculate reasonably, and then sort the defect levels of the modules according to the software defect level assessment results, which can reflect the safety status comprehensively and accurately.

Acknowledgment. This work was supported by the National Natural Science Foundation of China (No. U1833107).

References

1. Lin, G.F., Wen, S.S., Han, Q.L.T.: Software vulnerability detection using deep neural networks: a survey. Proc. IEEE **108**(10), 1825–1848 (2020)
2. Thota, M.K.F., Shajin, F.H.S., Rajesh, P.T.: Survey on software defect prediction techniques. Int. J. Appl. Sci. Eng. **17**(4), 331–344 (2020)
3. Yu, X.F., Jacky, K.S., Xiao, Y.T.: Predicting the precise number of software defects are we there yet. Inf. Softw. Technol. **146**(1), 106847–106863 (2022)
4. Wang, S.F., Liu, T.Y.S., Tan, L.T.: Automatically learning semantic features for defect prediction. In: Dillon, L.F., Visser, W.S. (eds.) IEEE/ACM 38th International Conference on Software Engineering 2016, ICSE, vol. 38, pp. 297–308. Association for Computing Machinery, New York (2016)
5. Li, J.F., He, P.J.S., Zhu, J.M.T.: Software defect prediction via convolutional neural network. In: Bilof, R.F. (ed.) IEEE International Conference on Software Quality Reliability and Security 2017, QRS, vol. 3, pp. 318–328. IEEE, Piscataway (2017)
6. Zhou, T.C.F., Sun, X.B.S., Xia, X.T.: Improving defect prediction with deep forest. Inf. Softw. Technol. **114**(1), 204–216 (2019)
7. Issam, H.L.F., Mohammad, A.S., Lahouari, G.T.: Software defect prediction using ensemble learning on selected features. Inf. Softw. Technol. **58**(1), 388–402 (2015)
8. Chen, H.W.F., Jing, X.Y.S., Li, Z.Q.T.: An empirical study on heterogeneous defect prediction approaches. IEEE Trans. Softw. Eng. **47**(12), 2803–2822 (2020)
9. The Standardization Administration of China: Information security risk assessment specification: GB/T 20984. Standards Press of China, Beijing (2007)
10. Shepperd, M.F., Song, Q.S., Sun, Z.T.: Data quality: some comments on the NASA software defect datasets. IEEE Trans. Softw. Eng. **39**(9), 1208–1215 (2013)
11. Jurecako, M.F., Madeyski, L.S.: Towards identifying software project clusters with regard to defect prediction. In: Menzies, T.F., Koru, G.S. (eds.) Proceedings of the 6th International Conference on Predictive Models in Software Engineering 2010, ICSE, vol. 5, pp. 1–10. Association for Computing Machinery, New York (2010)
12. D'Ambros, M.F., Lanza, M.S., Robbes, R.T.: Evaluating defect prediction approaches: a benchmark and an extensive comparison. Empir. Softw. Eng. **17**(4), 531–577 (2012)
13. Wu, R.F., Zhang, H.S., Kim, S.T.: Relink: recovering links between bugs and changes. In: Gyimóthy, T.F., Zeller, A.S. (eds.) Proceedings of the 19th ACM SIGSOFT Symposium and the 13th European Conference on Foundations of Software Engineering 2011, ESEC/FSE 2011, vol. 13, pp. 15–25. Association for Computing Machinery, New York (2011)

A Decentralized Ride-Hailing Mode Based on Blockchain and Attribute Encryption

Yifan Zhang[1], Yuping Zhou[1,2](✉), Yu Hu[1], and Hui Huang[1]

[1] Minnan Normal University, Zhangzhou 363000, People's Republic of China
[2] Key Laboratory of Data Science and Intelligence Application,
Fujian Province University, Zhangzhou 363000, People's Republic of China
1021784165@qq.com

Abstract. With the development of smart transportation, ride-hailing applications have become an essential part of people's lives. These ride-hailing apps provide convenience of contacting taxi for passengers. However, most present ride-hailing or ride-sharing systems rely on a trusted third party. It makes them be attacked vulnerably. A decentralized blockchain-based ride-hailing mode with attribute encryption is proposed in this paper. Attribute-based encryption is applied to ensure the drivers who meet the passenger's requirements can obtain the passenger's order in this mode. After the transaction has completed, the transaction information is saved on the blockchain. This mode supports the investigation of historical records via the blockchain technology. Besides, a new payment protocol is used in this mode. The new payment protocol is based on trip distance. It applies smart contract and zero-knowledge set membership proof. The reputation of drivers based on drivers' past behavior is designed. The driver's reputation will be updated after the transaction is completed. Passengers can choose a driver with high reputation. Each phase of this mode is simulated in our test net of Ethereum. The results prove that this ride-hailing mode is efficient.

Keywords: Blockchain · Ciphertext policy attribute-based encryption (CP-ABE) · Zero-knowledge proof · Smart contract · Ride-hailing service

1 Introduction

Ride-hailing refers to the provision of transportation services for passengers. In the past decade, online ride-hailing [1,2] has gradually replaced the traditional taxi mode. Existing research focuses on route planning for ride-hailing services and security privacy [3–9]. The advantages of online ride-hailing are reflected in the following points. First, people can choose the location which they are picked up by the driver. Second, people can confirm whether the driver's trip is correct in real-time. Third, all transactions will be saved in the database. People can check their history at any time.

© The Author(s), under exclusive license to Springer Nature Switzerland AG 2022
X. Chen et al. (Eds.): CSS 2022, LNCS 13547, pp. 301–313, 2022.
https://doi.org/10.1007/978-3-031-18067-5_22

Most of the current ride-hailing modes are based on third-party platforms. Relying on centralized services makes the system more vulnerable. The centralized modes suffer denial of service (DoS) attacks easily. And if one single point is attacked, the system will crash. In addition, the centralized modes lack transparency. Some malicious third-party platforms sell the private data of users. These points prove that it is not safe to store information on a third-party platform. Furthermore, third-party platforms require high service costs.

Compare with the current centralized ride-hailing mode, blockchain technology provides a distributed storage solution. Data is stored distributed with blockchain. This can avoid the situation where the data is completely controlled by someone. Meanwhile, blockchain can avoid the problem of single-point failure and DoS attacks by the decentralized structure. However, there are few works using blockchain to build a decentralized ride-hailing mode. They are working on transparency and privacy.

In this paper, we propose a decentralized ride-hailing mode with attribute encryption. Compared with other ride-hailing modes, our mode does not rely on third-party platforms. Moreover, we used attribute encryption to satisfy passenger's choice. Passengers can choose the attributes of the driver. Passengers encrypt their taxi information by the attributes tree and send it to drivers. Each vehicle will receive taxi information encrypted by ciphertext-policy attribute-based encryption (CP-ABE). Drivers with specific attributes have the right to decrypt taxi information. Then the passengers will choose the driver based on the unit price and reputation of the driver.

In general, we make the following contributions.

1. We proposed a decentralized blockchain-based ride-hailing mode with attribute encryption. Attribute-based encryption is used in this mode. It guarantees that users can choose the drivers which they need.
2. Attribute-based encryption is different from identity-based encryption. A fine-grained access control policy is built for the drivers. The two parties can complete more secure transactions without exposing their identity.
3. To ensure trust between a rider and a selected driver, we propose a deposit protocol for ride-hailing services based on the zero-knowledge set membership.

2   Related Works

2.1   Ride-Hailing Systems

In the early days of the study, centralized taxi modes were proposed. Aïvodji et al. [10] have proposed SRide in 2018. It's a ride-sharing system based on homomorphic encryption. Because of the complex process and homomorphic encryption, SRide does not work well. He et al. [11] have proposed a matching system based on the real distance between the drivers and the passengers. Sherif et al. [1] used group signature in their system in 2017.

Different from these previous research. Many researchers are focusing on the blockchain. Yuan et al. [12] researched the effects of blockchain in ride-hailing.

Li et al. [13] used private Blockchain to build the system. The system consists of a large number of Road Side Units(RSUs). So it is costly owing to the large number of RSUs required in the system. Baza et al. [14,15] have proposed a ride-sharing system named B-Ride.

B-Ride is deployed in Ethereum. They used cloaking technology to ensure the privacy of users' locations. Passengers and drivers communicate via blockchain.

2.2 Blockchain Technology and Smart Contract

Satoshi created Bitcoin in 2008 [16]. As the core technology of Bitcoin, blockchain technology builds the framework of Bitcoin. The blockchain is composed of data blocks in chronological order. The data block consists of a data area and a pointer. The pointer shows the location of the previous block. There are much research about the blockchain network. Myers et al. [17] and Ben-Sasson et al. [18] proposed decentralized anonymous Bitcoin payment systems. The zero-knowledge proof technology was used in these systems to protect users' privacy. A new protocol consensus algorithm was proposed by Ripple [19].The algorithm based on UNLs However, the data on the blockchain is open to everyone or open to the data owner. It doesn't have an efficient fine-grained control method to the data of the blockchain.

2.3 Attribute-Based Encryption

The fuzzy identity-based encryption (IBE) was proposed by Sahai and Waters [20] in 2005. Goyal et al. defines attribute-based encryption(ABE). Fine-grained access control was allowed by attribute-based encryption. If the attributes of the user conforms to the access control, user will decrypt ciphertext. The user's identity is no longer important in the decryption process, instead of his attributes. So, ABE implements fine-grained access control to data.

Both ciphertext policy attribute-based encryption(CP-ABE) and key policy attribute-based encryption(KP-ABE) belong to ABE. In CP-ABE, the ciphertext is related to the access control policies, and attribute is related to the key. The situation is just on the contrary in KP-ABE. Thus, Bethencourt et al. [11] And Ibraimi et al. [21] used tree structure to build access policy. However, the complexity of the tree structure is proportional to the time spent on encryption and decryption.

2.4 Zero Knowledge Set Membership Proof (ZKSM)

Zero Knowledge Proofs (ZKP) is an essential cryptographic technique. Many researchers have tried to implement ZKP by computer. ING [22] proposed Zero Knowledge Range Proofs (ZKRP) in 2017. In ZKRP, secret values were permitted in a certain interval. But ZKRP does not support generic collections.

ZKSM solves this problem perfectly. Camenisch et al. [23] use the generic set as the secret value to build ZKSM. In other word, ZKSM has a wide range of applications as opposed to ZKRP.

3   System Mode

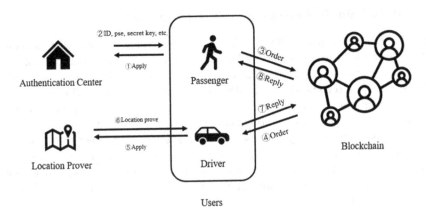

Fig. 1. Decentralized blockchain-based ride-hailing mode.

A decentralized blockchain-based ride-hailing mode is illustrated in Fig. 1. There are three roles in our system mode:

1. Passenger: The passenger means someone who needs ride-hailing service. The passenger generates a ride-hailing message which contains an attribute access tree and ciphertext. The tree contains the attributes of the driver that the passenger is looking for. The ciphertext contains the passenger's location information and contact information.

2. Driver: The drivers means someone who provides ride-hailing service. The driver is responsible for receiving the order of passenger from the blockchain. After obtaining the passenger's information, if the driver's attributes meet the passenger's requirement, the driver will decrypt the requirement to decide whether take the order. If the driver takes the order, the driver will add a random number to the end of the decrypted message.

3. Location Prover(LP): The LP is deployed in different locations of the road as an equipment. In general, the Road Side Unit (RSU) is always used as the LP. The responsibility of the LP is to verify the location of the driver. After the driver arrives at the location, the driver requests confirmation of the location from the LP. If the address is correct, then the LP will sign the location of the driver.

4. Authentication Center(AC): AC is a trusted third party. Each user in the system can initiate a request to the AC. AC distributes attribute sets and secret keys to the users of this mode. It can also authenticate the user's identity.

4   Method

This mode consists of the following four phases: matching phase, deposit payment phase, fair payment phase, and reputation calculation phase.

4.1   Matching Phase

This section proposes the way how passengers match drivers on public blockchain. Otherwise, there are three necessary steps for bidding and selection. This section proposes the way how passengers match drivers on public blockchain. Algorithm 1 and Algorithm 2 summarizes the process of the encryption and decryption.

Algorithm 1. Encryption of information

Require: security parameter λ, κ; a set of attribute sets of drivers S_{system}; a new message m; the identity of driver id; the pseudonym of driver pse.
Ensure: The ciphertext C.
1: $Setup_{att}(1^\lambda) \rightarrow (PK, MK)$
2: $Setup_{sig}(1^\kappa) \rightarrow pp$ // pp means a public parameter which is used to generate sercet key and public key
3: $Keygen_{att}(MK, S) \rightarrow SK$ // S means a set of attributes. SK is the attribute sercet key related to S.
4: If the id is verified and pse is unique then $Keygen(pp, pse) \rightarrow (pk, sk)$
5: Selecting $S_{passenger} \in S_{system}$, $S_{passenger} \rightarrow T$ // $S_{passenger}$ means a set of the driver's attributes which the passenger want. T means the tree structure. Using attributes to construct tree structure.
6: $Enc_{att}(PK, m, T) \rightarrow C$

Algorithm 2. Decryption of information

Require: the master key MK, a set of driver's attributes S_{driver}. The ciphertext C
Ensure: The message m.
1: $Keygen_{att}(MK, S_{driver}) \rightarrow SK_{driver}$
2: $Dec_{att}(C, SK_{driver}) \rightarrow m$ //If S_{driver} meet the requirement of the passenger , then the driver can decrypt the information

---

Request from the Passenger. The passenger generates their ride information. The information includes the starting point of the trip, end point of the trip, and the passenger's location. Then the passenger chooses the set of attributes of the driver who they want. They utilize it to build an access policy with a tree structure. This structure is used to encrypt the ride information. After getting the ciphertext, the passenger submits ride information to the blockchain.

Reply from the Driver. If the driver's attributes match the access policy, the driver can decrypt the ciphertext and get the ride information from the passenger. The driver has the right to decide whether to accept the order or not. If the driver decides to accept the order, the driver will encrypt the unit price and the ride information with the public key of the passenger. Then the driver submits the ciphertext to the blockchain.

Matching Completed. After the passenger obtains the driver's unit price from the blockchain, the passenger compares all drivers' unit price and past reputation. Finally, the passengers select a qualified driver to communicate via blockchain.

4.2 Deposit Payment Phase

This section introduces a deposit payment protocol that prohibits malicious drivers and passengers from giving their respective ride offers or requests. The cost of malicious behavior increases due to the deposit. In most schemes, this part is supervised by a trusted third party. However, the third party is not always credible. In other words, the entire system cannot remain secure when the third party is attacked. Based on this situation, a ride-hailing deposit payment scheme was proposed. The Passenger publishes deposit payment contract on the blockchain. The driver sends D deposit to the smart contract when the driver arrives at the designated location. After paying the D deposit, the driver sends the request of the location authentication to the LP. If the driver doesn't arrive the designated location, the passenger will receive the deposit directly from the contract. This workflow of the deposit phase is shown in Fig. 2.

Initialization. The passenger plans to generate their deposit payments by these following steps:

1) The passenger defines a location set ϕ , let $\phi \in \{ l_1, \cdots, l_k \}$. The set ϕ should include all pick-up locations.
2) The passenger chooses a number $x \in Z_p$ randomly, then compute $y \in g^x$, g is the generator of Z_p.
3) Computes $A_i = g^{\frac{1}{(x+i)}}, i \in \phi$.
4) Generates a contract.

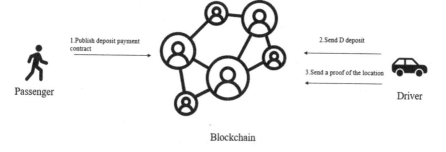

Fig. 2. Workflow of the deposit payment phase.

Driver Deposit and Claim. Upon arrival at the pick-up location, the driver uses Zero Knowledge member Set Membership Proof to prove that he or she has arrived:

1) Driver picks $v \in Z_p$ and computes $V = (A_{l_0^{(p)}})^v$, $A_{l_0^{(p)}}$ is the signature on $l_0^{(p)}$. Then, the driver computes $C = g^{l_0^{(p)}} h^l$.

2) The location is confirmed by the LP. If the location is correct, then LP will compute $C' = Cg^{-l_0^{(r)}} = g^{l_0^{(r)}} h^l g^{-l_0^{(r)}} = h^l$.

3) Driver chooses three numbers $s, t, m \in Z_p$ randomly, then computes $a = e(V, g)^{-s} \cdot e(g, g)^t$, $Q = g^s h^m$.

4) When the proof is received, the proof will be verified. If the proof belongs to the driver selected by the passenger and the time is validated. the commitment C is proved by the following statement : $PK \left\{ (l_0^{(r)}, \iota, v) : C = g^{l_0^{(r)}} h^\iota \wedge V = g^{\frac{v}{x+l_0^{(r)}}} \right\}$.

Blockchain will check the following equation: $Q = C^c h^{z_\iota} g^{z_l}$ and $a = e(V, y)^c \cdot e(V, g)^{-z_l} \cdot e(g, g)^{z_v}$. If the equation is correct, then this proof is correct

Users Authentication. The public key signature is used to prevent impersonation. The driver picks an integer $S \in Z_p$ randomly as a secret number then sends it to the passenger. The passenger uses the private key to sign S then generates $(\sigma_{sk(p)}(S))$. The passenger sends $(S \,||\, \sigma_{sk(p)}(S))$ to the driver. The driver verifies whether the signature is valid.

4.3 Fair Payment Phase

The journey is divided into many small parts. For each part traveled, the passenger must pay the driver the corresponding amount of money. The deposit stored previously by the passenger is paid as the price of the first part. After this, the driver asks the passenger for payment for every part traveled. The passenger confirms whether the driving distance is correct. If the distance is correct, the driver and the passenger sign this message and upload it to the smart contract. At the same time, the fare is transferred to the driver's account. If the passenger does not pay the money, the driver can terminate the trip at any time. This payment method ensures fairness for both users.

4.4 Reputation Calculation Phase

In this mode, the smart contract is also used to calculate the user's reputation value. We define the reputation score as β_d its value consists by β_d^{AP} and β_d^{AD}. When the driver arrives at the agreed location, β_d^{AP} increases. the second one β_d^{AD} increases after the trip is finished. Then the system calculates $\beta_d = \frac{\beta_d^{AP}}{\beta_d^{AD}}$. If $\beta_d = 1$ holds , then $\beta_d^{AP} = \beta_d^{AD}$. It indicates that the driver complete all orders. If $\beta_d < 1$, then some orders of the driver are not completed.

5 Performance Evaluations

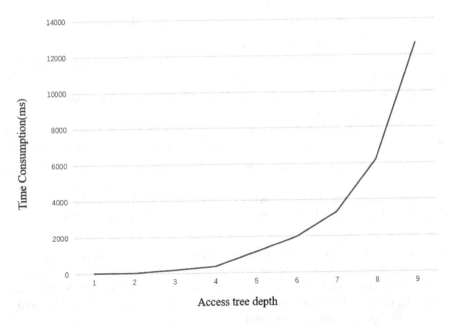

Fig. 3. Time of CP-ABE with a different access tree depth.

In this section, the performance of attribute encryption and smart contracts is evaluated. For attribute encryption, the time spent on encryption is a very important metric. We tested the encryption time for different depths of the attribute access tree and the different attribute complexities. However, the most important metric for smart contracts in Ethereum is the consumption of gas. The consumption gas represents the fee which is required in the contract. The gas value in the contract should be as low as possible.

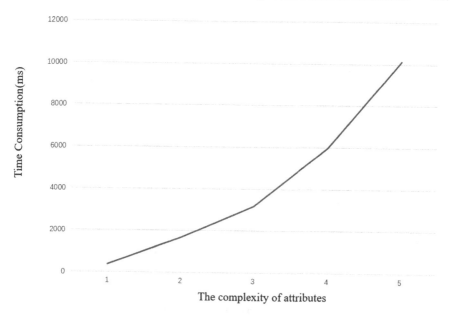

Fig. 4. Time of CP-ABE with different complexity of attributes.

Table 1. Precompiled contract name and address

Precompiled contract name	Features	Address	Gas cost
bn256Add()	Addition on elliptic curve	0×6	500
bn256ScalarMul()	Scalar multiplication on elliptic curve	0×7	40000
bn256Pairing()	Checking pairing equation on curve	0×8	100000 + 80000 * k

5.1   The Time Cost of the Attribute Encryption

We simulated the encryption phase on a personal computer with a 2.80 GHz Core i7-7700 CPU Intel, 24.0 GB RAM and 64-bit version of the Windows 10 operating system. The code of CP-ABE is coded in Java. We develop CP-ABE in Java Runtime Environment 1.8. The bilinear pairs in this mode are constructed with elliptic curves. We define all parent nodes in the access tree to have two child nodes. Tree access structure control is used for the encryption of our taxi solution. The relationship between the time consumption of CP-ABE and the depth of access tree is shown in Fig. 3. For instance, the depth of the access policy [[Man and 7 years driving experience] or [Woman and 7 years driving experience]] is three. The depth of [Man and 7 years driving experience] is two. It is easy to see that the time consumption of CP-ABE increases with the increasing

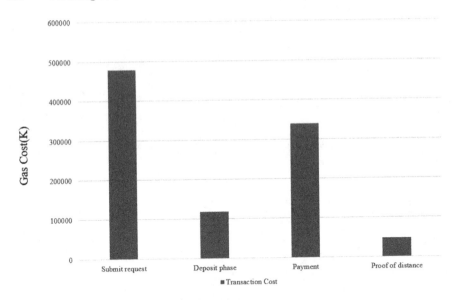

Fig. 5. Passenger's gas cost.

Table 2. Comparison of various taxi models

	Architecture	Rider's privacy	Trust	Fair payment	Transparency	Select the driver's attributes
Current RSS	Centralized	✗	✓	✗	✗	✗
SRide	Centralized	✓	✗	✗	✗	✗
Co-utile	Decentralized	✓	✗	✗	✗	✗
DACSEE	Blockchain	✗	✗	✗	✓	✗
Arcade City	Blockchain	✗	✗	✗	✓	✗
B-Ride	Blockchain	✓	✓	✓	✓	✗
Our mode	Blockchain	✓	✓	✓	✓	✓

depth of the attribute tree. For passengers, if they choose too many attributes of driver. The time consumption of the system will increase significantly. Therefore, passengers should choose the number of attributes appropriately according to their time cost. The relationship between the time consumption of CP-ABE and the complexity of the attributes is shown in Fig. 4. The complexity of the attributes represents the number of nodes other than the root and leaf nodes. It is simple to see the exponential growth between the encryption time and the complexity of attributes.

5.2 The Gas Cost of This Mode

Gas is used as the cost of the transaction in Ethereum. All smart contracts in this mode are coded in Solidity. However, if ZKSM is coded into the contract, it will

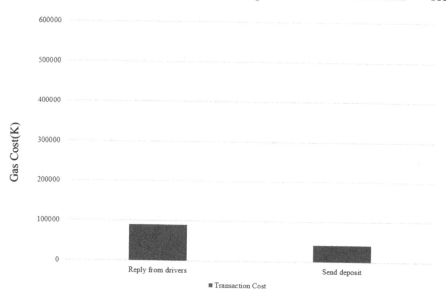

Fig. 6. Driver's gas cost.

consume a lot of gas. We can save a lot of gas by using the precompiled contracts of Ethereum Virtual Machine. The precompiled contracts are shown in Table 1. Gas is spent respectively on the transaction cost and execution cost. Execution cost includes the overhead of storing global variables and the cost of method calls. But, transaction cost is related to the length of the compiled contract code. The value of transaction cost and execution cost should be constant for each execution of the same contract. The gas consumption of drivers and passengers is shown in Fig. 5 and Fig. 6. The cost of the matching phase is about 560K gas. The cost of the deposit phase is about 150K. The cost of the payment phase is about 330K. The cost of the distance proof is about 30K. The mode is used to compare with other modes. The result is shown in Table 2. It is not difficult to see that this mode ensures privacy when it can select the attributes of the driver.

6   Conclusions

In this paper, we propose a decentralized blockchain-based ride-hailing mode with attribute encryption. The blockchain and smart contract are applied to improve the transparency of system. The attribute encryption technology is used to make passengers can select the driver who they want. Passengers can choose the driver's attributes according to their needs. The Experiments and analysises are conducted to evaluate this mode. The results indicate that mode is practical and efficient.

References

1. Sherif, A.B., Rabieh, K., Mahmoud, M.M., Liang, X.: Privacy-preserving ride sharing scheme for autonomous vehicles in big data era. IEEE IoT J. **4**(2), 611–618 (2016)
2. Cao, B., Alarabi, L., Mokbel, M. F., Basalamah, A.: SHAREK: a scalable dynamic ride sharing system. In 2015 16th IEEE International Conference on Mobile Data Management, vol. 1, pp. 4–13. IEEE (2015)
3. Engelhardt, R., Dandl, F., Bilali, A., Bogenberger, K.: Quantifying the benefits of autonomous on-demand ride-pooling: a simulation study for Munich, Germany. In: 2019 IEEE Intelligent Transportation Systems Conference (ITSC), pp. 2992–2997. IEEE (2019)
4. Dandl, F., Bogenberger, K.: Comparing future autonomous electric taxis with an existing free-floating carsharing system. IEEE Trans. Intell. Transp. Syst. **20**(6), 2037–2047 (2018)
5. Shi, J., Gao, Y., Wang, W., Yu, N., Ioannou, P.A.: Operating electric vehicle fleet for ride-hailing services with reinforcement learning. IEEE Trans. Intell. Transp. Syst. **21**(11), 4822–4834 (2019)
6. Guo, G., Xu, Y.: A deep reinforcement learning approach to ride-sharing vehicle dispatching in autonomous mobility-on-demand systems. IEEE Intell. Transp. Syst. Mag. **14**(1), 128–140 (2022)
7. Lam, A.Y., Leung, Y.W., Chu, X.: Autonomous-vehicle public transportation system: scheduling and admission control. IEEE Trans. Intell. Transp. Syst. **17**(5), 1210–1226 (2016)
8. Zhu, M., Liu, X.Y., Wang, X.: An online ride-sharing path-planning strategy for public vehicle systems. IEEE Trans. Intell. Transp. Syst. **20**(2), 616–627 (2018)
9. Zeng, W., Han, Y., Sun, W., Xie, S.: Exploring the ridesharing efficiency of taxi services. IEEE Access **8**, 160396–160406 (2020)
10. Aïvodji, U.M., Huguenin, K., Huguet, M.J., Killijian, M.O.: SRide: a privacy-preserving ridesharing system. In: Proceedings of the 11th ACM Conference on Security and Privacy in Wireless and Mobile Networks, pp. 40–50 (2018)
11. He, Y., Ni, J., Wang, X., Niu, B., Li, F., Shen, X.: Privacy-preserving partner selection for ride-sharing services. IEEE Trans. Veh. Technol. **67**(7), 5994–6005 (2018)
12. Yuan, Y., Wang, F.Y.: Towards blockchain-based intelligent transportation systems. In: 2016 IEEE 19th international conference on intelligent transportation systems (ITSC), pp. 2663–2668. IEEE (2016)
13. Li, M., Zhu, L., Lin, X.: Efficient and privacy-preserving carpooling using blockchain-assisted vehicular fog computing. IEEE IoT J. **6**(3), 4573–4584 (2018)
14. Baza, M., Lasla, N., Mahmoud, M.M., Srivastava, G., Abdallah, M.: B-ride: ride sharing with privacy-preservation, trust and fair payment atop public blockchain. IEEE Trans. Netw. Sci. Eng. **8**(2), 1214–1229 (2019)
15. Baza, M., Mahmoud, M., Srivastava, G., Alasmary, W., Younis, M.: A light blockchain-powered privacy-preserving organization scheme for ride sharing services. In: 2020 IEEE 91st Vehicular Technology Conference (VTC2020-Spring), pp. 1–6. IEEE. (2020)
16. Nakamoto, S.: Bitcoin: A peer-to-peer electronic cash system (2008)
17. Miers, I., Garman, C., Green, M., Rubin, A.D.: Zerocoin: anonymous distributed e-cash from bitcoin. In: 2013 IEEE Symposium on Security and Privacy, pp. 397–411. IEEE (2013)

18. Sasson, E.B., et al.: Zerocash: decentralized anonymous payments from bitcoin. In 2014 IEEE Symposium on Security and Privacy, pp. 459–474. IEEE (2014)
19. Schwartz, D., Youngs, N., Britto, A.: The ripple protocol consensus algorithm. Ripple Labs Inc White Pap. 5(8), 151 (2014)
20. Sahai, A., Waters, B.: Fuzzy identity-based encryption. In: Cramer, R. (ed.) EURO-CRYPT 2005. LNCS, vol. 3494, pp. 457–473. Springer, Heidelberg (2005). https://doi.org/10.1007/11426639_27
21. Ibraimi, L., Petkovic, M., Nikova, S., Hartel, P., Jonker, W.: Ciphertext-policy attribute-based threshold decryption with flexible delegation and revocation of user attributes. IEEE Trans. Image process (2009)
22. Koens, T., Ramaekers, C., Van Wijk, C.: Efficient zero-knowledge range proofs in ethereum. ING, blockchain@ing.com (2018)
23. Camenisch, J., Chaabouni, R., Shelat, A.: Efficient protocols for set membership and range proofs. In: Pieprzyk, J. (ed.) ASIACRYPT 2008. LNCS, vol. 5350, pp. 234–252. Springer, Heidelberg (2008). https://doi.org/10.1007/978-3-540-89255-7_15

Post-quantum Privacy-Preserving Aggregation in Federated Learning Based on Lattice

Ruozhou Zuo[1,2], Haibo Tian[1,2], Zhiyuan An[1,2], and Fangguo Zhang[1,2(✉)]

[1] School of Computer Science and Engineering, Sun Yat-sen University,
Guangzhou 510006, China
`isszhfg@mail.sysu.edu.cn`
[2] Guangdong Key Laboratory of Information Security Technology,
Guangzhou 510006, China

Abstract. With the fast growth of quantum computers in recent years, the use of post-quantum cryptography has steadily become vital. In the privacy-preserving aggregation of federated learning, different cryptographic primitives, such as encryption, key agreement, digital signature, secret-sharing, and pseudorandom generator, may be used to protect users' privacy. However, in the original privacy-preserving aggregation protocol, the classical cryptographic primitives are vulnerable to quantum attacks. Bonawitz et al. presented the SecAgg (Secure Aggregation) protocol, which is based on double-masking MPC (Multi-Party Computation). On this basis, we took advantage of the structure of the original protocol and the properties of lattice cryptography to apply lattice cryptography schemes to the protocol and presented a lattice-based post-quantum privacy-preserving aggregation protocol, which can withstand quantum attacks.

Keywords: Privacy-preserving · Secure aggregation · Post-quantum cryptography · Federated learning · Lattice cryptography

1 Introduction

Federated learning [1] is a model of machine learning in which multiple parties participate in joint computation. There is a whole set of users and a central server in this configuration. In federated learning, the central server has a global model that has been educated over numerous learning cycles. The global model is first given to all users during one learning round. Users then update the local model with the global model, train the local model with local data, and send the model gradient back to the central server for aggregation while maintaining anonymity, a process known as secure aggregation [2].

In the protocol of SecAgg, a series of cryptography primitives are used, including secret-sharing, key agreement, digital signature, authenticated encryption, pseudo-random generator, etc. However, attacks on the cryptographic primitives involved were not given any thought in the original protocol. Over recent years, quantum computers have developed rapidly, and different quantum computing algorithms, such as the Shor algorithm [3], have been able to pose significant threats to some mathematical problems which are used to build classical cryptography schemes, such as large integer decomposition and discrete logarithm problem. The secure aggregation protocol (SecAgg) introduced by Bonawitz et al. includes two variants of the protocol, the semi-honest model and the malicious model. The digital signature is included in the malicious model to confirm the user's identity. In the remainder of the study, we shall concentrate on the malicious model for simplicity. Several post-quantum cryptography algorithms are examined to post-quantum secure the privacy-preserving aggregation protocol. The realization of quantum cryptography mainly includes the following four approaches [4]: hash-based, code-based, multivariate-based, and lattice-based. The representative cryptographic algorithms of these four methods are Merkle hash tree signature, McEliece, Rainbow, and NTRU series. Other techniques, like isogeny-based cryptography [5], are also available. We chose lattice-based encryption techniques to create the post-quantum privacy-preserving aggregation protocol because they are faster to compute, have reduced communication costs, and can be utilized to build a variety of cryptographic applications.

Our Contributions: We attempted to improve the original privacy-preserving aggregation protocol using lattice-based cryptographic methods, encountered and addressed several adaption issues, and eventually proposed a secure aggregation protocol with an anti-quantum attacks function.

Organization: The rest of this research is organized as follows. The Sect. 2 presents the primitives of cryptography that we used. Section 3 describes an enhanced lattice-based privacy-preserving aggregation approach for the post-quantum period. Section 4 simulates the protocol and compares its security and performance to the original protocol.

2   Cryptographic Primitives

2.1   Secret Sharing

To address the issues of dropping out, we need to use the secret-sharing technology. In this study, we take Shamir's secret-sharing algorithm [6] as an example. The algorithm consists of two parts. The first is the secret distribution, that is $(u, s_u)_{u \in U} \leftarrow SS.share(s, t, u)$. It separates the user's secret s into n pieces and distributes them to n users. It is specifically implemented in the following ways:

$$F(x_i) = [s + a_1 x_i^1 + a_2 x_i^2 + ... + a_{t-1} x_i^{t-1}] \ mod \ (p), \ i = 1, 2, ..., n \quad (1)$$

where s is the secret, a_i is a random number less than p, x_i is the user ID, and $f(x_i)$ is the secret share of each user. The second part is reconstruction, that is, $s \leftarrow SS.Recon((u, s_u)_{u \in U})$. To reconstruct secret s, at least t users need to provide their shares of the secret s, i.e. $|U| \geq t$. To be specific, the following equations should be constructed first:

$$\begin{cases} F(x_{i_1}) = [s + a_1 x_{i_1}^1 + a_2 x_{i_1}^2 + ... + a_{t-1} x_{i_1}^{t-1}] \bmod (p), \\ F(x_{i_2}) = [s + a_1 x_{i_2}^1 + a_2 x_{i_2}^2 + ... + a_{t-1} x_{i_2}^{t-1}] \bmod (p), \\ ... \\ F(x_{i_t}) = [s + a_1 x_{i_t}^1 + a_2 x_{i_t}^2 + ... + a_{t-1} x_{i_t}^{t-1}] \bmod (p). \end{cases} \quad (2)$$

By solving the above equations, we can obtain the secret s.

2.2 Key Agreement

We apply the Frodo [7] key exchange based on reconciliation. In this study, we take the algorithm in [8] as an example. The key agreement algorithm is as follows (Fig. 1):

Initiator		Responder
Generate small private key S_i		
Generate small private noise E_i		
Compute public key $B_i = A \cdot S_i + E_i$	$\xrightarrow{B_i}$	Generate small private key S_r
		Generate small private noise E_r
		Compute public key $B_r = S_r \cdot A + E_r$
		Generate small private noise E_r'
		Compute value $V_r = S_r \cdot B_i + E_r'$
Compute value $V_i = B_r \cdot S_i$	$\xleftarrow{B_r, C}$	Compute check field $C = KA.check(V_r)$
Extract secret key $K = KA.rec(V_i, C)$		Extract secret key $K = KA.extract(V_r)$

Fig. 1. LWE key exchange with public matrix A

Where S_i, E_i, S_r, E_r and E_r' are all matrix with small entries sampled from a probability distribution χ over $\mathbb{Z}/q\mathbb{Z}$.

The key extraction is executed by the function $K_r \leftarrow KA.extract(V_r)$, and the (i, j)-th entry of the shared secret key is computed as follows:

$$K_r[i, j] = Round\left(\frac{2^B}{q} V_r[i, j]\right) \bmod 2^B \quad (3)$$

The check field is computed by the function $C \leftarrow KA.check(V_r)$, and the (i, j)-th entry of the check field is computed as follows:

$$C[i, j] = Floor\left(\frac{2^{B+1}}{q} V_r[i, j]\right) \bmod 2 \quad (4)$$

The reconciliation is executed by the function $K_i \leftarrow KA.rec(V_i, C)$, and the (i, j)-th entry of the shared secret key obtained from reconciliation is computed as follows:

$$K_i[i, j] = Round\left(\frac{2^B}{q} V_i[i, j] + \frac{1}{4}(2C[i, j] - 1)\right) \bmod 2^B \quad (5)$$

So that $K = Rec(V_i, C) = Extract(V_r)$, the key agreement is completed.

As shown above, there is a considerable difference between the lattice-based key agreement algorithm and the classical Diffie-Hellman [9] key agreement algorithm: It cannot be completed in a single round of communication, which is the primary issue to be addressed, and may result in a greater cost of communication and a higher percentage of drop-out. Section 3 will explain how to solve it.

2.3 Digital Signature

A digital signature employs asymmetric cryptography (public-key cryptography), in which the sender uses the private key to encrypt data and the recipient uses the matching public key to decode data. In this article, we use a lattice-based post-quantum digital signature, called FALCON [10]. For simplicity, we suppose it has the following functions: packet identification, denial prevention, and forgery prevention. It is made up of three algorithms. First is the parameter generation algorithm, i.e. $(d_u^{SK}, d_u^{PK}) \leftarrow SIG.gen(\kappa)(\kappa$ is a security parameter), which is used to produce a pair of keys (d_u^{SK}, d_u^{PK}) for a user $u \in U$. Second is the sign algorithm, i.e. $\sigma_u \leftarrow SIG.sign(d_u^{SK}, m)$(m is the message), which produces a signature σ_u. Third is the verification algorithm, i.e. $\{True, False\} \leftarrow SIG.ver(d_u^{PK}, m, \sigma_u)$, which is used to verify the signature.

2.4 Authenticated Encryption

Authentication encryption is used to offer identity authentication while also ensuring data confidentiality and integrity during encryption. The majority of authentication encryption systems employ both encryption and MAC. The Grover algorithm [11] can root the complexity of the symmetric cryptographic scheme, i.e. reduce the effective length of the key to half of the original, and reduce the computational complexity of the original $O(2^n)$ to $O(2^{n/2})$. As a result, it still needs a calculation cost of the order of 2^{128} using quantum computers to crack AES-256, i.e. AES-256 still has 128-bit security under quantum attacks. In this study, we used AES-256 [12] as the cryptographic primitive of authentication encryption.

This section contains two algorithms. First is the encryption algorithm, i.e. $c \leftarrow AE.enc(k, m)$, which is applied to encrypt data m with a key k and get the encrypted data c. Second is the decryption algorithm, i.e. $\{m, \bot\} \leftarrow AE.dec(k, c)$(where $\bot$ means decryption failed), which is used to decrypt the ciphertext c with the same key k in encryption.

2.5 Pseudorandom Generator

The pseudorandom generator is primarily dependent on a seed to create as many uniformly random pseudorandom sequences as feasible. The main algorithm is $o \leftarrow PRG(s)$, whose output is a vector of values o while taking a seed s as input. For the same reason, we apply a post-quantum PRG, e.g. in [13].

3   PPABoL

We call our protocol PPABoL (Privacy-Preserving Aggregation Based on Lattice). We met a problem while trying to apply the lattice-based key agreement scheme. SecAgg uses the standard Diffie-Hellman Key Agreement, which may be completed in a single round of communication. However, as demonstrated in Sect. 2.2, we were unable to find a lattice-based scheme that could complete key agreement in one round of communication while ensuring efficiency and security, resulting in our protocol having one more round of communication than the baseline in [2], thus increasing communication cost and drop rate. We will discuss how to address this issue.

3.1   The SecAgg

For comparison, we will first introduce SecAgg, which is the original protocol based on double-masking MPC (Multi-Party Computation), as follows:

The SecAgg (Secure Aggregation)

Round 1:

User u:

1) $(c_u^{PK}, c_u^{SK}) \leftarrow KA.gen(pp)$.

2) $(s_u^{PK}, s_u^{SK}) \leftarrow KA.gen(pp)$.

3) $\sigma_u \leftarrow SIG.sign(d_u^{SK}, c_u^{PK}||s_u^{PK})$.

4) Send $(c_u^{PK}||s_u^{PK}||\sigma_u) \rightarrow$ server.

Server:

1) Collect at least t messages, i.e. $\{(c_v^{PK}||s_v^{PK}||\sigma_v)|v \in U_1, |U_1| \geq t\}$.

2) And broadcast the messages to all users.

Round 2:

User u:

1) Receive the messages, ensure that $|U_1| \geq t$, and verify every σ_v.

2) Generate the seed $b_u \leftarrow \mathbb{F}$.

3) $\{(v, s_{u,v}^{sk})\}_{v \in U_1} \leftarrow SS.share(s_u^{SK}, t, U_1)$.

4) $\{(v, b_{u,v})\}_{v \in U_1} \leftarrow SS.share(b_u, t, U_1)$.

5) For every $v \in U_1 \setminus u$,

encrypt $e_{u,v} \leftarrow AE.enc(KA.agree(c_u^{SK}, c_v^{PK}), u||v||s_{u,v}^{sk}||b_{u,v})$.

6) Send $e_{u,v} \rightarrow$ server.

Server:

1) Collect at least $t \times (|U_1 - 1|)$ messages,

i.e. $\{e_{u,v}|u \in U_2, |U_2| \geq t, v \in U_1 \setminus u\}$.

2) For every $v \in U_2 \setminus u$, send$\{e_{u,v}|u \in U_2, |U_2| \geq t\}$.

The SecAgg (Secure Aggregation) Part.2

Round 3:

User u:

1) Receive the messages, ensure that $|U_2| \geq t$.

2) For every $v \in U_2 \setminus u$, compute $s_{u,v} \leftarrow KA.agree(s_u^{SK}, s_v^{PK})$.

3) Compute $p_{u,v} = \Delta_{u,v} \cdot PRG(s_{u,v})$,

where $\Delta_{u,v} = 1$ when $u < v$ and -1 otherwise. Let $p_{u,u} = 0$.

4) Compute $p_u = PRG(b_u)$, $y_u \leftarrow x_u + p_u + \sum_{v \in U_2} p_{u,v}(\bmod R)$.

5) Send $y_u \rightarrow$ server.

Server:

1) Collect at least t messages, i.e. $\{y_u | u \in U_3, |U_3| \geq t\}$.

2) Broadcast the list U_3 to all users.

Round 4:

User u:

1) Receive the messages, ensure that $|U_3| \geq t$.

2) Compute $\sigma_u' \leftarrow SIG.sign(d_u^{SK}, U_3)$.

3) Send $\sigma_u' \rightarrow server$.

Server:

1) Collect at least t messages, i.e. $\{(v, \sigma_v') | v \in U_4, |U_4| \geq t\}$.

2) For every $v \in U_4$, send $\{(u, \sigma_u') | u \in U_4, |U_4| \geq t\}$.

Round 5:

User u:

1) Receive the messages, ensure that $|U_4| \geq t$, and verify every σ_v'.

2) For every $v \in U_2 \setminus u$,

decrypt $v' || u' || s_{v,u}^{sk} || b_{v,u} \leftarrow AE.dec(KA.agree(c_u^{SK}, c_v^{PK}), e_{v,u})$.

3) Send $\{s_{v,u}^{sk} | v \in U_2 \setminus U_3\} and \{b_{v,u} | v \in U_3\} \rightarrow$ server.

Server:

1) Collect at least t messages,

i.e. $\{s_{v,u}^{sk} | v \in U_2 \setminus U_3, u \in U_5\} \{b_{v,u} | v \in U_3, u \in U_5\}$.

2) For every $u \in U_2 \setminus U_3$, reconstruct $s_u^{SK}, compute\{p_{v,u} | v \in U_3\}$.

3) For every $u \in U_3$, reconstruct b_u, compute $p_u = PRG(b_u)$.

4) Compute $z = \sum_{u \in U_3} x_u = \sum_{u \in U_3} y_u - \sum_{u \in U_3} p_u + \sum_{u \in U_3, v \in U_2 \setminus U_3} p_{v,u}$.

As depicted in Sect. 3.1, assuming that there is a user u and a user v and there is no drop in the whole process, the five rounds of indirect communication between the two users through the server are approximate as follows:

- Round 1: User u sends its two public keys (referred to here as the first and second key pair for convenience) to user v.
- Round 2: User u splits his first private key (for masking) into n shares through secret-sharing. Then, user u uses the second private key to complete the key agreement with the second public key sent by user v in Round 1, then encrypts n shares with the second key, and sends one of the encrypted shares to user v.

- Round 3: User u completes the first key agreement by using his first private key and user v's first public key and then utilizes this key (i.e. the key created by the first key agreement) to complete a layer of masking and eventually calculates the vector y after two masking rounds.
- Round 4: User u signs the current online user list and sends it to user v.
- Round 5: User u validates user v's signature, decrypts the ciphertext delivered to user u in the second round, reconstructs the secret with shares, and delivers the secret to the server.

We can see from the aforementioned communication process that the first pair of keys create the masking vector by completing the first key agreement in Round 3, whereas the second pair of keys create the communication key by completing the second key agreement. Simultaneously, we discovered that under the key agreement in Sect. 2.2, the responder can acquire the key in the first round of communication, whereas the initiator can obtain the key in the second round. This temporal sequence is identical to the two main agreements in SecAgg, which inspires us.

3.2 PPABoL

To graphically discuss our solution to this problem, we show in Fig. 2 that Alice and Bob conduct one set of key agreement in Sect. 2.2 at the same time and can complete the final key exchange without splitting users into groups of two. This is significant for our PPBoL since it allows us to implement lattice-based key agreements without increasing communication rounds. In Fig. 2, we assume that the user ID of Alice u_A is lower than Bob's ID u_B, and all secret keys are $m \times n$ matrices. The public key pk_A is computed by the equation $pk_A = sk_A \cdot A + E_A$, and the other public key pk'_A is computed by the equation $pk'_A = A \cdot sk_A + E'_A$, where pk_A is an $m \times n$ matrix and pk'_A is an $n \times m$ matrix.

	Alice		Bob
Round 1:	Generate (sk_A, pk_A, pk'_A) if $u_A > u_B$, then $K_A = KA.Extract(sk_A, pk'_B)$ $C_{A \to B} = KA.Check(sk_A, pk_B)$	$\xrightarrow{pk_A,pk'_A}$ $\xleftarrow{pk_B,pk'_B}$	Generate (sk_B, pk_B, pk'_B) if $u_A < u_B$, then $K_B = KA.Extract(sk_B, pk'_A)$ $C_{A \to B} = KA.Check(sk_B, pk'_A)$
Round 2:	if $u_A < u_B$, then $K_A = KA.Rec((sk_A)^T, pk_B, C_{A \leftarrow B})$ So that $K_A == K_B$	$\xrightarrow{C_{A \to B}(u_A > u_B)}$ $\xleftarrow{C_{A \to B}(u_A < u_B)}$	if $u_A > u_B$, then $K_B = KA.Rec((sk_B)^T, pk_A, C_{A \to B})$ So that $K_B == K_A$

Fig. 2. The LWE key exchange in the masking period of PPABoL

In [2], each user is given two pairs of keys for key agreement, one for creating the private key of the symmetric encryption algorithm used to communicate with other users, and the other for generating the first masking code. In the second round of the protocol, symmetric encryption happens, and the masking code is formed in the third round. The key agreement protocol in [7] includes an initiator and a responder. The responder can get the outcome of the key agreement during the first round of communication, but the initiator can only obtain the outcome during the second round. We assume that a user generates two pairs of keys based on the LWE key agreement, which are all in the form of the responder ($m \times n$ matrices). When user u needs to compute the masking vector based on LWE key agreements, he will use the $n \times m$ public key pk_v' received from the other user v if his ID is higher than user v. In this manner, the user can encrypt in the first round of communication using the key agreement result acquired by the key group as a responder and mask private data in the second round of communication using the key agreement result obtained by the key group as an initiator. Aggregation can therefore be achieved without affecting the protocol's communication cycles or security, while applying the same program for all users. The specific protocol is as follows:

The Privacy-Preserving Aggregation Based on Lattice Part.1

Round 1:

User u:

1) Generate two sets of keys for key agreement as in Fig.2,

i.e. $\{(i_u^{PK}, i_u^{PK'}, i_u^{SK}) || (r_u^{PK}, r_u^{PK'}, r_u^{SK})\}$.

2) Compute $\sigma_u \leftarrow SIG.sign(d_u^{SK}, i_u^{PK} || i_u^{PK'} || r_u^{PK} || r_u^{PK'})$.

3) Send$(i_u^{PK} || i_u^{PK'} || r_u^{PK} || r_u^{PK'} || \sigma_u) \rightarrow$ server.

Server:

1) Collect at least t messages.

2) And broadcast the messages to all users.

Round 2:

User u:

1) Receive the messages, ensure that $|U_1| \geq t$, and verify every σ_v.

2) Generate the seed $b_u \leftarrow \mathbb{F}$.

3) Compute $\{(v, i_{u,v}^{sk})\}_{v \in U_1} \leftarrow SS.share(i_u^{SK}, t, U_1)$.

4) Compute $\{(v, E_{u,v})\}_{v \in U_1} \leftarrow SS.share(E_i', t, U_1)$.

(E_i' is the error used in computing the check field $C_{u,v}'$, which is necessary for reconstruction of key in Round 5.)

5) Compute $\{(v, b_{u,v})\}_{v \in U_1} \leftarrow SS.share(b_u, t, U_1)$.

6) For every $v \in U_1 \setminus u$, encrypt

$e_{u,v} \leftarrow AE.enc(KA.extract(r_u^{SK}, r_v^{PK'}, u || v || i_{u,v}^{sk} || E_{u,v} || b_{u,v})$.

7) For every $v \in U_1 \setminus u$, compute $C_{u,v} \leftarrow KA.check(r_u^{SK}, r_v^{PK'})$ and if $u > v$, compute $C_{u,v}' \leftarrow KA.check(i_u^{SK}, i_v^{PK'})$.

8) Send $\{e_{u,v} || C_{u,v} || C_{u,v}' | v \in U_1 \setminus u\} \rightarrow$ server.

The Privacy-Preserving Aggregation Based on Lattice Part.2

Server:
1) Collect at least t messages.
2) For every $v \in U_2 \setminus u$, send$\{(e_{u,v}||C_{u,v}||C'_{u,v})|u \in U_2, |U_2| \geq t\}$.

Round 3:
User u:
1) Receive the messages, ensure that $|U_2| \geq t$.
2) For every $v \in U_2 \setminus u$, if $u > v$, compute $r_{u,v} \leftarrow KA.extract(i_u^{SK}, i_v^{PK'})$,
and if $u < v$, compute $r_{u,v} \leftarrow KA.rec((i_u^{SK})^T, i_v^{PK}, C'_{v,u})$.
3) Compute $p_{u,v} = \Delta_{u,v} \cdot PRG(r_{u,v})$,
where $\Delta_{u,v} = 1$ when $u < v$ and -1 otherwise. Let $p_{u,u} = 0$.
4) Compute $p_u = PRG(b_u)$, $y_u \leftarrow x_u + p_u + \sum_{v \in U_2} p_{u,v}(\mod R)$.
5) Send $y_u \rightarrow$ server.
Server:
1) Collect at least t messages, i.e. $\{y_u|u \in U_3, |U_3| \geq t\}$.
2) Broadcast the list U_3 to all users.

Round 4:
User u:
1) Receive the messages, ensure that $|U_3| \geq t$.
2) Compute $\sigma'_u \leftarrow (d_u^{SK}, U_3)$.
3) Send $\sigma'_u \rightarrow server$.
Server:
1) Collect at least t messages, i.e. $\{(v, \sigma'_v)|v \in U_4, |U_4| \geq t\}$.
2) For every $v \in U_4$, send $\{(u, \sigma'_u)|u \in U_4, |U_4| \geq t\}$.

Round 5:
User u:
1) Receive the messages, ensure that $|U_4| \geq t$, and verify every σ'_v.
2) For every $v \in U_2 \setminus u$, decrypt
$v'||u'||i_{v,u}^{sk}||E_{v,u}||b_{v,u} \leftarrow AE.dec(KA.rec((r_u^{SK})^T, r_v^{PK}, C_{v,u}), e_{v,u})$.
3) Send $\{i_{v,u}^{sk}||E_{v,u}|v \in U_2 \setminus U_3\} and \{b_{v,u}|v \in U_3\} \rightarrow$ server.
Server:
1) Collect at least t messages,
i.e. $\{r_{v,u}^{sk}|v \in U_2 \setminus U_3, u \in U_5\}\{b_{v,u}|v \in U_3, u \in U_5\}$.
2) For every $u \in U_2 \setminus U_3$, reconstruct $i_u^{SK}||E'_i, compute\{p_{v,u}|v \in U_3\}$.
3) For every $u \in U_3$, reconstruct b_u, compute $p_u = PRG(b_u)$.
4) Compute $z = \sum_{u \in U_3} x_u = \sum_{u \in U_3} y_u - \sum_{u \in U_3} p_u + \sum_{u \in U_3, v \in U_2 \setminus U_3} p_{v,u}$.

4 Security Estimates and Performance

4.1 Security Estimates

The components of the key agreement application in our protocol change significantly from those in the original protocol. Because the security of the other aspects has been thoroughly examined in [2], we will focus just on the LWE (Learning with Errors) problem and the security of the cryptographic schemes based on it. Because the key agreement and digital signature schemes in our protocol are predicated on the LWE problem, we shall focus on its security. The LWE problem is defined as:

Definition 1. *Given a uniformly randomly generated matrix $A \in \mathbb{Z}_q^{n \times m}$, $s \in \mathbb{Z}_q^n$ and $e \in \mathbb{Z}_q^m$ obey the disturbance distribution χ, $b_i = A_i s + e_i$.*
The Search version of the LWE problem (Search LWE) is: Given multiple sets of (A_i, b_i), find s.
The Decisional LWE problem is to differentiate b_i from uniformly randomly generated vectors.

The LWE problem was proposed by Regev in 2005 [14]. Simultaneously, Regev also proved that under quantum reduction, it is as difficult as variants of SVP (Shortest Vector Problem) with the approximate factor $\widetilde{O}(n/\alpha)$ under the worst-case, where α is a parameter associated with the variance of the disturbance distribution in the LWE instance. Specifically, if there is an effective algorithm for solving LWE problems, then an effective quantum algorithm for solving SVP problems with an approximate factor of $\widetilde{O}(n/\alpha)$ can be discovered. As a result, we consider cryptography schemes based on the LWE problem to be quantum-safe.

4.2 Performance

We made an implementation of both PPABoL and SecAgg in python by the following modules.

- The SS is Shamir's secret-sharing scheme with a 256-bit secret as input which is provided by the "secretsharing" python module.
- The KA is Frodo over the settings in [7] which is executed by ourselves.
- The AE is AES-GCM [15] authenticated encryption with a 256-bit key which is provided by the "Crypto" python module.
- The PRG is the algorithm in [13] where the seed s is taken as the encryption key, which is implemented by ourselves.
- The SIG is the FALCON [10] signature scheme with FALCON-512 settings which are provided by the author.

We run these modules in a 64-bit "Windows 10" system. The CPU is 11th Gen Intel(R) Core(TM) i5-11400H (2.70 GHz, 2.69 GHz) and the RAM is 16 GB. We use the python time evaluation function "time.process_time()" to estimate

324   R. Zuo et al.

the time cost of each module. Under different settings of user number and dimensions, the performance comparison for one round of training is shown below.

As depicted in Table 1, compared with SecAgg, our protocol can resist quantum attacks, and under the maximum setting, the running time of one round is reduced by 23.5% due to the speed of matrix computing. As a matrix is taken as the public key, the communication cost increases by 42.6% under the maximum setting. To decrease communication costs, the key length can be further lowered by using the Ring-LWE-based system. Furthermore, the performance can be improved by DAG and other methods in the future.

Table 1. Comparisons with baseline.

Scheme	Settings		Communication	Running time
	Users number	Dimensions		
PPABoL	50	20000	14,384,936 Bytes	53,238 ms
SecAgg	50	20000	5,056,814 Bytes	64,131 ms
PPABoL	100	40000	38,048,123 Bytes	99,867 ms
SecAgg	100	40000	19,986,715 Bytes	123,293 ms
PPABoL	150	60000	70,989,850 Bytes	186,994 ms
SecAgg	150	60000	44,790,314 Bytes	205,812 ms
PPABoL	200	80000	113,210,753 Bytes	238,421 ms
SecAgg	200	80000	79,466,983 Bytes	294,358 ms
PPABoL	250	100000	179,738,364 Bytes	344,881 ms
SecAgg	250	100000	126,024,836 Bytes	450,826 ms

5   Discussion and Future Work

We proposed a quantum-safe privacy-preserving aggregation protocol, although it can still be improved in several ways.

Reduce the Key Length: In our experiment, the public key is a 752×752 matrix, whose size is too big for large-scale communications. We may minimize the key size even further by improving the parameter selection process. Furthermore, we may employ Ring-LWE-based cryptographic primitives to shorten the length of a public key.

Unite Parameters: In our experiment, We selected the default parameters of chosen schemes without optimization. It is evident that if the parameters of the related cryptographic primitives are unified using acceptable methods, the protocol's cost may be greatly decreased and the security level may be enhanced.

Simplify Communication Network: Our protocol's communication network is as sophisticated as the original version, which surely raises the cost of the communication network and lowers the fault tolerance rate of dropping out.

In [16], B. Choi et al. proposed a communication computation effective secure aggregation for federated learning, which uses an Erdös-Rényi graph to construct the spark random graph. Each pair of FL users is connected with the probability P in such a network. As a result, selecting P results in a trade-off between security and protocol efficiency. Furthermore, we also note that there are other studies on post-quantum privacy-preserving aggregation over lattice.

In [17,18], a cryptography scheme based on HE (Homomorphic Encryption) is applied. In federated learning, aggregation based on HE is simpler in implementation than that based on masking. To aggregate the user's vector, they just need to encrypt it using the HE system and send it to the server. Because of HE's additive homomorphism, the aggregation may be completed by directly adding and decrypting the ciphertext.

6 Conclusion

We proposed a post-quantum privacy-preserving aggregation protocol in federated learning with lattice-based cryptography primitives based on SecAgg and encountered some difficulties along the way, such as the difficulty of completing the key agreement based on the LWE problem in one round of communication. Finally, we were able to fix these issues and make our privacy-preserving aggregation protocol quantum-safe. Furthermore, there are still certain issues with our protocol, such as a huge public-key size, a complex communication network, and so on, that will be addressed in the future.

Acknowledgements. This work is supported by Guangdong Major Project of Basic and Applied Basic Research (2019B030302008) and the National Natural Science Foundation of China (No. 61972429).

References

1. Yang, Q., et al.: Federated machine learning: concept and applications. ACM Trans. Intell. Syst. Technol. (TIST) **10**(2), 1–19 (2019)
2. Bonawitz, K., et al.: Practical secure aggregation for privacy-preserving machine learning. In: Proceedings of the 2017 ACM SIGSAC Conference on Computer and Communications Security (2017)
3. Shor, P.W.: Polynomial-time algorithms for prime factorization and discrete logarithms on a quantum computer. SIAM Rev. **41**(2), 303–332 (1999)
4. Bernstein, D.J.: Introduction to post-quantum cryptography. In: Bernstein, D.J., Buchmann, J., Dahmen, E. (eds.) Post-Quantum Cryptography, pp. 1–14. Springer, Berlin, Heidelberg (2009) . https://doi.org/10.1007/978-3-540-88702-7_1
5. De Feo, L.: Mathematics of isogeny based cryptography. arXiv preprint arXiv:1711.04062 (2017)
6. Shamir, A.: How to share a secret. Commun. ACM **22**(11), 612–613 (1979)
7. Bos, J., et al.: Frodo: Take off the ring! Practical, quantum-secure key exchange from LWE. In: Proceedings of the 2016 ACM SIGSAC Conference on Computer and Communications Security (2016)

8. CYBER: Quantum-Safe Key Exchanges (V1.1.1). ETSI TR 103 570–2017 (2017)
9. Diffie, W., Hellman, M.E.: New directions in cryptography. IEEE Trans. Inf. Theory **22**(6), 644–654 (1976)
10. Fouque, P.-A., et al.: Falcon: fast-Fourier lattice-based compact signatures over NTRU. Submiss. NIST's Post-quantum Cryptogr. Standard. Process. **36**(5), 1–7 (2018)
11. Grover, L.K.: From Schrödinger's equation to the quantum search algorithm. Pramana **56**(2), 333–348 (2001)
12. Dworkin, M.J., et al.: Advanced encryption standard (AES) (2001)
13. Applebaum, B., Cash, D., Peikert, C., Sahai, A.: Fast cryptographic primitives and circular-secure encryption based on hard learning problems. In: Halevi, S. (ed.) CRYPTO 2009. LNCS, vol. 5677, pp. 595–618. Springer, Heidelberg (2009). https://doi.org/10.1007/978-3-642-03356-8_35
14. Regev, O.: On lattices, learning with errors, random linear codes, and cryptography. J. ACM (JACM) **56**(6), 1–40 (2009)
15. Dworkin, M.J.: Recommendation for block cipher modes of operation: Galois/Counter Mode (GCM) and GMAC (2007)
16. Choi, B., et al.: Communication-computation efficient secure aggregation for federated learning. arXiv preprint arXiv:2012.05433 (2020)
17. Alexandru, A.B., Pappas, G.J.: Private weighted sum aggregation for distributed control systems. IFAC-PapersOnLine **53**(2), 11081–11088 (2020)
18. Stripelis, D., et al.: Secure neuroimaging analysis using federated learning with homomorphic encryption. In: 17th International Symposium on Medical Information Processing and Analysis, vol. 12088. SPIE (2021)

Improvised Model for Blockchain in Distributed Cloud Environment

Meeraj Mahendra Gawde[1], Gaurav Choudhary[2], Shishir Kumar Shandilya[1], Rizwan Ur Rahman[1], Hoonyong Park[3], and Ilsun You[4(✉)]

[1] SECURE, Center of Excellence for Cyber Security, VIT University, Bhopal, India
rizwan.ur@vitbhopal.ac.in
[2] DTU Compute, Technical University of Denmark, 2800 Kgs. Lyngby, Denmark
[3] Department of Information Security Engineering, Soonchunhyang University, Asan-si 31538, Korea
[4] Department of Financial Information Security, Kookmin University, Seoul 02707, South Korea
ilsunu@gmail.com

Abstract. In the current era, Blockchain Technology is blooming and growing faster. Blockchain is currently used in soft computing, agriculture, cloud network, healthcare, electronics, and electrical fields. Older technologies are upgraded to increase their reach using Distributed Cloud networks and blockchain. Implementing security for heterogeneous 5G services-based technologies of the MEC is challenging.

In this paper, we propose a blockchain-based distributed cloud security solution that uses technologies such as Digital Signature, RSA algorithm, AES encryption, and a Lookup table to improve the security of blockchain and decrease the traversal time of data in the blockchain. This proposed model is adept at solving the primary concern related to storage and confidentiality in a Distributed Cloud environment.

Keywords: Blockchain · Distributed cloud security · Digital signature · Rivest-Shamir-Adleman (RSA) algorithm · Advanced Encryption Standard (AES) algorithm

1 Introduction

Blockchain, since its launch, has seen a lot of direct and indirect applications. According to a report generated by statista.com, it was found that currently there are more than 80 million active blockchain wallets, whereas, in 2016, there were around 10 million blockchain wallets. Currently, Blockchain is being used in healthcare, supply chain management, Digital markets, and many other private cloud environments. Government of countries like Australia, China, and Japan, are also using Blockchain for identity management, record management, Non-profit organizations, and compliance and regulatory oversights. On the other hand, Distributed Cloud is a newer technology. It is a cloud environment whose infrastructure is dispersed globally and primarily runs services at the network edge [1].

Blockchain is an ever-evolving architecture, and many researchers are modifying this architecture to fit into their existing networks. Recently, technical giants like Amazon and Microsoft have adopted Blockchain as a service architecture for enhancing their products. In the pandemic situation, Blockchain was also used for tracking vaccinations. Several cryptocurrencies, such as Bitcoin, Litecoin, and Altcoin, have also been developed on Blockchain and are currently accepted as digital currency in some foreign countries. On the other hand, the Distributed cloud is used in several systems and software such as InterGrid, Bellagio, Tycoon, Amazon EC2, and Azure. Companies currently implementing distributed cloud are witnessing increased functionality, reliability, and retrieval capacity [2,3].

MEC and other edge computing paradigms facilitate the infrastructure for enhancing the access interfaces to cater to the mobile network's ultra-low latency, real-time ubiquity, security, and privacy aspects. Significant challenges faced by decentralized distributed systems are security and trust. Implementing a secure decentralized distributed system requires solutions that can efficiently ensure the authenticity of participants, provide robust authorization, preserve the participants' privacy, and route messages securely between distributed services. The integration of technology such as Blockchain has solved some of these significant issues, such as creating an immutable distributed ledger, maintaining proper timestamps, and establishing a fault-tolerant network. However, it lacks in maintaining confidentiality and privacy of the information entered into the Blockchain. All the nodes in the network are aware of what information has entered into the Blockchain. Also, the storage requirements for maintaining a distributed ledger such as a blockchain are enormous [4,5].

1.1 Problem Statements and Contributions

Extensive usage of cloud services gave rise to Distributed Cloud Environment, bringing together the power of Edge computing, On-prem environments, and public/private cloud environments. There has been a more significant storage requirement for using blockchain due to which small organizations are not able to use blockchain. Since blockchain uses distributed ledger, there can be some problems related to data privacy. Some researchers have proposed models involving specific alliance standards and privacy extensions, including HD wallets, to anonymize transactions into the network to tackle these issues.

Blockchain has features like immutability, transparency, distributed ledger, and decentralized technology, but it lacks adequate privacy. Though data in blockchain comes with a hash embedded within the blocks to verify the authenticity of the blockchain, this message is visible to everyone present in the network. Companies face problems while sending sensitive information across regions using blockchain.

After doing an in-depth survey about recent developments related to distributed cloud security and blockchain architecture for storing data in the cloud, we can conclude that there are still several weak points, such as the requirement for trusted third-party support, low data security, and large data storage requirements. Unfortunately, there are still no effective and completely optimized solutions available for improving security in the distributed cloud environment.

To solve the problems mentioned above in an optimized manner, we have designed three algorithms. In the Algorithm 1, we used a look-up table to compare the recurring hash values of the data. In the 2 and 3 algorithm, we used the concept of multiple encryption, encoding, and digital signature to improve security while transferring a piece of confidential information through blockchain.

2 Related Work

Due to the increased amount of user data in the cloud, cloud service providers use distributed cloud technology to improve data usability and accessibility [24]. In the current situation, the storage of confidential data is a more significant challenge. The Table 1 presents related work of existing solutions and mechanisms in the field of blockchain and distributed cloud computing. Below are some valuable contributions of some previous research papers.

Amin et al. [6] used AVISPA tool and BAN logic model to perform cryptanalysis on all possible Security threats. Carbone et al. [14] used state of the art ICT technologies to foster a high quality of products, contributing to better supply chain management. Cristea et al. [7] valuable insights for maritime transportation business are discussed, including the persistent data storage and analysis services for large maritime ships. A customized genetic algorithm is created to solve the file block replica placement problem between multi-user and multiple data centers in [9]. Li et al. [10] addressed problems related to reducing communication overhead whenever the file is encrypted traditionally. An exciting proposal of an intelligent cryptographic approach based on security-aware efficient distributed storage is contributed by [15]. It focused on problems of cloud data storage and aimed to provide a better approach that could avoid cloud operators reaching users' sensitive data. Ricci et al. [12] discussed research that has been conducted in cloud storage forensics and how it is different from distributed blockchain-based cloud forensics. Saia et al. [11] discussed the exploitation of wireless-based ecosystems and it is performed where some existing devices are used to track the activity of other devices.

Novel blockchain-based distributed cloud architecture with software-defined networking (SDN) enable controller is discussed in [25]. This paper also presented ongoing research on implementing function blocks as intelligent contracts executed on a supervision level. Sharma et al. [13] Proposed innovative hybrid architecture for intelligent city networks using Software Defined Networking and blockchain. They used memory hardened Proof-of-Work scheme to ensure security and privacy and avoid tampering with information by hackers. In [8] hyperledger fabric was selected as a blockchain solution where function blocks could be implemented as smart contracts on the supervisor level. This paper also explained the importance of edge computing and its application in the Internet

Table 1. The related work of existing solutions and mechanisms in the field of blockchain and distributed cloud computing. C1: Attack Consideration, C2: Authentication Consideration, C3: Edge Computing, C4: Integrity Consideration, C5: Software Defined Networking, C6: File Backup Consideration and C7: File Security Consideration

Authors	Key contribution	C1	C2	C3	C4	C5	C6	C7
Amin et al. [6]	Security Vulnerability of Multi-server Cloud Environment		Yes	Yes				
Cristea et al. [7]	Continuous data storage and analysis		Yes	Yes		Yes		Yes
Alexandru Stanciu [8]	Distributed control system based on IEC standards	Yes	Yes					
Li et al. [9]	Solving File Block replica placement problem		Yes			Yes		Yes
Wu et al. [10]	Reducing communication overhead while encryption		Yes	Yes		Yes		Yes
Saia et al. [11]	Exploitation of wireless based devices		Yes	Yes				
Ricci et al. [12]	Distinguish between cloud storage and distributed blockchain based forensics		Yes	Yes		Yes		Yes
Park et al. [13]	Hybrid architecture for smart city		Yes	Yes	Yes		Yes	
Davcev et al. [14]	Better Supply chain management for increasing performing value	Yes				Yes		Yes
Gai et al. [15]	Security Aware Efficient Distributed Storage		Yes	Yes		Yes		Yes
White et al. [16]	Framework for PingER for monitoring agents in permssioned blockchain		Yes	Yes		Yes		Yes
Chen et al. [17]	Design storage system to manage personal and medical data	Yes	Yes	Yes	Yes	Yes	Yes	Yes
Cheng et al. [18]	Solving problems of counterfeiting certificates	Yes	Yes		Yes		Yes	Yes
Wei et al. [19]	Securing cognitive vehicular Ad Hoc Network	Yes	Yes	Yes		Yes		
Liang et al. [20]	Data provenance system for cloud auditing	Yes	Yes	Yes	Yes	Yes		Yes
Sharma et al. [21]	DMM solution for flattened fog network	Yes	Yes	Yes	Yes	Yes	Yes	Yes
Wang et al. [2]	Public provable data possession scheme for cloud service providers	Yes	Yes	Yes	Yes	Yes	Yes	Yes
Zhang et al. [22]	High performance consensus for solving tokendependancy problems	Yes	Yes		Yes			
Cha et al. [23]	Secret Dispersion algorithm for storing data in distributed cloud	Yes	Yes	Yes	Yes			Yes

of Things, smart grids, healthcare, smart contract, etc. This paper also presented how blockchain can be integrated with edge nodes to perform process control.

Liang et al. [20] proposed a decentralized and trusted cloud data provenance architecture using blockchain technology. It also provides tamper-proof records that enable data accountability transparency in the cloud environment. This paper also presents the implementation of a data provenance system for cloud auditing, which would lead to increased availability and security related to privacy. Wang et al. [2] deeply addresses the issue of data outsourcing in the cloud by adopting blockchain-based fair payment smart contracts for public cloud storage auditing and developing blockchain-based payment methods for cloud storage. It also introduced a publicly provable data possession scheme to ensure that the cloud service provider provides proof of data possession. Although the proposed solution considers multiple aspects, as per the related work table, the solution is only applicable to a public cloud environment, also the time required for data processing is increased. Chen et al. [17] gives us in-depth knowledge about how to design a storage scheme to manage personal medical data based on blockchain and cloud and how to share these through a secure medium. Although the proposed model considers multiple aspects in the related work table, the proposed model is completely based on a private cloud network and implementing this model in a larger network will increase its complexity and data retrieval time. [19] provided an innovative method of securing cognitive radio vehicular Ad hoc network by using fog-based distributed blockchain cloud architecture. It also consolidated blockchain with edge computing in cognitive vehicular ad-hoc networks to protect the vehicular ecosystem's critical data.

Zang et al. [22] did research related to high-performance consensus for cloud architecture and also developed a new incentive mechanism for solving the problem of token dependency. They also analyzed energy consumption between Proof-of-Work and Proof-of-Stake mechanisms and developed a new consensus named Proof-of-Service Power. Ali et al. [16] designed a specialized framework for PingER using the permission blockchain, which removed the need for a centralized repository for monitoring agents and replaced it by writing access data entries on the permission blockchain. This research decentralized the PingER framework, removing the significant project dependencies. This resulted in a sustainable, scalable, and reliable prototype embedded in other APIs using the PingER framework.

Cheng et al. [18] created awareness related to the importance of digital certificates for solving the problem of counterfeiting certificates. They provided a literature review highlighting the use cases of digital certificates and how they can be implemented in the blockchain [26]. Did an in-depth analysis of RSA and ECC algorithms based on their crucial size, performance, key generation, and signature verification performance and concluded a result that Elliptic Curve Cryptography is better than Rivest-Shamir-Adleman algorithm. Also, the conclusion drawn was verified using TOPSIS and GRA models.

Sharma et al. [21] provided an innovative Distributed Mobility Management (DMM) solution for the flattened fog network architecture and developed technology to embed it in the blockchain. The proposed model can defend against malicious MAARs, CMDs, and malicious MNs. The distributed cloud model also helps counterfeit cyberattacks, such as Denial of Service, Impersonation, Session Hijacking, and backward broadcasting. Although the proposed model considers multiple aspects as per the related work table, it requires much more data processing time, since the data undergoes a series of security checks, interlinked with one another. Cha et al. [23] developed an innovative method for sharing secret information in a public cloud environment using distributed cloud technology, improving overall storage efficiency and privacy capabilities. Azzaoui et al. [27] Proposed an information hiding technique in the blockchain using smart contracts for increasing the privacy and security of healthcare supply chain networks.

3   Proposed Solution

Several methodologies are developed for improving security solutions and storage capabilities for the distributed cloud environment. However, they are not optimized for providing better security in the enterprise-level cloud environment and may not work correctly for many users. Here we attempt to solve the significant issue of improving the storage capabilities in a public cloud environment and improving the security in an enterprise-level private cloud environment using a blockchain-based model. The whole process is described in Fig. 1, where Bob needs to share confidential information with Alice.

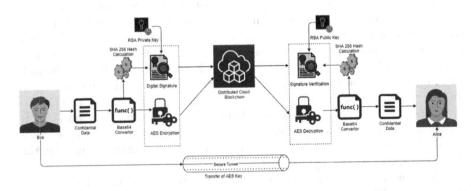

Fig. 1. Secure transfer of confidential information through a blockchain based distributed cloud model

3.1   Storage Solution

Here we are dealing with confidential data, including efficiency-related data from a particular machine, data about the transaction details, etc. This data may get repeated after a certain amount of time. In the traditional blockchain system, new data is stored as a separate entry in a newer node, but due to this, a large amount of storage space is going to waste, and it also takes a long time to search for particular information in the long blockchain. Instead, we propose a better solution for improving the storage capability, which would also decrease the information searching time for a particular node in the blockchain.

Creating a Better Blockchain. As we know, a blockchain is a chain of nodes bound together by a smart contract, whose information is known to each member of the decentralized network [28,29]. A primary blockchain contains transaction details. In our case, it is a series of information about a machine, nonce, and previous block hash.

Now, for the newer technology blockchain, we will add two more components, named "count" and "Hash of data of current block" this component will be initially set to zero. However, whenever a new block is generated, first it will traverse to the last ten blocks and check if the current block hash value of the data occurs anywhere between the last ten blocks, add a pointer to that to that block, also increment the count value of the last block by 1 in the lookup table. This lookup table will be used for future reference. This will help other users to track the repeated or recurrent values faster.

Whenever a new block is added, the lookup table is updated in a FIFO manner, the first value is deleted, and the newer value is added. The lookup table is traversed from bottom to up for finding the same hash value. If the same hash value is caught, the last value is deleted, and a pointer is created for that block. At last, the count value in the lookup table is also incremented. The whole process is described in the Fig. 2.

The lookup table stores ten values since time complexity is our primary concern. If time and space complexity is not the primary concern, the size of the lookup table can easily be increased. This will reduce the space complexity for adding newer blocks and gradually increase the time complexity for searching an element. For larger lookup tables, to reduce the time complexity, a special algorithm may be implemented, where the data entered in the blockchain is sorted when a new block is added, using the merge sort technique since it has an optimized time complexity for all kinds of data.

3.2   Security Solution

Blockchain works on a decentralized network where, when a new block is added, all the users in the network will get an alert, and a new mathematically complex problem will be generated, which needs to be solved faster. Here, the main problem is that when a new block is added, the information related to that block is broadcast to all the other nodes to maintain transparency and update the hash tables. The problem comes when we have to transfer confidential information through a distributed ledger to a particular user and authenticate ourselves as

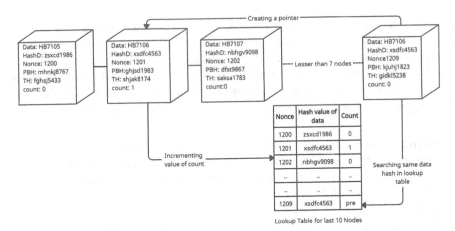

Fig. 2. Block diagram. HashD: hash of the data present in the block, PBH: previous Block Hash value TH: hash value of the current block.

Algorithm 1. Optimising Storage Capabilities

1: **Input**: Data, Nonce, Hash of current Data, Total Hash, Previous Block Hash
2: **Output**: Optimised Storage Solution
3: **while** (Data_Addition!=NULL) **do**
4:     **if** (New_Entity==TRUE && Modifications==False) **then**
5:         Initiate the pointer
6:         Update the count value in Lookup Table
7:         Ensure the same security policies as previous nodes.
8:     **else**
9:         Remove the first entry in the Lookup Table
10:        Accept next data
11:        Operate data addition and keep tracking
12:        **if** (LookupTable== FULL) **then**
13:            Delete the first entry
14:        **else**
15:            Add newer data at the bottom of LookupTable
16:            Validate and continue
17:        **end if**
18:    **end if**
19: **end while**
20: Update network, keep track and store results

---

potential bearers of this confidential information. It becomes difficult for a potential user to authenticate himself/herself in a large-scale organization, probably a Multinational Company, running on a blockchain. Though blockchain uses a key pair to authenticate a user and add the user to the blockchain, it is not entirely secure and may lead to an insider threat.

To address this issue, we propose a solution for transferring a piece of confidential information through a decentralized system such as a blockchain embedded in a distributed cloud environment.

Adding a Security Layer. Once a user enters a blockchain environment, no separate authentication mechanism is implemented to check whether he is the same user, even after one month. This gives rise to an insider threat in a large-scale organization, and if a potential user is unaware that his/her account details are stolen/used by a malicious intruder, it can create huge losses. The malicious user may also add daughter nodes to the blockchain network and mask another user. This faulty network can also lead to cyber-terrorism, passing fake news, achieving ideological or political gain through threat or intimidation, etc.

To solve this issue, we propose an innovative solution that will include the usage of AES encryption, SHA-256 hashing and RSA algorithm for creating digital signatures. This will surely help users authenticate themselves securely when they need to send a piece of confidential information.

Improvised Consensus. When a user wants to transfer confidential information, the user should follow the below steps:

1. Calculate a Base64 bytecode of the information
2. Calculate SHA-256 hash value of the bytecode
   (a) Use RSA algorithm to sign the hash value using the private key, to create a digital signature to the confidential information.
3. Perform AES encryption on the Base64 bytecode
4. Transfer the AES encrypted text along with the Digital Signature in the distributed network.

When another potential user wants to extract confidential data and wants to check whether the extracted data is authentic he/she must follow the below steps:-

1. Decrypt the message using the AES key.
2. Calculate the SHA-256 Hash value of the bytecode.
   (a) Use RSA public key to perform digital signature validation on the hash value.
3. Convert the Base64 Bytecode to text format.
4. Validate the confidential information by comparing it with hash and Digital Signature.

Algorithms 2 and 3 for the process of transferring the confidential information from the sender to the receiver's end are explained below.

Algorithm 2. Enhancing Security for Addition of Confidential Information in Blockchain: Sender's End

---
1: **Input**: Confidential Text, AES key
2: **Output**: Cipher Text, Digital Signature
3: Generate a separate public and private key pair and transfer the public key through a secure medium to the intended receiver.
4: **while** (ConfidentialText!=NULL) **do**
5:    **if** (Key_Transfer==TRUE) **then**
6:        Convert the plain text to Base64 Bytecode.
7:        Encrypt the Bytecode using Symmetric AES Encryption key.
8:        Calculate SHA-256 Hash value of the Bytecode.
9:        Apply Digital Signature to the Hash value using RSA private key.
10:       Initiate block creation.
11:   **else**
12:       Establish a secure medium to transfer keys.
13:       Complete the key transfer procedure.
14:   **end if**
15: **end while**
16: Update network, keep track and store results

Algorithm 3. Enhancing Security for Addition of Confidential Information in Blockchain: Receiver's End

---
1: **Input**: Cipher Text, AES key, Digital Signature
2: **Output**: Authentic Information
3: **while** (CipherText!=NULL) **do**
4:    **if** (Key_Transfer==TRUE) **then**
5:        Decrypt the Cipher text using AES key.
6:        Convert the Base64 Bytecode to Plaintext
7:        Calculate SHA-256 Hash value of the Bytecode.
8:        Verify the Digital Signature using Public key
9:    **else**
10:       Establish a secure medium to transfer keys.
11:       Complete the key transfer procedure.
12:   **end if**
13: **end while**
14: Update network, keep track and store results

---

4   Discussions and Result Analysis

The solutions discussed in this paper are developed to enhance the security of the current blockchain model. The security solution presented in the paper and the storage solution will efficiently store and transfer confidential information through blockchain. The proposed model is a specialized technique in which small-scale industries can use blockchain technology to enhance their transaction capabilities.

The second proposed model can help organizations with multiple nodes share confidential information with a particular user without other users knowing about it.

Efficiency: There can be two ways to measure and compare efficiency. At first, we can evaluate efficiency based on storage requirements. The proposed model is designed to decrease the storage requirement for storing recurring values in the blockchain. This enables small-scale industries with less storage capabilities to start using blockchain. For example, suppose using the traditional blockchain model requires 100 MB of storage. Our model can help reduce to 80MB, thus utilizing 20% lesser storage. This model will help small-scale industries to build an energy-efficient blockchain with better storage capabilities. Secondly, the efficiency can be measured using the time required to encrypt and decrypt the whole package. The time required for encryption and decryption is slightly more, but when compared to the increase in security architecture, the increase in processing time is passable.

Table 2 shows how the total package size increases after applying each algorithm. The base 64 encodings will increase the size by 0.37th multiple of the original data. The AES encryption value will be approximately the same. Combining the hash value and digital signature, the total size of the package will be approximately 0.4th multiple of the original data. Compared to the traditional blockchain model, the overhead here is approximately 35%, but the proposed model offers a 40% increase in the overall security architecture of blockchain. Therefore the proposed model is more efficient in terms of security and storage requirements than the older blockchain model.

Table 2. Comparison of Size Increment after applying each algorithm.

Data size	Base 64	AES	Digital signature	Total package size
1 MB	0.37 MB	0.001 MB	0.03 MB	1.40 MB
5 MB	1.85 MB	0.005 MB	0.15 MB	7.00 MB
10 MB	3.7 MB	0.01 MB	0.3 MB	14.01 MB
15 MB	5.55 MB	0.015 MB	0.45 MB	21.01 MB
20 MB	7.4 MB	0.02 MB	0.6 MB	28.02 MB

Scalability: The proposed solution can adjust the storage capacity of a network. The look-up table used in the solution is of adjustable length, scalable vertically, and adjusted according to the organization's needs. One shortcoming of this model is that it will be challenging to embed it in the existing blockchain model since adding information about previous blocks is not possible. However, it will benefit a small-scale industry that wants to start using blockchain. This blockchain will be able to intelligently sense the storage capacity of an existing system and adjust the look-up table accordingly to enhance the storage capabilities of the distributed blockchain network.

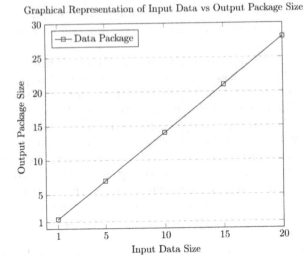

Fig. 3. Graphical representation of input data vs output package size graph

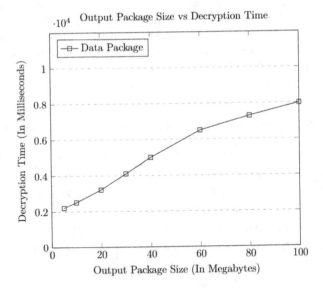

Fig. 4. Output package size vs decryption time

Privacy: The proposed model is adept at increasing confidentiality while sharing a piece of secret information through blockchain. The encryption process requires increased time but implementing multiple encryptions, hashing, and digital signatures makes the data more secure.

Decryption time becomes a significant comparison factor whenever privacy is concerned. The more decryption time, the more will be the privacy. Input

Data vs Output Package Size Graph is shown in Fig. 3. Figure 4 represents a graphical comparison of how the time required to decrypt the algorithm using the brute-force technique increases with the increase in output data size.

When a piece of private information is to be sent through the blockchain, at first, a secret key is to be sent through a dedicated secure tunnel. This process needs to be done with caution since if the attacker sniffs this key, he can efficiently perform cryptanalysis and decipher the confidential data. After the secure transfer of this long key, the user has to convert the secret information into Base64 byte-code, and then it gets converted to ciphertext using the previous AES key. The SHA-256 hash value of the byte-code is also calculated, and at last, a digital certificate is generated for verifying the authenticity of the digital document. At last, the Digital Signature and encrypted text are added to the blockchain-based distributed cloud. This data can be easily extracted and verified by the intended receiver.

5 Conclusion and Future Works

Here we discussed blockchain technology and how to create an improvised blockchain model, specifically for transferring confidential data in a decentralized medium. The major challenge in this sector is transparency. In a decentralized network such as a blockchain, each member of the blockchain sees all the data added to the blockchain. It becomes difficult to share confidential files intended to be shared only with a specific group. This problem may create havoc when a particular confidential message is transferred to an unintended user.

To tackle this issue, we have created a specialized consensus mechanism for transferring confidential data while maintaining the integrity, confidentiality, and availability of the information. We have also proposed a solution for faster traversal and mapping of recurrent data using a Lookup table. These models can be merged into a distinguished cloud environment for creating a more improvised version. This futuristic model would be more reliable, convenient, and faster. This model can also be integrated with other IoT devices in 5G based Mobile edge computing services. These devices continuously send recurrent data to their APIs, which may consume unnecessary memory. Therefore, the proposed model is best suited for such devices. Furthermore, the security architecture can be implemented in the healthcare sector for transferring medical reports through blockchain.

Acknowledgement. This work was supported by Institute of Information & communications Technology Planning & Evaluation (IITP) grant funded by the Korea government (MSIT) (No. 2020-0-00952, Development of 5G Edge Security Technology for Ensuring 5G+ Service Stability and Availability, 100%)

References

1. KodriÄ, Å., Vrhovec, S., JelovÄan, L.: Securing edge-enabled smart healthcare systems with blockchain: a systematic literature review. J. Internet Serv. Inf. Secur. (JISIS) **11**(4), 19–32 (2021)

2. Wang, H., Qin, H., Zhao, M., Wei, X., Shen, H., Susilo, W.: Blockchain-based fair payment smart contract for public cloud storage auditing. Inf. Sci. **519**, 348–362 (2020)
3. Narteni, S., Vaccari, I., Mongelli, M., Aiello, M., Cambiaso, E.: Evaluating the possibility to perpetrate tunneling attacks exploiting short-message-service. J. Internet Serv. Inf. Secur. (JISIS) **11**(3), 30–46 (2021)
4. Rahmadika, S., Firdaus, M., Lee, Y.-H., Rhee, K.-H.: An investigation of pseudonymization techniques in decentralized transactions. J. Internet Serv. Inf. Secur. (JISIS) **11**(4), 1–18 (2021)
5. Ribalta, C.N., Lombard-Platet, M., Salinesi, C., Lafourcade, P.: Blockchain mirage or silver bullet? A requirements-driven comparative analysis of business and developers' perceptions in the accountancy domain. J. Wirel. Mob. Netw. Ubiquit. Comput. Dependable Appl. (JoWUA) **12**(1), 85–110 (2021)
6. Amin, R., Kumar, N., Biswas, G.P., Iqbal, R., Chang, V.: A light weight authentication protocol for IoT-enabled devices in distributed cloud computing environment. Future Gener. Comput. Syst. **78**, 1005–1019 (2018)
7. Cristea, D.S., Moga, L.M., Neculita, M., Prentkovskis, O., Nor, K.M., Mardani, A.: Operational shipping intelligence through distributed cloud computing. J. Bus. Econ. Manag. **18**(4), 695–725 (2017)
8. Stanciu, A.: Blockchain based distributed control system for edge computing. In: 2017 21st International Conference on Control Systems and Computer Science (CSCS), pp. 667–671 (2017)
9. Li, J., Liu, Z., Chen, L., Chen, P., Wu, J.: Blockchain-based security architecture for distributed cloud storage. In: 2017 IEEE International Symposium on Parallel and Distributed Processing with Applications and 2017 IEEE International Conference on Ubiquitous Computing and Communications (ISPA/IUCC), pp. 408–411 (2017)
10. Li, J., Jigang, W., Chen, L.: Block-secure: blockchain based scheme for secure P2P cloud storage. Inf. Sci. **465**, 219–231 (2018)
11. Saia, R., Carta, S., Recupero, D.R., Fenu, G.: Internet of entities (IoE): a blockchain-based distributed paradigm for data exchange between wireless-based devices (2019)
12. Ricci, J., Baggili, I., Breitinger, F.: Blockchain-based distributed cloud storage digital forensics: where's the beef? IEEE Secur. Priv. **17**(1), 34–42 (2019)
13. Sharma, P.K., Park, J.H.: Blockchain based hybrid network architecture for the smart city. Futur. Gener. Comput. Syst. **86**, 650–655 (2018)
14. Davcev, D., Kocarev, L., Carbone, A., Stankovski, V., Mitresk, K.: Blockchain based distributed cloud fog platform for IoT supply chain management, pp. 51–58 (2018)
15. Li, Y., Gai, K., Qiu, L., Qiu, M., Zhao, H.: Intelligent cryptography approach for secure distributed big data storage in cloud computing. Inf. Sci. **387**, 103–115 (2017)
16. Ali, S., Wang, G., White, B., Cottrell, R.L.: A blockchain-based decentralized data storage and access framework for pinger. In: 2018 17th IEEE International Conference on Trust, Security and Privacy in Computing and Communications/12th IEEE International Conference on Big Data Science and Engineering (TrustCom/BigDataSE), pp. 1303–1308 (2018)
17. Chen, Y., Ding, S., Zheng, X., Zheng, H., Yang, S.: Blockchain-based medical records secure storage and medical service framework. J. Med. Syst. **43**, 11 (2018)
18. Cheng, J.-C., Lee, N.-Y., Chi, C., Chen, Y.-H.: Blockchain and smart contract for digital certificate. In: 2018 IEEE International Conference on Applied System Invention (ICASI), pp. 1046–1051 (2018)

19. He, Y., Wei, Z., Guangzheng, D., Li, J., Zhao, N., Yin, H.: Securing cognitive radio vehicular ad hoc networks with fog computing. Ad Hoc Sens. Wirel. Netw. **40**, 01 (2018)
20. Liang, X., Shetty, S., Tosh, D., Kamhoua, C., Kwiat, K., Njilla, L.: Provchain: a blockchain-based data provenance architecture in cloud environment with enhanced privacy and availability. In: 2017 17th IEEE/ACM International Symposium on Cluster, Cloud and Grid Computing (CCGRID), pp. 468–477 (2017)
21. Sharma, V., You, I., Palmieri, F., Jayakody, D.N.K., Li, J.: Secure and energy-efficient handover in fog networks using blockchain-based DMM. IEEE Commun. Mag. **56**(5), 22–31 (2018)
22. Zhang, Y., Zhang, L., Liu, Y., Luo, X.: Proof of service power: a blockchain consensus for cloud manufacturing. J. Manuf. Syst. **59**, 1–11 (2021)
23. Cha, J., Singh, S.K., Kim, T., Park, J.: Blockchain-empowered cloud architecture based on secret sharing for smart city. J. Inf. Secur. Appl. **57**, 102686 (2021)
24. Kumar, A., Dhurandher, S.K., Woungang, I., Rodrigues, J.J.P.C.: Securing opportunistic networks: an encounter-based trust-driven barter mechanism. J. Wirel. Mob. Netw. Ubiquit. Comput. Dependable Appl. (JoWUA) **12**(2), 99–113 (2021)
25. Sharma, P.K., Chen, M., Park, J.H.: A software defined fog node based distributed blockchain cloud architecture for IoT. IEEE Access **6**, 115–124 (2018)
26. Chandel, S., Cao, W., Sun, Z., Yang, J., Zhang, B., Ni, T.-Y.: A multi-dimensional adversary analysis of RSA and ECC in blockchain encryption. In: Arai, K., Bhatia, R. (eds.) FICC 2019. LNNS, vol. 70, pp. 988–1003. Springer, Cham (2020). https://doi.org/10.1007/978-3-030-12385-7_67
27. El Azzaoui, A., Chen, H., Kim, S.H., Pan, Y., Park, J.H.: Blockchain-based distributed information hiding framework for data privacy preserving in medical supply chain systems. Sensors **22**(4), 1371 (2022)
28. Reja, K., Choudhary, G., Shandilya, S.K., Sharma, D.M., Sharma, A.K.: Blockchain in logistics and supply chain monitoring. In: Utilizing Blockchain Technologies in Manufacturing and Logistics Management, pp. 104–121. IGI Global (2022)
29. Singh, S., Choudhary, G., Shandilya, S.K., Sihag, V., Choudhary, A.: Counterfeited product identification in a supply chain using blockchain technology. Res. Briefs Inf. Commun. Technol. Evol. **7**, 3 (2021)

Multi-hop Multi-key Homomorphic Encryption with Less Noise Under CRS Model

Hui Li[1]([✉]), Xuelian Li[1], Juntao Gao[2], and Runsong Wang[1]

[1] School of Mathematics and Statistics, Xidian University, Xi'an 710071, China
hui0921@stu.xidian.edu.cn
[2] State Key Laboratory of Integrated Services Networks, Xidian University, Xi'an 710071, China
jtgao@mail.xidian.edu.cn

Abstract. The application of information technologies such as big data, artificial intelligence, and cloud computing in the Internet environment makes protecting personal privacy and preventing data leakage an important issue. Homomorphic encryption (HE) supports the calculation and processing on ciphertexts and provides a technical guarantee for the security of personal information. Multi-key homomorphic encryption (MKHE) can perform cooperative calculation on ciphertexts under different keys, and is one of the solutions for secure computing in multi-user scenario. But the homomorphic multiplication after ciphertext extension makes the ciphertext dimension increase quadratically with respect to the number of users, so relinearization with noise is needed to reduce the dimension. In this paper, we propose an efficient multi-hop MKHE scheme with less relinearization noise under the common reference string (CRS) model, which supports real-time joining of new users. First, we propose an auxiliary coding scheme by introducing a random matrix instead of the encryption with noise. On this basis, we further propose how to construct the relinearization key, which can be pre-computed before the ciphertext input. In our MKHE scheme, the preprocessing of the ciphertext is cancelled to reduce the dimension of the ciphertext and the number of non-linear keys after homomorphic multiplication. In addition, we prove the semantic security of the scheme under the RLWE assumption, noise analysis and storage analysis also show that our scheme has smaller noise growth and storage space.

Keywords: Multi-key homomorphic encryption · Relinearization key · CRS model · Ciphertext extension · Less noise

1 Introduction

With the advent of the information age, costs and overhead can be reduced by outsourcing the storage of massive data and complex computing to cloud service providers [23]. The unlimited potential unleashed by digital information

© The Author(s), under exclusive license to Springer Nature Switzerland AG 2022
X. Chen et al. (Eds.): CSS 2022, LNCS 13547, pp. 342–357, 2022.
https://doi.org/10.1007/978-3-031-18067-5_25

technology has also revealed the other side of the same coin, that is, data leakage may cause enormous damage to personal privacy [9,27]. Therefore, cryptographic technology is usually used to ensure data security. Compared with traditional encryption schemes, homomorphic encryption not only guarantees the confidentiality of data, but also protects its availability, which provides a more reliable and effective way to protect individual privacy.

The concept of homomorphic encryption was first proposed by Rivest *et al.* in 1978 [25]. It means that we have $f(\text{Enc}(m_1, m_2)) = \text{Enc}(f(m_1, m_2))$ for any operation f. Until 2009, Gentry [17] proposed the first FHE scheme based on ideal lattice. The main principle is to design a homomorphic encryption scheme with limited ciphertext calculation, and perform reencryption operation when the ciphertext noise reaches the threshold, so as to realize bootstrapping. In 2010, Dijk *et al.* constructed the DGHV scheme [14] which is based on the approximate greatest common divisor problem. However, the public key size of this scheme is too large to implement, which is $O(\lambda^{10})$. Subsequently, Coron *et al.* [12,13] optimize the DGHV scheme used public key compression. Based on the ring learning with errors problem (RLWE), Brakersiki *et al.* proposed BGV scheme [3] with key-switching and modulo-switching techniques in 2012. Gentry *etal.* proposed the GSW scheme [18] in 2013, which flattened the ciphertext to reduce noise and improve the efficiency of the algorithm.

The above HE schemes are homomorphic only for a single key. However, the scattered and fragmented data in practical applications greatly restricts its application potential. For example, the data held by each operator is incomplete, and data fusion needs to be realized. Asharov *et al.* [1] extended this to the multiparty case for secure multiparty computation. The scheme includes a key generation protocol and a decryption protocol. The former is designed to jointly generate a common public key and each party encrypts its private data under the common public key. So in this case, the users participating in calculation are determined in advance. However, the cross-border integration of data is promoted so that it can play a greater role. This involves both the sharing of data across regions and departments, as well as data exchange between various types of enterprises.

In order to be more suitable for multiparty scenario, Lopez-Alt *et al.* [20] proposed the concept of multi-key homomorphic encryption (MKHE) in 2012 and constructed the first MKHE scheme based on NTRU cryptosystem [26]. MKHE supports homomorphic calculation on ciphertexts encrypted under different keys and is more suitable for outsourcing computing of multi-user data. Ciphertext extension is usually involved in the existing MKHE schemes, such as [5,7,11,19,22,24], which extends a single-key ciphertext to a multi-key ciphertext. A compact ciphertext extension is used in [6,7,19]. However, in the CDKS scheme [6], the ciphertext dimension after homomorphic multiplication and the storage space of the relinearization key are quadratic on the number of users. This further affects the noise growth when relinearizing the ciphertext with relinearization keys.

1.1 Our Motivation and Contribution

In the case of a single-key, the homomorphic schemes [2,3,8] based on R have an advantage over the homomorphic schemes [14,18] based on bit in the ciphertext/plaintext ratio. In the multi-key case, the BGV-type MKHE scheme [6,7,19] have a compact ciphertext extension than the GSW-type MKHE scheme [11,22,24]. In fact, the ciphertext $ct_\times$ obtained after the tensor product of the two multi-key ciphertexts ct_1, ct_2 under $sk = (1, s_i, \ldots, s_k)$ is a $(k + 1)^2$-dimensional ciphertext, which should be relinearized to a $(k + 1)$-dimensional ciphertext. At the same time, the key is transformed from $sk \otimes sk$ containing non-linear entries back to sk. Our main contributions are as follows:

1. According to RLWE problem and the encryption idea of GSW scheme [18], we propose an auxiliary coding scheme by introducing a random matrix. The scheme includes the encoding of the element over R by a random matrix and the commitment to the random matrix. On this basis, the user uses the auxiliary encoding scheme to generate the evaluation key and publish it together with public key. Using public information of two party, the relinearization key for the relinearization algorithm can be pre-computed. Finally we give the relinearization process after inputting a ciphertext.

2. We use the single-key BFV scheme [2,16] as the basic scheme to give the application of our relinearization algorithm in multi-party scenario. Similar to the previous multi-hop MKHE scheme, we describe the scheme construction under the CRS model, that is, all parties share a random vector. In our MKHE scheme, the preprocessing of the ciphertext is eliminated to reduce the dimension of the ciphertext after homomorphic multiplication and the number of nonlinear entries in the key. Furthermore, the relinearization key we need to construct is also only a subset of the scheme with ciphertext extension. Therefore, the storage of our relinearization key is about $O(k_1 k_2)$, where $\max\{k_1, k_2\} \le k$.

3. The security of multi-key encryption scheme is derived from its single-key scheme. In the security proof, we mainly discuss that our proposed auxiliary encoding scheme is semantically secure under the decisional-RLWE problem. In addition, we adopt the infinite norm to analyze the growth of noise during the relinearization process, and the results show that by using our proposed relinearization algorithm, less noise can be brought, which is only linearly related to the size of the noise distribution.

1.2   Related Work

Lopez-Alt *et al.* [20] first proposed an MKHE scheme and the parameters of the scheme are optimized in [10,15]. Besides, MKHE schemes [4,11,22,24] with ciphertext extension are constructed based on the GSW scheme [18]. In [22], before homomorphic operation, the ciphertext of different users needs to be preprocessed to generate auxiliary ciphertext. Peikert and Shiehian [24] provides two GSW-type multi-hop MKHE schemes, which are called large-ciphertext and small-ciphertext respectively. In the large-ciphertext construction, encryption will generate a ciphertext sequence, in which, in addition to the ciphertext, it also includes the commitment of the message and an encryption of the random value of the commitment. Therefore, the size of this type of ciphertext is large. Relatively speaking, there is only one ciphertext in small-ciphertext construction, but each user needs to generate related components required for ciphertext expansion in advance. In short, the ciphertext dimension of these GSW-type MKHE schemes increases too fast, the ciphertext expansion process is complex, and the calculation complexity is large.

In 2017, Chen *et al.* first put forward a BGV-type MKHE scheme [7] by introducing ring-GSW scheme. The scheme completes the ciphertext extension according to the index of the user set in the ciphertext. Although the process of ciphertext extension is relatively simple, the dimension of ciphertext increases at an exponential rate after homomorphic calculation. In order to control the dimension of the ciphertext, the key-switching technology is adopted. For this, the ring-GSW scheme is used to generate the evaluation key required in the transformation process. This also leads to the large size of the generated evaluation key. Li *et al.* [19] optimized Chen *et al.*'s scheme on ciphertext expansion, and used hybrid homomorphic multiplication between ciphertexts to generate evaluation key. In 2019, Chen *et al.* [6] proposed a new multi-key variant with the relinearization key based on RLWE problem, which has lower complexity and storage space than the above two ring-GSW-based schemes. These schemes all require the process of ciphertext extension before homomorphic operation.

2 Preliminaries

2.1 Basic Notation

We use lowercase bold $\mathbf{x}$ and uppercase bold $\mathbf{A}$ to represent the vector and the matrix, respectively. $\mathbf{x}[i]$ denotes the i-th entry of the vector $\mathbf{x}$. $\mathbf{A}[i]$ and $\mathbf{A}[j :]$ denote the i-th column and j-th row of matrix $\mathbf{A}$ respectively. $\langle \mathbf{x}, \mathbf{y} \rangle$ denotes the dot product of two vectors $\mathbf{x}, \mathbf{y}$. In this paper, we define the integral coefficient polynomial ring R as $Z[x]/(f(x))$, where $f(x)$ is a irreducible polynomial and has degree n. Generally, $f(x) = x^n + 1$ and $n = 2^m, m \in \mathbb{N}$. For a positive integer q, $R_q = R/qR$. For a polynomial $a \in R_q$, its coefficients lie in the interval $(-q/2, q/2]$. We assume $a = \sum_{i=0}^{n-1} a_i x^i$ and use $\|a\|_\infty = \max_{i \in \{0,1,\cdots,n-1\}} |a_i|$ to denote the infinite norm of a. For a vector $\mathbf{a} \in R_q^d$, the infinite norm is denoted by $\|\mathbf{a}\|_\infty = \max_{i \in \{1,\cdots,d\}} \|\mathbf{a}[i]\|$. In the rest of our paper, without specifically stating, the norm we refer to is infinite norm. In addition, we use λ represents the security parameter.

Definition 1 (B-Bounded Distribution). *For a distribution D and a specified norm space, we say D is B-bounded, where $B = B(\lambda)$ if:*

$$\Pr_{x \leftarrow D}[\|x\| > B] = \mathrm{negl}(\lambda)$$

In particular, the noise distribution χ over R_q is a B-bounded distribution.

2.2 Ring Learning With Errors

For security parameter λ and polynomial ring R_q, we define the noise distribution $\chi = \chi(\lambda)$ on the ring R. For $s \in R_q$, we first denote a distribution $A_{s,\chi} = (a, b)$, where $b = sa + e$ and a, e are randomly sampled on R_q and χ, respectively. Lyubashevsky *et al.* [21] first proposed the RLWE (ring learning with errors) problem and reduced it to the approximate SVP over ideal lattices. Below we describe the decisional version of RLWE.

Definition 2 (Decisional-RLWE Assumption). *The RLWE problem is to distinguish following two distributions. In one distribution, sample $(a, b) \leftarrow A_{s,\chi}$; In another distribution, sample $(a, b) \leftarrow R_q \times R_q$. The RLWE assumption means that the above two distributions are computationally indistinguishable. That is, for a PPT algorithm $\mathcal{B}$ and security parameter λ, We have*

$$Adv(\mathcal{B}) := \left| \Pr\left[\mathcal{B}^{A_{s,\chi}} \left(1^\lambda\right) = 1 \right] - \Pr\left[\mathcal{B}^{R_q \times R_q} \left(1^\lambda\right) = 1 \right] \right| = negl(\lambda)$$

2.3 Multi-key Homomorphic Encryption

Multi-key homomorphic encryption supports homomorphic evaluation of ciphertexts under different keys or user sets. A MKHE scheme $\mathcal{E}$ consists of five PPT algorithms (Setup, KeyGen, Enc, Eval, Dec). We define $\mathcal{M}$ as the plaintext space over R and each multi key ciphertext ct has a corresponding index set, which represents its corresponding users, such as $S = \{id_1, \ldots, id_k\}$. As new users are added, the user set corresponding to ciphertext ct becomes larger.

- $\mathcal{E}.Setup$ $(1^\lambda) \to pp$: Take the security parameter λ as input, output the public parameter pp for subsequent algorithms.
- $\mathcal{E}.KeyGen$ $(pp) \to (pk, sk)$: Given the public parameter pp and generate public and secret keys (pk, sk).
- $\mathcal{E}.Enc$ $(pk, m) \to ct$: For a message $m \in \mathcal{M}$ to be encrypted, given the public key pk and output a ciphertext ct.
- $\mathcal{E}.Eval$ $(\mathcal{C}, (ct_1, \ldots, ct_\ell), \{pk_i\}_{i \in S}) \to ct_S$: Given the circuit $\mathcal{C}$ with ℓ inputs, ℓ ciphertexts ct_i and a collection of public keys $\{pk_i\}_{i \in S}$, where $S = \bigcup_{i=1}^\ell S_i$, output a ciphertext ct.
- $\mathcal{E}.Dec$ $(ct, \{sk_i\}_{i \in S}) \to m'$: Given the ciphertext ct and the secret key sequence of corresponding users $\{sk_i\}_{i \in S}$, output the message m'.

2.4 Gadget Decomposition Technique

In homomorphic encryption, gadget decomposition function and gadget vector are used to control noise growth. For the integer q and a element $a \in R_q$, gadget vector is $\mathbf{g} = (g_1, \ldots, g_d) \in R_q^d$ and function $\mathbf{g}^{-1}(a) = (b_1, \ldots, b_d) \in R^d$, where each b_i is a polynomial with small coefficients and satisfies

$$a = \sum_{i=1}^d b_i \cdot g_i \pmod{q}.$$

The common gadget decomposition is bit decomposition technology [18], where d is the bit length of q.

3   Relinearization of Multi-key Ciphertexts

In a MKHE scheme from RLWE, it is necessary to preprocess two ciphertexts $ct_i \in R_q^{k_i+1}$ corresponding to different user sets $S_i = (id_1, \cdots, id_{k_i})$ to obtain extended ciphertexts $\widehat{ct_i} \in R_q^{k+1}$ corresponding to the same $\widehat{sk} = (1, s_1, \cdots, s_k)$ before homomorphic evaluation, where k is the number of all users involved in two user sets, so $\max\{k_1, k_2\} \leq k \leq k_1 + k_2$. Homomorphic multiplication is the tensor product of two extended ciphertexts. According to the property of homomorphism, we have $\langle ct_\times, sk_\times \rangle = \langle \widehat{ct_1}, \widehat{sk} \rangle \cdot \langle \widehat{ct_2}, \widehat{sk} \rangle$, so the decryption key of $ct_\times$ is $sk_\times = \widehat{sk} \otimes \widehat{sk}$. The ensuing problem is that the dimension of ciphertext has increased from $k+1$ to $(k+1)^2$ and $sk_\times$ includes some non-linear items, such as $s_i s_j (i \neq j)$ and s_i^2. If the operation continues, the dimension of the ciphertext will continue to increase, and the decryption key will be more complicated. Fortunately, relinearization technology can transform the key of encrypted plaintext without decryption and construct another ciphertext $ct_\times'$, which encrypts the same plaintext as $ct_\times$, but the dimension is reduced to $k+1$ and meets $\langle ct_\times', \widehat{sk} \rangle = \langle ct_\times, sk_\times \rangle$. In this section, we will describe how to generate relinearization keys to linearize entries in ciphertext $ct_\times$ encrypting under $s_i s_j$ and s_i^2 with less noise.

3.1   Auxiliary Coding Scheme

We will use the public information generated by the following auxiliary coding scheme to complete the relinearization process.

- **Setup**(1^λ) : Given the security parameter λ, denote n is the degree of polynomial, q is modulus, χ and ψ are key and noise distribution respectively. Output the public parameters $pp = \{n, q, \chi, \psi\}$.
- **KeyGen**(pp) : Randomly sample s from χ as the secret key and a random vectors $\mathbf{a} \leftarrow R_q^d, \mathbf{e} \leftarrow \psi^d$. Then calculate $\mathbf{b} = -s\mathbf{a} + \mathbf{e} \in R_q^d$. Let public key be $(\mathbf{a}, \mathbf{b}) \in R_q^{d \times 2}$.
- **Aux-Code**(pk, μ, s) : For a message $\mu \in R$, perform the following steps:
  - Select a random matrix $\mathbf{R} \in \{0, 1\}^{d \times d}$;
  - Encode μ with $\mathbf{R}$, set $\mathbf{d}_2 = \mathbf{R} \cdot \mathbf{a} + \mu \cdot \mathbf{g} \pmod{q}$;
  - Sample $\mathbf{d}_1 \leftarrow R_q^d, \mathbf{e}' \leftarrow \psi^d$, then calculate $\mathbf{d}_0 = -s \cdot \mathbf{d}_1 + \mathbf{e}' + \mathbf{R} \cdot \mathbf{g} \pmod{q}$.
  - Output $(\mathbf{d}_0, \mathbf{d}_1, \mathbf{d}_2)$.

The auxiliary coding algorithm contains a code of μ over R by introducing a random matrix and a commitment to the random matrix under secret key s. Random matrix $\mathbf{R}$ is used as a intermediate value in the subsequent verification. The final output of the algorithm is a matrix $\mathbf{D} = [\mathbf{d}_0 \,|\, \mathbf{d}_1 \,|\, \mathbf{d}_2] \in R_q^{d \times 3}$.

Security. The auxiliary coding scheme is IND-CPA secure under the RLWE assumption. We prove that for any polynomial time adversary $\mathcal{A}$, the advantage of $\mathcal{A}$ successfully distinguishing the distribution $(pk, \mathbf{D})$ from the uniform distribution over $(R_q^{d \times 2}, R_q^{d \times 3})$ for any message $\mu \in R$ is negligible. The detailed proof process is in Sect. 5.1.

3.2 Relinearization Key

The relinearization algorithm requires the evaluation key independently generated by each party as public information. Next, we first describe the generation of evaluation key by using the algorithm in Sect. 3.1.

- **Eval.KeyGen**(pk_i, s_i): For party i, consider the secret key s_i as a element on R, run **Aux-Code**(pk, s_i, s_i) and output $\mathbf{D}_i \in R_q^{d \times 3}$ as the evaluation key of party i.

Entries in the ciphertext after tensor product can be classified into three types, which correspond to the key s_i, $s_i s_j (i \neq j$, assuming $i < j)$ and s_i^2. Nonlinear entries need to be converted to s_i, s_j. We describe how to generate the relinearized key $rlk_{i,j}$ and rlk_i using evaluation keys and public keys respectively.

Relinearization Key About Two Parties. According to the CDKS scheme [6], we use the public information of i, j to generate $rlk_{i,j}$. It inherits the dimension advantage of a relinearized key in [6]. The algorithm is mainly based on the function between the matrix $\mathbf{B}_j \in R^{d \times d}$ decomposed by public key of j and the evaluation key of i. The generation process is shown in Algorithm 1.

Algorithm 1. Relinearization Key $rlk_{i,j}$

Input: Evaluation key $\mathbf{D}_i = [\mathbf{d}_{i,0} | \mathbf{d}_{i,1} | \mathbf{d}_{i,2}]$ and public key $\mathbf{b}_j = -s_j \mathbf{a} + \mathbf{e}_j$ for $i < j$.
Output: Relinearization key $rlk_{i,j}$.
1: **for** $t = 1$ to d **do**
2:     Let $\mathbf{B}_j[t:] = \mathbf{g}^{-1}(\mathbf{b}_j[t]) \in R^d$;
3: **end for**
4: Set $\mathbf{B}_j = \mathbf{g}^{-1}(\mathbf{b}_j)$;
5: Calculate $\mathbf{k}_1 = \mathbf{B}_j \cdot \mathbf{d}_{i,0} \pmod q) \in R_q^d$;
6: Calculate $\mathbf{k}_2 = \mathbf{B}_j \cdot \mathbf{d}_{i,1} \pmod q) \in R_q^d$;
7: Let $\mathbf{k}_3 = \mathbf{d}_{i,2} \in R_q^d$;
8: Arrange to get $rlk_{i,j} = \mathbf{K}_{i,j} = [\mathbf{k}_1 | \mathbf{k}_2 | \mathbf{k}_3] \in R_q^{d \times 3}$
9: Return $rlk_{i,j}$.

Relinearization Key About a Sngle Party. We describe how to generate rlk_i by using the above public information of party i without introducing the conversion key of s_i^2 or other information. The generation process is shown in Algorithm 2.

Correctness. The relinearization key can be calculated in advance before relinearizing a ciphertext, and we define $\widehat{rlk} = \{rlk_{i,j}, rlk_i\}_{1 \leq i < j \leq k}$. $\widehat{rlk}$ is generated to convert key components $s_i s_j$ and s_i^2 to s_i or s_j. Therefore, we verify that

---

Algorithm 2. Relinearization Key rlk_i

Input: The public key and evaluation key $\mathbf{b}_i = -s_i\mathbf{a} + \mathbf{e}_i, \mathbf{D}_i$ of party i.
Output: Relinearization key rlk_i.
1: **for** $t = 1$ to d **do**
2:    Let $\mathbf{B}_i[t :] = \mathbf{g}^{-1}(\mathbf{b}_i[t]) \in R^d$;
3: **end for**
4: Set $\mathbf{B}_i = \mathbf{g}^{-1}(\mathbf{b}_i)$;
5: Calculate $\mathbf{k}'_1 = \mathbf{B}_i \cdot \mathbf{d}_{i,0} \pmod{q} \in R_q^d$;
6: Calculate $\mathbf{k}'_2 = \mathbf{d}_{i,2} + \mathbf{B}_i \cdot \mathbf{d}_{i,1} \pmod{q} \in R_q^d$;
7: Arrange to get $rlk_i = \mathbf{K}_i = [\mathbf{k}'_1|\mathbf{k}'_2] \in R_q^{d \times 2}$
8: Return rlk_i.

$\widetilde{rlk}$ obtained through public keys and evaluation keys generated by our auxiliary coding scheme are the encryption of $s_i s_j$ and s_i^2 under corresponding linear entries.

- Correctness of $rlk_{i,j}$ about two parties:

$$\mathbf{k}_1 + s_i \cdot \mathbf{k}_2 = \mathbf{B}_j \cdot (\mathbf{d}_{i,0} + s_i \cdot \mathbf{d}_{i,1}) \approx \mathbf{R}_i \mathbf{b}_j \pmod{q}$$

$$s_j \cdot \mathbf{k}_3 = s_j \cdot \mathbf{d}_{i,2} = \mathbf{R}_i s_j \cdot \mathbf{a} + s_i s_j \cdot \mathbf{g} \approx -\mathbf{R}_i \cdot \mathbf{b}_j + s_i s_j \cdot \mathbf{g} \pmod{q}$$

$$\mathbf{K}_{i,j} \cdot (1, s_i, s_j) = \mathbf{k}_1 + s_i \cdot \mathbf{k}_2 + s_j \cdot \mathbf{k}_3 \approx s_i s_j \cdot \mathbf{g} \pmod{q}$$

- Correctness of rlk_i about a single party:

$$\begin{aligned}
\mathbf{K}_i \cdot (1, s_i) = \mathbf{k}'_1 + s_i \cdot \mathbf{k}'_2 &= \mathbf{B}_i \cdot \mathbf{d}_{i,0} + s_i \cdot \mathbf{d}_{i,2} + s_i \mathbf{B}_i \cdot \mathbf{d}_{i,1} \\
&= s_i \cdot \mathbf{d}_{i,2} + \mathbf{B}_i \cdot (\mathbf{d}_{i,0} + s_i \cdot \mathbf{d}_{i,1}) \\
&\approx -\mathbf{R}_i \cdot \mathbf{b}_i + s_i^2 \cdot \mathbf{g} + \mathbf{R}_i \cdot \mathbf{b}_i \\
&= s_i^2 \cdot \mathbf{g} \pmod{q}
\end{aligned}$$

3.3 Relinearization

The relinearization key $\widetilde{rlk}$ allows us to linearize a ciphertext $ct_\times \in R_q^{(k+1)^2}$ after homomorphic multiplication to the key $\widetilde{sk} = (1, s_1, \cdots, s_k)$. If we rearrange $ct_\times$ in the form of matrix, we will obtain a $(k + 1) \times (k + 1)$-dimensional matrix. In the relinearization algorithm, we use $\mathbf{ct}$ to represent the initial ciphertext after homomorphic multiplication, $\mathbf{ct}'$ represents the linearized ciphertext. $\mathbf{ct}[i, j]$ denotes the element of i-th row and j-th column arranged in the form of matrix, which are related to parties i, j. By using the relinearization key, the elements in $\mathbf{ct}$ are linearized and each component of $\mathbf{ct}'$ is updated step by step. The detailed process is shown in Algorithm 3.

Correctness. Through the relinearization algorithm, the decryption key is transformed from $\widetilde{sk} \otimes \widetilde{sk}$ to secret key $\widetilde{sk}$, and a $(k + 1)$-dimensional ciphertext

---

Algorithm 3. Relinearize the Ciphertext

Input: The relinearization key $\widehat{rlk} = \{rlk_{i,j}, rlk_i\}_{1 \leq i < j \leq k}$ and a ciphertext **ct**.

Output: Ciphertext $\mathbf{ct'} \in R_q^{k+1}$.

1: $\mathbf{ct'}[0] = \mathbf{ct}[0,0]$;
2: **for** $i = 1$ to k **do**
3:     $\mathbf{ct'}[i] = \mathbf{ct}[0,i] + \mathbf{ct}[i,0]$;
4: **end for**
5: **for** $i = 1$ to k **do**
6:     $(\mathbf{ct'}[0], \mathbf{ct'}[i]) = (\mathbf{ct'}[0], \mathbf{ct'}[i]) + \mathrm{g}^{-1}(\mathbf{ct}[i,i]) \cdot \mathbf{K}_i$;
7: **end for**
8: **for** $1 \leq i \neq j \leq k$ **do**
9:     $(\mathbf{ct'}[0], \mathbf{ct'}[i], \mathbf{ct'}[j]) = (\mathbf{ct'}[0], \mathbf{ct'}[i], \mathbf{ct'}[j]) + \mathrm{g}^{-1}(\mathbf{ct}[i,j]) \cdot \mathbf{K}_{i,j}$;
10: **end for**
11: Return $\mathbf{ct'}$.

---

encrypting the same message is output. According to the verification of the correctness of $rlk_{i,j}$ and rlk_i in Sect. 3.2, we further confirm the correctness of the above algorithm.

$$\langle \mathbf{ct'}, \widehat{sk} \rangle = \mathbf{ct'}[0] + \sum_{i=1}^{k} \mathbf{ct'}[i] \cdot s_i = \mathbf{ct}[0,0] + \sum_{i=1}^{k} (\mathbf{ct}[0,i] + \mathbf{ct}[i,0]) \cdot s_i$$

$$+ \sum_{i=1}^{k} \mathrm{g}^{-1}(\mathbf{ct}[i,i]) \cdot \mathbf{K}_i \cdot (1, s_i) + \sum_{i,j=1; i \neq j}^{k} \mathrm{g}^{-1}(\mathbf{ct}[i,j]) \cdot \mathbf{K}_{i,j} \cdot (1, s_i, s_j)$$

$$\approx \mathbf{ct}[0,0] + \sum_{i=1}^{k} (\mathbf{ct}[0,i] + \mathbf{ct}[i,0]) \cdot s_i + \sum_{i=1}^{k} \mathbf{ct}[i,i] \cdot s_i^2 + \sum_{i,j=1; i \neq j}^{k} \mathbf{ct}[i,j] \cdot s_i s_j$$

$$= \langle \mathbf{ct}, \widehat{sk} \otimes \widehat{sk} \rangle \pmod{q}$$

4   Multi-key Homomorphic Encryption Scheme

We use the BFV scheme [2,16] based on RLWE problem as the single-key scheme and give a multi-key variant, which further includes the optimization of the dimension growth in the process of homomorphic multiplication. We work on ring $R_q = R/qR$, where $R = Z[x]/(x^n + 1)$, n is a power of 2. In addition, the plaintext space is defined as R_p and $\Delta = \lfloor q/p \rfloor$, where p, q are the modulus. χ, ψ represent the key and error distribution.

- **MKHE.Setup(1^λ)** : Take the security parameter λ as input and output the public parameters $pp = \{n, q, \chi, \psi\}$ and a random vector $\mathbf{a} \leftarrow R_q^d$.
- **MKHE.KeyGen(pp)** : Each participant run **KeyGen** with $\mathbf{a}$ as a common random vector and output $sk_i = s_i, pk_i = (\mathbf{a}, \mathbf{b}_i)$. Then run **Eval.KeyGen** and return $\mathbf{D}_i$ as the evaluation key of party i.

– **MKHE.Enc**(m, pk_i) : Given message $m \in R_p$ and public key $pk_i = (\mathbf{a}, \mathbf{b}_i)$:
  - Set $a = \mathbf{a}[0], b_i = \mathbf{b}_i[0]$;
  - Randomly select $r \leftarrow \chi, e_1, e_2 \leftarrow \psi$;
  - Calculate $ct_{i,0} = r \cdot b_i + e_1 + \Delta \cdot m \pmod{q}$ and $ct_{i,1} = r \cdot a + e_2 \pmod{q}$;
  - Output $ct'_i = (ct_{i,0}, ct_{i,1}) \in R_q^2$.
– **MKHE.Dec**$(ct, sk_i, i \in \{1, \dots k\})$: Given ciphertext $ct = (ct_0, ct_1, \dots, ct_k) \in R_p^{k+1}$ related to k users and secret keys sk_i:
  - Let $\widehat{sk} = (1, s_1, \dots, s_k)$;
  - Calculate $m' \leftarrow \lfloor (1/\Delta) \cdot \langle ct, \widehat{sk} \rangle \rceil \pmod{p}$.
– **MKHE.Eval**(ct_1, ct_2) : The ciphertexts $ct_i \in R_q^{k_i+1}$ are related to k_1 and k_2 parties respectively. We directly carry out homomorphic evaluation on two ciphertexts without preprocessing, that is, without ciphertext extension. Suppose that the user sets of the two ciphertexts are $S_i = (id_1, \cdots, id_{k_i}) \subseteq \{id_1, \cdots, id_k\}$.
  - **MKHE.Add**(ct_1, ct_2):

$$ct_+ = \begin{cases} ct_+[0] = ct_1[0] + ct_2[0] \pmod{q} \\ ct_+[i] = ct_1[i] + ct_2[i] \pmod{q} & \text{if } id_i \in S_1 \cap S_2 \\ ct_+[j] = ct_1[j] & \text{if } id_j \notin S_2 \\ ct_+[h] = ct_2[h] & \text{if } id_h \notin S_1 \end{cases}$$

  Return $ct_+ \in R_q^{k+1}$.
  - **MKHE.Mult**(ct_1, ct_2):
    1. Calculate $ct_\times = \lfloor (1/\Delta) \cdot (ct_1 \otimes ct_2) \rceil \pmod{q} \in R_q^{(k_1+1)(k_2+1)}$;
    2. Run the relinearization algorithm and return $ct'_\times \in R_q^{k+1}$.

It is worth noting that since there is no ciphertext extension, the key corresponding to the tensor product $ct_1 \otimes ct_2$ of two ciphertexts in homomorphic multiplication is $sk_1 \otimes sk_2$ rather than $\widehat{sk} \otimes \widehat{sk}$, which satisfies

$$\langle ct_1 \otimes ct_2, sk_1 \otimes sk_2 \rangle = \langle ct_1, sk_1 \rangle \cdot \langle ct_2, sk_2 \rangle .$$

Although the corresponding user set after relinearization is still the union of the two user sets, the nonlinear entries contained in $sk_1 \otimes sk_2$ are only a subset of the scheme of adding ciphertext extension.

5 Scheme Analysis and Comparison

5.1 Security

Theorem 1. *The above auxiliary coding scheme is semantically secure under the RLWE assumption.*

Proof. We prove that for any polynomial time adversary $\mathcal{A}$, the advantage of $\mathcal{A}$ successfully distinguishing the output in the auxiliary coding scheme from the uniform distribution for any message μ is negligible. Given public parameters $pp = \{n, q, \chi, \psi\}$ and a randomly selected public vector $\mathbf{a}$, let $pk = (\mathbf{a}, \mathbf{b}) \leftarrow$

KeyGen(pp) and $\mathbf{D} = [\mathbf{d}_0 | \mathbf{d}_1 | \mathbf{d}_2] \leftarrow$ **Aux-Code**(pk, μ, s), where $\mu \in R$, $pk' = (\mathbf{a}, \mathbf{b}')$ where $\mathbf{b}' \leftarrow R_q^d$ and $\mathbf{D}' = [\mathbf{d}_0' | \mathbf{d}_1 | \mathbf{d}_2'] \leftarrow R_q^{d \times 3}$. That is to prove that $(pk, \mathbf{D})$ and $(pk', \mathbf{D}')$ are computationally indistinguishable for adversary $\mathcal{A}$. We make use of a series of hybrid arguments to illustrate:

$$Adv(\mathcal{A}) := \left| \Pr\left[\mathcal{A}\left(1^\lambda, pk, \mathbf{D}\right) = 1 \right] - \Pr\left[\mathcal{A}\left(1^\lambda, pk', \mathbf{D}'\right) = 1 \right] \right| = negl(\lambda)$$

Hybrid 0 : We denote the distribution $(pk, \mathbf{D})$ as follows, given the public parameter $pp = \{n, q, \chi, \psi\}$ and a public vector $\mathbf{a} \leftarrow R_q^d$, let $pk = (\mathbf{a}, \mathbf{b})$ generated by the key generation algorithm satisfing $\mathbf{b} = s\mathbf{a} + \mathbf{e}$ and $\mathbf{D} = [\mathbf{d}_0 | \mathbf{d}_1 | \mathbf{d}_2]$ is the ciphertext of the μ output by **Aux-Code**. So the distribution of $(pk, \mathbf{D})$ is consistent with our scheme at this phase.

Hybrid 1 : We redefine the distribution $(pk, \mathbf{D})$ as follows, given the public parameter $pp = \{n, q, \chi, \psi\}$ and the vector $\mathbf{a}$ as *Hybrid 0*, let $pk = (\mathbf{a}, \mathbf{b}')$, where $\mathbf{b}' \leftarrow R_q^d$, and $\mathbf{D} = [\mathbf{d}_0 | \mathbf{d}_1 | \mathbf{d}_2]$ is generated by **Aux-Code**(pk, μ, s). According to the RLWE assumption, $(pk, \mathbf{D})_{H_0}$ and $(pk, \mathbf{D})_{H_1}$ are computationally indistinguishable in this case, because $\mathbf{b}'$ and $\mathbf{b}$ are indistinguishable, so we have:

$$\left| \Pr_{H_0}\left[\mathcal{A}\left(1^\lambda, pk, \mathbf{D}\right) = 1 \right] - \Pr_{H_1}\left[\mathcal{A}\left(1^\lambda, pk, \mathbf{D}\right) = 1 \right] \right| = negl_1(\lambda).$$

Hybrid 2 : In this *Hybrid*, we define the distribution $(pk, \mathbf{D})$ as below. Given the public parameter $pp = \{n, q, \chi, \psi\}$ and vector $\mathbf{a}$, let $pk = (\mathbf{a}, \mathbf{b}')$ as *Hybrid 1*. For $\mathbf{D} = [\mathbf{d}_0 | \mathbf{d}_1 | \mathbf{d}_2]$, denote $(\mathbf{d}_0, \mathbf{d}_1)$ is generated by **Aux-Code** and $\mathbf{d}_2 = \mathbf{d}_2' + \mu \cdot \mathbf{g}$, where $\mathbf{d}_2' \leftarrow R_q^d$ rather than $\mathbf{d}_2 = \mathbf{R} \cdot \mathbf{a} + \mu \cdot \mathbf{g}$. Since $\mathbf{a}$ is a randomly vector and $\mathbf{R}$ is a randomly matrix, $\mathbf{d}_2'$ and $\mathbf{R} \cdot \mathbf{a}$ are statistically indistinguishable. Since $\mathbf{d}_2'$ is completely random, the probability of adversary $\mathcal{A}$'s success in this step is $1/2$, and we have

$$\left| \Pr_{H_1}\left[\mathcal{A}\left(1^\lambda, pk, \mathbf{D}\right) = 1 \right] - \Pr_{H_2}\left[\mathcal{A}\left(1^\lambda, pk, \mathbf{D}\right) = 1 \right] \right| = negl_2(\lambda).$$

Hybrid 3 : We denote the distribution $(pk, \mathbf{D})$ as follows, given the public parameter $pp = \{n, q, \chi, \psi\}$, vector $\mathbf{a}$ and $pk = (\mathbf{a}, \mathbf{b}')$ and $\mathbf{D} = [\mathbf{d}_0 | \mathbf{d}_1 | \mathbf{d}_2] \leftarrow R_q^{d \times 3}$ is a matrix independent of algorithm **Aux-Code**. In this case, the distribution of $(pk, \mathbf{D})$ is consistent with $(pk', \mathbf{D}')$. According to the RLWE assumption, we have

$$\left| \Pr_{H_2}\left[\mathcal{A}\left(1^\lambda, pk, \mathbf{D}\right) = 1 \right] - \Pr_{H_3}\left[\mathcal{A}\left(1^\lambda, pk, \mathbf{D}\right) = 1 \right] \right| = negl_3(\lambda).$$

Finally, we come to the conclusion that

$$\left| \Pr_{H_0}\left[\mathcal{A}\left(1^\lambda, pk, \mathbf{D}\right) = 1 \right] - \Pr_{H_3}\left[\mathcal{A}\left(1^\lambda, pk', \mathbf{D}'\right) = 1 \right] \right|$$
$$\leq negl_1(\lambda) + negl_2(\lambda) + negl_3(\lambda)$$
$$= negl(\lambda).$$

5.2 Noise Growth

In this part, we provide an analysis of the noise caused by our relinearization algorithm, and we use norm to measure and compare the size of noise. We denote χ and ψ are B-bounded distributions and assume that the gadget decomposition adopts bit decomposition, where $d = \log q$ is the bit length of q.

When decrypting $rlk_{i,j}, rlk_i$ with $(1, s_i, s_j), (1, s_i)$ respectively, we obtain:

$$\mathbf{K}_{i,j} \cdot (1, s_i, s_j) = \mathbf{k}_1 + s_i \cdot \mathbf{k}_2 + s_j \cdot \mathbf{k}_3 = s_i s_j \cdot \mathbf{g} + \ \mathbf{g}^{-1}(\mathbf{b}_j) \cdot \mathbf{e}'_i + \mathbf{R}_i \cdot \mathbf{e}_j \ (\mathrm{mod}\, q)$$

$$\mathbf{K}_i \cdot (1, s_i) = \mathbf{k}'_1 + s_i \cdot \mathbf{k}'_2 = s_i^2 \cdot \mathbf{g} + \ \mathbf{g}^{-1}(\mathbf{b}_i) \cdot \mathbf{e}'_i + \mathbf{R}_i \cdot \mathbf{e}_i \ (\mathrm{mod}\, q)$$

The noise in $rlk_{i,j}$ is $\mathbf{g}^{-1}(\mathbf{b}_j)\mathbf{e}'_i + \mathbf{R}_i\mathbf{e}_j$ and the noise in rlk_i is $\mathbf{g}^{-1}(\mathbf{b}_i)\mathbf{e}'_i + \mathbf{R}_i\mathbf{e}_i$. According to the property of norm, for any $a, b \in R$, there is $\|ab\| \leq n\|a\|\|b\|$. Therefore, the noise in the relinearized key is $(n + 1)\log q B$.

Table 1. Comparison of noise growth in relinearization key

Algorithm	Noise components	The norm of noise
CDKS [6]	$\mathbf{g}^{-1}(\mathbf{b}_j)\mathbf{e}_{i,1} + r_i\mathbf{e}_j + s_j\mathbf{e}_{i,2}$	$2nB^2 + n\log q B$
Our	$\mathbf{g}^{-1}(\mathbf{b}_j)\mathbf{e}'_i + \mathbf{R}_i\mathbf{e}_j$	$(n + 1)\log q B$

Table 2. Comparison of noise growth in relinearizing a ciphertext

Algorithm	Noise in relinearization	The norm of noise
CDKS [6]	$\sum_{i,j=1}^{k} \left\langle \mathbf{g}^{-1}\left(c_{i,j}\right), \mathbf{e}_{CDKS}^{rlk} \right\rangle$	$k^2 n \log q \cdot \|\mathbf{e}_{CDKS}^{rlk}\|$
Our	$\sum_{i=1}^{k_1} \sum_{j=1}^{k_2} \left\langle \mathbf{g}^{-1}\left(c_{i,j}\right), \mathbf{e}_{Our}^{rlk} \right\rangle$	$k_1 k_2 n \log q \cdot \|\mathbf{e}_{Our}^{rlk}\|$

In Table 1, we compare the noise in the relinearization key. In Table 2, we take the one-time relinearization algorithm to compare the increase of noise generated by relinearizing a ciphertext. According to the idea in [18], we encode $\mu \in R$ by a random matrix $\mathbf{R}$ and ensure the indistinguishability from random vectors. Due to the randomness of the matrix, no noise vector is introduced in $\mathbf{R} \cdot \mathbf{a} + \mu \cdot \mathbf{g}$. The generation of the relinearization key is affected by the auxiliary encoding scheme, and the results show that the noise in rlk of our scheme is smaller, which further reduces the noise in the process of ciphertext relinearization.

5.3 Storage Analysis

In the CDKS scheme, the relinearization key is proposed according to the RLWE problem, and the relinearization key can be calculated in advance according to the user's public information. Therefore, after knowing the ciphertext, it can have lower computational complexity. However, the relinearization keys need

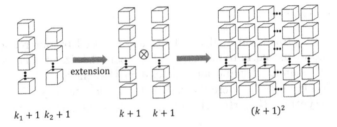

$k_1 + 1$ $k_2 + 1$ $k + 1$ $k + 1$ $(k + 1)^2$

Fig. 1. Previous MKHE scheme with ciphertext extension

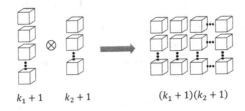

$k_1 + 1$ $k_2 + 1$ $(k_1 + 1)(k_2 + 1)$

Fig. 2. Our scheme without ciphertext extension

to consume storage space. The ciphertext extension increases the dimension of ciphertexts. After the tensor product operation, the dimension of the decryption key increases simultaneously with the ciphertext, which contains k^2 non-linear entries. We illustrate the processes in Fig. 1. Therefore, the storage space of relinearization keys is about $O(k^2)$.

In the construction of our multi-key scheme, the preprocessing of the ciphertext is cancelled and the homomorphic operation is carried out directly on two ciphertexts. In this way, while the dimension of the tensor product ciphertext is reduced, the dimension of the decryption key is also reduced. Furthermore, the non-linear entries involved are reduced to $k_1 k_2$. We illustrate the processes in Fig. 2. Therefore, the storage space of our relinearization keys is about $O(k_1 k_2)$, which is less than $O(k^2)$.

6   Conclusion

In the past few years, homomorphic encryption has received more and more attention and applications in the fields of machine learning, secure multiparty computing, and data sharing due to its good cryptographic nature. Multi-hop MKHE supports information sharing and federated computing with real-time participation of multiple users, which has important practical significance. However, the dimensional expansion in homomorphic multiplication ciphertexts and the noise growth weaken the MKHE scheme to a certain extent. In this paper, an efficient relinearization key generation algorithm with less noise is proposed, which converts a nonlinear key into linear entries. At the same time, a multi-hop multi-key variant is given based on the single-key BFV scheme. In our MKHE scheme, we propose a homomorphic evaluation without preprocessing the ciphertext, that is, without ciphertext expansion, to reduce the dimension expansion problem of ciphertexts. In addition, the number of non-linear entries of key in the multi-key scheme is reduced. This is also an improvement for the relinearization algorithm that needs to pre-calculate the relinearization keys, which can effectively reduce the calculation and storage space of relinearization keys. Therefore, we provide an option for efficiently realizing multi-user secure computing, and efforts should still be made to make MKHE better applicable to real-world environments.

Acknowledgements. This work is supported in part by the Key Research and Development Program of Shaanxi (No. 2021ZDLGY06-04) and by the Guangxi Key Laboratory of Cryptography and Information Security (No. GCIS201802).

References

1. Asharov, G., Jain, A., López-Alt, A., Tromer, E., Vaikuntanathan, V., Wichs, D.: Multiparty computation with low communication, computation and interaction via threshold FHE. In: Pointcheval, D., Johansson, T. (eds.) EUROCRYPT 2012. LNCS, vol. 7237, pp. 483–501. Springer, Heidelberg (2012). https://doi.org/10.1007/978-3-642-29011-4_29
2. Brakerski, Z.: Fully homomorphic encryption without modulus switching from classical GapSVP. In: Safavi-Naini, R., Canetti, R. (eds.) CRYPTO 2012. LNCS, vol. 7417, pp. 868–886. Springer, Heidelberg (2012). https://doi.org/10.1007/978-3-642-32009-5_50
3. Brakerski, Z., Gentry, C., Vaikuntanathan, V.: (Leveled) fully homomorphic encryption without bootstrapping. In: Goldwasser, S. (ed.) Innovations in Theoretical Computer Science 2012. pp. 309–325. ACM (2012)
4. Brakerski, Z., Perlman, R.: Lattice-based fully dynamic multi-key FHE with short ciphertexts. In: Robshaw, M., Katz, J. (eds.) CRYPTO 2016. LNCS, vol. 9814, pp. 190–213. Springer, Heidelberg (2016). https://doi.org/10.1007/978-3-662-53018-4_8
5. Chen, H., Chillotti, I., Song, Y.: Multi-key homomorphic encryption from TFHE. In: Galbraith, S.D., Moriai, S. (eds.) ASIACRYPT 2019. LNCS, vol. 11922, pp. 446–472. Springer, Cham (2019). https://doi.org/10.1007/978-3-030-34621-8_16
6. Chen, H., Dai, W., Kim, M., Song, Y.: Efficient multi-key homomorphic encryption with packed ciphertexts with application to oblivious neural network inference. In: Proceedings of the 2019 ACM SIGSAC Conference on Computer and Communications Security. pp. 395–412. ACM (2019)
7. Chen, L., Zhang, Z., Wang, X.: Batched multi-hop multi-key FHE from ring-LWE with compact ciphertext extension. In: Kalai, Y., Reyzin, L. (eds.) TCC 2017. LNCS, vol. 10678, pp. 597–627. Springer, Cham (2017). https://doi.org/10.1007/978-3-319-70503-3_20
8. Cheon, J.H., Kim, A., Kim, M., Song, Y.: Homomorphic encryption for arithmetic of approximate numbers. In: Takagi, T., Peyrin, T. (eds.) ASIACRYPT 2017. LNCS, vol. 10624, pp. 409–437. Springer, Cham (2017). https://doi.org/10.1007/978-3-319-70694-8_15
9. Chettri, L., Bera, R.: A comprehensive survey on Internet of Things (IoT) toward 5G wireless systems. IEEE Internet Things J. **7**(1), 16–32 (2020)

10. Chongchitmate, W., Ostrovsky, R.: Circuit-private multi-key FHE. In: Fehr, S. (ed.) PKC 2017. LNCS, vol. 10175, pp. 241–270. Springer, Heidelberg (2017). https://doi.org/10.1007/978-3-662-54388-7_9

11. Clear, M., McGoldrick, C.: Multi-identity and multi-key leveled FHE from learning with errors. In: Gennaro, R., Robshaw, M. (eds.) CRYPTO 2015. LNCS, vol. 9216, pp. 630–656. Springer, Heidelberg (2015). https://doi.org/10.1007/978-3-662-48000-7_31

12. Coron, J.-S., Mandal, A., Naccache, D., Tibouchi, M.: Fully homomorphic encryption over the integers with shorter public keys. In: Rogaway, P. (ed.) CRYPTO 2011. LNCS, vol. 6841, pp. 487–504. Springer, Heidelberg (2011). https://doi.org/10.1007/978-3-642-22792-9_28

13. Coron, J.-S., Naccache, D., Tibouchi, M.: Public key compression and modulus switching for fully homomorphic encryption over the integers. In: Pointcheval, D., Johansson, T. (eds.) EUROCRYPT 2012. LNCS, vol. 7237, pp. 446–464. Springer, Heidelberg (2012). https://doi.org/10.1007/978-3-642-29011-4_27

14. van Dijk, M., Gentry, C., Halevi, S., Vaikuntanathan, V.: Fully homomorphic encryption over the integers. In: Gilbert, H. (ed.) EUROCRYPT 2010. LNCS, vol. 6110, pp. 24–43. Springer, Heidelberg (2010). https://doi.org/10.1007/978-3-642-13190-5_2

15. Doröz, Y., Hu, Y., Sunar, B.: Homomorphic AES evaluation using the modified LTV scheme. Des. Codes Crypt. 80(2), 333–358 (2015). https://doi.org/10.1007/s10623-015-0095-1

16. Fan, J., Vercauteren, F.: Somewhat practical fully homomorphic encryption. Cryptology ePrint Archive, Report 2012/144 (2012). https://ia.cr/2012/144

17. Gentry, C.: Fully homomorphic encryption using ideal lattices. In: Proceedings of the 41st ACM Symposium on Theory of Computing, pp. 169–178. ACM (2009), https://doi.org/10.1145/1536414.1536440

18. Gentry, C., Sahai, A., Waters, B.: Homomorphic encryption from learning with errors: conceptually-simpler, asymptotically-faster, attribute-based. In: Canetti, R., Garay, J.A. (eds.) CRYPTO 2013. LNCS, vol. 8042, pp. 75–92. Springer, Heidelberg (2013). https://doi.org/10.1007/978-3-642-40041-4_5

19. Li, N.B., Zhou, T.P., Yang, X.Y., Han, Y.L., Liu, W.C., Tu, G.S.: Efficient multi-key FHE with short extended ciphertexts and directed decryption protocol. IEEE Access 7, 56724–56732 (2019)

20. López-Alt, A., Tromer, E., Vaikuntanathan, V.: On-the-fly multiparty computation on the cloud via multikey fully homomorphic encryption. In: Proceedings of the 44th Symposium on Theory of Computing, pp. 1219–1234. ACM (2012)

21. Lyubashevsky, V., Peikert, C., Regev, O.: On ideal lattices and learning with errors over rings. In: Gilbert, H. (ed.) EUROCRYPT 2010. LNCS, vol. 6110, pp. 1–23. Springer, Heidelberg (2010). https://doi.org/10.1007/978-3-642-13190-5_1

22. Mukherjee, Pratyay, Wichs, Daniel: Two round multiparty computation via multi-key FHE. In: Fischlin, M., Coron, J.S. (eds.) EUROCRYPT 2016. LNCS, vol. 9666, pp. 735–763. Springer, Heidelberg (2016). https://doi.org/10.1007/978-3-662-49896-5_26

23. Parast, F.K., Sindhav, C., Nikam, S., Yekta, H.I., Kent, K.B., Hakak, S.: Cloud computing security: a survey of service-based models. Comput. Secur. 114, 102580 (2022)

24. Peikert, C., Shiehian, S.: Multi-key FHE from LWE, revisited. In: Hirt, M., Smith, A. (eds.) TCC 2016. LNCS, vol. 9986, pp. 217–238. Springer, Heidelberg (2016). https://doi.org/10.1007/978-3-662-53644-5_9

25. Rivest, R.L., Adleman, L.M., Dertouzos, M.L.: On data banks and privacy homomorphisms. Found. Secur. Compuat. **4**(11), 169–178 (1978)
26. Stehlé, D., Steinfeld, R.: Making NTRU as secure as worst-case problems over ideal lattices. In: Paterson, K.G. (ed.) EUROCRYPT 2011. LNCS, vol. 6632, pp. 27–47. Springer, Heidelberg (2011). https://doi.org/10.1007/978-3-642-20465-4_4
27. Williams, P., Dutta, I.K., Daoud, H., Bayoumi, M.: A survey on security in internet of things with a focus on the impact of emerging technologies. Internet of Things **19**, 100564 (2022)

Design of Anti Machine Learning Malicious Node System Based on Blockchain

Yuanzhen Liu[1]([✉]), Yanbo Yang[1], Jiawei Zhang[2], and Baoshan Li[1]

[1] School of Information Engineering, Inner Mongolia University of Science and Technology,
Bao Tou 014010, China
`lz@stu.imust.edu.cn`
[2] School of Cyber Engineering, Xidian University, Xi'an 710071, China

Abstract. In order to solve the problem of security and privacy in machine learning, researchers have proposed many distributed solutions to protect data security and privacy, but the problem of anti malicious nodes in distributed machine learning system is still an open problem. Most of the existing distributed learning schemes solve the problem of malicious nodes by adding a disciplinary mechanism to the protocol. This method is based on two assumptions: 1. Participants give up the assumption of malicious behavior to maximize their own interests, and the calculation results can be verified only after the event occurs, which is not suitable for some scenarios requiring immediate verification; 2. Based on the assumption of a trusted third party, however, in practice, the credibility of the third party cannot be fully guaranteed. Using the trust mechanism of blockchain, this paper proposes an anti malicious node scheme based on smart contract, which realizes the whole process of model training in machine learning through smart contract to ensure that the machine learning model is not damaged by malicious nodes. This scheme takes the distributed model based on secure multi-party computing as the research model, stores the data involved in machine learning in the blockchain system, uses the smart contract of the blockchain to realize the data sharing, verification and training process, and writes the training results into the blockchain, so that the authorized users can aggregate the final model by obtaining the calculation results of each participant, Through experiments, compared with the traditional distributed machine learning model based on secure multi-party computing, and showed the advantages of this scheme.

Keywords: Blockchain · Smart contract · Distributed learning · Malicious nodes · Secure multi-party computation · Ring signature

1 Introduction

Machine learning effectively simulates human learning activities by using computers. Through learning the data, it generates useful models to make decisions and judgments on future behavior. It has brought revolutionary changes in the application fields of computer vision, natural language processing, speech recognition, data mining and information retrieval, and has become an indispensable tool in the research and technical application of various fields [1]. However, the booming machine learning technology makes data security and privacy face more severe challenges. According to the information disclosure research released by infowatch, there were about 2500 privacy data and payment data leaks worldwide in 2019, resulting in the exposure of more than 14.8 billion important records. On May 25, 2020, the European Union officially implemented the General Data Protection Regulation (GDPR), which is considered to be the strictest personal data protection regulation and puts forward strict requirements for data security and privacy protection. Machine learning needs to use a large amount of data for training, but the protection of data and privacy makes it difficult for data to circulate and form the isolated data island, which can not release the greater value of data. In order to solve the problems of data security and privacy protection in machine learning, researchers have proposed many distributed learning schemes with data security and privacy protection [2–4]. Among them, the machine learning model based on secure multi-party computing (as shown in Fig. 1) distributes the data to each node for calculation through garbled circuit, secret sharing, homomorphic encryption and other methods, and the node cannot infer the real data directly from the allocated data. It breaks the isolated data island, realizes the safe circulation of data, and provides a reliable guarantee for data security and privacy protection in machine learning.

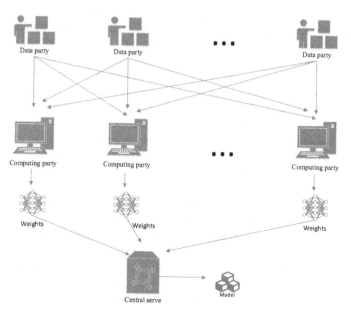

Fig. 1. Machine learning model of secure multi-party computing

Secure multi-party computing solutions solve the problems of data security and privacy protection in machine learning, but such solutions still need a centralized server to distribute and process the data. Once the centralized server is attacked, it will affect the whole learning process; At the same time, the central server itself may infer user privacy and destroy data security according to the obtained data; In addition, in the distributed learning process, not all participants are trusted, and the participants will steal user privacy, destroy data security, and even interfere with the learning process.

The untrusted participants include semi-honest participants and malicious participants: the semi-honest participants will execute according to the requirements of the agreement, only eavesdropping or obtaining all inputs of other participants in the process of the agreement; Malicious participants not only eavesdrop or obtain all the inputs of dishonest participants in the process of the agreement, but also control participants to participate in the agreement in their own way. Malicious attackers aim to destroy the correct implementation of the agreement or obtain the private inputs of other participants. The existing security computing schemes can only meet the security characteristics when dealing with semi-honest attackers or most of the participants are honest. In the face of malicious attacks, they cannot guarantee fairness, security or correctness [5].

Blockchain provides a trusted environment in an untrusted network. The consensus mechanism of blockchain ensures the correctness of execution results, and users do not need to perform any additional authentication operations. In addition, the invariance and traceability of blockchain can provide responsibility for malicious acts. Blockchain decentralization effectively avoids server failure and single node attack. At the same time, the encryption provides a strong guarantee for users' data security and privacy protection. When the smart contract in the blockchain meets the contract trigger conditions, the contract can be executed automatically without human control. Through the training of machine learning through smart contract, the participants in the training can only execute according to the agreement specified in the contract, that is, all attackers can be regarded as semi-honest attackers, so as to avoid the interference of malicious behavior to the normal execution of machine learning training to a great extent.

The transaction address of blockchain is usually generated by the user's public key and has nothing to do with the user's identity information. The transaction address has anonymity. At the same time, in the blockchain, transaction records are usually public and can be viewed arbitrarily. When users use blockchain addresses to participate in blockchain business, they may disclose some sensitive information, which may be used to speculate the real identity of the user corresponding to the address.

The openness and transparency of all transaction data is the advantage of blockchain for data without privacy protection, which makes it easy for people to trace the data. For private data that needs to be protected, this has become a defect of blockchain. The necessary privacy protection has become the key to the application of blockchain technology in various industries.

Ring signature technology mixes its own public key into multiple public keys. When verifying the signature, it is impossible to determine who signed it, so as to hide the identity of the transaction initiator. Ring signature is a simplified group signature. In ring signature, only ring members have no manager, and there is no need for cooperation among ring members. The signer can sign independently by using his private key and the public key of other members in the set, and other members in the set may not know that they are included. The advantage of ring signature is that in addition to the unconditional anonymity of the former, other members of the ring cannot forge the real signer's signature.

Blockchain provides a trusted environment in untrusted networks. It can provide secure and trusted services in many scenarios and solve the problems faced by traditional centralized servers. The comprehensive use of blockchain and distributed learning effectively improves the confidentiality of data and the security of computing, which can meet different application scenarios. The smart contract of blockchain converts malicious participants into semi-honest participants, which improves the ability of anti malicious nodes in machine learning; In the blockchain, ring signature technology is used to hide the participant's data address and protect the participant's identity privacy.

The main contributions of this paper are as follows:

(1) This paper designs a distributed machine learning protocol based on secure multi-party computing (SMPC), and analyzes the security of the protocol and the possible malicious behavior of malicious nodes.

(2) Design smart contract multi-party computing (SCMPC), realize distributed machine learning in the smart contract of blockchain, solve the problem of malicious nodes in secure multi-party computing, encrypt the data address with ring signature to protect user privacy, verify the feasibility of the scheme and analyze the security of the scheme through experiments.

2 Related Work

Since Nakamoto create blockchain in 2008, blockchain technology has been developing continuously. Now blockchain has been far more than used in the financial field to provide decentralized solutions for all walks of life. The comprehensive use of blockchain and distributed learning provides a new solution for data security and privacy protection of machine learning.

Xiao [6] uses the trust mechanism of blockchain to solve the edge attack and forged service record attack in mobile edge computing. Hua [7] regards the blockchain as a trusted third party and shares federal learning and training weights through the blockchain. Huang [8] used the blockchain smart contract to construct a punishment mechanism. Participants need to pay a deposit before executing the agreement. Participants who terminate the agreement or send error messages will be confiscated of the deposit. Gao [9] assumes that all participants are rational and selfish, punishes the uncooperative party and rewards the honest participants. At the same time, blockchain is introduced as a trusted third party to maintain the reputation system, and the party with high reputation is more likely to be selected to participate in the calculation.

The above scheme takes the blockchain as a trusted third party, enhances security and privacy protection, and uses the blockchain to protect data privacy and ensure data storage; The main idea of fighting against malicious nodes is to introduce the concept and method of game theory into secure multi-party computing, assuming that the participants are rational and selfish, only pay attention to how to obtain more benefits, add a disciplinary mechanism to the agreement, and use the incentive mechanism of blockchain to verify the behavior of the participants after the calculation and deduct the deposit or reputation value, All participants give up doing evil for the maximization of their own interests. Such methods need to verify the calculation of each participant after the results occur, which cannot meet some scenarios that need to use the calculation results immediately.

In order to meet these challenges, this paper proposes a training scheme of machine learning model against malicious nodes based on blockchain. By using blockchain, trust is established between nodes without relying on a trusted third party. Taking advantage of the automatic execution characteristics of smart contract, the execution process cannot be interfered by human beings, so as to solve the problem of malicious nodes; In the process of introducing blockchain, the openness and transparency of blockchain makes the training of machine learning face serious privacy problems. Ring signature is used to hide the data address in the execution process to protect the privacy problems in the execution process of blockchain.

3   Preliminaries

3.1   Secure Multi-party Computing

Secure multi-party computing is a very active research field in modern cryptography. It enables multiple parties to complete a computing task in a collaborative way, and maintains the privacy of inputs from all parties and the consistency of computing results [8–10]. There are n participants $P_1, P_2, \ldots, P_n$ who want to jointly calculate a function in a secure way. Security here refers to the correctness of output results and the confidentiality of input and output information. Specifically, each participant P_i has its own input information X_i, and n participant should jointly calculate a function

$$f(X_1, X_2, \ldots, X_n) = (Y_1, Y_2, \ldots Y_n) \tag{1}$$

At the end of the calculation, each participant P_i can only get Y_i and cannot understand any information of other parties. As a sub field of cryptography, secure multi-party computing protocol allows multiple data owners to perform collaborative computing and output computing results without mutual trust, and ensures that no party can get any information other than the due computing results. In other words, secure multi-party computing can obtain the use value of data without disclosing the original data content. Secure multi-party computing breaks the isolated data island and realizes the safe flow of data.

3.2   Ring Signature

Ring signature is a simplified group signature, Ring signature does not need to establish a signature group, which provides a clever method to hide the signer's identity [11, 12]. For the verifier, it is impossible to confirm the signer's identity information. This unconditional anonymity of ring signature is very useful in some special environments where information needs long-term protection.

In the ring signature, it is assumed that there are n users, each user has a public key pk_i and a corresponding private key sk_i, the signer generates $n-1$ random numbers $x_1, x_2, \cdots, x_{s-1}, x_{s+1}, \cdots, x_n, y_i = E_{pk_i}(x_i)$ is obtained by encrypting the random number with each user's public key pk_i respectively, and generates a random number v, which is calculated y_s according to the equation:

$$C_{k,y}(y_1, y_2, \cdots, y_s, \cdots, y_n) = E_k(y_n \oplus E_k(y_{n-1} \oplus E_k(\cdots \oplus E_k(y_1 \oplus v)))))) = v$$

The user uses the private key sk_i to decrypt y_s and get $x_s = D_{sk_s}(y_s)$.

Get ring signature $signature(pk_1, \cdots pk_s, \cdots pk_n; v; x_1, \cdots, x_s, \cdots x_n)$.

In the ring signature, there is no need for the group administrator to avoid the characteristics of excessive authority of the group administrator and realize the unconditional anonymity of the signer. With its unique properties, ring signature can be widely used in anonymous e-election, e-government, e-money system, key distribution and multi-party secure computing, so it has become a hot spot of current research.

In ring signature, the attacker cannot determine which member of the set. The generated signature can be verified by all others. Anyone cannot forge the signature of the real signer.

3.3 Blockchain

In the blockchain, users jointly create a public ledger for block verification and recording transactions [13, 14]. Blockchain technology has laid a solid foundation of "trust" and created a reliable cooperation mechanism, which has broad application prospects [7, 15, 16]. Its core technologies include:

3.3.1 Smart Contract

Smart contract is a contract defined in digital form that can automatically enforce terms. It puts the contract on the blockchain in the form of code and automatically executes it under the agreed conditions. The unchangeable and traceable characteristics of the blockchain provide a safe and reliable operation environment for smart contracts. Smart contracts are placed on the blockchain. Due to the characteristics of the blockchain, the data written into the blockchain cannot be changed or deleted. The whole process is transparent and traceable, and the contract execution is permanently recorded, which can effectively prevent piracy and tampering. When the smart contract meets the contract trigger conditions, the contract can be executed automatically without human control. Avoid the interference of malicious acts on the normal execution of the contract to a great extent.

3.3.2 Decentralization

Blockchain is a distributed ledger on a peer-to-peer network, and each node stores complete ledger information. Each node backs up the complete ledger information, which can avoid data loss caused by single node failure. Blockchain technology does not rely on additional third-party management institutions or hardware facilities, and there is no central control. In addition to the self-contained blockchain itself, each node realizes information self verification, transmission and management through distributed accounting and storage. Decentralization is the most essential feature of blockchain.

3.3.3 Consensus

Consensus mechanism is the process of reaching an agreement on a proposal to ensure the consistency of the contents of each node without a central node. It maintains the operation order and fairness of the system, so that each irrelevant node can verify and confirm the data in the network, so as to generate trust and reach a consensus.

3.3.4 Encryption

Many classical algorithms of modern cryptography are used in the application of blockchain, including hash algorithm, symmetric encryption, asymmetric encryption, digital signature, etc. the encryption algorithm protects the anonymity, tamperability and forgeability of blockchain, and is the bottom line of whether a public chain is trustworthy and has basic security.

The smart contract based on blockchain technology can not only give play to the advantages of smart contract in cost efficiency, but also avoid the interference of malicious behavior on the normal execution of the contract. The smart contract is written into the blockchain in digital form. The characteristics of blockchain technology ensure that the storage, reading and the whole execution process are transparent, traceable and tamperable.

4   System overview

4.1   System Model

As shown in Fig. 2, the whole system consists of four parts: blockchain network, data party, miner and management center. The specific description is as follows:

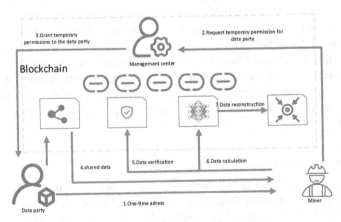

Fig. 2. System model

1) Blockchain network,ensures the reliable operation of smart contracts, stores data, manages the access of data accounts, the call of smart contracts and other permissions.

2) Data party, the provider of training data, shares its own data to different data addresses.
3) Miners,use the data shared by the data party to train on the smart contract, and save the calculation results in the data address. Miners are randomly selected by the system.
4) Management center, manages the training process of machine learning and assigns read-write permissions for data sharing.

In the system, the data party first confirms the miner who calculates the shared data at one time, and the management center grants the corresponding authority; After obtaining the corresponding permissions, share data with different miners through smart contracts; After obtaining the data, the miner verifies the shared data through the smart contract, trains the machine learning, and saves the training results in the data address; When using the model, the training weight saved by the miner is obtained from the data address and aggregated into the final model through the smart contract.

4.2   Threat Model

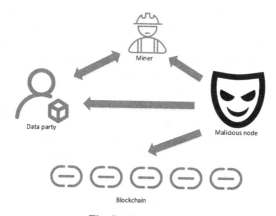

Fig. 3. Threat model

In the secure multi-party computing scheme (see Fig. 1), data share data with the computing party, and the data party may distribute wrong data in order to obtain results beneficial to itself; After receiving the data, the computing party will carry out machine learning training locally. The malicious computing party will constantly send data requests to the data party, so that the machine learning training process cannot be carried out smoothly. After the calculation results are calculated, it may not publish the calculation results in time based on its own interests, or publish the wrong results, destroy the model aggregation, and cause other parties to be unable to obtain the output.

In the system scheme designed based on blockchain, miners replace the computing party to become the specific executor of machine learning training. Blockchain provides a safe and trusted computing environment and avoids the malicious behavior of malicious participants, but the transparency of blockchain still faces the risk of user data and privacy being attacked. Figure 3 shows the threats faced by the blockchain system: miners will try to infer the user's identity information and obtain the privacy of the data party during the calculation process; Outside the system, malicious nodes will attack the data party, obtain the identity and privacy of the data party, attack miners, obtain training results, recover real data, monitor network links, expose user identities according to the transaction records of blockchain.

4.3 Scheme Principle

In the secure multi-party computing scheme, the data share data with the computing party; After receiving the data, the computing party carries out machine learning training locally; When users need to use the model, they request the training results from each computing party and aggregate them locally into the final model.

Machine learning needs to face the problem of malicious nodes in distributed training. Malicious nodes will steal user privacy, destroy data and destroy model data in various ways in the process of training and prediction. In the process of sharing, the distributor may send wrong data to other participants; Malicious participants in distributed machine learning will constantly send data requests to the data party, making the machine learning training process unable to proceed smoothly. After calculating the results, the malicious node may not publish the calculation results in time based on its own interests, or publish the wrong results, which destroys the model aggregation, resulting in the failure of other parties to obtain the output; Users will access data through collusive attacks and other illegal means to obtain training models and data privacy. During the execution of the smart contract, due to the transparency of blockchain technology, the parameters invoked by the user will be obtained by malicious adversaries, revealing the user's privacy.

In the anti malicious node scheme designed in this paper, secure multi-party computing is used to protect data security and privacy. Shamir secret sharing is used to complete the distribution of training data. Each miner can only obtain part of the original data. Malicious participants need to attack more than one participant to obtain the original data to ensure the data privacy in the process of data sharing. The characteristics of smart contracts in the blockchain can treat all participants in the system as semi-honest nodes. Each node automatically trains data through the contract and writes the training results into the blockchain to avoid the possibility of malicious nodes doing evil. Using ring signature technology to hide data operation address, malicious participants cannot obtain the correct address of the transaction party, protect user identity, and avoid privacy disclosure and conspiracy attack in the training process.

4.4 Scheme Construction

Scheme construction the scheme of this paper include system initialization stage, data distribution stage, data verification stage, data calculation stage and data reconstruction stage.

4.4.1 System Initialization Stage

Before data sharing, the data party needs to confirm which data addresses to share the data to. The confirmation process is as follows: first, the data party generates a random number r_i and randomly selects the miner's public key pk_j. $E_j(H(r_i))$ is the data party encrypts the hash value $H(r_i)$ of the random number r_i with the public key pk_j and saves $H(r_i)$ in its own data account; Secondly, generate a one-time address $P_i = H(H(r_i)||pk_j)$ and ring sign the data $Sign(P_i, E_j(H(r_i)))$ to be broadcast; Finally, after receiving the data, the miner decrypts the broadcast information $E_j(H(r_i))$ with the private key sk_j, $R' = D_j(E_j(H(r_i)))$.

If $H(R'||pk_j)$ equal to P_i, it indicates that the data party is about to share data with its own account. If agreed, the miner will send $H(r_i)$ to the authority center.

In the initialization stage, the data $Sign(P_i, E_j(H(r_i)))$ broadcast to the network by the data is that any node cannot confirm who sent and signed the data after receiving the data, and only the designated receiver can decrypt the information with its own private key. In the initialization process, it ensures that the data address of the data party is not found, thus ensuring the identity of the data party. At the same time, the miner receiving the data cannot judge other data receivers, Avoiding collusive attacks.

4.4.2 Data Distribution Stage

The data party calls the shared smart contract and saves the shared data to the miner's account address.

The contract first verifies the data $H(r_i)$ and requests the authority to write data to the miner's account address from the authority center. If the authority center does not receive $H(r_i)$ from the miner, it cannot write data to the miner's account address.

In this paper, the shared smart contract completes the distribution of training data based on Shamir secret sharing[8].

1. Assign a unique identifier x_i to each participant, t is the minimum threshold required to recover data.
2. The data side randomly generates $t - 1$ random numbers $a_1, a_2,...,$ $a_{t-1}, b_1, b_2, ..., b_{t-1}$.
3. Construct two random polynomials, a_0 is the shared secret value

$$a(x) = a_0 + a_1 x + a_2 x^2 + ... + a_{t-1} x^{t-1} \qquad (2)$$

$$b(x) = b_0 + b_1 x + b_2 x^2 + ... + b_{t-1} x^{t-1} \qquad (3)$$

Store the data $a(x_i)$, $b(x_i)$ in the data address.

In the blockchain, the data stored on the blockchain cannot be changed arbitrarily. In the process of data sharing, it can ensure that the data party cannot destroy the data source; The smart contract can be executed automatically without being controlled by human beings. The data is shared through the smart contract, which ensures that the data calculation is executed according to the specified protocol in the sharing process, and ensures the accuracy of the calculation process. The security of data source and computing process ensures the security of data sharing. In order to ensure data security, the blockchain requires the operator to sign the operation. However, due to the transparency of the blockchain, the signature can be seen by anyone, so it is easy to connect the operation with the signature, and then disclose the identity information of the participants. However, we use ring signature for signature, which makes the malicious participants unable to confirm the specific signer, and ensures the identity information of the data party.

4.4.3   Data Verification Stage

The miner calls the verification smart contract to verify whether the data distribution is correct.

1. The data distributor calculates the commitment A_k and writes it into the data address respectively

$$A_k = g^{a(k)} h^{b(k)} \bmod p \tag{4}$$

2. After receiving the data, the miner calculates

$$A_\delta' = \prod_{i=0}^{t} (A_i)^{\sum_{i=0}^{t} \lambda_{ji}\delta^j} \bmod p \tag{5}$$

V is the order matrix formed by $x_1, x_2, ..., x_t$, and λ_{mn} is the element in row m and column n of V^{-1}.

3. Participant P_i and calculation results will be compared with A_{x_i} published in the blockchain. If it is consistent, it means that the distributed data and the received data are in the same polynomial. Otherwise, request the distributor to redistribute the data.

In the distributed learning scheme, malicious nodes will still send request data to the data party when they obtain the correct data. On the one hand, it will increase the computing consumption of the data party and hinder the start of machine learning training; On the other hand, malicious nodes using different identities to request data will obtain multiple shared data, so as to recover the original data, which poses a threat to the data privacy of the data party. The use of smart contract for verification enables miners to send data retransmission requests only when the data verification fails, so as to avoid malicious participants requesting data from the data party for many times, destroy the training process of machine learning, and enhance the protection of the data privacy of the data party.

4.4.4   Data Calculation Stage

Miners call the training smart contract to train the data in the data address.

1. Obtain data from the blockchain's data account and complete data preprocessing.

2. To construct the machine learning neural network model, this paper uses the linear regression algorithm to calculate

$$z = \sum w_i x + b \tag{6}$$

3. Using the sigmoid activation function $\sigma(z) = \frac{1}{1+e^{-z}}$, the descent gradient is calculated

$$\sigma'(z) = \sigma(z)(1 - \sigma(z)) \tag{7}$$

4. Update the value of the weight sum of the model and calculate

$$\theta = \theta - \alpha \cdot \sigma'(z) \tag{8}$$

4. Repeat 2–4, iterate and update the model weight.
5. Store the calculated w and b into the blockchain data account.

In the data calculation stage, the smart contract uses the data in the miner's data address for machine learning training; Although the blockchain records all data operations of the user, and the content of the smart contract, that is, the training method of machine learning, can be viewed arbitrarily, the smart contract obtains data from the executor's data account. The malicious node cannot get the real data and machine learning model parameters of machine learning training, so the training data cannot be inferred from the model parameters; At the same time, miners use ring signature to sign the operation of calling smart contract. Malicious participants cannot judge the real address of executing the contract, so as to further protect data security. In general distributed machine learning, after training the model, malicious nodes find that the model is not conducive to them, and they will give up publishing the model, or they will not publish the model in time to destroy the machine learning training. Due to the automatic execution of smart contracts in the blockchain, miners will publish the model immediately after training, and malicious behavior is prevented.

4.4.5 Data Reconstruction Stage

At this stage, the data user reconstructs the final result by using the results calculated by the miners. Send a request to the management center to obtain the permission to read the results of the miner's data account model $y_1, y_2, ..., y_n$ in the blockchain. The result $y_1, y_2, ..., y_n$ is generated by the secret shared data through linear calculation, so it has the same properties as the shared data, and the real model can be recovered through the inverse matrix formed by the unique identification of the participants:

$$\left(y_1', y_2', ..., y_n'\right) = V^{-1}(y_1, y_2, ..., y_n) \tag{9}$$

The machine learning model is reconstructed by using $y_1', y_2', ..., y_n'$, and the model is used in the next step.

5 Security Analysis

The anti malicious node scheme proposed in this paper meets the requirements of data security and privacy protection in the process of machine learning and training, avoids the destruction of model data by malicious nodes, and greatly improves the anti malicious node ability of secure multi-party computing.

In the system initialization stage, the data party uses the one-time encrypted address to obtain the permission to write data to the miner's data address. Through the use of public key encryption, only the designated miner can obtain the encrypted address, and the data address of the data party is hidden through the ring signature technology. Any party in the calculation cannot judge the data address of the data party, so as to ensure the identity privacy of the data party.

In the data sharing stage, Shamir secret sharing is used to complete the distribution of training data. Each miner can only obtain part of the original data. In order to recover the original data, malicious participants need to attack participants to obtain the original data. In the process of data transmission, the encrypted data address is transmitted. Only the designated miner can decrypt the private key to obtain the correct data address, so as to ensure data security. Through the smart contract to share data, the smart contract can restrict the participants who upload data, so as to prevent malicious data parties from sending a large amount of useless data to designated miners, causing DDoS attacks, bringing miners' services offline and paralyzing the whole system.

The data parties share data through smart contracts, which avoids the distribution of wrong data by the distributor and ensures the integrity and correctness of the data obtained by the participants. After obtaining the data, the miner verifies the data. Only when the verification result is incorrect, can he request to resend the data from the data party, avoiding the situation that the participants continue to send request attacks and interfere with the training. After the miner verifies the data, he runs the smart contract trained by the model and automatically stores the calculation results in the blockchain, avoiding the situation that the malicious node does not publish or send the wrong results in time when calculating the adverse results. If the data user wants to use the calculation results, he must obtain the permission to read the calculation results stored in the blockchain by the participants, and can only use them after aggregating them into a model locally.

In the improved scheme, the ring signature ensures that no one knows which user the data comes from, and Shamir secret sharing ensures the data security under multi-party collaborative computing. The data distribution, verification and model training process in the scheme are automatically completed by the smart contract in the blockchain and cannot be controlled manually, and the calculation results are written into the blockchain. Due to the tamperability of the blockchain, malicious nodes cannot destroy the training model.

The operations in the blockchain are jointly confirmed by all nodes, so there is no need to review and verify the calculation results. The traditional trusted third party undertakes the tasks of key distribution management, role assignment and so on, and can obtain additional computing related information. If it colludes with malicious participants, it is likely to lead to data privacy disclosure. The authority center in the blockchain is jointly maintained by all nodes, avoiding the problems caused by the traditional third party.In addition, due to the introduction of blockchain network, there is no need to find another transmission channel to transfer information between parties, which greatly strengthens the transmission security and reduces the network traffic.

6 Performance Evaluation

In the system initialization stage, the data party uses the one-time encrypted address to obtain the permission to write data to the miner's data address. Through the use of public key encryption, only the designated miner can obtain the encrypted address, and the data address of the data party is hidden through the ring signature technology. Any party in the calculation cannot judge the data address of the data party, so as to ensure the identity privacy of the data party. In the ring signature, the more the number of signatures, the more difficult it is to judge the real data address. However, the larger the size of the ring signature, the longer the signature takes, as shown in Fig. 4.

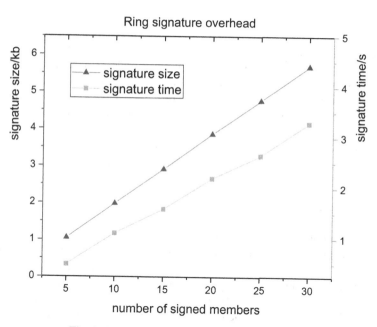

Fig. 4. Performance comparison of ring signature

In the data training stage, miners use the received data for machine learning training. In SMC scheme, miners need to transmit the results to a centralized node after calculating the results, but a single node is easy to be attacked, which poses a threat to the security of the model; In the SCMPC scheme, after the participants calculate the results, they directly write the results into the data account and wait for the user with permission to obtain them.

In the data reconstruction stage, the user obtains the calculation results of the calculation participants and aggregates the final model. At this stage, the SMC scheme requires all computing participants to send calculation results to users, but malicious participants will send wrong results, and security problems will occur in the transmission process, posing a serious threat to the security of the model. In the smart contract scheme, users with permissions can obtain real and reliable data through the blockchain without worrying about transmission security. Therefore, in the aggregation phase, less time cost is worth it.

Table 1. System model diagram and scheme performance comparison

Scheme	Distribution /ms	Verification /ms	Calculation /ms	Reconstruction /ms
SMC	65856	5	7767	5
SCMPC4	12915	135	10311	69
SCMPC8	28689	125	8275	92
SCMPC12	36670	123	9821	99

Table 1 shows the performance comparison between the SMC scheme and the SCMPC scheme with different number of consensus nodes. Compared with the SMC scheme, SCMPC scheme takes a certain time to complete the consensus when obtaining data, but it saves the communication cost of participants in the system and avoids the security problems in the transmission process; At the same time, due to the automatic execution of smart contract and the unchangeable nature of blockchain, malicious nodes obtain data privacy and destroy model training, which greatly enhances the anti malicious node ability of machine learning while ensuring privacy security.

7 Conclusion

Aiming at the problem of malicious nodes in machine learning, this paper proposes a machine learning training scheme based on blockchain smart contract. The key steps of this scheme are completed by smart contract. The operation of smart contract can not be interfered by human and the participants can not carry out malicious behavior. Therefore, there is no need to verify the results. The trust mechanism of blockchain provides a reliable trust environment, The scheme solves the problem that malicious nodes steal data privacy and destroy the training model in distributed machine learning, and provides a good solution to the problem of malicious nodes in distributed learning.

Acknowledgments. This research is supported by Natural Science Foundation of Inner Mongolia Autonomous Region (2020LH06006); Major science and technology projects of Inner Mongolia Autonomous Region (2019ZD025); Inner Mongolia discipline inspection and supervision big data open project (IMDBD2020021); Innovation fund of Inner Mongolia University of science and Technology (2019QDL-B51); Kundulun District Science and technology plan of Baotou City, Inner Mongolia (YF2021011).

References

1. Liu, W., Shen, C., Liu, W.: Survey on fairness in trustworthy machine learning. J. Softw. **32**(5), 1404–1426 (2021)
2. Liu, Y., Yu, F.R., Li, X., Ji, H., Leung, V.: Blockchain and machine learning for communications and networking systems. IEEE Commun. Surv. Tutorials **22**(2), 1392–1431 (2020)
3. Rathore, S., Pan, Y., Park, J.H.: BlockDeepNet: a blockchain-based secure deep learning for IoT network. Sustainability-Basel **11**(11), 1–15 (2019)
4. Liu, B., Ding, M., Shaham, S., Rahayu, W., Lin, Z.: When machine learning meets privacy: a survey and outlook. ACM Comput. Surv. **54**(2), 1–36 (2020)
5. Zhang, D., Yu, F.R., Yang, R.: Blockchain-based distributed software-defined vehicular networks: a dueling deep q-learning approach. IEEE Trans. Cogn. Commun. Netw. **5**(4), 1086–1100 (2019)
6. Xiao, L., Ding, Y., Jiang, D., Huang, J., Poor, H.V.: A reinforcement learning and blockchain-based trust mechanism for edge networks. IEEE Trans. Commun. **68**(9), 5460–5470 (2020)
7. Hua, G., Zhu, L., Wu, J., Shen, C., Lin, Q.: Blockchain-based federated learning for intelligent control in heavy haul railway. IEEE Access **8**, 176830–176839 (2020)
8. Huang, J., Huiya, J., Li, Z.: Constructing fair secure multi-party computation based on blockchain. App. Res. Comput. **37**(1), 225–230 (2020)
9. Gao, H., Ma, Z., Luo, S., Wang, Z.: BFR-MPC: a blockchain-based fair and robust multi-party computation scheme. IEEE Access **7**, 110439–110450 (2019)
10. Yang, Y., Wei, L., Wu, J., Long, C.: Block-SMPC: a blockchain-based secure multi-party computation for privacy-protected data sharing. In: ICBCT 2020: 2020 The 2nd International Conference on Blockchain Technology, pp. 46–51 (2020)
11. Guan, Z., Zhou, X., Liu, P., Wu, L., Yang, W.: A blockchain based dual side privacy preserving multi party computation scheme for edge enabled smart grid. IEEE Internet Things. 1–14 (2021)
12. Chow, S.S.M., Yiu, S.-M., Hui, L.C.K.: Efficient identity based ring signature. In: Ioannidis, J., Keromytis, A., Yung, M. (eds.) Applied Cryptography and Network Security. LNCS, vol. 3531, pp. 499–512. Springer, Heidelberg (2005). https://doi.org/10.1007/11496137_34
13. Casino, F., Dasaklis, T.K., Patsakis, C.: A systematic literature review of blockchain-based applications: current status, classification and open issues. ScienceDirect. Telemat. Inform. **36**, 55–81 (2019)
14. Zheng, Z., Xie, S., Dai, H., Chen, X., Wang, H.: An overview of blockchain technology: architecture, consensus, and future trends. In: 6th IEEE International Congress on Big Data, vol. 85, pp. 557–564 (2017)
15. Qiu, C., Yu, F.R., Yao, H., Jiang, C., Xu, F., Zhao, C.: Blockchain-based software-defined industrial internet of things: a dueling deep q-learning approach. IEEE Internet Things. 1–7 (2018)
16. Zerka, F., Urovi, V., Vaidyanathan, A., Barakat, S., Lambin, P.: Blockchain for privacy preserving and trustworthy distributed machine learning in multicentric medical imaging (C-DistriM). IEEE Access **8**, 183939–183951 (2020)